THE
WORD
TOPICAL
BIBLE
OF ISSUES
AND ANSWERS

WILLIAM PINSON

THE WORD TOPICAL BIBLE

OF ISSUES AND ANSWERS

CARMEL • NEW YORK 10512

This Guideposts edition is published by special arrangement with Word Books, Incorporated.

THE WORD TOPICAL BIBLE OF ISSUES AND ANSWERS
Copyright © 1981 by Word, Incorporated
ISBN 0–8499–0295–9
Library of Congress Catalog Number 80–54554
Printed in the United States of America

PREFACE

When a Christian deals with an issue, a subject, or a problem, he usually asks, "What does the Bible say about that?" Finding an answer at least begins with determining what the Bible sets forth on an issue. Here is a guide to discover what the Scriptures say about scores of topics from A to Z. These topics are the stuff daily life is made of—family life, daily work, government, and sexuality, for example. Others deal with controversial issues which demand our attention—homosexuality, drugs and alcohol, war, witchcraft. The book majors on ethical and moral issues. Thus, more theological subjects such as faith, heaven, or regeneration are not included nor are personal crisis subjects such as depression, grief, or death found here.

This volume is an aid to Bible study, both for the serious student and the casual inquirer. Designed for lay persons as well as professional church leaders, this volume can be of help to all Christians. Bible study leaders, Sunday school teachers, pastors, students in seminary and college classes in Bible, religion and ethics, writers, denominational leaders, and missionaries should find this work a useful tool.

Each section deals with a separate topic and is organized as follows: The name of the subject with which the section deals is followed by cross references to related subjects for further study. Next a group of Bible verses on the subject is printed followed by two lists of scripture references, one of biblical examples of the subject, and the other of additional passages on the subject. For the convenience of the reader enough scriptures are printed on each subject to supply basic biblical insight. Those desiring more complete biblical information can look up the additional references. The scriptures are in the familiar King James Version. This translation was selected primarily because it is the most widely used. In-depth study calls for the use of the Hebrew and Greek texts or recent translations.

No interpretation is given of the biblical material except the placement of Scriptures under particular subject headings. Some of the placement is subject to dispute. I realize this and in some instances I personally believe certain passages do not relate to the subject (some under Race Relations, for example), but because of widespread usage of these scriptures in connection with the subject they are included there anyway.

Discovering what the Bible says about an issue does not necessarily provide an automatic answer to what ought to be done about it. Seldom can an answer be found for an issue simply by listing all the scriptures which deal with it. The Bible may contain little or no direct teaching on the subject or the biblical material may require careful interpretation.

The reader should use this book as an aid to interpretation. It is important to know what the Bible *says* about a subject. It is just as important to discover what the Bible *teaches* about a subject. As a person reads the passages in this volume he should be constantly asking, "What does this mean? In light of this material, what am I to do today?" One's view of the Bible and of biblical interpretation will, of course, affect how one uses this volume, but whatever view is held, this collection

PREFACE

and arrangement of biblical material should be helpful.

This book is the product of the labor of many persons. Professors T. B. Maston and C. W. Scudder made valuable suggestions on subjects to include and the format. I am especially indebted to Bill Tillman, who did much of the early research and directed the team of persons who prepared the initial copy; they were Stan Beall, Sherri Briggs, Steve Fish, Ron Kurtz, Pam Kurtz, Beverly Lee, Norris Partridge, Gwen Partridge, Meredith Pinson, Mark Vinson, Susie Vinson, Tim Walker and Leta Tillman. A revised and expanded plan for the book caused the format and content to be changed with each section totally reworked. Of particular assistance to me in the total revision and final preparation of the material were Mrs. Treva Wilson, Janis McCracken, Wanda Phifer Bundy, and Bonnie Chap-

pell. Assisting them were Jan Franklin, Allison Pinson, Kathy Wills, Louanne Smith, Pam Tate, Vicky Darden, Tad Bundy, Jackie Barling and Gary Floyd. Mr. Vester T. Hughes, Jr., and Mr. Earl Rose made possible the completion of the project. Mr. Floyd W. Thatcher provided superb editorial guidance, suggestions and encouragement.

Our whole family was involved in the process of writing. Bobbie, charming wife and mother, encouraged all of us involved in the project. Meredith and Allison, delightful daughters, worked in the mechanics of book production. Without the loving support of these three beautiful Christians this volume would never have been completed.

W. M. Pinson, Jr.
Golden Gate Baptist Theological Seminary
Mill Valley, California

HOW TO USE THIS BOOK

Step One: Look through the Index of Subjects to locate the subject you want to investigate. If you do not find it, check related subjects in the Index.

Step Two: Turn to the page indicated for the selection of materials on the subject. For many subjects you will find a "See Also" listing of related subjects. Turn to these and scan them to determine if you want to use them.

Step Three: Read through the passages of Scripture printed in the section, noting the references. The references are abbreviated according to the pattern listed on the next page. The printed passages are primarily instructions or teachings, not examples.

Step Four: If you are interested in examples of the subject in the Bible, look up the passages indicated by the references under "Biblical Examples."

Step Five: If you are interested in a more exhaustive study than the printed passages make possible, look up the passages indicated by the references under "Further References." These passages are primarily instructional, some being parallel passages to those printed in the section.

ABBREVIATIONS USED
IN REFERENCES

Old Testament	Authorized	New Testament	Authorized and Douay
Genesis	Gen.	Matthew	Matt.
Exodus	Exod.	Mark	Mark
Leviticus	Lev.	Luke	Luke
Numbers	Num.	John	John
Deuteronomy	Deut.	Acts of the Apostles	Acts
Joshua	Josh.	Romans	Rom.
Judges	Judg.	1 Corinthians	1 Cor.
Ruth	Ruth	2 Corinthians	2 Cor.
1 Samuel	1 Sam.	Galatians	Gal.
2 Samuel	2 Sam.	Ephesians	Eph.
1 Kings	1 Kings	Philippians	Phil.
2 Kings	2 Kings	Colossians	Col.
1 Chronicles	1 Chron.	1 Thessalonians	1 Thess.
2 Chronicles	2 Chron.	2 Thessalonians	2 Thess.
Ezra	Ezra	1 Timothy	1 Tim.
Nehemiah	Neh.	2 Timothy	2 Tim.
Esther	Esth.	Titus	Titus
Job	Job	Philemon	Philem.
Psalms	Ps.	Hebrews	Heb.
Proverbs	Prov.	James	James
Ecclesiastes	Eccles.	1 Peter	1 Peter
Song of Solomon	Song of Sol.	2 Peter	2 Peter
Isaiah	Isa.	1 John	1 John
Jeremiah	Jer.	2 John	2 John
Lamentations	Lam.	3 John	3 John
Ezekiel	Ezek.	Jude	Jude
Daniel	Dan.	Revelation	Rev.
Hosea	Hos.		
Joel	Joel		
Amos	Amos		
Obadiah	Obad.		
Jonah	Jonah		
Micah	Mic.		
Nahum	Nah.		
Habakkuk	Hab.		
Zephaniah	Zeph.		
Haggai	Hag.		
Zechariah	Zech.		
Malachi	Mal.		

CONTENTS

CONTENTS

INDEX OF ISSUES

INDEX OF ISSUES

INDEX OF ISSUES

-A-

ABORTION (See Life, Sacredness of)

ABSTINENCE (See also Alcohol and Alcoholism; Self-control; Self-denial)

And the LORD spake unto Aaron, saying, do not drink wine nor strong drink, thou, nor thy sons with thee, when ye go into the tabernacle of the congregation, lest ye die: *it shall be* a statute for ever throughout your generations: and that ye may put difference between holy and unholy, and between unclean and clean (Lev 10:8–10).

And the LORD spake unto Moses, saying, Speak unto the children of Israel, and say unto them, When either man or woman shall separate *themselves* to vow a vow of a Nazarite, to separate *themselves* unto the LORD: he shall separate *himself* from wine and strong drink, and shall drink no vinegar of wine, or vinegar of strong drink, neither shall he drink any liquor of grapes, nor eat moist grapes, or dried. All the days of his separation shall he eat nothing that is made of the vine tree, from the kernels even to the husk. All the days of the vow of his separation there shall no razor come upon his head: until the days be fulfilled, in the which he separateth *himself* unto the LORD, he shall be holy, *and* shall let the locks of the hair of his head grow. All the days that he separateth *himself* unto the LORD he shall come at no dead body. He shall not make himself unclean for his father, or for his mother, for his brother, or for his sister, when they die: because the consecration of his God *is* upon his head. All the days of his separation he *is* holy unto the LORD (Num 6:1–8).

I have refrained my feet from every evil way, that I might keep thy word (Ps 119:101).

Be not among winebibbers; among riotous eaters of flesh (Prov 23:20).

Who hath woe? who hath sorrow? who hath contentions? who hath babbling? who hath wounds without cause? who hath redness of eyes? They that tarry long at the wine; they that go to seek mixed wine. Look not thou upon the wine when it is red, when it giveth his colour in the cup, *when* it moveth itself aright. At the last it biteth like a serpent, and stingeth like an adder. Thine eyes shall behold strange women, and thine heart shall utter perverse things. Yea, thou shalt be as he that lieth down in the midst of the sea, or as he that lieth upon the top of a mast. They have stricken me, *shalt thou say, and* I was not sick; they have beaten me, *and* I felt *it* not: when shall I awake? I will seek it yet again (Prov 23:29–35).

For it seemed good to the Holy Ghost, and to us, to lay upon you no greater burden than these necessary things; that ye abstain from meats offered to idols, and from blood, and from things strangled, and from fornication; from which if ye keep yourselves, ye shall do well. Fare ye well (Acts 15:28, 29).

Defraud ye not one the other, except *it be* with consent for a time, that ye may give yourselves to fasting and prayer; and come together again, that Satan tempt you not for your incontinency (1 Cor 7:5).

Wherefore, if meat make my brother to offend, I will eat no flesh while the world standeth, lest I make my brother to offend (1 Cor 8:13).

All things are lawful for me, but all things are not expedient: all things are lawful for me, but all things edify not. Let no man seek his own, but every man another's *wealth*. Whatsoever is sold in the shambles, *that* eat, asking no question for conscience sake: for the earth *is* the Lord's, and the fulness thereof. If any of them that believe not bid you *to a feast*, and ye be disposed to go; whatsoever is set before you, eat, asking no question for conscience sake. But if any man say unto you, This is offered in sacrifice unto idols, eat not for his sake that shewed it, and for conscience sake: for the earth *is* the Lord's, and the fulness thereof: conscience, I say, not thine own, but of the other: for why is my liberty judged of another *man's* conscience? For if I by grace be a partaker, why am I evil spoken of for that for which I give thanks? Whether therefore ye eat, or drink, or whatsoever ye do, do all to the glory of God. Give none offence, neither to the Jews, nor to the Gentiles, nor to the church of God: even as I please all *men* in all *things*, not seeking mine own profit, but the *profit* of many, that they may be saved (1 Cor 10:23–33).

And be not drunk with wine, wherein is excess; but be filled with the Spirit (Eph 5:18).

Wherefore if ye be dead with Christ from the rudiments of the world, why, as though living in the world, are ye subject to ordinances, (touch not; taste not; handle not; which all are to perish with the using;) after the commandments and doctrines of men? Which things have indeed a shew of wisdom in will-worship, and humility, and neglecting of the body; not in any honour to the satisfying of the flesh (Col 2:20–23).

Mortify therefore your members which are upon the earth; fornication, uncleanness, inordinate affection, evil concupiscence, and covetousness, which is idolatry (Col 3:5).

For this is the will of God, *even* your sanctification, that ye should abstain from fornication (1 Thess 4:3).

Abstain from all appearance of evil (1 Thess 5:22).

Now the Spirit speaketh expressly, that in the latter times some shall depart from the faith, giving heed to seducing spirits, and doctrines of devils; speaking lies in hypocrisy; having their conscience seared with a hot iron; forbidding to marry, *and commanding* to abstain from meats, which God hath created to be received with thanksgiving of them which believe and know the truth (1 Tim 4:1–3).

Dearly beloved, I beseech *you* as strangers and pilgrims, abstain from fleshly lusts, which war against the soul (1 Pet 2:11).

Biblical Examples: Deut 29:6; Judg 16:17; 2 Sam 1:12; Jer 35:6–14; Dan 1:8, 12; Matt 11:18; Luke 1:15; 7:33.

Further References: Lev 11:1–47; Judg 13:4, 13, 14; Prov 31:4, Jer 35:6–8; Ezek 44:21.

ADDICTION (See Drugs)

ADOPTION (See Orphans)

ADULTERY (See also Sex and Sexuality)
Thou shalt not commit adultery (Exod 20:14).

Thou shalt not covet thy neighbour's house, thou shalt not covet thy neighbour's wife, nor his manservant, nor his maidservant, nor his ox, nor his ass, nor any thing that *is* thy neighbour's (Exod. 20:17).

Moreover thou shalt not lie carnally with thy neighbour's wife, to defile thyself with her (Lev 18:20).

If a man be found lying with a woman married to an husband, then they shall both of them die, *both* the man that lay with the woman, and the woman: so shalt thou put away evil from Israel (Deut 22:22).

The eye also of the adulterer waiteth for the twilight, saying, No eye shall see me: and disguiseth *his* face. In the dark they dig through houses, *which* they had marked for themselves in the daytime: they know not the light. For the morning *is* to them even as the shadow of death: if *one* know *them, they are in* the terrors of the shadow of death (Job 24:15–17).

I made a covenant with mine eyes; why then should I think upon a maid? (Job 3:1).

If mine heart have been deceived by a woman, or *if* I have laid wait at my neighbour's door; *then* let my wife grind unto another, and let others bow down upon her. For this *is* an heinous crime; yea, it *is* an iniquity *to be punished by* the judges. For it *is* a fire *that* consumeth to destruction, and would root out all mine increase (Job 31:9–12).

For the commandment *is* a lamp; and the law *is* light; and reproofs of instruction *are* the way of life: to keep thee from the evil woman, from the flattery of the tongue of a strange woman. Lust not after her beauty in thine heart; neither let her take thee with her eyelids. For by means of a whorish woman *a man is brought* to a piece of bread: and the adulteress will hunt for the precious life. Can a man take fire in his bosom, and his clothes not be burned? Can one go upon hot coals, and his feet not be burned? So he that goeth in to his neighbour's wife; whosoever toucheth her shall not be innocent. *Men* do not despise a thief, if he steal to satisfy his soul when he is hungry; but *if* he be found, he shall restore sevenfold; he shall give all the substance of his house. *But* whoso committeth adultery with a woman lacketh understanding: he *that* doeth it destroyeth his own soul. A wound and dishonour shall he get; and his reproach shall not be wiped away (Prov 6:23–33).

Say unto wisdom, Thou *art* my sister; and call understanding *thy* kinswoman: that they may keep thee from the strange woman, from the stranger *which* flattereth with her words.

For at the window of my house I looked through my casement, and beheld among the simple ones, I discerned among the youths, a young man void of understanding, passing through the street near her corner; and he went the way to her house, in the twilight, in the evening, in the black and dark night: and, behold, there met him a woman *with* the attire of an harlot, and subtil of heart. (She *is* loud and stubborn; her feet abide not in her house: now *is she* without, now in the streets, and lieth in wait at every corner.) So she caught him, and kissed him, *and* with an impudent face said unto him, I *have* peace offerings with me; this day have I payed my vows. Therefore came I forth to meet thee, diligently to seek thy face, and I have found thee. I have decked my bed with coverings of tapestry, with carved *works,* with fine linen of Egypt. I have perfumed my bed with myrrh, aloes, and cinnamon. Come, let us take our fill of love until the morning: let us solace ourselves with loves. For the goodman *is* not at home, he is gone a long journey: he hath taken a bag of money with him, *and* will come home at the day appointed. With her much fair speech she caused him to yield, with the flattering of her lips she forced him. He goeth after her straightway, as an ox goeth to the slaughter, or as a fool to the correction of the stocks; till a dart strike through his liver; as a bird hasteth to the snare, and knoweth not that it *is* for his life (Prov 7:4–23).

Such *is* the way of an adulterous woman; she eateth, and wipeth her mouth, and saith, I have done no wickedness (Prov 30:20).

Ye have heard that it was said by them of old time, Thou shalt not commit adultery: but I say unto you, That whosoever looketh on a woman to lust after her hath committed adultery with her already in his heart. And if thy right eye offend thee, pluck it out, and cast *it* from thee: for it is profitable for thee that one of thy members should perish, and not *that* thy whole body should be cast into hell. And if thy right hand offend thee, cut it off, and cast *it* from thee: for it is profitable for thee that one of thy members should perish, and not *that* thy whole body should be cast into hell. It hath been said, Whosoever shall put away his wife, let him give her a writing of divorcement: but I say unto you, That whosoever shall put away his wife, saving for the cause of fornication, causeth her to commit adultery: and whosoever shall marry her that is divorced committeth adultery (Matt 5:27–32).

And I say unto you, Whosoever shall put away his wife, except *it be* for fornication, and shall marry another, committeth adultery: and whoso marrieth her which is put away doth commit adultery (Matt 19:9).

But from the beginning of the creation God made them male and female. For this cause shall a man leave his father and mother, and cleave to his wife; and they twain shall be one flesh: so then they are no more twain, but one flesh. What therefore God hath joined together, let not man put asunder. And in the house his disciples asked him again of the same *matter.* And he saith unto them, Whosoever shall put away his wife, and marry another, committeth adultery against her. And if a woman shall put away her husband, and be married to another, she committeth adultery (Mark 10:6–12).

For the woman which hath an husband is bound by the law to *her* husband so long as he liveth; but if the husband be dead, she is loosed from the law of *her* husband. So then if, while *her* husband liveth, she be married to another man, she shall be called an adulteress: but if her husband be dead, she is free from that law; so that she is no adulteress, though she be married to another man (Rom 7:2, 3).

Biblical Examples: Gen 19:5–8, 31–38; 20:3; 38:24; Judg 19:2, 22–25; 1 Sam 2:22; 2 Sam 11:1–5; 13:1–20; 16:22; Matt 14:3; John 8:4–11; 1 Cor 5:1–5; Eph 4:17–19; 1 Peter 4:3

Further References: Exod 22:16, 17; Lev 19:20–29; 20:10–12; Num 5:11–30; Deut 22:13–29; 23:17; 27:20–23; Prov 9:13–18; 22:14; 23:27, 28; 29:3; Jer 3:1; 5:7; 7:9, 10; 29:22, 23; Ezek 16:38–41; 18:5, 6, 9; 23:45–48; Hos 4:1, 2, 11; Matt 15:19; Mark 7:21; 10:19; Rom 1:28, 29, 32; 1 Cor 5:1–13; 6:9–18; 10:8; 12:21; Gal 5:19, 21; Eph 4:17–20; 1 Tim 1:9, 10; Heb 13:4; 2 Peter 2:9, 10, 14; Jude 7; Rev 3:20–22; 9:21; 21:8; 22:15.

ADVERTISING (See Daily Work; Honesty)

AFFLUENCE (See Economics; Extravagance; Materialism)

AGING

Honour thy father and thy mother: that thy days may be long upon the land which the LORD thy God giveth thee (Exod 20:12).

Thou shalt rise up before the hoary head, and honour the face of the old man, and fear thy God: I *am* the LORD (Lev 19:32).

Thou shalt keep therefore his statutes, and his commandments, which I command thee this day, that it may go well with thee, and with thy children after thee, and that thou mayest prolong *thy* days upon the earth, which the LORD thy God giveth thee, for ever (Deut 4:40).

Ye shall walk in all the ways which the LORD your God hath commanded you, that ye may live, and *that it may be* well with you, and *that* ye may prolong *your* days in the land which ye shall possess (Deut 5:33).

The LORD shall bring a nation against thee from far, from the end of the earth, *as swift* as the eagle flieth; a nation whose tongue thou shalt not understand; a nation of fierce countenance, which shall not regard the person of the old, nor shew favour to the young (Deut 28:49, 50).

Remember the days of old, consider the years of many generations: ask thy father, and he will shew thee; thy elders, and they will tell thee (Deut 32:7).

And the women said unto Naomi, Blessed *be* the LORD, which hath not left thee this day without a kinsman, that his name may be famous in Israel. And he shall be unto thee a restorer of *thy* life, and a nourisher of thine old age: for thy daughter in law, which loveth thee, which is better to thee than seven sons, hath borne him (Ruth 4:14, 15).

With the ancient *is* wisdom; and in length of days understanding (Job 12:12).

Cast me not off in the time of old age; forsake me not when my strength faileth (Ps 71:9).

O God, thou hast taught me from my youth: and hitherto have I declared thy wondrous works. Now also when I am old and greyheaded, O God, forsake me not; until I have shewed thy strength unto *this* generation, *and* thy power to every one *that* is to come (Ps 71:17, 18).

With long life will I satisfy him, and shew him my salvation (Ps 91:16).

The righteous shall flourish like the palm tree: he shall grow like a cedar in Lebanon. Those that be planted in the house of the LORD shall flourish in the courts of our God. They shall still bring forth fruit in old age; they shall be fat and flourishing; to shew that the LORD *is* upright: *he is* my rock, and *there is* no unrighteousness in him (Ps 92:12–15).

My son, forget not my law; but let thine heart keep my commandments; for length of days, and long life, and peace, shall they add to thee (Prov 3:1, 2).

Happy *is* the man *that* findeth wisdom, and the man *that* getteth understanding. For the merchandise of it *is* better than the merchandise of silver, and the gain thereof than fine gold. She *is* more precious than rubies: and all the things thou canst desire are not to be compared unto her. Length of days *is* in her right hand; *and* in her left hand riches and honour (Prov 3:13–16).

For by me thy days shall be multiplied, and the years of thy life shall be increased (Prov 9:11).

The fear of the LORD prolongeth days: but the years of the wicked shall be shortened (Prov 10:27).

The hoary head *is* a crown of glory, *if* it be found in the way of righteousness (Prov 16:31).

The glory of young men *is* their strength: and the beauty of old men *is* the grey head (Prov 20:29).

Hearken unto thy father that begat thee, and despise not thy mother when she is old (Prov 23:22).

Hearken unto me, O house of Jacob, and all the remnant of the house of Israel, which are borne *by me* from the belly, which are carried from the womb: and *even* to *your* old age I *am* he; and *even* to hoar hairs will I carry *you:* I have made, and I will bear; even I will carry, and will deliver *you* (Isa 46:3, 4).

I was wroth with my people, I have polluted mine inheritance, and given them into thine hand: thou didst shew them no mercy; upon the ancient hast thou very heavily laid thy yoke (Isa 47:6).

The anger of the LORD hath divided them; he will no more regard them: they respected not the persons of the priests, they favoured not the elders (Lam 4:16).

Then came to Jesus scribes and Pharisees, which were of Jerusalem, saying, Why do thy disciples transgress the tradition of the elders? for they wash not their hands when they eat bread. But he answered and said unto them, Why do ye also transgress the commandment of God by your tradition? For God commanded, saying, Honour thy father and mother: and, He that curseth father or mother, let him die the death. But ye say, Whosoever shall say to *his* father or *his* mother, *It is* a gift, by whatsoever thou mightest be profited by me; and honour not his father or his mother, *he shall be free.* Thus have ye made the commandment of God of none effect by your tradition. *Ye* hypocrites, well did Esaias prophesy of you, saying, This people draweth nigh unto me with their mouth, and honoureth me with *their* lips; but their heart is far from me. But in vain they do worship me, teaching *for* doctrines the commandments of men (Matt 15:1–9).

Verily, verily, I say unto thee, When thou wast young, thou girdedst thyself, and walkedst whither thou wouldest: but when thou shalt be old, thou shalt stretch forth thy hands, and another shall gird thee, and carry *thee* whither thou wouldest not (John 21:18).

Honour thy father and mother; which is the first commandment with promise; that it may be well with thee, and thou mayest live long on the earth (Eph 6:2, 3).

Rebuke not an elder, but entreat *him* as a father; *and* the younger men as brethren; the elder women as mothers; the younger as sisters, with all purity (1 Tim 5:1, 2).

But if any provide not for his own, and specially for those of his own house, he hath denied the faith, and is worse than an infidel (1 Tim 5:8).

Against an elder receive not an accusation, but before two or three witnesses (1 Tim 5:19).

That the aged men be sober, grave, temperate, sound in faith, in charity, in patience (Titus 2:2).

Likewise, ye younger, submit yourselves unto the elder. Yea, all *of you* be subject one to another, and be clothed with humility: for God resisteth the proud, and giveth grace to the humble (1 Peter 5:5).

Biblical Examples: Gen 17:1, 2; 18:11–13; 25:8; 27;1, 2; 47:9; Deut 34:7; Judg 8:32; 2 Sam 19:31–40; 1 Kings 12:6–13; 1 Chron 29:26–28; 2 Chron 10:6–13; Ps 71:17–19; Luke 2:36, 37; Philem 9.

Further References: Gen 15:15; Exod 3:16–18; 4:29; Lev 19:32; Deut 28:49, 50; 1 Kings 3:14; 1 Chron 29:28; Job 5:26; 15:7–11; 32:4–10; 42:16, 17; Ps 148:12, 13; Prov 10:27; 17:6; Eccl 12:1–7; Isa 3:5; 65:17–20; Rev 4:4; 5:14.

AGGRESSION (See Revenge; Vengeance; Violence)

ALCOHOL AND ALCOHOLISM (See also Abstinence; Drugs; Drunkenness; Wine)

Do not drink wine nor strong drink, thou, nor thy sons with thee, when ye go into the tabernacle of the congregation, lest ye die: *it shall be* a statute for ever throughout your generations (Lev 10:9).

Speak unto the children of Israel, and say unto them, When either man or woman shall separate *themselves* to vow a vow of a Nazarite, to separate *themselves* unto the LORD: he shall separate *himself* from wine and strong drink, and shall drink no vinegar of wine, or vinegar of strong drink, neither shall he drink any liquor of grapes, nor eat moist grapes, or dried. All the days of his separation shall he eat nothing that is made of the vine tree, from the kernels even to the husk (Num 6:2–4).

Wine *is* a mocker, strong drink *is* raging: and whosoever is deceived thereby is not wise (Prov 20:1).

Hear thou, my son, and be wise, and guide thine heart in the way. Be not among winebibbers; among riotous eaters of flesh: for the drunkard and the glutton shall come to poverty: and drowsiness shall clothe *a man* with rags (Prov 23:19–21).

Who hath woe? who hath sorrow? who hath contentions? who hath babbling? who hath wounds without cause? who hath redness of eyes? They that tarry long at the wine; they that go to seek mixed wine. Look not thou upon the wine when it is red, when it giveth his colour in the cup, *when* it moveth itself aright (Prov 23:29–31).

I sought in mine heart to give myself unto wine, yet acquainting mine heart with wisdom; and to lay hold on folly, till I might see what *was* that good for the sons of men, which they should do under the heaven all the days of their life (Eccl 2:3).

Woe unto them that rise up early in the morning, *that* they may follow strong drink; that continue until night, *till* wine inflame them (Isa 5:11).

Woe unto *them that are* mighty to drink wine, and men of strength to mingle strong drink: which justify the wicked for reward, and take away the righteousness of the righteous from him (Isa 5:22, 23).

That the aged men be sober, grave, temperate, sound in faith, in charity, in patience. The aged women likewise, that *they be* in behaviour as becometh holiness, not false accusers, not given to much wine, teachers of good things; that they may teach the young women to be sober, to love their husbands, to love their children, *to be* discreet, chaste, keepers at home, good, obedient to their own husbands, that the word of God be not blasphemed. Young men likewise exhort to be sober minded (Titus 2:2–6).

Biblical Examples: Jer 35:2–14; Matt 26:27–29; Luke 1:13–15; John 2:1–10.

Further References: Judg 13:12–14; Isa 28:1–8; 56:12; Ezek 44:21; Hos 4:11; Hab 2:15, 16.

ALLEGIANCE (See Citizenship; Government; Patriotism)

ALMS AND ALMSGIVING (See Charity)

ALTRUISM (See also Charity; Kindness; Ministry; Unselfishness)

But it shall not be so among you: but whosoever will be great among you, let him be your minister (Matt 20:26).

And he sat down, and called the twelve, and saith unto them, If any man desire to be first, *the same* shall be last of all, and servant of all (Mark 9:35).

So after he had washed their feet, and had taken his garments, and was set down again, he said unto them, Know ye what I have done to you? Ye call me Master and Lord: and ye say well; for *so* I am. If I then, *your* Lord and Master, have washed your feet; ye also ought to wash one another's feet. For I have given you an example, that you should do as I have done to you (John 13:12–15).

And now, brethren, I commend you to God, and to the word of his grace, which is able to build you up, and to give you an inheritance among all them which are sanctified. I have coveted no man's silver, or gold, or apparel. Yea, ye yourselves know, that these hands have ministered unto my necessities, and to them that were with me. I have shewed you all things, how that so labouring ye ought to support the weak, and to remember the words of the Lord Jesus, how he said, It is more blessed to give than to receive (Acts 20:32–35).

We then that are strong ought to bear the infirmities of the weak, and not to please ourselves. Let every one of us please *his* neighbour for *his* good to edification. For even Christ pleased not himself; but, as it is written, The reproaches of them that reproached thee fell on me (Rom 15:1–3).

What is my reward then? *Verily* that, when I preach the gospel, I may make the gospel of Christ without charge, that I abuse not my power in the gospel. For though I be free from all *men,* yet have I made myself servant unto all, that I might gain the more. And unto the Jews I became as a Jew, that I might gain the Jews; to them that are under the law, as under the law, that I might gain them that are under the law; to them that are without law, as without law, (being not without law to God, but under the law to Christ,) that I might gain them that are without law. To the weak became I as weak, that I might gain the weak: I am made all things to all *men,* that I might by all means save some (1 Cor 9:18–22).

Let no man seek his own, but every man another's *wealth.* Whatsoever is sold in the shambles, *that* eat, asking no question for conscience sake: for the earth *is* the Lord's, and the fulness thereof. If any of them that believe not bid you *to a feast,* and ye be disposed to go; whatsoever is set before you, eat, asking no question for conscience sake. But if any man say unto you, This is offered in sacrifice unto idols, eat not for his sake that shewed it, and for conscience sake: for the earth *is* the

Lord's, and the fulness thereof: conscience, I say, not thine own, but of the other: for why is my liberty judged of another *man's* conscience? For if I by grace be a partaker, why am I evil spoken of for that for which I give thanks? Whether therefore ye eat, or drink, or whatsoever ye do, do all to the glory of God. Give none offence, neither to the Jews, nor to the Gentiles, nor to the church of God: even as I please all *men* in all *things,* not seeking mine own profit, but the *profit* of many, that they may be saved (1 Cor 10:24–33).

As we have therefore opportunity, let us do good unto all *men,* especially unto them who are of the household of faith (Gal 6:10).

Let nothing *be done* through strife or vainglory; but in lowliness of mind let each esteem other better than themselves. Look not every man on his own things, but every man also on the things of others. Let this mind be in you, which was also in Christ Jesus: who, being in the form of God, thought it not robbery to be equal with God: but made himself of no reputation, and took upon him the form of a servant, and was made in the likeness of men: and being found in fashion as a man, he humbled himself, and became obedient unto death, even the death of the cross (Phil 2:3–8).

Biblical Examples: John 19:38–41; Acts 2:44–47; 2 Cor 8:1–9.

Further References: Mark 10:43–45; Luke 22:26, 27; 2 Cor 4:5; 6:10.

AMBITION (See also Pride)

Nevertheless man *being* in honour abideth not: he is like the beasts *that* perish. This their way *is* their folly: yet their posterity approve their sayings. Selah (Ps 49:12, 13).

Yea also, because he transgresseth by wine, *he is* a proud man, neither keepeth at home, who enlargeth his desire as hell, and *is* as death, and cannot be satisfied, but gathereth unto him all nations, and heapeth unto him all people: shall not all these take up a parable against him, and a taunting proverb against him, and say, Woe to him that increaseth *that which is* not his! how long? and to him that ladeth himself with thick clay! Shall they not rise up suddenly that shall bite thee, and awake that shall vex thee, and thou shalt be for booties unto them? Because thou hast spoiled many nations, all the remnant of the people shall spoil thee; because of men's blood, and *for* the violence of the land, of the city, and of all that dwell therein. Woe to him that coveteth an evil covetousness to his house, that he may set his nest on high, that he may be delivered from the power of evil! (Hab 2:5–9).

Again, the devil taketh him up into an exceeding high mountain, and sheweth him all the kingdoms of the world, and the glory of them; and saith unto him, All these things will I give thee, if thou wilt fall down and worship me. Then saith Jesus unto him, Get thee hence, Satan: for it is written, Thou shalt worship the Lord thy God, and him only shalt thou serve (Matt 4:8–10).

For what is a man profited, if he shall gain the whole world, and lose his own soul? or what shall a man give in exchange for his soul? (Matt 16:26).

But all their works they do for to be seen of men: they make broad their phylacteries, and enlarge the borders of their garments, and love the uppermost rooms at feasts, and the chief seats in the synagogues, and greetings in the markets, and to be called of men, Rabbi, Rabbi. But be not ye called Rabbi: for one is your Master, *even* Christ; and all ye are brethren. And call no *man* your father upon the earth: for one is your Father, which is in heaven. Neither be ye called masters: for one is your Master, *even* Christ. But he that is greatest among you shall be your servant. And whosoever shall exalt himself shall be abased; and he that shall humble himself shall be exalted (Matt 23:5–12).

And he came to Capernaum: and being in the house he asked them, What was it that ye disputed among yourselves by the way? But they held their peace: for by the way they had disputed among themselves, who *should be* the greatest. And he sat down, and called the twelve, and saith unto them, If any man desire to be first, *the same* shall be last of all, and servant of all. And he took a child, and set him in the midst of them: and when he had taken him in his arms, he said unto them, Whosoever shall receive one of such children in my name, receiveth me: and whosoever shall receive me, receiveth not me, but him that sent me (Mark 9:33–37).

And James and John, the sons of Zebedee, come unto him, saying, Master, we would that thou shouldest do for us whatsoever we shall desire. And he said unto them, What would ye that I should do for you? They said unto him, Grant unto us that we may sit, one on thy right hand, and the other on thy left hand, in thy glory. But Jesus said unto them, Ye know not what ye ask: can ye drink of the cup that I drink of? and be baptized with the baptism that I am baptized with? And they said unto him, We can. And Jesus said unto them, Ye shall indeed drink of the cup that I drink of; and with the baptism that I am baptized withal shall ye be baptized: but to sit on my right hand and on my left hand is not mine to give; but *it shall be given to them* for whom it is prepared. And when the ten heard *it*, they began to be much displeased with James and John. But Jesus called them *to him*, and saith unto them, Ye know that they which are accounted to rule over the Gentiles exercise lordship over them; and their great ones exercise authority upon them. But so shall it not be among you: but whosoever will be great among you, shall be your minister: and whosoever of you will be the chiefest, shall be servant of all. For even the Son of man came not to be ministered unto, but to minister, and to give his life a ransom for many (Mark 10:35–45).

From whence *come* wars and fightings among you? *come they* not hence, *even* of your lusts that war in your members? Ye lust, and have not: ye kill, and desire to have, and cannot obtain: ye fight and war, yet ye have not, because ye ask not (James 4:1, 2).

For all that *is* in the world, the lust of the flesh, and the lust of the eyes, and the pride of life, is not of the Father, but is of the world (1 John 2:16).

Biblical Examples: Gen. 3:5, 6; 11:4; Num 12:2–10; 2 Sam 15:1–13; 2 Kings 19:23; Esth 5:9–13; 6:6–9.

Further References: Isa 5:8; Matt 8:1;

Mark 12:38, 39; Luke 4:5–8; 9:25, 46; 11:43; 22:26; 1 Tim 3:1.

AMNESTY (See Forgiveness)

AMUSEMENTS (See Leisure; Pleasure, Lover of)

ANARCHY (See also Revolution; Selfishness)

In those days *there was* no king in Israel: every man did *that which was* right in his own eyes (Judg 21:25).

And I will give children *to be* their princes, and babes shall rule over them. And the people shall be oppressed, every one by another, and every one by his neighbour: the child shall behave himself proudly against the ancient, and the base against the honourable. When a man shall take hold of his brother of the house of his father, *saying,* Thou hast clothing, be thou our ruler, and *let* this ruin *be* under thy hand: in that day shall he swear, saying, I will not be an healer; for in my house *is* neither bread nor clothing: make me not a ruler of the people (Isa 3:4–7).

For, brethren, ye have been called unto liberty; only *use* not liberty for an occasion to the flesh, but by love serve one another. For all the law is fulfilled in one word, *even* in this; Thou shalt love thy neighbour as thyself. But if ye bite and devour one another, take heed that ye be not consumed one of another (Gal. 5:13–15).

But chiefly them that walk after the flesh in the lust of uncleanness, and despise government. Presumptuous *are they,* self-willed, they are not afraid to speak evil of dignities. Whereas angels, which are greater in power and might, bring not railing accusation against them before the Lord. But these, as natural brute beasts, made to be taken and destroyed, speak evil of the things that they understand not; and shall utterly perish in their own corruption; and shall receive the reward of unrighteousness, *as* they that count in pleasure to riot in the day time. Spots *they are* and blemishes, sporting themselves with their own deceivings while they feast with you; having eyes full of adultery, and that cannot cease from sin; beguiling unstable souls: an heart they

have exercised with covetous practices; cursed children: which have forsaken the right way, and are gone astray, following the way of Balaam *the son* of Bosor, who loved the wages of unrighteousness; but was rebuked for his iniquity: the dumb ass speaking with man's voice forbad the madness of the prophet. These are wells without water, clouds that are carried with a tempest; to whom the mist of darkness is reserved for ever. For when they speak great swelling *words* of vanity, they allure through the lusts of the flesh, *through much* wantonness, those that were clean escaped from them who live in error. While they promise them liberty, they themselves are the servants of corruption: for of whom a man is overcome, of the same is he brought in bondage (2 Peter 2:10–19).

Likewise also these *filthy* dreamers defile the flesh, despise dominion, and speak evil of dignities. Yet Michael the archangel, when contending with the devil he disputed about the body of Moses, durst not bring against him a railing accusation, but said, The Lord rebuke thee. But these speak evil of those things which they know not: but what they know naturally, as brute beasts, in those things they corrupt themselves. Woe unto them! for they have gone in the way of Cain, and ran greedily after the error of Balaam for reward, and perished in the gainsaying of Core. These are spots in your feasts of charity, when they feast with you, feeding themselves without fear: clouds *they are* without water, carried about of winds; trees whose fruit withereth, without fruit, twice dead, plucked up by the roots; raging waves of the sea, foaming out their own shame; wandering stars, to whom is reserved the blackness of darkness for ever (Jude 8–13).

ANGER (See also Hatred; Revenge; Vengeance; Violence)

And the LORD God of their fathers sent to them by his messengers, rising up betimes, and sending; because he had compassion on his people, and on his dwelling place: but they mocked the messengers of God, and despised his words, and misused his prophets, until the wrath of the LORD arose against his people, till *there was* no remedy (2 Chron 36:15, 16).

For wrath killeth the foolish man, and envy slayeth the silly one (Job 5:2).

But ye should say, Why persecute we him, seeing the root of the matter is found in me? Be ye afraid of the sword: for wrath *bringeth* the punishments of the sword, that ye may know *there is* a judgment (Job 19:28, 29).

Cease from anger, and forsake wrath: fret not thyself in any wise to do evil (Ps 37:8).

A fool's wrath is presently known: but a prudent *man* covereth shame (Prov 12:16).

He *that is* soon angry dealeth foolishly: and a man of wicked devices is hated (Prov 14:17).

He *that is* slow to wrath *is* of great understanding: but *he that is* hasty of spirit exalteth folly (Prov 14:29).

A soft answer turneth away wrath: but grievous words stir up anger (Prov 15:1).

A wrathful man stirreth up strife: but *he that is* slow to anger appeaseth strife (Prov 15:18).

He *that is* slow to anger *is* better than the mighty; and he that ruleth his spirit than he that taketh a city (Prov 16:32).

Make no friendship with an angry man; and with a furious man thou shalt not go: lest thou learn his ways, and get a snare to thy soul (Prov 22:24, 25).

If thou hast done foolishly in lifting up thyself, or if thou hast thought evil, *lay* thine hand upon thy mouth. Surely the churning of milk bringeth forth butter, and the wringing of the nose bringeth forth blood: so the forcing of wrath bringeth forth strife (Prov 30:32, 33).

Be not hasty in thy spirit to be angry: for anger resteth in the bosom of fools (Eccl 7:9).

But I say unto you, That whosoever is angry with his brother without a cause shall be in danger of the judgment: and whosoever shall say to his brother, Raca, shall be in danger of the council: but whosoever shall say, Thou fool, shall be in danger of hell fire (Matt 5:22).

And when he had looked round about on them with anger, being grieved for the hardness of their hearts, he saith unto the man, Stretch forth thine hand. And he stretched *it* out: and his hand was restored whole as the other (Mark 3:5).

But when Jesus saw *it,* he was much displeased, and said unto them, Suffer the little children to come unto me, and forbid them not: for of such is the kingdom of God (Mark 10:14).

And the Jews' passover was at hand, and Jesus went up to Jerusalem, and found in the temple those that sold oxen and sheep and doves, and the changers of money sitting: and when he had made a scourge of small cords, he drove them all out of the temple, and the sheep, and the oxen; and poured out the changers' money, and overthrew the tables; and said unto them that sold doves, Take these things hence; make not my Father's house an house of merchandise. And his disciples remembered that it was written, The zeal of thine house hath eaten me up (John 2:13–17).

Be ye angry, and sin not: let not the sun go down upon your wrath (Eph 4:26).

But now ye also put off all these; anger, wrath, malice, blasphemy, filthy communication out of your mouth (Col 3:8).

I will therefore that men pray every where, lifting up holy hands, without wrath and doubting (1 Tim 2:8).

Wherefore, my beloved brethren, let every man be swift to hear, slow to speak, slow to wrath: for the wrath of man worketh not the righteousness of God (James 1:19, 20).

Biblical Examples: Gen 4:5, 6; 31:36; Exod 11:8; Num 20:1–11; 1 Sam 20:30; 2 Kings 5:11; Mark 3:5; Luke 4:28; Acts 5:17; 7:54.

Further References: Prov 19:19; 25:28; 29:8; Rom 12:19; Gal 5:20; Eph 6:4; Col 3:21.

ANXIETY (See Mental Health)

APATHY (See Idleness)

ARROGANCE (See Pride)

ASCETICISM (See Abstinence; Celibacy; Fasting; Self-control; Self-denial; Temperance)

ASSASSINATION (See Homicide; Violence)

ASSAULT AND BATTERY (See Violence)

ASTROLOGY

And lest thou lift up thine eyes unto heaven, and when thou seest the sun, and the moon, and the stars, *even* all the host of heaven, shouldest be driven to worship them, and serve them, which the LORD thy God hath divided unto all nations under the whole heaven (Deut 4:19).

When thou art come into the land which the LORD thy God giveth thee, thou shalt not learn to do after the abominations of those nations. There shall not be found among you *any one* that maketh his son or his daughter to pass through the fire, *or* that useth divination, *or* an observer of times, or an enchanter, or a witch, or a charmer, or a consulter with familiar spirits, or a wizard, or a necromancer. For all that do these things *are* an abomination unto the LORD: and because of these abominations the LORD thy God doth drive them out from before thee. Thou shalt be perfect with the LORD thy God. For these nations, which thou shalt possess, hearkened unto observers of times, and unto diviners: but as for thee, the LORD thy God hath not suffered thee so *to do* (Deut 18:9–14).

Thou art wearied in the multitude of thy counsels. Let now the astrologers, the stargazers, the monthly prognosticators, stand up, and save thee from *these things* that shall come upon thee (Isa 47:13).

Daniel answered in the presence of the king, and said, The secret which the king hath demanded cannot the wise *men*, the astrologers, the magicians, the soothsayers, shew unto the king (Dan 2:27).

Then God turned, and gave them up to worship the host of heaven; as it is written in the book of the prophets, O ye house of Israel, have ye offered to me slain beasts and sacrifices *by the space of* forty years in the wilderness? Yea, ye took up the tabernacle of Moloch, and the star of your god Remphan, figures which ye made to worship them: and I will carry you away beyond Babylon (Acts 7:42, 43).

Biblical Examples: Dan 4:7; Matt 2:1, 2.

Further References: Isa 47:13; Jer 10:1, 2; Dan 1:20.

ASYLUM (See Crime and Punishment)

AUTHORITY (See also Citizenship; Decision-making; Government)

And God said, Let us make man in our image, after our likeness: and let them have dominion over the fish of the sea, and over the fowl of the air, and over the cattle, and over all the earth, and over every creeping thing that creepeth upon the earth. So God created man in his *own* image, in the image of God created he him; male and female created he them. And God blessed them, and God said unto them, Be fruitful, and multiply, and replenish the earth, and subdue it: and have dominion over the fish of the sea, and over the fowl of the air, and over every living thing that moveth upon the earth (Gen 1:26–28).

When I consider thy heavens, the work of thy fingers, the moon and the stars, which thou hast ordained; what is man, that thou art mindful of him? and the son of man, that thou visitest him? For thou hast made him a little lower than the angels, and hast crowned him with glory and honour. Thou madest him to have dominion over the works of thy hands; thou hast put all *things* under his feet: all sheep and oxen, yea, and the beasts of the field; the fowl of the air, and the fish of the sea, *and whatsoever* passeth through the paths of the seas (Ps 8:3–8).

And when he was come into the temple, the chief priests and the elders of the people came unto him as he was teaching, and said, By what authority doest thou these things? and who gave thee this authority? And Jesus answered and said unto them, I also will ask you one thing, which if ye tell me, I in like wise will tell you by what authority I do these things. The baptism of John, whence was it? from heaven, or of men? And they reasoned with themselves, saying, If we shall say, From heaven; he will say unto us, Why did ye not then believe him? But if we shall say, Of men; we fear the people; for all hold John as a prophet. And they answered Jesus, and said, We cannot tell.

And he said unto them, Neither tell I you by what authority I do these things (Matt 21:23–27).

And Jesus came and spake unto them, saying, All power is given unto me in heaven and in earth (Matt 28:18).

And they were astonished at his doctrine: for he taught them as one that had authority, and not as the scribes. And there was in their synagogue a man with an unclean spirit; and he cried out, saying, Let *us* alone; what have we to do with thee, thou Jesus of Nazareth? art thou come to destroy us? I know thee who thou art, the Holy One of God. And Jesus rebuked him, saying, Hold thy peace, and come out of him. And when the unclean spirit had torn him, and cried with a loud voice, he came out of him. And they were all amazed, insomuch that they questioned among themselves, saying, What thing is this? what new doctrine *is* this? for with authority commandeth he even the unclean spirits, and they do obey him (Mark 1:22–27).

Jesus answered them, and said, My doctrine is not mine, but his that sent me. If any man will do his will, he shall know of the doctrine, whether it be of God, or *whether* I speak of myself. He that speaketh of himself seeketh his own glory: but he that seeketh his glory that sent him, the same is true, and no unrighteousness is in him (John 7:16–18).

Then came the officers to the chief priests and Pharisees; and they said unto them, Why have ye not brought him? The officers answered, Never man spake like this man (John 7:45, 46).

Jesus answered, Thou couldest have no power *at all* against me, except it were given thee from above: therefore he that delivered me unto thee hath the greater sin (John 19:11).

But Peter and John answered and said unto them, Whether it be right in the sight of God to hearken unto you more than unto God, judge ye. For we cannot but speak the things which we have seen and heard. So when they had further threatened them, they let them go, finding nothing how they might punish them, because of the people: for all *men* glorified God for that which was done. For the man was

above forty years old, on whom this miracle of healing was shewed.

And being let go, they went to their own company, and reported all that the chief priests and elders had said unto them. And when they heard that, they lifted up their voice to God with one accord, and said, Lord, thou *art* God, which hast made heaven, and earth, and the sea, and all that in them is: who by the mouth of thy servant David hast said, Why did the heathen rage, and the people imagine vain things? The kings of the earth stood up, and the rulers were gathered together against the Lord, and against his Christ. For of a truth against thy holy child Jesus, whom thou hast anointed, both Herod, and Pontius Pilate, with the Gentiles, and the people of Israel, were gathered together, for to do whatsoever thy hand and thy counsel determined before to be done. And now, Lord, behold their threatenings: and grant unto thy servants, that with all boldness they may speak thy word, by stretching forth thine hand to heal; and that signs and wonders may be done by the name of thy holy child Jesus (Acts 4:19–30).

Then Peter and the *other* apostles answered and said, We ought to obey God rather than men (Acts 5:29).

For when the Gentiles, which have not the law, do by nature the things contained in the law, these, having not the law, are a law unto themselves: which shew the work of the law written in their hearts, their conscience also bearing witness, and *their* thoughts the mean while accusing or else excusing one another;) In the day when God shall judge the secrets of men by Jesus Christ according to my gospel (Rom 2:14–16).

Let every soul be subject unto the higher powers. For there is no power but of God: the powers that be are ordained of God. Whosoever therefore resisteth the power, resisteth the ordinance of God: and they that resist shall receive to themselves damnation. For rulers are not a terror to good works, but to the evil. Wilt thou then not be afraid of the power? do that which is good, and thou shalt have praise of the same: for he is the minister of God to thee for good. But if thou do that which is evil, be afraid; for he beareth not the sword in vain: for he is the minister of God, a revenger to *execute* wrath upon him that doeth evil. Wherefore *ye* must needs be subject, not only for wrath, but also for conscience sake. For for this cause pay ye tribute also: for they are God's ministers, attending continually upon this very thing. Render therefore to all their dues: tribute to whom tribute *is due;* custom to whom custom; fear to whom fear; honour to whom honour (Rom 13:1–7).

Submit yourselves to every ordinance of man for the Lord's sake: whether it be to the king, as supreme; or unto governors, as unto them that are sent by him for the punishment of evildoers, and for the praise of them that do well. For so is the will of God, that with well-doing ye may put to silence the ignorance of foolish men. As free, and not using *your* liberty for a cloak of maliciousness, but as the servants of God. Honour all *men.* Love the brotherhood. Fear God. Honour the king. Servants, *be* subject to *your* masters with all fear; not only to the good and gentle, but also to the froward. For this *is* thankworthy, if a man for conscience toward God endure grief, suffering wrongfully. For what glory *is it,* if, when ye be buffeted for your faults, ye shall take it patiently? but if, when ye do well, and suffer *for it,* ye take it patiently, this *is* acceptable with God. For even hereunto were ye called: because Christ also suffered for us, leaving us an example, that ye should follow his steps: who did not sin, neither was guile found in his mouth: who, when he was reviled, reviled not again; when he suffered, he threatened not; but committed *himself* to him that judgeth righteously: who his own self bare our sins in his own body on the tree, that we, being dead to sins, should live unto righteousness: by whose stripes ye were healed. For ye were as sheep going astray; but are now returned unto the Shepherd and Bishop of your souls.

Likewise, ye wives, *be* in subjection to your own husbands; that, if any obey not the word, they also may without the word be won by the conversation of the wives; while they behold your chaste conversation *coupled* with fear. Whose adorning let it not be that outward *adorning* of plaiting the hair, and of wearing of gold, or of putting on of apparel; but *let it be* the hidden man of the heart, in that which is not corruptible, *even the ornament* of a meek and quiet spirit, which is in the sight of God of great price. For after this manner in the old time the holy women also, who trusted in God, adorned themselves, being in subjection unto their own husbands: even as Sara obeyed Abraham, calling him lord: whose daughters ye are, as long as ye do well, and are not afraid with any amazement. Likewise, ye husbands, dwell with *them* according to knowledge, giving honour unto the wife, as unto the weaker vessel, and as being heirs together of the grace of life; that your prayers be not hindered (1 Pet 2:13–3:7).

Biblical Examples: Matt 8:9; Luke 7:8; 19:17; John 18:36; Acts 8:27; 26:12.

Further References: 1 Cor 7:3–7; 15:24; Eph 5:21–33.

AVARICE (See Greed)

– B –

BACKBITING (See Gossip)

BASTARD (See Birth Out of Wedlock)

BENEFICENCE (See Charity; Ministry)

BESTIALITY (See also Sex and Sexuality)

Whosoever lieth with a beast shall surely be put to death (Exod 22:19).

Neither shalt thou lie with any beast to defile thyself therewith: neither shall any woman stand before a beast to lie down thereto: it *is* confusion (Lev 18:23).

And if a man lie with a beast, he shall surely be put to death: and ye shall slay the beast. And if a woman approach unto any beast, and lie down thereto, thou shalt kill the woman, and the beast: they shall surely be put to death; their blood *shall be* upon them (Lev 20:15, 16).

Cursed *be* he that lieth with any manner of beast. And all the people shall say, Amen (Deut 27:21).

BIGOTRY (See Injustice; Race Relations)

BIRTH CONTROL (See also Children)

And God said, Let us make man in our image, after our likeness: and let them have dominion over the fish of the sea, and over the fowl of the air, and over the cattle, and over all the earth, and over every creeping thing that creepeth upon the earth. So God created man in his *own* image, in the image of God created he him; male and female created he them. And God blessed them, and God said unto them, Be fruitful, and multiply, and replenish the earth, and subdue it: and have dominion over the fish of the sea, and over the fowl of the air, and over every living thing that moveth upon the earth (Gen 1:26–28).

And Adam knew Eve his wife; and she conceived, and bare Cain, and said, I have gotten a man from the LORD (Gen 4:1).

And God blessed Noah and his sons, and said unto them, Be fruitful, and multiply, and replenish the earth. And the fear of you and the dread of you shall be upon every beast of the earth, and upon every fowl of the air, upon all that moveth *upon* the earth, and upon all the fishes of the sea; into your hand are they delivered. Every moving thing that liveth shall be meat for you; even as the green herb have I given you all things. But flesh with the life thereof, *which is* the blood thereof, shall ye not eat. And surely your blood of your lives will I require; at the hand of every beast will I require it, and at the hand of man; at the hand of every man's brother will I require the life of man. Whoso sheddeth man's blood, by man shall his blood be shed: for in the image of God made he man. And you, be ye fruitful, and multiply; bring forth abundantly in the earth, and multiply therein (Gen 9:1–7).

And God said, Sarah thy wife shall bear thee a son indeed; and thou shalt call his name Isaac: and I will establish my covenant with him for an everlasting covenant, *and* with his seed after him (Gen 17:19).

And when the LORD saw that Leah *was* hated, he opened her womb: but Rachel *was* barren (Gen 29:31).

And God remembered Rachel, and God hearkened to her, and opened her womb (Gen. 30:22).

And Judah said unto Onan, Go in unto thy brother's wife, and marry her, and raise up seed to thy brother. And Onan knew that the seed should not be his; and it came to pass, when he went in unto his brother's wife, that he spilled *it* on the ground, lest that he should give seed to his brother. And the thing which he did displeased the LORD: wherefore he slew him also (Gen 38:8–10).

So Boaz took Ruth, and she was his wife: and when he went in unto her, the LORD gave her conception, and she bare a son (Ruth 4:13).

Lo, children *are* an heritage of the LORD: *and* the fruit of the womb *is his* reward. As arrows *are* in the hand of a mighty man; so *are* children of the youth. Happy *is* the man that hath his quiver full of them: they shall not be ashamed, but they shall speak with the enemies in the gate (Ps 127:3–5).

Thy wife *shall be* as a fruitful vine by the sides of thine house: thy children like olive plants round about thy table. (Ps 128:3).

For thou hast possessed my reins: thou hast covered me in my mother's womb. I will praise thee; for I am fearfully *and* wonderfully made: marvellous *are* thy works; and *that* my soul knoweth right well. My substance was not hid from thee, when I was made in secret, *and* curiously wrought in the lowest parts of the earth. Thine eyes did see my substance, yet being unperfect; and in thy book all *my members* were written, *which* in continuance were fashioned, when *as yet there was* none of them. How precious also are thy thoughts unto me, O God! how great is the sum of them! *If* I should count them, they are more in number than the sand: when I awake, I am still with thee (Ps 139:13–18).

And did not he make one? Yet had he the residue of the spirit. And wherefore one? That he might seek a godly seed. Therefore take heed to your spirit, and let none deal treacherously against the wife of his youth (Mal 2:15).

Defraud ye not one the other, except *it be* with consent for a time, that ye may give yourselves to fasting and prayer; and come together again, that Satan tempt you not for your incontinency (1 Cor 7:5).

But if any provide not for his own, and specially for those of his own house, he hath denied the faith, and is worse than an infidel (1 Tim 5:8).

BIRTH OUT OF WEDLOCK

And Lot went up out of Zoar, and dwelt in the mountain, and his two daughters with him; for he feared to dwell in Zoar: and he dwelt in a cave, he and his two daughters. And the firstborn said unto the younger, Our father *is* old, and *there* is not a man in the earth to come in unto us after the manner of all the earth: come, let us make our father drink wine, and we will lie with him, that we may preserve seed of our father. And they made their father drink wine that night: and the firstborn went in, and lay with her father; and he perceived not when she lay down, nor when she arose. And it came to pass on the morrow, that the firstborn said unto the younger, Behold, I lay yesternight with my father: let us make him drink wine this night also; and go thou in, *and* lie with him, that we may preserve seed of our father. And they made their father drink wine that night also: and the younger arose, and lay with him; and he perceived not when she lay down, nor when she arose. Thus were both the daughters of Lot with child by their father. And the firstborn bare a son, and called his name Moab: the same *is* the father of the Moabites unto this day. And the younger, she also bare a son, and called his name Benammi: the same *is* the father of the children of Ammon unto this day (Gen 19:30–38).

A bastard shall not enter into the congregation of the LORD; even to his tenth generation shall he not enter into the congregation of the LORD (Deut 23:2).

But if ye be without chastisement, whereof all are partakers, then are ye bastards, and not sons (Heb 12:8).

Biblical Examples: Gen 16:1–16; 19:30–38; Judg 11:1, 2; 2 Sam 11:2–5.

BLASPHEMY (See also Cursing; Tongue)

And he that blasphemeth the name of the LORD, he shall surely be put to death, *and* all the congregation shall certainly stone him: as well the stranger, as he that is born in the land, when he blasphemeth the name *of the LORD,* shall be put to death (Lev 24:16).

O God, how long shall the adversary reproach? shall the enemy blaspheme thy name for ever? Why withdrawest thou thy hand, even thy right hand? pluck *it* out of thy bosom (Ps 74:10, 11).

Whom hast thou reproached and blasphemed? and against whom hast thou exalted *thy* voice, and lifted up thine eyes on high? *even* against the Holy One of Israel (Isa 37:23).

Now therefore, what have I here, saith the LORD, that my people is taken away for nought? they that rule over them make them to howl, saith the LORD; and my name continually every day *is* blasphemed (Isa 52:5).

Behold, *it is* written before me: I will not keep silence, but will recompense, even recompense into their bosom, Your iniquities, and the iniquities of your fathers together, saith the LORD, which have burned incense upon the mountains, and blasphemed me upon the hills: therefore will I measure their former work into their bosom (Isa 65:6, 7).

Verily I say unto you, All sins shall be forgiven unto the sons of men, and blasphemies wherewith soever they shall blaspheme: but he that shall blaspheme against the Holy Ghost hath never forgiveness, but is in danger of eternal damnation (Mark 3:28, 29).

Jesus answered them, Is it not written in your law, I said, Ye are gods? If he called them gods, unto whom the word of God came, and the scripture cannot be broken; say ye of him, whom the Father hath sanctified, and sent into the world, Thou blasphemest; because I said, I am the Son of God? If I do not the works of my Father, believe me not. But if I do, though ye believe not me, believe the works: that ye may know, and believe, that the Father *is* in me, and I in him (John 10:34–38).

For the name of God is blasphemed among the Gentiles through you, as it is written (Rom 2:24).

Let as many servants as are under the yoke count their own masters worthy of all honour, that the name of God and *his* doctrine be not blasphemed (1 Tim 6:1).

But ye have despised the poor. Do not rich men oppress you, and draw you before the judgment seats? Do not they blaspheme that worthy name by the which ye are called? (James 2:6, 7).

And there was given unto him a mouth speaking great things and blasphemies; and power was given unto him to continue forty *and* two months. And he opened his mouth in blasphemy against God, to blaspheme his name, and his tabernacle, and them that dwell in heaven (Rev 13:5, 6).

Biblical Examples: Lev 24:10–23; 1 Kings 21:13–14; 2 Kings 19:22; Job 1:5; Matt 26:74; 27:40–44; Acts 26:11; 1 Tim 1:20.

Further References: 2 Kings 19:6; Matt 15:9; 1 Tim 1:18–20; Titus 2:3–5; James 3:9, 10; Rev 16:19.

BOASTING (See Pride)

BODY, HUMAN (See also Health; Ministry; Sex and Sexuality)

This *is* my covenant, which ye shall keep, between me and you and thy seed after thee; Every man child among you shall be circumcised. And ye shall circumcise the flesh of your foreskin; and it shall be a token of the covenant betwixt me and you. And he that is eight days old shall be circumcised among you, every man child in your generations, he that is born in the house, or bought with money of any stranger, which *is* not of thy seed. He that is born in thy house, and he that is bought with thy money, must needs be circumcised: and my covenant shall be in your flesh for an everlasting covenant. And the uncircumcised man child whose flesh of his foreskin is not circumcised, that soul shall be cut off from his people; he hath broken my covenant (Gen 17:10–14).

Ye shall not make any cuttings in your flesh for the dead, nor print any marks upon you: I *am* the LORD (Lev 19:28).

He that is wounded in the stones, or hath his privy member cut off, shall not enter into the congregation of the LORD (Deut 23:1).

Know ye not that ye are the temple of God, and *that* the Spirit of God dwelleth in you? If any man defile the temple of

God, him shall God destroy; for the temple of God is holy, which *temple* ye are (1 Cor 3:16, 17).

What? know ye not that your body is the temple of the Holy Ghost *which is* in you, which ye have of God, and ye are not your own? (1 Cor 6:19).

But I keep under my body, and bring *it* into subjection: lest that by any means, when I have preached to others, I myself should be a castaway (1 Cor. 9:27).

Further References: Gen 2:25; 3:7–11; 9:22, 23; Exod 20:26; Lev 18:6–19; 20:11–21; Job 4:19; Matt 19:12; 25:36–43; Rom 1:24–27; 1 Cor 15:19–54.

BORROWING (See also Debt and Debtor)

And if a man borrow *aught* of his neighbour, and it be hurt, or die, the owner thereof *being* not with it, he shall surely make *it* good. *But* if the owner thereof *be* with it, he shall not make *it* good: if it *be* an hired *thing*, it came for his hire (Exod 22:14, 15).

And there was a great cry of the people and of their wives against their brethren the Jews. For there were that said, We, our sons, and our daughters, *are* many: therefore we take up corn *for them*, that we may eat, and live. *Some* also there were that said, We have mortgaged our lands, vineyards, and houses, that we might buy corn, because of the dearth. There were also that said, We have borrowed money for the king's tribute, *and that upon* our lands and vineyards. Yet now our flesh *is* as the flesh of our brethren, our children as their children: and, lo, we bring into bondage our sons and our daughters to be servants, and *some* of our daughters are brought unto bondage *already:* neither *is it* in our power *to redeem them;* for other men have our lands and vineyards.

And I was very angry when I heard their cry and these words. Then I consulted with myself, and I rebuked the nobles, and the rulers, and said unto them, Ye exact usury, every one of his brother. And I set a great assembly against them. And I said unto them, We after our ability have redeemed our brethren the Jews, which were sold unto the heathen; and will ye

even sell your brethren? or shall they be sold unto us? Then held they their peace, and found nothing *to answer.* Also I said, It *is* not good that ye do: ought ye not to walk in the fear of our God because of the reproach of the heathen our enemies? I likewise, *and* my brethren, and my servants, might exact of them money and corn: I pray you, let us leave off this usury. Restore, I pray you, to them, even this day, their lands, their vineyards, their oliveyards, and their houses, also the hundredth *part* of the money, and of the corn, the wine, and the oil, that ye exact of them. Then said they, We will restore *them,* and will require nothing of them; so will we do as thou sayest. Then I called the priests, and took an oath of them, that they should do according to this promise. Also I shook my lap, and said, So God shake out every man from his house, and from his labour, that performeth not this promise, even thus be he shaken out, and emptied. And all the congregation said, Amen, and praised the LORD. And the people did according to this promise (Neh 5:1–13).

The wicked borroweth, and payeth not again: but the righteous sheweth mercy, and giveth (Ps 37:21).

The rich ruleth over the poor, and the borrower *is* servant to the lender (Prov 22:7).

Give to him that asketh thee, and from him that would borrow of thee turn not thou away (Matt 5:42).

Owe no man any thing, but to love one another: for he that loveth another hath fulfilled the law (Rom 13:8).

Further References: Exod 3:22; 11:2; 12:35.

BRAVERY (See Courage)

BRIBES AND BRIBERY

Wherefore now let the fear of the LORD be upon you; take heed and do *it:* for *there is* no iniquity with the LORD our God, nor respect of persons, nor taking of gifts (2 Chron 19:7).

LORD, who shall abide in thy tabernacle? who shall dwell in thy holy hill? He that walketh uprightly, and worketh righteousness, and speaketh the truth in his heart. *He that* backbiteth not with his tongue, nor doeth evil to his neighbour, nor taketh up a reproach against his neighbour. In whose eyes a vile person is contemned; but he honoureth them that fear the LORD. *He that* sweareth to *his own* hurt, and changeth not. *He that* putteth not out his money to usury, nor taketh reward against the innocent. He that doeth these *things* shall never be moved (Ps 15).

A wicked *man* taketh a gift out of the bosom to pervert the ways of judgment (Prov 17:23).

He that walketh righteously, and speaketh uprightly; he that despiseth the gain of oppressions, that shaketh his hands from holding of bribes, that stoppeth his ears from hearing of blood, and shutteth his eyes from seeing evil; he shall dwell on high: his place of defence *shall be* the munitions of rocks: bread shall be given him; his waters *shall be* sure (Isa 33:15, 16).

Biblical Examples: Judg 16:5; 1 Sam 8:1–3; 1 Kings 15:19; Ezra 3:9; Matt 26:15; 27:3–9; 28:12–15; Mark 14:11; Luke 22:5; Acts 24:26.

Further References: Exod 23:8; Deut 16:18, 19; 27:25; Job 15:34; Ps 26:9, 10; Prov 18:16; 28:21; 29:4; Isa 1:23; 5:22, 23; Ezek 13:19; 22:12, 13; Amos 2:6; 5:12; Mic 7:3.

BUSINESS (See Daily Work; Labor Relations)

-C-

CALLING (See Vocation, Calling)

CAPITAL PUNISHMENT (See also Crime and Punishment)

And surely your blood of your lives will I require; at the hand of every beast will I require it, and at the hand of man; at the hand of every man's brother will I require the life of man. Whoso sheddeth man's blood, by man shall his blood be shed: for in the image of God made he man. And you, be ye fruitful, and multiply; bring forth abundantly in the earth, and multiply therein (Gen 9:5–7).

He that smiteth a man, so that he die, shall be surely put to death. . . . But if a man come presumptuously upon his neighbour, to slay him with guile; thou shalt take him from mine altar, that he may die.

And he that smiteth his father, or his mother, shall be surely put to death.

And he that stealeth a man, and selleth him, or if he be found in his hand, he shall surely be put to death.

And he that curseth his father, or his mother, shall surely be put to death (Exod 21:12, 14–17).

Thou shalt not suffer a witch to live.

Whosoever lieth with a beast shall surely be put to death.

He that sacrificeth unto *any* god, save unto the LORD only, he shall be utterly destroyed (Exod 22:18–20).

Six days shall work be done, but on the seventh day there shall be to you an holy day, a sabbath of rest to the LORD: whosoever doeth work therein shall be put to death (Exod 35:2).

And the LORD spake unto Moses, saying,

Again, thou shalt say to the children of Israel, Whosoever *he be* of the children of Israel, or of the strangers that sojourn in Israel, that giveth *any* of his seed unto Molech; he shall surely be put to death: the people of the land shall stone him with stones. And I will set my face against that man, and will cut him off from among his people; because he hath given of his seed unto Molech, to defile my sanctuary, and to profane my holy name. And if the people of the land do any ways hide their eyes from the man, when he giveth of his seed unto Molech, and kill him not: then I will set my face against that man, and against his family, and will cut him off, and all that go a-whoring after him, to commit whoredom with Molech, from among their people.

And the soul that turneth after such as have familiar spirits, and after wizards, to go a-whoring after them, I will even set my face against that soul, and will cut him off from among his people.

Sanctify yourselves therefore, and be ye holy: for I *am* the LORD your God. And ye shall keep my statutes, and do them: I *am* the LORD which sanctify you.

For every one that curseth his father or his mother shall be surely put to death: he hath cursed his father or his mother; his blood *shall be* upon him.

And the man that committeth adultery with *another* man's wife, *even he* that committeth adultery with his neighbour's wife, the adulterer and the adulteress shall surely be put to death. And the man that lieth with his father's wife hath uncovered his father's nakedness: both of them shall surely be put to death; their blood *shall be* upon them. And if a man lie with his daughter in law, both of them shall surely be put to death: they have wrought confusion; their blood *shall be* upon them. If a man also lie with mankind, as he lieth with a woman, both of them have committed an abomination: they shall surely be put to death; their blood *shall be* upon them. And if a man take a wife and her mother, it *is* wickedness: they shall be burnt with fire, both he and they; that there be no wickedness among you. And if a man lie with a beast, he shall surely be put to death: and ye shall slay the beast. And if a woman approach unto any beast, and lie down thereto, thou shalt kill the woman, and the beast: they shall surely be put to death; their blood *shall be* upon them (Lev 20:1–16).

And the daughter of any priest, if she profane herself by playing the whore, she profaneth her father: she shall be burnt with fire (Lev 21:9).

And the LORD spake unto Moses, saying, Bring forth him that hath cursed without the camp; and let all that heard *him* lay their hands upon his head, and let all the congregation stone him. And thou shalt speak unto the children of Israel, saying, Whosoever curseth his God shall bear his sin. And he that blasphemeth the name of the LORD, he shall surely be put to death, *and* all the congregation shall certainly stone him: as well the stranger, as he that is born in the land, when he blasphemeth the name *of the LORD,* shall be put to death.

And he that killeth any man shall surely be put to death. And he that killeth a beast shall make it good; beast for beast. And if a man cause a blemish in his neighbour; as he hath done, so shall it be done to him; breach for breach, eye for eye, tooth for tooth: as he hath caused a blemish in a man, so shall it be done to him *again.* And he that killeth a beast, he shall restore it: and he that killeth a man, he shall be put to death (Lev 24:13–21).

And if he smite him with an instrument of iron, so that he die, he *is* a murderer: the murderer shall surely be put to death. And if he smite him with throwing a stone, wherewith he may die, and he die, he *is* a murderer: the murderer shall surely be

put to death. Or *if* he smite him with an hand weapon of wood, wherewith he may die, and he die, he *is* a murderer: the murderer shall surely be put to death. The revenger of blood himself shall slay the murderer: when he meeteth him, he shall slay him. But if he thrust him of hatred, or hurl at him by laying of wait, that he die; or in enmity smite him with his hand, that he die: he that smote *him* shall surely be put to death; *for* he *is* a murderer: the revenger of blood shall slay the murderer, when he meeteth him (Num 35:16–21).

Whoso killeth any person, the murderer shall be put to death by the mouth of witnesses: but one witness shall not testify against any person *to cause him* to die (Num 35:30).

If there arise among you a prophet, or a dreamer of dreams, and giveth thee a sign or a wonder, and the sign or the wonder come to pass, whereof he spake unto thee, saying, Let us go after other gods, which thou hast not known, and let us serve them; thou shalt not hearken unto the words of that prophet, or that dreamer of dreams: for the LORD your God proveth you, to know whether ye love the LORD your God with all your heart and with all your soul. Ye shall walk after the LORD your God, and fear him, and keep his commandments, and obey his voice, and ye shall serve him, and cleave unto him. And that prophet, or that dreamer of dreams, shall be put to death; because he hath spoken to turn *you* away from the LORD your God, which brought you out of the land of Egypt, and redeemed you out of the house of bondage, to thrust thee out of the way which the LORD thy God commanded thee to walk in. So shalt thou put the evil away from the midst of thee.

If thy brother, the son of thy mother, or thy son, or thy daughter, or the wife of thy bosom, or thy friend, which *is* as thine own soul, entice thee secretly, saying, Let us go and serve other gods, which thou hast not known, thou, nor thy fathers; *namely,* of the gods of the people which *are* round about you, nigh unto thee, or far off from thee, from the *one* end of the earth even unto the *other* end of the earth; thou shalt not consent unto him, nor hearken unto him; neither shall thine eye pity him, neither shalt thou spare, neither shalt thou conceal him: but thou shalt surely kill him; thine hand shall be first upon him to put him to death, and afterwards the hand of all the people. And thou shalt stone him with stones, that he die; because he hath sought to thrust thee away from the LORD thy God, which brought thee out of the land of Egypt, from the house of bondage (Deut 13:1–10).

At the mouth of two witnesses, or three witnesses, shall he that is worthy of death be put to death; *but* at the mouth of one witness he shall not be put to death (Deut 17:6).

If a man have a stubborn and rebellious son, which will not obey the voice of his father, or the voice of his mother, and *that*, when they have chastened him, will not hearken unto them: then shall his father and his mother lay hold on him, and bring him out unto the elders of his city, and unto the gate of his place; and they shall say unto the elders of his city, This our son *is* stubborn and rebellious, he will not obey our voice; *he is* a glutton, and a drunkard. And all the men of his city shall stone him with stones, that he die: so shalt thou put evil away from among you; and all Israel shall hear, and fear (Deut 21:18–21).

If a man be found lying with a woman married to an husband, then they shall both of them die, *both* the man that lay with the woman, and the woman: so shalt thou put away evil from Israel.

If a damsel *that is* a virgin be betrothed unto an husband, and a man find her in the city, and lie with her; then ye shall bring them both out unto the gate of that city, and ye shall stone them with stones that they die; the damsel, because she cried not, *being* in the city; and the man, because he hath humbled his neighbour's wife: so thou shalt put away evil from among you (Deut 22:22–24).

If a man be found stealing any of his brethren of the children of Israel, and maketh merchandise of him, or selleth him; then that thief shall die; and thou shalt put evil away from among you (Deut 24:7).

And after that they had mocked him, they took the robe off from him, and put his own raiment on him, and led him away to crucify *him* (Matt 27:31).

For rulers are not a terror to good works, but to the evil. Wilt thou then not be afraid of the power? do that which is good, and thou shalt have praise of the same: for he is the minister of God to thee for good. But if thou do that which is evil, be afraid; for he beareth not the sword in vain: for he is the minister of God, a revenger to *execute* wrath upon him that doeth evil (Rom 13:3, 4).

Biblical Examples: Gen 38:24; Exod 32:15–29; Lev 24:10–23; Num 15:32–36; Josh 8:28, 29; 1 Kings 2:5; Esth 2:21–23; Dan 3:16–23; Matt 27:24–44; Mark 6:14–28; 15:15; John 19:1–16; Acts 7:54–8:1; 12:1–5; 16:16–24; 22:22–29.

Further References: Deut 17:12; 1 Kings 2:25; Esth 2:23; Zech 5:3, 4.

CASTRATION (See Celibacy; Body, Human)

CELIBACY (See also Abstinence; Chastity; Purity; Self-control; Self-denial)

And the LORD God said, *It is* not good that the man should be alone; I will make him an help meet for him (Gen 2:18).

For there are some eunuchs, which were so born from *their* mother's womb: and there are some eunuchs, which were made eunuchs of men: and there be eunuchs, which have made themselves eunuchs for the kingdom of heaven's sake. He that is able to receive *it*, let him receive *it* (Matt 19:12).

For I would that all men were even as I myself. But every man hath his proper gift of God, one after this manner, and another after that (1 Cor. 7:7).

Now concerning the things whereof ye wrote unto me: *It is* good for a man not to touch a woman. Nevertheless, *to avoid* fornication, let every man have his own wife, and let every woman have her own husband. Let the husband render unto the wife due benevolence: and likewise also the wife unto the husband. The wife hath not power of her own body, but the husband: and likewise also the husband hath not power of his own body, but the wife. Defraud ye not one the other, except *it be* with consent for a time, that ye may give yourselves to fasting and prayer; and come together again, that Satan tempt you not for your incontinency. But I speak this by permission, *and* not of commandment. For I would that all men were even as I myself. But every man hath his proper gift of God, one after this manner, and another after that.

I say therefore to the unmarried and widows, It is good for them if they abide even as I. But if they cannot contain, let them marry: for it is better to marry than to burn.

And unto the married I command, *yet* not I, but the Lord, Let not the wife depart from *her* husband: but and if she depart, let her remain unmarried, or be reconciled to *her* husband: and let not the husband put away *his* wife.

But to the rest speak I, not the Lord: If any brother hath a wife that believeth not, and she be pleased to dwell with him, let him not put her away. And the woman which hath an husband that believeth not, and if he be pleased to dwell with her, let her not leave him. For the unbelieving husband is sanctified by the wife, and the unbelieving wife is sanctified by the husband: else were your children unclean; but now are they holy. But if the unbelieving depart, let him depart. A brother or a sister is not under bondage in such *cases:* but God hath called us to peace. For what knowest thou, O wife, whether thou shalt save *thy* husband? or how knowest thou, O man, whether thou shalt save *thy* wife?

But as God hath distributed to every man, as the Lord hath called every one, so let him walk. And so ordain I in all churches. Is any man called being circumcised? let him not become uncircumcised. Is any called in uncircumcision? let him not be circumcised. Circumcision is nothing, and uncircumcision is nothing, but the keeping of the commandments of God. Let every man abide in the same calling wherein he was called. Art thou called *being* a servant? care not for it: but if thou mayest be made free, use *it* rather. For he that is called in the Lord, *being* a servant, is the Lord's freeman: likewise also he that is called, *being* free, is Christ's servant. Ye are bought with a price; be

not ye the servants of men. Brethren, let every man, wherein he is called, therein abide with God.

Now concerning virgins I have no commandment of the Lord: yet I give my judgment, as one that hath obtained mercy of the Lord to be faithful. I suppose therefore that this is good for the present distress, *I say,* that *it is* good for a man so to be. Art thou bound unto a wife? seek not to be loosed. Art thou loosed from a wife? seek not a wife. But and if thou marry, thou hast not sinned; and if a virgin marry, she hath not sinned. Nevertheless such shall have trouble in the flesh: but I spare you. But this I say, brethren, the time *is* short: it remaineth, that both they that have wives be as though they had none; and they that weep, as though they wept not; and they that rejoice, as though they rejoiced not; and they that buy, as though they possessed not; and they that use this world, as not abusing *it:* for the fashion of this world passeth away.

But I would have you without carefulness. He that is unmarried careth for the things that belong to the Lord, how he may please the Lord: but he that is married careth for the things that are of the world, how he may please *his* wife. There is difference *also* between a wife and a virgin. The unmarried woman careth for the things of the Lord, that she may be holy both in body and in spirit: but she that is married careth for the things of the world, how she may please *her* husband. And this I speak for your own profit; not that I may cast a snare upon you, but for that which is comely, and that ye may attend upon the Lord without distraction.

But if any man think that he behaveth himself uncomely toward his virgin, if she pass the flower of *her* age, and need so require, let him do what he will, he sinneth not: let them marry. Nevertheless he that standeth stedfast in his heart, having no necessity, but hath power over his own will, and hath so decreed in his heart that he will keep his virgin, doeth well. So then he that giveth *her* in marriage doeth well; but he that giveth *her* not in marriage doeth better.

The wife is bound by the law as long as her husband liveth; but if her husband be dead, she is at liberty to be married to whom she will; only in the Lord. But she is happier if she so abide, after my judgment: and I think also that I have the Spirit of God (1 Cor 7).

Now the Spirit speaketh expressly, that in the latter times some shall depart from the faith, giving heed to seducing spirits, and doctrines of devils; Speaking lies in hypocrisy; having their conscience seared with a hot iron; Forbidding to marry, *and commanding* to abstain from meats, which God hath created to be received with thanksgiving of them which believe and know the truth (1 Tim 4:1–3).

And I looked, and, lo, a Lamb stood on the mount Sion, and with him an hundred forty *and* four thousand, having his Father's name written in their foreheads. And I heard a voice from heaven, as the voice of many waters, and as the voice of a great thunder: and I heard the voice of harpers harping with their harps: and they sung as it were a new song before the throne, and before the four beasts, and the elders: and no man could learn that song but the hundred *and* forty *and* four thousand, which were redeemed from the earth. These are they which were not defiled with women; for they are virgins. These are they which follow the Lamb whithersoever he goeth. These were redeemed from among men, *being* the firstfruits unto God and to the Lamb (Rev 14:1–4).

CHARITY (See also Ministry; Poverty; Property)

If there be among you a poor man of one of thy brethren within any of thy gates in thy land which the LORD thy God giveth thee, thou shalt not harden thine heart, nor shut thine hand from thy poor brother: but thou shalt open thine hand wide unto him, and shalt surely lend him sufficient for his need, *in that* which he wanteth. Beware that there be not a thought in thy wicked heart, saying, The seventh year, the year of release, is at hand; and thine eye be evil against thy poor brother, and thou givest him nought; and he cry unto the LORD against thee, and it be sin unto thee. Thou shalt surely give him, and thine heart shall not be grieved when thou givest unto him: because that for this thing the LORD thy God shall bless thee in all thy works, and in all that thou puttest thine hand unto. For the poor shall never cease out of the land: therefore I command thee, saying, Thou shalt open thine hand wide unto thy brother, to thy poor, and to thy needy, in thy land (Deut 15:7–11).

Give to him that asketh thee, and from him that would borrow of thee turn not thou away (Matt 5:42).

Take heed that ye do not your alms before men, to be seen of them: otherwise ye have no reward of your Father which is in heaven. Therefore when thou doest *thine* alms, do not sound a trumpet before thee, as the hypocrites do in the synagogues and in the streets, that they may have glory of men. Verily I say unto you, They have their reward. But when thou doest alms, let not thy left hand know what thy right hand doeth: that thine alms may be in secret: and thy Father which seeth in secret himself shall reward thee openly (Matt 6:1–4).

Jesus said unto him, If thou wilt be perfect, go *and* sell that thou hast, and give to the poor, and thou shalt have treasure in heaven: and come *and* follow me (Matt 19:21).

Sell that ye have, and give alms; provide yourselves bags which wax not old, a treasure in the heavens that faileth not, where no thief approacheth, neither moth corrupteth (Luke 12:33).

Neither was there any among them that lacked: for as many as were possessors of lands or houses sold them, and brought the prices of the things that were sold, And laid *them* down at the apostles' feet: and distribution was made unto every man according as he had need. And Joses, who by the apostles was surnamed Barnabas, (which is, being interpreted, The son of consolation,) a Levite, *and* of the country of Cyprus, Having land, sold *it*, and brought the money, and laid *it* at the apostles' feet (Acts 4:34–37).

And in those days, when the number of the disciples was multiplied, there arose a murmuring of the Grecians against the Hebrews, because their widows were neglected in the daily ministration. Then the twelve called the multitude of the disciples *unto them,* and said, It is not reason that we should leave the word of God, and serve tables. Wherefore, brethren, look ye out among you seven men of honest report, full of the Holy Ghost and wisdom, whom we may appoint over this business (Acts 6:1–3).

For as we have many members in one body, and all members have not the same office: so we, *being* many, are one body in Christ, and every one members one of another. Having then gifts differing according to the grace that is given to us, whether prophecy, *let us prophesy* according to the proportion of faith; or ministry, *let us wait* on *our* ministering: or he that teacheth, on teaching; or he that exhorteth, on exhortation: he that giveth, *let him do it* with simplicity; he that ruleth, with diligence; he that sheweth mercy, with cheerfulness (Rom 12:4–8).

That they do good, that they be rich in good works, ready to distribute, willing to communicate; laying up in store for themselves a good foundation against the time to come, that they may lay hold on eternal life (1 Tim 6:18, 19).

For God *is* not unrighteous to forget your work and labour of love, which ye have shewed toward his name, in that ye have ministered to the saints, and do minister (Heb 6:10). But to do good and to communicate forget not: for with such sacrifices God is well pleased (Heb 13:16). But whoso hath this world's good, and seeth his brother have need, and shutteth up his bowels *of compassion* from him, how dwelleth the love of God in him? (1 John 3:17).

Biblical Examples: Judg 19:16–21; Ruth 2; Job 29:11–17; Luke 10:25–37; 19:8; Acts 2:44, 45; 9:36; 10:1–4; 11:29, 30; Rom 15:25–27; 1 Cor 16:1–4; 2 Cor 8:1–6; 9:1–15; Phil 4:10–18.

Further References: Ps 112:9; Prov 3:27, 28; 11:25; 22:9; 28:27; Isa 58:6–11; Ezek 18:5–9; Matt 25:35–45; Mark 10:21; Luke 3:11; 1 Cor 13:3; Gal 2:10; 1 Tim 5:8–16; James 2:15, 16.

CHASTITY (See also Purity; Sex and Sexuality)

Ye have heard that it was said by them of old time, Thou shalt not commit adultery: but I say unto you, That whosoever looketh on a woman to lust after her hath committed adultery with her already in his heart (Matt 5:27, 28).

Wherefore God also gave them up to uncleanness through the lusts of their own hearts, to dishonour their own bodies between themselves (Rom 1:24).

Know ye not that the unrighteous shall not inherit the kingdom of God? Be not deceived: neither fornicators, nor idolaters, nor adulterers, nor effeminate, nor abusers of themselves with mankind (1 Cor 6:9).

Know ye not that your bodies are the members of Christ? shall I then take the members of Christ, and make *them* the members of an harlot? God forbid. What? know ye not that he which is joined to an harlot is one body? for two, saith he, shall be one flesh. But he that is joined unto the Lord is one spirit. Flee fornication. Every sin that a man doeth is without the body; but he that committeth fornication sinneth against his own body. What? know ye not that your body is the temple of the Holy Ghost *which is* in you, which ye have of God, and ye are not your own? For ye are bought with a price: therefore glorify God in your body, and in your spirit, which are God's (1 Cor 6:15–20).

Now concerning the things whereof ye wrote unto me: *It is* good for a man not to touch a woman. Nevertheless, *to avoid* fornication, let every man have his own wife, and let every woman have her own husband (1 Cor 7:1, 2).

The aged women likewise, that *they be* in behaviour as becometh holiness, not false accusers, not given to much wine, teachers of good things; that they may teach the young women to be sober, to love their husbands, to love their children, *to be* discreet, chaste, keepers at home, good, obedient to their own husbands, that the word of God be not blasphemed (Titus 2:3–5).

Biblical Examples: Gen 39:7–20; Ruth 3:6–13; 1 Cor 7.

Further References: Exod 20:14; Prov 2:10, 11, 16–22; 5:15–21; 6:24, 25; Rom 13:13; Eph 5:3; Col 3:5; 1 Thess 4:3, 7; Rev 14:1–5.

CHEATING (See Dishonesty)

CHILD ABUSE (See Orphans; Parent-Child Relations)

CHILDREN (See also Parent-Child Relations)

Honour thy father and thy mother: that thy days may be long upon the land which the LORD thy God giveth thee (Exod 20:12).

And these words, which I command thee this day, shall be in thine heart: and thou shalt teach them diligently unto thy children, and shalt talk of them when thou sittest in thine house, and when thou walkest by the way, and when thou liest down, and when thou risest up (Deut 6:6, 7).

He maketh the barren woman to keep house, *and to be* a joyful mother of children. Praise ye the LORD (Ps 113:9).

Wherewithal shall a young man cleanse his way? by taking heed *thereto* according to thy word (Ps 119:9).

Lo, children *are* an heritage of the LORD: *and* the fruit of the womb *is his* reward. As arrows *are* in the hand of a mighty man; so *are* children of the youth. Happy *is* the man that hath his quiver full of them: they shall not be ashamed, but they shall speak with the enemies in the gate (Ps 127:3–5).

Both young men, and maidens; old men, and children: let them praise the name of the LORD: for his name alone is excellent; his glory *is* above the earth and heaven (Ps 148:12, 13).

My son, hear the instruction of thy father, and forsake not the law of thy mother (Prov 1:8).

My son, forget not my law; but let thine heart keep my commandments; for length of days, and long life, and peace, shall they add to thee. Let not mercy and truth forsake thee: bind them about thy neck; write them upon the table of thine heart: so shalt thou find favour and good understanding in the sight of God and man (Prov 3:1–4).

Hear, ye children, the instruction of a father, and attend to know understanding. For I give you good doctrine, forsake ye not my law. For I was my father's son, tender and only *beloved* in the sight of my mother. He taught me also, and said unto me, Let thine heart retain my words: keep my commandments, and live. Get wisdom, get understanding: forget *it* not; neither decline from the words of my mouth. Forsake her not, and she shall preserve thee: love her, and she shall keep thee. Wisdom *is* the principle thing; *therefore* get wisdom: and with all thy getting get understanding. Exalt her, and she shall promote thee: she shall bring thee to honour, when thou dost embrace her. She shall give to thine head an ornament of grace: a crown of glory shall she deliver to thee. Hear, O my son, and receive my sayings; and the years of thy life shall be many. I have taught thee in the way of wisdom; I have led thee in right paths. When thou goest, thy steps shall not be straitened; and when thou runnest, thou shalt not stumble. Take fast hold of instruction; let *her* not go: keep her; for she *is* thy life.

Enter not into the path of the wicked, and go not in the way of evil *men*. Avoid it, pass not by it, turn from it, and pass away. For they sleep not, except they have done mischief; and their sleep is taken away, unless they cause *some* to fall. For they eat the bread of wickedness, and drink the wine of violence. But the path of the just *is* as the shining light, that shineth more and more unto the perfect day. The way of the wicked *is* as darkness: they know not at what they stumble.

My son, attend to my words; incline thine ear unto my sayings. Let them not depart from thine eyes; keep them in the midst of thine heart. For they *are* life unto those that find them, and health to all their flesh (Prov 4:1–22).

Train up a child in the way he should go: and when he is old, he will not depart from it (Prov 22:6).

The rod and reproof give wisdom: but a child left *to himself* bringeth his mother to shame (Prov 29:15).

Remember now thy Creator in the days of thy youth, while the evil days come not, nor the years draw nigh, when thou shalt say, I have no pleasure in them (Eccl 12:1).

At the same time came the disciples unto Jesus, saying, Who is the greatest in the kingdom of heaven? And Jesus called a little child unto him, and set him in the midst of them, and said, Verily I say unto you, Except ye be converted, and become as little children, ye shall not enter into the kingdom of heaven. Whosoever therefore shall humble himself as this little child, the same is greatest in the kingdom of heaven. And whoso shall receive one such little child in my name receiveth me. But whoso shall offend one of these little ones which believe in me, it were better for him that a millstone were hanged about his neck, and *that* he were drowned in the depth of the sea (Matt 18:1–6).

Then were there brought unto him little children, that he should put *his* hands on them, and pray: and the disciples rebuked them. But Jesus said, Suffer little children, and forbid them not, to come unto me: for of such is the kingdom of heaven. And he laid *his* hands on them, and departed thence (Matt 19:13–15).

Children, obey your parents in the Lord: for this is right. Honour thy father and mother; which is the first commandment with promise; that it may be well with thee, and thou mayest live long on the earth. And, ye fathers, provoke not your children to wrath: but bring them up in the nature and admonition of the Lord (Eph 6:1–4).

Children, obey *your* parents in all things: for this is well pleasing unto the Lord. Fathers, provoke not your children *to anger,* lest they be discouraged (Col 3:20, 21).

Let no man despise thy youth; but be thou an example of the believers, in word, in conversation, in charity, in spirit, in faith, in purity (1 Tim 4:12).

Biblical Examples: Gen 21:1, 2; 25:21; Ruth 1:16–18; 1 Sam 1:9–20; 2:18; 3; Jer 1:5–7; Luke 1:15, 80; 2:40, 46–52; John 19:26, 27; Acts 22:3; 2 Tim 1:5; 3:15.

Further References: Care for: Deut 4:9, 10; 6:6–9; 11:19, 20; Ps 78:1–8; Col 3:21.

Discipline of: Prov 13:24; 19:18; 22:6, 15; 23:13, 14; 29:15–17; Isa 28:9, 10; Eph 6:4.

Gift from God: Gen 4:1, 25; 17:16, 20; 29:32–35; 33:5; Ruth 4:13; Job 1:21; Ps 113:9; 127:3.

Instructions to: Exod 20:12; Lev 19:3, 32; Deut 5:16; Ps 148:12, 13; Prov 1:8, 9;

3:1–3; 4:1–4, 10, 11, 20–22; 6:20–25; 23:22, 26; Eccl 12:1; Eph 6:1; Col 3:20; 1 Tim 4:12; Titus 2:6.

Worship Attendance of: Josh 8:34; 2 Chron 20:13; 31:16; Ezra 8:21; Neh 12:43; Matt 21:15; Luke 2:46.

CHURCH (See Ministry)

CHURCH DISCIPLINE

Moreover if thy brother shall trespass against thee, go and tell him his fault between thee and him alone: if he shall hear thee, thou hast gained thy brother. But if he will not hear *thee, then* take with thee one or two more, that in the mouth of two or three witnesses every word may be established. And if he shall neglect to hear them, tell *it* unto the church: but if he neglect to hear the church, let him be unto thee as an heathen man and a publican. Verily I say unto you, Whatsoever ye shall bind on earth shall be bound in heaven: and whatsoever ye shall loose on earth shall be loosed in heaven (Matt 18:15–18).

It is reported commonly *that there is* fornication among you, and such fornication as is not so much as named among the Gentiles, that one should have his father's wife. And ye are puffed up, and have not rather mourned, that he that hath done this deed might be taken away from among you. For I verily, as absent in body, but present in spirit, have judged already, as though I were present, *concerning* him that hath so done this deed, in the name of our Lord Jesus Christ, when ye are gathered together, and my spirit, with the power of our Lord Jesus Christ, to deliver such an one unto Satan for the destruction of the flesh, that the spirit may be saved in the day of the Lord Jesus. Your glorying *is* not good. Know ye not that a little leaven leaveneth the whole lump? Purge out therefore the old leaven, that ye may be a new lump, as ye are unleavened. For even Christ our passover is sacrificed for us: therefore let us keep the feast, not with old leaven, neither with the leaven of malice and wickedness; but with the unleavened *bread* of sincerity and truth.

I wrote unto you in an epistle not to

company with fornicators: yet not altogether with the fornicators of this world, or with the covetous, or extortioners, or with idolaters; for then must ye needs go out of the world. But now I have written unto you not to keep company, if any man that is called a brother be a fornicator, or covetous, or an idolater, or a railer, or a drunkard, or an extortioner; with such an one no not to eat. For what have I to do to judge them also that are without? do not ye judge them that are within? But them that are without God judgeth. Therefore put away from among yourselves that wicked person (1 Cor 5).

Of these things put *them* in remembrance, charging *them* before the Lord that they strive not about words to no profit, *but* to the subverting of the hearers. Study to shew thyself approved unto God, a workman that needeth not to be ashamed, rightly dividing the word of truth. But shun profane *and* vain babblings: for they will increase unto more ungodliness (2 Tim 2:14–16).

Biblical Examples: 1 Cor 5.

CHURCH AND STATE (See Citizenship; Government)

CITIZENSHIP (See also Government; Patriotism)

Thou shalt not revile the gods, nor curse the ruler of thy people (Exod 22:28).

Thou shalt not follow a multitude to *do* evil; neither shalt thou speak in a cause to decline after many to wrest *judgment* (Exod 23:2).

The land shall not be sold for ever: for the land *is* mine; for ye *are* strangers and sojourners with me (Lev 25:23).

When the LORD thy God shall cut off the nations from before thee, whither thou goest to possess them, and thou succeedest them, and dwellest in their land; take heed to thyself that thou be not snared by following them, after that they be destroyed from before thee; and that thou inquire not after their gods, saying, How did these nations serve their gods? even so will I do likewise (Deut 12:29, 30).

Nevertheless the people refused to obey the voice of Samuel; and they said, Nay; but we will have a king over us; that we also may be like all the nations; and that our king may judge us, and go out before us, and fight our battles (1 Sam 8:19, 20).

And whosoever will not do the law of thy God, and the law of the king, let judgment be executed speedily upon him, whether *it be* unto death, or to banishment, or to confiscation of goods, or to imprisonment (Ezra 7:26).

My son, fear thou the LORD and the king: *and* meddle not with them that are given to change (Prov 24:21).

For unto us a child is born, unto us a son is given: and the government shall be upon his shoulder: and his name shall be called Wonderful, Counsellor, The mighty God, The everlasting Father, The Prince of Peace (Isa 9:6).

And he changeth the times and the seasons: he removeth kings, and setteth up kings: he giveth wisdom unto the wise, and knowledge to them that know understanding (Dan 2:21).

This matter *is* by the decree of the watchers, and the demand by the word of the holy ones: to the intent that the living may know that the most High ruleth in the kingdom of men, and giveth it to whomsoever he will, and setteth up over it the basest of men (Dan 4:17).

Tell us therefore, What thinkest thou? Is it lawful to give tribute unto Cæsar, or not? But Jesus perceived their wickedness, and said, Why tempt ye me, *ye* hypocrites? Show me the tribute money. And they brought unto him a penny. And he saith unto them, Whose *is* this image and superscription? They say unto him, Cæsar's. Then saith he unto them, Render therefore unto Cæsar the things which are Cæsar's; and unto God the things that are God's (Matt 22:17–21).

Saying, The scribes and the Pharisees sit in Moses' seat: all therefore whatsoever they bid you observe, *that* observe and do; but do not ye after their works: for they say, and do not (Matt 23:2, 3).

If ye were of the world, the world would love his own: but because ye are not of the world, but I have chosen you out of the world, therefore the world hateth you (John 15:19).

I pray not that thou shouldest take them

out of the world, but that thou shouldest keep them from the evil. They are not of the world, even as I am not of the world (John 17:15, 16).

But Peter and John answered and said unto them, Whether it be right in the sight of God to hearken unto you more than unto God, judge ye (Acts 4:19).

Then Peter and the *other* apostles answered and said, We ought to obey God rather than men (Acts 5:29).

Let every soul be subject unto the higher powers. For there is no power but of God: the powers that be are ordained of God. Whosoever therefore resisteth the power, resisteth the ordinance of God: and they that resist shall receive to themselves damnation. For rulers are not a terror to good works, but to the evil. Wilt thou then not be afraid of the power? do that which is good, and thou shalt have praise of the same: for he is the minister of God to thee for good. But if thou do that which is evil, be afraid; for he beareth not the sword in vain: for he is the minister of God, a revenger to *execute* wrath upon him that doeth evil. Wherefore *ye* must needs be subject, not only for wrath, but also for conscience sake. For for this cause pay ye tribute also: for they are God's ministers, attending continually upon this very thing. Render therefore to all their dues: tribute to whom tribute *is due;* custom to whom custom; fear to whom fear; honour to whom honour (Rom 13:1–7).

Wherefore then *serveth* the law? It was added because of transgressions, till the seed should come to whom the promise was made; *and it was* ordained by angels in the hand of a mediator (Gal 3:19).

But we know that the law *is* good, if a man use it lawfully; knowing this, that the law is not made for a righteous man, but for the lawless and disobedient, for the ungodly and for sinners, for unholy and profane, for murderers of fathers and murderers of mothers, for manslayers, for whoremongers, for them that defile themselves with mankind, for menstealers, for liars, for perjured persons, and if there be any other thing that is contrary to sound doctrine (1 Tim 1:8–10).

I exhort therefore, that, first of all, supplications, prayers, intercessions, *and* giving of thanks, be made for all men; for kings, and *for* all that are in authority; that we may lead a quiet and peaceable life in all godliness and honesty. For this *is* good and acceptable in the sight of God our Saviour (1 Tim 2:1–3).

For here have we no continuing city, but we seek one to come (Heb 13:14).

But ye *are* a chosen generation, a royal priesthood, an holy nation, a peculiar people; that ye should shew forth the praises of him who hath called you out of darkness into his marvellous light: which in time past *were* not a people, but *are* now the people of God: which had not obtained mercy, but now have obtained mercy. Dearly beloved, I beseech *you* as strangers and pilgrims, abstain from fleshly lusts, which war against the soul; having your conversation honest among the Gentiles: that, whereas they speak against you as evildoers, they may by *your* good works, which they shall behold, glorify God in the day of visitation. Submit yourselves to every ordinance of man for the Lord's sake: whether it be to the king, as supreme; or unto governors, as unto them that are sent by him for the punishment of evildoers, and for the praise of them that do well. For so is the will of God, that with well-doing ye may put to silence the ignorance of foolish men (1 Pet 2:9–15).

Likewise also these *filthy* dreamers defile the flesh, despise dominion, and speak evil of dignities (Jude 1:8).

Biblical Examples: Josh 1:16–18; Judg 17:6; 2 Sam 3:36, 37; 18:12, 13; 19:5, 6; Dan 3:15; 6:6–10; Matt 17:24–27; Acts 16:37; 19:36–39; 22:25–29.

Further References: Ezra 6:10; 10:8; Prov 16:14, 15; 25:6–7, 15; Eccl 10:4, 20; Jer 29:7; Mark 12:14–17; Luke 20:22–25; Titus 3:1.

CIVIL DISOBEDIENCE (See Conscientious Objection)

CLAIRVOYANCE (See Witchcraft)

COERCION (See Violence)

COMMUNISM (See Economics; Property)

CONCEIT (See Pride)

CONSCIENCE

Yea, and why even of yourselves judge ye not what is right? (Luke 12:57).

For when the Gentiles, which have not the law, do by nature the things contained in the law, these, having not the law, are a law unto themselves: which shew the work of the law written in their hearts, their conscience also bearing witness, and *their* thoughts the mean while accusing or else excusing one another; in the day when God shall judge the secrets of men by Jesus Christ according to my gospel (Rom 2:14–16).

I say the truth in Christ, I lie not, my conscience also bearing me witness in the Holy Ghost (Rom 9:1).

Him that is weak in the faith receive ye, *but* not to doubtful disputations. For one believeth that he may eat all things: another, who is weak, eateth herbs. Let not him that eateth despise him that eateth not; and let not him which eateth not judge him that eateth: for God hath received him. Who art thou that judgest another man's servant? to his own master he standeth or falleth. Yea, he shall be holden up: for God is able to make him stand. One man esteemeth one day above another: another esteemeth every day *alike.* Let every man be fully persuaded in his own mind. He that regardeth the day, regardeth *it* unto the Lord; and he that regardeth not the day, to the Lord he doth not regard *it.* He that eateth, eateth to the Lord, for he giveth God thanks; and he that eateth not, to the Lord he eateth not, and giveth God thanks. For none of us liveth to himself, and no man dieth to himself. For whether we live, we live unto the Lord; and whether we die, we die unto the Lord: whether we live therefore, or die, we are the Lord's. For to this end Christ both died, and rose, and revived, that he might be Lord both of the dead and living. But why dost thou judge thy brother? or why dost thou set at nought thy brother? for we shall all stand before the judgment seat of Christ. For it is written, *As* I live, saith the Lord, every knee shall bow to me, and every tongue shall confess to God. So then every one of us shall give account of himself to God. Let us not therefore judge one another any more: but judge this rather, that no man put a stumblingblock or an occasion to fall in *his* brother's way. I know, and am persuaded by the Lord Jesus, that *there is* nothing unclean of itself: but to him that esteemeth any thing to be unclean, to him *it is* unclean. But if thy brother be grieved with *thy* meat, now walkest thou not charitably. Destroy not him with thy meat, for whom Christ died. Let not then your good be evil spoken of: for the kingdom of God is not meat and drink; but righteousness, and peace, and joy in the Holy Ghost. For he that in these things serveth Christ *is* acceptable to God, and approved of men. Let us therefore follow after the things which make for peace, and things wherewith one may edify another. For meat destroy not the work of God. All things indeed *are* pure; but *it is* evil for that man who eateth with offence. *It is* good neither to eat flesh, nor to drink wine, nor *any thing* whereby thy brother stumbleth, or is offended, or is made weak. Hast thou faith? have *it* to thyself before God. Happy *is* he that condemneth not himself in that thing which he alloweth. And he that doubteth is damned if he eat, because *he eateth* not of faith: for whatsoever *is* not of faith is sin (Rom 14:1–23).

For who hath known the mind of the Lord, that he may instruct him? But we have the mind of Christ (1 Cor 2:16).

For if any man see thee which hast knowledge sit at meat in the idol's temple, shall not the conscience of him which is weak be emboldened to eat those things which are offered to idols; and through thy knowledge shall the weak brother perish, for whom Christ died? But when ye sin so against the brethren, and wound their weak conscience, ye sin against Christ. Wherefore, if meat make my brother to offend, I will eat no flesh while the world standeth, lest I make my brother to offend (1 Cor 8:10–13).

If any of them that believe not bid you *to a feast,* and ye be disposed to go; whatsoever is set before you, eat, asking no question for conscience sake. But if any man say unto you, This is offered in sacrifice unto idols, eat not for his sake that shewed it, and for conscience sake: for the earth *is* the Lord's, and the fulness thereof: Conscience, I say, not thine own, but of the other: for why is my liberty judged of another *man's* conscience? For if I by grace be a partaker, why am I evil spoken of for that for which I give thanks? Whether therefore ye eat, or drink, or whatsoever ye do, do all to the glory of God. Give none offence, neither to the Jews, nor to the Gentiles, nor to the church of God (1 Cor 10:27–32).

For our rejoicing is this, the testimony of our conscience, that in simplicity and godly sincerity, not with fleshly wisdom, but by the grace of God, we have had our conversation in the world, and more abundantly to you-ward (2 Cor 1:12).

But have renounced the hidden things of dishonesty, not walking in craftiness, nor handling the word of God deceitfully; but by manifestation of the truth commending ourselves to every man's conscience in the sight of God (2 Cor 4:2).

Knowing therefore the terror of the Lord, we persuade men; but we are made manifest unto God; and I trust also are made manifest in your consciences (2 Cor 5:11).

Now the end of the commandment is charity out of a pure heart, and *of* a good conscience, and *of* faith unfeigned (1 Tim 1:5).

This charge I commit unto thee, son Timothy, according to the prophecies which went before on thee, that thou by them mightest war a good warfare; holding faith, and a good conscience; which some having put away concerning faith have made shipwreck (1 Tim 1:18, 19).

Speaking lies in hypocrisy; having their conscience seared with a hot iron (1 Tim 4:2).

Unto the pure all things *are* pure: but unto them that are defiled and unbelieving *is* nothing pure; but even their mind and conscience is defiled (Titus 1:15).

The Holy Ghost this signifying, that the way into the holiest of all was not yet made manifest, while as the first tabernacle was yet standing: which *was* a figure for the time then present, in which were offered both gifts and sacrifices, that could not

make him that did the service perfect, as pertaining to the conscience; *which stood* only in meats and drinks, and divers washings, and carnal ordinances, imposed *on them* until the time of reformation (Heb 9:8–10).

For if the blood of bulls and of goats, and the ashes of an heifer sprinkling the unclean, sanctifieth to the purifying of the flesh: how much more shall the blood of Christ, who through the eternal Spirit offered himself without spot to God, purge your conscience from dead works to serve the living God? (Heb 9:13, 14).

Having therefore, brethren, boldness to enter into the holiest by the blood of Jesus, by a new and living way, which he hath consecrated for us, through the veil, that is to say, his flesh; and *having* an high priest over the house of God; let us draw near with a true heart in full assurance of faith, having our hearts sprinkled from an evil conscience, and our bodies washed with pure water (Heb 10:19–22).

Pray for us: for we trust we have a good conscience, in all things willing to live honestly (Heb 13:18).

Having a good conscience; that, whereas they speak evil of you, as of evildoers, they may be ashamed that falsely accuse your good conversation in Christ. The like figure whereunto *even* baptism doth also now save us (not the putting away of the filth of the flesh, but the answer of a good conscience toward God,) by the resurrection of Jesus Christ (1 Pet 3:16, 21).

Biblical Examples: Gen 3:7, 8; 12:18; 31:39; 33:1–12; 39:7–12; Ps 51; 73:21; Dan 1:8; Matt 26:75; 27:3–5; John 8:9; Acts 2:37; 4:19, 20; 23:1; 24:16.

Further References: Rom 7:15–23; 1 Tim 3:9; Heb 10:26, 27; 1 Pet 2:19; 1 John 3:20, 21.

CONSCIENTIOUS OBJECTION

And the officers shall speak unto the people, saying, What man *is there* that hath built a new house, and hath not dedicated it? let him go and return to his house, lest he die in the battle, and another man dedicate it. And what man *is he* that hath planted a vineyard, and hath not *yet* eaten of it? let him *also* go and return unto his house, lest he die in the battle, and another man eat of it. And what man *is there* that hath betrothed a wife, and hath not taken her? let him go and return unto his house, least he die in the battle, and another man take her. And the officers shall speak further unto the people, and they shall say, What man *is there that is* fearful and fainthearted? let him go and return unto his house, lest his brethren's heart faint as well as his heart. And it shall be, when the officers have made an end of speaking unto the people, that they shall make captains of the armies to lead the people (Deut 20:5–9).

Tell us therefore, What thinkest thou? Is it lawful to give tribute unto Cæsar, or not?

But Jesus perceived their wickedness, and said, Why tempt ye me, *ye* hypocrites?

Show me the tribute money. And they brought unto him a penny.

And he saith unto them, Whose *is* this image and superscription?

They say unto him, Cæsar's. Then saith he unto them, Render therefore unto Cæsar the things which are Cæsar's; and unto God the things that are God's (Matt 22:17–21).

But Peter and John answered and said unto them, Whether it be right in the sight of God to hearken unto you more than unto God, judge ye (Acts 4:19).

Then Peter and the *other* apostles answered and said, We ought to obey God rather than men (Acts 5:29).

Whosoever therefore resisteth the power, resisteth the ordinance of God: and they that resist shall receive to themselves damnation (Rom 13:2).

Submit yourselves to every ordinance of man for the Lord's sake: whether it be to the king, as supreme; or unto governors, as unto them that are sent by him for the punishment of evildoers, and for the praise of them that do well. For so is the will of God, that with well-doing ye may put to silence the ignorance of foolish men: as free, and not using *your* liberty for a cloak of maliciousness, but as the servants of God (1 Pet 2:13–16).

Biblical Examples: Dan 6:12–15; Acts 5:29.

CONSUMER FRAUD (See also Deceit; Dishonesty; Honesty)

Just balances, just weights, a just ephah, and a just hin, shall ye have: I *am* the LORD your God, which brought you out of the land of Egypt (Lev 19:36).

Thou shalt not have in thy bag divers weights, a great and a small. Thou shalt not have in thine house divers measures, a great and a small. *But* thou shalt have a perfect and just weight, a perfect and just measure shalt thou have: that thy days may be lengthened in the land which the LORD thy God giveth thee. For all that do such things, *and* all that do unrighteously, *are* an abomination unto the LORD thy God (Deut 25:13–16).

A false balance *is* abomination to the LORD: but a just weight *is* his delight (Prov 11:1).

A just weight and balance *are* the LORD'S: all the weights of the bag *are* his work (Prov 16:11).

Divers weights, *and* divers measures, both of them *are* alike abomination to the LORD (Prov 20:10).

Here this, O ye that swallow up the needy, even to make the poor of the land to fail, saying, When will the new moon be gone, that we may sell corn? and the sabbath, that we may set forth wheat, making the ephah small, and the skekel great, and falsifying the balances by deceit? (Amos 8:4, 5).

He hath shewed thee, O man, what *is* good; and what doth the LORD require of thee, but to do justly, and to love mercy, and to walk humbly with thy God? The LORD'S voice crieth unto the city, and *the man of* wisdom shall see thy name: hear ye the rod, and who hath appointed it.

Are there yet the treasures of wickedness in the house of the wicked, and the scant measure *that is* abominable? Shall I count *them* pure with the wicked balances, and with the bag of deceitful weights? (Mic 6:8–11).

Biblical Examples: Ezek 22:9; Hos 4:1, 2.

Further References: Job 24:2–11; Isa 32:7; Jer 7:8–10; 9:4–6, 8; Hos 12:7; 1 Thess 4:6.

CONTENTMENT (See Mental Health)

CONTRACTS (See also Honesty; Labor Relations)

Unto Abraham for a possession in the presence of the children of Heth, before all that went in at the gate of his city (Gen 23:18).

Now therefore come thou, let us make a covenant, I and thou; and let it be for a witness between me and thee. And Jacob took a stone, and set it up *for* a pillar. And Jacob said unto his brethren, Gather stones; and they took stones, and made an heap: and they did eat there upon the heap. And Laban called it Jegarsahadutha: but Jacob called it Galeed. And Laban said, This heap *is* a witness between me and thee this day. Therefore was the name of it called Galeed; and Mizpah; for he said, The LORD watch between me and thee, when we are absent one from another. If thou shalt afflict my daughters, or if thou shalt take *other* wives beside my daughters, no man *is* with us; see, God *is* witness betwixt me and thee. And Laban said to Jacob, Behold this heap, and behold *this* pillar, which I have cast betwixt me and thee; This heap *be* witness, and *this* pillar *be* witness, that I will not pass over this heap to thee, and that thou shalt not pass over this heap and this pillar unto me, for harm. The God of Abraham, and the God of Nahor, the God of their father, judge betwixt us. And Jacob sware by the fear of his father Isaac. Then Jacob offered sacrifice upon the mount, and called his brethren to eat bread: and they did eat bread, and tarried all night in the mount (Gen 31:44–54).

If thou shalt afflict my daughters, or if thou shalt take *other* wives beside my daughters, no man *is* with us; see, God *is* witness betwixt me and thee (Gen 31:50).

If thou buy an Hebrew servant, six years he shall serve: and in the seventh he shall go out free for nothing. If he came in by himself, he shall go out by himself: if he were married, then his wife shall go out with him. If his master have given him a wife, and she have borne him sons or daughters; the wife and her children shall be her master's, and he shall go out by himself. And if the servant shall plainly say, I love my master, my wife, and my children; I will not go out free: then his master shall bring him unto the judges; he shall also bring him to the door, or unto the door post; and his master shall bore his ear through with an awl; and he shall serve him for ever (Exod 21:2–6).

And the LORD spake unto Moses, saying, If a soul sin, and commit a trespass against the LORD, and lie unto his neighbour in that which was delivered him to keep, or in fellowship, or in a thing taken away by violence, or hath deceived his neighbour; then it shall be, because he hath sinned, and is guilty, that he shall restore that which he took violently away, or the thing which he hath deceitfully gotten, or that which was delivered him to keep, or the lost thing which he found, or all that about which he hath sworn falsely; he shall even restore it in the principal, and shall add the fifth part more thereto, *and* give it unto him to whom it appertaineth, in the day of his trespass offering. And he shall bring his trespass offering unto the LORD, a ram without blemish out of the flock, with thy estimation, for a trespass offering, unto the priest: and the priest shall make an atonement for him before the LORD: and it shall be forgiven him for any thing of all that he hath done in trespassing therein (Lev 6:1, 2, 4–7).

And Moses spake unto the heads of the tribes concerning the children of Israel, saying, This *is* the thing which the LORD hath commanded. If a man vow a vow unto the LORD, or swear an oath to bind his soul with a bond; he shall not break his word, he shall do according to all that proceedeth out of his mouth (Num 30:1, 2).

And when the inhabitants of Gibeon heard what Joshua had done unto Jericho and to Ai, they did work wilily, and went and made as if they had been ambassadors, and took old sacks upon their asses, and wine bottles, old, and rent, and bound up; and old shoes and clouted upon their feet, and old garments upon them; and all the bread of their provision was dry *and* mouldy. And they went to Joshua unto the camp at Gilgal, and said unto him, and to the men of Israel, We be come from a far country: now therefore make ye a league with us. And the men of Israel said unto the Hivites, Peradventure ye dwell among us; and how shall we make a league with you? And they said unto Joshua, We *are* thy servants. And Joshua said unto them, Who *are* ye? and from whence come ye? And they said unto him, From a very far country thy servants are come because of the name of the LORD thy God: for we have heard the fame of him, and all that he did in Egypt. . . .

And Joshua made peace with them, and made a league with them, to let them live: and the princes of the congregation sware unto them.

And it came to pass at the end of three days after they had made a league with them, that they heard that they *were* their neighbours, and *that* they dwelt among them. And the children of Israel journeyed, and came unto their cities on the third day. Now their cities *were* Gibeon, and Chephirah, and Beeroth, and Kirjath-jearim. And the children of Israel smote them not, because the princes of the congregation had sworn unto them by the LORD God of Israel. And all the congregation murmured against the princes. But all the princes said unto all the congregation, We have sworn unto them by the LORD God of Israel: now therefore we may not touch them (Josh 9:3–9, 15–19).

But I say unto you, That ye resist not evil: but whosoever shall smite thee on thy right cheek, turn to him the other also. And if any man will sue thee at the law, and take away thy coat, let him have *thy* cloak also (Matt 5:39, 40).

For the kingdom of heaven is like unto a man *that is* an householder, which went out early in the morning to hire labourers into his vineyard. And when he had agreed with the labourers for a penny a day, he sent them into his vineyard. And he went out about the third hour, and saw others standing idle in the marketplace, and said unto them; Go ye also into the vineyard, and whatsoever is right I will give you. And they went their way. Again he went out about the sixth and ninth hour, and did likewise. And about the eleventh hour he went out, and found others standing idle, and saith unto them,

Why stand ye here all the day idle? They say unto him, Because no man hath hired us. He saith unto them, Go ye also into the vineyard; and whatsoever is right, *that* shall ye receive. So when even was come, the lord of the vineyard saith unto his steward, Call the labourers, and give them *their* hire, beginning from the last unto the first. And when they came that *were hired* about the eleventh hour, they received every man a penny. But when the first came, they supposed that they should have received more; and they likewise received every man a penny. And when they had received *it,* they murmured against the goodman of the house, Saying, These last have wrought *but* one hour, and thou hast made them equal unto us, which have borne the burden and heat of the day. But he answered one of them, and said, Friend, I do thee no wrong: didst not thou agree with me for a penny? Take *that* thine *is,* and go thy way: I will give unto this last, even as unto thee. Is it not lawful for me to do what I will with mine own? Is thine eye evil, because I am good? So the last shall be first, and the first last: for many be called, but few chosen (Matt 20:2–16).

Brethren, I speak after the manner of men; Though *it be* but a man's covenant, yet *if it be* confirmed, no man disannulleth, or addeth thereto (Gal 3:15).

Biblical Examples: Gen 21:25–32; 29:15–20, 27–30; 1 Kings 5:9–11; Jer 32:10–15.

Further References: Gen 30:27–29, 31–34; Ruth 4:6–8; Prov 6:11; 17:18.

CONVERSATION (See Tongue)

CORPORAL PUNISHMENT (See also Crime and Punishment)

If men strive, and hurt a woman with child, so that her fruit depart *from her,* and yet no mischief follow: he shall be surely punished according as the woman's husband will lay upon him; and he shall pay as the judges *determine.* And if *any* mischief follow, then thou shalt give life for life, eye for eye, tooth for tooth, hand for hand, foot for foot, burning for burning, wound for wound, stripe for stripe (Exod 21:22–25).

If any man take a wife, and go in unto her, and hate her, and give occasions of speech against her, and bring up an evil name upon her, and say, I took this woman, and when I came to her, I found her not a maid: then shall the father of the damsel, and her mother, take and bring forth *the tokens of* the damsel's virginity unto the elders of the city in the gate: and the damsel's father shall say unto the elders, I gave my daughter unto this man to wife, and he hateth her; and, lo, he hath given occasions of speech *against her*, saying, I found not thy daughter a maid; and yet these *are the tokens of* my daughter's virginity. And they shall spread the cloth before the elders of the city. And the elders of that city shall take that man and chastise him; and they shall amerce him in an hundred *shekels* of silver, and give *them* unto the father of the damsel, because he hath brought up an evil name upon a virgin of Israel: and she shall be his wife; he may not put her away all his days (Deut 22:13–19).

If there be a controversy between men, and they come unto judgment, that *the judges* may judge them; then they shall justify the righteous, and condemn the wicked. And it shall be, if the wicked man *be* worthy to be beaten, that the judge shall cause him to lie down, and to be beaten before his face, according to his fault, by a certain number. Forty stripes he may give him, *and* not exceed: lest, *if* he should exceed, and beat him above these with many stripes, then thy brother should seem vile unto thee (Deut 25:1–3).

He that spareth his rod hateth his son: but he that loveth him chasteneth him betimes (Prov 13:24).

Biblical Examples: Gen 39:20; Jer 37:11–21; 52:1–11; Matt 27:26; John 19:1–3; Acts 4:1–3; 5:17, 18; 22:24, 29.

Further References: Lev 19:20; Prov 17:10; 19:29; 20:30.

COURAGE

The wicked flee when no man pursueth: but the righteous are bold as a lion (Prov 28:1).

And he arose, and rebuked the wind, and said unto the sea, Peace, be still. And the wind ceased, and there was a great calm. And he said unto them, Why are ye so fearful? how is it that ye have no faith? And they feared exceedingly, and said one to another, What manner of man is this, that even the wind and the sea obey him? (Mark 4:39–41).

Watch ye, stand fast in the faith, quit you like men, be strong (1 Cor 16:13).

Only let your conversation be as it becometh the gospel of Christ: that whether I come and see you, or else be absent, I may hear of your affairs, that ye stand fast in one spirit, with one mind striving together for the faith of the gospel; and in nothing terrified by your adversaries: which is to them an evident token of perdition, but to you of salvation, and that of God (Phil 1:27, 28).

When I call to remembrance the unfeigned faith that is in thee, which dwelt first in thy grandmother Lois, and thy mother Eunice; and I am persuaded that in thee also. Wherefore I put thee in remembrance that thou stir up the gift of God, which is in thee by the putting on of my hands. For God hath not given us the spirit of fear; but of power, and of love, and of a sound mind (2 Tim 1:5–7).

Biblical Examples: Num 13:30; 14:6–12; Judg 7:7–23; 1 Sam 17:32–50; 2 Sam 19:5–7; Esth 4:8, 6; 5–7; Acts 5:21, 29–32; 20:22–24.

Further References: Deut 31:7, 8; 1 Chron 22:13; Ezek 2:6.

COURTS OF LAW (See Justice; Law)

COVETOUSNESS (See also Envy; Greed; Jealousy; Lust)

Thou shalt not covet thy neighbour's house, thou shalt not covet thy neighbour's wife, nor his manservant, nor his maidservant, nor his ox, nor his ass, nor any thing that *is* thy neighbour's (Exod 20:17).

For the wicked boasteth of his heart's desire, and blesseth the covetous, *whom* the LORD abhorreth (Ps 10:3).

He that is greedy of gain troubleth his own house; but he that hateth gifts shall live (Prov 15:27).

He that oppresseth the poor to increase his *riches, and* he that giveth to the rich, *shall* surely *come* to want (Prov 22:16).

He that loveth silver shall not be satisfied with silver; nor he that loveth abundance with increase: this *is* also vanity. When goods increase, they are increased that eat them: and what good *is there* to the owners thereof, saving the beholding *of them* with their eyes? (Eccl 5:10, 11).

As the partridge sitteth *on eggs,* and hatcheth *them* not; *so* he that getteth riches, and not by right, shall leave them in the midst of his days, and at his end shall be a fool (Jer 17:11).

Woe to them that devise iniquity, and work evil upon their beds! when the morning is light, they practise it, because it is in the power of their hand. And they covet fields, and take *them* by violence; and houses, and take *them* away: so they oppress a man and his house, even a man and his heritage. Therefore thus saith the LORD; Behold, against this family do I devise an evil, from which ye shall not remove your necks; neither shall ye go haughtily: for this time *is* evil.

In that day shall *one* take up a parable against you, and lament with a doleful lamentation, *and* say, We be utterly spoiled: he hath changed the portion of my people: how hath he removed *it* from me! turning away he hath divided our fields. Therefore thou shalt have none that shall cast a cord by lot in the congregation of the LORD (Mic 2:1–5).

Ye have sown much, and bring in little; ye eat, but ye have not enough; ye drink, but ye are not filled with drink; ye clothe you, but there is none warm; and he that earneth wages earneth wages *to put it* into a bag with holes (Hag 1:6).

Lay not up for yourselves treasures upon earth, where moth and rust doth corrupt, and where thieves break through and steal: but lay up for yourselves treasures in heaven, where neither moth nor rust doth corrupt, and where thieves do not break through nor steal:

For where your treasure is, there will your heart be also (Matt 6:19–21).

And he said unto them, Take heed, and beware of covetousness: for a man's life consisteth not in the abundance of the things which he possesseth (Luke 12:15).

(For many walk, of whom I have told you often, and now tell you even weeping, *that they are* the enemies of the cross of Christ: Whose end *is* destruction, whose God *is their* belly, and *whose* glory *is* in their shame, who mind earthly things) (Phil 3:18, 19).

Set your affection on things above, not on things on the earth.

For ye are dead, and your life is hid with Christ in God.

When Christ, *who is* our life, shall appear, then shall ye also appear with him in glory.

Mortify therefore your members which are upon the earth; fornication, uncleanness, inordinate affection, evil concupiscence, and covetousness, which is idolatry (Col 3:2–5).

Let your conversation *be* without covetousness; *and be* content with such things as ye have: for he hath said, I will never leave thee, nor forsake thee (Heb 13:5).

Feed the flock of God which is among you, taking the oversight *thereof,* not by constraint, but willingly; not for filthy lucre, but of a ready mind (1 Pet 5:2).

Love not the world, neither the things *that are* in the world. If any man love the world, the love of the Father is not in him (1 John 2:15).

Biblical Examples: Gen 3:6; 13:10–13; 2 Sam 11:2–5; 1 Kings 21:2–16; Jer 6:13; 8:10; 22:17; Ezek 33:31; Hab 2:5–9; Luke 12:15–21; Acts 16:19; 2 Tim 4:10.

Further References: Exod 18:21; Deut 5:21; Job 31:24, 25; Ps 119:36; Prov 21:25, 26; 23:4, 5; Isa 56:11; 57:17; Jer 51:13; Matt 16:26; Mark 7:21–23; Luke 12:15, 33, 34; Rom 1:29; 13:9; 1 Cor 5:11; Eph 5:3; 1 Thess 2:5; 1 Tim 3:3; 2 Tim 3:2; Titus 1:11; 2 Peter 2:3, 14.

COWARDICE (See Fear)

CREDITOR (See Debt and Debtor; Usury and Interest)

CRIME AND PUNISHMENT (See also Adultery; Bribes and Bribery; Capital Punishment; Consumer Fraud; Corporal Punishment; Dishonesty; Extortion; Fornication; Incest; Kidnapping; Lying; Perjury; Prostitution; Rape; Theft)

And surely your blood of your lives will I require; at the hand of every beast will I require it, and at the hand of man; at the hand of every man's brother will I require the life of man. Whoso sheddeth man's blood, by man shall his blood be shed: for in the image of God made he man (Gen 9:5, 6).

And if a man lie not in wait, but God deliver *him* into his hand; then I will appoint thee a place whither he shall flee. But if a man come presumptuously upon his neighbour, to slay him with guile; thou shalt take him from mine altar, that he may die (Exod 21:13, 14).

And if men strive together, and one smite another with a stone, or with *his* fist, and he die not, but keepeth *his* bed: if he rise again, and walk abroad upon his staff, then shall he that smote *him* be quit: only he shall pay *for* the loss of his time, and shall cause *him* to be thoroughly healed.

And if a man smite his servant, or his maid, with a rod, and he die under his hand; he shall be surely punished. Notwithstanding, if he continue a day or two, he shall not be punished: for he *is* his money.

If men strive, and hurt a woman with child, so that her fruit depart *from her,* and yet no mischief follow: he shall be surely punished, according as the woman's husband will lay upon him; and he shall pay as the judges *determine.* And if *any* mischief follow, then thou shalt give life for life, eye for eye, tooth for tooth, hand for hand, foot for foot, burning for burning, wound for wound, stripe for stripe.

And if a man smite the eye of his servant, or the eye of his maid, that it perish; he shall let him go free for his eye's sake. And if he smite out his manservant's tooth, or his maidservant's tooth; he shall let him go free for his tooth's sake (Exod 21:18–27).

And if a man shall open a pit, or if a man shall dig a pit, and not cover it, and an ox or an ass fall therein; the owner of the pit shall make *it* good, *and* give money unto the owner of them; and the dead *beast* shall be his.

And if one man's ox hurt another's, that he die; then they shall sell the live ox, and

divide the money of it; and the dead *ox* also they shall divide. Or if it be known that the ox hath used to push in time past, and his owner hath not kept him in; he shall surely pay ox for ox; and the dead shall be his own (Exod 21:33–36).

If a man shall steal an ox, or a sheep, and kill it, or sell it; he shall restore five oxen for an ox, and four sheep for a sheep. If a thief be found breaking up, and be smitten that he die, *there shall* no blood *be shed* for him. If the sun be risen upon him, *there shall be* blood *shed* for him; *for* he should make full restitution; if he have nothing, then he shall be sold for his theft. If the theft be certainly found in his hand alive, whether it be ox, or ass, or sheep; he shall restore double.

If a man shall cause a field or vineyard to be eaten, and shall put in his beast, and shall feed in another man's field; of the best of his own field, and of the best of his own vineyard, shall he make restitution.

If fire break out, and catch in thorns, so that the stacks of corn, or the standing corn, or the field, be consumed *therewith;* he that kindled the fire shall surely make restitution.

If a man shall deliver unto his neighbour money or stuff to keep, and it be stolen out of the man's house; if the thief be found, let him pay double. If the thief be not found, then the master of the house shall be brought unto the judges, *to see* whether he have put his hand unto his neighbour's goods. For all manner of trespass, *whether it be* for ox, for ass, for sheep, for raiment, *or* for any manner of lost thing, which *another* challengeth to be his, the cause of both parties shall come before the judges; *and* whom the judges shall condemn, he shall pay double unto his neighbour (Exod 22:1–9).

Thou shalt not suffer a witch to live.

Whosoever lieth with a beast shall surely be put to death.

He that sacrificeth unto *any* god, save unto the LORD only, he shall be utterly destroyed.

Thou shalt neither vex a stranger, nor oppress him: for ye were strangers in the land of Egypt.

Ye shall not afflict any widow, or fatherless child. If thou afflict them in any wise, and they cry at all unto me, I will surely hear their cry; and my wrath shall wax hot, and I will kill you with the sword; and your wives shall be widows, and your children fatherless (Exod 22:18–24).

And whosoever lieth carnally with a woman, that *is* a bondmaid, betrothed to an husband, and not at all redeemed, nor freedom given her; she shall be scourged; they shall not be put to death, because she was not free (Lev 19:20).

And the LORD spake unto Moses, saying, Again, thou shalt say to the children of Israel, Whosoever *he be* of the children of Israel, or of the strangers that sojourn in Israel, that giveth *any* of his seed unto Molech; he shall surely be put to death: the people of the land shall stone him with stones. And I will set my face against that man, and will cut him off from among his people; because he hath given of his seed unto Molech, to defile my sanctuary, and to profane my holy name. And if the people of the land do any ways hide their eyes from the man, when he giveth of his seed unto Molech, and kill him not: then I will set my face against that man, and against his family, and will cut him off, and all that go a-whoring after him, to commit whoredom with Molech, from among their people (Lev 20:1–5).

For every one that curseth his father or his mother shall be surely put to death: he hath cursed his father or his mother; his blood *shall be* upon him.

And the man that committeth adultery with *another* man's wife, *even he* that committeth adultery with his neighbour's wife, the adulterer and the adulteress shall surely be put to death. And the man that lieth with his father's wife hath uncovered his father's nakedness: both of them shall surely be put to death; their blood *shall be* upon them. And if a man lie with his daughter in law, both of them shall surely be put to death: they have wrought confusion; their blood *shall be* upon them. If a man also lie with mankind, as he lieth with a woman, both of them have committed an abomination: they shall surely be put to death; their blood *shall be* upon them. And if a man take a wife and her mother, it *is* wickedness: they shall be

burnt with fire, both he and they; that there be no wickedness among you. And if a man lie with a beast, he shall surely be put to death: and ye shall slay the beast. And if a woman approach unto any beast, and lie down thereto, thou shalt kill the woman, and the beast: they shall surely be put to death; their blood *shall be* upon them (Lev 20:9–16).

A man also or woman that hath a familiar spirit, or that is a wizard, shall surely be put to death: they shall stone them with stones: their blood *shall be* upon them (Lev 20:27).

And the daughter of any priest, if she profane herself by playing the whore, she profaneth her father: she shall be burnt with fire (Lev 21:9).

And he that killeth any man shall surely be put to death. And he that killeth a beast shall make it good; beast for beast. And if a man cause a blemish in his neighbour; as he hath done, so shall it be done to him; breach for breach, eye for eye, tooth for tooth: as he hath caused a blemish in a man, so shall it be done to him *again*. And he that killeth a beast, he shall restore it: and he that killeth a man, he shall be put to death. Ye shall have one manner of law, as well for the stranger, as for one of your own country: for I *am* the LORD your God (Lev 24:17–22).

But the soul that doeth *aught* presumptuously, *whether he be* born in the land, or a stranger, the same reproacheth the LORD; and that soul shall be cut off from among his people (Num 15:30).

And among the cities which ye shall give unto the Levites *there shall be* six cities for refuge, which ye shall appoint for the manslayer, that he may flee thither: and to them ye shall add forty and two cities. *So* all the cities which ye shall give to the Levites *shall be* forty and eight cities: them *shall ye give* with their suburbs. And the cities which ye shall give *shall be* of the possession of the children of Israel: from *them that have* many ye shall give many; but from *them that have* few ye shall give few: every one shall give of his cities unto the Levites according to his inheritance which he inheriteth.

And the LORD spake unto Moses, saying, Speak unto the children of Israel, and say unto them, When ye be come over Jordan into the land of Canaan; then ye shall appoint you cities to be cities of refuge for you; that the slayer may flee thither, which killeth any person at unawares. And they shall be unto you cities for refuge from the avenger; that the manslayer die not, until he stand before the congregation in judgment. And of these cities which ye shall give six cities shall ye have for refuge. Ye shall give three cities on this side Jordan, and three cities shall ye give in the land of Canaan, *which* shall be cities of refuge. These six cities shall be a refuge, *both* for the children of Israel, and for the stranger, and for the sojourner among them: that every one that killeth any person unawares may flee thither.

And if he smite him with an instrument of iron, so that he die, he *is* a murderer: the murderer shall surely be put to death. And if he smite him with throwing a stone, wherewith he may die, and he die, he *is* a murderer: the murderer shall surely be put to death. Or *if* he smite him with an hand weapon of wood, wherewith he may die, and he die, he *is* a murderer: the murderer shall surely be put to death. The revenger of blood himself shall slay the murderer: when he meeteth him, he shall slay him. But if he thrust him of hatred, or hurl at him by laying of wait, that he die; or in enmity smite him with his hand, that he die: he that smote *him* shall surely be put to death; *for* he *is* a murderer: the revenger of blood shall slay the murderer, when he meeteth him.

But if he thrust him suddenly without enmity, or have cast upon him any thing without laying of wait, or with any stone, wherewith a man may die, seeing *him* not, and cast *it* upon him, that he die, and *was* not his enemy, neither sought his harm: then the congregation shall judge between the slayer and the revenger of blood according to these judgments: and the congregation shall deliver the slayer out of the hand of the revenger of blood, and the congregation shall restore him to the city of his refuge, whither he was fled: and he shall abide in it unto the death of the high priest, which was anointed with the holy oil. But if the slayer shall at any time come without the border of the city of his refuge, whither he was fled;

and the revenger of blood find him without the borders of the city of his refuge, and the revenger of blood kill the slayer; he shall not be guilty of blood: because he should have remained in the city of his refuge until the death of the high priest: but after the death of the high priest the slayer shall return into the land of his possession.

So these *things* shall be for a statute of judgment unto you throughout your generations in all your dwellings. Whoso killeth any person, the murderer shall be put to death by the mouth of witnesses: but one witness shall not testify against any person *to cause him* to die. Moreover ye shall take no satisfaction for the life of a murderer, which *is* guilty of death: but he shall be surely put to death. And ye shall take no satisfaction for him that is fled to the city of his refuge, that he should come again to dwell in the land, until the death of the priest. So ye shall not pollute the land wherein ye *are:* for blood it defileth the land: and the land cannot be cleansed of the blood that is shed therein, but by the blood of him that shed it (Num 35:6–33).

Then Moses severed three cities on this side Jordan toward the sun rising; that the slayer might flee thither, which should kill his neighbour unawares, and hated him not in times past; and that fleeing unto one of these cities he might live: *namely,* Bezer in the wilderness, in the plain country, of the Reubenites; and Ramoth in Gilead, of the Gadites; and Golan in Bashan, of the Manassites (Deut 4:41–43).

If there arise among you a prophet, or a dreamer of dreams, and giveth thee a sign or a wonder, and the sign or the wonder come to pass, whereof he spake unto thee, saying, Let us go after other gods, which thou hast not known, and let us serve them; thou shalt not hearken unto the words of that prophet, or that dreamer of dreams: for the LORD your God proveth you, to know whether ye love the LORD your God with all your heart and with all your soul. Ye shall walk after the LORD your God, and fear him, and keep his commandments, and obey his voice, and ye shall serve him, and cleave unto him. And that prophet, or that dreamer of dreams, shall be put to death; because he hath spoken to turn *you* away from the LORD your God, which brought you out of the land of Egypt, and redeemed you out of the house of bondage, to thrust thee out of the way which the LORD thy God commanded thee to walk in. So shalt thou put the evil away from the midst of thee.

If thy brother, the son of thy mother, or thy son, or thy daughter, or the wife of thy bosom, or thy friend, which *is* as thine own soul, entice thee secretly, saying, Let us go and serve other gods, which thou hast not known, thou, nor thy fathers; *namely,* of the gods of the people which *are* round about you, nigh unto thee, or far off from thee, from the *one* end of the earth even unto the *other* end of the earth; thou shalt not consent unto him, nor hearken unto him; neither shall thine eye pity him, neither shalt thou spare, neither shalt thou conceal him: but thou shalt surely kill him; thine hand shall be first upon him to put him to death, and afterwards the hand of all the people. And thou shalt stone him with stones, that he die; because he hath sought to thrust thee away from the LORD thy God, which brought thee out of the land of Egypt, from the house of bondage. And all Israel shall hear, and fear, and shall do no more any such wickedness as this is among you.

If thou shalt hear *say* in one of thy cities, which the LORD thy God hath given thee to dwell there, saying, *Certain* men, the children of Belial, are gone out from among you, and have withdrawn the inhabitants of their city, saying, Let us go and serve other gods, which ye have not known; then shalt thou inquire, and make search, and ask diligently; and, behold, *if it be* truth, *and* the thing certain, *that* such abomination is wrought among you; thou shalt surely smite the inhabitants of that city with the edge of the sword, destroying it utterly, and all that *is* therein, and the cattle thereof, with the edge of the sword. And thou shalt gather all the spoil of it into the midst of the street thereof, and shalt burn with fire the city, and all the spoil thereof every whit, for the LORD thy God: and it shall be an heap for ever; it shall not be built again. And there shall cleave nought of the cursed thing to thine hand: that the LORD may turn from the fierceness of his anger, and shew thee

mercy, and have compassion upon thee, and multiply thee, as he hath sworn unto thy fathers; when thou shalt hearken to the voice of the LORD thy God, to keep all his commandments which I command thee this day, to do *that which is* right in the eyes of the LORD thy God (Deut 13:1–18).

If there be found among you, within any of thy gates which the LORD thy God giveth thee, man or woman, that hath wrought wickedness in the sight of the LORD thy God, in transgressing his covenant, and hath gone and served other gods, and worshipped them, either the sun, or moon, or any of the host of heaven, which I have not commanded; and it be told thee, and thou hast heard *of it,* and inquired diligently, and, behold, *it be* true, *and* the thing certain, *that* such abomination is wrought in Israel: then shalt thou bring forth that man or that woman, which have committed that wicked thing, unto thy gates, *even* that man or that woman, and shalt stone them with stones, till they die. At the mouth of two witnesses, or three witnesses, shall he that is worthy of death be put to death; *but* at the mouth of one witness he shall not be put to death. The hands of the witnesses shall be first upon him to put him to death, and afterward the hands of all the people. So thou shalt put the evil away from among you (Deut 17:2–7).

If there arise a matter too hard for thee in judgment, between blood and blood, between plea and plea, and between stroke and stroke, *being* matters of controversy within thy gates: then shalt thou arise, and get thee up into the place which the LORD thy God shall choose; and thou shalt come unto the priests the Levites, and unto the judge that shall be in those days, and inquire; and they shall shew thee the sentence of judgment: and thou shalt do according to the sentence, which they of that place which the LORD shall choose shall shew thee; and thou shalt observe to do according to all that they inform thee: according to the sentence of the law which they shall teach thee, and according to the judgment which they shall tell thee, thou shalt do: thou shalt not decline from the sentence which they shall shew thee, *to* the right hand, nor *to* the left. And the man that will do presumptuously, and will not hearken unto the priest that standeth to minister there before the LORD thy God, or unto the judge, even that man shall die: and thou shalt put away the evil from Israel. And all the people shall hear, and fear, and do no more presumptuously (Deut 17:8–13).

And this *is* the case of the slayer, which shall flee thither, that he may live: Whoso killeth his neighbour ignorantly, whom he hated not in time past; as when a man goeth into the wood with his neighbour to hew wood, and his hand fetcheth a stroke with the axe to cut down the tree, and the head slippeth from the helve, and lighteth upon his neighbour, that he die; he shall flee unto one of those cities, and live: lest the avenger of the blood pursue the slayer, while his heart is hot, and overtake him, because the way is long, and slay him; whereas he *was* not worthy of death, inasmuch as he hated him not in time past. Wherefore I command thee, saying, Thou shalt separate three cities for thee. And if the LORD thy God enlarge thy coast, as he hath sworn unto thy fathers, and give thee all the land which he promised to give unto thy fathers; if thou shalt keep all these commandments to do them, which I command thee this day, to love the LORD thy God, and to walk ever in his ways; then shalt thou add three cities more for thee, beside these three: that innocent blood be not shed in thy land, which the LORD thy God giveth thee *for* an inheritance, and *so* blood be upon thee.

But if any man hate his neighbour, and lie in wait for him, and rise up against him, and smite him mortally that he die, and fleeth into one of these cities: then the elders of his city shall send and fetch him thence, and deliver him into the hand of the avenger of blood, that he may die. Thine eye shall not pity him, but thou shalt put away *the guilt of* innocent blood from Israel, that it may go well with thee (Deut 19:4–13).

If a man have a stubborn and rebellious son, which will not obey the voice of his father, or the voice of his mother, and *that*, when they have chastened him, will not hearken unto them: then shall his fa-

ther and his mother lay hold on him, and bring him out unto the elders of his city, and unto the gate of his place; and they shall say unto the elders of his city, This our son *is* stubborn and rebellious, he will not obey our voice; *he is* a glutton, and a drunkard. And all the men of his city shall stone him with stones, that he die: so shalt thou put evil away from among you; and all Israel shall hear, and fear.

And if a man have committed a sin worthy of death, and he be to be put to death, and thou hang him on a tree: his body shall not remain all night upon the tree, but thou shalt in any wise bury him that day; (for he that is hanged *is* accursed of God;) that thy land be not defiled, which the LORD thy God giveth thee *for* an inheritance (Deut 21:18–23).

If any man take a wife, and go in unto her, and hate her, and give occasions of speech against her, and bring up an evil name upon her, and say, I took this woman, and when I came to her, I found her not a maid: then shall the father of the damsel, and her mother, take and bring forth *the tokens of* the damsel's virginity unto the elders of the city in the gate: and the damsel's father shall say unto the elders, I gave my daughter unto this man to wife, and he hateth her; and, lo, he hath given occasions of speech *against her*, saying, I found not thy daughter a maid; and yet these *are the tokens of* my daughter's virginity. And they shall spread the cloth before the elders of the city. And the elders of that city shall take that man and chastise him; and they shall amerce him in an hundred *shekels* of silver, and give *them* unto the father of the damsel, because he hath brought up an evil name upon a virgin of Israel: and she shall be his wife; he may not put her away all his days. But if this thing be true, *and the tokens of* virginity be not found for the damsel: then they shall bring out the damsel to the door of her father's house, and the men of her city shall stone her with stones that she die: because she hath wrought folly in Israel, to play the whore in her father's house: so shalt thou put evil away from among you.

If a man be found lying with a woman married to an husband, then they shall both of them die, *both* the man that lay with the woman, and the woman: so shalt thou put away evil from Israel.

If a damsel *that is* a virgin be betrothed unto an husband, and a man find her in the city, and lie with her; then ye shall bring them both out unto the gate of that city, and ye shall stone them with stones that they die; the damsel, because she cried not, *being* in the city; and the man, because he hath humbled his neighbour's wife: so thou shalt put away evil from among you.

But if a man find a betrothed damsel in the field, and the man force her, and lie with her: then the man only that lay with her shall die: but unto the damsel thou shalt do nothing; *there is* in the damsel no sin *worthy* of death: for as when a man riseth against his neighbour, and slayeth him, even so *is* this matter: for he found her in the field, *and* the betrothed damsel cried, and *there was* none to save her.

If a man find a damsel *that is* a virgin, which is not betrothed, and lay hold on her, and lie with her, and they be found; then the man that lay with her shall give unto the damsel's father fifty *shekels* of silver, and she shall be his wife; because he hath humbled her, he may not put her away all his days (Deut 22:13–29).

If a man be found stealing any of his brethren of the children of Israel, and maketh merchandise of him, or selleth him; then that thief shall die; and thou shalt put evil away from among you (Deut 24:7).

If there be a controversy between men, and they come unto judgment, that *the judges* may judge them; then they shall justify the righteous, and condemn the wicked. And it shall be, if the wicked man *be* worthy to be beaten, that the judge shall cause him to lie down, and to be beaten before his face, according to his fault, by a certain number. Forty stripes he may give him, *and* not exceed: lest, *if* he should exceed, and beat him above these with many stripes, then thy brother should seem vile unto thee (Deut 25:1–3).

Then said he unto me, This *is* the curse that goeth forth over the face of the whole earth: for every one that stealeth shall be cut off *as* on this side according to it; and every one that sweareth shall be cut off *as* on that side according to it. I will bring it forth, saith the LORD of hosts, and it shall enter into the house of the thief, and into the house of him that sweareth falsely by my name: and it shall remain in the midst of his house, and shall consume it with the timber thereof and the stones thereof (Zech 5:3, 4).

But I say unto you, That whosoever is angry with his brother without a cause shall be in danger of the judgment: and whosoever shall say to his brother, Raca, shall be in danger of the council: but whosoever shall say, Thou fool, shall be in danger of hell fire (Matt 5:22).

Ye have heard that it hath been said, An eye for an eye, and a tooth for a tooth: but I say unto you, That ye resist not evil: but whosoever shall smite thee on thy right cheek, turn to him the other also (Matt 5:38, 39).

For rulers are not a terror to good works, but to the evil. Wilt thou then not be afraid of the power? do that which is good, and thou shalt have praise of the same: for he is the minister of God to thee for good. But if thou do that which is evil, be afraid; for he beareth not the sword in vain: for he is the minister of God, a revenger to *execute* wrath upon him that doeth evil. Wherefore *ye* must needs be subject, not only for wrath, but also for conscience sake (Rom 13:3–5).

But now I have written unto you not to keep company, if any man that is called a brother be a fornicator, or covetous, or an idolater, or a railer, or a drunkard, or an extortioner; with such an one no not to eat. For what have I to do to judge them also that are without? do not ye judge them that are within? But them that are without God judgeth. Therefore put away from among yourselves that wicked person (1 Cor 5:11–13).

Be not deceived; God is not mocked: for whatsoever a man soweth, that shall he also reap. For he that soweth to his flesh shall of the flesh reap corruption; but he that soweth to the Spirit shall of the Spirit reap life everlasting (Gal 6:7, 8).

Biblical Examples: Exod 12:29; 32; Lev

24:10–23; Num 15:32–36; Josh 20:1–9; 1 Kings 2:13–46; Ezek 22:1–31; 23:1–49; Luke 23:18, 19; 23:33.

Further References: Lev 26:14–39; Hos 4:1, 2; Rom 3:14–18.

CRUELTY (See Violence)

CURSING (See also Blasphemy; Tongue)
And he that curseth his father, or his mother, shall surely be put to death (Exod 21:17).

For God commanded, saying, Honour thy father and mother: and, He that curseth father or mother, let him die the death (Matt 15:4).

Bless them that curse you, and pray for them which despitefully use you (Luke 6:28).

Bless them which persecute you: bless, and curse not (Rom 12:14).

Biblical Examples: Gen 9:24–27; 2 Sam 16:5–8; Matt 26:74.

Further References: Exod 22:28; Isa 65:15; Prov 20:20; 30:10; Eccl 10:20; Mark 7:10; Rom 3:14; James 3:9.

– D –

DAILY WORK (See also Economics; Labor Relations; Vocation)

And on the seventh day God ended his work which he had made; and he rested on the seventh day from all his work which he had made (Gen 2:2).

And the LORD God took the man, and put him into the garden of Eden to dress it and to keep it (Gen 2:15).

And unto Adam he said, Because thou hast hearkened unto the voice of thy wife, and hast eaten of the tree, of which I commanded thee, saying, Thou shalt not eat of it: cursed *is* the ground for thy sake; in sorrow shalt thou eat *of* it all the days of thy life; thorns also and thistles shall it bring forth to thee; and thou shalt eat the herb of the field; in the sweat of thy face shalt thou eat bread, till thou return unto the ground; for out of it wast thou taken: for dust thou *art,* and unto dust shalt thou return (Gen 3:17–19).

Six days shalt thou labour, and do all thy work: but the seventh day *is* the sabbath of the LORD thy God: *in it* thou shalt not do any work, thou, nor thy son, nor thy daughter, thy manservant, nor thy maidservant, nor thy cattle, nor thy stranger that *is* within thy gates: for *in* six days the LORD made heaven and earth, the sea, and all that in them *is,* and rested the seventh day: wherefore the LORD blessed the sabbath day, and hallowed it (Exod 20:9–11).

Six days thou shalt do thy work, and on the seventh day thou shalt rest: that thine ox and thine ass may rest, and the son of thy handmaid, and the stranger, may be refreshed (Exod 23:12).

Man goeth forth unto his work and to his labour until the evening (Ps 104:23).

Except the LORD build the house, they labour in vain that build it: except the LORD keep the city, the watchman walketh *but* in vain (Ps 127:1).

Go to the ant, thou sluggard; consider her ways, and be wise: which having no guide, overseer, or ruler, provideth her meat in the summer, *and* gathereth her food in the harvest. How long wilt thou sleep, O sluggard? when wilt thou arise out of thy sleep? *Yet* a little sleep, a little slumber, a little folding of the hands to sleep: so shall thy poverty come as one that travelleth, and thy want as an armed man (Prov 6:6–11).

He that tilleth his land shall be satisfied with bread: but he that followeth vain *persons is* void of understanding (Prov 12:11).

In all labour there is profit: but the talk of the lips *tendeth* only to penury (Prov 14:23).

Love not sleep, lest thou come to poverty; open thine eyes, *and* thou shalt be satisfied with bread (Prov 20:13).

Seest thou a man diligent in his business? he shall stand before kings; he shall not stand before mean *men* (Prov 22:29).

Prepare thy work without, and make it fit for thyself in the field; and afterwards build thine house (Prov 24:27).

Be thou diligent to know the state of thy flocks, *and* look well to thy herds (Prov 27:23).

He that tilleth his land shall have plenty of bread: but he that followeth after vain *persons* shall have poverty enough (Prov 28:19).

She seeketh wool, and flax, and worketh willingly with her hands. She is like the merchants' ships; she bringeth her food from afar. She riseth also while it is yet night, and giveth meat to her household, and a portion to her maidens. She considereth a field, and buyeth it: with the fruit of her hands she planteth a vineyard. She girdeth her loins with strength, and strengtheneth her arms. She perceiveth that her merchandise *is* good: her candle goeth not out by night. She layeth her hands to the spindle, and her hands hold the distaff. She stretcheth out her hand to the poor; yea, she reacheth forth her hands to the needy. She is not afraid of the snow for her household: for all her household *are* clothed with scarlet. She maketh herself coverings of tapestry; her clothing *is* silk and purple. Her husband is known in the gates, when he sitteth among the elders of the land. She maketh fine linen, and selleth *it;* and delivereth girdles unto the merchant. Strength and honour *are* her clothing; and she shall rejoice in time to come. She openeth her mouth with wisdom; and in her tongue *is* the law of kindness. She looketh well to the ways of her household, and eateth not the bread of idleness (Prov 31:13–27).

What profit hath a man of all his labour which he taketh under the sun? (Eccl 1:3).

And whatsoever mine eyes desired I kept not from them, I withheld not my heart from any joy; for my heart rejoiced in all my labour: and this was my portion of all my labour. Then I looked on all the works that my hands had wrought, and on the labour that I had laboured to do: and, behold, all *was* vanity and vexation of spirit, and *there was* no profit under the sun (Eccl 2:10, 11).

Therefore I hated life; because the work that is wrought under the sun *is* grievous unto me: for all *is* vanity and vexation of spirit.

Yea, I hated all my labour which I had taken under the sun: because I should leave it unto the man that shall be after me. And who knoweth whether he shall be a wise *man* or a fool? yet shall he have rule over all my labour wherein I have laboured, and wherein I have shewed myself wise under the sun. This *is* also vanity. Therefore I went about to cause my heart to despair of all the labour which I took

under the sun. For there is a man whose labour *is* in wisdom, and in knowledge, and in equity; yet to a man that hath not laboured therein shall he leave it *for* his portion. This also *is* vanity and a great evil. For what hath man of all his labour, and of the vexation of his heart, wherein he hath laboured under the sun? For all his days *are* sorrows, and his travail grief; yea, his heart taketh not rest in the night. This is also vanity (Eccl 2:17–23).

I know that *there is* no good in them, but for *a man* to rejoice, and to do good in his life. And also that every man should eat and drink, and enjoy the good of all his labour, it *is* the gift of God (Eccl 3:12, 13).

I said in mine heart, God shall judge the righteous and the wicked: for *there is* a time there for every purpose and for every work (Eccl 3:17).

The sleep of a labouring man *is* sweet, whether he eat little or much: but the abundance of the rich will not suffer him to sleep (Eccl 5:12).

Every man also to whom God hath given riches and wealth, and hath given him power to eat thereof, and to take his portion, and to rejoice in his labour; this *is* the gift of God (Eccl 5:19).

Whatsoever thy hand findeth to do, do *it* with thy might; for *there is* no work, nor device, nor knowledge, nor wisdom, in the grave, whither thou goest (Eccl 9:10).

For God shall bring every work into judgment, with every secret thing, whether *it be* good, or whether *it be* evil (Eccl 12:14).

Wherefore do ye spend money for *that which is* not bread? and your labour for *that which* satisfieth not? hearken diligently unto me, and eat ye *that which is* good, and let your soul delight itself in fatness (Isa 55:2).

Let your light so shine before men, that they may see your good works, and glorify your Father which is in heaven (Matt 5:16).

And the soldiers likewise demanded of him, saying, And what shall we do? And he said unto them, Do violence to no man, neither accuse *any* falsely; and be content with your wages (Luke 3:14).

And in the same house remain, eating and drinking such things as they give: for the labourer is worthy of his hire. Go not from house to house (Luke 10:7).

I have shewed you all things, how that so labouring ye ought to support the weak, and to remember the words of the Lord Jesus, how he said, It is more blessed to give than to receive (Acts 20:35).

Let every man abide in the same calling wherein he was called. Art thou called *being* a servant? care not for it: but if thou mayest be made free, use *it* rather. For he that is called in the Lord, *being* a servant, is the Lord's freeman: likewise also he that is called, *being* free, is Christ's servant. Ye are bought with a price; be not ye the servants of men. Brethren, let every man, wherein he is called, therein abide with God (1 Cor 7:20–24).

For it is written in the law of Moses, Thou shalt not muzzle the mouth of the ox that treadeth out the corn. Doth God take care for oxen? Or saith he *it* altogether for our sakes? For our sakes, no doubt, *this* is written: that he that ploweth should plow in hope; and that he that thresheth in hope should be partaker of his hope. If we have sown unto you spiritual things, *is it* a great thing if we shall reap your carnal things? If others be partakers of *this* power over you, *are* not we rather? Nevertheless we have not used this power; but suffer all things, lest we should hinder the gospel of Christ (1 Cor 9:9–12).

Whether therefore ye eat, or drink, or whatsoever ye do, do all to the glory of God (1 Cor 10:31).

Let him that stole steal no more: but rather let him labour, working with *his* hands the thing which is good, that he may have to give to him that needeth (Eph 4:28).

But as touching brotherly love ye need not that I write unto you: for ye yourselves are taught of God to love one another. And indeed ye do it toward all the brethren which are in all Macedonia: but we beseech you, brethren, that ye increase more and more; and that ye study to be quiet, and to do your own business, and to work with your own hands, as we commanded you; that ye may walk honestly toward them that are without, and *that* ye may have lack of nothing (1 Thess 4:9–12).

For yourselves know how ye ought to follow us: for we behaved not ourselves disorderly among you; neither did we eat any man's bread for nought; but wrought with labour and travail night and day, that we might not be chargeable to any of you: not because we have not power, but to make ourselves an ensample unto you to follow us. For even when we were with you, this we commanded you, that if any would not work, neither should he eat. For we hear that there are some which walk among you disorderly, working not at all, but are busybodies. Now them that are such we command and exhort by our Lord Jesus Christ, that with quietness they work, and eat their own bread. But ye, brethren, be not weary in well-doing (2 Thess 3:7–13).

Let as many servants as are under the yoke count their own masters worthy of all honour, that the name of God and *his* doctrine be not blasphemed. And they that have believing masters, let them not despise *them*, because they are brethren; but rather do *them* service, because they are faithful and beloved, partakers of the benefit. These things teach and exhort (1 Tim 6:1, 2).

Exhort servants to be obedient unto their own masters, *and* to please *them* well in all *things;* not answering again; not purloining, but shewing all good fidelity; that they may adorn the doctrine of God our Saviour in all things (Titus 2:9, 10).

Biblical Examples: Prov 30:24–28; Matt 20:1–15; Acts 18:2, 3.

Further References: Exod 34:21; Lev 23:3; Deut 5:13; Ps 90:17; Prov 10: 4, 5; 12:27; Eph 6:5–9; Col 3:22–24.

DAMAGES AND COMPENSATION
(See also Crime and Punishment; Honesty; Justice; Restitution)

And if men strive together, and one smite another with a stone, or with *his* fist, and he die not, but keepeth *his* bed: if he rise again, and walk abroad upon his staff, then shall he that smote *him* be quit: only he shall pay *for* the loss of his time, and shall cause *him* to be thoroughly healed.

And if a man smite his servant, or his maid, with a rod, and he die under his hand; he shall be surely punished. Notwithstanding, if he continue a day or two, he shall not be punished: for he *is* his money.

If men strive, and hurt a woman with child, so that her fruit depart *from her*, and yet no mischief follow: he shall be surely punished, according as the woman's husband will lay upon him; and he shall pay as the judges *determine*. And if *any* mischief follow, then thou shalt give life for life, eye for eye, tooth for tooth, hand for hand, foot for foot, burning for burning, wound for wound, stripe for stripe.

And if a man smite the eye of his servant, or the eye of his maid, that it perish; he shall let him go free for his eye's sake. And if he smite out his manservant's tooth, or his maidservant's tooth; he shall let him go free for his tooth's sake.

If an ox gore a man or a woman, that they die: then the ox shall be surely stoned, and his flesh shall not be eaten; but the owner of the ox *shall be* quit. But if the ox were wont to push with his horn in time past, and it hath been testified to his owner, and he hath not kept him in, but that he hath killed a man or a woman; the ox shall be stoned, and his owner also shall be put to death. If there be laid on him a sum of money, then he shall give for the ransom of his life whatsoever is laid upon him. Whether he have gored a son, or have gored a daughter, according to this judgment shall it be done unto him. If the ox shall push a manservant or a maidservant; he shall give unto their master thirty shekels of silver, and the ox shall be stoned.

And if a man shall open a pit, or if a man shall dig a pit, and not cover it, and an ox or an ass fall therein (Exod 21:18–33).

And the Lord spake unto Moses, saying, If a soul sin, and commit a trespass against the Lord, and lie unto his neighbour in that which was delivered him to keep, or in fellowship, or in a thing taken away by violence, or hath deceived his neigh-

bour; or have found that which was lost, and lieth concerning it, and sweareth falsely; in any of all these that a man doeth, sinning therein: then it shall be, because he hath sinned, and is guilty, that he shall restore that which he took violently away, or the thing which he hath deceitfully gotten, or that which was delivered him to keep, or the lost thing which he found, or all that about which he hath sworn falsely; he shall even restore it in the principal, and shall add the fifth part more thereto, *and* give it unto him to whom it appertaineth, and in the day of his trespass offering (Lev 6:1–5).

If any man take a wife, and go in unto her, and hate her, and give occasions of speech against her, and bring up an evil name upon her, and say, I took this woman, and when I came to her, I found her not a maid: then shall the father of the damsel, and her mother, take and bring forth *the tokens of* the damsel's virginity unto the elders of the city in the gate: and the damsel's father shall say unto the elders, I gave my daughter unto this man to wife, and he hateth her; and, lo, he hath given occasions of speech *against her*, saying, I found not thy daughter a maid; and yet these *are the tokens of* my daughter's virginity. And they shall spread the cloth before the elders of the city. And the elders of that city shall take that man and chastise him; and they shall amerce him in an hundred *shekels* of silver, and give *them* unto the father of the damsel, because he hath brought up an evil name upon a virgin of Israel: and she shall be his wife; he may not put her away all his days. But if this thing be true, *and the tokens of* virginity be not found for the damsel: then they shall bring out the damsel to the door of her father's house, and the men of her city shall stone her with stones that she die: because she hath wrought folly in Israel, to play the whore in her father's house: so shalt thou put evil away from among you.

If a man be found lying with a woman married to an husband, then they shall both of them die, *both* the man that lay with the woman, and the woman: so shalt thou put away evil from Israel.

If a damsel *that is* a virgin be betrothed

unto an husband, and a man find her in the city, and lie with her; then ye shall bring them both out unto the gate of that city, and ye shall stone them with stones that they die; the damsel, because she cried not, *being* in the city; and the man, because he hath humbled his neighbour's wife: so thou shalt put away evil from among you.

But if a man find a betrothed damsel in the field, and the man force her, and lie with her: then the man only that lay with her shall die: but unto the damsel thou shalt do nothing; *there is* in the damsel no sin *worthy* of death: for as when a man riseth against his neighbour, and slayeth him, even so *is* this matter: for he found her in the field, *and* the betrothed damsel cried, and *there was* none to save her.

If a man find a damsel *that is* a virgin, which is not betrothed, and lay hold on her, and lie with her, and they be found; then the man that lay with her shall give unto the damsel's father fifty *shekels* of silver, and she shall be his wife; because he hath humbled her, he may not put her away all his days (Deut 22:13–29).

DANCING

And it came to pass, as soon as he came nigh unto the camp, that he saw the calf, and the dancing: and Moses' anger waxed hot, and he cast the tables out of his hands, and brake them beneath the mount (Exod 32:19).

Then they said, Behold, *there is* a feast of the LORD in Shiloh yearly *in a place* which *is* on the north side of Bethel, on the east side of the highway that goeth up from Bethel to Shechem, and on the south of Lebonah. Therefore they commanded the children of Benjamin, saying, Go and lie in wait in the vineyards; and see, and, behold, if the daughters of Shiloh come out to dance in dances, then come ye out of the vineyards, and catch you every man his wife of the daughters of Shiloh, and go to the land of Benjamin (Judg 21:19–21).

And the servants of Achish said unto him, *Is* not this David the king of the land? did they not sing one to another of him in dances, saying, Saul hath slain his thou-sands, and David his ten thousands? (1 Sam 21:11).

They send forth their little ones like a flock, and their children dance (Job 21:11).

Thou hast turned for me my mourning into dancing: thou hast put off my sack-cloth, and girded me with gladness (Ps 30:11).

A time to weep, and a time to laugh; a time to mourn, and a time to dance (Eccl 3:4).

Again I will build thee, and thou shalt be built, O virgin of Israel: thou shalt again be adorned with thy tabrets, and shalt go forth in the dances of them that make merry. . . . Then shall the virgin rejoice in the dance, both young men and old together: for I will turn their mourning into joy, and will comfort them, and make them rejoice from their sorrow (Jer 31:4, 13).

And bring hither the fatted calf, and kill *it;* and let us eat, and be merry: For this my son was dead, and is alive again; he was lost, and is found. And they began to be merry. Now his elder son was in the field: and as he came and drew nigh to the house, he heard music and dancing (Luke 15:23–25).

Biblical Examples: Exod 15:20; 32:19, 25; Judg 11:34; 1 Sam 18:6; 30:16; 2 Sam 6:14–16; Matt 14:6; Mark 6:22.

Further References: Ps 149:3; 150:4; Lam 5:15; Matt 11:17.

DEBT AND DEBTOR (See also Borrowing; Usury and Interest)

If thou buy an Hebrew servant, six years he shall serve: and in the seventh he shall go out free for nothing. If he came in by himself, he shall go out by himself: if he were married, then his wife shall go out with him. If his master have given him a wife, and she have borne him sons or daughters; the wife and her children shall be her master's, and he shall go out by himself. And if the servant shall plainly say, I love my master, my wife, and my children; I will not go out free: then his master shall bring him unto the judges; he shall also bring him to the door, or unto the door post; and his master shall bore his ear through with an awl; and he shall serve him for ever (Exod 21:2–6).

If a man deliver unto his neighbour an ass, or an ox, or a sheep, or any beast, to keep; and it die, or be hurt, or driven away, no man seeing *it: then* shall an oath of the LORD be between them both, that he hath not put his hand unto his neighbour's goods; and the owner of it shall accept *thereof,* and he shall not make *it* good. And if it be stolen from him, he shall make restitution unto the owner thereof. If it be torn in pieces, *then* let him bring it *for* witness, *and* he shall not make good that which was torn.

And if a man borrow *aught* of his neighbour, and it be hurt, or die, the owner thereof *being* not with it, he shall surely make *it* good. *But* if the owner thereof *be* with it, he shall not make *it* good: if it *be* an hired *thing*, it came for his hire (Exod 22:10–15).

If thou lend money to *any of* my people *that is* poor by thee, thou shalt not be to him as an usurer, neither shalt thou lay upon him usury. If thou at all take thy neighbour's raiment to pledge, thou shalt deliver it unto him by that the sun goeth down: for that *is* his covering only, it *is* his raiment for his skin: wherein shall he sleep? and it shall come to pass, when he crieth unto me, that I will hear; for I *am* gracious (Exod 22:25–27).

If thy brother be waxen poor, and hath sold away *some* of his possession, and if any of his kin come to redeem it, then shall he redeem that which his brother sold. And if the man have none to redeem it, and himself be able to redeem it; then let him count the years of the sale thereof, and restore the overplus unto the man to whom he sold it; that he may return unto his possession. But if he be not able to restore *it* to him, then that which is sold shall remain in the hand of him that hath bought it until the year of jubilee: and in the jubilee it shall go out, and he shall return unto his possession. And if a man sell a dwelling house in a walled city, then he may redeem it within a whole year after it is sold; *within* a full year may he redeem it. And if it be not redeemed within the space of a full year, then the house that *is* in the walled city shall be established for ever to him that bought it throughout his generations: it shall not

go out in the jubilee, but the houses of the villages which have no wall round about them shall be counted as the fields of the country: they may be redeemed, and they shall go out in the jubilee. Notwithstanding the cities of the Levites, *and* the houses of the cities of their possession, may the Levites redeem at any time. And if a man purchase of the Levites, then the house that was sold, and the city of his possession, shall go out in *the year of* jubilee: for the houses of the cities of the Levites *are* their possession among the children of Israel. But the field of the suburbs of their cities may not be sold; for it *is* their perpetual possession.

And if thy brother be waxen poor, and fallen in decay with thee; then thou shalt relieve him: *yea, though he be* a stranger, or a sojourner; that he may live with thee. Take thou no usury of him, or increase: but fear thy God; that thy brother may live with thee. Thou shalt not give him thy money upon usury, nor lend him thy victuals for increase. I *am* the LORD your God, which brought you forth out of the land of Egypt, to give you the land of Canaan, *and* to be your God.

And if thy brother *that dwelleth* by thee be waxen poor, and be sold unto thee; thou shalt not compel him to serve as a bondservant: *but* as an hired servant, *and* as a sojourner, he shall be with thee, *and* shall serve thee unto the year of jubilee. And *then* shall he depart from thee, *both* he and his children with him, and shall return unto his own family, and unto the possession of his fathers shall he return. For they *are* my servants, which I brought forth out of the land of Egypt: they shall not be sold as bondmen. Thou shalt not rule over him with rigour; but shalt fear thy God. Both thy bondmen, and thy bondmaids, which thou shalt have, *shall be* of the heathen that are round about you; of them shall ye buy bondmen and bondmaids. Moreover of the children of the strangers that do sojourn among you, of them shall ye buy, and of their families that *are* with you, which they begat in your land: and they shall be your possession. And ye shall take them as an inheritance for your children after you, to inherit *them* for a possession; they shall be your bondmen for ever: but over your brethren the children of Israel, ye shall not rule one over another with rigour (Lev 25:25–46).

And if a sojourner or stranger wax rich by thee, and thy brother *that dwelleth* by him wax poor, and sell himself unto the stranger *or* sojourner by thee, or to the stock of the stranger's family: after that he is sold he may be redeemed again; one of his brethren may redeem him: either his uncle, or his uncle's son, may redeem him, or *any* that is nigh of kin unto him of his family may redeem him; or if he be able, he may redeem himself. And he shall reckon with him that bought him from the year that he was sold to him unto the year of jubilee: and the price of his sale shall be according unto the number of years, according to the time of an hired servant shall it be with him. If *there be* yet many years *behind,* according unto them he shall give again the price of his redemption out of the money that he was bought for. And if there remain but few years unto the year of jubilee, then he shall count with him, *and* according unto his years shall he give him again the price of his redemption. *And* as a yearly hired servant shall he be with him: *and the other* shall not rule with rigour over him in thy sight. And if he be not redeemed in these *years,* then he shall go out in the year of jubilee, *both* he, and his children with him. For unto me the children of Israel *are* servants; they *are* my servants whom I brought forth out of the land of Egypt: I *am* the LORD your God (Lev 25:47–55).

At the end of *every* seven years thou shalt make a release. And this *is* the manner of the release: Every creditor that lendeth *aught* unto his neighbour shall release *it;* he shall not exact *it* of his neighbour, or of his brother; because it is called the LORD's release. Of a foreigner thou mayest exact *it again:* but *that* which is thine with thy brother thine hand shall release; save when there shall be no poor among you; for the LORD shall greatly bless thee in the land which the LORD thy God giveth thee *for* an inheritance to possess it: only if thou carefully hearken unto the voice of the LORD thy God, to observe to do all these commandments which I command thee this day. For the LORD thy God blesseth thee, as he promised thee: and thou shalt lend unto many nations, but thou shalt not borrow; and thou shalt reign over many nations, but they shall not reign over thee (Deut 15:1–6).

When thou dost lend thy brother any thing, thou shalt not go into his house to fetch his pledge. Thou shalt stand abroad, and the man to whom thou dost lend shall bring out the pledge abroad unto thee. And if the man *be* poor, thou shalt not sleep with his pledge (Deut 24:10–12).

He that is surety for a stranger shall smart *for it:* and he that hateth suretyship is sure (Prov 11:15).

Agree with thine adversary quickly, whiles thou art in the way with him; lest at any time the adversary deliver thee to the judge, and the judge deliver thee to the officer, and thou be cast into prison. Verily I say unto thee, Thou shalt by no means come out thence, till thou hast paid the uttermost farthing (Matt 5:25, 26).

Ye have heard that it hath been said, An eye for an eye, and a tooth for a tooth: but I say unto you, That ye resist not evil: but whosoever shall smite thee on thy right cheek, turn to him the other also. And if any man will sue thee at the law, and take away thy coat, let him have *thy* cloak also (Matt 5:38–40).

Owe no man any thing, but to love one another: for he that loveth another hath fulfilled the law (Rom 13:8).

Biblical Examples: 2 Kings 4:1–7; Neh 5:1–13.

Further References: Deut 23:19, 20; 24:6; Neh 10:31; Job 20:18–20; 22:6; 24:9; Prov 22:6; Amos 2:8; Matt 5:42; 18:23–33; Luke 6:34.

DECEIT (See also Dishonesty)

For the congregation of hypocrites *shall be* desolate, and fire shall consume the tabernacles of bribery. They conceive mischief, and bring forth vanity, and their belly prepareth deceit (Job 15:34, 35).

Thou shalt destroy them that speak leasing: the LORD will abhor the bloody and deceitful man (Ps 5:6).

He that hath clean hands, and a pure heart; who hath not lifted up his soul unto vanity, nor sworn deceitfully. He shall receive the blessing from the LORD, and righteousness from the God of his salvation (Ps 24:4, 5).

Judge me, O God, and plead my cause against an ungodly nation: O deliver me from the deceitful and unjust man (Ps 43:1).

He that worketh deceit shall not dwell within my house: he that telleth lies shall not tarry in my sight (Ps 101:7).

Bread of deceit *is* sweet to a man; but afterwards his mouth shall be filled with gravel (Prov 20:17).

Be not a witness against thy neighbour without cause; and deceive *not* with thy lips (Prov 24:28).

Faithful *are* the wounds of a friend; but the kisses of an enemy *are* deceitful (Prov 27:6).

And he made his grave with the wicked, and with the rich in his death; because he had done no violence, neither *was any* deceit in his mouth (Isa 53:9).

The heart *is* deceitful above all *things,* and desperately wicked: who can know it? (Jer 17:9).

I will also leave in the midst of thee an afflicted and poor people, and they shall trust in the name of the LORD. The remnant of Israel shall not do iniquity, nor speak lies; neither shall a deceitful tongue be found in their mouth: for they shall feed and lie down, and none shall make *them* afraid (Zeph 3:12, 13).

For from within, out of the heart of men, proceed evil thoughts, adulteries, fornications, murders, thefts, covetousness, wickedness, deceit, lasciviousness, an evil eye, blasphemy, pride, foolishness (Mark 7:21, 22).

But have renounced the hidden things of dishonesty, not walking in craftiness, nor handling the word of God deceitfully; but by manifestation of the truth commending ourselves to every man's conscience in the sight of God (2 Cor 4:2).

But what I do, that I will do, that I may cut off occasion from them which desire occasion; that wherein they glory, they may be found even as we. For such *are* false apostles, deceitful workers, transforming themselves into the apostles of Christ (2 Cor 11:12, 13).

Let no man deceive you with vain words: for because of these things cometh the wrath of God upon the children of disobedience (Eph 5:6).

Beware lest any man spoil you through philosophy and vain deceit, after the tradition of men, after the rudiments of the world, and not after Christ (Col 2:8).

Even him, whose coming is after the working of Satan with all power and signs and lying wonders, and with all deceivableness of unrighteousness in them that perish; because they received not the love of the truth, that they might be saved (2 Thess 2:9, 10).

Yea, and all that will live godly in Christ Jesus shall suffer persecution. But evil men and seducers shall wax worse and worse, deceiving, and being deceived (2 Tim 3:12, 13).

Wherefore laying aside all malice, and all guile, and hypocrisies, and envies, and all evil speakings (1 Peter 2:1).

For he that will love life, and see good days, let him refrain his tongue from evil, and his lips that they speak no guile: let him eschew evil, and do good; let him seek peace, and ensue it (1 Peter 3:10, 11).

For many deceivers are entered into the world, who confess not that Jesus Christ is come in the flesh. This is a deceiver and an antichrist (2 John 7).

Biblical Examples: Gen 3:4; 12:11–13; 26:7; 27:6–23; 34:13–31; 37:29–35; Josh 9:3–15; Judg 16:4–20; 1 Sam 21:10–15; 2 Sam 13:6–14; Jer 14:14; Hos 11:12; Matt 2:8; 22:16; Luke 10:25; Acts 5:1, 2.

Further References: Job 31:5; Ps 10:7; 32:2; 72:14; 119:118; Prov 12:17; Jer 9:6; 14:14; 37:9; Rom 1:29; 3:13; 16:18; Eph 4:14; 1 Thess 2:3.

DECISION-MAKING (See also Vices and Virtues)

I call heaven and earth to record this day against you, *that* I have set before you life and death, blessing and cursing: therefore choose life, that both thou and thy seed may live: that thou mayest love the LORD thy God, *and* that thou mayest obey his voice, and that thou mayest cleave unto him: for he *is* thy life, and the length of thy days: that thou mayest dwell in the land which the LORD sware unto thy fathers, to Abraham, to Isaac, and to Jacob, to give them (Deut 30:19, 20).

And if it seem evil unto you to serve the LORD, choose you this day whom ye will serve; whether the gods which your fathers served that *were* on the other side of the flood, or the gods of the Amorites, in whose land ye dwell: but as for me and my house, we will serve the LORD (Josh 24:15).

For thou *art* my lamp, O LORD: and the LORD will lighten my darkness (2 Sam 22:29).

And now, O LORD my God, thou hast made thy servant king instead of David my father: and I *am but* a little child: I know not *how* to go out or come in. And thy servant *is* in the midst of thy people which thou hast chosen, a great people, that cannot be numbered nor counted for multitude. Give therefore thy servant an understanding heart to judge thy people, that I may discern between good and bad: for who is able to judge this thy so great a people? (1 Kings 3:7–9).

Seek the LORD and his strength, seek his face continually (1 Chron 16:11).

Blessed *is* the man that walketh not in the counsel of the ungodly, nor standeth in the way of sinners, nor sitteth in the seat of the scornful. But his delight *is* in the law of the LORD; and in his law doth he meditate day and night (Ps 1:1, 2).

Thou wilt shew me the path of life: in thy presence *is* fulness of joy; at thy right hand *there are* pleasures for evermore (Ps 16:11).

The law of the LORD *is* perfect, converting the soul: the testimony of the LORD *is* sure, making wise the simple. The statutes of the LORD *are* right, rejoicing the heart: the commandment of the LORD *is* pure, enlightening the eyes. The fear of the LORD *is* clean, enduring for ever: the judgments of the LORD *are* true *and* righteous altogether. More to be desired *are* *they* than gold, yea, than much fine gold: sweeter also than honey and the honeycomb (Ps 19:7–10).

What man *is* he that feareth the LORD? him shall he teach in the way *that* he shall choose (Ps 25:12).

Thou shalt guide me with thy counsel,

and afterward receive me *to* glory (Ps 73:24).

I will behave myself wisely in a perfect way. O when wilt thou come unto me? I will walk within my house with a perfect heart. I will set no wicked thing before mine eyes: I hate the work of them that turn aside; *it* shall not cleave to me. A froward heart shall depart from me: I will not know a wicked *person.* (Ps 101:2–4).

The fear of the LORD *is* the beginning of knowledge: *but* fools despise wisdom and instruction. My son, hear the instruction of thy father, and forsake not the law of thy mother: for they *shall be* an ornament of grace unto thy head, and chains about thy neck (Prov 1:7–9).

Trust in the LORD with all thine heart; and lean not unto thine own understanding. In all thy ways acknowledge him, and he shall direct thy paths (Prov 3:5, 6).

Envy thou not the oppressor, and choose none of his ways. For the froward *is* abomination to the LORD: but his secret *is* with the righteous (Prov 3:31, 32).

My son, keep thy father's commandment, and forsake not the law of thy mother: bind them continually upon thine heart, *and* tie them about thy neck. When thou goest, it shall lead thee: when thou sleepest, it shall keep thee; and *when* thou awakest, it shall talk with thee (Prov 6:20–22).

Hear instruction, and be wise, and refuse it not (Prov 8:33).

The fear of the LORD *is* the beginning of wisdom: and the knowledge of the holy *is* understanding (Prov 9:10).

The integrity of the upright shall guide them: but the perverseness of transgressors shall destroy them. Riches profit not in the day of wrath: but righteousness delivereth from death. The righteousness of the perfect shall direct his way: but the wicked shall fall by his own wickedness (Prov 11:3–5).

The way of a fool *is* right in his own eyes: but he that hearkeneth unto counsel *is* wise (Prov 12:15).

A wise son *heareth* his father's instruction: but a scorner heareth not rebuke (Prov 13:1).

Whoso despiseth the word shall be destroyed: but he that feareth the commandment shall be rewarded. The law of the wise *is* a fountain of life, to depart from the snares of death. Good understanding giveth favour: but the way of transgressors *is* hard. Every prudent *man* dealeth with knowledge: but a fool layeth open *his* folly (Prov 13:13–16).

Go from the presence of a foolish man, when thou perceivest not *in him* the lips of knowledge. The wisdom of the prudent *is* to understand his way: but the folly of fools *is* deceit (Prov 14:7, 8).

Without counsel purposes are disappointed: but in the multitude of counsellors they are established (Prov 15:22).

The ear that heareth the reproof of life abideth among the wise. He that refuseth instruction despiseth his own soul: but he that heareth reproof getteth understanding (Prov 15:31, 32).

The preparations of the heart in man, and the answer of the tongue, *is* from the LORD. All the ways of a man *are* clean in his own eyes; but the LORD weigheth the spirits. Commit thy works unto the LORD, and thy thoughts shall be established (Prov 16:1–3).

A good name *is* rather to be chosen than great riches, *and* loving favour rather than silver and gold (Prov 22:1).

Rejoice, O young man, in thy youth; and let thy heart cheer thee in the days of thy youth, and walk in the ways of thine heart (Eccl 11:9).

Let us hear the conclusion of the whole matter: Fear God, and keep his commandments: for this *is* the whole *duty* of man (Eccl 12:13).

And *though* the Lord give you the bread of adversity, and the water of affliction, yet shall not thy teachers be removed into a corner any more, but thine eyes shall see thy teachers: and thine ears shall hear a word behind thee, saying, This *is* the way, walk ye in it, when ye turn to the right hand, and when ye turn to the left (Isa 30:20, 21).

Seek good, and not evil, that ye may live: and so the LORD, the God of hosts, shall be with you, as ye have spoken (Amos 5:14).

No man can serve two masters: for either he will hate the one, and love the other; or else he will hold to the one, and despise the other. Ye cannot serve God and mammon (Matt 6:24).

He that is not with me is against me; and he that gathereth not with me scattereth abroad (Matt 12:30).

Watch and pray, that ye enter not into temptation: the spirit indeed *is* willing, but the flesh *is* weak (Matt 26:41).

For which of you, intending to build a tower, sitteth not down first, and counteth the cost, whether he have *sufficient* to finish *it?* (Luke 14:28).

If ye love me, keep my commandments. And I will pray the Father, and he shall give you another Comforter, that he may abide with you for ever; *even* the Spirit of truth; whom the world cannot receive, because it seeth him not, neither knoweth him: but ye know him; for he dwelleth with you, and shall be in you (John 14:15–17).

Howbeit when he, the Spirit of truth, is come, he will guide you into all truth: for he shall not speak of himself; but whatsoever he shall hear, *that* shall he speak: and he will shew you things to come (John 16:13).

And they gave forth their lots; and the lot fell upon Matthias; and he was numbered with the eleven apostles (Acts 1:26).

Then Peter and the *other* apostles answered and said, We ought to obey God rather than men (Acts 5:29).

What then? shall we sin, because we are not under the law, but under grace? God forbid. Know ye not, that to whom ye yield yourselves servants to obey, his servants ye are to whom ye obey; whether of sin unto death, or of obedience unto righteousness? But God be thanked, that ye were the servants of sin, but ye have obeyed from the heart that form of doctrine which was delivered you. Being then made free from sin, ye became the servants of righteousness. I speak after the manner of men because of the infirmity of your flesh: for as ye have yielded your members servants to uncleanness and to iniquity unto iniquity; even so now yield your members servants to righteousness unto holiness. For when ye were the servants of sin, ye were free from righteousness. What fruit had ye then in those things whereof ye are now ashamed? for the end of those things *is* death. But now being made free from sin, and become servants to God, ye have your fruit unto holiness, and the end everlasting life (Rom 6:15–22).

For that which I do I allow not: for what I would, that do I not; but what I hate, that do I. If then I do that which I would not, I consent unto the law that *it is* good. Now then it is no more I that do it, but sin that dwelleth in me. For I know that in me (that is, in my flesh,) dwelleth no good thing: for to will is present with me; but *how* to perform that which is good I find not. For the good that I would I do not: but the evil which I would not, that I do. Now if I do that I would not, it is no more I that do it, but sin that dwelleth in me (Rom 7:15–20).

And we know that all things work together for good to them that love God, to them who are the called according to *his* purpose (Rom 8:28).

I beseech you therefore, brethren, by the mercies of God, that ye present your bodies a living sacrifice, holy, acceptable unto God, *which is* your reasonable service. And be not conformed to this world: but be ye transformed by the renewing of your mind, that ye may prove what *is* that good, and acceptable, and perfect, will of God (Rom 12:1, 2).

Be not overcome of evil, but overcome evil with good (Rom 12:21).

I know, and am persuaded by the Lord Jesus, that *there is* nothing unclean of itself: but to him that esteemeth any thing to be unclean, to him *it is* unclean. But if thy brother be grieved with *thy* meat, now walkest thou not charitably. Destroy not him with thy meat, for whom Christ died. Let not then your good be evil spoken of: for the kingdom of God is not meat and drink; but righteousness, and peace, and joy in the Holy Ghost. For he that in these things serveth Christ *is* acceptable to God, and approved of men. Let us therefore follow after the things which make for peace, and things wherewith one may edify another. For meat destroy not the work of God. All things indeed *are* pure; but *it is* evil for that man who eateth with offence. *It is* good neither to eat flesh, nor to drink wine, nor *any thing* whereby

thy brother stumbleth, or is offended, or is made weak. Hast thou faith? have *it* to thyself before God. Happy *is* he that condemneth not himself in that thing which he alloweth. And he that doubteth is damned if he eat, because *he eateth* not of faith: for whatsoever *is* not of faith is sin (Rom 14:14–23).

Now as touching things offered unto idols, we know that we all have knowledge. Knowledge puffeth up, but charity edifieth. And if any man think that he knoweth any thing, he knoweth nothing yet as he ought to know. But if any man love God, the same is known of him. As concerning therefore the eating of those things that are offered in sacrifice unto idols, we know that an idol *is* nothing in the world, and that *there is* none other God but one. For though there be that are called gods, whether in heaven or in earth, (as there be gods many, and lords many,) but to us *there is but* one God, the Father, of whom *are* all things, and we in him; and one Lord Jesus Christ, by whom *are* all things, and we by him. Howbeit *there is* not in every man that knowledge: for some with conscience of the idol unto this hour eat *it* as a thing offered unto an idol; and their conscience being weak is defiled. But meat commendeth us not to God: for neither, if we eat, are we the better; neither, if we eat not, are we the worse. But take heed lest by any means this liberty of yours become a stumblingblock to them that are weak. For if any man see thee which hast knowledge sit at meat in the idol's temple, shall not the conscience of him which is weak be emboldened to eat those things which are offered to idols; and through thy knowledge shall the weak brother perish, for whom Christ died? But when ye sin so against the brethren, and wound their weak conscience, ye sin against Christ. Wherefore, if meat make my brother to offend, I will eat no flesh while the world standeth, lest I make my brother to offend (1 Cor 8:1–13).

For though I be free from all *men*, yet have I made myself servant unto all, that I might gain the more (1 Cor 9:19).

All things are lawful for me, but all things are not expedient: all things are lawful for me, but all things edify not. Let no man seek his own, but every man another's *wealth* (1 Cor 10:23, 24).

Whether therefore ye eat, or drink, or whatsoever ye do, do all to the glory of God. Give none offence, neither to the Jews, nor to the Gentiles, nor to the church of God: Even as I please all *men* in all *things,* not seeking mine own profit, but the *profit* of many, that they may be saved (1 Cor 10:31–33).

We are confident, *I say,* and willing rather to be absent from the body, and to be present with the Lord. Wherefore we labour, that, whether present or absent, we may be accepted of him. For we must all appear before the judgment seat of Christ; that every one may receive the things *done* in *his* body, according to that he hath done, whether *it be* good or bad (2 Cor 5:8–10).

This I say then, Walk in the Spirit, and ye shall not fulfil the lust of the flesh (Gal 5:16).

Be not deceived; God is not mocked: for whatsoever a man soweth, that shall he also reap. For he that soweth to his flesh shall of the flesh reap corruption; but he that soweth to the Spirit shall of the Spirit reap life everlasting (Gal 6:7, 8).

Let no man deceive you with vain words: for because of these things cometh the wrath of God upon the children of disobedience. Be not ye therefore partakers with them. For ye were sometimes darkness, but now *are ye* light in the Lord: walk as children of light: (for the fruit of the Spirit *is* in all goodness and righteousness and truth;) proving what is acceptable unto the Lord. And have no fellowship with the unfruitful works of darkness, but rather reprove *them* (Eph 5:6–11).

See then that ye walk circumspectly, not as fools, but as wise, redeeming the time, because the days are evil. Wherefore be ye not unwise, but understanding what the will of the Lord *is* (Eph 5:15–17).

If *there be* therefore any consolation in Christ, if any comfort of love, if any fellowship of the Spirit, if any bowels and mercies, fulfill ye my joy, that ye be likeminded, having the same love, *being* of one accord, of one mind. *Let* nothing *be done* through strife or vainglory; but in lowliness of mind let each esteem other better than themselves (Phil 2:1–3).

Finally, brethren, whatsoever things are true, whatsoever things *are* honest, whatsoever things *are* just, whatsoever things *are* pure, whatsoever things *are* lovely, whatsoever things *are* of good report; if *there be* any virtue, and if *there be* any praise, think on these things (Phil 4:8).

If ye then be risen with Christ, seek those things which are above, where Christ sitteth on the right hand of God. Set your affection on things above, not on things on the earth (Col 3:1, 2).

And whatsoever ye do in word or deed, *do* all in the name of the Lord Jesus, giving thanks to God and the Father by him (Col 3:17).

And we beseech you, brethren, to know them which labour among you, and are over you in the Lord, and admonish you; and to esteem them very highly in love for their work's sake. *And* be at peace among yourselves. Now we exhort you, brethren, warn them that are unruly, comfort the feebleminded, support the weak, be patient toward all *men.* See that none render evil for evil unto any *man;* but ever follow that which is good, both among yourselves, and to all *men.* Rejoice evermore. Pray without ceasing. In every thing give thanks: for this is the will of God in Christ Jesus concerning you. Quench not the Spirit. Despise not prophesyings. Prove all things; hold fast that which is good. Abstain from all appearance of evil (1 Thess 5:12–22).

Therefore, brethren, stand fast, and hold the traditions which ye have been taught, whether by word, or our epistle (2 Thess 2:15).

But thou, O man of God, flee these things; and follow after righteousness, godliness, faith, love, patience, meekness. Fight the good fight of faith, lay hold on eternal life, whereunto thou art also called, and hast professed a good profession before many witnesses (1 Tim 6:11, 12).

But foolish and unlearned questions avoid, knowing that they do gender strifes (2 Tim 2:23).

All scripture *is* given by inspiration of

God, and *is* profitable for doctrine, for re-proof, for correction, for instruction in righteousness: that the man of God may be perfect, throughly furnished unto all good works (2 Tim 3:16, 17).

In all things shewing thyself a pattern of good works: in doctrine *shewing* uncor-ruptness, gravity, sincerity, sound speech, that cannot be condemned; that he that is of the contrary part may be ashamed, having no evil thing to say of you (Titus 2:7, 8).

If any of you lack wisdom, let him ask of God, that giveth to all *men* liberally, and upbraideth not; and it shall be given him. But let him ask in faith, nothing wa-vering. For he that wavereth is like a wave of the sea driven with the wind and tossed (James 1:5, 6).

But be ye doers of the word, and not hearers only, deceiving your own selves. For if any be a hearer of the word, and not a doer, he is like unto a man beholding his natural face in a glass: for he beholdeth himself, and goeth his way, and straight-way forgetteth what manner of man he was. But whoso looketh into the perfect law of liberty, and continue *therein,* he being not a forgetful hearer, but a doer of the work, this man shall be blessed in his deed (James 1:22–25).

Therefore to him that knoweth to do good, and doeth *it* not, to him it is sin (James 4:17).

Wherefore gird up the loins of your mind, be sober, and hope to the end for the grace that is to be brought unto you at the revelation of Jesus Christ; as obedi-ent children, not fashioning yourselves ac-cording to the former lusts in your ignorance: but as he which hath called you is holy, so be ye holy in all manner of con-versation; because it is written, Be ye holy; for I am holy (1 Peter 1:13–16).

Love not the world, neither the things *that are* in the world. If any man love the world, the love of the Father is not in him. For all that *is* in the world, the lust of the flesh, and the lust of the eyes, and the pride of life, is not of the Father, but is of the world (1 John 2:15, 16).

Biblical Examples: Gen 28:20, 21; Exod 19:7, 8; 33:13–15; Lev 16:7–10; Deut 5:27; Josh 24:21–25; Judg 6:36–40; 7:1–7; 1 Sam 10:20, 21; 14:36–46; Ezra 10:3–5; Neh 10:28, 29; Isa 6:8; Jer 42:1–6; 50:4, 5; Jonah 1:7; Luke 9:59–62; 1 Cor 7:20–24; 2 Cor 9:7; Phil 3:12–14.

Further References: Lev 11:45; Josh 1:7–9; Ps 5:8; 16:8; 18:30; 23; 25:4, 5, 8, 9; 27:1–3, 11, 14; 32:8, 9; 34:4–8; 37:3–7, 23, 24, 34; 40:4; 43:3, 4; 51:6; 56:12; 62:5; 86:7, 11; 116:9–14; 119:9–16; Prov 2:6–8; 7:1–5; 13:18; 14:14, 15, 33; 16:9; 21:2, 3, 29; 22:3; 23:4, 12; 24:3, 4, 21, 22; 27:1; 29:25; Eccl 3:1–8; 4:13, 14; Isa 1:16–20; 26:3, 4; 41:8–10; 43:2; 48:17; 50:7, 8; 55:6–8; 58:9–11; Jer 17:7, 8; Joel 3:14; Mic 6:8; 7:7, 8; Nah 1:7; Matt 6:31; 18:19; Luke 12:8, 9; John 8:12; 15:7; Rom 12:9; 14:12, 13; 15:4; 1 Cor 2:12, 13; 6:12; 15:58; Gal 2:20; 5:19–25; Eph 1:15–23; 5:1, 2; Phil 4:13; Col 1:9, 10; 2:6–8; 1 Tim 4:11–16; 2 Tim 1:6, 7; 2:15; Titus 3:9; Heb 2:18; 4:14–16; 1 Peter 2:12–17; 2 Peter 1:3–9.

DEMONS

And they shall no more offer their sacri-fices unto devils, after whom they have gone a-whoring. This shall be a statute for ever unto them throughout their genera-tions (Lev 17:7).

They sacrificed unto devils, not to God; to gods whom they knew not, to new *gods that* came newly up, whom your fathers feared not (Deut 32:17).

Yea, they sacrificed their sons and their daughters unto devils, and shed innocent blood, *even* the blood of their sons and of their daughters, whom they sacrificed unto the idols of Canaan: and the land was polluted with blood (Ps 106:37, 38).

And his fame went throughout all Syria: and they brought unto him all sick people that were taken with divers diseases and torments, and those which were possessed with devils, and those which were lunatic, and those that had the palsy; and he healed them (Matt 4:24).

When the even was come, they brought unto him many that were possessed with devils: and he cast out the spirits with *his* word, and healed all that were sick (Matt 8:16).

Then goeth he, and taketh with himself seven other spirits more wicked than him-self, and they enter in and dwell there: and the last *state* of that man is worse than the first. Even so shall it be also unto this wicked generation (Matt 12:45).

And there was in their synagogue a man with an unclean spirit; and he cried out, saying, Let *us* alone; what have we to do with thee, thou Jesus of Nazareth? art thou come to destroy us? I know thee who thou art, the Holy One of God (Mark 1:23, 24).

But I *say*, that the things which the Gentiles sacrifice, they sacrifice to devils, and not to God: and I would not that ye should have fellowship with devils (1 Cor 10:20).

For we wrestle not against flesh and blood, but against principalities, against powers, against the rulers of the darkness of this world, against spiritual wickedness in high *places* (Eph 6:12).

Now the Spirit speaketh expressly, that in the latter times some shall depart from the faith, giving heed to seducing spirits, and doctrines of devils (1 Tim 4:1).

Thou believest that there is one God; thou doest well: the devils also believe, and tremble (James 2:19).

Beloved, believe not every spirit, but try the spirits whether they are of God: because many false prophets are gone out into the world. Hereby know ye the Spirit of God: Every spirit that confesseth that Jesus Christ is come in the flesh is of God (1 John 4:1, 2).

And the rest of the men which were not killed by these plagues yet repented not of the works of their hands, that they should not worship devils, and idols of gold, and silver, and brass, and stone, and of wood: which neither can see, nor hear, nor walk (Rev 9:20).

Biblical Examples: 1 Sam 16:14–23; 18:10, 11; 19:9, 10; Matt 8:28–34; 9:32; 12:22; 15:22–29; 17:14–18; Mark 5:2–20; 7:25–30; 9:17–27; 16:9; Luke 4:33–35; 9:37–42; 11:14.

Further References: Judg 9:23; 1 Kings 22:21–23; 2 Chron 11:15; Matt 4:9; 8:29; 10:1; 12:45; Mark 1:23, 24; 3:22–30; 5:7; 6:7; 9:18, 38; 16:17; Luke 4:41; 8:28; 10:17; John 7:20; 8:48; Acts 5:16; 8:7; 16:16–18; 19:12–16; 2 Peter 2:4; Rev 12:7–9; 13:14.

DEVIL (See Temptation)

DIET (See Health)

DILIGENCE (See also Patience; Perseverance)

And these words, which I command thee this day, shall be in thine heart: and thou shalt teach them diligently unto thy children, and shalt talk of them when thou sittest in thine house, and when thou walkest by the way, and when thou liest down, and when thou risest up (Deut 6:6, 7).

Ye shall diligently keep the commandments of the Lord your God, and his testimonies, and his statutes, which he hath commanded thee (Deut 6:17).

Now set your heart and your soul to seek the Lord your God; arise therefore, and build ye the sanctuary of the Lord God, to bring the ark of the covenant of the Lord, and the holy vessels of God, into the house that is to be built to the name of the Lord (1 Chron 22:19).

He becometh poor that dealeth *with* a slack hand: but the hand of the diligent maketh rich (Prov 10:4).

He that diligently seeketh good procureth favour: but he that seeketh mischief, it shall come unto him (Prov 11:27).

Wherefore do ye spend money for *that which is* not bread? and your labour for *that which* satisfieth not? hearken diligently unto me, and eat ye *that which is* good, and let your soul delight itself in fatness (Isa 55:2).

I must work the works of him that sent me, while it is day: the night cometh, when no man can work (John 9:4).

Therefore, my beloved brethren, be ye stedfast, unmoveable, always abounding in the work of the Lord, forasmuch as ye know that your labour is not in vain in the Lord (1 Cor 15:58).

Therefore, as ye abound in every *thing, in* faith, and utterance, and knowledge, and *in* all diligence, and *in* your love to us, *see* that ye abound in this grace also (2 Cor 8:7).

Brethren, I count not myself to have apprehended: but *this* one thing *I do*, forgetting those things which are behind, and reaching forth unto those things which are before, I press toward the mark for the prize of the high calling of God in Christ Jesus (Phil 3:13, 14).

I charge *thee* therefore before God, and the Lord Jesus Christ, who shall judge the quick and the dead at his appearing and his kingdom; preach the word; be instant in season, out of season; reprove, rebuke, exhort with all longsuffering and doctrine (2 Tim 4:1, 2).

Wherefore the rather, brethren, give diligence to make your calling and election sure: for if ye do these things, ye shall never fall (2 Peter 1:10).

Biblical Examples: Ruth 2:17; 2 Chron 31:21; Neh 4:6; Mark 1:35; Luke 2:49; Acts 5:42; 18:25; 2 Cor 8:22; 1 Thess 2:9; 2 Tim 1:17.

Further References: Exod 15:26; Deut 4:9; 11:13, 14; 19:18; Ps 77:6; Prov 4:23; 12:24; 1 Tim 3:10; Heb 6:10–12; 11:6; 12:15; 2 Peter 1:5; 3:14.

DISEASE (See Health)

DISCIPLINE (See Children; Church Discipline; Parent-Child Relations)

DISCRIMINATION (See Injustice)

DISHONESTY (See also Consumer Fraud; Deceit)

And the LORD spake unto Moses, saying, If a soul sin, and commit a trespass against the LORD, and lie unto his neighbour in that which was delivered him to keep, or in fellowship, or in a thing taken away by violence, or hath deceived his neighbour; or have found that which was lost, and lieth concerning it, and sweareth falsely; in any of all these that a man doeth, sinning therein: then it shall be, because he hath sinned, and is guilty, that he shall restore that which he took violently away, or the thing which he hath deceitfully gotten, or that which was delivered him to keep, or the lost thing which he found, or all that about which he hath sworn falsely; he shall even restore it in the principal, and shall add the fifth part more thereto, *and* give it unto him to whom it appertaineth, in the day of his trespass offering (Lev 6:1–5).

Ye shall not steal, neither deal falsely, neither lie one to another.

And ye shall not swear by my name falsely, neither shalt thou profane the name of thy God: I *am* the LORD.

Thou shalt not defraud thy neighbour,

neither rob *him:* the wages of him that is hired shall not abide with thee all night until the morning.

Thou shalt not curse the deaf, nor put a stumblingblock before the blind, but shalt fear thy God: I *am* the LORD (Lev 19:11–14).

Ye shall do no unrighteousness in judgment, in meteyard, in weight, or in measure. Just balances, just weights, a just ephah, and a just hin, shall ye have: I *am* the LORD your God, which brought you out of the land of Egypt (Lev 19:35, 36).

Thou shalt not have in thy bag divers weights, a great and a small. Thou shalt not have in thine house divers measures, a great and a small. *But* thou shalt have a perfect and just weight, a perfect and just measure shalt thou have: that thy days may be lengthened in the land which the LORD thy God giveth thee. For all that do such things, *and* all that do unrighteously, *are* an abomination unto the LORD thy God (Deut 25:13–16).

The wicked borroweth, and payeth not again: but the righteous sheweth mercy, and giveth. For *such as be* blessed of him shall inherit the earth; and *they that be* cursed of him shall be cut off (Ps 37:21, 22).

When thou sawest a thief, then thou consentedst with him, and hast been partaker with adulterers (Ps 50:18).

A false balance *is* abomination to the LORD: but a just weight *is* his delight (Prov 11:1).

Divers weights, *and* divers measures, both of them *are* alike abomination to the LORD (Prov 20:10).

Behold, the hire of the labourers who have reaped down your fields, which is of you kept back by fraud, crieth: and the cries of them which have reaped are entered into the ears of the Lord of sabaoth (James 5:4).

Biblical Examples: Gen 25:29–33; Josh 7:11–26; 2 Sam 14:2–20; Jer 7:8–10; 9:4–6, 8; Ezek 22:9; Hos 4:1, 2; 12:7; Amos 8:5; Mic 6:10.

Further References: Job 24:2–11; Ps 62:10; Prov 3:27; Isa 32:7; Jer 22:13; Luke 16:1–8; 1 Thess 4:6; James 5:4.

DIVISIONS (See Strife)

DIVORCE (See also Family; Husband-Wife Relations; Marriage; Remarriage)

And the LORD God said, *It is* not good that the man should be alone; I will make him an help meet for him. And out of the ground the LORD God formed every beast of the field, and every fowl of the air; and brought *them* unto Adam to see what he would call them: and whatsoever Adam called every living creature, that *was* the name thereof. And Adam gave names to all cattle, and to the fowl of the air, and to every beast of the field; but for Adam there was not found an help meet for him. And the LORD God caused a deep sleep to fall upon Adam, and he slept: and he took one of his ribs, and closed up the flesh instead thereof; and the rib, which the LORD God had taken from man, made he a woman, and brought her unto the man. And Adam said, This *is* now bone of my bones, and flesh of my flesh: she shall be called Woman, because she was taken out of Man. Therefore shall a man leave his father and his mother, and shall cleave unto his wife: and they shall be one flesh. And they were both naked, the man and his wife, and were not ashamed (Gen 2:18–25).

And if a man sell his daughter to be a maidservant, she shall not go out as the menservants do. If she please not her master, who hath betrothed her to himself, then shall he let her be redeemed: to sell her unto a strange nation he shall have no power, seeing he hath dealt deceitfully with her. And if he have betrothed her unto his son, he shall deal with her after the manner of daughters.

If he take him another *wife;* her food, her raiment, and her duty of marriage, shall he not diminish. And if he do not these three unto her, then shall she go out free without money. (Exod 21:7–11).

A widow, or a divorced woman, or profane, *or* an harlot, these shall he not take: but he shall take a virgin of his own people to wife. Neither shall he profane his seed among his people: for I the LORD do sanctify him (Lev 21:14, 15).

But if the priest's daughter be a widow, or divorced, and have no child, and is returned to her father's house, as in her youth, she shall eat of her father's meat: but there shall no stranger eat thereof (Lev 22:13).

But every vow of a widow, and of her that is divorced, wherewith they have bound their souls, shall stand against her (Num 30:9).

When thou goest forth to war against thine enemies, and the LORD thy God hath delivered them into thine hands, and thou hast taken them captive, and seest among the captives a beautiful woman, and hast a desire unto her, that thou wouldest have her to thy wife; then thou shalt bring her home to thine house; and she shall shave her head, and pare her nails; and she shall put the raiment of her captivity from off her, and shall remain in thine house, and bewail her father and her mother a full month: and after that thou shalt go in unto her, and be her husband, and she shall be thy wife. And it shall be, if thou have no delight in her, then thou shalt let her go whither she will; but thou shalt not sell her at all for money, thou shalt not make merchandise of her, because thou hast humbled her (Deut 21:10–14).

When a man hath taken a wife, and married her, and it come to pass that she find no favour in his eyes, because he hath found some uncleanness in her: then let him write her a bill of divorcement, and give *it* in her hand, and send her out of his house. And when she is departed out of his house, she may go and be another man's *wife.* And *if* the latter husband hate her, and write her a bill of divorcement, and giveth *it* in her hand, and sendeth her out of his house; or if the latter husband die, which took her *to be* his wife; her former husband, which sent her away, may not take her again to be his wife, after that she is defiled for that *is* abomination before the LORD: and thou shalt not cause the land to sin, which the LORD thy God giveth thee *for* an inheritance (Deut 24:1–4).

Now therefore let us make a covenant with our God to put away all the wives, and such as are born of them, according to the counsel of my lord, and of those that tremble at the commandment of our God; and let it be done according to the law (Ezra 10:3).

Thus saith the LORD, Where *is* the bill of your mother's divorcement, whom I have put away? or which of my creditors *is it* to whom I have sold you? Behold, for your iniquities have ye sold yourselves, and for your transgressions is your mother put away (Isa 50:1).

For the LORD hath called thee as a woman forsaken and grieved in spirit, and a wife of youth, when thou wast refused, saith thy God (Isa 54:6).

They say, If a man put away his wife, and she go from him, and become another man's, shall he return unto her again? shall not that land be greatly polluted? but thou hast played the harlot with many lovers; yet return again to me, saith the LORD (Jer 3:1).

And did not he make one? Yet had he the residue of the spirit. And wherefore one? That he might seek a godly seed. Therefore take heed to your spirit, and let none deal treacherously against the wife of his youth. For the LORD, the God of Israel, saith that he hateth putting away: for *one* covereth violence with his garment, saith the LORD of hosts: therefore take heed to your spirit, that ye deal not treacherously (Mal 2:15, 16).

It hath been said, Whosoever shall put away his wife, let him give her a writing of divorcement: but I say unto you, That whosoever shall put away his wife, saving for the cause of fornication, causeth her to commit adultery: and whosoever marry her that is divorced committeth adultery (Matt 5:31, 32).

The Pharisees also came unto him, tempting him, and saying unto him, Is it lawful for a man to put away his wife for every cause? And he answered and said unto them, Have ye not read, that he which made *them* at the beginning made them male and female, and said, For this cause shall a man leave father and mother, and shall cleave to his wife: and they twain shall be one flesh?

Wherefore they are no more twain, but one flesh. What therefore God hath joined together, let not man put asunder. They say unto him, Why did Moses then command to give a writing of divorcement, and to put her away?

He saith unto them, Moses because of the hardness of your hearts suffered you to put away your wives: but from the beginning it was not so.

And I say unto you, Whosoever shall put away his wife, except *it be* for fornication, and shall marry another, committeth adultery: and whoso marrieth her which is put away doth commit adultery (Matt 19:3–9).

And the Pharisees came to him, and asked him, Is it lawful for a man to put away *his* wife? tempting him. And he answered and said unto them, What did Moses command you? And they said, Moses suffered to write a bill of divorcement, and to put *her* away. And Jesus answered and said unto them, For the hardness of your heart he wrote you this precept. But from the beginning of the creation God made them male and female. For this cause shall a man leave his father and mother, and cleave to his wife; and they twain shall be one flesh: so then they are no more twain, but one flesh. What therefore God hath joined together, let not man put asunder.

And in the house his disciples asked him again of the same *matter*. And he saith unto them, Whosoever shall put away his wife, and marry another, committeth adultery against her. And if a woman shall put away her husband, and be married to another, she committeth adultery (Mark 10:2–12).

Whosoever putteth away his wife, and marrieth another, committeth adultery: and whosoever marrieth her that is put away from *her* husband committeth adultery (Luke 16:18).

Know ye not, brethren, (for I speak to them that know the law), how that the law hath dominion over a man as long as he liveth? For the woman which hath an husband is bound by the law to *her* husband so long as he liveth; but if the husband be dead, she is loosed from the law of *her* husband. So then if, while *her* husband liveth, she be married to another man, she shall be called an adulteress: but if her husband be dead, she is free from that law; so that she is no adulteress, though she be married to another man (Rom 7:1–3).

But to the rest speak I, not the Lord:

If any brother hath a wife that believeth not, and she be pleased to dwell with him, let him not put her away. And the woman which hath an husband that believeth not, and if he be pleased to dwell with her, let her not leave him. For the unbelieving husband is sanctified by the wife, and the unbelieving wife is sanctified by the husband; else were your children unclean; but now are they holy. But if the unbelieving depart, let him depart. A brother or a sister is not under bondage in such *cases:* but God hath called us to peace (1 Cor 7:12–15).

A bishop then must be blameless, the husband of one wife, vigilant, sober, of good behaviour, given to hospitality, apt to teach (1 Tim 3:2).

Biblical Examples: Ezra 10:1–6; Neh 13:23–30; Jer 3:1–10.

Further References: Esth 1:10–22; Mic 2:9.

DRESS

And the eyes of them both were opened, and they knew that they *were* naked; and they sewed fig leaves together, and made themselves aprons (Gen 3:7).

Unto Adam also and to his wife did the LORD God make coats of skins, and clothed them (Gen 3:21).

If thou at all take thy neighbour's raiment to pledge, thou shalt deliver it unto him by that the sun goeth down (Exod 22:26).

The woman shall not wear that which pertaineth unto a man, neither shall a man put on a woman's garment: for all that do so *are* abomination unto the LORD thy God (Deut 22:5).

Thou shalt not wear a garment of divers sorts, *as* of woollen and linen together (Deut 22:11).

Though he heap up silver as the dust, and prepare raiment as the clay (Job 27:16).

Let thy garments be always white; and let thy head lack no ointment (Eccl 9:8).

And why take ye thought for raiment. Consider the lilies of the field, how they grow; they toil not, neither do they spin: and yet I say unto you, That even Solomon in all his glory was not arrayed like one of these (Matt 6:28, 29).

I will therefore that men pray every where, lifting up holy hands, without wrath and doubting. In like manner also, that women adorn themselves in modest apparel, with shamefacedness and sobriety; not with braided hair, or gold, or pearls, or costly array (1 Tim 2:8, 9).

Whose adorning let it not be that outward *adorning* of plaiting the hair, and of wearing of gold, or of putting on of apparel; but *let it be* the hidden man of the heart, in that which is not corruptible, *even the ornament* of a meek and quiet spirit, which is in the sight of God of great price (1 Peter 3:3, 4).

Biblical Examples: Exod 28:40; 2 Sam 13:18; Isa 3:20–23; Ezek 24:17; 44:18; Dan 3:21; Matt 5:40; Luke 6:29; 2 Tim 4:13.

Further References: Lev 11:32; 13:47–59; Num 31:20.

DRUGS (See also Alcohol and Alcoholism; Wine)

And Reuben went in the days of wheat harvest, and found mandrakes in the field, and brought them unto his mother Leah. Then Rachel said to Leah, Give me, I pray thee, of thy son's mandrakes. And she said unto her, *Is it* a small matter that thou hast taken my husband? and wouldest thou take away my son's mandrakes also? And Rachel said, Therefore he shall lie with thee to-night for thy son's mandrakes. And Jacob came out of the field in the evening, and Leah went out to meet him, and said, Thou must come in unto me; for surely I have hired thee with my son's mandrakes. And he lay with her that night (Gen 30:14–16).

And ye shall take a bunch of hyssop, and dip *it* in the blood that *is* in the basin, and strike the lintel and the two side posts with the blood that *is* in the basin; and none of you shall go out at the door of his house until the morning (Exod 12:22).

Speak unto the children of Israel, and say unto them, When either man or woman shall separate *themselves* to vow a vow of a Nazarite, to separate *themselves* unto the LORD: he shall separate *himself* from wine and strong drink, and shall drink no vinegar of wine, or vinegar of strong drink, neither shall he drink any liquor of grapes, nor eat moist grapes, or dried (Num 6:2, 3).

There shall not be found among you *any one* that maketh his son or his daughter to pass through the fire, *or* that useth divination, *or* an observer of times, or an enchanter, or a witch (Deut 18:10).

Lest there should be among you man, or woman, or family, or tribe, whose heart turneth away this day from the LORD our God, to go *and* serve the gods of these nations; lest there should be among you a root that beareth gall and wormwood (Deut 29:18).

Give strong drink unto him that is ready to perish, and wine unto those that be of heavy hearts (Prov 31:6).

Is there no balm in Gilead; *is there* no physician there? why then is not the health of the daughter of my people recovered? (Jer 8:22).

Therefore thus saith the LORD of hosts concerning the prophets; Behold, I will feed them with wormwood, and make them drink the water of gall: for from the prophets of Jerusalem is profaneness gone forth into all the land (Jer 23:15).

Babylon is suddenly fallen and destroyed: howl for her; take balm for her pain, if so be she healed (Jer 51:8).

Shall horses run upon the rock? will *one* plow *there* with oxen? for ye have turned judgment into gall, and the fruit of righteousness into hemlock (Amos 6:12).

And they gave him to drink wine mingled with myrrh: but he received *it* not (Mark 15:23).

And one ran and filled a sponge full of vinegar, and put *it* on a reed, and gave him to drink, saying, Let alone; let us see whether Elias will come to take him down (Mark 15:36).

Now there was set a vessel full of vinegar: and they filled a sponge with vinegar, and put *it* upon hyssop, and put *it* to his mouth. When Jesus therefore had received the vinegar, he said, It is finished; and he bowed his head, and gave up the ghost (John 19:29, 30).

Biblical Examples: 2 Kings 21:6; Neh 3:8; Ps 69:21; Jer 9:15; 27:9; Lam 3:19; Matt 27:34, 48; Luke 23:36, 37.

Further References: Exod 7:22; Isa 47:9, 12; Gal 5:20; Rev 9:21; 18:23; 21:8; 22:15.

DRUNKENNESS (See also Alcohol and Alcoholism; Wine)

If a man have a stubborn and rebellious son, which will not obey the voice of his father, or the voice of his mother, and *that*, when they have chastened him, will not hearken unto them: Then shall his father and his mother lay hold on him, and bring him out unto the elders of his city, and unto the gate of his place; and they shall say unto the elders of his city, This our son *is* stubborn and rebellious, he will not obey our voice; *he is* a glutton, and a drunkard. And all the men of his city shall stone him with stones, that he die: so shalt thou put evil away from among you; and all Israel shall hear and fear (Deut 21:18–21).

Who hath woe? who hath sorrow? who hath contentions? who hath babbling? who hath wounds without cause? who hath redness of eyes? They that tarry long at the wine; they that go to seek mixed wine. Look not thou upon the wine when it is red, when it giveth his colour in the cup, *when* it moveth itself aright. At the last it biteth like a serpent, and stingeth like an adder. Thine eyes shall behold strange women, and thine heart shall utter perverse things. Yea, thou shalt be as he that lieth down in the midst of the sea, or as he that lieth upon the top of a mast. They have stricken me, *shalt thou say, and* I was not sick; they have beaten me, *and* I felt *it* not: when shall I awake? I will seek it yet again (Prov 23:29–35).

Blessed *art* thou, O land, when thy king *is* the son of nobles, and thy princes eat in due season, for strength, and not for drunkenness! (Eccl 10:17).

Whoredom and wine and new wine take away the heart (Hos 4:11).

The Son of man came eating and drinking, and they say, Behold a man gluttonous, and a winebibber, a friend of publicans and sinners. But wisdom is justified of her children (Matt 11:19).

And take heed to yourselves, lest at any time your hearts be overcharged with surfeiting, and drunkenness, and cares of his life, and *so* that day come upon you unawares (Luke 21:34).

But now I have written unto you not

to keep company, if any man that is called a brother be a fornicator, or covetous, or an idolater, or a railer, or a drunkard, or an extortioner; with such an one no not to eat (1 Cor 5:11).

Envyings, murders, drunkenness, revellings, and such like: of the which I tell you before, as I have also told *you* in time past, that they which do such things shall not inherit the kingdom of God (Gal 5:21).

And be not drunk with wine, wherein is excess; but be filled with the Spirit (Eph 5:18).

For they that sleep sleep in the night; and they that be drunken are drunken in the night (1 Thess 5:7).

Likewise *must* the deacons *be* grave, not double-tongued, not given to much wine, not greedy of filthy lucre (1 Tim 3:8).

Biblical Examples: Gen 9:20, 21; 19:30–33; 1 Sam 1:12–15; 25:36; 2 Sam 11:12, 13; 13:28; 1 Kings 16:8–10; 20:12–16; Esth 1:1–8; Dan 5:1–4; Joel 1:5–7; 3:3; Amos 6:1–6.

Further References: Deut 21:20, 21; 29:19–21; 1 Sam 1:14; Prov 23:20, 21; Isa 5:11–22; 19:14; 28:1–8; Jer 25:27; Nah 1:10; Hab 2:15, 16; Matt 24:49; Rom 13:13; 1 Cor 6:9–11.

– E –

ECOLOGY (See also Economics)

In the beginning God created the heaven and the earth. And the earth was without form, and void; and darkness *was* upon the face of the deep. And the spirit of God moved upon the face of the waters. And God said, Let there be light: and there was light. And God saw the light, that *it was* good: and God divided the light from the darkness. And God called the light Day, and the darkness he called Night. And the evening and the morning were the first day.

And God said, Let there be a firmament in the midst of the waters, and let it divide the waters from the waters. And God made the firmament, and divided the waters which *were* under the firmament from the waters which *were* above the firmament: and it was so. And God called the firmament Heaven. And the evening and the morning were the second day.

And God said, Let the waters under the heaven be gathered together unto one place, and let the dry *land* appear: and it was so. And God called the dry *land* Earth; and the gathering together of the waters called he Seas: and God saw that *it was* good. And God said, Let the earth bring forth grass, the herb yielding seed, *and* the fruit tree yielding fruit after his kind, whose seed *is* in itself, upon the earth: and it was so. And the earth brought forth grass, *and* herb yielding seed after his kind, and the tree yielding fruit, whose seed *was* in itself, after his kind: and God saw that *it was* good. And the evening and the morning were the third day.

And God said, Let there be lights in the firmament of the heaven to divide the day from the night; and let them be for signs, and for seasons, and for days, and years: and let them be for lights in the firmament of the heaven to give light upon the earth: and it was so. And God made two great lights; the greater light to rule the day, and the lesser light to rule the night: *he made* the stars also. And God set them in the firmament of the heaven to give light upon the earth, and to rule over the day and over the night, and to divide the light from the darkness: and God saw that *it was* good. And the evening and the morning were the fourth day.

And God said, Let the waters bring forth abundantly the moving creature that hath life, and fowl *that* may fly above the earth in the open firmament of heaven. And God created great whales, and every living creature that moveth, which the waters brought forth abundantly, after their kind, and every winged fowl after his kind: and God saw that *it was* good. And God blessed them, saying, Be fruitful, and multiply, and fill the waters in the seas, and let fowl multiply in the earth. And the evening and the morning were the fifth day.

And God said, Let the earth bring forth the living creature after his kind, cattle, and creeping thing, and beast of the earth after his kind: and it was so. And God made the beast of the earth after his kind, and cattle after their kind, and every thing that creepeth upon the earth after his kind: and God saw that *it was* good.

And God said, Let us make man in our image, after our likeness: and let them have dominion over the fish of the sea, and over the fowl of the air, and over the cattle, and over all the earth, and over every creeping thing that creepeth upon the earth. So God created man in his *own* image, in the image of God created he him; male and female created he them. And God blessed them, and God said unto them, Be fruitful, and multiply, and replenish the earth, and subdue it: and have dominion over the fish of the sea, and over the fowl of the air, and over every living thing that moveth upon the earth.

And God said, Behold, I have given you every herb bearing seed, which *is* upon the face of all the earth, and every tree, in which *is* the fruit of a tree yielding seed; to you it shall be for meat. And to every beast of the earth, and to every fowl of the air, and to every thing that creepeth upon the earth, wherein *there is* life, *I have given* every green herb for meat: and it was so. And God saw every thing that he had made, and, behold, *it was* very good. And the evening and the morning were the sixth day (Gen 1).

And six years thou shalt sow thy land, and shalt gather in the fruits thereof: but the seventh *year* thou shalt let it rest and lie still; that the poor of thy people may eat: and what they leave the beasts of the field shall eat. In like manner thou shalt deal with thy vineyard, *and* with thy olive-yard (Exod 23:10, 11).

And the LORD spake unto Moses in Mount Sinai, saying, Speak unto the children of Israel, and say unto them, When ye come into the land which I give you, then shall the land keep a sabbath unto the LORD. Six years thou shalt sow thy field, and six years thou shalt prune thy vineyard, and gather in the fruit thereof; but in the seventh year shall be a sabbath of rest unto the land, a sabbath for the LORD: thou shalt neither sow thy field, nor prune thy vineyard (Lev 25:1–4).

When thou shalt besiege a city a long time, in making war against it to take it, thou shalt not destroy the trees thereof by forcing an axe against them: for thou mayest eat of them, and thou shalt not cut them down (for the tree of the field *is* man's *life*) to employ *them* in the siege: only the trees which thou knowest that they *be* not trees for meat, thou shalt destroy and cut them down; and thou shalt

build bulwarks against the city that maketh war with thee, until it be subdued (Deut 20:19, 20).

Bless the LORD, O my soul. O LORD my God, thou art very great; thou art clothed with honour and majesty. Who coverest *thyself* with light as *with* a garment: who stretchest out the heavens like a curtain: who layeth the beams of his chambers in the waters: who maketh the clouds his chariot: who walketh upon the wings of the wind: who maketh his angels spirits; his ministers a flaming fire:

Who laid the foundations of the earth, *that* it should not be removed for ever. Thou coveredst it with the deep as *with* a garment: the waters stood above the mountains. At thy rebuke they fled; at the voice of thy thunder they hasted away. They go up by the mountains; they go down by the valleys unto the place which thou hast founded for them.

Thou hast set a bound that they may not pass over; that they turn not again to cover the earth.

He sendeth the springs into the valleys, *which* run among the hills. They give drink to every beast of the field: the wild asses quench their thirst. By them shall the fowls of the heaven have their habitation, *which* sing among the branches. He watereth the hills from his chambers: the earth is satisfied with the fruit of thy works.

He causeth the grass to grow for the cattle, and herb for the service of man: that he may bring forth food out of the earth; and wine *that* maketh glad the heart of man, *and* oil to make *his* face to shine, and bread *which* strengtheneth man's heart. The trees of the LORD are full *of sap;* the cedars of Lebanon, which he hath planted; where the birds make their nests; *as for* the stork, the fir trees *are* her house. The high hills *are* a refuge for the wild goats; *and* the rocks for the conies. He appointed the moon for seasons: the sun knoweth his going down. Thou makest darkness, and it is night: wherein all the beasts of the forest do creep *forth.* The young lions roar after their prey, and seek their meat from God. The sun ariseth, they gather themselves together, and lay them down in their dens.

Man goeth forth unto his work and to his labour until the evening.

O LORD, how manifold are thy works! in wisdom hast thou made them all: the earth is full of thy riches. *So is* this great and wide sea, wherein *are* things creeping innumerable, both small and great beasts. There go the ships: *there is* that leviathan, *whom* thou hast made to play therein.

These wait all upon thee; that thou mayest give *them* their meat in due season. *That* thou givest them they gather: thou openest thine hand, they are filled with good. Thou hidest thy face, they are troubled: thou takest away their breath, they die, and return to their dust. Thou sendest forth thy spirit, they are created: and thou renewest the face of the earth.

The glory of the LORD shall endure for ever: the LORD shall rejoice in his works. He looketh on the earth, and it trembleth: he toucheth the hills, and they smoke. I will sing unto the LORD as long as I live: I will sing praise to my God while I have my being.

My meditation of him shall be sweet: I will be glad in the LORD. Let the sinners be consumed out of the earth, and let the wicked be no more. Bless thou the LORD, O my soul. Praise ye the LORD (Ps 104).

Thus saith the LORD, thy redeemer, and he that formed thee from the womb, I *am* the LORD that maketh all *things;* that stretcheth forth the heavens alone; that spreadeth abroad the earth by myself (Isa 44:24).

For, behold, I create new heavens and a new earth: and the former shall not be remembered, nor come into mind (Isa 65:17).

Thus saith the LORD, The heaven *is* my throne, and the earth *is* my footstool: where *is* the house that ye build unto me? and where *is* the place of my rest? For all those *things* hath mine hand made, and all those *things* have been, saith the LORD: but to this *man* will I look, *even to him that is* poor and of a contrite spirit, and trembleth at my word (Isa 66:1, 2).

Therefore *as* I live, saith the LORD of hosts, the God of Israel, Surely Moab shall be as Sodom and the children of Ammon as Gomorrah, *even* the breeding of nettles, and saltpits, and a perpetual desolation:

the residue of my people shall spoil them, and the remnant of my people shall possess them. This shall they have for their pride, because they have reproached and magnified *themselves* against the people of the LORD of hosts. The LORD *will be* terrible unto them: for he will famish all the gods of the earth; and *men* shall worship him, every one from his place, *even* all the isles of the heathen (Zeph 2:9–11).

Behold the fowls of the air: for they sow not, neither do they reap, nor gather into barns; yet your heavenly Father feedeth them. Are ye not much better than they? (Matt 6:26).

In the beginning was the Word, and the Word was with God, and the Word was God. The same was in the beginning with God. All things were made by him; and without him was not any thing made that was made (John 1:1–3).

For the invisible things of him from the creation of the world are clearly seen, being understood by the things that are made, *even* his eternal power and Godhead; so that they are without excuse (Rom 1:20).

For the earnest expectation of the creature waiteth for the manifestation of the sons of God. For the creature was made subject to vanity, not willingly, but by reason of him who hath subjected *the same* in hope, because the creature itself also shall be delivered from the bondage of corruption into the glorious liberty of the children of God. For we know that the whole creation groaneth and travaileth in pain together until now. And not only *they,* but ourselves also, which have the firstfruits of the Spirit, even we ourselves groan within ourselves, waiting for the adoption, *to wit,* the redemption of our body (Rom 8:19–23).

For by him were all things created, that are in heaven, and that are in earth, visible and invisible, whether *they be* thrones, or dominions, or principalities, or powers: all things were created by him, and for him: and he is before all things, and by him all things consist. And he is the head of the body, the church: who is the beginning, the firstborn from the dead; that in all *things* he might have the preeminence. For it pleased *the Father* that in him should all fulness dwell; and, having made peace through the blood of his cross, by him to reconcile all things unto himself; by him, *I say,* whether *they be* things in earth, or things in heaven (Col 1:16–20).

God, who at sundry times and in divers manners spake in time past unto the fathers by the prophets, hath in these last days spoken unto us by *his* Son, whom he hath appointed heir of all things, by whom also he made the worlds; who being the brightness of *his* glory, and the express image of his person, and upholding all things by the word of his power, when he had by himself purged our sins, sat down on the right hand of the Majesty on high (Heb 1:1–3).

And I saw a new heaven and a new earth: for the first heaven and the first earth were passed away; and there was no more sea (Rev 21:1).

Further References: Gen 3:17–19; Deut 20:19, 20; Ps 50:9–12; Isa 24:1–6; 40:21–23; 66:2; Hag 2:8.

ECONOMICS (See also Borrowing; Charity; Contracts; Crime and Punishment; Daily Work; Damages and Compensation; Debt and Debtor; Dishonesty; Ecology; Extravagance; Frugality; Greed; Honesty; Hunger; Labor Relations; Leisure; Materialism; Poverty; Profit; Property; Stewardship; Taxes; Theft; Vocation; Wages; Wealth)

And when ye reap the harvest of your land, thou shalt not wholly reap the corners of thy field, neither shalt thou gather the gleanings of thy harvest. And thou shalt not glean thy vineyard, neither shalt thou gather *every* grape of thy vineyard; thou shalt leave them for the poor and stranger: I *am* the LORD your God (Lev 19:9, 10).

And all the tithe of the land, *whether* of the seed of the land, *or* of the fruit of the tree, *is* the LORD's: *it is* holy unto the LORD (Lev 27:30).

Beware that thou forget not the LORD thy God, in not keeping his commandments, and his judgments, and his statutes, which I command thee this day: lest *when* thou hast eaten and art full, and hast built goodly houses, and dwelt *therein;* and *when* thy herds and thy flocks multiply,

and thy silver and thy gold is multiplied, and all that thou hast is multiplied; then thine heart be lifted up, and thou forget the LORD thy God, which brought thee forth out of the land of Egypt, from the house of bondage (Deut 8:11–14).

But thou shalt remember the LORD thy God: for *it is* he that giveth thee power to get wealth, that he may establish his covenant which he sware unto thy fathers, as *it is* this day (Deut 8:18).

Thou shalt truly tithe all the increase of thy seed, that the field bringeth forth year by year (Deut 14:22).

Thou shalt not muzzle the ox when he treadeth out *the corn.* (Deut 25:4).

If I have made gold my hope, or have said to the fine gold, *Thou art* my confidence; if I rejoiced because my wealth *was* great, and because mine hand had gotten much; if I beheld the sun when it shined, or the moon walking *in* brightness; and my heart hath been secretly enticed, or my mouth hath kissed my hand: this also *were* an iniquity *to be punished by* the judge: for I should have denied the God *that is* above (Job 31:24–28).

The earth *is* the LORD's, and the fullness thereof; the world, and they that dwell therein (Ps 24:1).

Be not thou afraid when one is made rich, when the glory of his house is increased; for when he dieth he shall carry nothing away: his glory shall not descend after him (Ps 49:16, 17).

I will take no bullock out of thy house, *nor* he goats out of thy folds. For every beast of the forest *is* mine, *and* the cattle upon a thousand hills. I know all the fowls of the mountains: and the wild beasts of the field *are* mine. If I were hungry, I would not tell thee: for the world *is* mine, and the fulness thereof (Ps 50:9–12).

Riches profit not in the day of wrath: but righteousness delivereth from death (Prov 11:4).

There is that maketh himself rich, yet *hath* nothing: *there is* that maketh himself poor, yet *hath* great riches (Prov 13:7).

In the house of the righteous *is* much treasure: but in the revenues of the wicked is trouble (Prov 15:6).

Better *is* little with the fear of the LORD

than great treasure and trouble therewith (Prov 15:16).

Labour not to be rich: cease from thine own wisdom. Wilt thou set thine eyes upon that which is not? for *riches* certainly make themselves wings; they fly away as an eagle toward heaven (Prov 23:4, 5).

A faithful man shall abound with blessings: but he that maketh haste to be rich shall not be innocent. To have respect of persons *is* not good: for for a piece of bread *that* man will transgress. He that hasteth to be rich *hath* an evil eye, and considereth not that poverty shall come upon him (Prov 28:20–22).

He that loveth silver shall not be satisfied with silver; nor he that loveth abundance with increase: this *is* also vanity. When goods increase, they are increased that eat them: and what good *is there* to the owners thereof, saving the beholding *of them* with their eyes? The sleep of a labouring man *is* sweet, whether he eat little or much: but the abundance of the rich will not suffer him to sleep. There is a sore evil *which* I have seen under the sun, *namely,* riches kept for the owners thereof to their hurt. But those riches perish by evil travail: and he begetteth a son, and *there is* nothing in his hand. As he came forth of his mother's womb, naked shall he return to go as he came, and shall take nothing of his labour, which he may carry away in his hand (Eccl 5:10–15).

Every man also to whom God hath given riches and wealth, and hath given him power to eat thereof, and to take his portion, and to rejoice in his labour; this *is* the gift of God (Eccl 5:19).

For all those *things* hath mine hand made, and all those *things* have been, saith the LORD: but to this *man* will I look, *even* to *him that is* poor and of a contrite spirit, and trembleth at my word (Isa 66:2).

The silver *is* mine, and the gold *is* mine, saith the LORD of hosts (Hag 2:8).

No man can serve two masters: for either he will hate the one, and love the other; or else he will hold to the one, and despise the other. Ye cannot serve God and mammon.

Therefore I say unto you, Take no thought for your life, what ye shall eat, or what ye shall drink; nor yet for your body, what ye shall put on. Is not the life more than meat, and the body than raiment? Behold the fowls of the air: for they sow not, neither do they reap, nor gather into barns; yet your heavenly Father feedeth them. Are ye not much better than they? Which of you by taking thought can add one cubit unto his stature? And why take ye thought for raiment? Consider the lilies of the field, how they grow; they toil not, neither do they spin: and yet I say unto you, That even Solomon in all his glory was not arrayed like one of these. Wherefore, if God so clothe the grass of the field, which today is, and tomorrow is cast into the oven, *shall he* not much more *clothe* you, O ye of little faith? Therefore take no thought, saying, What shall we eat? or, What shall we drink? or, Wherewithal shall we be clothed? (For after all these things do the Gentiles seek:) for your heavenly Father knoweth that ye have need of all these things. But seek ye first the kingdom of God, and his righteousness; and all these things shall be added unto you. Take therefore no thought for the morrow: for the morrow shall take thought for the things of itself. Sufficient unto the day *is* the evil thereof (Matt 6:24–34).

He also that received seed among the thorns is he that heareth the word; and the care of this world, and the deceitfulness of riches, choke the word, and he becometh unfruitful (Matt 13:22).

And when they were come to Capernaum, they that received tribute *money* came to Peter, and said, Doth not your master pay tribute? He saith, Yes. And when he was come into the house, Jesus prevented him, saying, What thinkest thou, Simon? of whom do the kings of the earth take custom or tribute? of their own children, or of strangers? Peter saith unto him, Of strangers. Jesus saith unto him, Then are the children free. Notwithstanding, lest we should offend them, go thou to the sea, and cast an hook, and take up the fish that first cometh up; and when thou hast opened his mouth, thou shalt find a piece of money: that take, and give unto them for me and thee (Matt 17:24–27).

Then said Jesus unto his disciples, Verily

I say unto you, That a rich man shall hardly enter into the kingdom of heaven. And again I say unto you, It is easier for a camel to go through the eye of a needle, than for a rich man to enter into the kingdom of God (Matt 19:23, 24).

Is it not lawful for me to do what I will with mine own? Is thine eye evil, because I am good? (Matt 20:15).

Tell us therefore, What thinkest thou? Is it lawful to give tribute unto Cæsar, or not? But Jesus perceived their wickedness, and said, Why tempt ye me, *ye* hypocrites? Show me the tribute money. And they brought unto him a penny. And he saith unto them, Whose *is* this image and super-scription? They say unto him, Cæsar's. Then saith he unto them, Render therefore unto Cæsar the things which are Cæsar's; and unto God the things that are God's. When they had heard *these words*, they marvelled, and left him, and went their way (Matt 22:17–22).

Woe unto you, scribes and Pharisees, hypocrites! for ye pay tithe of mint and anise and cummin, and have omitted the weightier *matters* of the law, judgment, mercy, and faith: these ought ye to have done, and not to leave the other undone (Matt 23:23).

Now when Jesus was in Bethany, in the house of Simon the leper, there came unto him a woman having an alabaster box of very precious ointment, and poured it on his head, as he sat *at meat*. But when his disciples saw *it*, they had indignation, saying, To what purpose *is* this waste? For this ointment might have been sold for much, and given to the poor. When Jesus understood *it*, he said unto them, Why trouble ye the woman? for she hath wrought a good work upon me. For ye have the poor always with you; but me ye have not always. For in that she hath poured this ointment on my body, she did *it* for my burial. Verily I say unto you, Wheresoever this gospel shall be preached in the whole world, *there* shall also this, that this woman hath done, be told for a memorial of her (Matt 26:6–13).

And Jesus looked around about, and saith unto his disciples, How hardly shall they that have riches enter into the kingdom of God! And the disciples were aston-

ished at his words. But Jesus answereth again, and saith unto them, Children, how hard is it for them that trust in riches to enter into the kingdom of God! It is easier for a camel to go through the eye of a needle, than for a rich man to enter into the kingdom of God. And they were astonished out of measure, saying among themselves, Who then can be saved? And Jesus looking upon them saith, With men *it is* impossible, but not with God: for with God all things are possible (Mark 10:23–27).

And there came a certain poor widow, and she threw in two mites, which make a farthing. And he called *unto him* his disciples, and saith unto them, Verily I say unto you, That this poor widow hath cast more in, than all they which have cast into the treasury: for all *they* did cast in of their abundance; but she of her want did cast in all she had, *even* all her living (Mark 12:42–44).

He answereth and saith unto them, He that hath two coats, let him impart to him that hath none; and he that hath meat, let him do likewise (Luke 3:11)

But woe unto you that are rich! for ye have received your consolation (Luke 6:24).

Sell that ye have, and give alms; provide yourself bags which wax not old, a treasure in the heavens that faileth not, where no thief approacheth, neither moth corrupteth. For where your treasure is, there will your heart be also (Luke 12:33, 34).

So likewise, whosoever he be of you that forsaketh not all that he hath, he cannot be my disciple (Luke 14:33).

And as they heard these things, he added and spake a parable, because he was nigh to Jerusalem, and because they thought that the kingdom of God should immediately appear. He said therefore, A certain nobleman went into a far country to receive for himself a kingdom, and to return. And he called his ten servants, and delivered them ten pounds, and said unto them, Occupy till I come. But his citizens hated him, and sent a message after him, saying, We will not have this *man* to reign over us. And it came to pass, that when he was returned, having received the kingdom, then he commanded these servants to be called unto him, to whom he had given the money, that he might know how much every man had gained by trading. Then came the first, saying, Lord, thy pound hath gained ten pounds. And he said unto him, Well, thou good servant: because thou hast been faithful in a very little, have thou authority over ten cities. And the second came, saying, Lord, thy pound hath gained five pounds. And he said likewise to him, Be thou also over five cities. And another came, saying, Lord, behold, *here is* thy pound, which I have kept laid up in a napkin: for I feared thee, because thou art an austere man: thou takest up that thou layedst not down, and reapest that thou didst not sow. And he saith unto him, Out of thine own mouth will I judge thee, *thou* wicked servant. Thou knewest that I was an austere man, taking up that I laid not down, and reaping that I did not sow: wherefore then gavest not thou my money into the bank, that at my coming I might have required mine own with usury? And he said unto them that stood by, Take from him the pound, and give *it* to him that hath ten pounds. (And they said unto him, Lord, he hath ten pounds.) For I say unto you, That unto every one which hath shall be given; and from him that hath not, even that he hath shall be taken away from him. But those mine enemies, which would not that I should reign over them, bring hither, and slay *them* before me (Luke 19:11–27).

For it is written in the law of Moses, Thou shalt not muzzle the mouth of the ox that treadeth out the corn. Doth God take care for oxen? Or saith he *it* altogether for our sakes? For our sakes, no doubt, *this* is written: that he that ploweth should plow in hope; and that he that thresheth in hope should be partaker of his hope (1 Cor 9:9, 10).

Upon the first *day* of the week let every one of you lay by him in store, as *God* hath prospered him, that there be no gatherings when I come (1 Cor 16:2).

Every man according as he purposeth in his heart, *so let him give;* not grudgingly, or of necessity: for God loveth a cheerful giver (2 Cor 9:7).

Let him that stole steal no more: but rather let him labour, working with *his* hands the thing which is good, that he may have to give to him that needeth (Eph 4:28).

Not that I speak in respect of want: for I have learned, in whatsoever state I am, *therewith* to be content. I know both how to be abased, and I know how to abound: every where and in all things I am instructed both to be full and to be hungry, both to abound and to suffer need (Phil 4:11, 12).

Likewise *must* the deacons *be* grave, not double-tongued, not given to much wine, not greedy of filthy lucre (1 Tim 3:8).

But godliness with contentment is great gain. For we brought nothing into *this* world, *and it is* certain we can carry nothing out. And having food and raiment let us be therewith content. But they that will be rich fall into temptation and a snare, and *into* many foolish and hurtful lusts, which drown men in destruction and perdition. For the love of money is the root of all evil: which while some coveted after, they have erred from the faith, and pierced themselves through with many sorrows (1 Tim 6:6–10).

Charge them that are rich in this world, that they be not high-minded, nor trust in uncertain riches, but in the living God, who giveth us richly all things to enjoy (1 Tim 6:17).

Let your conversation *be* without covetousness; *and be* content with such things as ye have: for he hath said, I will never leave thee, nor forsake thee. So that we may boldly say, The Lord *is* my helper, and I will not fear what man shall do unto me (Heb 13:5, 6).

Let the brother of low degree rejoice in that he is exalted: but the rich, in that he is made low: because as the flower of the grass he shall pass away. For the sun is no sooner risen with a burning heat, but it withereth the grass, and the flower thereof falleth, and the grace of the fashion of it perisheth: so also shall the rich man fade away in his ways (James 1:9–11).

Love not the world, neither the things *that are* in the world. If any man love the world, the love of the Father is not in him (1 John 2:15).

Biblical Examples: Gen 29:16–30; 1 Kings 11:28; 21:1–24; Acts 2:42–47; 4:33–37; 18:3; 2 Cor 8:1–24; 2 Thess 3:8.

Further References: Gen 1:1, 31; 2:15; Exod 23:10–12; Prov 10:4; 11:24; 12:11, 24–27; 14:4; 22:9; 27:23; 28:19; 30:25, 26; 31:27; Eccl 8:10; 11:4–6; Luke 16:13; 18:22–25; Rom 12:11; 1 Thess 4:11, 12; 2 Thess 3:10–12; 1 Tim 5:8.

EMPLOYEE-EMPLOYER (See Labor Relations)

ENVY (See also Covetousness)

For wrath killeth the foolish man, and envy slayeth the silly one. I have seen the foolish taking root: but suddenly I cursed his habitation (Job 5: 2, 3).

Fret not thyself because of evildoers, neither be thou envious against the workers of iniquity (Ps 37:1).

Rest in the LORD, and wait patiently for him: fret not thyself because of him who prospereth in his way, because of the man who bringeth wicked devices to pass (Ps 37:7).

Be not thou afraid when one is made rich, when the glory of his house is increased (Ps 49:16).

Envy thou not the oppressor, and choose none of his ways (Prov 3:31).

A sound heart *is* the life of the flesh: but envy the rottenness of the bones (Prov 14:30).

Set me as a seal upon thine heart, as a seal upon thine arm: for love *is* strong as death; jealousy *is* cruel as the grave: the coals thereof *are* coals of fire, *which hath* a most vehement flame (Song of Sol 8:6).

Let us walk honestly, as in the day; not in rioting and drunkenness, not in chambering and wantonness, not in strife and envying (Rom 13:13).

For ye are yet carnal: for whereas *there is* among you envying, and strife, and divisions, are ye not carnal, and walk as men? (1 Cor 3:3).

But if ye have bitter envying and strife in your hearts, glory not, and lie not against the truth. This wisdom descendeth not from above, but *is* earthly, sensual, devilish. For where envying and strife *is,* there *is* confusion and every evil work (James 3:14–16).

Biblical Examples: Gen 4:4–8; 16:5, 6; 26:4; 37:4–11; Num 12:1–10; 1 Sam 18:8, 9; Dan 6:4; Acts 13:45.

Further References: Ps 73:3; Prov 23:17; 24:1, 19; 27:4; Eccl 4:4; Isa 26:11; Ezek 35:11; Rom 1:29; 1 Cor 13:4; 2 Cor 12:20; Gal 5:19–21, 26; 1 Tim 6:4, 5; Titus 3:3; James 4:5, 9; 1 Peter 2:1.

EQUALITY (See also Injustice; Justice)

For as the body is one, and hath many members, and all the members of that one body, being many, are one body: so also *is* Christ. For by one Spirit are we all baptized into one body, whether *we be* Jews or Gentiles, whether *we be* bond or free; and have been all made to drink into one Spirit. For the body is not one member, but many. If the foot shall say, Because I am not the hand, I am not of the body; is it therefore not of the body? And if the ear shall say, Because I am not the eye, I am not of the body; is it therefore not of the body? If the whole body *were* an eye, where *were* the hearing? If the whole *were* hearing, where *were* the smelling? But now hath God set the members every one of them in the body, as it hath pleased him. And if they were all one member, where *were* the body? But now *are they* many members, yet but one body (1 Cor 12:12–20).

For ye are all the children of God by faith in Christ Jesus. For as many of you as have been baptized into Christ have put on Christ. There is neither Jew nor Greek, there is neither bond nor free, there is neither male nor female: for ye are all one in Christ Jesus (Gal 3:26–28).

But now in Christ Jesus ye who sometimes were far off are made nigh by the blood of Christ. For he is our peace, who hath made both one, and hath broken down the middle wall of partition *between us;* having abolished in his flesh the enmity, *even* the law of commandments *contained* in ordinances; for to make in himself of twain one new man, *so* making peace; and that he might reconcile both unto God in one body by the cross, having slain the enmity thereby (Eph 2:13–16).

Where there is neither Greek nor Jew, circumcision nor uncircumcision, Barbarian, Scythian, bond *nor* free: but Christ *is* all, and in all (Col 3:11).

EUTHANASIA (See Suffering and Death)

EVIL COMPANY (See also Example, Bad; Influence)

Thou shalt not follow a multitude to *do* evil; neither shalt thou speak in a cause to decline after many to wrest *judgment* (Exod 23:2).

And he spake unto the congregation, saying, Depart, I pray you, from the tents of these wicked men, and touch nothing of theirs, lest ye be consumed in all their sins (Num 16:26).

Blessed *is* the man that walketh not in the counsel of the ungodly, nor standeth in the way of sinners, nor sitteth in the seat of the scornful (Ps 1:1).

I have not sat with vain persons, neither will I go in with dissemblers. I have hated the congregation of evildoers; and will not sit with the wicked (Ps 26:4, 5).

Draw me not away with the wicked, and with the workers of iniquity, which speak peace to their neighbours, but mischief *is* in their hearts (Ps 28:3).

My son, if sinners entice thee, consent thou not. If they say, Come with us, let us lay wait for blood, let us lurk privily for the innocent without cause: let us swallow them up alive as the grave; and whole, as those that go down into the pit: we shall find all precious substance, we shall fill our houses with spoil: cast in thy lot among us; let us all have one purse: my son, walk not thou in the way with them; refrain thy foot from their path (Prov 1:10–15).

I have taught thee in the way of wisdom; I have led thee in right paths. When thou goest, thy steps shall not be straitened; and when thou runnest, thou shalt not stumble. Take fast hold of instruction; let *her* not go: keep her; for she *is* thy life.

Enter not into the path of the wicked, and go not in the way of evil *men*. Avoid it, pass not by it, turn from it, and pass away. For they sleep not, except they have done mischief; and their sleep is taken away, unless they cause *some* to fall. For they eat the bread of wickedness, and drink the wine of violence. But the path of the just *is* as the shining light, that shineth more and more unto the perfect day. The way of the wicked *is* as darkness: they know not at what they stumble (Prov 4:11–19).

He that tilleth his land shall be satisfied with bread: but he that followeth vain *persons is* void of understanding (Prov 12:11).

The righteous *is* more excellent than his neighbour: but the way of the wicked seduceth them (Prov 12:26).

Be not thou envious against evil men, neither desire to be with them (Prov 24:1).

Whoso is partner with a thief hateth his own soul: he heareth cursing, and bewrayeth *it* not (Prov 29:24).

Now I beseech you, brethren, mark them which cause divisions and offences contrary to the doctrine which ye have learned; and avoid them (Rom 16:17).

Be not deceived: evil communications corrupt good manners (1 Cor 15:33).

Be ye not unequally yoked together with unbelievers: for what fellowship hath righteousness with unrighteousness? and what communion hath light with darkness? (2 Cor 6:14).

If any man teach otherwise, and consent not to wholesome words, *even* the words of our Lord Jesus Christ, and to the doctrine which is according to godliness; he is proud, knowing nothing, but doting about questions and strifes of words, whereof cometh envy, strife, railings, evil surmisings, perverse disputings of men of corrupt minds, and destitute of the truth, supposing that gain is godliness: from such withdraw thyself (1 Tim 6:3–5).

For men shall be lovers of their own selves, covetous, boasters, proud, blasphemers, disobedient to parents, unthankful, unholy, without natural affection, trucebreakers, false accusers, incontinent, fierce, despisers of those that are good, traitors, heady, highminded, lovers of pleasures more than lovers of God; having a form of godliness, but denying the power thereof: from such turn away (2 Tim 3:2–5).

Finally, *be ye* all of one mind, having compassion one of another, love as brethren, *be* pitiful, *be* courteous: not rendering evil for evil, or railing for railing: but contrariwise blessing; knowing that ye are thereunto called, that ye should inherit a blessing. For he that will love life, and see good days, let him refrain his tongue from evil, and his lips that they speak no guile: Let him eschew evil, and do good; let him seek peace, and ensue it. For the eyes of the Lord *are* over the righteous, and his ears *are open* unto their prayers: but the face of the Lord *is* against them that do evil (1 Peter 3:8–12).

Biblical Examples: Gen 19:15; Hos 7:5–9; Mic 6:16.

Further References: Lev 18:3; Num 33:55; Deut 7:2–4; Josh 23:6–13; Ezra 9:14; Ps 6:8; 84:10; 101:4; 139:19–22; Prov 2:11, 12, 16, 19; 9:6; 13:20; 14:7; 22:5, 10, 24, 25; 23:6, 20; 28:7, 19; Isa 6:5; 8:11, 12; Jer 2:25; 15:17; Hos 4:17; 1 Cor 5:6, 9–11; Gal 5:9; Eph 5:6–11; 2 Thess 3:6; 2 Peter 2:7, 8, 18; 2 John 10, 11.

EXAMPLE, BAD (See also Influence)

And be not ye like your fathers, and like your brethren, which trespassed against the Lord God of their fathers, *who* therefore gave them up to desolation, as ye see (2 Chron 30:7).

Make no friendship with an angry man; and with a furious man thou shalt not go: lest thou learn his ways, and get a snare to thy soul (Prov 22:24, 25).

Be ye not as your fathers, unto whom the former prophets have cried, saying, Thus saith the Lord of hosts; Turn ye now from your evil ways, and *from* your evil doings: but they did not hear, nor hearken unto me, saith the Lord (Zech 1:4).

Then spake Jesus to the multitude, and to his disciples, saying, The scribes and the Pharisees sit in Moses' seat: all therefore whatsoever they bid you observe, *that* observe and do; but do not ye after their works: for they say, and do not (Matt 23:1–3).

But take heed lest by any means this liberty of yours become a stumblingblock to them that are weak. For if any man see thee which hast knowledge sit at meat in the idol's temple, shall not the conscience of him which is weak be emboldened to eat those things which are offered to idols; and through thy knowledge shall the weak brother perish, for whom Christ died? But when ye sin so against the brethren, and wound their weak conscience, ye sin against Christ. Wherefore, if meat make my brother to offend, I will eat no flesh while the world standeth, lest I make my brother to offend (1 Cor 8:9–13).

Now these things were our examples, to the intent we should not lust after evil things, as they also lusted (1 Cor 10:6).

Beloved, follow not that which is evil, but that which is good. He that doeth good is of God: but he that doeth evil hath not seen God (3 John 11).

Biblical Examples: Jer 16:12; 17:1, 2; Hos 5:5.

Further References: Lev 18:2, 3; 20:23; Deut 18:19; Isa 8:11; Ezek 20:18; Eph 4:17.

EXAMPLE, GOOD (See also Influence)

Be ye therefore followers of God, as dear children; and walk in love, as Christ also hath loved us, and hath given himself for us an offering and a sacrifice to God for a sweet-smelling savour (Eph 5:1, 2).

And ye became followers of us, and of the Lord, having received the word in much affliction, with joy of the Holy Ghost: so that ye were ensamples to all that believe in Macedonia and Achaia (1 Thess 1:6, 7).

Let no man despise thy youth; but be thou an example of the believers, in word, in conversation, in charity, in spirit, in faith, in purity (1 Tim 4:12).

In all things shewing thyself a pattern of good works: in doctrine *shewing* uncorruptness, gravity, sincerity, sound speech, that cannot be condemned; that he that is of the contrary part may be ashamed, having no evil thing to say of you (Titus 2:7, 8).

Looking unto Jesus the author and finisher of *our* faith; who for the joy that was set before him endured the cross, despising the shame, and is set down at the right hand of the throne of God. For consider him that endured such contradiction of sinners against himself, lest ye be wearied and faint in your minds (Heb 12:2, 3).

Remember them which have the rule over you, who have spoken unto you the word of God: whose faith follow, considering the end of *their* conversation (Heb 13:7).

Take, my brethren, the prophets, who have spoken in the name of the Lord, for an example of suffering affliction, and of patience. Behold, we count them happy which endure. Ye have heard of the patience of Job, and have seen the end of the Lord; that the Lord is very pitiful, and of tender mercy (James 5:10, 11).

Dearly beloved, I beseech *you* as strangers and pilgrims, abstain from fleshly lusts, which war against the soul; having your conversation honest among the Gentiles: that, whereas they speak against you as evildoers, they may by *your* good works, which they shall behold, glorify God in the day of visitation. Submit yourselves to every ordinance of man for the Lord's sake: whether it be to the king, as supreme; or unto governors, as unto them that are sent by him for the punishment of evildoers, and for the praise of them that do well. For so is the will of God, that with well-doing ye may put to silence the ignorance of foolish men: as free, and not using *your* liberty for a cloak of maliciousness, but as the servants of God. Honour all *men*. Love the brotherhood. Fear God. Honour the king. Servants, *be* subject to *your* masters with all fear; not only to the good and gentle, but also to the froward. For this *is* thankworthy, if a man for conscience toward God endure grief, suffering wrongfully. For what glory *is it*, if, when ye be buffeted for your faults, ye shall take it patiently? but if, when ye do well, and suffer *for it*, ye take it patiently, this *is* acceptable with God. For even hereunto were ye called: because Christ also suffered for us, leaving us an example, that ye should follow his steps: who did no sin, neither was guile found in his mouth: who, when he was reviled, reviled not again; when he suffered, he threatened not; but committed *himself* to him that judgeth righteously: who his own self bare our sins in his own body on the tree, that we, being dead to sins, should live unto righteousness: by whose stripes ye were healed. For ye were as sheep going astray; but are now returned unto the Shepherd and Bishop of your souls (1 Peter 2:11–25).

Neither as being lords over *God's* heritage, but being ensamples to the flock (1 Peter 5:3).

Biblical Examples: Neh 5:8–19; Mark 10:43–45; Acts 20:35; 1 Cor 7:7, 8; Phil 4:9; 2 Thess 3:7–10.

Further References: Luke 22:27; John 13:13–17, 34; Rom 15:2–7; 2 Cor 8:9; Phil 2:5–8; Col 3:13; 1 John 3:16.

EXPEDIENCY

Him would Paul have to go forth with him; and took and circumcised him because of the Jews which were in those quarters: for they knew all that his father was a Greek (Acts 16:3).

I know, and am persuaded by the Lord Jesus, that *there* is nothing unclean of itself: but to him that esteemeth any thing to be unclean, to him *it is* unclean. But if thy brother be grieved with *thy* meat, now walkest thou not charitably. Destroy not him with thy meat, for whom Christ died. Let not then your good be evil spoken of: for the kingdom of God is not meat and drink; but righteousness, and peace, and joy in the Holy Ghost. For he that in these things serveth Christ *is* acceptable to God, and approved of men. Let us therefore follow after the things which make for peace, and things wherewith one may edify another. For meat destroy not the work of God. All things indeed *are* pure; but *it is* evil for that man who eateth with offence. *It is* good neither to eat flesh, nor to drink wine, nor *any thing* whereby thy brother stumbleth, or is offended, or is made weak. Hast thou faith? have *it* to thyself before God. Happy *is* he that condemneth not himself in that thing which he alloweth (Rom 14:14–22).

All things are lawful unto me, but all things are not expedient: all things are lawful for me, but I will not be brought under the power of any (1 Cor 6:12).

Now as touching things offered unto idols, we know that we all have knowledge. Knowledge puffeth up, but charity edifieth. And if any man think that he knoweth any thing, he knoweth nothing yet as he ought to know. But if any man love God, the same is known of him. As concerning therefore the eating of those things that are offered in sacrifice unto idols, we know that an idol *is* nothing in the world, and that *there is* none other God but one. For though there be that are called gods, whether in heaven or in earth, (as there by gods many, and lords many,) but to us *there is but* one God, the Father, of whom *are* all things, and we in him; and one Lord Jesus Christ, by whom *are* all things, and we by him. Howbeit *there is* not in every man that knowledge: for some with conscience of the idol unto this hour eat *it* as a thing offered unto an idol; and their conscience being weak is defiled. But meat commendeth us not to God: for neither, if we eat, are we the better; neither, if we eat not, are we the worse. But take heed lest by any means this liberty of yours become a stumblingblock to them that are weak. For if any man see thee which hast knowledge sit at meat in the idol's temple, shall not the conscience of him which is weak be emboldened to eat those things which are offered to idols; and through thy knowledge shall the weak brother perish, for whom Christ died? But when ye sin so against the brethren, and wound their weak conscience, ye sin against Christ. Wherefore, if meat make my brother to offend, I will eat no flesh while the world standeth, lest I make my brother to offend (1 Cor 8:1–13).

For though I be free from all *men,* yet have I made myself servant unto all, that I might gain the more. And unto the Jews I became as a Jew, that I might gain the Jews; to them that are under the law, as under the law, that I might gain them that are under the law; to them that are without law, as without law, (being not without law to God, but under the law to Christ,) that I might gain them that are without law. To the weak became I as weak, that I might gain the weak: I am made all things to all *men,* that I might by all means save some. And this I do for the gospel's sake, that I might be partaker thereof with *you* (1 Cor 9:19–23).

And things are lawful for me, but all things are not expedient: all things are lawful for me, but all things edify not. Let no man seek his own, but every man another's *wealth.* Whatsoever is sold in the shambles, *that* eat, asking no question for conscience sake: for the earth *is* the Lord's, and the fulness thereof. If any of them that believe not bid you *to a feast,* and ye be disposed to go; whatsoever is set before you, eat, asking no question for conscience sake. But if any man say unto you, This is offered in sacrifice unto idols,

eat not for his sake that shewed it, and for conscience sake: for the earth *is* the Lord's, and the fulness thereof: Conscience, I say, not thine own, but of the other: for why is my liberty judged of another *man's* conscience? For if I by grace be a partaker, why am I evil spoken of for that for which I give thanks? (1 Cor 10:23–30).

Forbidding to marry, *and commanding* to abstain from meats, which God hath created to be received with thanksgiving of them which believe and know the truth. For every creature of God *is* good, and nothing to be refused, if it be received with thanksgiving: for it is sanctified by the word of God and prayer (1 Tim 4:3–5).

EXTORTION (See also Deceit; Dishonesty; Theft)

Trust not in oppression, and become not vain in robbery: if riches increase, set not your heart *upon them* (Ps 62:10).

Let the extortioner catch all that he hath; and let the strangers spoil his labour (Ps 109:11).

Let mine outcasts dwell with thee, Moab; be thou a covert to them from the face of the spoiler: for the extortioner is at an end, the spoiler ceaseth, the oppressors are consumed out of the land (Isa 16:4).

In thee have they taken gifts to shed blood; thou hast taken usury and increase, and thou hast greedily gained of thy neighbours by extortion, and hast forgotten me, said the Lord GOD (Ezek 22:12).

Woe unto you, scribes and Pharisees, hypocrites! for ye make clean the outside of the cup and of the platter, but within they are full of extortion and excess. *Thou* blind Pharisee, cleanse first that *which is* within the cup and platter, that the outside of them may be clean also (Matt 23:25, 26).

The Pharisee stood and prayed thus with himself, God, I thank thee, that I am not as other men *are,* extortioners, unjust, adulterers, or even as this publican (Luke 18:11).

Biblical Examples: Gen 25:31; 47:13–26.

Further References: Mic 3:1–3; 1 Cor 5:9–13; 6:9, 10.

EXTRAVAGANCE (See also Economics; Materialism; Wealth)

He that loveth pleasure *shall be* a poor man: he that loveth wine and oil shall not be rich. The wicked *shall be* a ransom for the righteous, and the transgressor for the upright. *It is* better to dwell in the wilderness, than with a contentious and an angry woman. *There is* treasure to be desired and oil in the dwelling of the wise; but a foolish man spendeth it up (Prov 21:17–20).

And in that day did the Lord GOD of hosts call to weeping, and to mourning, and to baldness, and to girding with sackcloth: and behold joy and gladness, slaying oxen, and killing sheep, eating flesh, and drinking wine: let us eat and drink; for tomorrow we shall die (Isa 22:12, 13).

That lie upon beds of ivory, and stretch themselves upon their couches, and eat the lambs out of the flock, and the calves out of the midst of the stall; that chant to the sound of the viol, *and* invent to themselves instruments of music, like David; That drink wine in bowls, and anoint themselves with the chief ointments: but they are not grieved for the affliction of Joseph.

Therefore now shall they go captive with the first that go captive, and the banquet of them that stretched themselves shall be removed (Amos 6:4–7).

And I will say to my soul, Soul, thou hast much goods laid up for many years; take thine ease, eat, drink, *and* be merry. But God said unto him, *Thou* fool, this night thy soul shall be required of thee: then whose shall those things be, which thou has provided? (Luke 12:19, 20).

There was a certain rich man, which was clothed in purple and fine linen, and fared sumptuously every day (Luke 16:19).

Let us walk honestly, as in the day; not in rioting and drunkenness, not in chambering and wantonness, not in strife and envying (Rom 13:13).

Whose end *is* destruction, whose God *is their* belly, and *whose* glory *is* in their shame, who mind earthly things (Phil 3:19).

For the time past of *our* life may suffice us to have wrought the will of the Gentiles, when we walked in lasciviousness, lusts, excess of wine, revellings, banquetings, and abominable idolatries (1 Peter 4:3).

Biblical Examples: Gen 25:30–34; Dan 5:1; Amos 6:4–7

EXTREMISM (See Fanaticism)

– F –

FAITHFULNESS

Help, LORD; for the godly man ceaseth; for the faithful fail from among the children of men (Ps 12:1).

O love the LORD, all ye his saints: *for* the LORD preserveth the faithful, and plentifully rewardeth the proud doer (Ps 31:23).

Most men will proclaim every one his own goodness: but a faithful man who can find? (Prov 20:6).

A faithful man shall abound with blessings: but he that maketh haste to be rich shall not be innocent (Prov 28:20).

Who then is a faithful and wise servant, whom his lord hath made ruler over his household, to give them meat in due season? Blessed *is* that servant, whom his lord when he cometh shall find so doing. Verily I say unto you, That he shall make him ruler over all his goods (Matt 24:45–47).

For *the kingdom of heaven is* as a man travelling into a far country, *who* called his own servants, and delivered unto them his goods. And unto one he gave five talents, to another two, and to another one; to every man according to his several ability; and straightway took his journey. Then he that had received the five talents went and traded with the same, and made *them* other five talents. And likewise he that *had received* two, he also gained other two. But he that had received one went and digged in the earth, and hid his lord's money. After a long time the lord of those servants cometh, and reckoneth with them. And so he that had received five talents came and brought other five talents, saying, Lord, thou deliveredst unto me five talents: behold, I have gained beside them five talents more. His lord said unto him, Well done, *thou* good and faithful servant: thou hast been faithful over a few things, I will make thee ruler over many things: enter thou into the joy of thy lord. He also that had received two talents came and said, Lord, thou deliveredst unto me two talents: behold, I have gained two other talents beside them. His lord said unto him, Well done, good and faithful servant; thou hast been faithful over a few things, I will make thee ruler over many things: enter thou into the joy of thy lord (Matt 25:14–23).

He that is faithful in that which is least is faithful also in much: and he that is unjust in the least is unjust also in much. If therefore ye have not been faithful in the unrighteous mammon, who will commit to your trust the true *riches?* And if ye have not been faithful in that which is another man's, who shall give you that which is your own? (Luke 16:10–12).

Moreover it is required in stewards, that a man be found faithful (1 Cor 4:2).

Biblical Examples: 2 Sam 22:22–25; 1 Kings 19:10, 14; Gal 3:9; Heb 3:5.

Further References: Luke 12:42–44; 19:12–27; Col 3:22; Rev 2:10.

FALSEHOOD (See Lying; Tongue)

FALSE WITNESS (See Lying; Tongue)

FAMILY (See also Adultery; Aging; Birth Control; Children; Divorce; Husband-Wife Relations; Incest; Intermarriage; Marriage; Monogamy; Parent-Child Relations; Remarriage; Sex and Sexuality; Women; Youth)

Hear, O Israel: The LORD our God *is* one LORD: and thou shalt love the LORD thy God with all thine heart, and with all thy soul, and with all thy might. And these words, which I command thee this day, shall be in thine heart: and thou shalt teach them diligently unto thy children, and shalt talk of them when thou sittest in thine house, and when thou walkest by the way, and when thou liest down, and when thou risest up (Deut 6:4–7).

Except the LORD build the house, they labour in vain that build it: except the LORD keep the city, the watchman waketh *but* in vain (Ps 127:1).

Chasten thy son while there is hope, and let not thy soul spare for his crying (Prov 19:18).

Train up a child in the way he should go: and when he is old, he will not depart from it (Prov 22:6).

Live joyfully with the wife whom thou lovest all the days of the life of thy vanity, which he hath given thee under the sun, all the days of thy vanity: for that *is* thy portion in *this* life, and in thy labour which thou takest under the sun (Eccl 9:9).

And he answered and said unto them, Have ye not read, that he which made *them* at the beginning made them male and female, and said, For this cause shall a man leave father and mother, and shall cleave to his wife: and they twain shall be one flesh? Wherefore they are no more twain, but one flesh. What therefore God hath joined together, let not man put asunder (Matt 19:4–6).

There came then his brethren and his mother, and, standing without, sent unto him, calling him. And the multitude sat about him, and they said unto him, Behold, thy mother and thy brethren without seek for thee. And he answered them, saying, Who is my mother, or my brethren? And he looked round about on them which sat about him, and said, Behold my mother and my brethren! For whosoever shall do the will of God, the same is my brother, and my sister, and mother (Mark 3:31–35).

Then came to *him* certain of the Sadducees, which deny that there is any resurrection; and they asked him, saying,

Master, Moses wrote unto us, If any man's brother die, having a wife, and he die without children, that his brother should take his wife, and raise up seed unto his brother. There were therefore seven brethren: and the first took a wife, and died without children. And the second took her to wife, and he died childless. And the third took her; and in like manner the seven also: and they left no children, and died. Last of all the woman died also. Therefore in the resurrection whose wife of them is she? for seven had her to wife. And Jesus answering said unto them, The children of this world marry, and are given in marriage: but they which shall be accounted worthy to obtain that world, and the resurrection from the dead, neither marry, nor are given in marriage: neither can they die any more: for they are equal unto the angels; and are the children of God, being the children of the resurrection (Luke 20:27–36).

Wives, submit yourselves unto your own husbands, as it is fit in the Lord. Husbands, love *your* wives, and be not bitter against them. Children, obey *your* parents in all things: for this is well pleasing unto the Lord. Fathers, provoke not your children *to anger,* lest they be discouraged (Col 3:18–21).

Honour widows that are widows indeed. But if any widow have children or nephews, let them learn first to shew piety at home, and to requite their parents: for that is good and acceptable before God. Now she that is a widow indeed, and desolate, trusteth in God, and continueth in supplications and prayers night and day. But she that liveth in pleasure is dead while she liveth. And these things give in charge, that they may be blameless. But if any provide not for his own, and specially for those of his own house, he hath denied the faith, and is worse than an infidel (1 Tim 5:3–8).

The aged women likewise, that *they be* in behaviour as becometh holiness, not false accusers, not given to much wine, teachers of good things; that they may teach the young women to be sober, to love their husbands, to love their children, *to be* discreet, chaste, keepers at home, good, obedient to their own husbands, that the word of God be not blasphemed (Titus 2:3–5).

Likewise, ye wives, *be* in subjection to your own husbands; that, if any obey not the word, they also may without the word be won by the conversation of the wives; while they behold your chaste conversation *coupled* with fear. Whose adorning let it not be that outward *adorning* of plaiting the hair, and of wearing of gold, or of putting on of apparel; but *let it be* the hidden man of the heart, in that which is not corruptible, *even the ornament* of a meek and quiet spirit, which is in the sight of God of great price. For after this manner in the old time the holy women also, who trusted in God, adorned themselves, being in subjection unto their own husbands: even as Sara obeyed Abraham, calling him lord: whose daughters ye are, as long as ye do well, and are not afraid with any amazement. Likewise, ye husbands, dwell with *them* according to knowledge, giving honour unto the wife, as unto the weaker vessel, and as being heirs together of the grace of life; that your prayers be not hindered (1 Peter 3:1–7).

Biblical Examples: Gen 18:19; Josh 24:15; 2 Sam 6:20; John 11:1–5; Acts 10:1–6, 32, 44–48; 16:15; 16:31–34; 2 Tim 1:5.

Further References: Gen 2:23, 24; 3:16; Deut 11:19, 20; Esth 1:20–22; Prov 15:17; 19:13; 21:9, 19; 31:21, 23; Eph 5:22–6:4; 1 Tim 3:2–5.

FAMILY-PLANNING (See Birth Control)

FANATICISM

And they cried aloud, and cut themselves after their manner with knives and lancets, till the blood gushed out upon them (1 Kings 18:28).

But they cried out, Away with *him*, away with *him*, crucify him. Pilate saith unto them, Shall I crucify your King? The chief priests answered, We have no king but Cæsar (John 19:15).

Then they cried out with a loud voice, and stopped their ears, and ran upon him with one accord (Acts 7:57).

And Saul, yet breathing out threatenings and slaughter against the disciples of the Lord, went unto the high priests (Acts 9:1).

Further References: Acts 21:36; 22:23.

FASTING (See also Abstinence)

Cry aloud, spare not, lift up thy voice like a trumpet, and shew my people their transgression, and the house of Jacob their sins. Yet they seek me daily, and delight to know my ways, as a nation that did righteousness, and forsook not the ordinance of their God: they ask of me the ordinances of justice; they take delight in approaching to God.

Wherefore have we fasted, *say they,* and thou seest not? *wherefore* have we afflicted our soul, and thou takest no knowledge? Behold, in the day of your fast ye find pleasure, and exact all your labours. Behold, ye fast for strife and debate, and to smite with the fist of wickedness: ye shall not fast as *ye do this* day, to make your voice to be heard on high. Is it such a fast that I have chosen? a day for a man to afflict his soul? *is it* to bow down his head as a bulrush, and to spread sackcloth and ashes *under him?* wilt thou call this a fast, and an acceptable day to the LORD? *Is* not this the fast that I have chosen? to loose the bands of wickedness, to undo the heavy burdens, and to let the oppressed go free, and that ye break every yoke? *Is it* not to deal thy bread to the hungry, and that thou bring the poor that are cast out to thy house? when thou seest the naked, that thou cover him; and that thou hide not thyself from thine own flesh? (Isa 58:1–7).

Moreover when ye fast, be not, as the hypocrites, of a sad countenance; for they disfigure their faces, that they may appear unto men to fast. Verily I say unto you, They have their reward. But thou, when thou fastest, anoint thine head, and wash thy face; that thou appear not unto men to fast, but unto thy Father which is in secret: and thy Father, which seeth in secret, shall reward thee openly (Matt 6:16–18).

Then came to him the disciples of John, saying, Why do we and the Pharisees fast oft, but thy disciples fast not? And Jesus said unto them, Can the children of the bridechamber mourn, as long as the bridegroom is with them? but the days will come, when the bridegroom shall be taken from them, and then they shall fast. No man putteth a piece of new cloth unto an old garment, for that which is put in to fill it up taketh from the garment, and the rent is made worse. Neither do men put new wine into old bottles: else the bottles break, and the wine runneth out, and the bottles perish: but they put new wine into new bottles, and both are preserved (Matt 9:14–17).

Defraud ye not one the other, except *it be* with consent for a time, that ye may give yourselves to fasting and prayer; and come together again, that Satan tempt you not for your incontinency (1 Cor. 7:5).

Biblical Examples: Exod 24:18; 1 Sam 7:6; 2 Sam 1:11, 12; 1 Kings 19:8; Zech 7:5; Matt 4:1–4; Mark 1:12, 13; Luke 4:1, 2; 18:9–14; Acts 13:2, 3; 14:23.

Further References: 2 Sam 12:16; Ezra 8:21–23; Ps 35:13; 69:10; Jer 14:12; 36:6; Dan 9:3; 10:2, 3; Joel 2:12, 13; Zech 8:19; Mark 2:18; Luke 2:37; 18:12; Acts 10:30; 2 Cor 6:5.

FEAR

And they heard the voice of the LORD God walking in the garden in the cool of the day: and Adam and his wife hid themselves from the presence of the LORD God amongst the trees of the garden. And the LORD God called unto Adam, and said unto him, Where *art* thou? And he said, I heard thy voice in the garden, and I was afraid, because I *was* naked; and I hid myself. And he said, Who told thee that thou *wast* naked? Hast thou eaten of the tree, whereof I commanded thee that thou shouldest not eat? And the man said, The woman whom thou gavest *to be* with me, she gave me of the tree, and I did eat. And the LORD God said unto the woman, What *is* this *that* thou hast done? And the woman said, The serpent beguiled me, and I did eat (Gen 3:8–13).

Ye shall not respect persons in judgment; *but* ye shall hear the small as well as the great; ye shall not be afraid of the face of man; for the judgment *is* God's: and the cause that it is too hard for you, bring *it* unto me, and I will hear it (Deut 1:17).

How should one chase a thousand, and two put ten thousand to flight, except their Rock had sold them, and the LORD had shut them up? (Deut 32:30).

Now therefore go to, proclaim in the ears of the people, saying, Whosoever *is* fearful and afraid, let him return and depart early from mount Gilead. And there returned of the people twenty and two thousand; and there remained ten thousand (Judg 7:3).

The wicked man travaileth with pain all *his* days, and the number of years is hidden to the oppressor. A dreadful sound *is* in his ears: in prosperity the destroyer shall come upon him. He believeth not that he shall return out of darkness, and he is waited for of the sword. He wandereth abroad for bread, *saying*, Where *is it?* he knoweth that the day of darkness is ready at his hand. Trouble and anguish shall make him afraid; they shall prevail against him, as a king ready to the battle (Job 15:20–24).

The wicked flee when no man pursueth: but the righteous are bold as a lion (Prov 28:1).

The fear of man bringeth a snare: but whoso putteth his trust in the LORD shall be safe (Prov 29:25).

I, *even* I, *am* he that comforteth you: who *art* thou, that thou shouldest be afraid of a man *that* shall die, and of the son of man *which* shall be made *as* grass; and forgettest the LORD thy maker, that hath stretched forth the heavens, and laid the foundations of the earth; and hast feared continually every day because of the fury of the oppressor, as if he were ready to destroy? and where *is* the fury of the oppressor? (Isa 51:12, 13).

Fear them not therefore: for there is nothing covered, that shall not be revealed; and his, that shall not be known. What I tell you in darkness, *that* speak ye in light: and what ye hear in the ear, *that* preach ye upon the housetops. And fear not them which kill the body, but are not able to kill the soul: but rather fear him which is able to destroy both soul and body in hell. Are not two sparrows sold for a farthing? and one of them shall not fall on the ground without your Father. But the very hairs of your head are all numbered. Fear ye not therefore, ye are of more value than many sparrows (Matt 10:26–31).

Thou believest that there is one God; thou doest well: the devils also believe, and tremble (James 2:19).

There is no fear in love; but perfect love casteth out fear: because fear hath torment. He that feareth is not made perfect in love (1 John 4:18).

Biblical Examples: Gen 31:31; Num 13:28–33; Josh 7:5; 1 Sam 13:6, 7; 17:24; 2 Sam 15:13–17; Matt 8:26; 14:25, 26; 26:55, 56, 70–74; Mark 4:38; 6:50; 14:66–72; Luke 8:25; 22:54–60; John 6:19; Acts 16:27; 1 Tim 4:16.

Further References: Lev 26:36, 37; Deut 20:8; Job 18:11.

FEMINISM (See Women)

FLATTERY (See also Pride)

Let me not, I pray you, accept any man's person, neither let me give flattering titles unto man. For I know not to give flattering titles; *in so doing* my maker would soon take me away (Job 32:21, 22).

They speak vanity every one with his neighbour: *with* flattering lips *and* with a double heart do they speak. The LORD shall cut off all flattering lips, *and* the tongue that speaketh proud things (Ps 12:2, 3).

For the lips of a strange woman drop *as* an honeycomb, and her mouth *is* smoother than oil (Prov 5:3).

Say unto wisdom, Thou *art* my sister; and call understanding *thy* kinswoman: that they may keep thee from the strange woman, from the stranger *which* flattereth with her words (Prov 7:4, 5).

With her much fair speech she caused him to yield, with the flattering of her lips she forced him (Prov 7:21).

He that goeth about *as* a tale-bearer revealeth secrets: therefore meddle not with him that flattereth with his lips (Prov 20:19).

A lying tongue hateth *those that are* afflicted by it; and a flattering mouth worketh ruin (Prov 26:28).

He that rebuketh a man afterwards shall find more favour than he that flattereth with his tongue (Prov 28:23).

A man that flattereth his neighbour spreadeth a net for his feet (Prov 29:5).

Woe unto you, when all men shall speak well of you! for so did their fathers to the false prophets (Luke 6:26).

Biblical Examples: Gen 33:10; Judg 8:1–3; 2 Sam 9:8; 14:17–20; 15:2–6; 1 Kings 20:4; Luke 20:21; Acts 24:2–4; 26:2, 3; 1 Thess 2:4–6.

Further References: Job 17:5; Ps 5:8, 9; 36:2; 49:13, 18; 78:36; Prov 24:24; Dan 11:21, 34.

FORCE (See Violence)

FORGIVENESS

Hatred stirreth up strifes: but love covereth all sins (Prov 10:12).

He that covereth a transgression seeketh love; but he that repeateth a matter separateth *very* friends (Prov 17:9).

Therefore if thou bring thy gift to the altar, and there rememberest that thy brother hath aught against thee; leave there thy gift before the altar, and go thy way; first be reconciled to thy brother, and then come and offer thy gift (Matt 5:23, 24).

For if ye forgive men their trespasses, your heavenly Father will also forgive you: but if ye forgive not men their trespasses, neither will your Father forgive your trespasses (Matt 6:14, 15).

Judge not, that ye be not judged. For with what judgment ye judge, ye shall be judged: and with what measure ye mete, it shall be measured to you again. And why beholdest thou the mote that is in thy brother's eye, but considerest not the beam that is in thine own eye? Or how wilt thou say to thy brother, Let me pull out the mote out of thine eye; and, behold, a beam *is* in thine own eye? Thou hypocrite, first cast out the beam out of thine own eye; and then shalt thou see clearly to cast out the mote out of thy brother's eye (Matt 7:1–5).

Then came Peter to him, and said, Lord, how oft shall my brother sin against me, and I forgive him? till seven times? Jesus saith unto him, I say not unto thee, Until seven times: but, Until seventy times seven.

Therefore is the kingdom of heaven likened unto a certain king, which would take account of his servants. And when he had begun to reckon, one was brought unto him, which owed him ten thousand talents. But forasmuch as he had not to pay, his lord commanded him to be sold, and his wife, and children, and all that he had, and payment to be made. The servant therefore fell down, and worshipped him, saying, Lord, have patience with me, and I will pay thee all. Then the lord of that servant was moved with compassion, and loosed him, and forgave him the debt. But the same servant went out, and found one of his fellow-servants, which owed him an hundred pence: and he laid hands on him, and took *him* by the throat, saying, Pay me that thou owest. And his fellow-servant fell down at his feet, and besought him, saying, Have patience with me, and I will pay thee all. And he would not: but went and cast him into prison, till he should pay the debt. So when his fellow-servants saw what was done, they were very sorry, and came and told unto their lord all that was done. Then his lord, after that he had called him, said unto him, O thou wicked servant, I forgave thee all that debt, because thou desiredst me: shouldest not thou also have had compassion on thy fellow-servant, even as I had pity on thee?

And his lord was wroth, and delivered him to the tormentors, till he should pay all that was due unto him. So likewise shall my heavenly Father do also unto you, if ye from your hearts forgive not every one his brother their trespasses (Matt 18:21–35).

Be ye therefore merciful, as your Father also is merciful (Luke 6:36).

Take heed to yourselves: If thy brother trespass against thee, rebuke him; and if he repent, forgive him. And if he trespass against thee seven times in a day, and seven times in a day turn again to thee, saying, I repent; thou shalt forgive him (Luke 17:3, 4).

Brethren, if a man be overtaken in a fault, ye which are spiritual, restore such an one in the spirit of meekness; considering thyself, lest thou also be tempted (Gal 6:1).

Let all bitterness, and wrath, and anger, and clamour, and evil speaking, be put away from you, with all malice: and be ye kind one to another, tenderhearted, forgiving one another, even as God for Christ's sake hath forgiven you (Eph 4:31, 32).

Put on therefore, as the elect of God, holy and beloved, bowels of mercies, kindness, humbleness of mind, meekness, longsuffering; forbearing one another, and forgiving one another, if any man have a quarrel against any: even as Christ forgave you, so also *do* ye (Col 3:12, 13).

Biblical Examples: Gen 33:4, 11; 45:5–15; 50:19–21; Num 12:1–13; 1 Sam 24:10–12; 2 Sam 16:9–13; 1 Kings 1:53; Luke 23:34; Philem 10, 18.

Further References: Exod 23:4, 5; Prov 19:11; 24:17, 29; 25:21, 22; Matt 5:7, 39–41, 43, 46; Mark 11:25; 1 Peter 3:9.

FORNICATION (See also Adultery; Sex and Sexuality)

Know ye not that your bodies are the members of Christ? shall I then take the members of Christ, and make *them* the members of an harlot? God forbid. What? know ye not that he which is joined to an harlot is one body? for two, saith he, shall be one flesh. But he that is joined unto the Lord is one spirit. Flee fornication. Every sin that a man doeth is without the body; but he that committeth fornication sinneth against his own body. What? know ye not that your body is the temple of the Holy Ghost *which is* in you, which ye have of God, and ye are not your own? For ye are bought with a price: therefore glorify God in your body, and in your spirit, which are God's (1 Cor 6:15–20).

And lest, when I come again, my God will humble me among you, and *that* I shall bewail many which have sinned already, and have not repented of the uncleanness and fornication and lasciviousness which they have committed (2 Cor 12:21).

Now the works of the flesh are manifest, which are *these;* Adultery, fornication, uncleanness, lasciviousness, idolatry, witchcraft, hatred, variance, emulations, wrath, strife, seditions, heresies, envyings, murders, drunkenness, revellings, and such like: of the which I tell you before, as I have also told *you* in time past, that they which do such things shall not inherit the kingdom of God (Gal 5:19–21).

And the angels which kept not their first estate, but left their own habitation, he hath reserved in everlasting chains under darkness unto the judgment of the great day. Even as Sodom and Gomorrha, and the cities about them in like manner, giving themselves over to fornication, and going after strange flesh, are set forth for an example, suffering the vengeance of eternal fire (Jude 6, 7).

And after these things, I heard a great voice of much people in heaven, saying, Alleluia; Salvation, and glory, and honour, and power, unto the Lord our God: for true and righteous *are* his judgments: for he hath judged the great whore, which did corrupt the earth with her fornication, and hath avenged the blood of his servants at her hand (Rev 19:1, 2).

Further References: Matt 5:28; 15:19; 19:9; Acts 15:20; Rom 1:28, 29, 32; 1 Cor 5:9–11; 6:9, 10; 10:8; Eph 5:3, 11, 12; Col 3:5; Rev 3:20–22; 9:21.

FREEDOM

Then said Jesus to those Jews which believed on him, If ye continue in my word, *then* are ye my disciples indeed; and ye shall know the truth, and the truth shall make you free (John 8:31, 32).

If the Son therefore shall make you free, ye shall be free indeed (John 8:36).

Now the Lord is that Spirit: and where the Spirit of the Lord *is,* there *is* liberty (2 Cor 3:17).

Stand fast therefore in the liberty wherewith Christ hath made us free, and be not entangled again with the yoke of bondage (Gal 5:1).

I know both how to be abased, and I know how to abound: every where and in all things I am instructed both to be full and to be hungry, both to abound and to suffer need (Phil 4:12).

Further References: Exod 21:2–27; Lev 19:20; Num 5:19, 28; Deut 15:12–18; Josh 2:20; 1 Sam 17:25; 1 Chron 9:33; 2 Chron 29:31; Job 3:19; Ps 51:12; Isa 58:6; Jer 34:9–14; Amos 4:5; Matt 17:26; Mark 7:11; Luke 4:18; Acts 22:28; Rom 5:15–18; 6:18–22; 1 Cor 7:21, 22; Gal 3:13, 28.

Further References: Gal 4:26, 31; Eph 6:8; Col 3:11; 2 Thess 3:1; 1 Peter 2:16.

FRIENDSHIP

To him that is afflicted pity *should be shewed* from his friend; but he forsaketh the fear of the Almighty. My brethren have dealt deceitfully as a brook, *and* as the stream of brooks they pass away (Job 6:14, 15).

But as for me, when they were sick, my clothing *was* sackcloth: I humbled my soul with fasting; and my prayer returned into mine own bosom. I behaved myself as though *he had been* my friend *or* brother: I bowed down heavily, as one that mourneth *for his* mother (Ps 35:13, 14).

For *it was* not an enemy *that* reproached me; then I could have borne *it:* neither *was it* he that hated me *that* did magnify *himself* against me; then I would have hid myself from him: but *it was* thou, a man mine equal, my guide, and mine acquaintance. We took sweet counsel together, *and* walked unto the house of God in company (Ps 55:12–14).

A talebearer revealeth secrets: but he that is of a faithful spirit concealeth the matter (Prov 11:13).

He that covereth a transgression seeketh love; but he that repeateth a matter separateth *very* friends (Prov 17:9).

A man *that hath* friends must shew himself friendly: and there is a friend *that* sticketh closer than a brother (Prov 18:24).

Make no friendship with an angry man; and with a furious man thou shalt not go: lest thou learn his ways, and get a snare to thy soul. Be not thou *one* of them that strike hands, *or* of them that are sureties for debts. If thou hast nothing to pay, why should he take away thy bed from under thee? (Prov 22:24–27).

Faithful *are* the wounds of a friend; but the kisses of an enemy *are* deceitful. The full soul loatheth an honeycomb; but to the hungry soul every bitter thing is sweet. As a bird that wandereth from her nest, so *is* a man that wandereth from his place. Ointment and perfume rejoice the heart: so *doth* the sweetness of a man's friend by hearty counsel. Thine own friend, and thy father's friend, forsake not; neither go into thy brother's house in the day of thy calamity: *for* better *is* a neighbour *that is* near than a brother far off (Prov 27:6–10).

Biblical Examples: Ruth 1:16, 17; 1 Sam 18:1–4; 2 Sam 9; Job 16:2, 20; 19:13–22; Dan 2:49; Matt 27:55–61; Luke 10:38–42; Phil 2:19–25.

Further References: Deut 13:6–9; Ps 41:9; 88:8–18; Eccl 4:9–12; Amos 3:3.

FRUGALITY

He that loveth pleasure *shall be* a poor man: he that loveth wine and oil shall not be rich. *There is* treasure to be desired and oil in the dwelling of the wise; but a foolish man spendeth it up (Prov 21:17, 20).

Be not among winebibbers; among riotous eaters of flesh: For the drunkard and the glutton shall come to poverty: and drowsiness shall clothe *a man* with rags (Prov 23:20, 21).

She looketh well to the ways of her household, and eateth not the bread of idleness (Prov 31:27).

And they did all eat, and were filled: and they took up of the fragments that remained twelve baskets full (Matt 14:20).

And they did all eat, and were filled: and they took up of the broken *meat* that was left seven baskets full (Matt 15:37).

And there were some that had indignation within themselves, and said, Why was this waste of the ointment made? For it might have been sold for more than three hundred pence, and have been given to the poor. And they murmured against her (Mark 14:4, 5).

Biblical Examples: Gen 41:48–54; Exod 16:17–24.

Further References: 1 Kings 17:5–13; Prov 11:6; 12:27; 13:22; Mark 7:28; Eph 4:28.

-G-

GAMBLING (See Deceit; Dishonesty; Lots, Casting; Theft)

GENEROSITY (See Unselfishness)

GENTLENESS (See Vices and Virtues)

GIVING (See Unselfishness)

GLUTTONY (See also Abstinence; Temperance)

Notwithstanding they hearkened not unto Moses; but some of them left of it until the morning, and it bred worms, and stank: and Moses was wroth with them. And they gathered it every morning, every man according to his eating: and when the sun waxed hot, it melted. . . .

And it came to pass, *that* there went out *some* of the people on the seventh day for to gather, and they found none (Exod 16:20, 21, 27).

And the people stood up all that day, and all *that* night, and all the next day, and they gathered the quails: he that gathered least gathered ten homers: and they spread *them* all abroad for themselves round about the camp (Num 11:32).

For the drunkard and the glutton shall come to poverty: and drowsiness shall clothe *a man* with rags (Prov 23:21).

That lie upon beds of ivory, and stretch themselves upon their couches, and eat the lambs out of the flock, and the calves out of the midst of the stall (Amos 6:4).

The Son of man came eating and drinking, and they say, Behold a man gluttonous, and a winebibber, a friend of publicans and sinners. But wisdom is justified of her children (Matt 11:19).

And I will say to my soul, Soul, thou hast much goods laid up for many years; take thine ease, eat, drink, *and* be merry. But God said unto him, *Thou* fool, this night thy soul shall be required of thee: then whose shall those things be, which thou hast provided? (Luke 12:19, 20).

(For many walk, of whom I have told you often, and now tell you even weeping, *that they are* the enemies of the cross of Christ: whose end *is* destruction, whose God *is their* belly, and *whose* glory *is* in their shame, who mind earthly things) (Phil 3:18, 19).

Biblical Examples: Gen 25:30–34; Num 11:4; 1 Sam 2:12–17; Dan 5:1.

Further References: Deut 21:20–23; Prov 30:21, 22; Isa 22:13; Luke 21:34; Rom 13:13, 14; 1 Peter 4:3.

GODLINESS (See also Holiness; Righteousness)

But refuse profane and old wives' fables, and exercise thyself *rather* unto godliness. For bodily exercise profiteth little: but godliness is profitable unto all things, having promise of the life that now is, and of that which is to come (1 Tim 4:7, 8).

If any man teach otherwise, and consent not to wholesome words, *even* the words of our Lord Jesus Christ, and to the doctrine which is according to godliness; he is proud, knowing nothing, but doting about questions and strifes of words, whereof cometh envy, strife, railings, evil surmisings, perverse disputing of men of corrupt minds, and destitute of the truth, supposing that gain is godliness: from such withdraw thyself. But godliness with contentment is great gain. For we brought nothing into *this* world, *and it is* certain we can carry nothing out. And having food and raiment let us be therewith content. But they that will be rich fall into temptation and a snare, and *into* many foolish and hurtful lusts, which drown men in destruction and perdition. For the love of money is the root of all evil: which while some coveted after, they have erred from the faith, and pierced themselves through with many sorrows. But thou, O man of God, flee these things; and follow after righteousness, godliness, faith, love, patience, meekness (1 Tim 6:3–11).

Paul, a servant of God, and an apostle of Jesus Christ, according to the faith of God's elect, and the acknowledging of the truth which is after godliness; in hope of eternal life, which God, that cannot lie, promised before the world began; but hath in due times manifested his word through preaching, which is committed unto me according to the commandment of God our Saviour (Titus 1:1–3).

According as his divine power hath given unto us all things that *pertain* unto life and godliness, through the knowledge of him that hath called us to glory and virtue: whereby are given unto us exceeding great and precious promises: that by these ye might be partakers of the divine nature, having escaped the corruption that is in the world through lust. And beside this, giving all diligence, add to your faith virtue; and to virtue knowledge; and to knowledge temperance; and to temperance patience; and to patience godliness; and to godliness brotherly kindness; and to brotherly kindness charity (2 Peter 1:3–7).

Seeing then *that* all these things shall be dissolved, what manner *of persons* ought ye to be in *all* holy conversation and godliness, looking for and hasting unto the coming of the day of God, wherein the heavens being on fire shall be dissolved, and the elements shall melt with fervent heat? (2 Peter 3:11, 12).

Biblical Examples: Luke 2:25–38; Acts 3:12.

GOSSIP (See also Slander; Tongue)
Thou shalt not go up and down *as* a talebearer among thy people: neither shalt thou stand against the blood of thy neighbour: I *am* the LORD (Lev 19:16).

For we hear that there are some which walk among you disorderly, working not at all, but are busybodies (2 Thess 3:11).

But the younger widows refuse: for when they have begun to wax wanton against Christ, they will marry; Having damnation, because they have cast off their first faith. And withal they learn *to be* idle, wandering about from house to house; and not only idle, but tattlers also and busybodies, speaking things which they ought not (1 Tim 5:11–13).

Further References: Ps 15:1–3; 50:2; Prov 20:19; 25:23; Ezek 22:9; Rom 1:28–30; 2 Cor 12:20.

GOVERNMENT (See also Anarchy; Authority; Bribes and Bribery; Citizenship; Conscientious Objection; Crime and Punishment; Honesty; Injustice; Justice; Nonresistance; Patriotism; Peace; Revolution; Taxes; War)
And thou shalt take no gift: for the gift blindeth the wise, and perverteth the words of the righteous (Exod 23:8).

On this side Jordan, in the land of Moab, began Moses to declare this law, saying, The LORD our God spake unto us in Horeb, saying, Ye have dwelt long enough in this mount: turn you, and take your journey, and go to the mount of the Amorites, and unto all *the places* nigh thereunto, in the plain, in the hills, and in the vale, and in the south, and by the sea side, to the land of the Canaanites, and unto Lebanon, unto the great river, the river Euphrates. Behold, I have set the land before you: go in and possess the land which the LORD sware unto your fathers, Abraham, Isaac, and Jacob, to give unto them and to their seed after them.

And I spake unto you at that time, saying, I am not able to bear you myself alone: the LORD your God hath multiplied you, and, behold, ye *are* this day as the stars of heaven for multitude. (The LORD God of your fathers make you a thousand times so many more as ye *are*, and bless you, as he hath promised you!) How can I myself alone bear your cumbrance, and your burden, and your strife? Take your wise men, and understanding, and known among your tribes, and I will make them rulers over you. And ye answered me, and said, The thing which thou hast spoken *is* good *for us* to do. So I took the chief of your tribes, wise men, and known, and made them heads over you, captains over thousands, and captains over hundreds, and captains over fifties, and captains over tens, and officers among your tribes. And I charged your judges at that time, saying, Hear *the causes* between your brethren, and judge righteously between *every* man and his brother, and the stranger *that is* with him. Ye shall not respect persons in judgment; *but* ye shall hear the small as well as the great; ye shall not be afraid of the face of man; for the judgment *is* God's: and the cause that is too hard for you, bring *it* unto me, and I will hear it (Deut 1:5–17).

Judges and officers shalt thou make thee in all thy gates, which the LORD thy God giveth thee, throughout thy tribes: and they shall judge the people with just judgment. Thou shalt not wrest judgment; thou shalt not respect persons, neither take a gift: for a gift doth blind the eyes of the wise, and pervert the words of the righteous (Deut 16:18, 19).

When thou art come unto the land which the LORD thy God giveth thee, and shalt possess it, and shalt dwell therein, and shalt say, I will set a king over me, like as all the nations that *are* about me; thou shalt in any wise set *him* king over thee, whom the LORD thy God shall choose: *one* from among thy brethren shalt thou set king over thee: thou mayest not set a stranger over thee, which *is* not thy brother. But he shall not multiply horses to himself, nor cause the people to return to Egypt, to the end that he should multiply horses: forasmuch as the LORD hath said unto you, Ye shall henceforth return no more that way. Neither shall he multiply wives to himself, that his heart turn not away: neither shall he greatly multiply to himself silver and gold. And it shall be, when he sitteth upon the throne of his kingdom, that he shall write him a copy of this law in a book out of *that which is* before the priests the Levites: And it shall be with him, and he shall read therein all the days of his life:

that he may learn to fear the LORD his God, to keep all the words of this law and these statutes, to do them: That his heart be not lifted up above his brethren, and that he turn not aside from the commandment, *to* the right hand, or *to* the left: to the end that he may prolong *his* days in his kingdom, he, and his children, in the midst of Israel (Deut 17:14–20).

And the LORD sent Nathan unto David. And he came unto him, and said unto him, There were two men in one city; the one rich, and the other poor. The rich *man* had exceeding many flocks and herds: but the poor *man* had nothing, save one little ewe lamb, which he had bought and nourished up: and it grew up together with him, and with his children; it did eat of his own meat, and drank of his own cup, and lay in his bosom, and was unto him as a daughter. And there came a traveller unto the rich man, and he spared to take of his own flock and of his own herd, to dress for the wayfaring man that was come unto him; but took the poor man's lamb, and dressed it for the man that was come to him. And David's anger was greatly kindled against the man; and he said to Nathan, *As* the LORD liveth, the man that hath done this *thing* shall surely die: and he shall restore the lamb fourfold, because he did this thing, and because he had no pity.

And Nathan said to David, Thou *art* the man. Thus saith the LORD God of Israel, I anointed thee king over Israel, and I delivered thee out of the hand of Saul; and I gave thee thy master's house, and thy master's wives into thy bosom, and gave thee the house of Israel and of Judah; and if *that had been* too little, I would moreover have given unto thee such and such things. Wherefore hast thou despised the commandment of the LORD, to do evil in his sight? thou hast killed Uriah the Hittite with the sword, and hast taken his wife *to be* thy wife, and hast slain him with the sword of the children of Ammon. Now therefore the sword shall never depart from thine house; because thou hast despised me, and hast taken the wife of Uriah the Hittite to be thy wife (2 Sam 12:1–10).

Be wise now therefore, O ye kings: be

instructed, ye judges of the earth. Serve the LORD with fear, and rejoice with trembling (Ps 2:10, 11).

Kings of the earth, and all people; princes, and all judges of the earth: both young men, and maidens; old men, and children: let them praise the name of the LORD: for his name alone is excellent; his glory *is* above the earth and heaven (Ps 148:11–13).

A divine sentence *is* in the lips of the king: his mouth transgresseth not in judgment. A just weight and balance *are* the LORD's: all the weights of the bag *are* his work. *It is* an abomination to kings to commit wickedness: for the throne is established by righteousness. Righteous lips *are* the delight of kings; and they love him that speaketh right (Prov 16:10–13).

A king that sitteth in the throne of judgment scattereth away all evil with his eyes (Prov 20:8).

A wise king scattereth the wicked, and bringeth the wheel over them. The spirit of man *is* the candle of the LORD, searching all the inward parts of the belly. Mercy and truth preserve the king: and his throne is upholden by mercy (Prov 20:26–28).

It is not for kings, O Lemuel, *it is* not for kings to drink wine; nor for princes strong drink: lest they drink, and forget the law, and pervert the judgment of any of the afflicted (Prov 31:4, 5).

Thy princes *are* rebellious, and companions of thieves: every one loveth gifts, and followeth after rewards: they judge not the fatherless, neither doth the cause of the widow come unto them (Isa 1:23).

And when they were come to Capernaum, they that received tribute *money* came to Peter, and said, Doth not your master pay tribute? He saith, Yes. And when he was come into the house, Jesus prevented him, saying, What thinkest thou, Simon? of whom do the kings of the earth take custom or tribute? of their own children, or of strangers? (Matt 17:24, 25).

Then went the Pharisees, and took counsel how they might entangle him in *his* talk. And they sent out unto him their disciples with the Herodians, saying, Master, we know that thou art true, and teachest the way of God in truth, neither carest thou for any *man:* for thou regardest not the person of men. Tell us therefore, What thinkest thou? Is it lawful to give tribute unto Cæsar, or not? But Jesus perceived their wickedness, and said, Why tempt ye me, *ye* hypocrites? Show me the tribute money. And they brought unto him a penny. And he saith unto them, Whose *is* this image and superscription? They say unto him, Cæsar's. Then saith he unto them, Render therefore unto Cæsar the things which are Cæsar's; and unto God the things that are God's. When they had heard *these words,* they marvelled, and left him, and went their way (Matt 22:15–22).

And he charged them, saying, Take heed, beware of the leaven of the Pharisees, and *of* the leaven of Herod (Mark 8:15).

But Jesus called them to *him,* and saith unto them, Ye know that they which are accounted to rule over the Gentiles exercise lordship over them; and their great ones exercise authority upon them. But so shall it not be among you: but whosoever will be great among you, shall be your minister (Mark 10:42, 43).

And Jesus answering said unto them, Render to Cæsar the things that are Cæsar's, and to God the things that are God's. And they marvelled at him (Mark 12:17).

Then Peter and the *other* apostles answered and said, We ought to obey God rather than men (Acts 5:29).

Let every soul be subject unto the higher powers. For there is no power but of God: the powers that be are ordained of God. Whosoever therefore resisteth the power, resisteth the ordinance of God: and they that resist shall receive to themselves damnation. For rulers are not a terror to good works, but to the evil. Wilt thou then not be afraid of the power? do that which is good, and thou shalt have praise of the same: for he is the minister of God to thee for good. But if thou do that which is evil, be afraid; for he beareth not the sword in vain: for he is the minister of God, a revenger to *execute* wrath upon him that doeth evil. Wherefore *ye* must needs be subject, not only for wrath, but also for conscience sake. For for this cause pay ye tribute also: for they are God's ministers, attending continually upon this very thing. Render therefore to all their dues: tribute to whom tribute *is due;* custom to whom custom; fear to whom fear; honour to whom honour (Rom 13:1–7).

I exhort therefore, that, first of all, supplications, prayers, intercessions, *and* giving of thanks, be made for all men; for kings, and *for* all that are in authority; that we may lead a quiet and peaceable life in all godliness and honesty. For this *is* good and acceptable in the sight of God our Saviour (1 Tim 2:1–3).

Submit yourselves to every ordinance of man for the Lord's sake: whether it be to the king, as supreme; or unto governors, as unto them that are sent by him for the punishment of evildoers, and for the praise of them that do well. For so is the will of God, that with well-doing ye may put to silence the ignorance of foolish men: as free, and not using *your* liberty for a cloak of maliciousness, but as the servants of God. Honour all *men.* Love the brotherhood. Fear God. Honour the king (1 Peter 2:13–17).

And I stood upon the sand of the sea, and saw a beast rise up out of the sea, having seven heads and ten horns, and upon his horns ten crowns, and upon his heads the name of blasphemy. And the beast which I saw was like unto a leopard, and his feet were as *the feet* of a bear, and his mouth as the mouth of a lion: and the dragon gave him his power, and his seat, and great authority. And I saw one of his heads as it were wounded to death; and his deadly wound was healed: and all the world wondered after the beast. And they worshipped the dragon which gave power unto the beast: and they worshipped the beast, saying, Who *is* like unto the beast? who is able to make war with him?

And there was given unto him a mouth speaking great things and blasphemies; and power was given unto him to continue forty *and* two months. And he opened his mouth in blasphemy against God, to blaspheme his name, and his tabernacle, and them that dwell in heaven. And it was given unto him to make war with the saints, and to overcome them: and power was given him over all kindreds, and tongues, and nations. And all that dwell upon the earth shall worship him, whose names are not written in the book of life of the Lamb slain from the foundation of the world. If any man have an ear, let him hear. He that leadeth into captivity shall go into captivity: he that killeth with the sword must be killed with the sword. Here is the patience and the faith of the saints.

And I beheld another beast coming up out of the earth; and he had two horns like a lamb, and he spake as a dragon. And he exerciseth all the power of the first beast before him, and causeth the earth and them which dwell therein to worship the first beast, whose deadly wound was healed. And he doeth great wonders, so that he maketh fire come down from heaven on the earth in the sight of men, and deceiveth them that dwell on the earth by *the means of* those miracles which he had power to do in the sight of the beast; saying to them that dwell on the earth, that they should make an image to the beast, which had the wound by a sword, and did live. And he had power to give life unto the image of the beast, that the image of the beast should both speak, and cause that as many as would not worship the image of the beast should be killed. And he causeth all, both small and great, rich and poor, free and bond, to receive a mark in their right hand, or in their foreheads: and that no man might buy or sell, save he that had the mark, or the name of the beast, or the number of his name. Here is wisdom. Let him that hath understanding count the number of the beast: for it is the number of a man; and his number *is* Six hundred threescore *and* six (Rev 13).

Biblical Examples: Exod 18:13–26; Num 11:16, 17, 24, 25; 14:1–10; 27:18–23; Deut 29:15; Josh 23:2–6; 1 Sam 8:4–10, 19–22; 10:24; 14:44, 45; 22:6, 12–19; 2 Sam 3:17–21; 1 Kings 21:5–13; Dan 3:15; 5:18–28; Hos 8:4; John 19:10–16.

Further References: Ps 22:28; Prov 8:15, 16; Isa 9:6, 7; Jer 1:1–10; Dan 2:20, 21; 4:17; Luke 20:25; Titus 3:1.

GREED (See also Covetousness; Materialism)

Thou shalt not covet thy neighbour's house, thou shalt not covet thy neighbour's wife, nor his manservant, nor his maidservant, nor his ox, nor his ass, nor any thing that *is* thy neighbour's (Exod 20:17).

For the wicked boasteth of his heart's desire, and blesseth the covetous, *whom* the LORD abhorreth (Ps 10:3).

He that is of a proud heart stirreth up strife: but he that putteth his trust in the LORD shall be made fat (Prov 28:25).

Then I returned, and I saw vanity under the sun. There is one *alone*, and *there is* not a second; yea, he hath neither child nor brother: yet *is there* no end of all his labour; neither is his eye satisfied with riches; neither *saith he*, For whom do I labour, and bereave my soul of good? This *is* also vanity, yea, it *is* a sore travail (Eccl 4:7, 8).

He that loveth silver shall not be satisfied with silver; nor he that loveth abundance with increase: this *is* also vanity (Eccl 5:10).

And, behold, one came and said unto him, Good Master, what good thing shall I do, that I may have eternal life? And he said unto him, Why callest thou me good? *there is* none good but one, *that is*, God: but if thou wilt enter into life, keep the commandments. He saith unto him, Which? Jesus said, Thou shalt do no murder, Thou shalt not commit adultery, Thou shalt not steal, Thou shalt not bear false witness, honour thy father and *thy* mother: and, Thou shalt love thy neighbour as thyself. The young man saith unto him, All these things have I kept from my youth up: what lack I yet? Jesus said unto him, If thou wilt be perfect, go *and* sell that thou hast, and give to the poor, and thou shalt have treasure in heaven: and come *and* follow me. But when the young man heard that saying, he went away sorrowful: for he had great possessions (Matt 19:16–22).

And he said unto them, Take heed, and beware of covetousness: for a man's life consisteth not in the abundance of the things which he possesseth (Luke 12:15).

I wrote unto you in an epistle not to company with fornicators: yet not altogether with the fornicators of this world, or with the covetous, or extortioners, or with idolaters; for then must ye needs go out of the world. But now I have written unto you not to keep company, if any man that is called a brother be a fornicator, or covetous, or an idolater, or a railer, or a drunkard, or an extortioner; with such an one no not to eat (1 Cor 5:9–11).

Know ye not that the unrighteous shall not inherit the kingdom of God? Be not deceived: neither fornicators, nor idolaters, nor adulterers, nor effeminate, nor abusers of themselves with mankind, nor thieves, nor covetous, nor drunkards, nor revilers, nor extortioners, shall inherit the kingdom of God (1 Cor 6:9, 10).

But fornication, and all uncleanness, or covetousness, let it not be once named among you, as becometh saints (Eph 5:3).

But they that will be rich fall into temptation and a snare, and *into* many foolish and hurtful lusts, which drown men in destruction and perdition. For the love of money is the root of all evil: which while some coveted after, they have erred from the faith, and pierced themselves through with many sorrows (1 Tim 6:9, 10).

Biblical Examples: Gen 13:10–13; 27:6–29; Josh 7:21; 1 Sam 8:3; 1 Kings 21:2–16; Matt 21:12, 13; Luke 12:15–21; 19:45, 46; John 2:14–16.

Further References: Prov 1:19; 15:27; 21:25, 26; Isa 56:11; Matt 6:19–24; 1 Tim 3:3; Titus 1:11; Jude 11.

-H-

HAPPINESS (See Mental Health)

HATRED

Thou shalt not hate thy brother in thine heart: thou shalt in any wise rebuke thy neighbour, and not suffer sin upon him (Lev 19:17).

The foolish shall not stand in thy sight: thou hatest all workers of iniquity (Ps 5:5).

I hate, I despise your feast days, and I will not smell in your solemn assemblies. Though ye offer me burnt offerings and your meat offerings, I will not accept *them:* neither will I regard the peace offerings of your fat beasts. Take thou away from me the noise of thy songs; for I will not hear the melody of thy viols. But let judgment run down as waters, and righteousness as a mighty stream (Amos 5:21–24).

These *are* the things that ye shall do; Speak ye every man the truth to his neighbour; execute the judgment of truth and peace in your gates: and let none of you imagine evil in your hearts against his neighbour; and love no false oath: for all these *are things* that I hate, saith the LORD (Zech 8:16, 17).

I have loved you, saith the LORD. Yet ye say, Wherein hast thou loved us? *Was* not Esau Jacob's brother? saith the LORD: yet I loved Jacob, and I hated Esau, and laid his mountains and his heritage waste for the dragons of the wilderness (Mal 1:2, 3).

For the LORD, the God of Israel, saith that he hateth putting away: for *one* covereth violence with his garment, saith the LORD of hosts: therefore take heed to your spirit, that ye deal not treacherously (Mal 2:16).

Ye have heard that it was said by them of old time, Thou shalt not kill; and whosoever shall kill shall be in danger of the judgment: but I say unto you, That whosoever is angry with his brother without a cause shall be in danger of the judgment: and whosoever shall say to his brother, Raca, shall be in danger of the council: but whosoever shall say, Thou fool, shall be in danger of hell fire (Matt 5:21, 22).

Think not that I am come to send peace on earth: I came not to send peace, but a sword. For I am come to set a man at variance against his father, and the daughter against her mother, and the daughter in law against her mother in law. And a man's foes *shall be* they of his own household. He that loveth father or mother more than me is not worthy of me and he that loveth son or daughter more than me is not worthy of me (Matt 10:34–37).

If any *man* come to me, and hate not his father, and mother, and wife, and children, and brethren, and sisters, yea, and his own life also, he cannot be my disciple (Luke 14:26).

He that loveth his life shall lose it; and he that hateth his life in this world shall keep it unto life eternal (John 12:25).

He that hateth me hateth my Father also. If I had not done among them the works which none other man did, they had not had sin: but now have they both seen and hated both me and my Father. But *this cometh to pass,* that the word might be fulfilled that is written in their law, They hated me without a cause (John 15:23–25).

For we ourselves also were sometimes foolish, disobedient, deceived, serving divers lusts and pleasures, living in malice and envy, hateful, *and* hating one another (Titus 3:3).

He that saith he is in the light, and hateth his brother, is in darkness even until now. He that loveth his brother abideth in the light, and there is none occasion of stumbling in him. But he that hateth his brother is in darkness, and walketh in darkness, and knoweth not whither he goeth, because that darkness hath blinded his eyes (1 John 2:9–11).

If a man say, I love God, and hateth his brother, he is a liar: for he that loveth not his brother whom he hath seen, how can he love God whom he hath not seen? (1 John 4:20).

And of some have compassion, making a difference: and others save with fear, pulling *them* out of the fire; hating even the garment spotted by the flesh (Jude 22, 23).

Biblical Examples: Gen 29:3–31; 37; 42:21; Deut 12:31; 19:6–11; 1 Kings 19:1, 2; Ps 41:5–8; 69:4–26; 109:2–5, 16–18; Matt 14:3–10; Acts 17:5; Rev 2:6.

Further References: Job 31:29, 30; Ps 25:19; 35:19; 38:16–19; Prov 10:6, 12, 18; 14:17, 22; 15:17; 26:24–26; Matt 5:43, 44; 10:22; John 17:14; Rom 1:28–32; Gal 5:19, 20; 1 John 3:10–15.

HEALTH (See also Body, Human; Mental Health)

And said, If thou wilt diligently hearken to the voice of the LORD thy God, and wilt do that which is right in his sight, and wilt give ear to his commandments, and keep all his statutes, I will put none of these diseases upon thee, which I have brought upon the Egyptians: for I *am* the LORD that healeth thee (Exod 15:26).

It shall be a perpetual state for your generations throughout all your dwellings, that ye eat neither fat nor blood (Lev 3:17).

Or if a soul touch any unclean thing, whether *it be* a carcase of an unclean beast, or a carcase of unclean cattle, or the carcase of unclean creeping things, and *if* it be hidden from him; he also shall be unclean, and guilty. Or if he touch the uncleanness of man, whatsoever uncleanness *it be* that a man shall be defiled withal, and it be hid from him; when he knoweth *of it,* then he shall be guilty (Lev 5:2, 3).

And the flesh that toucheth any unclean *thing* shall not be eaten; it shall be burnt with fire; and as for the flesh, all that be clean shall eat thereof (Lev 7:19).

And he that beareth the carcase of them shall wash his clothes, and be unclean until the even: they *are* unclean unto you (Lev 11:28).

And upon whatsoever *any* of them, when they are dead, doth fall, it shall be unclean; whether *it be* any vessel of wood, or raiment, or skin, or sack, whatsoever vessel *it be,* wherein *any* work is done, it must be put into water, and it shall be unclean until the even; so it shall be cleansed. And every earthen vessel, whereinto *any* of them falleth, whatsoever *is* in it shall be unclean; and ye shall break it. Of all meat which may be eaten, *that* on which *such* water cometh shall be unclean: and all drink that may be drunk in every *such* vessel shall be unclean. And every *thing* whereupon *any part* of their carcase falleth shall be unclean; *whether it be* oven, or ranges for pots, they shall be broken down: *for* they *are* unclean, and shall be unclean unto you. Nevertheless a fountain or pit, *wherein there is* plenty of water, shall be clean: but that which toucheth their carcase shall be unclean (Lev 11:32–36).

And the LORD spake unto Moses, saying, Speak unto the children of Israel, saying, If a woman have conceived seed, and born a man child: then she shall be unclean seven days; according to the days of the separation for her infirmity shall she be unclean. And in the eighth day the flesh of his foreskin shall be circumcised. And she shall then continue in the blood of her purifying three and thirty days; she shall touch no hallowed thing, nor come into the sanctuary, until the days of her purifying be fulfilled. But if she bear a maid child, then she shall be unclean two weeks, as in her separation: and she shall continue in the blood of her purifying threescore and six days. And when the days of her purifying are fulfilled, for a son, or for a daughter, she shall bring a lamb of the first year for a burnt offering, and a young pigeon, or a turtledove, for a sin offering, unto the door of the tabernacle of the congregation, unto the priest: who shall offer it before the LORD, and make an atonement for her; and she shall be cleansed from the issue of her blood. This *is* the law for her that hath borne a male or a female. And if she be not able to bring a lamb, then she shall bring two turtles, or two young pigeons; the one for the burnt offering, and the other for a sin offering: and the priest shall make an atonement for her, and she shall be clean (Lev 12:1–8).

And when he that hath an issue is cleansed of his issue; then he shall number to himself seven days for his cleansing, and wash his clothes, and bathe his flesh in running water, and shall be clean. And on the eighth day he shall take to him two turtledoves, or two young pigeons, and come before the LORD unto the door of the tabernacle of the congregation, and give them unto the priest: and the priest shall offer them, the one *for* a sin offering, and the other *for* a burnt offering; and the priest shall make an atonement for him before the LORD for his issue (Lev 15:13–15).

And the LORD spake unto Moses, saying, Speak unto the children of Israel, and say unto them, I am the LORD your God. After the doings of the land of Egypt, wherein ye dwelt, shall ye not do: and after the doings of the land of Canaan, whither I bring you, shall ye not do: neither shall ye walk in their ordinances. Ye shall do my judgments, and keep mine ordinances, to walk therein: I *am* the LORD your God. Ye shall therefore keep my statutes, and my judgments: which if a man do, he shall live in them: I *am* the LORD.

None of you shall approach to any that is near of kin to him, to uncover *their* nakedness: I *am* the LORD. The nakedness of thy father, or the nakedness of thy mother, shalt thou not uncover: she *is* thy mother; thou shalt not uncover her nakedness. The nakedness of thy father's wife shalt thou not uncover: it *is* thy father's nakedness. The nakedness of thy sister, the daughter of thy father, or daughter of thy mother, *whether she be* born at home, or born abroad, *even* their nakedness thou shalt not uncover. The nakedness of thy son's daughter, or of thy daughter's daughter, *even* their nakedness thou shalt not uncover: for theirs *is* thine own nakedness. The nakedness of thy father's wife's daughter, begotten of thy father, she *is* thy sister, thou shalt not uncover her nakedness. Thou shalt not uncover the nakedness of thy father's sister: she *is* thy father's near kinswoman. Thou shalt not uncover the nakedness of thy mother's sister: for she *is* thy mother's near kinswoman. Thou shalt not uncover the nakedness of thy father's brother, thou shalt not approach to his wife: she *is* thine aunt. Thou shalt not uncover the nakedness of thy daughter in law: she *is* thy son's wife; thou shalt not uncover her nakedness. Thou shalt not uncover the nakedness of thy brother's wife: it *is* thy brother's nakedness. Thou shalt not uncover the nakedness of a woman and her daughter, neither shalt thou take her son's daughter, or her daughter's daughter, to uncover her nakedness; *for* they *are* her near kinswomen: it *is* wickedness. Neither shalt thou take a wife to her sister, to vex *her,* to uncover her nakedness, beside the other in her life *time.*

And thou shalt not approach unto a woman to uncover her nakedness, as long as she is put apart for her uncleanness. Moreover thou shalt not lie carnally with thy neighbor's wife, to defile thyself with her (Lev 18:1–20).

What man soever of the seed of Aaron *is* a leper, or hath a running issue; he shall not eat of the holy things, until he be clean. And whoso toucheth any thing *that is* unclean *by* the dead, or a man whose seed goeth from him; or whosoever toucheth any creeping thing, whereby he may be made unclean, or a man of whom he may take uncleanness, whatsoever uncleanness he hath; the soul which hath touched any such shall be unclean until even, and shall not eat of the holy things, unless he wash his flesh with water. And when the sun is down, he shall be clean, and shall afterward eat of the holy things; because it *is* his food. That which dieth of itself, or is torn *with beasts,* he shall not eat to defile himself therewith: I *am* the LORD (Lev 22:4–8).

He that toucheth the dead body of any man shall be unclean seven days. He shall purify himself with it on the third day, and on the seventh day he shall be clean: but if he purify not himself the third day, then the seventh day he shall not be clean. Whosoever toucheth the dead body of any man that is dead, and purifieth not himself, defileth the tabernacle of the LORD; and that soul shall be cut off from Israel: because the water of separation was not sprinkled upon him, he shall be unclean; his uncleanness *is* yet upon him. This *is* the law, when a man dieth in a tent: all that come into the tent, and all that *is* in the tent, shall be unclean seven days. And every open vessel, which hath no covering bound upon it, *is* unclean. And whosoever toucheth one that is slain with a sword in the open fields, or a dead body, or a bone of a man, or a grave, shall be unclean seven days (Num 19:11–16).

Thou shalt not eat any abominable thing. These *are* the beasts which ye shall eat: the ox, the sheep, and the goat, the hart, and the roebuck, and the fallow deer, and the wild goat, and the pygarg, and the wild ox, and the chamois. And every beast that parteth the hoof, and cleaveth the cleft into two claws, *and* cheweth the cud among the beasts, that ye shall eat. Nevertheless these ye shall not eat of them that chew the cud, or of them that divide the cloven hoof; *as* the camel, and the hare, and the coney: for they chew the cud, but divide not the hoof; *therefore* they *are* unclean unto you. And the swine, because it divideth the hoof, yet cheweth not the cud, it *is* unclean unto you: ye shall not eat of their flesh, nor touch their dead carcase.

These ye shall eat of all that *are* in the waters: all that have fins and scales shall ye eat: and whatsoever hath not fins and scales ye may not eat; it *is* unclean unto you.

Of all clean birds ye shall eat. But these *are they* of which ye shall not eat: the eagle, and the ossifrage, and the osprey, and the glede, and the kite, and the vulture after his kind, and every raven after his kind, and the owl, and the night hawk, and the cuckoo, and the hawk after his kind, the little owl, and the great owl, and the swan, and the pelican, and the gier eagle, and the cormorant, and the stork, and the heron after her kind, and the lapwing, and the bat. And every creeping thing that flieth *is* unclean unto you: they shall not be eaten. *But of* all clean fowls ye may eat.

You shall not eat *of* any thing that dieth of itself: thou shalt give it unto the stranger that *is* in thy gates, that he may eat it; or thou mayest sell it unto an alien: for thou *art* an holy people unto the LORD thy God. Thou shalt not seethe a kid in his mother's milk. Thou shalt truly tithe all the increase of thy seed, that the field bringeth forth year by year. And thou shalt eat before the LORD thy God, in the place which he shall choose to place his name there, the tithe of thy corn, of thy wine, and of thine oil, and the firstlings of thy herds and of thy flocks; that thou mayest learn to fear the LORD thy God always. And if the way be too long for thee, so that thou art not able to carry it; *or* if the place be too far from thee, which the LORD thy God shall choose to set his name there, when the LORD thy God hath blessed thee: then shalt thou turn *it* into money, and bind up the money in thine hand, and shalt go unto the place which the LORD thy God shall choose: and thou shalt bestow that money for whatsoever thy soul lusteth after, for oxen, or for sheep, or for wine, or for strong drink, or for whatsoever thy soul desireth: and thou shalt eat there before the LORD thy God, and thou shalt rejoice, thou, and thine household (Deut 14:3–26).

His body shall not remain all night upon the tree, but thou shalt in any wise bury him that day; (for he that is hanged *is* accursed of God;) that thy land be not defiled, which the LORD thy God giveth thee *for* an inheritance (Deut 21:23).

Thou shalt have a place also without the camp, whither thou shalt go forth abroad: and thou shalt have a paddle upon thy weapon; and it shall be, when thou wilt ease thyself abroad, thou shalt dig therewith, and shalt turn back and cover that which cometh from thee (Deut 23:12, 13).

My son, attend to my words; incline

thine ear unto my sayings. Let them not depart from thine eyes; keep them in the midst of thine heart. For they *are* life unto those that find them, and health to all their flesh (Prov 4:20–22).

Be not among winebibbers; among riotous eaters of flesh: for the drunkard and the glutton shall come to poverty: and drowsiness shall clothe *a man* with rags (Prov. 23:20, 21).

Biblical Examples: Lev 11–15; 14:34–48; 15:1–13.

Further References: Exod 22:31; Lev 12:3; 13:2–59; 14:2–57; 15:2–33; 17:10–15; Num 5:2–4; Deut 23:10, 11; 28:15–62; Mark 7:1–3; 1 Cor 10:31.

HEDONISM (See Pleasure, Lover of)

HOLINESS (See also Godliness; Righteousness)

And ye shall be holy men unto me: neither shall ye eat *any* flesh *that is* torn of beasts in the field; ye shall cast it to the dogs (Exod 22:31).

For I *am* the LORD your God: ye shall therefore sanctify yourselves, and ye shall be holy; for I *am* holy: neither shall ye defile yourselves with any manner of creeping thing that creepeth upon the earth. For I *am* the LORD that bringeth you up out of the land of Egypt, to be your God: ye shall therefore be holy, for I *am* holy (Lev 11:44, 45).

And the LORD spake unto Moses, saying, Speak unto all the congregation of the children of Israel, and say unto them, Ye shall be holy: for I the LORD your God *am* holy (Lev 19:1, 2).

And ye shall be holy unto me: for I the LORD *am* holy, and have severed you from *other* people, that ye should be mine (Lev 20:26).

Thou shalt be perfect with the LORD thy God (Deut 18:13).

Who shall ascend into the hill of the LORD? or who shall stand in his holy place? He that hath clean hands, and a pure heart; who hath not lifted up his soul unto vanity, nor sworn deceitfully (Ps 24:3, 4).

Blessed *is* the man unto whom the LORD imputeth not iniquity, and in whose spirit *there is* no guile (Ps 32:2).

Blessed *are* the undefiled in the way,

who walk in the law of the LORD. Blessed *are* they that keep his testimonies, *and that* seek him with the whole heart. They also do no iniquity: they walk in his ways (Ps 119:1–3).

Hearken unto me, ye that know righteousness, the people in whose heart *is* my law; fear ye not the reproach of men, neither be ye afraid of their revilings (Isa 51:7).

He hath shewed thee, O man, what *is* good; and what doth the LORD require of thee, but to do justly, and to love mercy, and to walk humbly with thy God? (Mic 6:8).

For if the firstfruit *be* holy, the lump *is* also *holy:* and if the root *be* holy, so *are* the branches (Rom 11:16).

I beseech you therefore, brethren, by the mercies of God, that ye present your bodies a living sacrifice, holy, acceptable unto God, *which is* your reasonable service. And be not conformed to this world: but be ye transformed by the renewing of your mind, that ye may prove what *is* that good, and acceptable, and perfect, will of God (Rom 12:1, 2).

Having therefore these promises, dearly beloved, let us cleanse ourselves from all filthiness of the flesh and spirit, perfecting holiness in the fear of God (2 Cor 7:1).

According as he hath chosen us in him before the foundation of the world, that we should be holy and without blame before him in love. . . . In whom ye also *trusted,* after that ye heard the word of truth, the gospel of your salvation: in whom also after that ye believed, ye were sealed with that holy Spirit of promise, which is the earnest of our inheritance until the redemption of the purchased possession, unto the praise of his glory (Eph 1:4, 13, 14).

But ye have not so learned Christ; if so be that ye have heard him, and have been taught by him, as the truth is in Jesus: that ye put off concerning the former conversation the old man, which is corrupt according to the deceitful lusts; and be renewed in the spirit of your mind; and that ye put on the new man, which after God is created in righteousness and true holiness (Eph 4:20–24).

For this is the will of God, *even* your

sanctification, that ye should abstain from fornication: that every one of you should know how to possess his vessel in sanctification and honour; not in the lust of concupiscence, even as the Gentiles which know not God: that no *man* go beyond and defraud his brother in *any* matter: because that the Lord *is* the avenger of all such, as we also have forewarned you and testified. For God hath not called us unto uncleanness, but unto holiness (1 Thess 4:3–7).

And to esteem them very highly in love for their work's sake. *And* be at peace among yourselves (1 Thess 5:13).

Wherefore seeing we also are compassed about with so great a cloud of witnesses, let us lay aside every weight, and the sin which doth so easily beset *us*, and let us run with patience the race that is set before us. . . . Follow peace with all *men*, and holiness, without which no man shall see the Lord: looking diligently lest any man fail of the grace of God; lest any root of bitterness springing up trouble *you*, and thereby many be defiled; lest there *be* any fornicator, or profane person, as Esau, who for one morsel of meat sold his birthright (Heb 12:1, 14–16).

Wherefore laying aside all malice, and all guile, and hypocrisies, and envies, and all evil speakings. . . . Ye also, as lively stones, are built up a spiritual house, an holy priesthood, to offer up spiritual sacrifices, acceptable to God by Jesus Christ. . . . But ye *are* a chosen generation, a royal priesthood, an holy nation, a peculiar people; that ye should shew forth the praises of him who hath called you out of darkness into his marvellous light: which in time past *were* not a people, but *are* now the people of God: which had not obtained mercy, but now have obtained mercy. Dearly beloved, I beseech *you* as strangers and pilgrims, abstain from fleshly lusts, which war against the soul. . . . Who his own self bare our sins in his own body on the tree, that we, being dead to sins, should live unto righteousness: by those stripes ye were healed (1 Pet 2:1, 5, 9–11, 24).

Further References: Exod 19:6; 39:30; Lev 10:8–10; Deut 14:2; 28:9; Isa 4:3; 35:8; Zech 14:20, 21; Rom 6:1–23; 1 Cor 3:16, 17; 6:12, 13, 19, 20; Eph 5:1–3, 8–11; Col 1:22; 3:5–10, 12–15; 1 Thess 5:5, 22, 23; 2 Tim 2:2, 19–22; James 1:21, 27; 2 Peter 3:11–14; 1 John 2:1, 5, 29; 3:3, 6, 9, 10.

HOMICIDE

And Cain talked with Abel his brother: and it came to pass, when they were in the field, that Cain rose up against Abel his brother, and slew him (Gen 4:8).

Whoso sheddeth man's blood, by man shall his blood be shed: for in the image of God made he man (Gen 9:6).

Thou shalt not kill (Exod 20:13).

He that smiteth a man, so that he die, shall be surely put to death. And if a man lie not in wait, but God deliver *him* into his hand; then I will appoint thee a place whither he shall flee. But if a man come presumptuously upon his neighbour, to slay him with guile; thou shalt take him from mine altar, that he may die.

And he that smiteth his father, or his mother, shall be surely put to death (Exod 21:12–15).

If a thief be found breaking up, and be smitten that he die, *there shall* no blood *be shed* for him. If the sun be risen upon him, *there shall be* blood *shed* for him; *for* he should make full restitution; if he have nothing, then he shall be sold for his theft (Exod 22:2, 3).

And he that killeth any man shall surely be put to death (Lev 24:17).

And the LORD spake unto Moses, saying, Speak unto the children of Israel, and say unto them, When ye be come over Jordan into the land of Canaan; Then ye shall appoint you cities to be cities of refuge for you; that the slayer may flee thither, which killeth any person at unawares. And they shall be unto you cities for refuge from the avenger; that the manslayer die not, until he stand before the congregation in judgment. And of these cities which ye shall give six cities shall ye have for refuge. Ye shall give three cities on this side Jordan, and three cities shall ye give in the land of Canaan, *which* shall be cities of refuge. These six cities shall be a refuge, *both* for the children of Israel, and for the stranger, and for the sojourner among them: that every one that killeth any person unawares may flee thither.

And if he smite him with an instrument of iron, so that he die, he *is* a murderer: the murderer shall surely be put to death. And if he smite him with throwing a stone, wherewith he may die, and he die, he *is* a murderer: the murderer shall surely be put to death. Or *if* he smite him with an hand weapon of wood, wherewith he may die, and he die, he *is* a murderer: the murderer shall surely be put to death. The revenger of blood himself shall slay the murderer: when he meeteth him, he shall slay him. But if he thrust him of hatred, or hurl at him by laying of wait, that he die; or in enmity smite him with his hand, that he die: he that smote *him* shall surely be put to death; *for* he *is* a murderer: the revenger of blood shall slay the murderer, when he meeteth him.

But if he thrust him suddenly without enmity, or have cast upon him any thing without laying of wait, or with any stone, wherewith a man may die, seeing *him* not, and cast *it* upon him, that he die, and *was* not his enemy, neither sought his harm: then the congregation shall judge between the slayer and the revenger of blood according to these judgments: and the congregation shall deliver the slayer out of the hand of the revenger of blood, and the congregation shall restore him to the city of his refuge, whither he was fled: and he shall abide in it unto the death of the high priest, which was anointed with the holy oil. But if the slayer shall at any time come without the border of the city of his refuge, whither he was fled; and the revenger of blood find him without the borders of the city of his refuge, and the revenger of blood kill the slayer; he shall not be guilty of blood: because he should have remained in the city of his refuge until the death of the high priest: but after the death of the high priest the slayer shall return into the land of his possession (Num 35:9–28).

Whoso killeth any person, the murderer shall be put to death by the mouth of witnesses: but one witness shall not testify against any person *to cause him* to die. Moreover ye shall take no satisfaction for the life of a murderer, which *is* guilty of death: but he shall be surely put to death (Num 35:30, 31).

Cursed *be* he that smiteth his neighbour secretly. And all the people shall say, Amen (Deut 27:24).

These six *things* doth the LORD hate: yea, seven *are* an abomination unto him: a proud look, a lying tongue, and hands that shed innocent blood (Prov 6:16, 17).

A man that doeth violence to the blood of *any* person shall flee to the pit; let no man stay him (Prov 28:17).

For your hands are defiled with blood, and your fingers with iniquity; your lips have spoken lies, your tongue hath muttered perverseness (Isa 59:3).

Will ye steal, murder, and commit adultery, and swear falsely, and burn incense unto Baal, and walk after other gods whom ye know not; and come and stand before me in this house, which is called by my name, and say, We are delivered to do all these abominations? (Jer 7:9, 10).

Ye have heard that it was said by them of old time, Thou shalt not kill; and whosoever shall kill shall be in danger of the judgment: but I say unto you, That whosoever is angry with his brother without a cause shall be in danger of the judgment: and whosoever shall say to his brother, Raca, shall be in danger of the council: but whosoever shall say, Thou fool, shall be in danger of hell fire. Therefore if thou bring thy gift to the altar, and there rememberest that thy brother hath aught against thee . . . be reconciled . . . and then come and offer thy gift (Matt 5:21–24).

For out of the heart proceed evil thoughts, murders, adulteries, fornications, thefts, false witness, blasphemies (Matt 15:19).

Ye are of *your* father the devil, and the lusts of your father ye will do. He was a murderer from the beginning, and abode not in the truth, because there is no truth in him. When he speaketh a lie, he speaketh of his own . . . (John 8:44).

Whosoever hateth his brother is a murderer: and ye know that no murderer hath eternal life abiding in him (1 John 3:15).

But the fearful, and unbelieving, and the abominable, and murderers, and whoremongers, and sorcerers, and idolaters, and all liars, shall have their part in the lake which burneth with fire and brimstone: which is the second death (Rev 21:8).

For without *are* dogs, and sorcerers, and whoremongers, and murderers, and idolaters, and whosoever loveth and maketh a lie (Rev 22:15).

Biblical Examples: Gen 4:8; Num 31:7, 8; 2 Sam 11:14–17; 12:9; 1 Kings 21:10–24; 2 Chron 24:22; Hos 4:1–3; Matt 2:16; Acts 12:2.

Further References: Exod 21:28–32; Deut 4:41–43; 5:17; 17:6; 19:1–10; 21:1–9; 22:8; Josh 20:1–9; Job 24:14; Ps 5:6; 10:2, 8; 16:9, 10; 94:3–6; Prov 1:11, 12, 15, 16; Matt 19:18; Mark 7:21; 10:19; Luke 18:20; Rom 13:9; Gal 5:19–21; 1 Tim 1:9; James 2:11; 1 Peter 4:15.

HOMOSEXUALITY (See also Sex and Sexuality)

Thou shalt not lie with mankind, as with womankind: it *is* abomination. Neither shalt thou lie with any beast to defile thyself therewith: neither shall any woman stand before a beast to lie down thereto: it *is* confusion.

Defile not ye yourselves in any of these things: for in all these the nations are defiled which I cast out before you: and the land is defiled: therefore I do visit the iniquity thereof upon it, and the land itself vomiteth out her inhabitants. Ye shall therefore keep my statutes and my judgments, and shall not commit *any* of these abominations; *neither* any of your own nation, nor any stranger that sojourneth among you: (for all these abominations have the men of the land done, which *were* before you, and the land is defiled;) that the land spue not you out also, when ye defile it, as it spued out the nations that *were* before you. For whosoever shall commit any of these abominations, even the souls that commit *them* shall be cut off from among their people. Therefore shall ye keep mine ordinance, that *ye* commit not *any one* of these abominable customs, which were committed before you, and that ye defile not yourselves therein: I *am* the LORD your God (Lev 18:22–30).

If a man also lie with mankind, as he lieth with a woman, both of them have committed an abomination: they shall surely be put to death; their blood *shall be* upon them (Lev 20:13).

There shall be no whore of the daughters of Israel, nor a sodomite of the sons of Israel. Thou shalt not bring the hire of a whore, or the price of a dog, into the house of the LORD thy God for any vow: for even both these *are* abomination unto the LORD thy God (Deut 23:17, 18).

And there were also sodomites in the land: *and* they did according to all the abominations of the nations which the LORD cast out before the children of Israel (1 Kings 14:24).

And he brake down the houses of the sodomites, that *were* by the house of the LORD, where the women wove hangings for the grove (2 Kings 23:7).

Wherefore God also gave them up to uncleanness through the lusts of their own hearts, to dishonour their own bodies between themselves: who changed the truth of God into a lie, and worshipped and served the creature more than the Creator, who is blessed for ever. Amen.

For this cause God gave them up unto vile affections: for even their women did change the natural use into that which is against nature: and likewise also the men, leaving the natural use of the woman, burned in their lust one toward another; men with men working that which is unseemly, and receiving in themselves that recompence of their error which was meet.

And even as they did not like to retain God in *their* knowledge, God gave them over to a reprobate mind, to do those things which are not convenient; being filled with all unrighteousness, fornication, wickedness, covetousness, maliciousness; full of envy, murder, debate, deceit, malignity; whisperers, backbiters, haters of God, despiteful, proud, boasters, inventors of evil things, disobedient to parents, without understanding, covenant-breakers, without natural affection, implacable, unmerciful: who knowing the judgment of God, that they which commit such things are worthy of death, not only do the same, but have pleasure in them that do them (Rom 1:24–32).

Know ye not that the unrighteous shall not inherit the kingdom of God? Be not deceived: neither fornicators, nor idolaters, nor adulterers, nor effeminate, nor abusers of themselves with mankind, nor thieves, nor covetous, nor drunkards, nor revilers, nor extortioners, shall inherit the kingdom of God (1 Cor 6:9, 10).

Knowing this, that the law is not made for a righteous man, but for the lawless and disobedient, for the ungodly and for sinners, for unholy and profane, for murderers of fathers and murderers of mothers, for manslayers, for whoremongers, for them that defile themselves with mankind, for menstealers, for liars, for perjured persons, and if there be any other thing that is contrary to sound doctrine (1 Tim 1:9, 10).

Biblical Examples: Gen 19:1–14; 1 Kings 14:24; 2 Kings 23:7.

HONESTY (See also Truth)

Ye shall do no unrighteousness in judgment, in meteyard, in weight, or in measure. Just balances, just weights, a just ephah, and a just hin, shall ye have: I *am* the LORD your God, which brought you out of the land of Egypt (Lev 19:35, 36).

Thou shalt not have in thy bag divers weights, a great and a small. Thou shalt not have in thine house divers measures, a great and a small. *But* thou shalt have a perfect and just weight, a perfect and just measure shalt thou have: that thy days may be lengthened in the land which the LORD thy God giveth thee. For all that do such things, *and* all that do unrighteously, *are* an abomination unto the LORD thy God (Deut 25:13–16).

Let thine eyes look right on, and let thine eyelids look straight before thee (Prov 4:25).

A false balance *is* abomination to the LORD: but a just weight *is* his delight (Prov 11:1).

He that walketh righteously, and speaketh uprightly; he that despiseth the gain of oppressions, that shaketh his hands from holding of bribes, that stoppeth his ears from hearing of blood, and shutteth his eyes from seeing evil; he shall dwell on high: his place of defence *shall be* the munitions of rocks: bread shall be given him; his waters *shall be* sure (Isa 33:15, 16).

Let your light so shine before men, that they may see your good works, and glorify your Father which is in heaven (Matt 5:16).

Woe unto you, scribes and Pharisees, hypocrites! for ye make clean the outside of the cup and of the platter, but within they are full of extortion and excess. *Thou* blind Pharisee, cleanse first that *which* is within the cup and platter, that the outside of them may be clean also. Woe unto you, scribes and Pharisees, hypocrites! for ye are like unto whited sepulchres, which indeed appear beautiful outward, but are within full of dead *men's* bones, and of all uncleanness. Even so ye also outwardly appear righteous unto men, but within ye are full of hypocrisy and iniquity (Matt 23:25–28).

Providing for honest things, not only in the sight of the Lord, but also in the sight of men (2 Cor 8:21).

Now I pray to God that ye do no evil; not that we should appear approved, but that ye should do that which is honest, though we be as reprobates (2 Cor 13:7).

And let us not be weary in well-doing: for in due season we shall reap, if we faint not (Gal 6:9).

Finally, brethren, whatsoever things are true, whatsoever things *are* honest, whatsoever things *are* just, whatsoever things *are* pure, whatsoever things *are* lovely, whatsoever things *are* of good report; if *there be* any virtue, and if *there be* any praise, think on these things (Phil 4:8).

And that ye study to be quiet, and to do your own business, and to work with your own hands, as we commanded you; that ye may walk honestly toward them that are without, and *that* we may have lack of nothing (1 Thess 4:11, 12).

Pray for us: for we trust we have a good conscience, in all things willing to live honestly (Heb 13:18).

Having your conversation honest among the Gentiles: that, whereas they speak against you as evildoers, they may by *your* good works, which they shall behold, glorify God in the day of visitation (1 Pet 2:12).

Biblical Examples: Gen 43:12; 2 Kings 12:15; 22:4–7; Neh 13:13.

Further References: Deut 16:20; Ps 24:4; Prov 12:23; 16:11; 20:10; Ezek 45:10; 10:19; Luke 3:12, 13; 2 Cor 4:1, 2; 8:21.

HOSPITALITY (See also Ministry; Unselfishness)

Thou shalt neither vex a stranger, nor oppress him: for ye were strangers in the land of Egypt (Exod 22:21).

Ye shall have one manner of law, as well for the stranger, as for one of your own country: for I *am* the LORD your God (Lev 24:22).

Love ye therefore the stranger: for ye were strangers in the land of Egypt (Deut 10:19).

When the Son of man shall come in his glory, and all the holy angels with him, then shall he sit upon the throne of his glory: and before him shall be gathered all nations: and he shall separate them one from another, as a shepherd divideth *his* sheep from the goats: and he shall set the sheep on his right hand, but the goats on the left. Then shall the King say unto them on his right hand, Come, ye blessed of my Father, inherit the kingdom prepared for you from the foundation of the world: for I was an hungered, and ye gave me meat: I was thirsty, and ye gave me drink: I was a stranger, and ye took me in: naked, and ye clothed me: I was sick, and ye visited me: I was in prison, and ye came unto me. Then shall the righteous answer him, saying, Lord, when saw we thee an hungered, and fed *thee?* or thirsty, and gave *thee* drink? When saw we thee a stranger, and took *thee* in? or naked, and clothed *thee?* Or when saw we thee sick, or in prison, and came unto thee? And the King shall answer and say unto them, Verily I say unto you, Inasmuch as ye have done *it* unto one of the least of these my brethren, ye have done *it* unto me. Then shall he say also unto them on the left hand, Depart from me, ye cursed, into everlasting fire, prepared for the devil and his angels: for I was an hungered, and ye gave me no meat: I was thirsty, and ye gave me no drink: I was a stranger, and ye took me not in: naked, and ye clothed me not: sick, and in prison, and ye visited me not. Then shall they also answer him, saying, Lord, when saw we thee an hungered, or

athirst, or a stranger, or naked, or sick, or in prison, and did not minister unto thee? Then shall he answer them, saying, Verily I say unto you, Inasmuch as ye did *it* not to one of the least of these, ye did *it* not to me. And these shall go away into everlasting punishment: but the righteous into life eternal (Matt 25:31–46).

And he called *unto him* the twelve, and began to send them forth by two and two; and gave them power over unclean spirits; and commanded them that they should take nothing for *their* journey, save a staff only; no scrip, no bread, no money in *their* purse: but *be* shod with sandals; and not put on two coats. And he said unto them, In what place soever ye enter into an house, there abide till ye depart from that place. And whosoever shall not receive you, nor hear you, when ye depart thence, shake off the dust under your feet for a testimony against them. Verily I say unto you, It shall be more tolerable for Sodom and Gomorrha in the day of judgment, than for that city (Mark 6:7–11).

And he said unto them, Which of you shall have a friend, and shall go unto him at midnight, and say unto him, Friend, lend me three loaves; for a friend of mine in his journey is come to me, and I have nothing to set before him? And he from within shall answer and say, Trouble me not: the door is now shut, and my children are with me in bed; I cannot rise and give thee. I say unto you, Though he will not rise and give him, because he is his friend, yet because of his importunity he will rise and give him as many as he needeth (Luke 11:5–8).

Then said he also to him that bade him, When thou makest a dinner or a supper, call not thy friends, nor thy brethren, neither thy kinsmen, nor *thy* rich neighbours; lest they also bid thee again, and a recompence be made thee. But when thou makest a feast, call the poor, the maimed, the lame, the blind: and thou shalt be blessed; for they cannot recompense thee: for thou shalt be recompensed at the resurrection of the just (Luke 14:12–14).

Distributing to the necessity of saints; given to hospitality (Rom 12:13).

A bishop then must be blameless, the husband of one wife, vigilant, sober, of good behaviour, given to hospitality, apt to teach; not given to wine, no striker, not greedy of filthy lucre; but patient, not a brawler, not covetous (1 Tim 3:2, 3).

Let brotherly love continue. Be not forgetful to entertain strangers: for thereby some have entertained angels unawares (Heb 13:1, 2).

Use hospitality one to another without grudging (1 Peter 4:9).

Biblical Examples: Gen 12:16; 18:1–8; 19:1–11; 43:31–34; Exod 2:20; Josh 2:1–16; 2 Sam 9:7–13; 1 Kings 17:10–24; 2 Kings 4:8; Matt 10:5–15; Luke 7:36; 10:34–38; 19:1–10; Acts 10:6; 16:14, 15; 28:7; Rom 16:1, 2.

Further References: Exod 23:9; Lev 19:10, 33, 34; Deut 26:12, 13; 27:10; 1 Tim 5:10; Titus 1:7, 8; 3 John 5–8.

HUMILITY

If my people, which are called by my name, shall humble themselves, and pray, and seek my face, and turn from their wicked ways; then will I hear from heaven, and will forgive their sin, and will heal their land (2 Chron 7:14).

When *men* are cast down, then thou shalt say, *There is* lifting up; and he shall save the humble person (Job 22:29).

Though the LORD *be* high, yet hath he respect unto the lowly: but the proud he knoweth afar off (Ps 138:6).

Surely he scorneth the scorners: but he giveth grace unto the lowly (Prov 3:34).

Better *it is to be* of an humble spirit with the lowly, than to divide the spoil with the proud (Prov 16:19).

Let another man praise thee, and not thine own mouth; a stranger, and not thine own lips (Prov 27:2).

Better *is* the end of a thing than the beginning thereof: *and* the patient in spirit *is* better than the proud in spirit (Eccl 7:8).

The meek also shall increase *their* joy in the LORD, and the poor among men shall rejoice in the Holy One of Israel (Isa 29:19).

For thus saith the high and lofty One that inhabiteth eternity, whose name *is* Holy; I dwell in the high and holy *place,* with him also *that is* of a contrite and hum-

ble spirit, to revive the spirit of the humble, and to revive the heart of the contrite ones (Isa 57:15).

He hath shewed thee, O man, what *is* good; and what doth the LORD require of thee, but to do justly, and to love mercy, and to walk humbly with thy God? (Mic 6:8).

Blessed *are* the poor in spirit: for theirs is the kingdom of heaven (Matt 5:3).

Blessed *are* the meek: for they shall inherit the earth (Matt 5:5).

Take my yoke upon you, and learn of me; for I am meek and lowly in heart: and ye shall find rest unto your souls (Matt 11:29).

And said, Verily I say unto you, Except ye be converted, and become as little children, ye shall not enter into the kingdom of heaven. Whosoever therefore shall humble himself as this little child, the same is greatest in the kingdom of heaven (Matt 18:3, 4).

But it shall not be so among you: but whosoever will be great among you, let him be your minister; and whosoever will be chief among you, let him be your servant (Matt 20:26, 27).

I tell you, this man went down to his house justified *rather* than the other: for every one that exalteth himself shall be abased; and he that humbleth himself shall be exalted (Luke 18:14).

For I say, through the grace given unto me, to every man that is among you, not to think of *himself* more highly than he ought to think; but to think soberly, according as God hath dealt to every man the measure of faith (Rom 12:3).

Be of the same mind one toward another. Mind not high things, but condescend to men of low estate. Be not wise in your own conceits (Rom 12:16).

And base things of the world, and things which are despised, hath God chosen, *yea,* and things which are not, to bring to nought things that are (1 Cor 1:28).

Let no man deceive himself. If any man among you seemeth to be wise in this world, let him become a fool, that he may be wise (1 Cor 3:18).

For ye know the grace of our Lord Jesus Christ, that, though he was rich, yet for your sakes he became poor, that ye through his poverty might be rich (2 Cor 8:9).

Of such an one will I glory: yet of myself I will not glory, but in mine infirmities (2 Cor 12:5).

Brethren, if a man be overtaken in a fault, ye which are spiritual, restore such an one in the spirit of meekness; considering thyself, lest thou also be tempted (Gal 6:1).

Let nothing *be done* through strife or vainglory; but in lowliness of mind let each esteem other better than themselves. Look not every man on his own things, but every man also on the things of others. Let this mind be in you, which was also in Christ Jesus: who, being in the form of God, thought it not robbery to be equal with God: but made himself of no reputation, and took upon him the form of a servant, and was made in the likeness of men: and being found in fashion as a man, he humbled himself, and became obedient unto death, even the death of the cross. Wherefore God also hath highly exalted him, and given him a name which is above every name: that at the name of Jesus every knee should bow, of *things* in heaven, and *things* in earth, and *things* under the earth; and *that* every tongue should confess that Jesus Christ *is* Lord, to the glory of God the Father (Phil 2:3–11).

Put on therefore, as the elect of God, holy and beloved, bowels of mercies, kindness, humbleness of mind, meekness, longsuffering (Col 3:12).

Let the brother of low degree rejoice in that he is exalted: but the rich, in that he is made low: because as the flower of the grass he shall pass away. Wherefore, my beloved brethren, let every man be swift to hear, slow to speak, slow to wrath (James 1:9, 10, 19).

But he giveth more grace. Wherefore he saith, God resisteth the proud, but giveth grace unto the humble. Humble yourselves in the sight of the Lord, and he shall lift you up (James 4:6, 10).

Neither as being lords over *God's* heritage, but being ensamples to the flock. Likewise, ye younger, submit yourselves unto the elder. Yea, all *of you* be subject one to another, and be clothed with hu-

mility: for God resisteth the proud, and giveth grace to the humble. Humble yourselves therefore under the mighty hand of God, that he may exalt you in due time (1 Peter 5:3, 5, 6).

Biblical Examples: Gen 18:27; 32:10; Exod 3:11; 1 Sam 18:18–23; 1 Kings 3:7; Job 42:4–6; Ps 8:3, 4; Prov 30:2, 3; Isa 6:5; Matt 3:14; Luke 1:46–55; 5:8; 7:6, 7; John 1:27; 3:29, 30; 13:3–17; Acts 20:17–23; 1 Cor 2:1; 15:10; 2 Cor 3:5; 12:7; Eph 3:8; Phil 3:12, 13; 1 Tim 1:15.

Further References: Ps 9:12; 10:17; 69:32; 131:1, 2; Prov 11:2; 15:33; 22:4; 29:23; Isa 66:12; Jer 45:5; Zeph 3:11, 12; Matt 23:12; Mark 9:33–37; 10:43, 44; Luke 1:52; 9:46–48; 10:21; 14:10, 11; 22:24–27; Gal 5:26; 6:14.

HUNGER (See also Poverty)

Defend the poor and fatherless: do justice to the afflicted and needy. Deliver the poor and needy: rid *them* out of the hand of the wicked (Ps 82:3, 4).

The full soul loatheth an honeycomb; but to the hungry soul every bitter thing is sweet (Prov 27:7).

Is not this the fast that I have chosen? to loose the bands of wickedness, to undo the heavy burdens, and to let the oppressed go free, and that ye break every yoke? *Is it* not to deal thy bread to the hungry, and that thou bring the poor that are cast out to thy house? when thou seest the naked, that thou cover him; and that thou hide not thyself from thine own flesh?

Then shall thy light break forth as the morning, and thine health shall spring forth speedily: and thy righteousness shall go before thee; the glory of the LORD shall be thy rereward. Then shalt thou call, and the LORD shall answer; thou shalt cry, and he shall say, Here I *am*. If thou take away from the midst of thee the yoke, the putting forth of the finger, and speaking vanity; and *if* thou draw out thy soul to the hungry, and satisfy the afflicted soul; then shall thy light rise in obscurity, and thy darkness *be* as the noon day (Isa 58:6–10).

They that be slain with the sword are better than *they that be* slain with hunger: for these pine away, stricken through for *want of* the fruits of the field. The hands of the pitiful women have sodden their own children: they were their meat in the destruction of the daughter of my people (Lam 4:9, 10).

What *doth it* profit, my brethren, though a man say he hath faith, and have not works? can faith save him? If a brother or sister be naked, and destitute of daily food, and one of you say unto them, Depart in peace, be *ye* warmed and filled; notwithstanding ye give them not those things which are needful to the body; what *doth it* profit? Even so faith, if it hath not works, is dead, being alone (James 2:14–17).

But whoso hath this world's good, and seeth his brother have need, and shutteth up his bowels *of compassion* from him, how dwelleth the love of God in him? (1 John 3:17).

Biblical Examples: Matt 4:2–4; 21:18; Mark 11:12; Luke 4:2–4; John 4:8.

Further References: Deut 28:53; 2 Kings 6:28; Job 5:20; Ps 33:19; 37:19; Prov 16:26; Matt 25:31–46; Luke 6:21; Rev 7:16, 17.

HUSBAND-WIFE RELATIONS (See also Family; Marriage; Sex and Sexuality)

Therefore shall a man leave his father and his mother, and shall cleave unto his wife: and they shall be one flesh (Gen 2:24).

Unto the woman he said, I will greatly multiply thy sorrow and thy conception; in sorrow thou shalt bring forth children; and thy desire *shall be* to thy husband, and he shall rule over thee (Gen 3:16).

They shall not take a wife *that is* a whore, or profane; neither shall they take a woman put away from her husband: for he *is* holy unto his God (Lev 21:7).

And *he that is* the high priest among his brethren, upon whose head the anointing oil was poured, and that is consecrated to put on the garments, shall not uncover his head, nor rend his clothes; neither shall he go in to any dead body, nor defile himself for his father, or for his mother; neither shall he go out of the sanctuary, nor profane the sanctuary of his God; for the crown of the anointing oil of his God *is* upon him: I *am* the LORD. And he shall take a wife in her virginity. A widow, or a divorced woman, or profane, *or* an har-

lot, these shall he not take: but he shall take a virgin of his own people to wife. Neither shall he profane his seed among his people: for I the LORD do sanctify him (Lev 21:10–15).

And the LORD spake unto Moses, saying, Speak unto the children of Israel, and say unto them, If any man's wife go aside, and commit a trespass against him, and a man lie with her carnally, and it be hid from the eyes of her husband, and be kept close, and she be defiled, and *there be* no witness against her, neither she be taken *with the manner;* and the spirit of jealousy come upon him, and he be jealous of his wife, and she be defiled: or if the spirit of jealousy come upon him, and he be jealous of his wife, and she be not defiled: then shall the man bring his wife unto the priest, and he shall bring her offering for her, the tenth *part* of an ephah of barley meal; he shall pour no oil upon it, nor put frankincense thereon; for it *is* an offering of jealousy, an offering of memorial, bringing iniquity to remembrance.

And the priest shall bring her near, and set her before the LORD: and the priest shall take holy water in an earthen vessel; and of the dust that is in the floor of the tabernacle the priest shall take, and put *it* into the water: and the priest shall set the woman before the LORD, and uncover the woman's head, and put the offering of memorial in her hands, which *is* the jealousy offering: and the priest shall have in his hand the bitter water that causeth the curse: and the priest shall charge her by an oath, and say unto the woman, If no man have lain with thee, and if thou hast not gone aside to uncleanness *with another* instead of thy husband, be thou free from this bitter water that causeth the curse: but if thou hast gone aside *to another* instead of thy husband, and if thou be defiled, and some man have lain with thee beside thine husband: then the priest shall charge the woman with an oath of cursing, and the priest shall say unto the woman, The LORD make thee a curse and an oath among thy people, when the LORD doth make thy thigh to rot, and thy belly to swell; and this water that causeth the curse shall go into thy bowels, to make *thy* belly to swell, and *thy* thigh to rot: And the woman shall say, Amen, amen (Num 5:11–22).

When a man hath taken a wife, and married her, and it come to pass that she find no favour in his eyes, because he hath found some uncleanness in her: then let him write her a bill of divorcement, and give *it* in her hand, and send her out of his house. And when she is departed out of his house, she may go and be another man's *wife.* And *if* the latter husband hate her, and write her a bill of divorcement, and giveth *it* in her hand, and sendeth her out of his house; or if the latter husband die, which took her *to be* his wife; her former husband, which sent her away, may not take her again to be his wife, after that she is defiled; for that *is* abomination before the LORD: and thou shalt not cause the land to sin, which the LORD thy God giveth thee *for* an inheritance.

When a man hath taken a new wife, he shall not go out to war, neither shall he be charged with any business: *but* he shall be free at home one year, and shall cheer up his wife which he hath taken (Deut 24:1–5).

If brethren dwell together; and one of them die, and have no child, the wife of the dead shall not marry without unto a stranger: her husband's brother shall go in unto her, and take her to him to wife, and perform the duty of an husband's brother unto her (Deut 25:5).

Drink waters out of thine own cistern, and running waters out of thine own well. Let thy fountains be dispersed abroad, *and* rivers of waters in the streets. Let them be only thine own, and not strangers' with thee. Let thy fountain be blessed: and rejoice with the wife of thy youth. *Let her be as* the loving hind and pleasant roe; let her breasts satisfy thee at all times; and be thou ravished always with her love. And why wilt thou, my son, be ravished with a strange woman, and embrace the bosom of a stranger? (Prov 5:15–20).

A virtuous woman *is* a crown to her husband: but she that maketh ashamed *is* as rottenness in his bones (Prov 12:4).

Whoso findeth a wife findeth a good *thing,* and obtaineth favour of the LORD (Prov 18:22).

A foolish son *is* the calamity of his father:

and the contentions of a wife *are* a continual dropping (Prov 19:13).

House and riches *are* the inheritance of fathers: and a prudent wife *is* from the LORD (Prov 19:14).

It is better to dwell in a corner of the housetop, than with a brawling woman in a wide house (Prov 21:9).

A continual dropping in a very rainy day and a contentious woman are alike. Whosoever hideth her hideth the wind, and the ointment of his right hand, *which* bewrayeth *itself* (Prov 27:15, 16).

Who can find a virtuous woman? for her price *is* far above rubies. The heart of her husband doth safely trust in her, so that he shall have no need of spoil. She will do him good and not evil all the days of her life. She seeketh wool, and flax, and worketh willingly with her hands. She is like the merchants' ships; she bringeth her food from afar. She riseth also while it is yet night, and giveth meat to her household, and a portion to her maidens. She considereth a field, and buyeth it: with the fruit of her hands she planteth a vineyard. She girdeth her loins with strength, and strengtheneth her arms. She perceiveth that her merchandise *is* good: her candle goeth not out by night. She layeth her hands to the spindle, and her hands hold the distaff. She stretcheth out her hand to the poor; yea, she reacheth forth her hands to the needy. She is not afraid of the snow for her household: for all her household *are* clothed with scarlet. She maketh herself coverings of tapestry; her clothing *is* silk and purple. Her husband is known in the gates, when he sitteth among the elders of the land. She maketh fine linen, and selleth *it;* and delivereth girdles unto the merchant. Strength and honour *are* her clothing; and she shall rejoice in time to come. She openeth her mouth with wisdom; and in her tongue *is* the law of kindness. She looketh well to the ways of her household, and eateth not the bread of idleness. Her children arise up, and call her blessed; her husband *also,* and he praiseth her. Many daughters have done virtuously, but thou excellest them all. Favour *is* deceitful, and beauty *is* vain: *but* a woman *that* feareth the LORD, she shall be praised. Give her of the fruit of her hands; and let her own works praise her in the gates (Prov 31:10–31).

Live joyfully with the wife whom thou lovest all the days of the life of thy vanity, which he hath given thee under the sun, all the days of thy vanity: for that *is* thy portion in *this* life, and in thy labour which thou takest under the sun (Eccl 9:9).

The Pharisees also came unto him, tempting him, and saying unto him, Is it lawful for a man to put away his wife for every cause? And he answered and said unto them, Have ye not read, that he which made *them* at the beginning made them male and female, and said, For this cause shall a man leave father and mother, and shall cleave to his wife: and they twain shall be one flesh? Wherefore they are no more twain, but one flesh. What therefore God hath joined together, let not man put asunder (Matt 19:3–6).

If any *man* come to me, and hate not his father, and mother, and wife, and children, and brethren, and sisters, yea, and his own life also, he cannot be my disciple (Luke 14:26).

Whosoever putteth away his wife, and marrieth another, committeth adultery: and whosoever marrieth her that is put away from *her* husband committeth adultery (Luke 16:18).

Now concerning the things whereof ye wrote unto me: *It is* good for a man not to touch a woman. Nevertheless, *to avoid* fornication, let every man have his own wife, and let every woman have her own husband. Let the husband render unto the wife due benevolence: and likewise also the wife unto the husband. The wife hath not power of her own body, but the husband: and likewise also the husband hath not power of his own body, but the wife. Defraud ye not one the other, except *it be* with consent for a time, that ye may give yourselves to fasting and prayer; and come together again, that Satan tempt you not for your incontinency (1 Cor 7:1–5).

But I would have you know, that the head of every man is Christ; and the head of the woman *is* the man; and the head of Christ *is* God (1 Cor 11:3).

Submitting yourselves one to another in the fear of God. Wives, submit your-selves unto your own husbands, as unto the Lord. For the husband is the head of the wife, even as Christ is the head of the church: and he is the saviour of the body. Therefore as the church is subject unto Christ, so *let* the wives *be* to their own husbands in every thing. Husbands, love your wives, even as Christ also loved the church, and gave himself for it; that he might sanctify and cleanse it with the washing of water by the word, that he might present it to himself a glorious church, not having spot, or wrinkle, or any such thing; but that it should be holy and without blemish. So ought men to love their wives as their own bodies. He that loveth his wife loveth himself. For no man ever yet hated his own flesh; but nourish-eth and cherisheth it, even as the Lord the church: for we are members of his body, of his flesh, and of his bones. For this cause shall a man leave his father and mother, and shall be joined unto his wife, and they two shall be one flesh. This is a great mystery: but I speak concerning Christ and the church. Nevertheless let every one of you in particular so love his wife even as himself; and the wife *see* that she reverence *her* husband (Eph 5:21–33).

Wives, submit yourselves unto your own husbands, as it is fit in the Lord. Husbands, love *your* wives, and be not bitter against them (Col 3:18, 19).

The aged women likewise, that *they be* in behaviour as becometh holiness, not false accusers, not given to much wine, teachers of good things; that they may teach the young women to be sober, to love their husbands, to love their children, *to be* discreet, chaste, keepers at home, good, obedient to their own husbands, that the word of God be not blasphemed (Titus 2:3–5).

Marriage *is* honourable in all, and the bed undefiled: but whoremongers and adulterers God will judge (Heb 13:4).

Likewise, ye wives, *be* in subjection to your own husbands; that, if any obey not the word, they also may without the word be won by the conversation of the wives; while they behold your chaste conversa-tion *coupled* with fear. Whose adorning let it not be that outward *adorning* of plaiting the hair, and of wearing of gold, or of putting on of apparel; but *let it be* the hidden man of the heart, in that which is not corruptible, *even the ornament* of a meek and quiet spirit, which is in the sight of God of great price. For after this manner in the old time the holy women also, who trusted in God, adorned themselves, being in subjection unto their own husbands: even as Sara obeyed Abraham, calling him lord: whose daughters ye are, as long as ye do well, and are not afraid with any amazement.

Likewise, ye husbands, dwell with *them* according to knowledge, giving honour unto the wife, as unto the weaker vessel, and as being heirs together of the grace of life; that your prayers be not hindered (1 Peter 3:1–7).

Biblical Examples: Gen 24; 28:1; 38:8–10; Matt 1:19.

Further References: Deut 22:13–21; Mal 2:14–16; 1 Cor 7:14, 16, 33.

HYPOCRISY (See also Deceit; Lying)

Lead me, O LORD, in thy righteousness because of mine enemies; make thy way straight before my face. For *there is* no faithfulness in their mouth; their inward part *is* very wickedness; their throat *is* an open sepulchre; they flatter with their tongue (Ps 5:8, 9).

They speak vanity every one with his neighbour: *with* flattering lips *and* with a double heart do they speak (Ps 12:2).

For *it was* not an enemy *that* reproached me; then I could have borne *it:* neither *was it* he that hated me *that* did magnify *himself* against me; then I would have hid myself from him: but *it was* thou, a man mine equal, my guide, and mine acquaintance. We took sweet counsel together, *and* walked unto the house of God in company (Ps 55:12–14).

He hath put forth his hands against such as be at peace with him: he hath broken his covenant. *The words* of his mouth were smoother than butter, but war *was* in his heart: his words were softer than oil, yet *were* they drawn swords. Cast thy burden upon the LORD, and he shall sustain thee: he shall never suffer the righteous to be moved. But thou, O God, shalt bring them down into the pit of destruction: bloody and deceitful men shall not live out half their days; but I will trust in thee (Ps 55:20–23).

Eat thou not the bread of *him that hath* an evil eye, neither desire thou his dainty meats: for as he thinketh in his heart, so *is* he: Eat and drink, saith he to thee; but his heart *is* not with thee. The morsel *which* thou hast eaten shalt thou vomit up, and lose thy sweet words (Prov 23:6–8).

All the men of thy confederacy have brought thee *even* to the border: the men that were at peace with thee have deceived thee, *and* prevailed against thee; *they that eat* thy bread have laid a wound under thee: *there is* none understanding in him (Obad 7).

Take heed that ye do not your alms before men, to be seen of them: otherwise ye have no reward of your Father which is in heaven. Therefore when thou doest *thine* alms, do not sound a trumpet before thee, as the hypocrites do in the synagogues and in the streets, that they may have glory of men. Verily I say unto you, They have their reward (Matt 6:1, 2).

And when thou prayest, thou shalt not be as the hypocrites *are:* for they love to pray standing in the synagogues and in the corners of the streets, that they may be seen of men. Verily I say unto you, They have their reward (Matt 6:5).

Moreover when ye fast, be not, as the hypocrites, of a sad countenance: for they disfigure their faces, that they may appear unto men to fast. Verily I say unto you, They have their reward (Matt 6:16).

And why beholdest thou the mote that is in thy brother's eye, but considerest not the beam that is in thine own eye? Or how wilt thou say to thy brother, Let me pull out the mote out of thine eye; and, behold, a beam *is* in thine own eye? Thou hypocrite, first cast out the beam out of thine own eye; and then shalt thou see clearly to cast out the mote out of thy brother's eye (Matt 7:3–5).

Ye hypocrites, well did Esaias prophesy of you, saying, This people draweth nigh unto me with their mouth, and honoureth me with *their* lips; but their heart is far from me. But in vain they do worship me, teaching *for* doctrines the commandments of men (Matt 15:7–9).

Saying, The scribes and the Pharisees sit in Moses' seat: all therefore whatsoever they bid you observe, *that* observe and do; but do not ye after their works: for they say, and do not. For they bind heavy burdens and grievous to be borne, and lay *them* on men's shoulders; but they *themselves* will not move them with one of their fingers (Matt 23:2–4).

But all their works they do for to be seen of men: they make broad their phylacteries, and enlarge the borders of their garments, and love the uppermost rooms at feasts, and the chief seats in the synagogues, and greetings in the markets, and to be called of men, Rabbi, Rabbi (Matt 23:5–7).

And he said unto them in his doctrine, Beware of the scribes, which love to go in long clothing, and *love* salutations in the marketplaces, and the chief seats in the synagogues, and the uppermost rooms at feasts: which devour widows' houses, and for a pretence make long prayers: these shall receive greater damnation (Mark 12:38–40).

And why call ye me, Lord, Lord, and do not the things which I say? (Luke 6:46).

Therefore thou art inexcusable, O man, whosoever thou art that judgest: for wherein thou judgest another, thou condemnest thyself; for thou that judgest doest the same things. But we are sure that the judgment of God is according to truth against them which commit such things. And thinkest thou this, O man, that judgest them which do such things, and doest the same, that thou shalt escape the judgment of God? (Rom 2:1–3).

They profess that they know God; but in works they deny *him,* being abominable, and disobedient, and unto every good work reprobate (Titus 1:16).

A double-minded man *is* unstable in all his ways (James 1:8).

What *doth it* profit, my brethren, though a man say he hath faith, and have not works? can faith save him? If a brother or sister be naked, and destitute of daily food, and one of you say unto them, Depart in peace, be *ye* warmed and filled; notwithstanding ye give them not those things which are needful to the body; what *doth it* profit? Even so faith, if it hath not works, is dead, being alone.

Yea, a man may say, Thou hast faith, and I have works: shew me thy faith without thy works, and I will shew thee my faith by my works. Thou believest that there is one God; thou doest well: the devils also believe, and tremble. But wilt thou know, O vain man, that faith without works is dead? Was not Abraham our father justified by works, when he had offered Isaac his son upon the altar? Seest thou how faith wrought with his works, and by works was faith made perfect? And the scripture was fulfilled which saith Abraham believed God, and it was imputed unto him for righteousness: and he was called the Friend of God. Ye see then how that by works a man is justified, and not by faith only. Likewise also was not Rahab the harlot justified by works, when she had received the messengers, and had sent *them* out another way? For as the body without the spirit is dead, so faith without works is dead also (James 2:14–26).

Draw nigh to God, and he will draw nigh to you. Cleanse *your* hands, *ye* sinners; and purify *your* hearts, *ye* double-minded (James 4:8).

If we say that we have fellowship with him, and walk in darkness, we lie, and do not the truth (1 John 1:6).

He that saith, I know him, and keepeth not his commandments, is a liar, and the truth is not in him (1 John 2:4).

Biblical Examples: Judg 16; Ezek 13:1–23; 33:30–32; Hos 7:14–16; Mic 3:11; Mal 1:6–8, 13, 14; Matt 2:8; 15:7–9; 16:3; 22:12; 23:2–33; 26:25; Mark 7:6; 12:38–40; Luke 12:54–56; John 12:5, 6; Rom 16:18; 1 Tim 4:2; Titus 1:16.

Further References: Job 8:13–15; 13:16; 15:31–34; 17:8; 20:4, 5; 27:8–10; 34:30; 36:13, 14; Ps 52:4; 78:34–37; 101:7; Prov 11:9; 26:18, 19, 23–26; Isa 9:17; 10:6; 29:13–16; 32:5, 6; 48:1, 2; Jer 7:4, 8–10; 9:4, 8; 17:9; Matt 24:50, 51; Mark 8:15; Luke 6:46; 11:39–44, 52; 12:1, 2; 13:13–17, 26, 27; 16:13–15; 18:11, 12; 20:46, 47; 2 Tim 3:5, 13; James 1:8, 22–24, 26; 3:17; 1 Peter 2:1, 16; 2 Peter 2:1–3, 17–19.

-I-

IDLENESS

Go to the ant, thou sluggard; consider her ways, and be wise: how long wilt thou sleep, O sluggard? when wilt thou arise out of thy sleep? *Yet* a little sleep, a little slumber, a little folding of the hands to sleep: so shall thy poverty come as one that travelleth, and thy want as an armed man (Prov 6:6, 9–11).

He becometh poor that dealeth *with* a slack hand: but the hand of the diligent maketh rich. He that gathereth in summer *is* a wise son: *but* he that sleepeth in harvest *is* a son that causeth shame. . . . As vinegar to the teeth, and as smoke to the eyes, so *is* the sluggard to them that send him (Prov 10:4, 5, 26).

In all labour there is profit: but the talk of the lips *tendeth* only to penury (Prov 14:23).

He also that is slothful in his work is brother to him that is a great waster (Prov 18:9).

Slothfulness casteth into a deep sleep; and an idle soul shall suffer hunger. . . . A slothful *man* hideth his hand in *his* bosom, and will not so much as bring it to his mouth again (Prov 19:15, 24).

The sluggard will not plow by reason of the cold; *therefore* shall he beg in harvest, and *have* nothing. . . . Love not sleep, lest thou come to poverty; open thine eyes, *and* thou shalt be satisfied with bread (Prov 20:4, 13).

The desire of the slothful killeth him; for his hands refuse to labour. He coveteth greedily all the day long: but the righteous giveth and spareth not (Prov 21:25, 26).

I went by the field of the slothful, and by the vineyard of the man void of understanding; and, lo, it was all grown over with thorns, *and* nettles had covered the face thereof, and the stone wall thereof was broken down. Then I saw, *and* considered *it* well: I looked upon *it, and* received instruction. *Yet* a little sleep, a little slumber, a little folding of the hands to sleep: so shall thy poverty come *as* one that travelleth; and thy want as an armed man (Prov 24:30–34).

The slothful *man* saith, *There is* a lion in the way; a lion *is* in the streets. *As* the door turneth upon his hinges, so *doth* the slothful upon his bed. The slothful hideth his hand in *his* bosom; it grieveth him to bring it again to his mouth. The sluggard *is* wiser in his own conceit than seven men that can render a reason (Prov 26:13–16).

By much slothfulness the building decayeth; and through idleness of the hands the house droppeth through (Eccl 10:18).

I beseech you therefore, brethren, by the mercies of God, that ye present your bodies a living sacrifice, holy, acceptable unto God, *which is* your reasonable service (Rom 12:1).

For even when we were with you, this we commanded you, that if any would not work, neither should he eat. For we hear that there are some which walk among you disorderly, working not at all, but are busybodies (2 Thess 3:10, 11).

That ye be not slothful, but followers of them who through faith and patience inherit the promises. (Heb 6:12).

Biblical Examples: Matt 20:6, 7; Acts 17:21; 1 Tim 5:13.

Further References: Prov 12:9, 24, 27; 13:4; 15:19; 23:21; Eccl 4:5.

IDOLATRY

Thou shalt have no other gods before me. Thou shalt not make unto thee any graven image, or any likeness *of any thing* that *is* in heaven above, or that *is* in the earth beneath, or that *is* in the water under the earth: thou shalt not bow down thyself to them, nor serve them: for I the LORD thy God *am* a jealous God, visiting the iniquity of the fathers upon the children unto the third and fourth *generation* of them that hate me; and shewing mercy unto thousands of them that love me, and keep my commandments (Exod 20:3–6).

Ye shall not make with me gods of silver, neither shall ye make unto you gods of gold. (Exod 20:23).

And thou shalt not let any of thy seed pass through *the fire* to Molech, neither shalt thou profane the name of thy God: I *am* the Lord (Lev 18:21).

Ye shall make you no idols nor graven image, neither rear you up a standing image, neither shall ye set up *any* image of stone in your land, to bow down unto it: for I *am* the LORD your God (Lev 26:1).

Speak unto the children of Israel, and say unto them, When ye are passed over Jordan into the land of Canaan; then ye shall drive out all the inhabitants of the land from before you, and destroy all their pictures, and destroy all their molten images, and quite pluck down all their high places: and ye shall dispossess *the inhabitants of* the land, and dwell therein: for I have given you the land to possess it (Num 33:51–53).

And lest thou lift up thine eyes unto heaven, and when thou seest the sun, and the moon, and the stars, *even* all of the host of heaven, shouldest be driven to worship them, and serve them, which the LORD thy God hath divided unto all nations under the whole heaven (Deut 4:19).

There shall no strange god be in thee; neither shalt thou worship any strange god (Ps 81:9).

Confounded be all they that serve graven images, that boast themselves of idols: worship him, all *ye* gods (Ps 97:7).

They shall be turned back, they shall be greatly ashamed, that trust in graven images, that say to the molten images, Ye *are* our gods (Isa 42:17).

Assemble yourselves and come; draw near together, ye *that are* escaped of the nations: they have no knowledge that set up the wood of their graven image, and pray unto a god *that* cannot save (Isa 45:20).

Thy calf, O Samaria, hath cast *thee* off; mine anger is kindled against them: how long *will it be* ere they attain to innocency? For from Israel *was* it also: the workman made it; therefore it *is* not God: but the calf of Samaria shall be broken in pieces (Hos 8:5, 6).

I will also stretch out mine hand upon Judah, and upon all the inhabitants of Jerusalem; and I will cut off the remnant of Baal from this place, *and* the name of the Chemarims with the priests; and them that worship the host of heaven upon the housetops; and them that worship *and* that swear by the LORD, and that swear by Malcham; and them that are turned back from the LORD; and *those* that have not sought the LORD, nor inquired for him (Zeph 1:4–6).

Professing themselves to be wise, they became fools, and changed the glory of the uncorruptible God into an image made like to corruptible man, and to birds, and fourfooted beasts, and creeping things (Rom 1:22, 23).

As concerning therefore the eating of those things that are offered in sacrifice unto idols, we know that an idol *is* nothing in the world, and that *there is* none other God but one (1 Cor 8:4).

Wherefore, my dearly beloved, flee from idolatry (1 Cor 10:14).

Howbeit then, when ye knew not God, ye did service unto them which by nature are no gods. But now, after that ye have known God, or rather are known of God, how turn ye again to the weak and beggarly elements, whereunto ye desire again to be in bondage? (Gal 4:8, 9).

Let no man beguile you of your reward in a voluntary humility and worshipping of angels, intruding into those things which he hath not seen, vainly puffed up by his fleshly mind (Col 2:18).

Mortify therefore your members which are upon the earth; fornication, uncleanness, inordinate affection, evil concupiscence, and covetousness, which is idolatry (Col 3:5).

Little children, keep yourselves from idols. Amen (1 John 5:21).

But the fearful, and unbelieving, and the abominable, and murderers, and whoremongers, and sorcerers, and idolaters, and all liars, shall have their part in the lake which burneth with fire and brimstone: which is the second death (Rev 21:8).

Biblical Examples: Gen 35:1–4; Exod 12:12; 32:1–4; 2 Kings 17:16; 18:1–4; Ezek 8:15, 16; Acts 17:16.

Further References: Exod 23:13; Deut 12:31; Jer 3; 7:17–20.

ILLEGITIMACY (See Birth Out of Wedlock)

IMPARTIALITY (See Race Relations)

INCEST

None of you shall approach to any that is near of kin to him, to uncover *their* nakedness: I *am* the LORD. The nakedness of thy father, or the nakedness of thy mother, shalt thou not uncover: she *is* thy mother; thou shalt not uncover her nakedness. The nakedness of thy father's wife shalt thou not uncover: it *is* thy father's nakedness. The nakedness of thy sister, the daughter of thy father, or daughter of thy mother, *whether she be* born at home, or born abroad, *even* their nakedness thou shalt not uncover. The nakedness of thy son's daughter, or of thy daughter's daughter, *even* their nakedness thou shalt not uncover: for theirs *is* thine own nakedness. The nakedness of thy father's wife's daughter, begotten of thy father, she *is* thy sister, thou shalt not uncover her nakedness. Thou shalt not uncover the nakedness of thy father's sister: she *is* thy father's near kinswoman. Thou shalt not uncover the nakedness of thy mother's sister: for she *is* thy mother's near kinswoman. Thou shalt not uncover the nakedness of thy father's brother, thou shalt not approach to his wife: she *is* thine aunt. Thou shalt not uncover the nakedness of thy daughter in law: she *is* thy son's wife; thou shalt not uncover her naked-

ness. Thou shalt not uncover the nakedness of thy brother's wife: it *is* thy brother's nakedness. Thou shalt not uncover the nakedness of a woman and her daughter, neither shalt thou take her son's daughter, or her daughter's daughter, to uncover her nakedness; *for* they *are* her near kinswomen: it *is* wickedness. Neither shalt thou take a wife to her sister, to vex *her,* to uncover her nakedness, beside the other in her life *time* (Lev 18:6–18).

And the man that lieth with his father's wife hath uncovered his father's nakedness: both of them shall surely be put to death; their blood *shall be* upon them. And if a man lie with his daughter in law, both of them shall surely be put to death: they have wrought confusion; their blood *shall be* upon them. If a man also lie with mankind, as he lieth with a woman, both of them have committed an abomination: they shall surely be put to death; their blood *shall be* upon them. And if a man take a wife and her mother, it *is* wickedness: they shall be burnt with fire, both he and they; that there be no wickedness among you. And if a man lie with a beast, he shall surely be put to death: and ye shall slay the beast. And if a woman approach unto any beast, and lie down thereto, thou shalt kill the woman, and the beast: they shall surely be put to death; their blood *shall be* upon them. And if a man shall take his sister, his father's daughter, or his mother's daughter, and see her nakedness, and she see his nakedness; it *is* a wicked thing; and they shall be cut off in the sight of their people: he hath uncovered his sister's nakedness; he shall bear his iniquity (Lev 20:11–17).

And thou shalt not uncover the nakedness of thy mother's sister, nor of thy father's sister: for he uncovereth his near kin: they shall bear their iniquity. And if a man shall lie with his uncle's wife, he hath uncovered his uncle's nakedness: they shall bear their sin; they shall die childless. And if a man shall take his brother's wife, it *is* an unclean thing: he hath uncovered his brother's nakedness; they shall be childless (Lev 20:19–21).

A man shall not take his father's wife, nor discover his father's skirt (Deut 22:30).

It is reported commonly *that there is*

fornication among you, and such fornication as is not so much as named among the Gentiles, that one should have his father's wife. And ye are puffed up, and have not rather mourned, that he that hath done this deed might be taken away from among you. For I verily, as absent in body, but present in spirit, have judged already, as though I were present, *concerning* him that hath so done this deed, in the name of our Lord Jesus Christ, when ye are gathered together, and my spirit, with the power of our Lord Jesus Christ, to deliver such an one unto Satan for the destruction of the flesh, that the spirit may be saved in the day of the Lord Jesus (1 Cor 5:1–5).

Biblical Examples: Gen 9:21–26; 19:30–38; 35:22; 2 Sam 13:7–14; 16:21, 22; Matt 14:3, 4; Mark 6:17, 18; Luke 3:19.

Further References: Deut 27:20–23; Ezek 22:10, 11.

INDECISION (See Decision-making)

INDUSTRY (See Daily Work; Diligence; Idleness)

INFIDELITY (See Adultery)

INFLUENCE (See also Example, Bad; Example, Good)

Make no friendship with an angry man; and with a furious man thou shalt not go: lest thou learn his ways, and get a snare to thy soul. (Prov 22:24, 25).

If a ruler hearken to lies, all his servants *are* wicked (Prov 29:12).

And there shall be, like people, like priest: and I will punish them for their ways, and reward them their doings (Hos 4:9).

Ye are the light of the world. A city that is set on an hill cannot be hid. Neither do men light a candle, and put it under a bushel, but on a candlestick; and it giveth light unto all that are in the house. Let your light so shine before men, that they may see your good works, and glorify your Father which is in heaven (Matt 5:14–16).

In the mean time, when there were gathered together an innumerable multitude of people, insomuch that they trode

one upon another, he began to say unto his disciples first of all, Beware ye of the leaven of the Pharisees, which is hypocrisy (Luke 12:1).

Your glorying *is* not good. Know ye not that a little leaven leaveneth the whole lump? Purge out therefore the old leaven, that ye may be a new lump, as ye are unleavened. For even Christ our passover is sacrificed for us (1 Cor 5:6, 7).

But now I have written unto you not to keep company, if any man that is called a brother be a fornicator, or covetous, or an idolater, or a railer, or a drunkard, or an extortioner; with such an one no not to eat (1 Cor 5:11).

But I keep under my body, and bring *it* into subjection: lest that by any means, when I have preached to others, I myself should be a castaway (1 Cor 9:27).

Biblical Examples: 1 Sam 19:1–6; 1 Kings 11:3, 4; 21:25; 2 Chron 22:3–5; 1 Thess 1:7, 8; 2 Tim 2:14–18; Heb 11:4.

Further References: Mark 4:21, 22; Luke 11:33–36; 1 Cor 7:16; Heb 12:15; 1 Peter 2:11, 12; 3:1, 2, 15, 16.

INJUSTICE

Thou shalt neither vex a stranger, nor oppress him: for ye were strangers in the land of Egypt (Exod 22:21).

Thou shalt not raise a false report: put not thine hand with the wicked to be an unrighteous witness. Thou shalt not follow a multitude to *do* evil; neither shalt thou speak in a cause to decline after many to wrest *judgment:* neither shalt thou countenance a poor man in his cause.

If thou meet thine enemy's ox or his ass going astray, thou shalt surely bring it back to him again. If thou see the ass of him that hateth thee lying under his burden, and wouldest forbear to help him, thou shalt surely help with him. Thou shalt not wrest the judgment of thy poor in his cause. Keep thee far from a false matter; and the innocent and righteous slay thou not: for I will not justify the wicked (Exod 23:1–7).

He that justifieth the wicked, and he that condemneth the just, even they both *are* abomination to the LORD. (Prov 17:15).

If thou seest the oppression of the poor,

and violent perverting of judgment and justice in a province, marvel not at the matter: for *he that is* higher than the highest regardeth; and *there be* higher than they (Eccl 5:8).

Forasmuch therefore as your treading *is* upon the poor, and ye take from him burdens of wheat: ye have built houses of hewn stone, but ye shall not dwell in them; ye have planted pleasant vineyards, but ye shall not drink wine of them. For I know your manifold transgressions, and your mighty sins: they afflict the just, they take a bribe, and they turn aside the poor in the gate *from their right* (Amos 5:11, 12).

And the soldiers likewise demanded of him, saying, And what shall we do? And he said unto them, Do violence to no man, neither accuse *any* falsely; and be content with your wages (Luke 3:14).

Biblical Examples: Matt 27:1–38; Mark 15:1–25; Luke 23:1–38; John 18:19–19:18; Acts 16:19–24; 17:5–9; 21:33–28:31.

Further References: Lev 19:35; Deut 16:19–20; Job 16:16, 17; Ps 12:5; 43:1; 82:2; Prov 11:7; 29:27; Jer 22:3–5; Mic 7:3; Zeph 3:5; Luke 16:10; 1 Thess 4:6; Rev 22:11.

INTEGRITY (See also Honesty)

And the LORD said, Shall I hide from Abraham that thing which I do; seeing that Abraham shall surely become a great and mighty nation, and all the nations of the earth shall be blessed in him? For I know him, that he will command his children and his household after him, and they shall keep the way of the LORD, to do justice and judgment; that the LORD may bring upon Abraham that which he hath spoken of him (Gen 18:17–19).

Moreover thou shalt provide out of all the people able men, such as fear God, men of truth, hating covetousness; and place *such* over them, *to be* rulers of thousands, *and* rulers of hundreds, rulers of fifties, and rulers of tens (Exod 18:21).

Thou shalt not wrest judgment; thou shalt not respect persons, neither take a gift: for a gift doth blind the eyes of the wise, and pervert the words of the righteous. That which is altogether just shalt thou follow, that thou mayest live, and in-

herit the land which the LORD thy God giveth thee (Deut 16:19, 20).

Moreover Job continued his parable, and said, As God liveth, *who* hath taken away my judgment; and the Almighty, *who* hath vexed my soul; all the while my breath *is* in me, and the spirit of God *is* in my nostrils; my lips shall not speak wickedness, nor my tongue utter deceit. God forbid that I should justify you: till I die I will not remove mine integrity from me. My righteousness I hold fast, and will not let it go: my heart shall not reproach *me* so long as I live (Job 27:1–6).

Lord, who shall abide in thy tabernacle? who shall dwell in thy holy hill? He that walketh uprightly, and worketh righteousness, and speaketh the truth in his heart. He *that* backbiteth not with his tongue, nor doeth evil in his neighbour, nor taketh up a reproach against his neighbour. In whose eyes a vile person is contemned; but he honoureth them that fear the LORD. *He that* sweareth to *his own* hurt, and changeth not. *He that* putteth not out his money to usury, nor taketh reward against the innocent. He that doeth these *things* shall never be moved (Ps 15:1–5).

Thou hast proved mine heart, thou hast visited *me* in the night; thou has tried me, *and* shalt find nothing; I am purposed *that* my mouth shall not transgress (Ps 17:3).

Who shall ascend into the hill of the LORD? or who shall stand in his holy place? He that hath clean hands, and a pure heart; who hath not lifted up his soul unto vanity, nor sworn deceitfully. He shall receive the blessing from the LORD, and righteousness from the God of his salvation (Ps 24:3–5).

Let not mercy and truth forsake thee: bind them about thy neck; write them upon the table of thine heart (Prov 3:3).

He that walketh uprightly walketh surely: but he that perverteth his ways shall be known (Prov 10:9).

Better *is* the poor that walketh in his integrity, than *he that is* perverse in his lips, and is a fool (Prov 19:1).

A faithful man shall abound with blessings: but he that maketh haste to be rich shall not be innocent (Prov 28:20).

He that walketh righteously, and speaketh uprightly; he that despiseth the gain of oppressions, that shaketh his hands from holding of bribes, that stoppeth his ears from hearing of blood, and shutteth his eyes from seeing evil; he shall dwell on high: his place of defence *shall be* the munitions of rocks: bread shall be given him; his waters *shall be* sure (Isa 33:15, 16).

He that is faithful in that which is least is faithful also in much: and he that is unjust in the least is unjust also in much (Luke 16:10).

Avoiding this, that no man should blame us in this abundance which is administered by us: providing for honest things, not only in the sight of the Lord, but also in the sight of men (2 Cor 8:20, 21).

Having your conversation honest among the Gentiles: that, whereas they speak against you as evildoers, they may by *your* good works, which they shall behold, glorify God in the day of visitation (1 Peter 2:12).

Biblical Examples: Gen 39:8–12; Num 16:15; 1 Sam 12:4; Ezra 8:24–30; Neh 5:14–19; Job 31:1–40; Luke 3:12, 13; Rom 9:1–3; 2 Cor 7:2.

Further References: Ps 7:3–5; 26:1–3; Prov 4:25–27; 11:3–5; 20:7; Ezek 18:5, 7–9; Mic 6:6–8; Mal 2:6; Rom 14:5, 14, 22; 2 Cor 4:2; Phil 4:8; 1 Tim 3:9; Heb 13:18.

INTEREST (see Usury and Interest)

INTERMARRIAGE

Observe thou that which I command thee this day: behold, I drive out before thee the Amorite, and the Canaanite, and the Hittite, and the Perizzite, and the Hivite, and the Jebusite. Take heed to thyself, lest thou make a covenant with the inhabitants of the land whither thou goest, lest it be for a snare in the midst of thee: but ye shall destroy their altars, break their images, and cut down their groves: for thou shalt worship no other god: for the LORD, whose name *is* jealous, *is* a jealous God: lest thou make a covenant with the inhabitants of the land, and they go a-whoring after their gods, and do sacrifice unto their gods, and *one* call thee, and thou eat of his sacrifice; and thou take of their daughters unto thy sons, and their

daughters go a-whoring after their gods, and make thy sons go a-whoring after their gods (Exod 34:11–16).

When the LORD thy God shall bring thee into the land whither thou goest to possess it, and hath cast out many nations before thee, the Hittites, and the Girgashites, and the Amorites, and the Canaanites, and the Perizzites, and the Hivites, and the Jebusites, seven nations greater and mightier than thou; and when the LORD thy God shall deliver them before thee; thou shalt smite them, *and* utterly destroy them; thou shalt make no covenant with them, nor shew mercy unto them: neither shalt thou make marriages with them; thy daughter thou shalt not give unto his son, nor his daughter shalt thou take unto thy son. For they will turn away thy son from following me, that they may serve other gods: so will the anger of the LORD be kindled against you, and destroy thee suddenly. But thus shall ye deal with them; ye shall destroy their altars, and break down their images, and cut down their groves, and burn their graven images with fire. For thou *art* an holy people unto the LORD thy God: the LORD thy God hath chosen thee to be a special people unto himself, above all people that *are* upon the face of the earth. The LORD did not set his love upon you, nor choose you, because ye were more in number than any people; for ye *were* the fewest of all people: but because the LORD loved you, and because he would keep the oath which he had sworn unto your fathers, hath the LORD brought you out with a mighty hand, and redeemed you out of the house of bondmen, from the hand of Pharaoh king of Egypt (Deut 7:1–8).

Now when these things were done, the princes came to me, saying, The people of Israel, and the priests, and the Levites, have not separated themselves from the people of the lands, *doing* according to their abominations, *even* of the Canaanites, the Hittites, the Perizzites, the Jebusites, the Ammonites, the Moabites, the Egyptians, and the Amorites. For they have taken of their daughters for themselves, and for their sons: so that the holy seed have mingled themselves with the people of *those* lands: yea, the hand of the princes and rulers hath been chief in this trespass (Ezra 9:1, 2).

Then all the men of Judah and Benjamin gathered themselves together unto Jerusalem within three days. It *was* the ninth month, on the twentieth *day* of the month; and all the people sat in the street of the house of God, trembling because of *this* matter, and for the great rain. And Ezra the priest stood up, and said unto them, Ye have transgressed, and have taken strange wives, to increase the trespass of Israel. Now therefore make confession unto the LORD God of your fathers, and do his pleasure: and separate yourselves from the people of the land, and from the strange wives (Ezra 10:9–11).

Judah hath dealt treacherously, and an abomination is committed in Israel and in Jerusalem; for Judah hath profaned the holiness of the LORD which he loved, and hath married the daughter of a strange god. The LORD will cut off the man that doeth this, the master and the scholar, out of the tabernacles of Jacob, and him that offereth an offering unto the LORD of hosts. And this have ye done again, covering the altar of the LORD with tears, with weeping, and with crying out, insomuch that he regardeth not the offering any more, or receiveth *it* with good will at your hand.

Yet ye say, Wherefore? Because the LORD hath been witness between thee and the wife of thy youth, against whom thou hast dealt treacherously: yet *is* she thy companion, and the wife of thy covenant. And did not he make one? Yet had he the residue of the spirit. And wherefore one? That he might seek a godly seed. Therefore take heed to your spirit, and let none deal treacherously against the wife of his youth. For the LORD, the God of Israel, saith that he hateth putting away: for *one* covereth violence with his garment, saith the LORD of hosts: therefore take heed to your spirit, that ye deal not treacherously (Mal 2:11–16).

Be ye not unequally yoked together with unbelievers: for what fellowship hath righteousness with unrighteousness? and what communion hath light with darkness? And what concord hath Christ with Belial? or what part hath he that believeth with an infidel? And what agreement hath the temple of God with idols? for ye are the temple of the living God; as God hath said, I will dwell in them, and walk in *them;* and I will be their God, and they shall be my people. Wherefore come out from among them, and be ye separate, saith the Lord, and touch not the unclean *thing;* and I will receive you (2 Cor 6:14–17).

Biblical Examples: Ezra 10:18–44.

Further References: 1 Chron 23:22; Neh 10:30; 13:26, 27; 1 Cor 7:39.

INTOXICANTS (See Abstinence; Alcohol and Alcoholism; Drunkenness; Wine)

– J –

JEALOUSY (See also Covetousness; Envy)

Thou shalt not make unto thee any graven image, or any likeness *of any thing* that *is* in heaven above, or that *is* in the earth beneath, or that *is* in the water under the earth: thou shalt not bow down thyself to them, nor serve them: for I the LORD thy God *am* a jealous God, visiting the iniquity of the fathers upon the children unto the third and fourth *generation* of them that hate me; and shewing mercy unto thousands of them that love me, and keep my commandments (Exod 20:4–6).

Take heed unto yourselves, lest ye forget the covenant of the LORD your God, which he made with you, and make you a graven image, *or* the likeness of any *thing*, which the LORD thy God hath forbidden thee. For the LORD thy God *is* a consuming fire, *even* a jealous God (Deut 4:23, 24).

For jealousy *is* the rage of a man: therefore he will not spare in the day of vengeance (Prov 6:34).

Set me as a seal upon thine heart, as a seal upon thine arm: for love *is* strong as death; jealousy *is* cruel as the grave: the coals thereof *are* coals of fire, *which hath a* most vehement flame (Song of Sol 8:6).

Therefore thus saith the Lord GOD; Now will I bring again the captivity of Jacob, and have mercy upon the whole house of Israel, and will be jealous for my holy name (Ezek 39:25).

God *is* jealous, and the LORD revengeth; the LORD revengeth, and *is* furious; the LORD will take vengeance on his adversaries, and he reserveth *wrath* for his enemies (Nah 1:2).

For I am jealous over you with godly jealousy: for I have espoused you to one husband, that I may present *you as* a chaste virgin to Christ (2 Cor 11:2).

Now the works of the flesh are manifest, which are *these;* Adultery, fornication, uncleanness, lasciviousness, idolatry, witchcraft, hatred, variance, emulations, wrath, strife, seditions, heresies, envyings, murders, drunkenness, revellings, and such like: of the which I tell you before, as I have also told *you* in time past, that they which do such things shall not inherit the kingdom of God (Gal 5:19–21).

Biblical Examples: Gen 16:5; 37:5–11; 1 Sam 18:8, 9; Luke 15:25–32; Acts 13:45–50.

Further References: Num 5:11–31; Prov 27:4; Eccl 4:4; Ezek 8:3, 4; Rom 13:13.

JOY (See Mental Health)

JUDICIAL SYSTEM (See Justice; Law)

JUSTICE

Thou shalt not defraud thy neighbour, neither rob *him:* the wages of him that is hired shall not abide with thee all night until the morning (Lev 19:13).

He doth execute the judgment of the fatherless and widow, and loveth the stranger, in giving him food and raiment (Deut 10:18).

Judges and officers shalt thou make thee in all thy gates, which the LORD thy God giveth thee, throughout thy tribes: and they shall judge the people with just judgment. Thou shalt not wrest judgment; thou shalt not respect persons, neither take a gift: for a gift doth blind the eyes of the wise, and pervert the words of the righteous. That which is altogether just shalt thou follow, that thou mayest live, and inherit the land which the LORD thy God giveth thee (Deut 16:18–20).

If there be a controversy between men, and they come unto judgment, that *the judges* may judge them; then they shall justify the righteous, and condemn the wicked. And it shall be, if the wicked man *be* worthy to be beaten, that the judge shall cause him to lie down, and to be beaten before his face, according to his fault, by a certain number. Forty stripes he may give him, *and* not exceed: lest, *if* he should exceed, and beat him above these with many stripes, then thy brother should seem vile unto thee.

Thou shalt not muzzle the ox when he treadeth out *the corn* (Deut 25:1–4).

And whosoever will not do the law of thy God, and the law of the king, let judgment be executed speedily upon him, whether *it be* unto death, or to banishment, or to confiscation of goods, or to imprisonment (Ezra 7:26).

He loveth righteousness and judgment: the earth is full of the goodness of the LORD (Ps 33:5).

God standeth in the congregation of the mighty; he judgeth among the gods. How long will ye judge unjustly, and accept the persons of the wicked? Selah. Defend the poor and fatherless: do justice to the afflicted and needy. Deliver the poor and needy: rid *them* out of the hand of the wicked (Ps 82:1–4).

To receive the instruction of wisdom, justice, and judgment, and equity (Prov 1:3).

To do justice and judgment *is* more acceptable to the LORD than sacrifice (Prov 21:3).

It is joy to the just to do judgment: but destruction *shall be* to the workers of iniquity (Prov 21:15).

These *things* also *belong* to the wise. *It is* not good to have respect of persons in judgment (Prov 24:23).

Thus saith the LORD, Keep ye judgment, and do justice: for my salvation *is* near to come, and my righteousness to be revealed (Isa 56:1).

For if ye throughly amend your ways

and your doings; if ye throughly execute judgment between a man and his neighbour; if ye oppress not the stranger, the fatherless, and the widow, and shed not innocent blood in this place, neither walk after other gods to your hurt: then will I cause you to dwell in this place, in the land that I gave to your fathers, for ever and ever (Jer 7:5–7).

But if a man be just, and do that which is lawful and right, *and* hath not eaten upon the mountains, neither hath lifted up his eyes to the idols of the house of Israel, neither hath defiled his neighbour's wife, neither hath come near to a menstruous woman, and hath not oppressed any, *but* hath restored to the debtor his pledge, hath spoiled none by violence, hath given his bread to the hungry, and hath covered the naked with a garment; he *that* hath not given forth upon usury, neither hath taken any increase, *that* hath withdrawn his hand from iniquity, hath executed true judgment between man and man. Hath walked in my statutes, and hath kept my judgments, to deal truly; he *is* just, he shall surely live, saith the Lord GOD (Ezek 18:5–9).

Hate the evil, and love the good, and establish judgment in the gate: it may be that the LORD God of hosts will be gracious unto the remnant of Joseph (Amos 5:15).

He hath shewed thee, O man, what *is* good; and what doth the LORD require of thee, but to do justly, and to love mercy, and to walk humbly with thy God? (Mic 6:8).

Thus speaketh the LORD of hosts, saying, Execute true judgment, and shew mercy and compassions every man to his brother: and oppress not the widow, nor the fatherless, the stranger, nor the poor; and let none of you imagine evil against his brother in your heart (Zech 7:9, 10).

These *are* the things that ye shall do; Speak ye every man the truth to his neighbour; execute the judgment of truth and peace in your gates (Zech 8:16).

Agree with thine adversary quickly, whiles thou art in the way with him; lest at any time the adversary deliver thee to the judge, and the judge deliver thee to the officer, and thou be cast into prison. Verily I say unto thee, Thou shalt by no means come out thence, till thou hast paid the uttermost farthing (Matt 5:25, 26).

Judge not according to the appearance, but judge righteous judgment (John 7:24).

Biblical Examples: Exod 18:21, 22; Deut 1:12–17; 2 Chron 19:5–10; Acts 18:12–16.

Further References: Exod 23:1–7; Lev 19:14, 15; Deut 19:16–19; Ps 72:1, 2; Prov 17:15, 26; 18:5, 17; 29:26; Isa 1:17; Jer 22:1–4; Mal 3:5.

JUVENILE DELINQUENCY (See Youth)

– K –

KIDNAPPING

And he that stealeth a man, and selleth him, or if he be found in his hand, he shall surely be put to death (Exod 21:16).

If a man be found stealing any of his brethren of the children of Israel, and maketh merchandise of him, or selleth him; then that thief shall die; and thou shalt put evil away from among you (Deut 24:7).

Biblical Examples: Gen 37:12–36; Judg 21:20–23.

Further References: 1 Tim 1:8–10.

KINDNESS

And if a stranger sojourn with thee in your land, ye shall not vex him. *But* the stranger that dwelleth with you shall be unto you as one born among you, and thou shalt love him as thyself; for ye were strangers in the land of Egypt: I *am* the LORD your God (Lev 19:33, 34).

Thou shalt not see thy brother's ox or his sheep go astray, and hide thyself from them: thou shalt in any case bring them again unto thy brother. And if thy brother *be* not nigh unto thee, or if thou know him not, then thou shalt bring it unto thine own house, and it shall be with thee until thy brother seek after it, and thou shalt restore it to him again. In like manner shalt thou do with his ass; and so shalt thou do with his raiment; and with all lost thing of thy brother's, which he hath lost, and thou hast found, shalt thou do likewise: thou mayest not hide thyself.

Thou shalt not see thy brother's ass or his ox fall down by the way, and hide thyself from them: thou shalt surely help him to lift *them* up again (Deut 22:1–4).

He that despiseth his neighbour sinneth: but he that hath mercy on the poor, happy *is* he (Prov 14:21).

And the word of the LORD came unto Zechariah saying, Thus speaketh the LORD of hosts, saying, Execute true judgment, and shew mercy and compassions every man to his brother: And oppress not the widow, nor the fatherless, the stranger, nor the poor; and let none of you imagine evil against his brother in your heart (Zech 7:8–10).

Blessed *are* the merciful: for they shall obtain mercy (Matt 5:7).

Give to him that asketh thee, and from him that would borrow of thee turn not thou away (Matt 5:42).

Then shall the King say unto them on his right hand, Come, ye blessed of my Father, inherit the kingdom prepared for you from the foundation of the world: for I was an hungered, and ye gave me meat: I was thirsty, and ye gave me drink: I was a stranger, and ye took me in: naked, and ye clothed me: I was sick, and ye visited me: I was in prison, and ye came unto me (Matt 25:34–36).

For if ye love them which love you, what thank have ye? for sinners also love those that love them. And if ye do good to them which do good to you, what thank have ye? for sinners also do even the same. And if ye lend *to them* of whom ye hope to receive, what thank have ye? for sinners also lend to sinners, to receive as much again. But love ye your enemies, and do good, and lend, hoping for nothing again; and your reward shall be great, and ye shall be the children of the Highest: for he is kind unto the unthankful and *to the* evil. Be ye therefore merciful, as your Father also is merciful (Luke 6:32–36).

We then that are strong ought to bear the infirmities of the weak, and not to please ourselves. Let every one of us please *his* neighbour for *his* good to edification (Rom 15:1, 2).

Charity suffereth long, *and* is kind; charity envieth not; charity vaunteth not itself, is not puffed up, doth not behave itself unseemly, seeketh not her own, is not easily provoked, thinketh no evil; rejoiceth not in iniquity, but rejoiceth in the truth; beareth all things, believeth all things, hopeth all things, endureth all things (1 Cor 13:4–7).

Brethren, if a man be overtaken in a fault, ye which are spiritual, restore such an one in the spirit of meekness, considering thyself, lest thou also be tempted. Bear ye one another's burdens, and so fulfil the law of Christ (Gal 6:1, 2).

As we have therefore opportunity, let us do good unto all *men,* especially unto them who are of the household of faith (Gal 6:10).

Let all bitterness, and wrath, and anger, and clamour, and evil speaking, be put away from you, with all malice: and be ye kind one to another, tenderhearted, forgiving one another, even as God for Christ's sake hath forgiven you (Eph 4:31, 32).

Put on therefore, as the elect of God, holy and beloved, bowels of mercies, kindness, humbleness of mind, meekness, longsuffering; forbearing one another, and forgiving one another, if any man have a quarrel against any: even as Christ forgave you, so also *do* ye. And above all these things *put on* charity, which is the bond of perfectness (Col 3:12–14).

Not rendering evil for evil, or railing for railing: but contrariwise blessing; knowing that ye are thereunto called, that ye should inherit a blessing (1 Peter 3:9).

But whoso hath this world's good, and seeth his brother have need, and shutteth up his bowels *of compassion* from him, how dwelleth the love of God in him? My little children, let us not love in word, neither in tongue; but in deed and in truth (1 John 3:17, 18).

Biblical Examples: Gen 45:16–20; Josh 2:6–16; 1 Sam 31:11, 12; 2 Sam 9:1–13; Jer 39:11, 12; Acts 27:3, 43; Gal 6:10.

Further References: Prov 19:22; 31:26; Acts 20:35; Rom 12:15; 1 Tim 5:9, 10; 2 Peter 1:7.

-L-

LABOR RELATIONS (See also Daily Work; Wages)

Thou shalt not defraud thy neighbour, neither rob *him:* the wages of him that is hired shall not abide with thee all night until the morning (Lev 19:13).

And the sabbath of the land shall be meat for you; for thee, and for thy servant, and for thy maid, and for thy hired servant, and for thy stranger that sojourneth with thee (Lev 25:6).

But the seventh day *is* the sabbath of the LORD thy God: *in it* thou shalt not do any work, thou, nor thy son, nor thy daughter, nor thy manservant, nor thy maidservant, nor thine ox, nor thine ass, nor any of thy cattle, nor thy stranger that *is* within thy gates; that thy manservant and thy maidservant may rest as well as thou (Deut 5:14).

Thou shalt not oppress an hired servant *that is* poor and needy, *whether he be* of thy brethren, or of thy strangers that *are* in thy land within thy gates: at his day thou shalt give *him* his hire, neither shall the sun go down upon it; for he *is* poor, and setteth his heart upon it: lest he cry against thee unto the LORD, and it be sin unto thee (Deut 24:14, 15).

He that oppresseth the poor to increase his *riches, and* he that giveth to the rich, *shall* surely *come* to want (Prov 22:16).

Woe unto him that buildeth his house by unrighteousness, and his chambers by wrong; *that* useth his neighbour's service without wages, and giveth him not for his work (Jer 22:13).

And I will come near to you to judgment; and I will be a swift witness against the sorcerers, and against the adulterers, and against false swearers, and against those that oppress the hireling in *his* wages, the widow, and the fatherless, and that turn aside the stranger *from his right,* and fear not me, saith the LORD of hosts (Mal 3:5).

Provide neither gold, nor silver, nor brass in your purses, nor scrip for *your* journey, neither two coats, neither shoes, nor yet staves: for the workman is worthy of his meat (Matt 10:9, 10).

Servants, be obedient to them that are *your* masters according to the flesh, with fear and trembling, in singleness of your heart, as unto Christ; not with eye-service, as menpleasers but as the servants of Christ, doing the will of God from the heart; with good will doing service, as to the Lord, and not to men: knowing that whatsoever good thing any man doeth, the same shall he receive of the Lord, whether *he be* bond or free. And, ye masters, do the same things unto them, forbearing threatening: knowing that your Master also is in heaven; neither is there respect of persons with him (Eph 6:5–9).

And whatsoever ye do, do *it* heartily, as to the Lord, and not unto men (Col 3:23).

Masters, give unto *your* servants that which is just and equal; knowing that ye also have a Master in heaven (Col 4:1).

But as touching brotherly love ye need not that I write unto you: for ye yourselves are taught of God to love one another. And indeed ye do it toward all the brethren which are in all Macedonia: but we beseech you, brethren, that ye increase more and more; and that ye study to be quiet, and to do your own business, and to work with your own hands, as we commanded you; that ye may walk honestly toward them that are without, and *that* ye may have lack of nothing (1 Thess 4:9–12).

Behold, the hire of the labourers who have reaped down your fields, which is of you kept back by fraud, crieth: and the cries of them which have reaped are entered into the ears of the Lord of sabaoth (James 5:4).

Servants, *be* subject to *your* masters with all fear; not only to the good and gentle, but also to the froward. For this *is* thankworthy, if a man for conscience toward God endure grief, suffering wrongfully. For what glory *is it,* if, when ye be buffeted for your faults, ye shall take it patiently? but if, when ye do well, and suffer *for it,* ye take it patiently, this *is* acceptable with God. For even hereunto were ye called: because Christ also suffered for us, leaving us an example, that ye should follow his steps: who did no sin, neither was guile found in his mouth: who, when he was reviled, reviled not again; when he suffered, he threatened not; but committed *himself* to him that judgeth righteously (1 Peter 2:18–23).

Biblical Examples: Gen 30:37–43; Job 31:13–15; Matt 20:1–15.

Further References: Exod 20:9–11; 23:12; Ps 128:2; Matt 10:10; Luke 10:7; Acts 20:35; 1 Tim 5:18.

LAW

Thou shalt have no other gods before me. Thou shalt not make unto thee any graven image, or any likeness *of any thing* that *is* in heaven above, or that *is* in the earth beneath, or that *is* in the water under the earth: thou shalt not bow down thyself to them, nor serve them: for I the LORD thy God *am* a jealous God, visiting the iniquity of the fathers upon the children unto the third and fourth *generation* of them that hate me; and shewing mercy unto thousands of them that love me, and keep my commandments. Thou shalt not take the name of the LORD thy God in vain; for the LORD will not hold him guiltless that taketh his name in vain. Remember the sabbath day, to keep it holy. Six days shalt thou labour, and do all thy work:

but the seventh day *is* the sabbath of the LORD thy God: *in it* thou shalt not do any work, thou, nor thy son, nor thy daughter, thy manservant, nor thy maidservant, nor thy cattle, nor thy stranger that *is* within thy gates: for *in* six days the LORD made heaven and earth, the sea, and all that in them *is,* and rested the seventh day: wherefore the LORD blessed the sabbath day, and hallowed it.

Honour thy father and thy mother: that thy days may be long upon the land which the LORD thy God giveth thee. Thou shalt not kill. Thou shalt not commit adultery. Thou shalt not steal. Thou shalt not bear false witness against thy neighbour. Thou shalt not covet thy neighbour's wife, nor his manservant, nor his maidservant, nor his ox, nor his ass, nor any thing that *is* thy neighbour's (Exod 20:3–17).

And it shall be, when he sitteth upon the throne of his kingdom, that he shall write him a copy of this law in a book out of *that which is* before the priests the Levites: and it shall be with him, and he shall read therein all the days of his life: that he may learn to fear the LORD his God, to keep all the words of this law and these statutes, to do them: that his heart be not lifted up above his brethren, and that he turn not aside from the commandment, *to* the right hand, or *to* the left: to the end that he may prolong *his* days in his kingdom, he, and his children, in the midst of Israel (Deut 17:18–20).

And he brought forth the king's son, and put the crown upon him, and *gave him* the testimony; and they made him king, and anointed him; and they clapped their hands, and said, God save the king (2 Kings 11:12).

Then they brought out the king's son, and put upon him the crown, and *gave him* the testimony and made him king. And Jehoiada and his sons anointed him, and said, God save the king (2 Chron 23:11).

The law of the LORD *is* perfect, converting the soul: the testimony of the LORD *is* sure, making wise the simple. The statutes of the LORD *are* right, rejoicing the heart: the commandment of the LORD *is* pure, enlightening the eyes. The fear of the LORD *is* clean, enduring for ever: the judgments of the LORD *are* true *and* righteous altogether (Ps 19:7–9).

They that forsake the law praise the wicked: but such as keep the law contend with them. Evil men understand not judgment: but they that seek the LORD understand all *things* (Prov 28:4, 5).

Think not that I am come to destroy the law, or the prophets: I am not come to destroy, but to fulfil. For verily I say unto you, Till heaven and earth pass, one jot or one tittle shall in no wise pass from the law, till all be fulfilled. Whosoever therefore shall break one of these least commandments, and shall teach men so, he shall be called the least in the kingdom of heaven: but whosoever shall do and teach *them,* the same shall be called great in the kingdom of heaven. For I say unto you, That except your righteousness shall exceed *the righteousness* of the scribes and Pharisees, ye shall in no case enter into the kingdom of heaven.

Ye have heard that it was said by them of old time, Thou shalt not kill; and whosoever shall kill shall be in danger of the judgment: but I say unto you, That whosoever is angry with his brother without a cause shall be in danger of the judgment: and whosoever shall say to his brother, Raca, shall be in danger of the council: but whosoever shall say, Thou fool, shall be in danger of hell fire. Therefore if thou bring thy gift to the altar, and there rememberest that thy brother hath aught against thee; leave there thy gift before the altar, and go thy way; first be reconciled to thy brother, and then come and offer thy gift. Agree with thine adversary quickly, whiles thou art in the way with him; lest at any time the adversary deliver thee to the judge, and the judge deliver thee to the officer, and thou be cast into prison. Verily I say unto thee, Thou shalt by no means come out thence, till thou hast paid the uttermost farthing.

Ye have heard that it was said by them of old time, Thou shalt not commit adultery: but I say unto you, That whosoever looketh on a woman to lust after her hath committed adultery with her already in his heart. And if thy right eye offend thee, pluck it out, and cast *it* from thee: for it is profitable for thee that one of thy mem-

bers should perish, and not *that* thy whole body should be cast into hell. And if thy right hand offend thee, cut it off, and cast *it* from thee: for it is profitable for thee that one of thy members should perish, and not *that* thy whole body should be cast into hell. It hath been said, Whosoever shall put away his wife, let him give her a writing of divorcement: but I say unto you, That whosoever shall put away his wife, saving for the cause of fornication, causeth her to commit adultery: and whosoever shall marry her that is divorced committeth adultery.

Again, ye have heard that it hath been said by them of old time, Thou shalt not forswear thyself, but shalt perform unto the Lord thine oaths: but I say unto you, Swear not at all; neither by heaven; for it is God's throne: nor by the earth; for it is his footstool: neither by Jerusalem; for it is the city of the great King. Neither shalt thou swear by thy head, because thou canst not make one hair white or black. But let your communication be, Yea, yea; Nay, nay: for whatsoever is more than these cometh of evil.

Ye have heard that it hath been said, An eye for an eye, and a tooth for a tooth: but I say unto you, That ye resist not evil: but whosoever shall smite thee on thy right cheek, turn to him the other also. And if any man will sue thee at the law, and take away thy coat, let him have *thy* cloak also. And whosoever shall compel thee to go a mile, go with him twain. Give to him that asketh thee, and from him that would borrow of thee turn not thou away.

Ye have heard that it hath been said, Thou shalt love thy neighbour, and hate thine enemy. But I say unto you, Love your enemies, bless them that curse you, do good to them that hate you, and pray for them which despitefully use you, and persecute you; that ye may be the children of your Father which is in heaven: for he maketh his sun to rise on the evil and on the good, and sendeth rain on the just and on the unjust. For if ye love them which love you, what reward have ye? do not even the publicans the same? And if ye salute your brethren only, what do ye more *than others?* do not even the publicans so? Be ye therefore perfect, even as your Father which is in heaven is perfect (Matt 5:17–48).

They say unto him, Cæsar's. Then saith he unto them, Render therefore unto Cæsar the things which are Cæsar's; and unto God the things that are God's (Matt 22:21).

Then one of them, *which was* a lawyer, asked *him a question*, tempting him, and saying, Master, which *is* the great commandment in the law? Jesus said unto him, Thou shalt love the Lord thy God with all thy heart, and with all thy soul, and with all thy mind. This is the first and great commandment. And the second *is* like unto it, Thou shalt love thy neighbour as thyself. On these two commandments hang all the law and the prophets (Matt 22:35–40).

For when the Gentiles, which have not the law, do by nature the things contained in the law, these, having not the law, are a law unto themselves: which shew the work of the law written in their hearts, their conscience also bearing witness, and *their* thoughts the mean while accusing or else excusing one another (Rom 2:14, 15).

What shall we say then? *Is* the law sin? God forbid. Nay, I had not known sin, but by the law: for I had not known lust, except the law had said, Thou shalt not covet. . . . Wherefore the law *is* holy, and the commandment holy, and just, and good. Was then that which is good made death unto me? God forbid. But sin, that it might appear sin, working death in me by that which is good; that sin by the commandment might become exceeding sinful. For we know that the law is spiritual: but I am carnal, sold under sin (Rom 7:7, 12–14).

Wherefore the law was our schoolmaster *to bring us* unto Christ, that we might be justified by faith (Gal 3:24).

But whoso looketh into the perfect law of liberty, and continueth *therein,* he being not a forgetful hearer, but a doer of the work, this man shall be blessed in his deed (James 1:25).

Whosover committeth sin transgresseth also the law: for sin is the transgression of the law (1 John 3:4).

For this is the love of God, that we keep his commandments: and his commandments are not grievous (1 John 5:3).

Biblical Examples: Exod; Lev; Num; Deut.

Further References: Deut 5:6–21; Ps 19; 119:1–8; Matt 5:17–45; Luke 20:22–25.

LEISURE

And on the seventh day God ended his work which he had made; and he rested on the seventh day from all his work which he had made. And God blessed the seventh day, and sanctified it: because that in it he had rested from all his work which God created and made (Gen 2:2, 3).

Six days shalt though labour, and do all thy work: but the seventh day *is* the sabbath of the LORD thy God: *in it* thou shalt not do any work, thou, nor thy son, nor thy daughter, thy manservant, nor thy maidservant, nor thy cattle, nor thy stranger that *is* within thy gates: for *in* six days the LORD made heaven and earth, the sea, and all that in them *is,* and rested the seventh day: wherefore the LORD blessed the sabbath day, and hallowed it (Exod 20:9–11).

And six years thou shalt sow thy land, and shalt gather in the fruits thereof: but the seventh *year* thou shalt let it rest and lie still; that the poor of thy people may eat: and what they leave the beasts of the field shall eat. In like manner thou shalt deal with thy vineyard, *and* with thy oliveyard (Exod 23:10, 11).

And the LORD spake unto Moses, saying, Speak unto the children of Israel, and say unto them, *Concerning* the feasts of the LORD, which ye shall proclaim *to be* holy convocation, *even* these *are* my feasts. Six days shall work be done: but the seventh day *is* the sabbath of rest, an holy convocation; ye shall do no work *therein:* it *is* the sabbath of the LORD in all your dwellings.

These *are* the feasts of the LORD, *even* holy convocations, which ye shall proclaim in their seasons. In the fourteenth *day* of the first month at even *is* the LORD's passover. And on the fifteenth day of the same month *is* the feast of unleavened bread unto the LORD: seven days ye must eat unleavened bread. In the first day ye shall have an holy convocation: ye shall do no servile work therein. But ye shall offer an offering made by fire unto the LORD seven days: in the seventh day *is* an holy convocation: ye shall do no servile work *therein* (Lev 23:1–8).

And keep the feast of unleavened bread seven days with joy: for the LORD had made them joyful, and turned the heart of the king of Assyria unto them, to strengthen their hands in the work of the house of God, the God of Israel (Ezra 6:22).

It is vain for you to rise up early, to sit up late, to eat the bread of sorrows: *for* so he giveth his beloved sleep (Ps 127:2).

Love not sleep, lest thou come to poverty; open thine eyes, *and* thou shalt be satisfied with bread (Prov 20:13).

And also that every man should eat and drink, and enjoy the good of all his labour, it *is* the gift of God (Eccl 3:13).

By much slothfulness the building decayeth; and through idleness of the hands the house droppeth through (Eccl 10:18).

Ye shall have a song, as in the night *when* a holy solemnity is kept; and gladness of heart, as when one goeth with a pipe to come into the mountain of the LORD, to the mighty One of Israel (Isa 30:29).

And the word of the LORD of hosts came unto me, saying, Thus saith the LORD of hosts; The fast of the fourth *month,* and the fast of the fifth, and the fast of the seventh, and the fast of the tenth, shall be to the house of Judah joy and gladness, and cheerful feasts; therefore love the truth and peace (Zech 8:18, 19).

And the apostles gathered themselves together unto Jesus, and told him all things, both what they had done, and what they had taught. And he said unto them, Come ye yourselves apart into a desert place, and rest a while: for there were many coming and going, and they had no leisure so much as to eat. And they departed into a desert place by ship privately (Mark 6:30–32).

What? know ye not that your body is the temple of the Holy Ghost *which is* in you, which ye have of God, and ye are not your own? For ye are bought with a price: therefore glorify God in your body,

and in your spirit, which are God's (1 Cor 6:19, 20).

Whether therefore ye eat, or drink, or whatsoever ye do, do all to the glory of God (1 Cor 10:31).

Let no man therefore judge you in meat, or in drink, or in respect of an holyday, or of the new moon, or of the sabbath *days* (Col 2:16).

Now we command you, brethren, in the name of our Lord Jesus Christ, that ye withdraw yourselves from every brother that walketh disorderly, and not after the tradition which he received us. For yourselves know how ye ought to follow us: for we behaved not ourselves disorderly among you; neither did we eat any man's bread for nought; but wrought with labour and travail night and day, that we might not be chargeable to any of you: not because we have not power, but to make ourselves an ensample unto you to follow us. For even when we were with you, this we commanded you, that if any would not work, neither should he eat. For we hear that there are some which walk among you disorderly, working not at all, but are busybodies. Now them that are such we command and exhort by our Lord Jesus Christ, that with quietness they work, and eat their own bread. But ye, brethren, be not weary in well-doing (2 Thess 3:6–13).

Biblical Examples: Exod 12:1–28; 13:1–7; Lev 23:34–42; 25:2–7; 25:8–16; 26:34, 35; 27:16–25; Num 10:10; 29:1–12; 29:35; Deut 16:11–14; 2 Sam 2:13, 14; 2 Chron 30:21–26; Neh 8:1–18; Job 41:5; Ps 42:4; 122:1–4; Prov 31:27; Mark 6:31, 32; 7:24.

Further References: Num 28:18–25; 1 Cor 3:13–15; Eph 5:15–17; 1 Tim 4:7, 8.

LENDING (See Borrowing; Debt and Debtor)

LESBIANISM (See Homosexuality)

LIBERALITY (See Unselfishness)

LICENTIOUSNESS

And he said, That which cometh out of the man, that defileth the man. For from within, out of the heart of men, proceed evil thoughts, adulteries, fornications, murders, thefts, covetousness, wickedness, deceit, lasciviousness, an evil eye, blasphemy, pride, foolishness: all these evil things come from within, and defile the man (Mark 7:20–23).

And that, knowing the time, that now *it is* high time to awake out of sleep: for now *is* our salvation nearer than when we believed. The night is far spent, the day is at hand: let us therefore cast off the works of darkness, and let us put on the armour of light. Let us walk honestly, as in the day; not in rioting and drunkenness, not in chambering and wantonness, not in strife and envying (Rom 13:11–13).

Flee fornication. Every sin that a man doeth is without the body; but he that committeth fornication sinneth against his own body. What? know ye not that your body is the temple of the Holy Ghost *which is* in you, which ye have of God, and ye are not your own? For ye are bought with a price: therefore glorify God in your body, and in your spirit, which are God's (1 Cor 6:18–20).

Whether therefore ye eat, or drink, or whatsoever ye do, do all to the glory of God. Give none offence, neither to the Jews, nor to the Gentiles, nor to the church of God: even as I please all *men* in all *things,* not seeking mine own profit, but the *profit* of many, that they may be saved (1 Cor 10:31–33).

And lest, when I come again, my God will humble me among you, and *that* I shall bewail many which have sinned already, and have not repented of the uncleanness and fornication and lasciviousness which they have committed (2 Cor 12:21).

For, brethren, ye have been called unto liberty; only *use* not liberty for an occasion to the flesh, but by love serve one another (Gal 5:13).

Now the works of the flesh are manifest, which are *these;* Adultery, fornication, uncleanness, lasciviousness, idolatry, witchcraft, hatred, variance, emulations, wrath, strife, seditions, heresies, envyings, murders, drunkenness, revellings, and such like: of the which I tell you before, as I have also told *you* in time past, that they which do such things shall not inherit the kingdom of God (Gal 5:19–21).

This I say therefore, and testify in the Lord, that ye henceforth walk not as other Gentiles walk, in the vanity of their mind, having the understanding darkened, being alienated from the life of God through the ignorance that is in them, because of the blindness of their heart: who being past feeling have given themselves over unto lasciviousness, to work all uncleanness with greediness (Eph 4:17–19).

But fornication, and all uncleanness, or covetousness, let it not be once named among you, as becometh saints (Eph 5:3).

Biblical Examples: Gen 19:5, 30–38; Exod 32; Judg 19:22–25; 2 Sam 11:2–27; Esth 2:2–19.

Further References: Joel 3:3; 1 Peter 2:16; 2 Peter 2:4–9.

LIFE, SACREDNESS OF (See also Homicide)

Whoso sheddeth man's blood, by man shall his blood be shed: for in the image of God made he man (Gen 9:6).

Thou shalt not kill (Exod 20:13).

If men strive, and hurt a woman with child, so that her fruit depart *from her,* and yet no mischief follow: he shall be surely punished, according as the woman's husband will lay upon him; and he shall pay as the judges *determine* (Exod 21:22).

Keep thee far from a false matter; and the innocent and righteous slay thou not: for I will not justify the wicked (Exod 23:7).

For thou hast possessed my reins: thou hast covered me in my mother's womb. I will praise thee; for I am fearfully *and* wonderfully made: marvellous *are* thy works; and *that* my soul knoweth right well. My substance was not hid from thee, when I was made in secret, *and* curiously wrought in the lowest parts of the earth. Thine eyes did see my substance, yet being unperfect; and in thy book all *my members* were written, *which* in continuance were fashioned, when *as yet there was* none of them (Ps 139:13–16).

As thou knowest not what *is* the way of the spirit, *nor* how the bones *do grow* in the womb of her that is with child: even so thou knowest not the works of God who maketh all (Eccl 11:5).

Before I formed thee in the belly, I knew thee; and before thou comest forth out of the womb I sanctified thee, *and* I ordained thee a prophet unto the nations (Jer 1:5).

The burden of the word of the LORD for Israel, saith the LORD, which stretcheth forth the heavens, and layeth the foundation of the earth, and formeth the spirit of man within him (Zech 12:1).

Therefore I say unto you, Take no thought for your life, what ye shall eat, or what ye shall drink; nor yet for your body, what ye shall put on. Is not the life more than meat, and the body than raiment? Behold the fowls of the air: for they sow not, neither do they reap, nor gather into barns; yet your heavenly Father feedeth them. Are ye not much better than they? Which of you by taking thought can add one cubit unto his stature? And why take ye thought for raiment? Consider the lilies of the field, how they grow; they toil not, neither do they spin: and yet I say unto you, That even Solomon in all his glory was not arrayed like one of these. Wherefore, if God so clothe the grass of the field, which today is, and tomorrow is cast into the oven, *shall he* not much more *clothe* you, O ye of little faith? Therefore take no thought, saying, What shall we eat? or, What shall we drink? or, Wherewithal shall we be clothed? (For after all these things do the Gentiles seek:) for your heavenly Father knoweth that ye have need of all these things. But seek ye first the kingdom of God, and his righteousness; and all these things shall be added unto you (Matt 6:25–33).

And it came to pass, that, when Elisabeth heard the salutation of Mary, the babe leaped in her womb; and Elisabeth was filled with the Holy Ghost (Luke 1:41).

Jesus answered, Neither hath this man sinned, nor his parents: but that the works of God should be made manifest in him (John 9:3).

Neither is worshipped with men's hands, as though he needed any thing, seeing he giveth to all life, and breath, and all things; and hath made of one blood all nations of men for to dwell on all the face of the earth, and hath determined the times before appointed, and the bounds of their habitation; that they should seek the Lord, if haply they might feel after him, and find him, though he be not far from every one of us: for in him we live, and move, and have our being; as certain also of your own poets have said, For we are also his offspring (Acts 17:25–28).

And last of all he was seen of me also, as of one born out of due time (1 Cor 15:8).

For we are his workmanship, created in Christ Jesus unto good works, which God hath before ordained that we should walk in them (Eph. 2:10).

For every creature of God *is* good, and nothing to be refused, if it be received with thanksgiving (1 Tim 4:4).

I give thee charge in the sight of God, who quickeneth all things, and *before* Christ Jesus, who before Pontius Pilate witnessed a good confession (1 Tim 6:13).

Biblical Examples: Gen 4:3–15.

Further References: Gen 2:7; Deut 30:20; Judg 13:2–5; Ps 22:29; 51:5; Eccl 12:7; Isa 38:16–20; Eph 1:3, 4.

LONGSUFFERING (See Diligence; Patience; Perseverance)

LOTS, CASTING

And the LORD spake unto Moses, saying, Unto these the land shall be divided for an inheritance according to the number of names. To many thou shalt give the more inheritance, and to few thou shalt give the less inheritance: to every one shall his inheritance be given according to those that were numbered of him. Notwithstanding the land shall be divided by lot: according to the names of the tribes of their fathers they shall inherit. According to the lot shall the possession thereof be divided between many and few (Num 26:52–56).

Thus were they divided by lot, one sort with another; for the governors of the sanctuary, and governors *of the house* of God, were of the sons of Eleazar, and of the sons of Ithamar (1 Chron 24:5).

And they crucified him, and parted his garments, casting lots: that it might be fulfilled which was spoken by the prophet, They parted my garments among them, and upon my vesture did they cast lots (Matt 27:35).

Then the soldiers, when they had crucified Jesus, took his garments, and made four parts, to every soldier a part; and also *his* coat: now the coat was without seam, woven from the top throughout. They said therefore among themselves, Let us not rend it, but cast lots for it, whose it shall be: that the scripture might be fulfilled, which saith, They parted my raiment among them, and for my vesture they did cast lots. These things therefore the soldiers did (John 19:23, 24).

Biblical Examples: Lev 16:8; Josh 7:14–18; 15; 18:10; 1 Sam 14:41, 42; 1 Chron 6:61–65; Ps 22:18; Prov 16:33; 18:18; Isa 34:17; 65:12; Ezek 45:1; Matt 27:35; Mark 15:24; Luke 1:9; Acts 1:26.

LOVE

Thou shalt not avenge, nor bear any grudge against the children of thy people, but thou shalt love thy neighbour as thyself: I *am* the LORD (Lev 19:18).

Hear, O Israel: The LORD our God *is* one LORD: and thou shalt love the LORD thy God with all thine heart, and with all thy soul, and with all thy might (Deut 6:4, 5).

And now, Israel, what doth the LORD thy God require of thee, but to fear the LORD thy God, to walk in all his ways, and to love him, and to serve the LORD thy God with all thy heart and with all thy soul, to keep the commandments of the LORD, and his statutes, which I command thee this day for thy good? (Deut. 10:12, 13).

Therefore thou shalt love the LORD thy God, and keep his charge, and his statutes, and his judgments, and his commandments, alway (Deut 11:1).

Hatred stirreth up strifes: but love covereth all sins (Prov 10:12).

Better *is* a dinner of herbs where love is, than a stalled ox and hatred therewith (Prov 15:17).

He that covereth a transgression seeketh love; but he that repeateth a matter separateth *very* friends. . . . A friend loveth at all times, and a brother is born for adversity (Prov 17:9, 17).

Set me as a seal upon thine heart, as a seal upon thine arm: for love *is* strong as death; jealousy *is* cruel as the grave: the coals thereof *are* coals of fire, *which hath*

a most vehement flame. Many waters cannot quench love, neither can the floods drown it: if *a* man would give all the substance of his house for love, it would utterly be contemned (Song of Sol 8:6, 7).

Ye have heard that it hath been said, Thou shalt love thy neighbour, and hate thine enemy. But I say unto you, Love your enemies, bless them that curse you, do good to them that hate you, and pray for them which despitefully use you, and persecute you: that ye may be the children of your Father which is in heaven: for he maketh his sun to rise on the evil and on the good, and sendeth rain on the just and on the unjust. For if ye love them which love you, what reward have ye? do not even the publicans the same? And if ye salute your brethren only, what do ye more *than others?* do not even the publicans so? Be ye therefore perfect, even as your Father which is in heaven is perfect. (Matt 5:43–48).

Then one of them, *which was* a lawyer, asked *him a question,* tempting him, and saying, Master, which *is* the great commandment in the law? Jesus said unto him, Thou shalt love the Lord thy God with all thy heart, and with all thy soul, and with all thy mind. This is the first and great commandment. And the second *is* like unto it, Thou shalt love thy neighbour as thyself. On these two commandments hang all the law and the prophets (Matt 22:35–40).

But I say unto you which hear, Love your enemies, do good to them which hate you, bless them that curse you, and pray for them which despitefully use you. And unto him that smiteth thee on the *one* cheek offer also the other; and him that taketh away thy cloak forbid not *to take thy* coat also. Give to every man that asketh of thee; and of him that taketh away thy goods ask *them* not again. And as ye would that men should do to you, do ye also to them likewise. For if ye love them which love you, what thank have ye? for sinners also love those that love them. And if ye do good to them which do good to you, what thank have ye? for sinners also do even the same. And if ye lend *to them* of whom ye hope to receive, what thank have ye? for sinners also lend to sinners, to receive as much again. But love ye your enemies, and do good, and lend, hoping for nothing again; and your reward shall be great, and ye shall be the children of the Highest: for he is kind unto the unthankful and *to* the evil (Luke 6:27–35).

But woe unto you, Pharisees! for ye tithe mint and rue and all manner of herbs, and pass over judgment and the love of God: these ought ye to have done, and not to leave the other undone (Luke 11:42).

For God so loved the world, that he gave his only begotten Son, that whosoever believeth in him should not perish, but have everlasting life (John 3:16).

A new commandment I give unto you, That ye love one another; as I have loved you, that ye also love one another. By this shall all *men* know that ye are my disciples, if ye have love one to another (John 13:34, 35).

If ye love me, keep my commandments. And I will pray the Father, and he shall give you another Comforter, that he may abide with you for ever; *even* the Spirit of truth; whom the world cannot receive, because it seeth him not, neither knoweth him: but ye know him; for he dwelleth with you, and shall be in you. I will not leave you comfortless: I will come to you. Yet a little while, and the world seeth me no more; but ye see me: because I live, ye shall live also. At that day ye shall know that I *am* in my Father, and ye in me, and I in you. He that hath my commandments, and keepeth them, he it is that loveth me: and he that loveth me shall be loved of my Father, and I will love him, and will manifest myself to him (John 14:15–21).

And the glory which thou gavest me I have given them; that they may be one, even as we are one: I in them, and thou in me, that they may be made perfect in one; and that the world may know that thou hast sent me, and hast loved them, as thou hast loved me (John 17:22, 23).

Let love be without dissimulation. Abhor that which is evil; cleave to that which is good. *Be* kindly affectioned one to another with brotherly love; in honour preferring one another (Rom 12:9, 10).

Owe no man any thing, but to love one another: for he that loveth another hath fulfilled the law. For this, Thou shalt not commit adultery, Thou shalt not kill, Thou shalt not steal, Thou shalt not bear false witness, Thou shalt not covet; and if *there be* any other commandment, it is briefly comprehended in this saying, namely, Thou shalt love thy neighbour as thyself. Love worketh no ill to his neighbour: therefore love *is* the fulfilling of the law (Rom 13:8–10).

Though I speak with the tongues of men and of angels, and have not charity, I am become *as* sounding brass, or a tinkling cymbal. And though I have *the gift of* prophecy, and understand all mysteries, and all knowledge; and though I have all faith, so that I could remove mountains, and have not charity, I am nothing. And though I bestow all my goods to feed *the poor,* and though I give my body to be burned, and have not charity, it profiteth me nothing. Charity suffereth long, *and* is kind; charity envieth not; charity vaunteth not itself, is not puffed up, doth not behave itself unseemly, seeketh not her own, is not easily provoked, thinketh no evil; rejoiceth not in iniquity, but rejoiceth in the truth; beareth all things, believeth all things, hopeth all things, endureth all things. Charity never faileth: but whether *there be* prophecies, they shall fail; whether *there be* tongues, they shall cease; whether *there be* knowledge, it shall vanish away. For we know in part, and we prophesy in part. But when that which is perfect is come, then that which is in part shall be done away. When I was a child, I spake as a child, I understood as a child, I thought as a child: but when I became a man, I put away childish things. For now we see through a glass, darkly; but then face to face: now I know in part; but then shall I know even as also I am known. And now abideth faith, hope, charity, these three; but the greatest of these *is* charity (1 Cor 13).

For God hath not given us the spirit of fear; but of power, and of love, and of a sound mind (2 Tim 1:7).

Seeing ye have purified your souls in obeying the truth through the Spirit unto unfeigned love of the brethren, *see that ye* love one another with a pure heart fervently (1 Peter 1:22).

And above all things have fervent charity among yourselves: for charity shall cover the multitude of sins (1 Peter 4:8).

And to godliness brotherly kindness; and to brotherly kindness charity (2 Peter 1:7).

For this is the message that ye heard from the beginning, that we should love one another. Not as Cain, *who* was of that wicked one, and slew his brother. And wherefore slew he him? Because his own works were evil, and his brother's righteous. Marvel not, my brethren, if the world hate you. We know that we have passed from death unto life, because we love the brethren. He that loveth not *his* brother abideth in death. Whosoever hateth his brother is a murderer: and ye know that no murderer hath eternal life abiding in him. Hereby perceive we the love *of God,* because he laid down his life for us: and we ought to lay down *our* lives for the brethren. But whoso hath this world's good, and seeth his brother have need, and shutteth up his bowels *of compassion* from him, how dwelleth the love of God in him? My little children, let us not love in word, neither in tongue; but in deed and in truth (1 John 3:11–18).

Beloved, let us love one another: for love is of God; and every one that loveth is born of God, and knoweth God. He that loveth not knoweth not God; for God is love. In this was manifested the love of God toward us, because that God sent his only begotten Son into the world, that we might live through him. Herein is love, not that we loved God, but that he loved us, and sent his Son *to be* the propitiation for our sins. Beloved, if God so loved us, we ought also to love one another. No man hath seen God at any time. If we love one another, God dwelleth in us, and his love is perfected in us.

Hereby know we that we dwell in him, and he in us, because he hath given us of his Spirit. And we have seen and do testify that the Father sent the Son *to be* the Savior of the world. Whosoever shall confess that Jesus is the Son of God, God dwelleth in him, and he in God. And we have known and believed the love that God hath to us. God is love; and he that dwelleth in love dwelleth in God, and God

in him. Herein is our love made perfect, that we may have boldness in the day of judgment: because as he is, so are we in this world. There is no fear in love; but perfect love casteth out fear: because fear hath torment. He that feareth is not made perfect in love. We love him, because he first loved us. If a man say, I love God, and hateth his brother, he is a liar: for he that loveth not his brother whom he hath seen, how can he love God whom he hath not seen? And this commandment have we from him, That he who loveth God love his brother also (1 John 4:7–21).

Whosoever believeth that Jesus is the Christ is born of God: and every one that loveth him that begat loveth him also that is begotten of him. By this we know that we love the children of God, when we love God, and keep his commandments. For this is the love of God, that we keep his commandments: and his commandments are not grievous (1 John 5:1–3).

And now I beseech thee, lady, not as though I wrote a new commandment unto thee, but that which we had from the beginning, that we love one another (2 John 5).

Biblical Examples: Gen 14:14–16; Exod 32:31, 32; Ruth 1–3; 1 Sam 20; Neh 5:10–15; Luke 7:36–50; John 3:16; 21:17; Acts 21:13; Rom 9:3; 2 Cor 2:4; Phil 1:3–5, 7, 8, 23–26; Col 1:8; Philem 5, 12, 16–21.

Further References: Exod 20:6; Deut 5:10; 7:9, 10:19; 13:13; 30:6; Josh 22:5; 23:6–8, 11; Ps 18:1; 31:23; 91:14; 97:10; 145:20; Isa 56:6, 7; Matt 10:37; Mark 12:29–33; John 8:42; 15:9, 12, 13; Rom 5:5; 8:28; 1 Cor 16:22; 2 Cor 5:8, 14, 15; Gal 5:6, 22; Eph 3:17–19; 4:3, 15; 5:2; Phil 1:9; 2:2; Col 2:2; 3:12–14; 1 Thess 3:12; 4:9; 1 Tim 1:5, 14; 6:2, 11; Heb 10:24; James 2:8; 1 John 2:10.

LUST (See also Covetousness)

Thou shalt not covet thy neighbour's house, thou shalt not covet thy neighbour's wife, nor his manservant, nor his maidservant, nor his ox, nor his ass, nor any thing that *is* thy neighbour's (Exod 20:17).

So I gave them up unto their own hearts' lust: *and* they walked in their own counsels (Ps 81:12).

To keep thee from the evil woman, from the flattery of the tongue of a strange woman. Lust not after her beauty in thine heart; neither let her take thee with her eyelids (Prov 6:24, 25).

But I say unto you, That whosoever looketh on a woman to lust after her hath committed adultery with her already in his heart (Matt 5:28).

And the cares of this world, and the deceitfulness of riches, and the lusts of other things entering in, choke the word, and it becometh unfruitful (Mark 4:19).

Wherefore God also gave them up to uncleanness through the lusts of their own hearts, to dishonour their own bodies between themselves: mortify therefore your members which are upon the earth; fornication, uncleanness, inordinate affection, evil concupiscence, and covetousness, which is idolatry (Col 3:5).

Flee also youthful lusts: but follow righteousness, faith, charity, peace, with them that call on the Lord out of a pure heart. (2 Tim 2:22).

But every man is tempted, when he is drawn away of his own lusts, and enticed. Then when lust hath conceived, it bringeth forth sin: and sin, when it is finished, bringeth forth death (James 1:14, 15).

Dearly beloved, I beseech *you* as strangers and pilgrims, abstain from fleshly lusts, which war against the soul (1 Peter 2:11).

According as his divine power hath given unto us all things that *pertain* unto life and godliness, through the knowledge of him that hath called us to glory and virtue: whereby are given unto us exceeding great and precious promises: that by these ye might be partakers of the divine nature, having escaped the corruption that is in the world through lust (2 Peter 1:3, 4).

For all that *is* in the world, the lust of the flesh, and the lust of the eyes, and the pride of life, is not of the Father, but is of the world. And the world passeth away, and the lust thereof: but he that doeth the will of God abideth for ever (1 John 2:16, 17).

Biblical Examples: Gen 13:5–14; 2 Sam 11:2–5; 13:1–33.

Further References: Ezek 16:23; John 8:44; 1 Cor 10: 6, 7; Eph 4:22; 1 Tim 6:9;

2 Tim 4:3, 4; Titus 1:12; James 4:1–3; 1 Peter 4:3; 2 Peter 2:4–10, 18; 3:3; Jude 16–18.

LYING (See also Deceit; Dishonesty)

Thou shalt not bear false witness against thy neighbour (Exod 20:16).

Thou shalt not raise a false report: put not thine hand with the wicked to be an unrighteous witness (Exod 23:1).

If a soul sin, and commit a trespass against the LORD, and lie unto his neighbour in that which was delivered him to keep, or in fellowship, or in a thing taken away by violence, or hath deceived his neighbour; or have found that which was lost, and lieth concerning it, and sweareth falsely; in any of all these that a man doeth, sinning therein: then it shall be, because he hath sinned, and is guilty, that he shall restore that which he took violently away, or the thing which he hath deceitfully gotten, or that which was delivered him to keep, or the lost thing which he found, or all that about which he hath sworn falsely; he shall even restore it in the principal, and shall add the fifth part more thereto, *and* give it unto him to whom it appertaineth, in the day of his trespass offering. And he shall bring his trespass offering unto the LORD, a ram without blemish out of the flock, with thy estimation, for a trespass offering, unto the priest: and the priest shall make an atonement for him before the LORD: and it shall be forgiven him for any thing of all that he hath done in trespassing therein (Lev 6:2–7).

God *is* not a man, that he should lie; neither the son of man, that he should repent: hath he said, and shall he not do *it?* or hath he spoken, and shall he not make it good? (Num 23:19).

For truly my words *shall* not *be* false: he that is perfect in knowledge *is* with thee (Job 36:4).

Thou shalt destroy them that speak leasing: the LORD will abhor the bloody and deceitful man. . . . For *there is* no faithfulness in their mouth; their inward part *is* very wickedness; their throat *is* an open sepulchre; they flatter with their tongue (Ps 5:6, 9).

His mouth is full of cursing and deceit

and fraud: under his tongue *is* mischief and vanity (Ps 10:7).

Thy tongue deviseth mischiefs; like a sharp razor, working deceitfully. Thou lovest evil more than good; *and* lying rather than to speak righteousness. Selah. Thou lovest all devouring words, O *thou* deceitful tongue. God shall likewise destroy thee for ever, he shall take thee away, and pluck thee out of *thy* dwelling place, and root thee out of the land of the living. Selah (Ps 52:2–5).

For the sin of their mouth *and* the words of their lips let them even be taken in their pride: and for cursing and lying *which* they speak. Consume *them* in wrath, consume *them,* that they *may* not *be:* and let them know that God ruleth in Jacob unto the ends of the earth. Selah (Ps 59:12, 13).

But the king shall rejoice in God; every one that sweareth by him shall glory: but the mouth of them that speak lies shall be stopped (Ps 63:11).

He that worketh deceit shall not dwell within my house: he that telleth lies shall not tarry in my sight (Ps 101:7).

Remove from me the way of lying: and grant me thy law graciously. . . . The proud have forged a lie against me: *but* I will keep thy precepts with *my* whole heart. . . . I hate and abhor lying: *but* thy law do I love (Ps 119:29, 69, 163).

These six *things* doth the LORD hate: yea, seven *are* an abomination unto him: a proud look, a lying tongue, and hands that shed innocent blood, an heart that deviseth wicked imaginations, feet that be swift in running to mischief, a false witness *that* speaketh lies, and he that soweth discord among brethren (Prov 6:16–19).

He that hideth hatred *with* lying lips, and he that uttereth a slander, *is* a fool (Prov 10:18).

The lip of truth shall be established for ever: but a lying tongue *is* but for a moment (Prov 12:19).

Lying lips *are* abomination to the LORD: but they that deal truly *are* his delight (Prov 12:22).

A righteous *man* hateth lying: but a wicked *man* is loathsome, and cometh to shame (Prov 13:5).

A true witness delivereth souls: but a deceitful *witness* speaketh lies (Prov 14:25).

Wherefore hear the word of the LORD, ye scornful men, that rule this people which *is* in Jerusalem. Because ye have said, We have made a covenant with death, and with hell are we at agreement; when the overflowing scourge shall pass through, it shall not come unto us: for we have made lies our refuge, and under falsehood have we hid ourselves: therefore thus saith the Lord GOD, Behold, I lay in Zion for a foundation a stone, a tried stone, a precious corner *stone,* a sure foundation: he that believeth shall not make haste. Judgment also will I lay to the line, and righteousness to the plummet: and the hail shall sweep away the refuge of lies, and the waters shall overflow the hiding place (Isa 28:14–17).

The instruments also of the churl *are* evil: he deviseth wicked devices to destroy the poor with lying words, even when the needy speaketh right (Isa 32:7).

And of whom hast thou been afraid or feared, that thou hast lied, and hast not remembered me, nor laid *it* to thy heart? have not I held my peace even of old, and thou fearest me not? (Isa 57:11).

Ye are of *your* father the devil, and the lusts of your father ye will do. He was a murderer from the beginning, and abode not in the truth, because there is no truth in him. When he speaketh a lie, he speaketh of his own: for he is a liar, and the father of it (John 8:44).

Wherefore putting away lying, speak every man truth with his neighbour: for we are members one of another. . . . Let no corrupt communication proceed out of your mouth, but that which is good to the use of edifying, that it may minister grace unto the hearers (Eph 4:25, 29).

Lie not one to another, seeing that ye have put off the old man with his deeds; and have put on the new *man,* which is renewed in knowledge after the image of him that created him (Col 3:9, 10).

Knowing this, that the law is not made for a righteous man, but for the lawless and disobedient, for the ungodly and for sinners, for unholy and profane, for murderers of fathers and murderers of mothers, for manslayers, for whoremongers, for them that defile themselves with mankind, for menstealers, for liars, for perjured persons, and if there be any other thing that is contrary to sound doctrine (1 Tim 1:9, 10).

Speaking lies in hypocrisy; having their conscience seared with a hot iron (1 Tim 4:2).

But the fearful, and unbelieving, and the abominable, and murderers, and whoremongers, and sorcerers, and idolaters, and all liars, shall have their part in the lake which burneth with fire and brimstone: which is the second death (Rev 21:8).

For without *are* dogs, and sorcerers, and whoremongers, and murderers, and idolaters, and whosoever loveth and maketh a lie (Rev 22:15).

Biblical Examples: Gen 3:4, 5; 4:9; 12:11–19; 26:7–10; 39:14–17; Exod 1:15–20; 32:1–24; 1 Sam 15:1–20; 19:12–17; 2 Kings 5:20–27; Job 13:4; Isa 59:3–13; Jer 9:3–8; Hos 4:1, 2; Mic 6:12; Nah 3:1; Matt 2:8; 26:69–75; 28:13–15; Mark 14:68–71; Acts 5:1–10; 16:20, 21.

Further References: Ps 31:18; 34:13; 50:19, 20; 55:21, 23; 58:3; 62:4; 109:2; 120:2–4; 144:8, 11; Prov 17:4, 7; 19:5, 22, 28; 21:6; 26:18–19, 24–28; 30:8, 9; Isa 28:14–17, 63:8; Jer 7:8, 28; 50:36, Zeph 3:13.

– M –

MAGIC (See also Astrology, Sorcery; Witchcraft)

And it came to pass in the morning that his spirit was troubled; and he sent and called for all the magicians of Egypt, and all the wise men thereof: and Pharaoh told them his dream; but *there was* none that could interpret them unto Pharaoh. And the thin ears devoured the seven good ears: and I told *this* unto the magicians; but *there was* none that could declare *it* to me (Gen 41:8, 24).

Then Pharaoh also called the wise men and the sorcerers: now the magicians of Egypt, they also did in like manner with their enchantments. And the magicians of Egypt did so with their enchantments: and Pharaoh's heart was hardened, neither did he hearken unto them; as the LORD had said (Exod 7:11, 22).

And the magicians did so with their enchantments, and brought up frogs upon the land of Egypt. . . . And the magicians did so with their enchantments to bring forth lice, but they could not: so there were lice upon man, and upon beast (Exod 8:7, 18).

And Saul disguised himself, and put on other raiment, and he went, and two men with him, and they came to the woman by night: and he said, I pray thee, divine unto me by the familiar spirit, and bring me *him* up, whom I shall name unto thee (1 Sam 28:8).

For the king of Babylon stood at the parting of the way, at the head of the two ways, to use divination: he made *his* arrows bright, he consulted with images, he looked in the liver (Ezek 21:21).

And in all matters of wisdom *and* under-standing, that the king inquired of them, he found them ten times better than all the magicians *and* astrologers that *were* in all his realm (Dan 1:20).

Then the king commanded to call the magicians, and the astrologers, and the sorcerers, and the Chaldeans, for to shew the king his dreams. So they came and stood before the king. And the king said unto them, I have dreamed a dream, and my spirit was troubled to know the dream. Then spake the Chaldeans to the king in Syriac, O king, live for ever: tell thy servants the dream, and we will shew the interpretation. The king answered and said to the Chaldeans, The thing is gone from me: if ye will not make known unto me the dream, with the interpretation thereof, ye shall be cut in pieces, and your houses shall be made in dunghill. But if ye shew the dream, and the interpretations thereof, ye shall receive of me gifts and rewards and great honour: therefore shew me the dream, and the interpretation thereof. They answered again and said, Let the king tell his servants the dream, and we will shew the interpretation of it. The king answered and said, I know of certainty that ye would gain the time, because ye see the thing is gone from me. But if ye will not make known unto me the dream, *there is but* one decree for you: for ye have prepared lying and corrupt words to speak before me, till the time be changed: therefore tell me the dream, and I shall know that ye can shew me the interpretation thereof.

The Chaldeans answered before the king, and said, There is not a man upon the earth that can shew the king's matter:

therefore *there is* no king, lord, nor ruler, *that* asked such things at any magician, or astrologer, or Chaldean. And *it is* a rare thing that the king requireth, and there is none other that can shew it before the king, except the gods, whose dwelling is not with flesh. For this cause the king was angry and very furious, and commanded to destroy all the wise *men* of Babylon. And the decree went forth that the wise *men* should be slain; and they sought Daniel and his fellows to be slain (Dan 2:2–13).

Then came in the magicians, the astrologers, the Chaldeans, and the soothsayers: and I told the dream before them; but they did not make known unto me the interpretation thereof (Dan 4:7).

But there was a certain man, called Simon, which beforetime in the same city used sorcery, and bewitched the people of Samaria, giving out that himself was some great one (Acts 8:9).

And when they had gone through the isle unto Paphos, they found a certain sorcerer, a false prophet, a Jew, whose name *was* Bar-jesus: Which was with the deputy of the country, Sergius Paulus, a prudent man; who called for Barnabas and Saul, and desired to hear the word of God. But Elymas the sorcerer (for so is his name by interpretation) withstood them, seeking to turn away the deputy from the faith (Acts 13:6–8).

And it came to pass, as we went to prayer, a certain damsel possessed with a spirit of divination met us, which brought her masters much gain by soothsaying (Acts 16:16).

Many of them also which used curious arts brought their books together, and burned them before all *men:* and they counted the price of them, and found *it* fifty thousand *pieces* of silver (Acts 19:19).

MALICE (See also Anger; Hatred; Revenge; Vengeance)

Thou shalt not raise a false report: put not thine hand with the wicked to be an unrighteous witness (Exod 23:1).

Thou shalt not curse the deaf, nor put a stumblingblock before the blind, but shalt fear thy God: I *am* the LORD.

Thou shalt not hate thy brother in thine heart: thou shalt in any wise rebuke thy neighbour, and not suffer sin upon him.

Thou shalt not avenge, nor bear any grudge against the children of thy people, but thou shalt love thy neighbour as thyself: I *am* the LORD (Lev 19:14, 17, 18).

Cursed *be* he that removeth his neighbour's landmark. And all the people shall say, Amen (Deut 27:17).

Mine enemies speak evil of me, When shall he die, and his name perish? (Ps 41:5).

They are corrupt, and speak wickedly *concerning* oppression: they speak loftily (Ps 73:8).

Surely thou wilt slay the wicked, O God: depart from me therefore, ye bloody men. For they speak against thee wickedly, *and* thine enemies take *thy name* in vain (Ps 139:19, 20).

Frowardness *is* in his heart, he deviseth mischief continually; he soweth discord. Therefore shall his calamity come suddenly; suddenly shall he be broken without remedy.

These six *things* doth the LORD hate: yea, seven *are* an abomination unto him: A proud look, a lying tongue, and hands that shed innocent blood, an heart that deviseth wicked imaginations, feet that be swift in running to mischief, a false witness *that* speaketh lies, and he that soweth discord among brethren (Prov 6:14–19).

He shutteth his eyes to devise froward things: moving his lips he bringeth evil to pass (Prov 16:30).

He that deviseth to do evil shall be called a mischievous person. . . . Rejoice not when thine enemy falleth, and let not thine heart be glad when he stumbleth: lest the LORD see *it,* and it displease him, and he turn away his wrath from him. . . . Say not, I will do so to him as he hath done to me: I will render to the man according to his work (Prov 24:8, 17, 18, 29).

As for his father, because he cruelly oppressed, spoiled his brother by violence, and did *that* which *is* not good among his people, lo, even he shall die in his iniquity (Ezek 18:18).

Woe to them that devise iniquity, and work evil upon their beds! when the morning is light, they practise it, because it is in the power of their hand (Mic 2:1).

Ye have heard that it hath been said, An eye for an eye, and a tooth for a tooth: but I say unto you, That ye resist not evil: but whosoever shall smite thee on thy right cheek, turn to him the other also. And if any man will sue thee at the law, and take away thy coat, let him have *thy* cloak also. And whosoever shall compel thee to go a mile, go with him twain (Matt 5:38–41).

But Jesus perceived their wickedness, and said, Why tempt ye me, *ye* hypocrites? (Matt 22:18).

And even as they did not like to retain God in *their* knowledge, God gave them over to a reprobate mind, to do those things which are not convenient; being filled with all unrighteousness, fornication, wickedness, covetousness, maliciousness; full of envy, murder, debate, deceit, malignity; whisperers, backbiters, haters of God, despiteful, proud, boasters, inventors of evil things, disobedient to parents, without understanding, covenant-breakers, without natural affection, implacable, unmerciful: who knowing the judgment of God, that they which commit such things are worthy of death, not only do the same, but have pleasure in them that do them (Rom 1:28–32).

Dearly beloved, avenge not yourselves, but *rather* give place unto wrath: for it is written, Vengeance *is* mine; I will repay, saith the Lord (Rom 12:19).

Therefore let us keep the feast, not with old leaven, neither with the leaven of malice and wickedness; but with the unleavened *bread* of sincerity and truth (1 Cor 5:8).

Brethren, be not children in understanding: howbeit in malice be ye children, but in understanding be men (1 Cor 14:20).

Now the works of the flesh are manifest, which are *these;* Adultery, fornication, uncleanness, lasciviousness, idolatry, witchcraft, hatred, variance, emulations, wrath, strife, seditions, heresies, envyings, murders, drunkenness, revellings, and such like: of the which I tell you before, as I have also told *you* in time past, that they which do such things shall not inherit the kingdom of God (Gal 5:19–21).

Let all bitterness, and wrath, and anger, and clamour, and evil speaking, be put away from you, with all malice: and be ye kind one to another, tenderhearted, forgiving one another, even as God for Christ's sake hath forgiven you (Eph 4:31, 32).

But now ye also put off all these; anger, wrath, malice, blasphemy, filthy communication out of your mouth (Col 3:8).

For we ourselves also were sometimes foolish, disobedient, deceived, serving divers lusts and pleasures, living in malice and envy, hateful, *and* hating one another (Titus 3:3).

Wherefore laying aside all malice, and all guile, and hypocrisies, and envies, and all evil speakings. . . . offer up spiritual sacrifices, acceptable to God by Christ Jesus (1 Peter 2:1, 5).

He that saith he is in the light, and hateth his brother, is in darkness even until now. He that loveth his brother abideth in the light, and there is none occasion of stumbling in him. But he that hateth his brother is in darkness, and walketh in darkness, and knoweth not whither he goeth, because that darkness hath blinded his eyes (1 John 2:9–11).

Biblical Examples: Gen 4:8; 21:10; 37; 1 Kings 19:1, 2; Ps 10:7–10, 14; 35:15–21; 55:3, 10, 11; 59:3–7; 64:2–6; 69:4, 10–12; 109:2–5, 16–18; 140:1–4; Isa 59:4–6; Ezek 25:3–17; 26:2, 3; Amos 1:11; Matt 14:3–10; John 18:22, 23; Acts 17:5; 23:12–14; 25:3.

Further References: Job 31:29, 30; Ps 74:20; Prov 26:2, 27; 30:14; Isa 29:20, 21; 32:6; Matt 18:28–35; Luke 6:29, 30; 1 John 3:10–15; 4:20; 3 John 10.

MARRIAGE (See also Adultery; Birth Control; Children; Divorce; Family; Husband-Wife Relations; Intermarriage; Monogamy; Sex and Sexuality)

And the LORD God said, *It is* not good that the man should be alone; I will make him an help meet for him. And out of the ground the LORD God formed every beast of the field, and every fowl of the air; and brought *them* unto Adam to see what he would call them: and whatsoever Adam called every living creature, that *was* the name thereof. And Adam gave names to all cattle, and to the fowl of the air, and to every beast of the field; but for Adam there was not found an help meet for him. And the LORD God caused a deep sleep to fall upon Adam, and he slept: and he took one of his ribs, and closed up the flesh instead thereof; and the rib, which the LORD God had taken from man, made he a woman, and brought her unto the man. And Adam said, This *is* now bone of my bones, and flesh of my flesh: she shall be called Woman, because she was taken out of Man. Therefore shall a man leave his father and his mother, and shall cleave unto his wife: and they shall be one flesh (Gen 2:18–24).

Thou shalt not commit adultery (Exod 20:14).

Whoso findeth a wife findeth a good *thing,* and obtaineth favour of the LORD (Prov 18:22).

It is better to dwell in a corner of the housetop, than with a brawling woman in a wide house. . . . *It is* better to dwell in the wilderness, than with a contentious and an angry woman (Prov 21:9, 19).

Take ye wives, and beget sons and daughters; and take wives for your sons, and give your daughters to husbands, that they may bear sons and daughters; that ye may be increased there, and not diminished (Jer 29:6).

And this have ye done again, covering the altar of the LORD with tears, with weeping, and with crying out, insomuch that he regardeth not the offering any more, or receiveth *it* with good will at your hand.

Yet ye say, Wherefore? Because the LORD hath been witness between thee and the wife of thy youth, against whom thou hast dealt treacherously: yet *is* she thy companion, and the wife of thy covenant. And did not he make one? Yet had he the residue of the spirit. And wherefore one? That he might seek a godly seed. Therefore take heed to your spirit, and let none deal treacherously against the wife of his youth. For the LORD, the God of Israel, saith that he hateth putting away: for *one* covereth violence with his garment, saith the LORD of hosts: therefore take heed to your spirit, that ye deal not treacherously (Mal 2:13–16).

The Pharisees also came unto him,

tempting him, and saying unto him, Is it lawful for a man to put away his wife for every cause? And he answered and said unto them, Have ye not read, that he which made *them* at the beginning made them male and female, and said, For this cause shall a man leave father and mother, and shall cleave to his wife: and they twain shall be one flesh? Wherefore they are no more twain, but one flesh. What therefore God hath joined together, let no man put asunder. They say unto him, Why did Moses then command to give a writing of divorcement, and to put her away? He saith unto them, Moses because of the hardness of your hearts suffered you to put away your wives: but from the beginning it was not so. And I say unto you, Whosoever shall put away his wife, except *it be* for fornication, and shall marry another, committeth adultery, and whoso marrieth her which is put away doth commit adultery.

His disciples say unto him, If the case of the man be so with *his* wife, it is not good to marry. But he said unto them, All *men* cannot receive this saying, save *they* to whom it is given. For there are some eunuchs, which were so born from *their* mother's womb: and there are some eunuchs, which were made eunuchs of men: and there be eunuchs, which have made themselves eunuchs for the kingdom of heaven's sake. He that is able to receive *it,* let him receive *it* (Matt 19:3–12).

The same day came to him the Sadducees, which say that there is no resurrection, and asked him, saying, Master, Moses said, If a man die, having no children, his brother shall marry his wife, and raise up seed unto his brother. Now there were with us seven brethren: and the first, when he had married a wife, deceased, and, having no issue, left his wife unto his brother: likewise the second also, and the third, unto the seventh. And last of all the woman died also. Therefore in the resurrection whose wife shall she be of the seven? for they all had her. Jesus answered and said unto them, Ye do err, not knowing the scriptures, nor the power of God. For in the resurrection they neither marry, nor are given in marriage, but are as the angels of God in heaven (Matt 22:23–30).

Whosoever putteth away his wife, and marrieth another, committeth adultery: and whosoever marrieth her that is put away from *her* husband committeth adultery (Luke 16:18).

Know ye not, brethren, (for I speak to them that know the law,) how that the law hath dominion over a man as long as he liveth? For the woman which hath an husband is bound by the law to *her* husband so long as he liveth; but if the husband be dead, she is loosed from the law of *her* husband. So then if, while *her* husband liveth, she be married to another man, she shall be called an adulteress: but if her husband be dead, she is free from that law; so that she is no adulteress, though she be married to another man (Rom 7:1–3).

Now concerning the things whereof ye wrote unto me: *It is* good for a man not to touch a woman. Nevertheless, *to avoid* fornication, let every man have his own wife, and let every woman have her own husband. Let the husband render unto the wife due benevolence: and likewise also the wife unto the husband. The wife hath not power of her own body, but the husband: and likewise also the husband hath not power of his own body, but the wife. Defraud ye not one the other, except *it be* with consent for a time, that ye may give yourselves to fasting and prayer; and come together again, that Satan tempt you not for your incontinency. But I speak this by permission, *and* not of commandment. For I would that all men were even as I myself. But every man hath his proper gift of God, one after this manner, and another after that.

I say therefore to the unmarried and widows, It is good for them if they abide even as I. But if they cannot contain, let them marry: for it is better to marry than to burn.

And unto the married I command, *yet* not I, but the Lord, Let not the wife depart from *her* husband: but and if she depart, let her remain unmarried, or be reconciled to *her* husband: and let not the husband put away *his* wife.

But to the rest speak I, not the Lord:

If any brother hath a wife that believeth not, and she be pleased to dwell with him, let him not put her away. And the woman which hath an husband that believeth not, and if he be pleased to dwell with her, let her not leave him. For the unbelieving husband is sanctified by the wife, and the unbelieving wife is sanctified by the husband: else were your children unclean; but now are they holy. But if the unbelieving depart let him depart. A brother or a sister is not under bondage in such *cases:* but God hath called us to peace. For what knowest thou, O wife, whether thou shalt save *thy* husband? or how knowest thou, O man, whether thou shalt save *thy* wife? But as God hath distributed to every man, as the Lord hath called every one, so let him walk. And so ordain I in all churches. Is any man called being circumcised? let him not become uncircumcised. Is any called in uncircumcision? let him not be circumcised. Circumcision is nothing, and uncircumcision is nothing, but the keeping of the commandments of God. Let every man abide in the same calling wherein he was called. Art thou called *being* a servant? care not for it: but if thou mayest be made free, use *it* rather. For he that is called in the Lord, *being* a servant, is the Lord's freeman: likewise also he that is called, *being* free, is Christ's servant. Ye are bought with a price; be not ye the servants of men. Brethren, let every man, wherein he is called, therein abide with God.

Now concerning virgins I have no commandment of the Lord: yet I give my judgment, as one that hath obtained mercy of the Lord to be faithful. I suppose therefore that this is good for the present distress, *I say,* that *it is* good for a man so to be. Art thou bound unto a wife? seek not to be loosed. Art thou loosed from a wife? seek not a wife. But and if thou marry, thou hast not sinned; and if a virgin marry, she hath not sinned. Nevertheless such shall have trouble in the flesh: but I spare you. But this I say, brethren, the time *is* short: it remaineth, that both they that have wives be as though they had none; and they that weep, as though they wept not; and they that rejoice, as though they rejoiced not; and they that buy, as though they possessed not; and they that use this world, as not abusing *it:* for the fashion of this world passeth away.

But I would have you without carefulness. He that is unmarried careth for the things that belong to the Lord, how he may please the Lord: but he that is married careth for the things that are of the world, how he may please *his* wife. There is difference *also* between a wife and a virgin. The unmarried woman careth for the things of the Lord, that she may be holy both in body and in spirit: but she that is married careth for the things of the world, how she may please *her* husband. And this I speak for your own profit; not that I may cast a snare upon you, but for that which is comely, and that ye may attend upon the Lord without distraction.

But if any man think that he behaveth himself uncomely toward his virgin, if she pass the flower of *her* age, and need so require, let him do what he will, he sinneth not: let them marry. Nevertheless he that standeth stedfast in his heart, having no necessity, but hath power over his own will, and hath so decreed in his heart that he will keep his virgin, doeth well. So then he that giveth *her* in marriage doeth well; but he that giveth *her* not in marriage doeth better.

The wife is bound by the law as long as her husband liveth; but if her husband be dead, she is at liberty to be married to whom she will; not in the Lord. But she is happier if she so abide, after my judgment: and I think also that I have the Spirit of god (1 Cor 7).

Submitting yourselves one to another in the fear of God. Wives, submit yourselves unto your own husbands, as unto the lord. For the husband is the head of the wife, even as Christ is the head of the church: and he is the savior of the body. Therefore as the church is subject unto Christ, so *let* the wives *be* to their own husbands in every thing. Husbands, love your wives, even as Christ also loved the church, and gave himself for it; that he might sanctify and cleanse it with the washing of water by the word, that he might present it to himself a glorious church, not having spot, or wrinkle, or any

such thing; but that it should be holy and without blemish. So ought men to love their wives as their own bodies. He that loveth his wife loveth himself. For no man ever yet hated his own flesh; but nourisheth and cherisheth it, even as the Lord the church: for we are members of his body, of his flesh, and of his bones. For this cause shall a man leave his father and mother, and shall be joined unto his wife, and they two shall be one flesh. This is a great mystery: but I speak concerning Christ and the church. Nevertheless let every one of you in particular so love his wife even as himself; and the wife *see* that she reverence *her* husband (Eph 5:21–33).

Wives, submit yourselves unto your own husbands, as it is fit in the Lord. Husbands, love *your* wives, and be not bitter against them. (Col 3:18, 19).

A bishop then must be blameless, the husband of one wife, vigilant, sober, of good behavior, given to hospitality, apt to teach; Not given to wine, no striker, not greedy of filthy lucre; but patient, not a brawler, not covetous; One that ruleth well his own house, having his children in subjection with all gravity; (for if a man know not how to rule his own house, how shall he take care of the church of God?) (1 Tim 3:2–5).

I will therefore that the younger women marry, bear children, guide the house, give none occasion to the adversary to speak reproachfully (1 Tim 5:14).

Marriage *is* honourable in all, and the bed undefiled: but whoremongers and adulterers God will judge (Heb. 13:4).

Likewise, ye wives, *be* in subjection to your own husbands; that, if any obey not the word, they also may without the word be won by the conversation of the wives; while they behold your chaste conversation *coupled* with fear. Whose adorning let it not be that outward *adorning* of plaiting the hair, and of wearing of gold, or of putting on of apparel; but *let it be* the hidden man of the heart, in that which is not corruptible, *even the ornament* of a meek and quiet spirit, which is in the sight of God of great price. For after this manner in the old time the holy women also, who trusted in God, adorned themselves, being in subjection unto their own husbands: even as Sara obeyed Abraham, calling him lord: whose daughters ye are, as long as ye do well, and are not afraid with any amazement. Likewise, ye husbands, dwell with *them* according to knowledge, giving honour unto the wife, as unto the weaker vessel, and as being heirs together of the grace of life; that your prayers be not hindered (1 Peter 3: 1–7).

Biblical Examples: Gen 4:19; 11:29; 21:21; 24:3; 25:1; 29:15–30; 38:8; Deut 21:11–15; 25:5–10; Judg 8:30; 14:2; 21:21–23; Ruth 4:1–11; 1 Sam 17:25; 27:3; 2 Sam 3:14; 1 Kings 11:1–3; 2 Chron 11:18–21; Matt 1:18; 22:11, 12; 25:6; Mark 6:17, 18; Luke 1:27; John 2:1–5.

Further References: Exod 22:17; Lev 20:19–21; 21:1, 7, 13–15; Deut 13:6–10; 21:10–14; 24:1–5; Matt 19:29; Mark 10:2–12; 12:19, 20, 24, 25; Luke 14:26; 20:28; 1 Cor 9:5; 11:11, 12; 1 Thess 4:3–6; 1 Tim 4:1–3.

MATERIALISM (See also Economics: Extravagance; Pleasure, Lover of; Property; Wealth)

He hath swallowed down riches, and he shall vomit them up again: God shall cast them out of his belly (Job 20:15).

If I have made gold my hope, or have said to the fine gold, *Thou art* my confidence; if I rejoiced because my wealth *was* great, and because mine hand had gotten much; if I beheld the sun when it shined, or the moon walking *in* brightness; and my heart hath been secretly enticed, or my mouth hath kissed my hand: this also *were* an iniquity *to be punished by* the judge: for I should have denied the God *that is* above (Job 31:24–28).

So *are* the ways of every one that is greedy of gain; *which* taketh away the life of the owners thereof (Prov 1:19).

He that is greedy of gain troubleth his own house; but he that hateth gifts shall live (Prov 15:27).

He that loveth pleasure *shall be* a poor man: he that loveth wine and oil shall not be rich. The wicked *shall be* a ransom for the righteous, and the transgressor for the upright. *It is* better to dwell in the wilderness, than with a contentious and an angry woman. *There is* treasure to be desired

and oil in the dwelling of the wise; but a foolish man spendeth it up (Prov 21:17–20).

Labour not to be rich: cease from thine own wisdom. Wilt thou set thine eyes upon that which is not? for *riches* certainly make themselves wings; they fly away as an eagle toward heaven (Prov 23:4, 5).

There is one *alone,* and *there is* not a second; yea, he hath neither child nor brother: yet *is there* no end of all his labour; neither is his eye satisfied with riches; neither *saith he,* For whom do I labour, and bereave my soul of good? This *is* also vanity, yea, it *is* a sore travail (Eccl 4:8).

He that loveth silver shall not be satisfied with silver; nor he that loveth abundance with increase: this *is* also vanity. When goods increase, they are increased that eat them: and what good *is there* to the owners thereof, saving the beholding *of them* with their eyes? (Eccl 5:10, 11).

Woe unto them that join house to house, *that* lay field to field, till *there be* no place, that they may be placed alone in the midst of the earth! (Isa 5:8).

Lay not up for yourselves treasures upon earth, where moth and rust doth corrupt, and where thieves break through and steal: but lay up for yourselves treasures in heaven, where neither moth nor rust doth corrupt, and where thieves do not break through nor steal: for where your treasure is, there will your heart be also (Matt 6:19–21).

No man can serve two masters: for either he will hate the one, and love the other; or else he will hold to the one, and despise the other. Ye cannot serve God and mammon. Therefore I say unto you, Take no thought for your life, what ye shall eat, or what ye shall drink; nor yet for your body, what ye shall put on. Is not the life more than meat, and the body than raiment? (Matt 6:24, 25).

Therefore take no thought, saying, What shall we eat? or, What shall we drink? or, Wherewithal shall we be clothed? (For after all these things do the Gentiles seek:) for your heavenly Father knoweth that ye have need of all these things. But seek ye first the kingdom of God, and his righteousness; and all these things shall be added unto you (Matt 6:31–33).

He also that received seed among the thorns is he that heareth the word; and the care of this world, and the deceitfulness of riches, choke the word, and he becometh unfruitful (Matt 13:22).

For what is a man profited, if he shall gain the whole world, and lose his own soul? or what shall a man give in exchange for his soul? (Matt 16:26).

But they that will be rich fall into temptation and a snare, and *into* many foolish and hurtful lusts, which drown men in destruction and perdition. For the love of money is the root of all evil: which while some coveted after, they have erred from the faith, and pierced themselves through with many sorrows (1 Tim 6:9, 10).

Ye lust, and have not: ye kill, and desire to have, and cannot obtain: ye fight and war, yet ye have not, because ye ask not (James 4:2).

Go to now, ye that say, Today or tomorrow we will go into such a city, and continue there a year, and buy and sell, and get gain: Whereas ye know not what *shall be* on the morrow. For what *is* your life? It is even a vapour, that appeareth for a little time, and then vanisheth away (James 4:13, 14).

Love not the world, neither the things *that are* in the world. If any man love the world, the love of the Father is not in him (1 John 2:15).

Biblical Examples: Jer 8:10; Ezek 22:12, 13; Mic 3:11; Luke 12:16–31; 16:19–31; Acts 5:1–11.

Further References: Neh 5:1–13; Job 21:7–15; Prov 21:25, 26; 30:8, 9; Jer 17:11; 51:13; Hab 2:15, 16; Matt 19:16–25; Mark 4:19; 10:17–25; Luke 8:14; 12:15, 33, 34; 16:9–13; 18:18–25; Phil 3:18, 19; Col 3:2, 5, 6; 1 Peter 5:2; Jude 11.

MATURITY (See Aging)

MEEKNESS (See Humility)

MENTAL HEALTH (See also Anger; Courage; Covetousness; Envy; Gluttony; Godliness; Greed; Hatred; Humility; Jealousy; Love; Malice; Patience; Pride; Self-Control; Unselfishness)

Thou wilt keep *him* in perfect peace, *whose* mind *is* stayed *on thee:* because he trusteth in thee (Isa 26:3).

Take therefore no thought for the morrow: for the morrow shall take thought for the things of itself. Sufficient unto the day *is* the evil thereof (Matt 6:34).

And be not conformed to this world: but be ye transformed by the renewing of your mind, that ye may prove what *is* that good, and acceptable, and perfect, will of God (Rom 12:2).

Let this mind be in you, which was also in Christ Jesus: who, being in the form of God, thought it not robbery to be equal with God: but made himself of no reputation, and took upon him the form of a servant, and was made in the likeness of men: and being found in fashion as a man, he humbled himself, and became obedient unto death, even the death of the cross (Phil 2:5–8).

Be careful for nothing; but in every thing by prayer and supplication with thanksgiving let your requests be made known unto God. And the peace of God, which passeth all understanding, shall keep your hearts and minds through Christ Jesus. Finally, brethren, whatsoever things are true, whatsoever things *are* honest, whatsoever things *are* just, whatsoever things *are* pure, whatsoever things *are* lovely, whatsoever things *are* of good report; if *there be* any virtue, and if *there be* any praise, think on these things (Phil 4:6–8).

Not that I speak in respect of want: for I have learned, in whatsoever state I am; *therewith* to be content. I know both how to be abased, and I know how to abound: every where and in all things I am instructed both to be full and to be hungry, both to abound and to suffer need. I can do all things through Christ which strengtheneth me (Phil 4:11–13).

But godliness with contentment is great gain. For we brought nothing into *this* world, *and it is* certain we can carry nothing out. And having food and raiment let us be therewith content (1 Tim 6:6–8).

Further References: Ps 23:1–6; Luke

12:11, 12, 25, 26; 1 Cor 7:32; Phil 4:6; 1 Peter 5:7.

MINISTRY (See also Aging; Alcohol and Alcoholism; Charity; Daily Work; Economics; Family; Orphans; Poverty; Race Relations; Sex and Sexuality; Suffering and Death; Widows)

If I have withheld the poor from *their* desire, or have caused the eyes of the widow to fail; or have eaten my morsel myself alone, and the fatherless hath not eaten thereof; (for from my youth he was brought up with me, as *with* a father, and I have guided her from my mother's womb;) if I have seen any perish for want of clothing, or any poor without covering; if his loins have not blessed me, and *if* he were *not* warmed with the fleece of my sheep; if I have lifted up my hand against the fatherless, when I saw my help in the gate: *then* let mine arm fall from my shoulder blade, and mine arm be broken from the bone. For destruction *from* God *was* a terror to me, and by reason of his highness I could not endure (Job 31:16–23).

For I was an hungered, and ye gave me meat: I was thirsty, and ye gave me drink: I was a stranger, and ye took me in: naked, and ye clothed me: I was sick, and ye visited me: I was in prison, and ye came unto me. Then shall the righteous answer him, saying, Lord, when saw we thee an hungered, and fed *thee?* or thirsty, and gave *thee* drink? When saw we thee a stranger, and took *thee* in? or naked, and clothed thee? Or when saw we thee sick, or in prison, and came unto thee? And the King shall answer and say unto them, Verily I say unto you, Inasmuch as ye have done *it* unto one of the least of these my brethren, ye have done *it* unto me (Matt 25:35–40).

But Jesus called them *to him,* and saith unto them, Ye know that they which are accounted to rule over the Gentiles exercise lordship over them; and their great ones exercise authority upon them. But so shall it not be among you: but whosoever will be great among you, shall be your minister: and whosoever of you will be the chiefest, shall be servant of all. For even the Son of man came not to be minis-

tered unto, but to minister, and to give his life a ransom for many (Mark 10:42–45).

Then said he also to him that bade him, When thou makest a dinner or a supper, call not thy friends, nor thy brethren, neither thy kinsmen, nor *thy* rich neighbours; lest they also bid thee again, and a recompence be made thee. But when thou makest a feast, call the poor, the maimed, the lame, the blind: and thou shalt be blessed; for they cannot recompense thee: for thou shalt be recompensed at the resurrection of the just (Luke 14:12–14).

I have shewed you all things, how that so labouring ye ought to support the weak, and to remember the words of the Lord Jesus, how he said, It is more blessed to give than to receive (Acts 20:35).

Having then gifts differing according to the grace that is given to us, whether prophecy, *let us prophesy* according to the proportion of faith; or ministry, *let us wait* on *our* ministering: or he that teacheth, on teaching; or he that exhorteth, on exhortation: he that giveth, *let him do it* with simplicity; he that ruleth, with diligence; he that sheweth mercy, with cheerfulness. *Let* love be without dissimulation. Abhor that which is evil; cleave to that which is good. *Be* kindly affectioned one to another with brotherly love; in honour preferring one another; not slothful in business; fervent in spirit; serving the Lord; rejoicing in hope; patient in tribulation; continuing instant in prayer; distributing to the necessity of saints; given to hospitality (Rom 12:6–13).

Bless them which persecute you: bless, and curse not. Rejoice with them that do rejoice, and weep with them that weep (Rom 12:14, 15).

And he gave some, apostles; and some, prophets; and some, evangelists; and some, pastors and teachers; for the perfecting of the saints, for the work of the ministry, for the edifying of the body of Christ: till we all come in the unity of the faith, and of the knowledge of the Son of God, unto a perfect man, unto the measure of the stature of the fulness of Christ: that we *henceforth* be no more children, tossed to and fro, and carried about with every wind of doctrine, by the sleight of men, *and* cunning craftiness, whereby they lie in wait to deceive (Eph 4:11–14).

But be ye doers of the word, and not hearers only, deceiving your own selves. For if any be a hearer of the word, and not a doer, he is like unto a man beholding his natural face in a glass: for he beholdeth himself, and goeth his way, and straightway forgetteth what manner of man he was. But whoso looketh into the perfect law of liberty, and continueth *therein,* he being not a forgetful hearer, but a doer of the work, this man shall be blessed in his deed. If any man among you seem to be religious, and bridleth not his tongue, but deceiveth his own heart, this man's religion *is* vain. Pure religion and undefiled before God and the Father is this, To visit the fatherless and widows in their affliction, *and* to keep himself unspotted from the world (James 1:22–27).

If a brother or sister be naked, and destitute of daily food, and one of you say unto them, Depart in peace, but *ye* warmed and filled; notwithstanding ye give them not those things which are needful to the body; what *doth it* profit? (James 2:15, 16).

But whoso hath this world's good, and seeth his brother have need, and shutteth up his bowels *of compassion* from him, how dwelleth the love of God in him? (1 John 3:17).

Biblical Examples: Judg 19:16–21; Ruth 2; Jesus' Ministry in the Gospels; Luke 10:33–35; 14:8; Acts 2:44–46; 4:32–37; 6:1–4; 11:29, 30; Rom 15:25–27; 1 Cor 16:1–3; 2 Cor 8:1–15, 24; 9:1–15; Gal 2:10; Phil 4:10–18; Heb 6:10.

Further References: Ps 41:1; 112:9; Prov 22:9; Isa 58:6, 7, 10, 11; Mark 9:41; Luke 3:11; 11:41; 1 Cor 13:13; 2 Cor 8:8–15; 1 Tim 5:16; 6:18; James 5:14.

MINORITY RIGHTS (See Injustice; Race Relations)

MIXED MARRIAGES (See Husband-Wife Relations; Intermarriage; Marriage)

MODERATION (See Temperance)

MODESTY (See Body, Human; Dress)

MONOGAMY (See also Husband-Wife Relations; Marriage)

And the LORD God said, *It is* not good that the man should be alone; I will make him an help meet for him. And out of the ground the LORD God formed every beast of the field, and every fowl of the air; and brought *them* unto Adam to see what he would call them: and whatsoever Adam called every living creature, that *was* the name thereof. And Adam gave names to all cattle, and to the fowl of the air, and to every beast of the field; but for Adam there was not found an help meet for him. And the LORD God caused a deep sleep to fall upon Adam, and he slept: and he took one of his ribs, and closed up the flesh instead thereof; and the rib, which the LORD God had taken from man, made he a woman, and brought her unto the man. And Adam said, This *is* now bone of my bones, and flesh of my flesh: she shall be called Woman, because she was taken out of Man. Therefore shall a man leave his father and his mother, and shall cleave unto his wife: and they shall be one flesh (Gen 2:18–24).

The Pharisees also came unto him, tempting him, and saying unto him, Is it lawful for a man to put away his wife for every cause? And he answered and said unto them, Have ye not read, that he which made *them* at the beginning made them male and female, and said, For this cause shall a man leave father and mother, and shall cleave to his wife: and they twain shall be one flesh? Wherefore they are no more twain, but one flesh. What therefore God hath joined together, let not man put asunder (Matt 19:3–6).

For I am jealous over you with godly jealousy: for I have espoused you to one husband, that I may present *you as* a chaste virgin to Christ (2 Cor 11:2).

Submitting yourselves one to another in the fear of God. Wives, submit yourselves unto your own husbands, as unto the Lord. For the husband is the head of the wife, even as Christ is the head of the church: and he is the saviour of the body. Therefore as the church is subject unto Christ, so *let* the wives *be* to their own husbands in every thing. Husbands, love your wives, even as Christ also loved the church, and gave himself for it; that he might sanctify and cleanse it with the washing of water by the word, that he might present it to himself a glorious church, not having spot, or wrinkle, or any such thing; but that it should be holy and without blemish. So ought men to love their wives as their own bodies. He that loveth his wife loveth himself. For no man ever yet hated his own flesh; but nourisheth and cherisheth it, even as the Lord the church: for we are members of his body, of his flesh, and of his bones. For this cause shall a man leave his father and mother, and shall be joined unto his wife, and they two shall be one flesh. This is a great mystery: but I speak concerning Christ and the church. Nevertheless let every one of you in particular so love his wife even as himself; and the wife *see* that she reverence *her* husband (Eph 5:21–33).

A bishop then must be blameless, the husband of one wife, vigilant, sober, of good behaviour, given to hospitality, apt to teach; not given to wine, no striker, not greedy of filthy lucre; but patient, not a brawler, not covetous; one that ruleth well his own house, having his children in subjection with all gravity; (for if a man know not how to rule his own house, how shall he take care of the church of God?) (1 Tim 3:2–5).

Biblical Examples: Hos 2; Matt 9:15.
Further References: Isa 4:1; Jer 3:1–20.

MURDER (See Homicide)

– N –

NARCOTICS (See Drugs)

NEIGHBOR

Thou shalt not bear false witness against thy neighbour (Exod 20:16).

If thou meet thine enemy's ox or his ass going astray, thou shalt surely bring it back to him again. If thou see the ass of him that hateth thee lying under his burden, and wouldest forbear to help him, thou shalt surely help with him (Exod 23:4, 5).

And ye shall not swear by my name falsely, neither shalt thou profane the name of thy God: I *am* the LORD.

Thou shalt not defraud thy neighbour, neither rob *him:* the wages of him that is hired shall not abide with thee all night until the morning.

Thou shalt not curse the deaf, nor put a stumblingblock before the blind, but shalt fear thy God: I *am* the LORD.

Ye shall do no unrighteousness in judgment: thou shalt not respect the person of the poor, nor honour the person of the mighty: *but* in righteousness shalt thou judge thy neighbour.

Thou shalt not go up and down *as* a talebearer among thy people: neither shalt thou stand against the blood of thy neighbour: I *am* the LORD.

Thou shalt not hate thy brother in thine heart: thou shalt in any wise rebuke thy neighbour, and not suffer sin upon him.

Thou shalt not avenge, nor bear any grudge against the children of thy people, but thou shalt love thy neighbour as thyself: I *am* the LORD (Lev 19:12–18).

Lord, who shall abide in thy tabernacle? who shall dwell in thy holy hill? He that walketh uprightly, and worketh righteousness, and speaketh the truth in his heart. *He that* backbiteth not with his tongue, nor doeth evil to his neighbour, nor taketh up a reproach against his neighbour (Ps 15:1–3).

Say not unto thy neighbour, Go, and come again, and tomorrow I will give; when thou hast it by thee. Devise not evil against thy neighbour, seeing he dwelleth securely by thee (Prov 3:28, 29).

Therefore all things whatsoever ye would that men should do to you, do ye even so to them: for this is the law and the prophets (Matt 7:12).

And, behold, a certain lawyer stood up, and tempted him, saying, Master, what shall I do to inherit eternal life? He said unto him, What is written in the law? how readest thou? And he answering said, Thou shalt love the Lord thy God with all thy heart, and with all thy soul, and with all thy strength, and with all thy mind; and thy neighbour as thyself. And he said unto him, Thou hast answered right: this do, and thou shalt live (Luke 10:25–28).

As we have therefore opportunity, let us do good unto all *men,* especially unto them who are of the household of faith (Gal 6:10).

If ye fulfil the royal law according to the scripture, Thou shalt love thy neighbour as thyself, ye do well (James 2:8).

Biblical Examples: Matt 25:34–46; Luke 10:25–37.

Further References: Lev 6:2–5; Deut 22:1–4; Jer 22:13; Zech 8:16; Matt 19:19; 22:39; Mark 12:31; Rom 13:9, 10; 16:2; Gal 5:14; 6:10; James 2:8, 9.

NONRESISTANCE

Thou shalt not kill (Exod 20:13). Blessed *are* they which are persecuted for righteousness' sake: for theirs is the kingdom of heaven (Matt 5:10).

Ye have heard that it hath been said, An eye for an eye, and a tooth for a tooth: but I say unto you, That ye resist not evil: but whosoever shall smite thee on thy right cheek, turn to him the other also. And if any man will sue thee at the law, and take away thy coat, let him have *thy* cloak also. And whosoever shall compel thee to go a mile, go with him twain (Matt 5:38–41).

But I say unto you which hear, Love your enemies, do good to them which hate you, bless them that curse you, and pray for them which despitefully use you. And unto him that smiteth thee on the *one* cheek offer also the other; and him that taketh away thy cloak forbid not *to take thy* coat also. Give to every man that asketh of thee; and of him that taketh away thy goods ask *them* not again. And as ye would that men should do to you, do ye also to them likewise (Luke 6:27–31).

Be of the same mind one toward another. Mind not high things, but condescend to men of low estate. Be not wise in your own conceits. Recompense to no man evil for evil. Provide things honest in the sight of all men. If it be possible, as much as lieth in you, live peaceably with all men. Dearly beloved, avenge not yourselves, but *rather* give place unto wrath: for it is written, Vengeance *is* mine; I will repay, saith the Lord. Therefore if thine enemy hunger, feed him; if he thirst, give him drink: for in so doing thou shalt heap coals of fire on his head. Be not overcome of evil, but overcome evil with good (Rom 12:16–21).

Servants, *be* subject to *your* masters with all fear; not only to the good and gentle, but also to the froward. For this *is* thankworthy, if a man for conscience toward God endure grief, suffering wrongfully. For what glory *is it*, if, when ye be buffeted for your faults, ye shall take it patiently? but if, when ye do well, and suffer *for it*, ye take it patiently, this *is* acceptable with God. For even hereunto were ye called: because Christ also suffered for us, leaving us an example, that ye should follow his steps: who did no sin, neither was guile found in his mouth: who, when he was reviled, reviled not again; when he suffered, he threatened not; but committed *himself* to him that judgeth righteously (1 Peter 2:18–23).

Biblical Examples: Matt 26:52, 53; Mark 14:46–50; Luke 22:50–54; John 18:10–12.

Further References: Rom 13:1, 2.

– O –

OATHS (See also Tongue)

Or if a soul swear, pronouncing with *his* lips to do evil, or to do good, whatsoever *it be* that a man shall pronounce with an oath, and it be hid from him; when he knoweth *of it*, then he shall be guilty in one of these (Lev 5:4).

And the LORD spake unto Moses, saying, If a soul sin, and commit a trespass against the LORD, and lie unto his neighbour in that which was delivered him to keep, or in fellowship, or in a thing taken away by violence, or hath deceived his neighbour; or have found that which was lost, and lieth concerning it, and sweareth falsely; in any of all these that a man doeth, sinning therein: then it shall be, because he hath sinned, and is guilty, that he shall restore that which he took violently away, or the thing which he hath deceitfully gotten, or that which was delivered him to keep, or the lost thing which he found, or all that about which he hath sworn falsely; he shall even restore it in the principal, and shall add the fifth part more thereto, *and* give it unto him to whom it appertaineth, in the day of his trespass offering. (Lev 6:1–5).

When thou vowest a vow unto God, defer not to pay it; for *he hath* no pleasure in fools: pay that which thou hast vowed. Better *is it* that thou shouldest not vow, than that thou shouldest vow and not pay. Suffer not thy mouth to cause thy flesh to sin; neither say thou before the angel, that it *was* an error: wherefore should God be angry at thy voice, and destroy the work of thine hands? (Eccl 5:4–6).

Again, ye have heard that it hath been said by them of old time, Thou shalt not forswear thyself, but shalt perform unto the Lord thine oaths: but I say unto you, Swear not at all; neither by heaven; for it is God's throne: nor by the earth; for it is his footstool: neither by Jerusalem; for it is the city of the great King. Neither shalt thou swear by thy head, because thou canst not make one hair white or black. But let your communication be, Yea, yea; Nay, nay: for whatsoever is more than these cometh of evil (Matt 5:33–37).

And, Whosoever shall swear by the altar, it is nothing; but whosoever sweareth by the gift that is upon it, he is guilty. *Ye* fools and blind: for whether *is* greater, the gift, or the altar that sanctifieth the gift? Whoso therefore shall swear by the altar, sweareth by it, and by all things thereon. And whoso shall swear by the temple, sweareth by it, and by him that dwelleth therein. And he that shall swear by heaven, sweareth by the throne of God, and by him that sitteth thereon (Matt 23:18–22).

But above all things, my brethren, swear not, neither by heaven, neither by the earth, neither by any other oath: but let your yea be yea; and *your* nay, nay; lest ye fall into condemnation (James 5:12).

Biblical Examples: Gen 24:2, 3; Exod 13:19; Josh 9:18–20; 1 Sam 14:24; Isa 45:23; Jer 7:8, 9; Dan 12:7; Matt 14:7–9; 26:63; 6:26; Acts 23:12–14; Gal 1:20; Heb 6:13; Rev 10:5, 6.

Further References: Exod 22:10, 11; 23:1; Num 5:19–24; 1 Kings 8:31, 32; Ps 15:1–4; Jer 4:2; Heb 6:16.

OBEDIENCE (See Authority; Decision-making)

OBSCENITY (See Cursing; Sex and Sexuality)

OCCULT (See Astrology; Demons; Sorcery; Witchcraft)

OPPRESSION (See also Violence)

Now therefore, behold, the cry of the children of Israel is come unto me: and I have also seen the oppression wherewith the Egyptians oppress them (Exod 3:9).

Thou shalt neither vex a stranger, nor oppress him: for ye were strangers in the land of Egypt.

Ye shall not afflict any widow, or fatherless child. If thou afflict them in any wise, and they cry at all unto me, I will surely hear their cry; and my wrath shall wax hot, and I will kill you with the sword; and your wives shall be widows, and your children fatherless (Exod 22:21–24).

Thou shalt not deliver unto his master the servant which is escaped from his master unto thee: he shall dwell with thee, *even* among you, in that place which he shall choose in one of thy gates, where it liketh him best: thou shalt not oppress him (Deut 23:15, 16).

Thou shalt not oppress an hired servant *that is* poor and needy, *whether he be* of thy brethren, or of thy strangers that *are* in thy land within thy gates (Deut 24:14).

LORD, thou hast heard the desire of the humble: thou wilt prepare their heart, thou wilt cause thine ear to hear: to judge the fatherless and the oppressed, that the man of the earth may no more oppress (Ps 10:17, 18).

Thine enemies roar in the midst of thy congregations; they set up their ensigns *for* signs (Ps 74:4).

He that oppresseth the poor reproacheth his Maker: but he that honoureth him hath mercy on the poor (Prov 14:31).

Rob not the poor, because he *is* poor: neither oppress the afflicted in the gate (Prov 22:22).

A poor man that oppresseth the poor *is like* a sweeping rain which leaveth no food (Prov 28:3).

So I returned, and considered all the oppressions that are done under the sun: and behold the tears of *such as were* oppressed, and they had no comforter; and on the side of their oppressors *there was* power; but they had no comforter (Eccl 4:1).

Wash you, make you clean; put away the evil of your doings from before mine eyes; cease to do evil; learn to do well; seek judgment, relieve the oppressed, judge the fatherless, plead for the widow (Isa 1:16, 17).

For if ye throughly amend your ways and your doings; if ye throughly execute judgment between a man and his neighbour; *if* ye oppress not the stranger, the fatherless, and the widow, and shed not innocent blood in this place, neither walk after other gods to your hurt: then will I cause you to dwell in this place, in the land that I gave to your fathers, for ever and ever (Jer 7:5–7).

In the land shall be his possession in Israel: and my princes shall no more oppress my people; and *the rest of* the land shall they give to the house of Israel according to their tribes (Ezek 45:8).

Hear this word, ye kine of Bashan, that *are* in the mountain of Samaria, which oppress the poor, which crush the needy, which say to their masters, Bring, and let us drink (Amos 4:1).

Hearken, my beloved brethren, Hath not God chosen the poor of this world rich in faith, and heirs of the kingdom which he hath promised to them that love him? But ye have despised the poor. Do not rich men oppress you, and draw you before the judgment seats? Do not they blaspheme that worthy name by the which ye are called? (James 2:5–7).

Biblical Examples: Gen 16:6; Exod 1:10–22; 1 Kings 12:14; Ezek 22:29; Amos 5:11, 12; 8:4–6; Mic 2:1–3; Hab 2:5–11; Matt 23:2–4.

Further References: Job 27:13–23; Ps 9:9; 12:5; 62:10; 119:134; Eccl 5:8; 7:7; Isa 33:15, 16; 58:6.

ORPHANS (See also Ministry; Widows; Youth)

Ye shall not afflict any widow, or fatherless child. If thou afflict them in any wise, and they cry at all unto me, I will surely hear their cry; and my wrath shall wax hot, and I will kill you with the sword; and your wives shall be widows, and your children fatherless (Exod 22:22–24).

When thou hast made an end of tithing all the tithes of thine increase the third year, *which is* the year of tithing, and hast given *it* unto the Levite, the stranger, the fatherless, and the widow, that they may eat within thy gates, and be filled (Deut 26:12).

Thou hast seen *it:* for thou beholdest mischief and spite, to requite *it* with thy hand: the poor committeth himself unto thee; thou art the helper of the fatherless (Ps 10:14).

A father of the fatherless, and a judge of the widows, *is* God in his holy habitation. God setteth the solitary in families: he bringeth out those which are bound with chains: but the rebellious dwell in a dry *land* (Ps 68:5, 6).

The Lord preserveth the strangers; he relieveth the fatherless and widow: but the way of the wicked he turneth upside down (Ps 146:9).

Wash you, make you clean; put away the evil of your doings from before mine eyes; cease to do evil; learn to do well; seek judgment, relieve the oppressed, judge the fatherless, plead for the widow (Isa 1:16, 17).

They are waxen fat, they shine: yea, they overpass the deeds of the wicked: they judge not the cause, the cause of the fatherless, yet they prosper; and the right of the needy do they not judge (Jer 5:28).

For if ye throughly amend your ways and your doings; if ye throughly execute judgment between a man and his neighbour; *if* ye oppress not the stranger, the fatherless, and the widow, and shed not innocent blood in this place, neither walk after other gods to your hurt: then will I cause you to dwell in this place, in the land that I gave to your fathers, for ever and ever (Jer 7:5–7).

In thee have they set light by father and mother; in the midst of thee have they dealt by oppression with the stranger: in thee have they vexed the fatherless and the widow (Ezek 22:7).

And I will come near to you to judgment; and I will be a swift witness against the sorcerers, and against the adulterers, and against false swearers, and against those that oppress the hireling in *his* wages, the widow, and the fatherless, and that turn aside the stranger *from his right,* and fear not me, saith the Lord of hosts (Mal 3:5).

Pure religion and undefiled before God and the Father is this, To visit the fatherless and widows in their affliction, *and* to keep himself unspotted from the world (James 1:27).

Biblical Examples: Gen 11:27, 28; Num 27:1–5; Judg 9:16–21; 2 Sam 9:3; 2 Kings 11:1–12; Esth 2:7.

Further References: Deut 10:18; 14:28, 29; 16:11, 14; 24:17–22; 27:19; Job 6:27; 22:9; 24:3, 9; 29:12, 13; 31:16–18, 21; Ps 27:10; 82:3; 94:6; Prov 23:10; Isa 10:1, 2; Jer 22:3; 49:11; Hos 14:3.

OWING (See Borrowing)

– P –

PACIFISM (See Nonresistance; Peace; War)

PARENT-CHILD RELATIONS (See also Family)

And Adam knew Eve his wife; and she conceived, and bare Cain, and said, I have gotten a man from the LORD (Gen 4:1).

Now Israel loved Joseph more than all his children, because he *was* the son of his old age: and he made him a coat of *many* colours. And when his brethren saw that their father loved him more than all his brethren, they hated him, and could not speak peaceably unto him (Gen 37: 3, 4).

Honour thy father and thy mother: that thy days may be long upon the land which the LORD thy God giveth thee (Exod 20:12).

And he that smiteth his father, or his mother, shall be surely put to death (Exod 21:15).

And he that curseth his father, or his mother, shall surely be put to death (Exod 21:17).

Ye shall fear every man his mother, and his father, and keep my sabbaths: I *am* the LORD your God (Lev 19:3).

Thou shalt rise up before the hoary head, and honour the face of the old man, and fear thy God: I *am* the LORD (Lev 19:32).

For every one that curseth his father or his mother shall be surely put to death: he hath cursed his father or his mother; his blood *shall be* upon him (Lev 20:9).

And these words, which I command thee this day, shall be in thine heart: and thou shalt teach them diligently unto thy children, and shalt talk of them when thou sittest in thine house, and when thou walkest by the way, and when thou liest down, and when thou risest up (Deut 6:6, 7).

If a man have two wives, one beloved, and another hated, and they have born him children, *both* the beloved and the hated; and *if* the firstborn son be hers that was hated: then it shall be, when he maketh his sons to inherit *that* which he hath, *that* he may not make the son of the beloved firstborn before the son of the hated, *which is indeed* the firstborn: but he shall acknowledge the son of the hated *for* the firstborn, by giving him a double portion of all that he hath: for he *is* the beginning of his strength; the right of the firstborn *is* his.

If a man have a stubborn and rebellious son, which will not obey the voice of his father, or the voice of his mother, and *that*, when they have chastened him, will not hearken unto them: then shall his father and his mother lay hold on him, and bring him out unto the elders of his city, and unto the gate of his place; and they shall say unto the elders of his city, This our son *is* stubborn and rebellious, he will not obey our voice; *he is* a glutton, and a drunkard. And all the men of his city shall stone him with stones, that he die: so shalt thou put evil away from among you; and all Israel shall hear, and fear (Deut 21:15–21).

A bastard shall not enter into the congregation of the LORD; even to his tenth generation shall he not enter into the congregation of the LORD (Deut 23:2).

Cursed *be* he that setteth light by his

father or his mother. And all the people shall say, Amen (Deut 27:16).

And Ruth said, Entreat me not to leave thee, *or* to return from following after thee: for whither thou goest, I will go; and where thou lodgest, I will lodge: thy people *shall be* my people, and thy God my God: where thou diest, will I die, and there will I be buried: the LORD do so to me, and more also, *if aught* but death part thee and me. When she saw that she was stedfastly minded to go with her, then she left speaking unto her (Ruth 1:16–18).

Give ear, O my people, *to* my law: incline your ears to the words of my mouth. I will open my mouth in a parable: I will utter dark sayings of old: which we have heard and known, and our fathers have told us. We will not hide *them* from their children, shewing to the generation to come the praises of the LORD, and his strength, and his wonderful works that he hath done.

For he established a testimony in Jacob, and appointed a law in Israel, which he commanded our fathers, that they should make them known to their children: that the generation to come might know *them,* *even* the children *which* should be born; *who* should arise and declare *them* to their children: that they might set their hope in God, and not forget the works of God, but keep his commandments: and might not be as their fathers, a stubborn and rebellious generation; a generation *that* set not their heart aright, and whose spirit was not stedfast with God (Ps 78: 1–8).

Like as a father pitieth *his* children, *so* the LORD pitieth them that fear him (Ps 103:13).

Lo, children *are* an heritage of the LORD: *and* the fruit of the womb *is his* reward. As arrows *are* in the hand of a mighty man; so *are* children of the youth. Happy *is* the man that hath his quiver full of them: they shall not be ashamed, but they shall speak with the enemies in the gate (Ps 127:3–5).

My son, hear the instruction of thy father, and forsake not the law of thy mother: for they *shall be* an ornament of grace unto thy head, and chains about thy neck (Prov 1:8, 9).

My son, despise not the chastening of the LORD; neither be weary of his correction: for whom the LORD loveth he correcteth; even as a father the son *in whom* he delighteth (Prov 3:11, 12).

Hear, ye children, the instruction of a father, and attend to know understanding. For I give you good doctrine, forsake ye not my law. For I was my father's son, tender and only *beloved* in the sight of my mother. He taught me also, and said unto me, Let thine heart retain my words: keep my commandments, and live (Prov 4:1–4).

My son, attend to my words; incline thine ear unto my sayings. Let them not depart from thine eyes; keep them in the midst of thine heart (Prov 4:20, 21).

The proverbs of Solomon. A wise son maketh a glad father: but a foolish son *is* the heaviness of his mother (Prov 10:1).

A wise son *heareth* his father's instruction: but a scorner heareth not rebuke (Prov 13:1).

A good *man* leaveth an inheritance to his children's children: and the wealth of the sinner *is* laid up for the just (Prov 13:22).

He that spareth his rod hateth his son: but he that loveth him chasteneth him betimes (Prov 13:24).

Children's children *are* the crown of old men; and the glory of children *are* their fathers (Prov 17:6).

Chasten thy son while there is hope, and let not thy soul spare for his crying (Prov 19:18).

He that wasteth *his* father, *and* chaseth away *his* mother, *is* a son that causeth shame, and bringeth reproach. Cease, my son, to hear the instruction *that causeth* to err from the words of knowledge (Prov 19:26, 27).

Train up a child in the way he should go: and when he is old, he will not depart from it (Prov 22:6).

Foolishness *is* bound in the heart of a child; *but* the rod of correction shall drive it far from him (Prov 22:15).

Withhold not correction from the child: for *if* thou beatest him with the rod, he shall not die (Prov 23:13).

Hearken unto thy father that begat

thee, and despise not thy mother when she is old (Prov 23:22).

Whoso robbeth his father or his mother, and saith, *It is* no transgression; the same *is* the companion of a destroyer (Prov 28:24).

Correct thy son, and he shall give thee rest; yea, he shall give delight unto thy soul (Prov 29:17).

The eye *that* mocketh at *his* father, and despiseth to obey *his* mother, the ravens of the valley shall pick it out, and the young eagles shall eat it (Prov 30:17).

In those days they shall say no more, The fathers have eaten a sour grape, and the children's teeth are set on edge. But every one shall die for his own iniquity: every man that eateth the sour grape, his teeth shall be set on edge (Jer 31:29, 30).

Think not that I am come to send peace on earth: I came not to send peace, but a sword. For I am come to set a man at variance against his father, and the daughter against her mother, and the daughter in law against her mother in law. And a man's foes *shall be* they of his own household. He that loveth father or mother more than me is not worthy of me: and he that loveth son or daughter more than me is not worthy of me. And he that taketh not his cross, and followeth after me is not worthy of me. He that findeth his life shall lose it: and he that loseth his life for my sake shall find it (Matt 10:34–39).

Then were there brought unto him little children, that he should put *his* hands on them, and pray: and the disciples rebuked them. But Jesus said, Suffer little children, and forbid them not, to come unto me: for of such is the kingdom of heaven. And he laid *his* hands on them, and departed thence (Matt 19:13–15).

When Jesus therefore saw his mother, and the disciple standing by, whom he loved, he saith unto his mother, Woman, behold thy son! Then saith he to the disciple, Behold thy mother! And from that hour that disciple took her unto his own *home* (John 19:26, 27).

Behold, the third time I am ready to come to you; and I will not be burdensome to you: for I seek not yours, but you: for the children ought not to lay up for the parents, but the parents for the children. And I will very gladly spend and be spent for you; though the more abundantly I love you, the less I be loved (2 Cor 12:14, 15).

Children, obey your parents in the Lord: for this is right. Honour thy father and mother; which is the first commandment with promise; that it may be well with thee, and thou mayest live long on the earth. And, ye fathers, provoke not your children to wrath: but bring them up in the nurture and admonition of the Lord (Eph 6:1–4).

Children, obey *your* parents in all things: for this is well pleasing unto the Lord. Fathers, provoke not your children *to anger,* lest they be discouraged (Col 3:20, 21).

One that ruleth well his own house, having his children in subjection with all gravity; (for if a man know not how to rule his own house, how shall he take care of the church of God?) (1 Tim 3:4, 5).

Let the deacons be the husbands of one wife, ruling their children and their own houses well (1 Tim 3:12).

But if any widow have children or nephews, let them learn first to shew piety at home, and to requite their parents: for that is good and acceptable before God (1 Tim 5:4).

But if any provide not for his own, and specially for those of his own house, he hath denied the faith, and is worse than an infidel (1 Tim 5:8).

That they may teach the young women to be sober, to love their husbands, to love their children (Titus 2:4).

Biblical Examples: Gen 4:1; 4:25; 15:2, 3; 21:10–14; 24:1–4; 28:1, 2; 29:32–35; 45:9–11; 47:12; Judg 11; 2 Kings 4:1–37; Neh 5:3–9; Job 1:5; 32:6, 7; 42:15; Mark 5:23, 24, 35–42; John 4:46–53.

Further References: Gen 18:19; Exod 21:15–17; Deut 4:9–11; 31:9–13; 32:46; 1 Sam 1; 1 Chron 28:9; 29:19; Job 1:21; Ps 112:1, 2; 113:9; Prov 4:10, 11; 7:1, 2; 8:32, 33; 15:5; 20:20, 21; 30:11; 31:21; Eccl 12:1; Isa 49:15; Ezek 18:1–32; 20:18–21; Joel 1:2, 3; Matt 15:1–9; Luke 11:11–13; 2 Cor 12:14; Gal 4:30, 31; 1 Thess 2:11; Titus 1:5, 6; 2:2–5; Heb 12:7–10; 1 Peter 5:5.

PATIENCE (See also Diligence; Perseverance)

Rest in the LORD, and wait patiently for him: fret not thyself because of him who prospereth in his way, because of the man who bringeth wicked devices to pass (Ps 37:7).

A wrathful man stirreth up strife: but *he that is* slow to anger appeaseth strife (Prov 15:18).

Why sayest thou, O Jacob, and speakest, O Israel, My way is hid from the LORD, and my judgment is passed over from my God?

Hast thou not known? hast thou not heard, *that* the everlasting God, the LORD, the Creator of the ends of the earth, fainteth not, neither is weary? *there is* no searching of his understanding. He giveth power to the faint; and to *them that have* no might he increaseth strength. Even the youths shall faint and be weary, and the young men shall utterly fall: But they that wait upon the LORD shall renew *their* strength; they shall mount up with wings as eagles; they shall run, and not be weary; *and* they shall walk, and not faint (Isa 40:27–31).

In your patience possess ye your souls (Luke 21:19).

And not only *so*, but we glory in tribulations also: knowing that tribulation worketh patience (Rom 5:3).

For whatsoever things were written aforetime were written for our learning, that we through patience and comfort of the scriptures might have hope (Rom 15:4).

Charity suffereth long, *and* is kind; charity envieth not; charity vaunteth not itself, is not puffed up, doth not behave itself unseemly, seeketh not her own, is not easily provoked, thinketh no evil; rejoiceth not in iniquity, but rejoiceth in the truth; beareth all things, believeth all things, hopeth all things, endureth all things (1 Cor 13:4–7).

And let us not be weary in well-doing: for in due season we shall reap, if we faint not (Gal 6:9).

Strengthened with all might, according to his glorious power, unto all patience and longsuffering with joyfulness; giving thanks unto the Father, which hath made us meet to be partakers of the inheritance of the saints in light (Col 1:11, 12).

Put on therefore, as the elect of God, holy and beloved, bowels of mercies, kindness, humbleness of mind, meekness, longsuffering; forbearing one another, and forgiving one another, if any man have a quarrel against any: even as Christ forgave you, so also *do* ye (Col 3:12, 13).

This *is* a faithful saying, and worthy of all acceptation, that Christ Jesus came into the world to save sinners; of whom I am chief. Howbeit for this cause I obtained mercy, that in me first Jesus Christ might shew forth all longsuffering, for a pattern to them which should hereafter believe on him to life everlasting (1 Tim 1:15, 16).

I charge *thee* therefore before God, and the Lord Jesus Christ, who shall judge the quick and the dead at his appearing and his kingdom; preach the word; be instant in season, out of season; reprove, rebuke, exhort with all longsuffering and doctrine (2 Tim 4:1, 2).

For ye have need of patience, that, after ye have done the will of God, ye might receive the promise (Heb 10:36).

My brethren, count it all joy when ye fall into divers temptations; knowing *this*, that the trying of your faith worketh patience. But let patience have *her* perfect work, that ye may be perfect and entire, wanting nothing (James 1:2–4).

For this *is* thankworthy, if a man for conscience toward God endure grief, suffering wrongfully. For what glory *is it*, if, when ye be buffeted for your faults, ye shall take it patiently? but if, when ye do well, and suffer *for it*, ye take it patiently, this *is* acceptable with God. For even hereunto were ye called: because Christ also suffered for us, leaving us an example, that ye should follow his steps: who did no sin, neither was guile found in his mouth: who, when he was reviled, reviled not again; when he suffered, he threatened not; but committed *himself* to him that judgeth righteously (1 Peter 2:19–23).

And beside this, giving all diligence, add to your faith virtue; and to virtue knowledge; and to knowledge temperance; and to temperance patience; and to patience godliness (2 Peter 1:5, 6).

Biblical Examples: Gen 26:15–22; Exod

16:7, 8; Job 1:21; Ps 40:1; Luke 2:25; 2 Tim 3:10; James 5:11; Rev 1:9; 2:2, 3; 13:10; 14:12.

Further References: Eccl 7:8, 9; Lam 3:26, 27; Luke 8:15; Rom 2:7; 8:25; 12:12; 2 Cor 6:4–6; 12:12; Eph 4:1, 2; 1 Thess 1:3; 5:14; 2 Thess 3:5; 1 Tim 3:2; 6:11; 2 Tim 2:24, 25; Titus 2:1, 2, 9; Heb 6:12, 15; 12:1; James 5:7, 8.

PATRIOTISM (See also Citizenship; Government)

And when we cried unto the LORD God of our fathers, the LORD heard our voice, and looked on our affliction, and our labour, and our oppression: and the LORD brought us forth out of Egypt with a mighty hand, and with an outstretched arm, and with great terribleness, and with signs, and with wonders: and he hath brought us into this place, and hath given us this land, *even* a land that floweth with milk and honey (Deut 26:7–9).

Do good in thy good pleasure unto Zion: build thou the walls of Jerusalem (Ps 51:18).

Pray for the peace of Jerusalem: they shall prosper that love thee. Peace be within thy walls, *and* prosperity within thy palaces (Ps 122:6, 7).

The LORD shall bless thee out of Zion: and thou shalt see the good of Jerusalem all the days of thy life. Yea, thou shalt see thy children's children *and* peace upon Israel (Ps 128:5, 6).

By the rivers of Babylon, there we sat down, yea, we wept, when we remembered Zion. We hanged our harps upon the willows in the midst thereof. For there they that carried us away captive required of us a song; and they that wasted us *required of us* mirth, *saying,* Sing us *one* of the songs of Zion. How shall we sing the LORD's song in a strange land? If I forget thee, O Jerusalem, let my right hand forget *her cunning.* If I do not remember thee, let my tongue cleave to the roof of my mouth; if I prefer not Jerusalem above my chief joy (Ps 137:1–6).

For Zion's sake will I not hold my peace, and for Jerusalem's sake I will not rest, until the righteousness thereof go forth as brightness, and the salvation thereof as a lamp *that* burneth (Isa 62:1).

Biblical Examples: Judg 5:1–31; 1 Sam 4:17, 18; 4:19–22; 2 Sam 10:12; 11:11; 2 Kings 7:9; Neh 1:1–11; 2:1–20; 5:1–18; Ps 85:1–13; Jer 9:1, 2; Heb 11:24–26.

Further References: Ecc 8:2–4; 10:4, 20; Jer 8:11, 21, 22; Lam 5:1–22.

PEACE (See also War)

And I will give peace in the land, and ye shall lie down, and none shall make *you* afraid: and I will rid evil beasts out of the land, neither shall the sword go through your land (Lev 26:6).

I will both lay me down in peace, and sleep: for thou, LORD, only makest me dwell in safety (Ps 4:8).

The LORD will give strength unto his people; the LORD will bless his people with peace (Ps 29:11).

Depart from evil, and do good; seek peace, and pursue it (Ps 34:14).

There is no soundness in my flesh because of thine anger; neither *is there any* rest in my bones because of my sin (Ps 38:3).

Rebuke the company of spearmen, the multitude of the bulls, with the calves of the people, *till every one* submit himself with pieces of silver: scatter thou the people *that* delight in war (Ps 68:30).

My soul hath long dwelt with him that hateth peace. I *am for* peace: but when I speak, they *are* for war (Ps 120:6, 7).

Pray for the peace of Jerusalem: they shall prosper that love thee (Ps 122:6).

Better *is* a dry morsel, and quietness therewith, than an house full of sacrifices *with* strife (Prov 17:1).

It is an honour for a man to cease from strife: but every fool will be meddling (Prov 20:3).

Better *is* an handful *with* quietness, than both the hands full *with* travail and vexation of spirit (Eccl 4:6).

And he shall judge among the nations, and shall rebuke many people: and they shall beat their swords into plowshares, and their spears into pruninghooks: nation shall not lift up sword against nation, neither shall they learn war any more (Isa 2:4).

Thou wilt keep *him* in perfect peace, *whose* mind *is* stayed *on thee:* because he trusteth in thee (Isa 26:3).

And thou hast removed my soul far off from peace: I forgat prosperity (Lam 3:17).

And in that day will I make a covenant for them with the beasts of the field, and with the fowls of heaven, and *with* the creeping things of the ground: and I will break the bow and the sword and the battle out of the earth, and will make them to lie down safely (Hos 2:18).

And he shall judge among many people, and rebuke strong nations afar off; and they shall beat their swords into plowshares, and their spears into pruninghooks: nation shall not lift up a sword against nation, neither shall they learn war any more. But they shall sit every man under his vine and under his fig tree; and none shall make *them* afraid: for the mouth of the LORD of hosts hath spoken *it* (Mic 4:3, 4).

Thus saith the LORD of hosts; The fast of the fourth *month*, and the fast of the fifth, and the fast of the seventh, and the fast of the tenth, shall be to the house of Judah joy and gladness, and cheerful feasts; therefore love the truth and peace (Zech 8:19).

Blessed *are* the peacemakers: for they shall be called the children of God (Matt 5:9).

But I say unto you, That ye resist not evil: but whosoever shall smite thee on thy right cheek, turn to him the other also. And if any man will sue thee at the law, and take away thy coat let him have *thy* cloak also. And whosoever shall compel thee to go a mile, go with him twain (Matt 5:39–41).

Then said Jesus unto him, Put up again thy sword into his place: for all they that take the sword shall perish with the sword (Matt 26:52).

Glory to God in the highest and on earth peace, good will toward men (Luke 2:14).

Suppose ye that I am come to give peace on earth? I tell you, Nay; but rather division: for from henceforth there shall be five in one house divided, three against two, and two against three. The father shall be divided against the son, and the son against the father; the mother against the daughter, and the daughter against the mother; the mother in law against her daughter in law, and the daughter in law against her mother in law (Luke 12:51–53).

And when he was come near, he beheld the city, and wept over it, saying, If thou hadst known, even thou, at least in this thy day, the things *which belong* unto thy peace! but now they are hid from thine eyes (Luke 19:41, 42).

If it be possible, as much as lieth in you, live peaceably with all men (Rom 12:18).

Therefore if thine enemy hunger, feed him; if he thirst, give him drink: for in so doing thou shalt heap coals of fire on his head. Be not overcome of evil, but overcome evil with good (Rom 12:20, 21).

But if the unbelieving depart, let him depart. A brother or a sister is not under bondage in such *cases:* but God hath called us to peace (1 Cor 7:15).

For God is not *the author* of confusion, but of peace, as in all churches of the saints (1 Cor 14:33).

And the fruit of righteousness is sown in peace of them that make peace (James 3:18).

For he that will love life, and see good days, let him refrain his tongue from evil, and his lips that they speak no guile: let him eschew evil, and do good; let him seek peace, and ensue it (1 Peter 3:10, 11).

Biblical Examples: Gen 15:15; Exod 18:23; 1 Sam 20:42; Isa 11:6–9, 13; 32:2, 17, 18; 55:2, 12; Jer 29:7; 33:9; Ezek 34:25; Zech 8:12, 19; 1 Cor 11:18.

Further References: Job 5:23, 24; Ps 125:1, 5; 133:1; Prov 12:20; Isa 9:6; 45:7; 53:5; 54:1, 10, 13; 57:1, 2, 19; Hag 2:9; Mal 2:5; Matt 5:9; 6:14, 15; 10:21, 22, 34–36; 18:15; Mark 9:50; Luke 1:79; John 12:14, 15; 14:27; 16:33; 20:19; Rom 5:1; 14:19; 15:13, 33; 2 Cor 4:7; 13:11; Gal 1:3; 5:22; Eph 2:14–17; 4:1–3; 6:15; Phil 4:7–9; Col 1:19–22; 3:15; 1 Thess 5:13; 2 Thess 3:16; 2 Tim 2:22; Heb 12:11, 14; James 3:17, 18; 2:16; 1 Peter 3:11.

PERJURY (See also Dishonesty; Lying; Oaths; Truth)

And the LORD spake unto Moses, saying, If a soul sin, and commit a trespass against the LORD, and lie unto his neighbour in that which was delivered him to keep, or in fellowship, or in a thing taken away by violence, or hath deceived his neighbour; or have found that which was lost, and lieth concerning it, and sweareth falsely; in any of all these that a man doeth, sinning therein: then it shall be, because he hath sinned, and is guilty, that he shall restore that which he took violently away, or the thing which he hath deceitfully gotten, or that which was delivered him to keep, or the lost thing which he found, or all that about which he hath sworn falsely; he shall even restore it in the principal, and shall add the fifth part more thereto, *and* give it unto him to whom it appertaineth, in the day of his trespass offering. And he shall bring his trespass offering unto the LORD, a ram without blemish out of the flock, with thy estimation, for a trespass offering, unto the priest: and the priest shall make an atonement for him before the LORD: and it shall be forgiven him for any thing of all that he hath done in trespassing therein (Lev 6:1–7).

And ye shall not swear by my name falsely, neither shalt thou profane the name of thy God: I *am* the LORD (Lev 19:12).

Will ye steal, murder, and commit adultery, and swear falsely, and burn incense unto Baal, and walk after other gods whom ye know not (Jer 7:9).

They have spoken words, swearing falsely in making a covenant: thus judgment springeth up as hemlock in the furrows of the field (Hos 10:4).

Again, ye have heard that it hath been said by them of old time, Thou shalt not forswear thyself, but shalt perform unto the Lord thine oaths (Matt 5:33).

But we know that the law *is* good, if a man use it lawfully; knowing this, that the law is not made for a righteous man, but for the lawless and disobedient, for the ungodly and for sinners, for unholy and profane, for murderers of fathers and murderers of mothers, for manslayers, for whoremongers, for them that defile themselves with mankind, for menstealers, for liars, for perjured persons, and if there be any other thing that is contrary to sound doctrine; according to the glorious gospel of the blessed God, which was committed to my trust (1 Tim 1:8–11).

Biblical Examples: 2 Chron 36:13; Isa 48:1; Jer 5:2.

Further References: Zech 5:4; 8:17; Mal 3:5.

PERSEVERANCE (See also Diligence; Patience)

So they brought the ark of God, and set it in the midst of the tent that David had pitched for it: and they offered burnt sacrifices and peace offerings before God (1 Chron 16:1).

The righteous also shall hold on his way, and he that hath clean hands shall be stronger and stronger (Job 17:9).

The steps of a *good* man are ordered by the LORD: and he delighteth in his way. Though he fall, he shall not be utterly cast down: for the LORD upholdeth *him with* his hand. I have been young, and *now* am old; yet have I not seen the righteous forsaken, nor his seed begging bread. *He is* ever merciful, and lendeth; and his seed *is* blessed. Depart from evil, and do good; and dwell for evermore. For the LORD loveth judgment, and forsaketh not his saints; they are preserved for ever: but the seed of the wicked shall be cut off (Ps 37:23–28).

Therefore turn thou to thy God: keep mercy and judgment, and wait on thy God continually (Hos 12:6).

But he that shall endure unto the end, the same shall be saved (Matt 24:13).

Then said Jesus to those Jews which believed on him, If ye continue in my word, *then* are ye my disciples indeed; And ye shall know the truth, and the truth shall make you free (John 8:31, 32).

And I give unto them eternal life; and they shall never perish, neither shall any *man* pluck them out of my hand. My Father, which gave *them* me, is greater than all; and no *man* is able to pluck *them* out of my Father's hand. I and *my* Father are one (John 10:28–30).

Abide in me, and I in you. As the branch cannot bear fruit of itself, except it abide in the vine; no more can ye, except ye abide in me. I am the vine, ye *are* the branches: He that abideth in me, and I in him, the same bringeth forth much fruit: for without me ye can do nothing. If a man abide not in me, he is cast forth as a branch, and is withered; and men gather them, and cast *them* into the fire, and they are burned. If ye abide in me, and my words abide in you, ye shall ask what ye will, and it shall be done unto you. Herein is my Father glorified, that ye bear much fruit; so shall ye be my disciples. As the Father hath loved me, so have I loved you: continue ye in my love (John 15:4–9).

Therefore, my beloved brethren, be ye stedfast, unmoveable, always abounding in the work of the Lord, forasmuch as ye know that your labour is not in vain in the Lord (1 Cor 15:58).

Stand fast therefore in the liberty wherewith Christ hath made us free, and be not entangled again with the yoke of bondage (Gal 5:1).

And let us not be weary in well-doing: for in due season we shall reap, if we faint not (Gal 6:9).

Only let your conversation be as it becometh the gospel of Christ: that whether I come and see you, or else be absent, I may hear of your affairs, that ye stand fast in one spirit, with one mind striving together for the faith of the gospel (Phil 1:27).

Quench not the Spirit. Despise not prophesyings. Prove all things; hold fast that which is good. Abstain from all appearance of evil (1 Thess 5:19–22).

But continue thou in the things which thou hast learned and hast been assured of, knowing of whom thou hast learned *them* (2 Tim 3:14).

Therefore we ought to give the more earnest heed to the things which we have heard, lest at any time we should let *them* slip (Heb 2:1).

Seeing then that we have a great high priest, that is passed into the heavens, Jesus the Son of God, let us hold fast *our* profession (Heb 4:14).

Let us hold fast the profession of *our* faith without wavering; (for he *is* faithful that promised) (Heb 10:23).

Cast not away therefore your confidence, which hath great recompence of reward. For ye have need of patience, that, after ye have done the will of God, ye might receive the promise (Heb 10:35, 36).

They went out from us, but they were not of us; for if they had been of us, they would *no doubt* have continued with us: but *they went out,* that they might be made manifest that they were not all of us (1 John 2:19).

These *things* have I written unto you concerning them that seduce you. But the anointing which ye have received of him abideth in you, and ye need not that any man teach you: but as the same anointing teacheth you of all things, and is truth, and is no lie, and even as it hath taught you, ye shall abide in him (1 John 2:26, 27).

To him that overcometh will I grant to sit with me in my throne, even as I also overcame, and am set down with my Father in his throne (Rev 3:21).

Biblical Examples: Gen 32:24–26; Num 14:24, 38; Luke 22:31, 32; Acts 13:43; James 5:10, 11.

Further References: Ps 138:8; Prov 4:18; Mark 4:3–8; 13:13; Luke 22:31, 32; John 6:37–40; Rom 2:6, 7; 8:30–39; Eph 4:11–16; 6:13, 18; Phil 4:1; Col 1:10, 22, 23; 2 Thess 3:13; 2 Tim 1:12, 13; 2:1–3, 12; 4:18; Heb 3:5–16; 6:1, 11, 12, 15–18; 12:1–15; 13:9; James 1:4, 12, 25; 1 Peter 1:4–7; 2 Peter 1:10, 11; Rev 2:7–28; 3:5.

PHILANTHROPY (See Charity; Ministry)

PLEASURE, LOVER OF

He that loveth pleasure *shall be* a poor man: he that loveth wine and oil shall not be rich (Prov 21:17).

And I gave my heart to know wisdom, and to know madness and folly: I perceived that this also is vexation of spirit (Eccl 1:17).

I said in mine heart, Go to now, I will prove thee with mirth, therefore enjoy pleasure: and, behold, this also *is* vanity. I said of laughter, *It is* mad: and of mirth, What doeth it? I sought in mine heart to give myself unto wine, yet acquainting mine heart with wisdom; and to lay hold on folly, till I might see what *was* that good for the sons of men, which they should do under the heaven all the days of their life. I made me great works; I builded me houses; I planted me vineyards: I made me gardens and orchards, and I planted trees in them of all *kind of* fruits: I made me pools of water, to water therewith the wood that bringeth forth trees: I got *me* servants and maidens, and had servants born in my house; also I had great possessions of great and small cattle above all that were in Jerusalem before me: I gathered me also silver and gold, and the peculiar treasure of kings and of provinces: I got me men singers and women singers, and the delights of the sons of men, *as* musical instruments, and that of all sorts. So I was great, and increased more than all that were before me in Jerusalem: also my wisdom remained with me. And whatsoever mine eyes desired I kept not from them, I withheld not my heart from any joy; for my heart rejoiced in all my labour: and this was my portion of all my labour. Then I looked on all the works that my hands had wrought, and on the labour that I had laboured to do: and, behold, all *was* vanity and vexation of spirit, and *there was* no profit under the sun.

And I turned myself to behold wisdom, and madness, and folly: for what *can* the man *do* that cometh after the king? *even* that which hath been already done. Then I saw that wisdom excelleth folly, as far as light excelleth darkness (Eccl 2:1–13).

There is nothing better for a man, *than* that he should eat and drink, and *that* he should make his soul enjoy good in his labour. This also I saw, that it *was* from the hand of God (Eccl 2:24).

Rejoice, O young man, in thy youth; and let thy heart cheer thee in the days of thy youth, and walk in the ways of thine heart, and in the sight of thine eyes: but know thou, that for all these *things* God will bring thee into judgment (Eccl 11:9).

Woe unto them that rise up early in the morning, *that* they may follow strong drink; that continue until night, *till* wine inflame them! And the harp, and the viol, the tabret, and pipe, and wine, are in their feasts: but they regard not the work of the LORD, neither consider the operation of his hands (Isa 5:11, 12).

And in that day did the Lord GOD of hosts call to weeping, and to mourning, and to baldness, and to girding with sackcloth: and behold joy and gladness, slaying oxen, and killing sheep, eating flesh, and drinking wine: let us eat and drink; for tomorrow we shall die (Isa 22:12, 13).

Therefore hear now this, *thou that art* given to pleasures, that dwellest carelessly, that sayest in thine heart, I *am*, and none else beside me; I shall not sit *as* a widow, neither shall I know the loss of children: but these two *things* shall come to thee in a moment in one day, the loss of children, and widowhood: they shall come upon thee in their perfection for the multitude of thy sorceries, *and* for the great abundance of thine enchantments (Isa 47:8, 9).

Woe to them *that are* at ease in Zion, and trust in the mountain of Samaria, *which are* named chief of the nations, to whom the house of Israel came! Pass ye unto Calneh, and see; and from thence go ye to Hamath the great: then go down to Gath of the Philistines: *be they* better than these kingdoms? or their border greater than your border? Ye that put far away the evil day, and cause the seat of violence to come near (Amos 6:1–3).

That lie upon beds of ivory, and stretch themselves upon their couches, and eat the lambs out of the flock, and the calves out of the midst of the stall; that chant to the sound of the viol, *and* invent to themselves instruments of music, like David: that drink wine in bowls, and anoint themselves with the chief ointments: but they are not grieved for the affliction of Joseph (Amos 6:4–6).

But I say unto you, That whosoever looketh on a woman to lust after her hath committed adultery with her already in his heart (Matt 5:28).

Woe unto you that are full! for ye shall hunger. Woe unto you that laugh now! for ye shall mourn and weep. Woe unto you, when all men shall speak well of you! for so did their fathers to the false prophets (Luke 6:25, 26).

And that which fell among thorns are they, which, when they have heard, go forth, and are choked with cares and riches and pleasures of *this* life, and bring no fruit to perfection (Luke 8:14).

And I will say to my soul, Soul, thou hast much goods laid up for many years; take thine ease, eat, drink, *and* be merry.

But God said unto him, *Thou* fool, this night thy soul shall be required of thee: then whose shall those things be, which thou hast provided? (Luke 12:19, 20).

Let not sin therefore reign in your mortal body, that ye should obey it in the lusts thereof. Neither yield ye your members *as* instruments of unrighteousness unto sin: but yield yourselves unto God, as those that are alive from the dead, and your members *as* instruments of righteousness unto God. For sin shall not have dominion over you: for ye are not under the law, but under grace (Rom 6:12–14).

This I say then, Walk in the Spirit, and ye shall not fulfil the lust of the flesh (Gal 5:16).

Among whom also we all had our conversation in times past in the lusts of our flesh, fulfilling the desires of the flesh and of the mind; and were by nature the children of wrath, even as others (Eph 2:3).

Now she that is a widow indeed, and desolate, trusteth in God, and continueth in supplications and prayers night and day. But she that liveth in pleasure is dead while she liveth (1 Tim 5:5, 6).

Dearly beloved, I beseech *you* as strangers and pilgrims, abstain from fleshly lusts, which war against the soul (1 Peter 2:11).

Forasmuch then as Christ hath suffered for us in the flesh, arm yourselves likewise with the same mind: for he that hath suffered in the flesh hath ceased from sin; That he no longer should live the rest of *his* time in the flesh to the lusts of men, but to the will of God (1 Peter 4:1, 2).

For all that *is* in the world, the lust of the flesh, and the lust of the eyes, and the pride of life, is not of the Father, but is of the world (1 John 2:16).

But, beloved, remember ye the words which were spoken before of the apostles of our Lord Jesus Christ; How that they told you there should be mockers in the last time, who should walk after their own ungodly lusts (Jude 17, 18).

Biblical Examples: Eccl 2:1–13; Amos 6:4–6.

Further References: Job 20:12–14; 21:12, 13; Prov 9:17; 15:21; Rom 1:32; 2 Thess 2:12; 2 Tim 3:4; Titus 3:3; Heb 11:25, 26; 2 Peter 2:4–10, 13.

POLITICS (See Citizenship; Government)

POLLUTION (See Ecology)

POLYGAMY (See Adultery; Family; Husband-Wife Relations; Marriage; Monogamy)

POOR (See Economics; Hunger; Poverty)

POVERTY (See also Economics; Hunger)

If thou lend money to *any of* my people *that is* poor by thee, thou shalt not be to him as an usurer, neither shalt thou lay upon him usury (Exod 22:25).

And six years thou shalt sow thy land, and shalt gather in the fruits thereof: But the seventh *year* thou shalt let it rest and lie still; that the poor of thy people may eat: and what they leave the beasts of the field shall eat. In like manner thou shalt deal with thy vineyard, *and* with thy olive-yard (Exod 23:10, 11).

And when ye reap the harvest of your land, thou shalt not wholly reap the corners of thy field, neither shalt thou gather the gleanings of thy harvest. And thou shalt not glean thy vineyard, neither shalt thou gather *every* grape of thy vineyard; thou shalt leave them for the poor and stranger: I *am* the LORD your God (Lev 19:9, 10).

Ye shall do no unrighteousness in judgment: thou shalt not respect the person of the poor, nor honour the person of the mighty: *but* in righteousness shalt thou judge thy neighbour (Lev 19:15).

And when ye reap the harvest of your land, thou shalt not make clean riddance of the corners of thy field when thou reapest, neither shalt thou gather any gleaning of thy harvest: thou shalt leave them unto the poor, and to the stranger: I *am* the LORD your God (Lev 23:22).

If thy brother be waxen poor, and hath sold away *some* of his possession, and if any of his kin come to redeem it, then shall he redeem that which his brother sold. And if the man have none to redeem it, and himself be able to redeem it; Then let him count the years of the sale thereof, and restore the overplus unto the man to whom he sold it; that he may return unto his possession. But if he be not able to restore *it* to him, then that which is sold shall remain in the hand of him that hath bought it until the year of jubilee: and in the jubilee it shall go out, and he shall return unto his possession (Lev 25:25–28).

And if thy brother be waxen poor, and fallen in decay with thee; then thou shalt relieve him: *yea, though he be* a stranger, or a sojourner; that he may live with thee. Take thou no usury of him, or increase: but fear thy God; that thy brother may live with thee (Lev 25:35, 36).

And if thy brother *that dwelleth* by thee be waxen poor, and be sold unto thee; thou shalt not compel him to serve as a bondservant (Lev 25:39).

Save when there shall be no poor among you; for the LORD shall greatly bless thee in the land which the LORD thy God giveth thee *for* an inheritance to possess it: only if thou carefully hearken unto the voice of the LORD thy God, to observe to do all these commandments which I command thee this day. For the LORD thy God blesseth thee, as he promised thee: and thou shalt lend unto many nations, but thou shalt not borrow; and thou shalt reign over many nations, but they shall not reign over thee.

If there be among you a poor man of one of thy brethren within any of thy gates in thy land which the LORD thy God giveth thee, thou shalt not harden thine heart, nor shut thine hand from thy poor brother: but thou shalt open thine hand wide unto him, and shalt surely lend him sufficient for his need, *in that* which he wanteth. Beware that there be not a thought in thy wicked heart, saying, The seventh year, the year of release, is at hand; and thine eye be evil against thy poor brother, and thou givest him nought; and he cry unto the LORD against thee, and it be sin unto thee. Thou shalt surely give him, and thine heart shall not be grieved when thou givest unto him: because that for this thing the LORD thy God shall bless thee in all thy works, and in all that thou puttest thine hand unto. For the poor shall never cease out of the land: therefore I command thee, saying, Thou shalt open thine hand wide unto thy

brother, to thy poor, and to thy needy, in thy land (Deut 15:4–11).

Thou shalt not oppress an hired servant *that is* poor and needy, *whether he be* of thy brethren, or of thy strangers that *are* in thy land within thy gates (Deut 24:14).

Blessed *is* he that considereth the poor: the LORD will deliver him in time of trouble. The LORD will preserve him, and keep him alive; *and* he shall be blessed upon the earth: and thou wilt not deliver him unto the will of his enemies (Ps 41:1, 2).

How long will ye judge unjustly, and accept the persons of the wicked? Selah. Defend the poor and fatherless: do justice to the afflicted and needy. Deliver the poor and needy: rid *them* out of the hand of the wicked (Ps 82:2–4).

I know that the LORD will maintain the cause of the afflicted, *and* the right of the poor (Ps 140:12).

Much food *is in* the tillage of the poor: but there is *that is* destroyed for want of judgment (Prov 13:23).

Whoso mocketh the poor reproacheth his Maker: *and* he that is glad at calamities shall not be unpunished (Prov 17:5).

He that hath pity upon the poor lendeth unto the LORD; and that which he hath given will he pay him again (Prov 19:17).

Rob not the poor, because he *is* poor: neither oppress the afflicted in the gate: for the LORD will plead their cause, and spoil the soul of those that spoiled them (Prov 22:22, 23).

He that giveth unto the poor shall not lack: but he that hideth his eyes shall have many a curse (Prov 28:27).

Learn to do well; seek judgment, relieve the oppressed, judge the fatherless, plead for the widow (Isa 1:17).

The LORD will enter into judgment with the ancients of his people, and the princes thereof: for ye have eaten up the vineyard; the spoil of the poor *is* in your houses. What mean ye *that ye* beat my people to pieces, and grind the faces of the poor? saith the Lord GOD of hosts (Isa 3:14, 15).

Woe unto them that decree unrighteous decrees, and that write grievousness *which* they have prescribed; to turn aside the needy from judgment, and to take away the right from the poor of my people, that widows may be their prey, and *that* they may rob the fatherless! (Isa 10: 1, 2).

And *if* thou draw out thy soul to the hungry, and satisfy the afflicted soul; then shall thy light rise in obscurity, and thy darkness *be* as the noon day (Isa 58:10).

Behold, this was the iniquity of thy sister Sodom, pride, fulness of bread, and abundance of idleness was in her and in her daughters, neither did she strengthen the hand of the poor and needy (Ezek 16:49).

Thus saith the LORD; For three transgressions of Israel, and for four, I will not turn away *the punishment* thereof; because they sold the righteous for silver, and the poor for a pair of shoes; that pant after the dust of the earth on the head of the poor, and turn aside the way of the meek: and a man and his father will go in unto the *same* maid, to profane my holy name (Amos 2:6, 7).

Hear this word, ye kine of Bashan, that *are* in the mountain of Samaria, which oppress the poor, which crush the needy, which say to their masters, Bring, and let us drink. The Lord GOD hath sworn by his holiness, that, lo, the days shall come upon you, that he will take you away with hooks, and your posterity with fishhooks. And ye shall go out at the breaches, every *cow at that which is* before her; and ye shall cast *them* into the palace, saith the LORD (Amos 4:1–3).

Forasmuch therefore as your treading *is* upon the poor, and ye take from him burdens of wheat: ye have built houses of hewn stone, but ye shall not dwell in them; ye have planted pleasant vineyards, but ye shall not drink wine of them For I know your manifold transgressions, and your mighty sins: they afflict the just, they take a bribe, and they turn aside the poor in the gate *from their right* (Amos 5:11, 12).

Hear this, O ye that swallow up the needy, even to make the poor of the land to fail, saying, When will the new moon be gone, that we may sell corn? and the sabbath, that we may set forth wheat, making the ephah small, and the shekel great, and falsifying the balances by de-

ceit? That we may buy the poor for silver, and the needy for a pair of shoes; *yea,* and sell the refuse of the wheat? The LORD hath sworn by the excellency of Jacob, Surely I will never forget any of their works. Shall not the land tremble for this, and every one mourn that dwelleth therein? and it shall rise up wholly as a flood; and it shall be cast out and drowned, as *by* the flood of Egypt (Amos 8:4–8).

Lay not up for yourselves treasures upon earth, where moth and rust doth corrupt, and where thieves break through and steal (Matt 6:19).

No man can serve two masters: for either he will hate the one, and love the other; or else he will hold to the one, and despise the other. Ye cannot serve God and mammon. Therefore I say unto you, Take no thought for your life, what ye shall eat, or what ye shall drink; nor yet for your body, what ye shall put on. Is not the life more than meat, and the body than raiment? Behold the fowls of the air: for they sow not, neither do they reap, nor gather into barns; yet your heavenly Father feedeth them. Are ye not much better than they? Which of you by taking thought can add one cubit unto his stature? And why take ye thought for raiment? Consider the lilies of the field, how they grow; they toil not, neither do they spin: and yet I say unto you, That even Solomon in all his glory was not arrayed like one of these. Wherefore, if God so clothe the grass of the field, which today is, and tomorrow is cast into the oven, *shall he* not much more *clothe* you, O ye of little faith? Therefore take no thought, saying, What shall we eat? or, What shall we drink? or, Wherewithal shall we be clothed? (For after all these things do the Gentiles seek:) for your heavenly Father knoweth that ye have need of all these things. But seek ye first the kingdom of God, and his righteousness; and all these things shall be added unto you. Take therefore no thought for the morrow: for the morrow shall take thought for the things of itself. Sufficient unto the day *is* the evil thereof (Matt 6:24–34).

If ye then, being evil, know how to give good gifts unto your children, how much more shall your Father which is in heaven give good things to them that ask him? (Matt 7:11).

Jesus said unto him, If thou wilt be perfect, go *and* sell that thou hast, and give to the poor, and thou shalt have treasure in heaven: and come *and* follow me (Matt 19:21).

Then said Jesus unto his disciples, Verily I say unto you, That a rich man shall hardly enter into the kingdom of heaven. And again I say unto you, It is easier for a camel to go through the eye of a needle, than for a rich man to enter into the kingdom of God (Matt 19:23, 24).

Then shall the King say unto them on his right hand, Come, ye blessed of my Father, inherit the kingdom prepared for you from the foundation of the world: for I was an hungered, and ye gave me meat: I was thirsty, and ye gave me drink: I was a stranger, and ye took me in: naked, and ye clothed me: I was sick, and ye visited me: I was in prison, and ye came unto me (Matt 25:34–36).

For ye have the poor always with you; but me ye have not always (Matt 26:11).

And there came a certain poor widow, and she threw in two mites, which make a farthing. And he called *unto him* his disciples, and saith unto them, Verily I say unto you, That this poor widow hath cast more in, than all they which have cast into the treasury: for all *they* did cast in of their abundance; but she of her want did cast in all that she had, *even* all her living (Mark 12:42–44).

And being in Bethany in the house of Simon the leper, as he sat at meat, there came a woman having an alabaster box of ointment of spikenard very precious; and she brake the box, and poured *it* on his head. And there were some that had indignation within themselves and said, Why was this waste of the ointment made? For it might have been sold for more than three hundred pence, and have been given to the poor. And they murmured against her. And Jesus said, Let her alone; why trouble ye her? she hath wrought a good work on me. For ye have the poor with you always, and whensoever ye will ye may do them good: but me ye have not always (Mark 14:3–7).

He answereth and saith unto them, He

that hath two coats, let him impart to him that hath none; and he that hath meat, let him do likewise (Luke 3:11).

And when they had brought their ships to land, they forsook all, and followed him. (Luke 5:11).

And he lifted up his eyes on his disciples, and said, Blessed *be ye* poor: for yours is the kingdom of God (Luke 6:20).

And Jesus said unto him, Foxes have holes, and birds of the air *have* nests; but the Son of man hath not where to lay *his* head (Luke 9:58).

And he spake a parable unto them, saying, The ground of a certain rich man brought forth plentifully: and he thought within himself, saying, What shall I do, because I have no room where to bestow my fruits? And he said, This will I do: I will pull down my barns, and build greater; and there will I bestow all my fruits and my goods. And I will say to my soul, Soul, thou hast much goods laid up for many years; take thine ease, eat, drink, *and* be merry. But God said unto him, *Thou* fool, this night thy soul shall be required of thee: then whose shall those things be, which thou hast provided? So *is* he that layeth up treasure for himself, and is not rich toward God (Luke 12:16–21).

Sell that ye have, and give alms; provide yourselves bags which wax not old, a treasure in the heavens that faileth not, where no thief approacheth, neither moth corrupteth (Luke 12:33).

But when thou makest a feast, call the poor, the maimed, the lame, the blind: and thou shalt be blessed; for they cannot recompense thee: for thou shalt be recompensed at the resurrection of the just (Luke 14:13, 14).

For which of you, intending to build a tower, sitteth not down first, and counteth the cost, whether he have *sufficient* to finish it?

Lest haply, after he hath laid the foundation, and is not able to finish *it*, all that behold *it* begin to mock him, saying, This man began to build, and was not able to finish. Or what king, going to make war against another king, sitteth not down first, and consulteth whether he be able with ten thousand to meet him that cometh against him with twenty thousand? Or else, while the other is yet a great way off, he sendeth an ambassage, and desireth conditions of peace. So likewise, whosoever he be of you that forsaketh not all that he hath, he cannot be my disciple (Luke 14:28–33).

Now when Jesus heard these things, he said unto him, Yet lackest thou one thing: sell all that thou hast, and distribute unto the poor, and thou shalt have treasure in heaven: and come, follow me (Luke 18:22).

And all that believed were together, and had all things common; and sold their possessions and goods, and parted them to all *men*, as every man had need (Acts 2:44, 45).

I have shewed you all things, how that so labouring ye ought to support the weak, and to remember the words of the Lord Jesus, how he said, It is more blessed to give than to receive (Acts 20:35).

What is my reward then? *Verily* that, when I preach the gospel, I may make the gospel of Christ without charge, that I abuse not my power in the gospel (1 Cor 9:18).

Moreover, brethren, we do you to wit of the grace of God bestowed on the churches of Macedonia; how that in a great trial of affliction the abundance of their joy and their deep poverty abounded unto the riches of their liberality. For to *their* power, I bear record, yea, and beyond *their* power *they were* willing of themselves; praying us with much entreaty that you would receive the gift, and *take upon us* the fellowship of the ministering to the saints. And *this they did*, not as we hoped, but first gave their own selves to the Lord, and unto us by the will of God (2 Cor 8:1–5).

Pure religion and undefiled before God and the Father is this, To visit the fatherless and widows in their affliction, *and* to keep himself unspotted from the world (James 1:27).

Go to now, *ye* rich men, weep and howl for your miseries that shall come upon *you*. Your riches are corrupted, and your garments are motheaten. Your gold and silver is cankered; and the rust of them shall be a witness against you, and shall

eat your flesh as it were fire. Ye have heaped treasure together for the last days. Behold, the hire of the labourers who have reaped down your fields, which is of you kept back by fraud, crieth: and the cries of them which have reaped are entered into the ears of the Lord of sabaoth. Ye have lived in pleasure on the earth, and been wanton; ye have nourished your hearts, as in the day of slaughter. Ye have condemned *and* killed the just; *and* he doth not resist you (James 5:1–6).

But whoso hath this world's good, and seeth his brother have need, and shutteth up his bowels *of compassion* from him, how dwelleth the love of God in him? My little children, let us not love in word, neither in tongue; but in deed and in truth (1 John 3:17, 18).

Biblical Examples: Neh 5:1–13; Job 20:19–21; 22:6–11; 24:4, 7–10; Ps 10:2, 8–10; Isa 3:14, 15; 41:17; Ezek 18:12; Matt 11:5; Mark 12:43, 44; Luke 9:58; 16:20–22; James 2:2–9, 15, 16.

Further References: Exod 23:3, 6; Deut 14:28, 29; 24:12–21; 26:12, 13; 1 Sam 2:7; Neh 8:10–12; Job 29:11–13, 15, 16; 31:15–22; 34:19; Ps 72:2, 4, 12–14; 73:12–17; 107:9, 36, 41; 109:16; 113:7, 8; Prov 13:7, 8; 14:20, 21, 31; 19:1, 4, 7, 22; 20:13; 21:13; 22:2, 9; 23:21; 28:6, 8, 11, 19; 29:7, 14; Eccl 6:8; 9:15, 16; Isa 1:17; Jere 22:16; Ezek 18:7; Zech 7:10; Matt 13:22; Luke 12:22–29; 19:8; John 12:2–8; Rom 12:8, 13, 20; 1 Cor 13:3; 2 Cor 9:5–7; Gal 2:10; 6:10; Eph 4:28; 2 Thess 3:8; 1 Tim 5:9, 10, 16.

PORNOGRAPHY (See Pleasure, Lover of; Sex and Sexuality)

POSSESSIONS (See Property)

PREJUDICE (See Injustice; Race Relations)

PRIDE (See also Ambition)
And I will break the pride of your power; and I will make your heaven as iron, and your earth as brass (Lev 26:19).

Talk no more so exceeding proudly; let *not* arrogancy come out of your mouth: for the LORD *is* a God of knowledge, and by him actions are weighed (1 Sam 2:3).

Put them in fear, O LORD: *that* the nations may know themselves *to be but* men. Selah (Ps 9:20).

The wicked in *his* pride doth persecute the poor: let them be taken in the devices that they have imagined. For the wicked boasteth of his heart's desire, and blesseth the covetous, *whom* the LORD abhorreth. The wicked, through the pride of his countenance, will not seek *after God:* God *is* not in all his thoughts (Ps 10:2–4).

Whoso privily slandereth his neighbour, him will I cut off: him that hath an high look and a proud heart will not I suffer (Ps 101:5).

Though the LORD *be* high, yet hath he respect unto the lowly: but the proud he knoweth afar off (Ps 138:6).

Trust in the LORD with all thine heart; and lean not unto thine own understanding. In all thy ways acknowledge him, and he shall direct thy paths.

Be not wise in thine own eyes: fear the LORD, and depart from evil (Prov. 3:5–7).

These six *things* doth the LORD hate: yea, seven *are* an abomination unto him: a proud look, a lying tongue, and hands that shed innocent blood, an heart that deviseth wicked imaginations, feet that be swift in . . . mischief, a false witness . . . and he that soweth discord among brethren (Prov 6:16, 19).

The fear of the LORD *is* to hate evil: pride, and arrogancy, and the evil way, and the froward mouth, do I hate (Prov 8:13).

The wicked is snared by the transgression of *his* lips: but the just shall come out of trouble (Prov 12:13).

Every one *that is* proud in heart *is* an abomination to the LORD: *though* hand *join* in hand, he shall not be unpunished (Prov 16:5).

Pride *goeth* before destruction, and an haughty spirit before a fall. Better *it is to be* of an humble spirit with the lowly, than to divide the spoil with the proud (Prov 16:18, 19).

Whoso boasteth himself of a false gift *is like* clouds and wind without rain (Prov. 25:14).

Woe unto *them that are* wise in their own eyes, and prudent in their own sight! (Isa 5:21).

And I will punish the world for *their* evil, and the wicked for their iniquity; and I will cause the arrogancy of the proud to cease, and will lay low the haughtiness of the terrible (Isa 13:11).

Thus saith the LORD, Let not the wise *man* glory in his wisdom, neither let the mighty *man* glory in his might, let not the rich *man* glory in his riches: but let him that glorieth glory in this, that he understandeth and knoweth me, that I *am* the LORD which exercise lovingkindness, judgment, and righteousness, in the earth: for in these *things* I delight, saith the LORD (Jer 9:23, 24).

Behold, I *am* against thee, *O thou* most proud, saith the Lord GOD of hosts: for thy day is come, the time *that* I will visit thee. And the most proud shall stumble and fall, and none shall raise him up: and I will kindle a fire in his cities, and it shall devour all round about him (Jer 50:31, 32).

The pride of thine heart hath deceived thee, thou that dwellest in the clefts of the rock, whose habitation *is* high; that saith in his heart, Who shall bring me down to the ground? Though thou exalt *thyself* as the eagle, and though thou set thy nest among the stars, thence will I bring thee down, saith the LORD (Obad 3, 4).

For, behold the day cometh, that shall burn as an oven; and all the proud, yea, and all that do wickedly, shall be stubble: and the day that cometh shall burn them up, saith the LORD of hosts, that it shall leave them neither root nor branch (Mal 4:1).

And love the uppermost rooms at feasts, and the chief seats in the synagogues, and greetings in the markets, and to be called of men, Rabbi, Rabbi. But be not ye called Rabbi: for one is your Master, *even* Christ; and all ye are brethren. And call no *man* your father upon the earth: for one is your Father, which is in heaven. Neither be ye called masters: for one is your Master, *even* Christ. But he that is greatest among you shall be your servant. And whosoever shall exalt himself shall be abased; and he that shall humble himself shall be exalted (Matt 23:6–12).

Bring forth therefore fruits worthy of

repentance, and begin not to say within yourselves, We have Abraham to *our* father: for I say unto you, That God is able of these stones to raise up children unto Abraham (Luke 3:8).

When thou art bidden of any *man* to a wedding, sit not down in the highest room; lest a more honourable man than thou be bidden of him; and he that bade thee and him come and say to thee, Give this man place; and thou begin with shame to take the lowest room (Luke 14:8, 9).

For I say, through the grace given unto me, to every man that is among you, not to think *of himself* more highly than he ought to think; but to think soberly, according as God hath dealt to every man the measure of faith (Rom 12:3).

Be of the same mind one toward another. Mind not high things, but condescend to men of low estate. Be not wise in your own conceits (Rom 12:16).

Let no man deceive himself. If any man among you seemeth to be wise in this world, let him become a fool, that he may be wise (1 Cor 3:18).

And these things, brethren, I have in a figure transferred to myself and *to* Apollos for your sakes; that ye might learn in us not to think *of men* above that which is written, that no one of you be puffed up for one against another. For who maketh thee to differ *from another?* and what hast thou that thou didst not receive? now if thou didst receive *it*, why dost thou glory, as if thou hadst not received *it?* Now ye are full, now ye are rich, ye have reigned as kings without us: and I would to God ye did reign, that we also might reign with you. For I think that God hath set forth us the apostles last, as it were appointed to death: for we are made a spectacle unto the world, and to angels, and to men. We *are* fools for Christ's sake, but ye *are* wise in Christ; we *are* weak, but ye *are* strong; ye *are* honourable, but we *are* despised (1 Cor 4:6–10).

Now as touching things offered unto idols, we know that we all have knowledge. Knowledge puffeth up, but charity edifieth. And if any man think that he knoweth any thing, he knoweth nothing yet as he ought to know (1 Cor 8:1, 2).

Wherefore let him that thinketh he standeth take heed lest he fall (1 Cor 10:12).

Casting down imaginations, and every high thing that exalteth itself against the knowledge of God, and bringing into captivity every thought to the obedience of Christ (2 Cor 10:5).

For we dare not make ourselves of the number, or compare ourselves with some that commend themselves: but they measuring themselves by themselves, and comparing themselves among themselves, are not wise (2 Cor 10:12).

For not he that commendeth himself is approved, but whom the Lord commendeth (2 Cor 10:18).

For this thing I besought the Lord thrice, that it might depart from me. And he said unto me, My grace is sufficient for thee: for my strength is made perfect in weakness. Most gladly therefore will I rather glory in my infirmities, that the power of Christ may rest upon me (2 Cor 12:8, 9).

For if a man think himself to be something, when he is nothing, he deceiveth himself (Gal 6:3).

Let nothing *be done* through strife or vainglory; but in lowliness of mind let each esteem other better than themselves (Phil 2:3).

Do ye think that the scripture saith in vain, The spirit that dwelleth in us lusteth to envy? But he giveth more grace. Wherefore he saith, God resisteth the proud, but giveth grace unto the humble. Submit yourselves therefore to God. Resist the devil, and he will flee from you (James 4:5–7).

For all that *is* in the world, the lust of the flesh, and the lust of the eyes, and the pride of life, is not of the Father, but is of the world (1 John 2:16).

Biblical Examples: 2 Kings 5:11–13; 2 Chron 26:16–19; Job 32:9–13; Ps 49:11; 52:7; 73:6–9; Isa 3:16–26; 5:8, 15; 9:9, 10; 10:5–16; 14:12–16; 47:7–10; Jer 48:7–15; 49:4, 16; Ezek 28:2–9, 17; 30:6; Dan 4:30–34; Zeph 2:10, 15; Luke 18:11; Rev 3:17, 18; 18:7, 8.

Further References: Deut 8:11–14, 17–20; 1 Kings 20:11; Job 15:1–13; Ps 12:3, 4; 18:27; 119:21, 69, 70, 78; Prov 11:2, 12;

13:10; 18:11, 12; 21:4, 24; 26:5, 12, 16; 27:2; 29:8; 30:12, 13; Isa 2:11–17; 23:7–9; 24:4, 21; Jer 13:9, 15, 17; Dan 4:37; Mark 7:21, 22; 10:43; Luke 1:51, 52; 9:46; 14:8, 9; 18:14; Rom 1:22, 29, 30; 11:17–21, 25; Eph 4:17; 1 Tim 3:6; 6:3, 4, 17; 2 Tim 3:2–4.

PROCRASTINATION (See also Idleness)

Thou shalt not delay *to offer* the first of thy ripe fruits, and of thy liquors: the firstborn of thy sons shalt thou give unto me. Likewise shalt thou do with thine oxen, *and* with thy sheep: seven days it shall be with his dam; on the eighth day thou shalt give it me (Exod 22:29, 30).

Boast not thyself of tomorrow; for thou knowest not what a day may bring forth (Prov 27:1).

And another of his disciples said unto him, Lord, suffer me first to go and bury my father (Matt 8:21).

Then shall the kingdom of heaven be likened unto ten virgins, which took their lamps, and went forth to meet the bridegroom. And five of them were wise, and five *were* foolish. They that *were* foolish took their lamps, and took no oil with them: but the wise took oil in their vessels with their lamps. While the bridegroom tarried, they all slumbered and slept. And at midnight there was a cry made, Behold, the bridegroom cometh; go ye out to meet him.

Then all those virgins arose, and trimmed their lamps. And the foolish said unto the wise, Give us of your oil; for our lamps are gone out. But the wise answered, saying, *Not so;* lest there be not enough for us and you: but go ye rather to them that sell, and buy for yourselves. And while they went to buy, the bridegroom came; and they that were ready went in with him to the marriage: and the door was shut. Afterward came also the other virgins, saying, Lord, Lord, open to us. But he answered and said, Verily I say unto you, I know you not. Watch therefore, for ye know neither the day nor the hour wherein the Son of man cometh (Matt 25:1–13).

And another also said, Lord, I will follow thee; but let me first go bid them farewell, which are at home at my house. And Jesus said unto him, No man, having put his hand to the plough, and looking back, is fit for the kingdom of God (Luke 9:61, 62).

But of the times and the seasons, brethren, ye have no need that I write unto you. For yourselves know perfectly that the day of the Lord so cometh as a thief in the night. For when they shall say, Peace and safety; then sudden destruction cometh upon them, as travail upon a woman with child; and they shall not escape. But ye, brethren, are not in darkness, that that day should overtake you as a thief. Ye are all the children of light, and the children of the day: we are not of the night, nor of darkness. Therefore let us not sleep, as *do* others; but let us watch and be sober (1 Thess 5:1–6).

Biblical Examples: Exod 8:10; 1 Kings 19:20, 21; Esth 5:8; Acts 24:25.

Further References: Ezek 12:22–28; Matt 24:48–51; Luke 12:43–48; Heb 3:7–19.

PROCREATION (See Children; Husband-Wife Relations; Sex and Sexuality)

PROFANITY (See Cursing; Tongue)

PROFIT (See also Economics)

Honour the LORD with thy substance, and with the firstfruits of all thine increase: so shall thy barns be filled with plenty, and thy presses shall burst out with new wine (Prov 3:9, 10).

The soul of the sluggard desireth, and *hath* nothing: but the soul of the diligent shall be made fat (Prov 13:4).

Wealth *gotten* by vanity shall be diminished: but he that gathereth by labour shall increase (Prov 13:11).

In all labour there is profit: but the talk of the lips *tendeth* only to penury (Prov 14:23).

Bread of deceit *is* sweet to a man; but afterwards his mouth shall be filled with gravel (Prov 20:17).

The getting of treasures by a lying tongue *is* a vanity tossed to and fro of them that seek death (Prov 21:6).

He that by usury and unjust gain increaseth his substance, he shall gather it for him that will pity the poor (Prov 28:8).

A faithful man shall abound with blessings: but he that maketh haste to be rich shall not be innocent (Prov 28:20).

He that hasteth to be rich *hath* an evil eye, and considereth not that poverty shall come upon him (Prov 28:22).

What profit hath a man of all his labour which he taketh under the sun? (Eccl 1:3).

Wisdom *is* good with an inheritance: and *by it there is* profit to them that see the sun (Eccl 7:11).

Woe unto them that join house to house, *that* lay field to field, till *there be* no place, that they may be placed alone in the midst of the earth? (Isa 5:8).

And they covet fields, and take *them* by violence; and the houses, and take *them* away: so they oppress a man and his house, even a man and his heritage (Mic 2:2).

Ye have said, It *is* vain to serve God: and what profit *is it* that we have kept his ordinance, and that we have walked mournfully before the LORD of hosts? (Mal 3:14).

Biblical Examples: Gen 14:22, 23; 24:34, 35; 32:9, 10; Neh 5:14–16.

PROMISCUITY (See Pleasure, Lover of; Prostitution; Sex and Sexuality)

PROPERTY (See also Economics; Stewardship; Wealth)

Thou shalt not steal (Exod 20:15).

If a man shall deliver unto his neighbour money or stuff to keep, and it be stolen out of the man's house; if the thief be found, let him pay double. If the thief be not found, then the master of the house shall be brought unto the judges, *to see* whether he have put his hand unto his neighbour's goods (Exod 22:7, 8).

The land shall not be sold for ever: for the land *is* mine; for ye *are* strangers and sojourners with me (Lev 25:23).

If a man have two wives, one beloved, and another hated, and they have born him children, *both* the beloved and the hated; and *if* the firstborn son be hers that was hated: then it shall be, when he maketh his sons to inherit *that* which he hath, *that* he may not make the son of the beloved firstborn before the son of the hated, *which is indeed* the firstborn: but he shall acknowledge the son of the hated *for* the firstborn, by giving him a double portion of all that he hath; for he *is* the beginning of his strength; the right of the firstborn *is* his (Deut 21:15–17).

Thine, O LORD, *is* the greatness, and the power, and the glory, and the victory, and the majesty: for all *that is* in the heaven and in the earth *is thine;* thine *is* the kingdom, O LORD, and thou art exalted as head above all (1 Chron 29:11).

The earth *is* the LORD'S, and the fulness thereof; the world, and they that dwell therein (Ps 24:1).

A little that a righteous man hath *is* better than the riches of many wicked. For the arms of the wicked shall be broken: but the LORD upholdeth the righteous (Ps 37:16, 17).

The rich man's wealth *is* his strong city: the destruction of the poor *is* their poverty (Prov 10:15).

He that trusteth in his riches shall fall: but the righteous shall flourish as a branch (Prov 11:28).

Better *is* little with the fear of the LORD than great treasure and trouble therewith (Prov 15:16).

Better *is* a little with righteousness than great revenues without right (Prov 16:8).

House and riches *are* the inheritance of fathers: and a prudent wife *is* from the LORD (Prov 19:14).

There is treasure to be desired and oil in the dwelling of the wise; but a foolish man spendeth it up (Prov 21:20).

There is a sore evil *which* I have seen under the sun, *namely,* riches kept for the owners thereof to their hurt. But those riches perish by evil travail: and he begetteth a son, and *there is* nothing in his hand. As he came forth of his mother's womb, naked shall he return to go as he came, and shall take nothing of his labour, which he may carry away in his hand. And this also *is* a sore evil, *that* in all points as he came, so shall he go: and what profit hath he that hath laboured for the wind? All his days also he eateth in darkness, and *he hath* much sorrow and wrath with his sickness (Eccl 5:13–17).

Woe unto them that join house to house, *that* lay field to field, till *there be* no place, that they may be placed alone in the midst of the earth! (Isa 5:8).

Thus saith the LORD, The heaven *is* my throne, and the earth *is* my footstool: where *is* the house that ye build unto me? and where *is* the place of my rest? For all those *things* hath mine hand made, and all those *things* have been, saith the LORD: but to this *man* will I look, *even* to *him that is* poor and of a contrite spirit, and trembleth at my word (Isa 66:1, 2).

Woe to them that devise iniquity, and work evil upon their beds! when the morning is light, they practise it, because it is in the power of their hand. And they covet fields, and take *them* by violence; and houses, and take *them* away: so they oppress a man and his house, even a man and his heritage. Therefore thus saith the LORD; Behold, against this family do I devise an evil, from which ye shall not remove your necks; neither shall ye go haughtily: for this time *is* evil (Mic 2: 1–3).

Wherefore, if God so clothe the grass of the field, which today is, and tomorrow is cast into the oven, *shall he* not much more *clothe* you, O ye of little faith? Therefore take no thought, saying, What shall we eat? or, What shall we drink? or, Wherewithal shall we be clothed? (For after all these things do the Gentiles seek:) for your heavenly Father knoweth that ye have need of all these things. But seek ye first the kingdom of God, and his righteousness; and all these things shall be added unto you (Matt 6:30–33).

And he spake a parable unto them, saying, The ground of a certain rich man brought forth plentifully: and he thought within himself, saying, What shall I do, because I have no room where to bestow my fruits? And he said, This will I do: I will pull down my barns, and build greater; and there will I bestow all my fruits and my goods. And I will say to my soul, Soul, thou hast much goods laid up for many years; take thine ease, eat, drink, *and* be merry. But God said unto him, *Thou* fool, this night thy soul shall be required of thee: then whose shall those things be, which thou hast provided? So *is* he that layeth up treasure for himself, and is not rich toward God.

And he said unto his disciples, Therefore I say unto you, Take no thought for your life, what ye shall eat; neither for the body, what ye shall put on. The life is more than meat, and the body *is more* than raiment. Consider the ravens: for they neither sow nor reap; which neither have storehouse nor barn; and God feedeth them: how much more are ye better than the fowls? And which of you with taking thought can add to his stature one cubit? If ye then be not able to do that thing which is least, why take ye thought for the rest? Consider the lilies how they grow: they toil not, they spin not; and yet I say unto you, that Solomon in all his glory was not arrayed like one of these. If then God so clothe the grass, which is today in the field, and tomorrow is cast into the oven; how much more *will he clothe* you, O ye of little faith? And seek not ye what ye shall eat, or what ye shall drink, neither be ye of doubtful mind. For all these things do the nations of the world seek after: and your Father knoweth that ye have need of these things.

But rather seek ye the kingdom of God; and all these things shall be added unto you. Fear not, little flock; for it is your Father's good pleasure to give you the kingdom. Sell that ye have, and give alms; provide yourselves bags which wax not old, a treasure in the heavens that faileth not, where no thief approacheth, neither moth corrupteth. For where your treasure is, there will your heart be also (Luke 12:16–34).

And all that believed were together, and had all things common; and sold their possessions and goods, and parted them to all *men,* as every man had need (Acts 2:44, 45).

And the multitude of them that believed were of one heart and of one soul: neither said any *of them* that aught of the things which he possessed was his own; but they had all things common. And with great power gave the apostles witness of the resurrection of the Lord Jesus: and great grace was upon them all. Neither was there any among them that lacked: for as many as were possessors of lands or houses sold them, and brought the prices of the things that were sold, and laid *them* down at the apostles' feet: and distribution was made unto every man according as he had need (Acts 4:32–35).

Biblical Examples: 1 Kings 21:1–29; Matt 20:1–16; Luke 19:11–27.

Further References: Gen 1:28–30; Exod 21:28–36; 22:9; Lev 27:9–13, 16–33; Deut 19:14; 22:1–3; 27:17; Amos 5:11; Mark 12:38–40.

PROSTITUTION (See also Adultery; Sex and Sexuality)

Do not prostitute thy daughter, to cause her to be a whore; lest the land fall to whoredom, and the land become full of wickedness (Lev 19:29).

There shall be no whore of the daughters of Israel, nor a sodomite of the sons of Israel (Deut 23:17).

To deliver thee from the strange woman, *even* from the stranger *which* flattereth with her words; which forsaketh the guide of her youth, and forgetteth the covenant of her God. For her house inclineth unto death, and her paths unto the dead. None that go unto her return again, neither take they hold of the paths of life (Prov 2:16–19).

Say unto wisdom, Thou *art* my sister; and call understanding *thy* kinswoman: that they may keep thee from the strange woman, from the stranger *which* flattereth with her words.

For at the window of my house I looked through my casement, and beheld among the simple ones, I discerned among the youths, a young man void of understanding, passing through the street near her corner; and he went the way to her house, in the twilight, in the evening, in the black and dark night: and, behold, there met him a woman *with* the attire of an harlot, and subtil of heart. (She *is* loud and stubborn; her feet abide not in her house: Now *is she* without, now in the streets, and lieth in wait at every corner.) So she caught him, and kissed him, *and* with an impudent face said unto him, *I have* peace offerings with me; this day have I payed my vows. Therefore came I forth to meet thee, diligently to seek thy face, and I have found thee. I have decked my bed with coverings of tapestry, with carved *works,* with fine linen of Egypt. I have perfumed my bed with myrrh, aloes, and cinnamon. Come, let us take our fill of love until the morning: let us solace ourselves with loves. For the goodman *is* not at home, he is gone a long journey: he hath taken a bag of money with him, *and* will come home at the day appointed. With her much fair speech she caused him to yield, with the flattering of her lips she forced him. He goeth after her straightway, as an ox goeth to the slaughter, or as a fool to the correction of the stocks; till a dart strike through his liver; as a bird hasteth to the snare, and knoweth not that it *is* for his life.

Hearken unto me now therefore, O ye children, and attend to the words of my mouth. Let not thine heart decline to her ways, go not astray in her paths. For she hath cast down many wounded: yea, many strong *men* have been slain by her. Her house *is* the way to hell, going down to the chambers of death (Prov 7:4–27).

A foolish woman *is* clamorous: *she is* simple, and knoweth nothing. For she sitteth at the door of her house, on a seat in the high places of the city, To call passengers who go right on their ways: whoso *is* simple, let him turn in hither: and *as for* him that wanteth understanding, she saith to him, stolen waters are sweet, and bread *eaten* in secret is pleasant (Prov 9:13–17).

The mouth of strange women *is* a deep pit: he that is abhorred of the LORD shall fall therein (Prov 22:14).

For a whore *is* a deep ditch; and a strange woman *is* a narrow pit (Prov 23:27).

Whoso loveth wisdom rejoiceth his father: but he that keepeth company with harlots spendeth *his* substance (Prov 29:3).

Know ye not that your bodies are the members of Christ? shall I then take the members of Christ, and make *them* the members of an harlot? God forbid. What? know ye not that he which is joined to an harlot is one body? for two, saith he, shall be one flesh. But he that is joined unto the Lord is one spirit. Flee fornication. Every sin that a man doeth is without the body; but he that committeth fornication sinneth against his own body. What? know ye not that your body is the temple of the Holy Ghost *which is* in you, which ye have of God, and ye are not your own? For ye are bought with a price: therefore glorify God in your body, and in your spirit, which are God's (1 Cor 6:15–20).

Biblical Examples: Lev 19:29; Deut 31:16; Josh 2:3–6; 6:17–25; Judg 2:17; 2 Kings 9:22.

Further References: Gen 38:24; Lev 21:9; Prov 5:3–20; Isa 23:15, 16; Hos 2:13; Heb 11:31.

PRUDENCE

Hear my words, O ye wise *men:* and give ear unto me, ye that have knowledge. For the ear trieth words, as the mouth tasteth meat. Let us choose to us judgment: let us know among ourselves what *is* good (Job 34:2–4).

A good man sheweth favour, and lendeth: he will guide his affairs with discretion (Ps 112:5).

A talebearer revealeth secrets: but he that is of a faithful spirit concealeth the matter (Prov 11:13).

A man shall be commended according to his wisdom: but he that is of a perverse heart shall be despised (Prov 12:8).

A fool's wrath is presently known: but a prudent *man* covereth shame (Prov 12:16).

A prudent man concealeth knowledge: but the heart of fools proclaimeth foolishness (Prov 12:23).

Every prudent *man* dealeth with knowledge: but a fool layeth open *his* folly (Prov 13:16).

The wisdom of the prudent *is* to understand his way: but the folly of fools *is* deceit (Prov 14:8).

The simple believeth every word: but the prudent *man* looketh well to his going. A wise *man* feareth, and departeth from evil: but the fool rageth, and is confident (Prov 14:15, 16).

The simple inherit folly: but the prudent are crowned with knowledge (Prov 14:18).

The heart of the prudent getteth knowledge; and the ear of the wise seeketh knowledge. A man's gift maketh room for him, and bringeth him before great men (Prov 18:15, 16).

A prudent *man* foreseeth the evil, and hideth himself: but the simple pass on, and are punished (Prov 22:3).

For I know your manifold transgressions, and your mighty sins: they afflict the just, they take a bribe, and they turn aside the poor in the gate *from their right.* Therefore the prudent shall keep silence in that time; for it *is* an evil time (Amos 5:12, 13).

Agree with thine adversary quickly, whiles thou art in the way with him; lest at any time the adversary deliver thee to the judge, and the judge deliver thee to the officer, and thou be cast into prison. Verily I say unto thee, Thou shalt by no means come out thence, till thou hast paid the uttermost farthing (Matt 5:25, 26).

Give not that which is holy unto the dogs, neither cast ye your pearls before swine, lest they trample them under their feet, and turn again and rend you (Matt 7:6).

For which of you, intending to build a tower, sitteth not down first, and counteth the cost, whether he have *sufficient* to finish it? Lest haply, after he hath laid the foundation, and is not able to finish *it,* all that behold *it* begin to mock him, saying, This man began to build, and was not able to finish. Or what king, going to make war against another king, sitteth not down first, and consulteth whether he be able with ten thousand to meet him that cometh against him with twenty thousand? Or else, while the other is yet a great way off, he sendeth an ambassage, and desireth conditions of peace (Luke 14:28–32).

All things are lawful unto me, but all things are not expedient: all things are lawful for me, but I will not be brought under the power of any (1 Cor 6:12).

Biblical Examples: Gen 32:3–21; 34:5, 30; 41:33–57; Exod 18:17–23; 1 Sam 11:13; 18:5–30; 25:18–31; 1 Kings 19:3, 4; Dan 1:8–14; Acts 19:29–41; 21:20–26; 2 Cor 8:20.

Further References: Prov 8:12; 15:5, 22; 16:20, 21; 17:2, 18; 24:6, 27; 27;12; Hos 14:9; 1 Cor 8:8–13; 10:25–33; Col 4:5.

PUNISHMENT (See Capital Punishment; Corporal Punishment; Crime and Punishment; Parent-Child Relations; Rewards)

PURITY (See also Chastity)

The law of the LORD *is* perfect, converting the soul: the testimony of the LORD *is* sure, making wise the simple. The statutes of the LORD *are* right, rejoicing the heart: the commandment of the LORD *is* pure, enlightening the eyes. The fear of the LORD *is* clean, enduring for ever: the judgments of the LORD *are* true *and* righteous altogether (Ps 19:7–9).

Who shall ascend into the hill of the LORD? or who shall stand in his holy place? He that hath clean hands, and a pure heart; who hath not lifted up his soul unto vanity, nor sworn deceitfully (Ps 24:3, 4).

Behold, thou desirest truth in the inward parts: and in the hidden *part* thou shalt make me to know wisdom. Purge me with hyssop, and I shall be clean: wash me, and I shall be whiter than snow. Make me to hear joy and gladness; *that* the bones *which* thou hast broken may rejoice. Hide thy face from my sins, and blot out all mine iniquities. Create in me a clean heart, O God; and renew a right spirit within me (Ps 51:6–10).

The thoughts of the wicked *are* an abomination to the LORD: but *the words* of the pure *are* pleasant words (Prov 15:26).

Come now, and let us reason together, saith the LORD: though your sins be as scarlet, they shall be as white as snow; though they be red like crimson, they shall be as wool (Isa 1:18).

Blessed *are* the pure in heart: for they shall see God (Matt 5:8).

And he saith unto them, Are ye so without understanding also? Do ye not perceive, that whatsoever thing from without entereth into the man, *it* cannot defile him; because it entereth not into his heart, but into the belly, and goeth out into the draught, purging all meats? And he said, That which cometh out of the man, that defileth the man (Mark 7:18–20).

A good man out of the good treasure of his heart bringeth forth that which is good; and an evil man out of the evil treasure of his heart bringeth forth that which is evil: for of the abundance of the heart his mouth speaketh (Luke 6:45).

Finally, brethren, whatsoever things are true, whatsoever things *are* honest, whatsoever things *are* just, whatsoever things *are* pure, whatsoever things *are* lovely, whatsoever things *are* of good report; if *there be* any virtue, and if *there be* any praise, think on these things (Phil 4:8).

As I besought thee to abide still at Ephesus, when I went into Macedonia, that thou mightest charge some that they teach no other doctrine, neither give heed to fables and endless genealogies, which minister questions, rather than godly edifying which is in faith: *so do.* Now the end of the commandment is charity out of a pure heart, and *of* a good conscience, and *of* faith unfeigned (1 Tim 1:3–5).

Unto the pure all things *are* pure: but unto them that are defiled and unbelieving *is* nothing pure; but even their mind and conscience is defiled (Titus 1:15).

Seeing ye have purified your souls in obeying the truth through the Spirit unto unfeigned love of the brethren, *see that ye* love one another with a pure heart fervently (1 Peter 1:22).

Biblical Examples: Isa 6:6, 7; 1 John 1:7–9.

Further References: Ps 119:140; Prov 20:9; 21:8; 30:12; Dan 12:10; Mal 3:2, 3; 1 Tim 1:5; 3: 9; 5:22; 2 Tim 1:3; 2:21, 22; Heb 9:13, 14; James 4:8; 1 John 3:3.

– R –

RACE RELATIONS (See also Slavery)

So God created man in his *own* image, in the image of God created he him; male and female created he them (Gen 1:27).

And Adam called his wife's name Eve; because she was the mother of all living (Gen 3:20).

And Noah awoke from his wine, and knew what his younger son had done unto him. And he said, Cursed *be* Canaan; a servant of servants shall he be unto his brethren. And he said, Blessed *be* the LORD God of Shem; and Canaan shall be his servant. God shall enlarge Japheth, and he shall dwell in the tents of Shem; and Canaan shall be his servant (Gen. 9:24–27).

And the whole earth was of one language, and of one speech. And it came to pass, as they journeyed from the east, that they found a plain in the land of Shinar; and they dwelt there. And they said one to another, Go to, let us make brick, and burn them throughly. And they had brick for stone, and slime had they for mortar. And they said, Go to, let us build us a city and a tower, whose top *may reach* unto heaven; and let us make us a name, lest we be scattered abroad upon the face of the whole earth. And the LORD came down to see the city and the tower, which the children of men builded. And the LORD said, Behold, the people *is* one, and they have all one language; and this they begin to do: and now nothing will be restrained from them, which they have imagined to do. Go to, let us go down, and there confound their language, that they may not understand one another's speech. So the LORD scattered them abroad from thence upon the face of all the earth: and they left off to build the city. Therefore is the name of it called Babel; because the LORD did there confound the language of all the earth: and from thence did the LORD scatter them abroad upon the face of all the earth (Gen 11:1–9).

Thou shalt neither vex a stranger, nor oppress him: for ye were strangers in the land of Egypt (Exod 22:21).

Also thou shalt not oppress a stranger: for ye know the heart of a stranger, seeing ye were strangers in the land of Egypt (Exod 23:9).

Defile not ye yourselves in any of these things: for in all these the nations are defiled which I cast out before you: and the land is defiled: therefore I do visit the iniquity thereof upon it, and the land itself vomiteth out her inhabitants (Lev 18:24, 25).

And if a stranger sojourn with thee in your land, ye shall not vex him. *But* the stranger that dwelleth with you shall be unto you as one born among you, and thou shalt love him as thyself; for ye were strangers in the land of Egypt: I *am* the LORD your God (Lev 19:33, 34).

But I have said unto you, Ye shall inherit their land, and I will give it unto you to possess it, a land that floweth with milk and honey: I *am* the LORD your God, which have separated you from *other* people (Lev 20:24).

When the LORD thy God shall bring thee into the land whither thou goest to possess it, and hath cast out many nations before thee, the Hittites, and the Girgashites, and the Amorites, and the Canaanites, and the Perizzites, and the Hivites, and the Jebusites, seven nations greater and mightier than thou; and when the LORD thy God shall deliver them before thee; thou shalt smite them, *and* utterly destroy them; thou shalt make no covenant with them, nor shew mercy unto them: neither shalt thou make marriages with them; thy daughter thou shalt not give unto his son, nor his daughter shalt thou take unto thy son (Deut 7:1–3).

Ye shall not eat *of* any thing that dieth of itself: thou shalt give it unto the stranger that *is* in thy gates, that he may eat it; or thou mayest sell it unto an alien: for thou *art* an holy people unto the LORD thy God. Thou shalt not seethe a kid in his mother's milk (Deut 14:21).

And the seed of Israel separated themselves from all strangers, and stood and confessed their sins, and the iniquities of their fathers (Neh 9:2).

On that day they read in the book of Moses in the audience of the people; and therein was found written, that the Ammonite and the Moabite should not come into the congregation of God for ever; because they met not the children of Israel with bread and with water, but hired Balaam against them, that he should curse them: howbeit our God turned the curse into a blessing. Now it came to pass, when they had heard the law, that they separated from Israel all the mixed multitude (Neh 13:1–3).

The people of the land have used oppression, and exercised robbery, and have vexed the poor and needy: yea, they have oppressed the stranger wrongfully (Ezek 22:29).

He hath shewed thee, O man, what *is* good; and what doth the LORD require of thee, but to do justly, and to love mercy, and to walk humbly with thy God? (Mic 6:8).

Have we not all one father? hath not one God created us? why do we deal treacherously every man against his brother, by profaning the covenant of our fathers? (Mal 2:10).

Therefore all things whatsoever ye would that men should do to you, do ye even so to them: for this is the law and the prophets (Matt 7:12).

Then Jesus went thence, and departed into the coasts of Tyre and Sidon. And, behold a woman of Canaan came out of the same coasts, and cried unto him, saying, Have mercy on me, O Lord, *thou* son of David; my daughter is grievously vexed with a devil. But he answered her not a word. And his disciples came and besought him, saying, Send her away; for she crieth after us. But he answered and said, I am not sent but unto the lost sheep of the house of Israel. Then came she and worshipped him, saying, Lord, help me. But he answered and said, It is not meet to take the children's bread, and to cast *it* to dogs. And she said, Truth, Lord: yet the dogs eat of the crumbs which fall from their masters' table. Then Jesus answered and said unto her, O woman, great *is* thy faith: be it unto thee even as thou wilt. And her daughter was made whole from that very hour (Matt 15:21–28).

Jesus said unto him, Thou shalt love the Lord thy God with all thy heart, and with all thy soul, and with all thy mind. This is the first and great commandment. And the second *is* like unto it, Thou shalt love thy neighbour as thyself. On these two commandments hang all the law and the prophets (Matt 22:37–40).

And Jesus came and spake unto them, saying, All power is given unto me in heaven and in earth.

Go ye therefore, and teach all nations, baptizing them in the name of the Father, and of the Son, and of the Holy Ghost: Teaching them to observe all things whatsoever I have commanded you: and, lo, I am with you alway, *even* unto the end of the world. Amen (Matt 28:18–20).

Now when he had ended all his sayings in the audience of the people, he entered into Capernaum. And a certain centurion's servant, who was dear unto him, was sick, and ready to die. And when he heard of Jesus, he sent unto him the elders of the Jews, beseeching him that he would come and heal his servant. And when they came to Jesus, they besought him instantly, saying, That he was worthy for whom he should do this: for he loveth our nation, and he hath built us a synagogue. Then Jesus went with them. And when he was now not far from the house, the centurion sent friends to him, saying unto him, Lord, trouble not thyself: for I am not worthy that thou shouldest enter under my roof: wherefore neither thought I myself worthy to come unto thee: but say in a word, and my servant shall be healed. For I also am a man set under authority, having under me soldiers, and I say unto one, Go, and he goeth; and to another, Come, and he cometh; and to my servant, Do this, and he doeth *it.* When Jesus heard these things, he marvelled at him, and turned him about, and said unto the people that followed him, I say unto you, I have not found so great faith, no, not in Israel. And they that were sent, returning to the house, found the servant whole that had been sick (Luke 7:1–10).

But he, willing to justify himself, said unto Jesus, And who is my neighbour? And Jesus answering said, A certain *man* went down from Jerusalem to Jericho, and fell among thieves which stripped him of his raiment, and wounded *him,* and departed, leaving *him* half dead. And by chance there came down a certain priest that way: and when he saw him, he passed by on the other side. And likewise a Levite, when he was at the place, came and looked *on him,* and passed by on the other side. But a certain Samaritan, as he journeyed, came where he was: and when he saw him, he had compassion *on him,* and went to *him,* and bound up his wounds, pouring in oil and wine, and set him on his own beast, and brought him to an inn, and took care of him. And on the morrow when he departed, he took out two pence, and gave *them* to the host, and said unto him, Take care of him; and whatsoever thou spendest more, when I come again, I will repay thee. Which now of these three, thinkest thou, was neighbour unto him that fell among the thieves? And he said, He that shewed mercy on him. Then said Jesus unto him, Go, and do thou likewise (Luke 10:29–37).

For God so loved the world, that he gave his only begotten Son, that whosoever believeth in him should not perish, but have everlasting life (John 3:16).

But ye shall receive power, after that the Holy Ghost is come upon you: and ye shall be witnesses unto me both in Jerusalem, and in all Judaea, and in Samaria, and unto the uttermost part of the earth (Acts 1:8).

And how hear we every man in our own tongue, wherein we were born? Parthians, and Medes and Elamites, and the dwellers in Mesopotamia, and in Judæa, and Cappadocia, in Pontus, and Asia, Phrygia, and Pamphylia, in Egypt, and in the parts of Libya about Cyrene, and strangers of Rome, Jews and proselytes, Cretes and Arabians, we do hear them speak in our tongues the wonderful works of God (Acts 2:8–11).

And it shall come to pass, *that* whosoever shall call on the name of the Lord shall be saved (Acts 2:21).

And as he talked with him, he went in, and found many that were come together. And he said unto them, Ye know how that it is an unlawful thing for a man that is a Jew to keep company, or come unto one of another nation; but God hath shewed me that I should not call any man common or unclean (Acts 10:27, 28).

Then Peter opened *his* mouth, and said, Of a truth I perceive that God is no respecter of persons: but in every nation he that feareth him, and worketh righteousness, is accepted with him (Acts 10:34, 35).

And hath made of one blood all nations of men for to dwell on all the face of the earth, and hath determined the times before appointed, and the bounds of their habitation (Acts 17:26).

Tribulation and anguish, upon every soul of man that doeth evil, of the Jew first, and also of the Gentile; but glory, honour, and peace, to every man that worketh good, to the Jew first, and also to the Gentile: for there is no respect of persons with God (Rom 2:9–11).

For when we were yet without strength, in due time Christ died for the ungodly. For scarcely for a righteous man will one die: yet peradventure for a good man some would even dare to die. But God commendeth his love toward us, in that, while we were yet sinners, Christ died for us. Much more then, being now justified by his blood, we shall be saved from wrath through him. For if, when we were enemies, we were reconciled to God by the death of his Son, much more, being reconciled, we shall be saved by his life. And not only *so,* but we also joy in God through our Lord Jesus Christ, by whom we have now received the atonement (Rom 5:6–11).

For as we have many members in one body, and all members have not the same office: so we, *being* many, are one body in Christ, and every one members one of another (Rom 12:4, 5).

For as the body is one, and hath many members, and all the members of that one body, being many, are one body: so also *is* Christ. For by one Spirit are we all baptized into one body, whether *we be* Jews or Gentiles, whether *we be* bond or free; and have been all made to drink into one Spirit (1 Cor 12:12, 13).

There is neither Jew nor Greek, there is neither bond nor free, there is neither male nor female: for ye are all one in Christ Jesus (Gal 3:28).

But now in Christ Jesus ye who sometimes were far off are made nigh by the blood of Christ. For he is our peace, who hath made both one, and hath broken down the middle wall of partition *between us;* having abolished in his flesh the enmity, *even* the law of commandments *contained* in ordinances, for to make in himself of twain one new man, *so* making peace; and that he might reconcile both unto God in one body by the cross, having slain the enmity thereby (Eph 2:13–16).

Now therefore ye are no more strangers and foreigners, but fellow-citizens with the saints, and of the household of God (Eph 2:19).

Whereby, when ye read, ye may understand my knowledge in the mystery of Christ) which in other ages was not made known unto the sons of men, as it is now revealed unto his holy apostles and prophets by the Spirit; that the Gentiles should be fellow-heirs, and of the same body and partakers of his promise in Christ by the gospel (Eph 3:4–6).

There is one body, and one Spirit, even as ye are called in one hope of your calling; one Lord, one faith, one baptism, one God and Father of all, who *is* above all, and through all, and in you all (Eph 4:4–6).

Wherefore putting away lying, speak every man truth with his neighbour: for we are members one of another (Eph 4:25).

But we see Jesus, who was made a little lower than the angels for the suffering of death, crowned with glory and honour; that he by the grace of God should taste death for every man (Heb 2:9).

My brethren, have not the faith of our Lord Jesus Christ, *the Lord* of glory, with respect of persons (James 2:1).

But if ye have respect to persons, ye commit sin, and are convinced of the law as transgressors (James 2:9).

And if ye call on the Father, who without respect of persons judgeth according to every man's work, pass the time of your sojourning *here* in fear (1 Peter 1:17).

He that saith he is in the light, and hateth his brother, is in darkness even until now. He that loveth his brother abideth in the light, and there is none occasion of stumbling in him. But he that hateth his brother is in darkness, and walketh in darkness, and knoweth not whither he goeth, because that darkness hath blinded his eyes (1 John 2:9–11).

But whoso hath this world's good, and seeth his brother have need, and shutteth up his bowels *of compassion* from him, how dwelleth the love of God in him? (1 John 3:17).

Biblical Examples: Acts 11:1–18.

Further References: Num 22:1–6; Ezra 9:10; Ps 136:21, 22; John 4:1–42; Rom 3:21–26; Phil 2.

RAILING (See Slander)

RAPE
But if a man find a betrothed damsel in the field, and the man force her, and lie with her: then the man only that lay with her shall die: but unto the damsel thou shalt do nothing; *there is* in the damsel no sin *worthy* of death: for as when a man riseth against his neighbour, and slayeth him, even so *is* this matter: for he found her in the field, *and* the betrothed damsel cried, and *there was* none to save her.

If a man find a damsel *that is* a virgin, which is not betrothed, and lay hold on her, and lie with her, and they be found; then the man that lay with her shall give unto the damsel's father fifty *shekels* of silver, and she shall be his wife; because he hath humbled her, and he may not put her away all his days. (Deut 22:25–29).

Biblical Examples: Gen 34:1, 2; Judg 19:22–30; 2 Sam 13:6–29; 32, 33; Isa 13:16; Lam 5:11; Zech 14:2.

RASHNESS

He that is slow to wrath *is* of great understanding: but *he that is* hasty of spirit exalteth folly (Prov 14:29).

Also, *that* the soul *be* without knowledge, *it is* not good; and he that hasteth with *his* feet sinneth (Prov 19:2).

Put not forth thyself in the presence of the king, and stand not in the place of great *men:* for better *it is* that it be said unto thee, Come up hither; than that thou shouldest be put lower in the presence of the prince whom thine eyes have seen. Go not forth hastily to strive, lest *thou know not* what to do in the end thereof, when thy neighbour hath put thee to shame (Prov 25:6–8).

Seest thou a man *that is* hasty in his words? *there is* more hope of a fool than of him (Prov 29:20).

Keep thy foot when thou goest to the house of God, and be more ready to hear, than to give the sacrifice of fools: for they consider not that they do evil. Be not rash with thy mouth, and let not thine heart be hasty to utter *any* thing before God: for God *is* in heaven, and thou upon earth: therefore let thy words be few. For a dream cometh through the multitude of business; and a fool's voice is *known* by multitude of words (Eccl 5:1–3).

Be not hasty in thy spirit to be angry: for anger resteth in the bosom of fools (Eccl 7:9).

Biblical Examples: Exod 2:11, 12; Num 20:10–12; Judg 21:1–23; 1 Kings 12:8–15; 2 Chron 35:20–24; Luke 9:54.

Further References: Ps 116:11; Prov 21:5.

REBELLION (See Revolution)

RECREATION (See Leisure)

REMARRIAGE (See also Divorce; Marriage)

It hath been said, Whosoever shall put away his wife, let him give her a writing of divorcement: but I say unto you, That whosoever shall put away his wife, saving for the cause of fornication, causeth her to commit adultery: and whosoever shall marry her that is divorced committeth adultery (Matt 5:31, 32).

He saith unto them, Moses because of the hardness of your hearts suffered you to put away your wives: but from the beginning it was not so. And I say unto you, Whosoever shall put away his wife, except *it be* for fornication, and shall marry another, committeth adultery: and whoso marrieth her which is put away doth commit adultery (Matt 19:8, 9).

And he saith unto them, Whosoever shall put away his wife, and marry another, committeth adultery against her. And if a woman shall put away her husband, and be married to another, she committeth adultery (Mark 10:11, 12).

Know ye not, brethren, (for I speak to them that know the law,) how that the law hath dominion over a man as long as he liveth? For the woman which hath an husband is bound by the law to *her* husband so long as he liveth; but if the husband be dead, she is loosed from the law of *her* husband. So then if, while *her* husband liveth, she be married to another man, she shall be called an adulteress: but if her husband be dead, she is free from that law; so that she is no adulteress, though she be married to another man (Rom 7:1–3).

And unto the married I command, *yet* not I, but the Lord, Let not the wife depart from *her* husband: but and if she depart, let her remain unmarried, or be reconciled to *her* husband: and let not the husband put away *his* wife. But to the rest speak I, not the Lord: If any brother hath a wife that believeth not, and she be pleased to dwell with him, let him not put her away. And the woman which hath an husband that believeth not, and if he be pleased to dwell with her, let her not leave him. For the unbelieving husband is sanctified by the wife, and the unbelieving wife is sanctified by the husband: else were your children unclean; but now are they holy. But if the unbelieving depart, let him depart. A brother or a sister is not under bondage in such *cases:* but God hath called us to peace (1 Cor 7:10–15).

The wife is bound by the law as long as her husband liveth; but if her husband is dead, she is at liberty to be married to whom she will; only in the Lord. But she is happier if she so abide, after my judgment: and I think also that I have the Spirit of God (1 Cor 7:39, 40).

Biblical Example: Mal 2:13–16.

Further References: Lev 21:1, 7, 13–15; Deut 24:1–5.

RESPONSIBILITY

Again the word of the LORD came unto me, saying, Son of man, speak to the children of thy people, and say unto them, When I bring the sword upon a land, if the people of the land take a man of their coasts, and set him for their watchman: if when he seeth the sword come upon the land, he blow the trumpet, and warn the people; then whosoever heareth the sound of the trumpet, and taketh not warning; if the sword come, and take him away, his blood shall be upon his own head. He heard the sound of the trumpet, and took not warning; his blood shall be upon him. But he that taketh warning shall deliver his soul. But if the watchman see the sword come, and blow not the trumpet, and the people be not warned; if the sword come, and take *any* person from among them, he is taken away in his iniquity; but his blood will I require at the watchman's hand (Ezek 33:1–6)

And into whatsoever city or town ye shall enter, inquire who in it is worthy; and there abide till ye go thence. And when ye come into an house, salute it. And if the house be worthy, let your peace come upon it: but if it be not worthy, let your peace return to you. And whosoever shall not receive you, nor hear your words, when ye depart out of that house or city, shake off the dust of your feet. Verily I say unto you, It shall be more tolerable for the land of Sodom and Gomorrha in the day of judgment, than for that city (Matt 10:11–15).

For God sent not his Son into the world

to condemn the world; but that the world through him might be saved.

He that believeth on him is not condemned: but he that believeth not is condemned already, because he hath not believed in the name of the only begotten Son of God (John 3:17, 18).

If I had not come and spoken unto them, they had not had sin: but now they have no cloak for their sin. He that hateth me hateth my Father also. If I had not done among them the works which none other man did, they had not had sin: but now have they both seen and hated both me and my Father (John 15:22–24).

For I say, through the grace given unto me, to every man that is among you, not to think of *himself* more highly than he ought to think; but to think soberly, according as God hath dealt to every man the measure of faith. For as we have many members in one body, and all members have not the same office: so we, *being* many, are one body in Christ, and every one members one of another. Having then gifts differing according to the grace that is given to us, whether prophecy, *let us prophesy* according to the proportion of faith; Or ministry, *let us wait* on *our* ministering: or he that teacheth, on teaching. Or he that exhorteth, on exhortation: he that giveth, *let him do it* with simplicity; he that ruleth, with diligence; he that sheweth mercy, with cheerfulness (Rom 12:3–8).

But unto every one of us is given grace according to the measure of the gift of Christ (Eph 4:7).

Biblical Examples: Gen 3:12, 13; Exod 32:22–24; 1 Sam 15:20, 21; Matt 25:14–30; 27:24; 1 Tim 6:20, 21.

Further References: Ezek 18:1–32; Matt 11:20–24; Mark 6:11; Luke 9:5; 10:10–15; 19:12–27; John 12:47, 48.

RESTITUTION

And if men strive together, and one smite another with a stone, or with *his* fist, and he die not, but keepeth *his* bed: if he rise again, and walk abroad upon his staff, then shall he that smote *him* be quit: only he shall pay *for* the loss of his time, and shall cause *him* to be thoroughly healed.

And if a man smite his servant, or his maid, with a rod, and he die under his hand; he shall be surely punished. Notwithstanding, if he continue a day or two, he shall not be punished: for he *is* his money.

If men strive, and hurt a woman with child, so that her fruit depart *from her,* and yet no mischief follow: he shall be sure punished, according as the woman's husband will lay upon him; and he shall pay as the judges *determine.* And if *any* mischief follow, then thou shalt give life for life, eye for eye, tooth for tooth, hand for hand, foot for foot, burning for burning, wound for wound, stripe for stripe.

And if a man smite the eye of his servant, or the eye of his maid, that it perish; he shall let him go free for his eye's sake. And if he smite out his manservant's tooth, or his maidservant's tooth; he shall let him go free for his tooth's sake.

If an ox gore a man or a woman, that they die: then the ox shall be surely stoned, and his flesh shall not be eaten; but the owner of the ox *shall be* quit. But if the ox were wont to push with his horn in time past, and it hath been testified to his owner, and he hath not kept him in, but that he hath killed a man or a woman; the ox shall be stoned, and his owner also shall be put to death. If there be laid on him a sum of money, then he shall give for the ransom of his life whatsoever is laid upon him. Whether he have gored a son, or have gored a daughter, according to this judgment shall it be done unto him. If the ox shall push a manservant or a maidservant; he shall give unto their master thirty shekels of silver, and the ox shall be stoned.

And if a man shall open a pit, or if a man shall dig a pit, and not cover it, and an ox or an ass fall therein; the owner of the pit shall make *it* good, *and* give money unto the owner of them; and the dead *beast* shall be his.

And if one man's ox hurt another's, that he die; then they shall sell the live ox, and divide the money of it; and the dead *ox* also they shall divide. Or if it be known that the ox hath used to push in time past, and his owner hath not kept him in; he

shall surely pay ox for ox; and the dead shall be his own (Exod 21:18–36).

And he that killeth a beast shall make it good; beast for beast. And if a man cause a blemish in his neighbour; as he hath done, so shall it be done to him; breach for breach, eye for eye, tooth for tooth: as he hath caused a blemish in a man, so shall it be done to him *again.* And he that killeth a beast, he shall restore it: and he that killeth a man, he shall be put to death (Lev. 24:18–21).

Men do not despise a thief, if he steal to satisfy his soul when he is hungry; but *if* he be found, he shall restore sevenfold; he shall give all the substance of his house (Prov 6:30, 31).

Therefore if thou bring thy gift to the altar, and there rememberest that thy brother hath aught against thee; leave there thy gift before the altar, and go thy way; first be reconciled to thy brother, and then come and offer thy gift. Agree with thine adversary quickly, whiles thou art in the way with him; lest at any time the adversary deliver thee to the judge, and the judge deliver thee to the officer, and thou be cast into prison. Verily I say unto thee, Thou shalt by no means come out thence, till thou hast paid the uttermost farthing (Matt 5:23–26).

And Zacchæus stood, and said unto the Lord; Behold, Lord, the half of my goods I give to the poor; and if I have taken any thing from any man by false accusation, I restore *him* fourfold. And Jesus said unto him, This day is salvation come to this house, forsomuch as he also is a son of Abraham. For the Son of man is come to seek and to save that which was lost (Luke 19:8–10).

Further References: Exod 22:1–4; Lev 6:2–5; Num 5:7; Deut 19:15–21; Ezra 5:3–6:17; Job 20:18; Ezek 33:15.

RETALIATION (See also Revenge; Vengeance)

And if *any* mischief follow, then thou shalt give life for life, eye for eye, tooth for tooth, hand for hand, foot for foot, burning for burning wound for wound, stripe for stripe (Exod 21:23–25).

Thou shalt not avenge, nor bear any grudge against the children of thy people, but thou shalt love thy neighbour as thyself: I *am* the LORD (Lev 19:18).

And he that killeth any man shall surely be put to death. And he that killeth a beast shall make it good; beast for beast. And if a man cause a blemish in his neighbour; as he hath done, so shall it be done to him; breach for breach, eye for eye, tooth for tooth: as he hath caused a blemish in a man, so shall it be done to him *again.* And he that killeth a beast, he shall restore it: and he that killeth a man, he shall be put to death. Ye shall have one manner of law, as well for the stranger, as for one of your own country: for I *am* the LORD your God (Lev 24:17–22).

Say not, I will do so to him as he hath done to me: I will render to the man according to his work (Prov 24:29).

Ye have heard that it hath been said, An eye for an eye, and a tooth for a tooth: but I say unto you, That ye resist not evil: but whosoever shall smite thee on thy right cheek, turn to him the other also. And if any man will sue thee at the law, and take away thy coat, let him have *thy* cloak also. And whosoever shall compel thee to go a mile, go with him twain. Give to him that asketh thee, and from him that would borrow of thee turn not thou away.

Ye have heard that it hath been said, Thou shalt love thy neighbour, and hate thine enemy. But I say unto you, Love your enemies, bless them that curse you, do good to them that hate you, and pray for them which despitefully use you, and persecute you (Matt 5:38–44).

Recompense to no man evil for evil. Provide things honest in the sight of all men. If it be possible, as much as lieth in you, live peaceably with all men. Dearly beloved, avenge not yourselves, but *rather* give place unto wrath: for it is written, Vengeance *is* mine; I will repay, saith the Lord (Rom 12:17–19).

See that none render evil for evil unto any *man;* but ever follow that which is good, both among yourselves, and to all *men* (1 Thess 5:15).

Not rendering evil for evil, or railing for railing: but contrariwise blessing; knowing that ye are thereunto called, that ye should inherit a blessing (1 Peter 3:9).

Biblical Examples: Deut 25:17–19; Judg 8:7, 13–16; 2 Sam 3:27–30; 6:21–23; 1 Kings 2:5, 6; Esth 9; Luke 9:52–56.

Further References: Deut 19:19–21; Prov 20:22; 26:27; 1 Cor 6:7, 8.

REVENGE (See also Vengeance)

If a false witness rise up against any man to testify against him *that which is* wrong; then both the men, between whom the controversy *is,* shall stand before the LORD, before the priests and the judges, which shall be in those days; and the judges shall make diligent inquisition: and, behold, *if* the witness *be* a false witness, *and* hath testified falsely against his brother; then shall ye do unto him, as he had thought to have done unto his brother: so shalt thou put the evil away from among you. And those which remain shall hear, and fear, and shall hence forth commit no more any such evil among you. And thine eye shall not pity; *but* life *shall* go for life, eye for eye, tooth for tooth, hand for hand, foot for foot (Deut 19:16–21).

The wicked in *his* pride doth persecute the poor: let them be taken in the devices that they have imagined (Ps 10:2).

For jealousy *is* the rage of a man: therefore he will not spare in the day of vengeance (Prov 6:34).

Say not thou, I will recompense evil; *but* wait on the LORD, and he shall save thee (Prov 20:22).

Say not, I will do so to him as he hath done to me: I will render to the man according to his work (Prov 24:29).

Woe to thee that spoilest, and thou *wast* not spoiled; and dealest treacherously, and they dealt not treacherously with thee! when thou shalt cease to spoil, thou shalt be spoiled; *and* when thou shalt make an end to deal treacherously, they shall deal treacherously with thee (Isa 33:1).

Ye have heard that it hath been said, An eye for an eye, and a tooth for a tooth: but I say unto you, That ye resist not evil: but whosoever shall smite thee on thy right cheek, turn to him the other also. And if any man will sue thee at the law, and take away thy coat, let him have *thy* cloak also. And whosoever shall compel thee to go a mile, go with him twain. Give to him that asketh thee, and from him that would borrow of thee turn not thou away.

Ye have heard that it hath been said, Thou shalt love thy neighbour, and hate thine enemy. But I say unto you, Love your enemies, bless them that curse you, do good to them that hate you, and pray for them which despitefully use you, and persecute you; that ye may be the children of your Father which is in heaven: for he maketh his sun to rise on the evil and on the good, and sendeth rain on the just and on the unjust. For if ye love them which love you, what reward have ye? do not even the publicans the same? And if ye salute your brethren only, what do ye more *than others?* do not even the publicans so? Be ye therefore perfect, even as your Father which is in heaven is perfect (Matt 5:38–48).

Judge not, that ye be not judged. For with what judgment ye judge, ye shall be judged: and with what measure ye mete, it shall be measured to you again (Matt 7:1, 2).

And it came to pass, when the time was come that he should be received up, he stedfastly set his face to go to Jerusalem, and sent messengers before his face: and they went, and entered into a village of the Samaritans, to make ready for him. And they did not receive him, because his face was as though he would go to Jerusalem. And when his disciples James and John saw *this,* they said, Lord, wilt thou that we command fire to come down from heaven, and consume them, even as Elias did? But he turned, and rebuked them, and said, Ye know not what manner of spirit ye are of. For the Son of man is not come to destroy men's lives, but to save *them.* And they went to another village (Luke 9:51–56).

Recompense to no man evil for evil. Provide things honest in the sight of all men. If it be possible, as much as lieth in you, live peaceably with all men. Dearly beloved, avenge not yourselves, but *rather* give place unto wrath: for it is written, Vengeance *is* mine; I will repay, saith the Lord (Rom 12:17–19).

See that none render evil for evil unto any *man;* but ever follow that which is good, both among yourselves, and to all *men* (1 Thess 5:15).

Not rendering evil for evil, or railing for railing: but contrariwise blessing; knowing that ye are thereunto called, that ye should inherit a blessing (1 Peter 3:9).

Biblical Examples: Gen 34:25; Judg 15:7, 8; 16:28–30; 2 Sam 3:27; 13:23–29; 1 Kings 19:2; 22:27; Mark 6:19–24; Acts 5:33; 7:54–59.

Further Reference: Ezek 25:15–17; Amos 1:11, 12; 1 Cor 6:7, 8.

REVOLUTION

(See also Anarchy; Conscientious Objection; Strife; War)

And when inquisition was made of the matter, it was found out; therefore they were both hanged on a tree: and it was written in the book of the chronicles before the king (Esth 2:23).

Ye have heard that it hath been said, An eye for an eye, and a tooth for a tooth: but I say unto you, That ye resist not evil: but whosoever shall smite thee on thy right cheek, turn to him the other also. And if any man will sue thee at the law, and take away thy coat, let him have *thy* cloak also. And whosoever shall compel thee to go a mile, go with him twain. Give to him that asketh thee, and from him that would borrow of thee turn not thou away (Matt 5:38–42).

And Jesus stood before the governor: and the governor asked him, saying, Art thou the King of the Jews? And Jesus said unto him, Thou sayest.

And when they had platted a crown of thorns, they put *it* upon his head, and a reed in his right hand: and they bowed the knee before him, and mocked him, saying, Hail, King of the Jews! And they spit upon him, and took the reed, and smote him on the head (Matt 27:11, 29, 30).

And they come again to Jerusalem: and as he was walking in the temple, there come to him the chief priests, and the scribes, and the elders, and say unto him, By what authority doest thou these things? and who gave thee this authority to do these things? (Mark 11:27, 28).

And they send unto him certain of the Pharisees and of the Herodians, to catch him in *his* words. And when they were come, they say unto him, Master, we know that thou are true, and carest for no man: for thou regardest not the person of men, but teachest the way of God in truth: Is it lawful to give tribute to Cæsar, or not? Shall we give, or shall we not give? But he, knowing their hypocrisy, said unto them, Why tempt ye me? bring me a penny, that I may see *it*. And they brought *it*. And he saith unto them, Whose *is* this image and superscription? And they said unto him, Cæsar's. And Jesus answering said unto them, Render to Cæsar the things that are Cæsar's, and to God the things that are God's. And they marvelled at him (Mark 12:13–17).

And the whole multitude of them arose, and led him unto Pilate. And they began to accuse him saying, We found this *fellow* perverting the nation, and forbidding to give tribute to Cæsar, saying that he himself is Christ a King. And Pilate asked him, saying, Art thou the King of the Jews? And he answered him and said, Thou sayest *it*. Then said Pilate to the chief priests and *to* the people, I find no fault in this man. And they were the more fierce, saying, He stirreth up the people, teaching throughout all Jewry, beginning from Galilee to this place (Luke 23:1–5).

And they called them, and commanded them not to speak at all nor teach in the name of Jesus. But Peter and John answered and said unto them, Whether it be right in the sight of God to hearken unto you more than unto God, judge ye. For we cannot but speak the things which we have seen and heard (Acts 4:18–20).

And when they had brought them, they set *them* before the council: and the high priest asked them, saying, Did not we straitly command you that ye should not teach in this name? and, behold, ye have filled Jerusalem with your doctrine, and intend to bring this man's blood upon us.

Then Peter and the *other* apostles answered and said, We ought to obey God rather than men (Acts 5:27–29).

Let every soul be subject unto the higher powers. For there is no power but of God: the powers that be are ordained of God.

Whosoever therefore resisteth the power, resisteth the ordinance of God: and they that resist shall receive to themselves damnation. For rulers are not a terror to good works, but to the evil. Wilt thou then not be afraid of the power? do that which is good, and thou shalt have praise of the same: for he is the minister of God to thee for good. But if thou do that which is evil, be afraid; for he beareth not the sword in vain: for he is the minister of God, a revenger to *execute* wrath upon him that doeth evil. Wherefore *ye* must needs be subject, not only for wrath, but also for conscience sake. For for this cause pay ye tribute also: for they are God's ministers, attending continually upon this very thing. Render therefore to all their dues: tribute to whom tribute *is due;* custom to whom custom; fear to whom fear; honour to whom honour (Rom 13:1–7).

Put them in mind to be subject to principalities and powers, to obey magistrates, to be ready to every good work, to speak evil of no man, to be no brawlers, *but* gentle, shewing all meekness unto all men. For we ourselves also were sometimes foolish, disobedient, deceived, serving divers lusts and pleasures, living in malice and envy, hateful, *and* hating one another. But after that the kindness and love of God our Saviour toward man appeared, not by works of righteousness which we have done, but according to his mercy he saved us, by the washing of regeneration, and renewing of the Holy Ghost; which he shed on us abundantly through Jesus Christ our Saviour; that being justified by his grace, we should be made heirs according to the hope of eternal life (Titus 3:1–7).

Having your conversation honest among the Gentiles: that, whereas they speak against you as evildoers, they may by *your* good works, which they shall behold, glorify God in the day of visitation. Submit yourselves to every ordinance of man for the Lord's sake: whether it be to the king, as supreme; or unto governors, as unto them that are sent by him for the punishment of evildoers, and for the praise of them that do well. For so is the will of God, that with well-doing ye may put to silence the ignorance of foolish men: as free, and not using *your* liberty for a cloak of maliciousness, but as the servants of God. Honour all *men.* Love the brotherhood. Fear God. Honour the king (1 Peter 2:12–17).

Biblical Examples: Num 12:1–11; 16:1–33; Isa 10:26; 2 Sam 15–17; 19:16–23; 15:7.

Further References: Matt 10:34–36; 27:1–56; Mark 8:29–33; Luke 22:35–38; John 6:15; 18:28–19:16; Acts 1:6, 7; 17:7.

REWARDS

Wherefore ye shall do my statutes, and keep my judgments, and do them; and ye shall dwell in the land in safety (Lev. 25:18).

If ye walk in my statutes, and keep my commandments, and do them; then I will give you rain in due season, and the land shall yield her increase, and the trees of the field shall yield their fruit. And your threshing shall reach unto the vintage, and the vintage shall reach unto the sowing time: and ye shall eat your bread to the full, and dwell in your land safely. And I will give peace in the land, and ye shall lie down, and none shall make *you* afraid: and I will rid evil beasts out of the land, neither shall the sword go through your land. And ye shall chase your enemies, and they shall fall before you by the sword. And five of you shall chase an hundred, and an hundred of you shall put ten thousand to flight: and your enemies shall fall before you by the sword. For I will have respect unto you, and make you fruitful, and multiply you, and establish my covenant with you. And ye shall eat old store, and bring forth the old because of the new. And I will set my tabernacle among you: and my soul shall not abhor you. And I will walk among you, and will be your God, and ye shall be my people. I *am* the LORD your God, which brought you forth out of the land of Egypt, that ye should not be their bondmen; and I have broken the bands of your yoke, and made you go upright (Lev 26:3–13).

If they shall confess their iniquity, and the iniquity of their fathers, with their trespass which they trespassed against me, that also they have walked contrary unto me; and *that* I also have walked contrary

unto them, and have brought them into the land of their enemies; if then their uncircumcised hearts be humbled, and they then accept of the punishment of their iniquity: then I will remember my covenant with Jacob, and also my covenant with Isaac, and also my covenant with Abraham will I remember; and I will remember the land. The land also shall be left of them, and shall enjoy her sabbaths, while she lieth desolate without them: and they shall accept of the punishment of their iniquity: because, even because they despised my judgments, and because their soul abhorred my statutes. And yet for all that, when they be in the land of their enemies, I will not cast them away, neither will I abhor them, to destroy them utterly, and to break my covenant with them: for I *am* the LORD their God. But I will for their sakes remember the covenant of their ancestors, whom I brought forth out of the land of Egypt in the sight of the heathen, that I might be their God: I *am* the LORD (Lev 26:40–45).

Thou shalt keep therefore his statutes, and his commandments, which I command thee this day, that it may go well with thee, and with thy children after thee, and that thou mayest prolong *thy* days upon the earth, which the LORD thy God giveth thee, for ever (Deut 4:40).

Thou shalt not muzzle the ox when he treadeth out *the corn* (Deut 25:4).

Wash you, make you clean; put away the evil of your doings from before mine eyes; cease to do evil; learn to do well; seek judgment, relieve the oppressed, judge the fatherless, plead for the widow. Come now, and let us reason together, saith the LORD: though your sins be as scarlet, they shall be as white as snow; though they be red like crimson, they shall be as wool. If ye be willing and obedient, ye shall eat the good of the land: but if ye refuse and rebel, ye shall be devoured with the sword: for the mouth of the LORD hath spoken *it* (Isa 1:16–20).

Behold, the Lord GOD will come with strong *hand,* and his arm shall rule for him: behold, his reward *is* with him, and his work before him. He shall feed his flock like a shepherd: he shall gather the lambs with his arm, and carry *them* in his bosom, *and* shall gently lead those that are with young (Isa 40:10, 11).

For the Son of man shall come in the glory of his Father with his angels; and then he shall reward every man according to his works (Matt 16:27).

And Jesus answered and said, Verily I say unto you, There is no man that hath left house, or brethren, or sisters, or father, or mother, or wife, or children, or lands, for my sake, and the gospel's, but he shall receive an hundredfold now in this time, houses, and brethren, and sisters, and mothers, and children, and lands, with persecutions; and in the world to come eternal life. But many *that are* first shall be last; and the last first (Mark 10:29–31).

Blessed are ye, when men shall hate you, and when they shall separate you *from their company,* and shall reproach *you,* and cast out your name as evil, for the Son of man's sake. Rejoice ye in that day, and leap for joy: for, behold, your reward *is* great in heaven: for in the like manner did their fathers unto the prophets (Luke 6:22, 23).

But love ye your enemies, and do good, and lend, hoping for nothing again; and your reward shall be great, and ye shall be the children of the Highest: for he is kind unto the unthankful and *to* the evil (Luke 6:35).

Now he that planteth and he that watereth are one: and every man shall receive his own reward according to his own labour (1 Cor 3:8).

If any man's work abide which he hath built thereupon, he shall receive a reward (1 Cor 3:14).

Wherefore the rather, brethren, give diligence to make your calling and election sure: for if ye do these things, ye shall never fall: for so an entrance shall be ministered unto you abundantly into the everlasting kingdom of our Lord and Saviour Jesus Christ (2 Peter 1:10, 11).

Biblical Examples: Matt 20:1–16; 25:34–46.

Further References: Exod 20:6, 12; Deut 6:3; 11:13–16, 18–21, 26–29; 24:19; Jer 22:3, 4; Acts 26:18; Rom 2:10; Heb 11:26; 12:1, 2, 28; Rev 2:10, 17, 25–28; 7:14–17; 22:12.

RICHES (See Economics; Wealth)

RIGHTEOUSNESS (See also Godliness; Holiness)

And it shall be our righteousness, if we observe to do all these commandments before the LORD our God, as he hath commanded us (Deut 6:25).

Blessed *is* the man that walketh not in the counsel of the ungodly, nor standeth in the way of sinners, nor sitteth in the seat of the scornful. But his delight *is* in the law of the LORD; and in his law doth he mediate day and night. And he shall be like a tree planted by the rivers of water, that bringeth forth his fruit in his season; his leaf also shall not wither; and whatsoever he doeth shall prosper (Ps 1:1–3).

LORD, who shall abide in thy tabernacle? who shall dwell in thy holy hill? He that walketh uprightly, and worketh righteousness, and speaketh the truth in his heart. *He that* backbiteth not with his tongue, nor doeth evil to his neighbour, nor taketh up a reproach against his neighbour. In whose eyes a vile person is contemned; but he honoureth them that fear the LORD. *He that* sweareth to *his own* hurt, and changeth not. *He that* putteth not out his money to usury, nor taketh reward against the innocent. He that doeth these *things* shall never be moved (Ps 15:1–5).

Who shall ascend into the hill of the LORD? or who shall stand in his holy place? He that hath clean hands, and a pure heart, who hath not lifted up his soul unto vanity, nor sworn deceitfully. He shall receive the blessing from the LORD, and righteousness from the God of his salvation (Ps 24:3–5).

Blessed *are* they that keep judgment, *and* he that doeth righteousness at all times (Ps 106:3).

Treasures of wickedness profit nothing: but righteousness delivereth from death (Prov 10:2).

Though hand *join* in hand, the wicked shall not be unpunished: but the seed of the righteous shall be delivered (Prov 11:21).

Righteousness exalteth a nation: but sin *is* a reproach to any people (Prov 14:34).

The righteous considereth the cause of the poor: *but* the wicked regardeth not to know *it* (Prov 29:7).

And the work of righteousness shall be peace; and the effect of righteousness quietness and assurance for ever (Isa 32:17).

He that walketh righteously and speaketh uprightly; he that despiseth the gain of oppressions, that shaketh his hands from holding of bribes, that stoppeth his ears from hearing of blood, and shutteth his eyes from seeing evil; He shall dwell on high: his place of defence *shall be* the munitions of rocks: bread shall be given him; his waters *shall be* sure (Isa 33:15, 16).

But if a man be just, and do that which is lawful and right, *and* hath not eaten upon the mountains, neither hath lifted up his eyes to the idols of the house of Israel, neither hath defiled his neighbour's wife, neither hath come near to a menstruous woman, and hath not oppressed any, *but* hath restored to the debtor his pledge, hath spoiled none by violence, hath given his bread to the hungry, and hath covered the naked with a garment; he *that* hath not given forth upon usury, neither hath taken any increase, *that* hath withdrawn his hand from iniquity, hath executed true judgment between man and man, hath walked in my statutes, and hath kept my judgments, to deal truly; he *is* just, he shall surely live, saith the Lord GOD (Ezek 18:5–9).

Blessed *are* they which do hunger and thirst after righteousness: for they shall be filled (Matt 5:6).

For I say unto you, That except your righteousness shall exceed *the righteousness* of the scribes and Pharisees, ye shall in no case enter into the kingdom of heaven (Matt 5:20).

I speak after the manner of men because of the infirmity of your flesh: for as ye have yielded your members servants to uncleanness and to iniquity unto iniquity; even so now yield your members servants to righteousness unto holiness. For when ye were the servants of sin, ye were free from righteousness. What fruit had ye then in those things whereof ye are now ashamed? for the end of those things *is* death. But now being made free from sin, and become servants to God, ye have your fruit unto holiness, and the end everlasting life (Rom 6:19–22).

That the righteousness of the law might be fulfilled in us, who walk not after the flesh, but after the Spirit. For they that are after the flesh do mind the things of the flesh; but they that are after the Spirit the things of the Spirit. For to be carnally minded *is* death; but to be spiritually minded *is* life and peace (Rom 8:4–6).

For the kingdom of God is not meat and drink; but righteousness, and peace, and joy in the Holy Ghost. For he that in these things serveth Christ *is* acceptable to God, and approved of men. Let us therefore follow after the things which make for peace, and things wherewith one may edify another (Rom 14:17–19).

Now he that ministereth seed to the sower both minister bread for *your* food, and multiply your seed sown, and increase the fruits of your righteousness (2 Cor 9:10).

For the fruit of the Spirit *is* in all goodness and righteousness and truth (Eph 5:9).

Flee also youthful lusts: but follow righteousness, faith, charity, peace, with them that call on the Lord out of a pure heart (2 Tim 2:22).

And the fruit of righteousness is sown in peace of them that make peace (James 3:18).

But and if ye suffer for righteousness' sake, happy *are ye:* and be not afraid of their terror, neither be troubled (1 Peter 3:14).

Biblical Examples: 1 John 2:24–29; 3:3–24.

Further References: Ps 112:4–9; Prov 11:5, 6, 18, 19, 30; 12:28; 13:6; Isa 28:17; 58:6–14; Dan 12:3; Hos 10:12; Mal 3:3; 4:2; Phil 1:11, 27–29; 2 Tim 4:6–8; James 2:14–26.

RULERS (See Authority; Government)

– S –

SABBATH

And on the seventh day God ended his work which he had made; and he rested on the seventh day from all his work which he had made. And God blessed the seventh day, and sanctified it: because that in it he had rested from all his work which God created and made (Gen 2:2, 3).

Remember the sabbath day, to keep it holy. Six days shalt thou labour, and do all thy work: but the seventh day *is* the sabbath of the LORD thy God: *in it* thou shalt not do any work, thou, nor thy son, nor thy daughter, thy manservant, nor thy maidservant, nor thy cattle, nor thy stranger that *is* within thy gates: For *in* six days the LORD made heaven and earth, the sea, and all that in them *is*, and rested the seventh day: wherefore the LORD blessed the sabbath day, and hallowed it (Exod 20:8–11).

Six days thou shalt do thy work, and on the seventh day thou shalt rest: that thine ox and thine ass may rest, and the son of thy handmaid, and the stranger, may be refreshed (Exod 23:12).

Speak thou also unto the children of Israel, saying, Verily my sabbaths ye shall keep: for it *is* a sign between me and you throughout your generations; that *ye* may know that I *am* the LORD that doth sanctify you. Ye shall keep the sabbath therefore; for it *is* holy unto you: every one that defileth it shall surely be put to death: for whosoever doeth *any* work therein, that soul shall be cut off from among his people.

Six days may work be done; but in the seventh *is* the sabbath of rest, holy to the LORD: whosoever doeth *any* work in the sabbath day, he shall surely be put to death. Wherefore the children of Israel shall keep the sabbath, to observe the sabbath throughout their generations, *for* a perpetual covenant. It *is* a sign between me and the children of Israel for ever: for *in* six days the LORD made heaven and earth, and on the seventh day he rested, and was refreshed (Exod 31:13–17).

Ye shall fear every man his mother, and his father, and keep my sabbaths: I *am* the LORD your God (Lev 19:3).

Keep the sabbath day to sanctify it, as the LORD thy God hath commanded thee. Six days thou shalt labour, and do all thy work: but the seventh day *is* the sabbath of the LORD thy God: *in it* thou shalt not do any work, thou, nor thy son, nor thy daughter, nor thy manservant, nor thy maidservant, nor thine ox, nor thine ass, nor any of thy cattle, nor thy stranger that *is* within thy gates; that thy manservant and thy maidservant may rest as well as thou. And remember that thou wast a servant in the land of Egypt, and *that* the LORD thy God brought thee out thence through a mighty hand and by a stretched out arm: therefore the LORD thy God commanded thee to keep the sabbath day (Deut 5:12–15).

Blessed *is* the man *that* doeth this, and the son of man *that* layeth hold on it; that keepeth the sabbath from polluting it, and keepeth his hand from doing any evil (Isa 56:2).

Thus saith the LORD; Take heed to yourselves, and bear no burden on the sabbath day, nor bring *it* in by the gates of Jerusalem; neither carry forth a burden out of your houses on the sabbath day, neither do ye any work, but hallow ye the sabbath day, as I commanded your fathers. But they obeyed not, neither inclined their ear, but made their neck stiff, that they might not hear, nor receive instruction.

And it shall come to pass, if ye diligently hearken unto me, saith the LORD, to bring in no burden through the gates of this city on the sabbath day, but hallow the sabbath day, to do no work therein; then shall there enter into the gates of this city kings and princes sitting upon the throne of David, riding in chariots and on horses, they, and their princes, the men of Judah, and the inhabitants of Jerusalem: and this city shall remain for ever. And they shall come from the cities of Judah, and from the places about Jerusalem, and from the land of Benjamin, and from the plain, and from the mountains, and from the south, bringing burnt offerings, and sacrifices, and meat offerings, and incense, and bringing sacrifices of praise, unto the house of the LORD. But if ye will not hearken unto me to hallow the sabbath day, and not to bear a burden, even entering in at the gates of Jerusalem on the sabbath day; then will I kindle a fire in the gates thereof, and it shall devour the palaces of Jerusalem, and it shall not be quenched (Jer 17:21–27).

Moreover also I gave them my sabbaths, to be a sign between me and them, that they might know that I *am* the LORD that sanctify them. But the house of Israel rebelled against me in the wilderness: they walked not in my statutes, and they despised my judgments, which *if* a man do, he shall even live in them; and my sabbaths they greatly polluted: then I said, I would pour out my fury upon them in the wilderness, to consume them (Ezek 20:12, 13).

At that time Jesus went on the sabbath day through the corn; and his disciples were an hungered, and began to pluck the ears of corn, and to eat. But when the Pharisees saw *it*, they said unto him, Behold, thy disciples do that which is not lawful to do upon the sabbath day. But he said unto them, Have ye not read what David did, when he was an hungered, and they that were with him; how he entered into the house of god, and did eat the shewbread, which was not lawful for him to eat, neither for them which were with him, but only for the priests? Or have ye not read in the law, how that on the sabbath days the priests in the temple profane the sabbath, and are blameless? But I say unto you, That in this place is *one* greater than the temple. But if ye had known what *this* meaneth, I will have mercy, and not sacrifice, ye would not have condemned the guiltless. For the Son of man is Lord even of the sabbath day (Matt 12:1–8).

And he said unto them, The sabbath was made for man, and not man for the sabbath: therefore the Son of man is Lord also of the sabbath (Mark 2:27, 28).

And it came to pass, as he went into the house of one of the chief Pharisees to eat bread on the sabbath day, that they watched him. And, behold, there was a certain man before him which had the dropsy. And Jesus answering spake unto the lawyers and Pharisees, saying, Is it lawful to heal on the sabbath day? And they held their peace. And he took *him*, and healed him, and let him go; and answered them, saying, Which of you shall have an ass or an ox fallen into a pit, and will not straightway pull him out on the sabbath day? And they could not answer him again to these things (Luke 14:1–6).

But Jesus answered them, My Father worketh hitherto, and I work. Therefore the Jews sought the more to kill him, because he not only had broken the sabbath, but said also that God was his Father, making himself equal with God. Then answered Jesus and said unto them, Verily, verily, I say unto you, The Son can do nothing of himself, but what he seeth the Father do: for what things soever he doeth, these also doeth the Son likewise (John 5:17–19).

Jesus answered and said unto them, I have done one work, and ye all marvel. Moses therefore gave unto you circumcision; (not because it is of Moses, but of the fathers;) and ye on the sabbath day circumcise a man. If a man on the sabbath day receive circumcision, that the law of Moses should not be broken; are ye angry at me, because I have made a man every whit whole on the sabbath day? Judge not according to the appearance, but judge righteous judgment (John 7:21–24).

Biblical Examples: Exod 16:22–30; Num 15:32–34; 2 Kings 4:23; 2 Chron 36:21; Neh 13:15–22; Lam 1:7; Ezek 23:38; Amos 8:5; Matt 27:62; Mark 2:28; 16:1–9; Luke 4:16–31; 6:6; 13:10–17; 23:54–56; John 5:5–14; 19:31; 20:19–26; Acts 13:14, 27, 42, 44; 15:21; 16:13; 17:2; 18:4; 20:7; 1 Cor 16:2.

Further References: Exod 35:2, 3; Lev 23:1–3, 27–32; 24:8; 26:2, 34, 35; Num 15:32–36; 28:9, 10; Neh 9:13, 14; 10:31; Isa 1:13; 58:13, 14; 66:23; Ezek 22:8; 44:24; 46:1–3; Hos 2:11; Matt 28:1–9; Mark 6:2; Luke 6:1–10; 14:1–6; John 7:21–24; Col 2:16; Heb 4:4.

SACRIFICE, HUMAN

And thou shalt not let any of thy seed pass through *the fire* to Molech, neither shalt thou profane the name of thy God: I *am* the LORD (Lev 18:21).

Again, thou shalt say to the children of Israel, Whosoever *he be* of the children of Israel, or of the strangers that sojourn in Israel, that giveth *any* of his seed unto Molech; he shall surely be put to death: the people of the land shall stone him with stones. And I will set my face against that man, and will cut him off from among his people; because he hath given of his seed unto Molech, to defile my sanctuary, and to profane my holy name. And if the people of the land do any ways hide their eyes from the man, when he giveth of his seed unto Molech, and kill him not: then I will set my face against that man, and against his family, and will cut him off, and all that go a-whoring after him, to commit whoredom with Molech, from among their people (Lev 20:2–5).

Thou shalt not do so unto the LORD thy God: for every abomination to the LORD, which he hateth, have they done unto their gods; for even their sons and their daughters they have burnt in the fire to their gods (Deut 12:31).

There shall not be found among you *any one* that maketh his son or his daughter to pass through the fire, *or* that useth divination, *or* an observer of times, or an enchanter, or a witch, or a charmer, or a consulter with familiar spirits, or a wizard,

or a necromancer. For all that do these things *are* an abomination unto the LORD: and because of these abominations the LORD thy God doth drive them out from before thee. Thou shalt be perfect with the LORD thy God. For these nations, which thou shalt possess, hearkened unto observers of times, and unto diviners: but as for thee, the LORD thy God hath not suffered thee so *to do* (Deut 18:10–14).

Yea, they sacrificed their sons and their daughters unto devils, and shed innocent blood, *even* the blood of their sons and of their daughters, whom they sacrificed unto the idols of Canaan: and the land was polluted with blood (Ps. 106:37, 38).

Against whom do ye sport yourselves? against whom make ye a wide mouth, *and* draw out the tongue? *are* ye not children of transgression, a seed of falsehood, enflaming yourselves with idols under every green tree, slaying the children in the valleys under the clifts of the rocks? (Isa 57:4, 5).

And they have built the high places of Tophet, which *is* in the valley of the son of Hinnom, to burn their sons and their daughters in the fire; which I commanded *them* not, neither came it into my heart (Jer 7:31).

That they have committed adultery, and blood *is* in their hands, and with their idols have they committed adultery, and have also caused their sons, whom they bare unto me, to pass for them through *the fire*, to devour *them*. Moreover this they have done unto me: they have defiled my sanctuary in the same day, and have profaned my sabbaths. For when they had slain their children to their idols, then they came the same day into my sanctuary to profane it; and, lo, thus have they done in the midst of mine house (Ezek 23:37–39).

By faith Abraham, when he was tried, offered up Isaac; and he that had received the promises offered up his only begotten *son,* of whom it was said, That in Isaac shall thy seed be called: accounting that God *was* able to raise *him* up, even from the dead; from whence also he received him in a figure (Heb 11:17–19).

Biblical Examples: Gen 22:19; 2 Kings 16:1–3; 17:24–31; 21:1–6; 23:1–10; 2

Chron 28:3; Jer 19:5, 6; 32:35; Ezek 16:20, 21; 20:22–25.

SANITATION (See Health)

SATAN (See Temptation)

SCOFFING

And the LORD God of their fathers sent to them by his messengers, rising up betimes, and sending; because he had compassion on his people, and on his dwelling place: but they mocked the messengers of God, and despised his words and misused his prophets, until the wrath of the LORD arose against his people, till *there was* no remedy (2 Chron 36:15, 16).

Blessed *is* the man that walketh not in the counsel of the ungodly, nor standeth in the way of sinners, nor sitteth in the seat of the scornful (Ps 1:1).

My tears have been my meat day and night, while they continually say unto me, Where *is* thy God? (Ps 42:3).

And they say, How doth God know? and is there knowledge in the most High? (Ps 73:11).

Yea, they spake against God; they said, Can God furnish a table in the wilderness? (Ps 78:19).

The thought of foolishness *is* sin: and the scorner *is* an abomination to men (Prov 24:9).

Of how much sorer punishment, suppose ye, shall he be thought worthy, who hath trodden under foot the Son of God, and hath counted the blood of the covenant, wherewith he was sanctified, an unholy thing, and hath done despite unto the Spirit of grace? (Heb 10:29).

Knowing this first, that there shall come in the last days scoffers, walking after their own lusts, and saying, Where is the promise of his coming? for since the fathers fell asleep, all things continue as *they were* from the beginning of the creation (2 Peter 3:3, 4).

Biblical Examples: 2 Kings 2:23; 2 Chron 30:6–10; Neh 4:1; Ps 35:15; Isa 5:18–25; 57:4; Jer 17:15; Hos 7:5; Matt 12:24; 27:28–30, 41; Luke 4:23; 16:14; Acts 2:13; 13:45; 17:18, 32.

Further References: Prov 1:22–25; 3:34;

9:12; 13:1; 19:29; 21:11; 22:10; 2 Peter 3:3, 4.

SEDUCTION (See also Fornication)

And if a man entice a maid that is not betrothed, and lie with her, he shall surely endow her to be his wife. If her father utterly refuse to give her unto him, he shall pay money according to the dowry of virgins (Exod 22:16, 17).

If a damsel *that is* a virgin be betrothed unto an husband, and a man find her in the city, and lie with her; then ye shall bring them both out unto the gate of that city, and ye shall stone them with stones that they die; the damsel, because she cried not, *being* in the city; and the man, because he hath humbled his neighbour's wife: so thou shalt put away evil from among you.

But if a man find a betrothed damsel in the field, and the man force her, and lie with her: then the man only that lay with her shall die: but unto the damsel thou shalt do nothing; *there is* in the damsel no sin *worthy* of death: for as when a man riseth against his neighbour, and slayeth him, even so *is* this matter: for he found her in the field, *and* the betrothed damsel cried, and *there was* none to save her.

If a man find a damsel *that is* a virgin, which is not betrothed, and lay hold on her, and lie with her, and they be found; then the man that lay with her shall give unto the damsel's father fifty *shekels* of silver, and she shall be his wife; because he hath humbled her, he may not put her away all his days (Deut 22:23–29).

For the commandment *is* a lamp; and the law *is* light; and reproofs of instruction *are* the way of life: to keep thee from the evil woman, from the flattery of the tongue of a strange woman.

Lust not after her beauty in thine heart; neither let her take thee with her eyelids. For by means of a whorish woman *a man is brought* to a piece of bread: and the adulteress will hunt for the precious life (Prov 6:23–26).

Say unto wisdom, Thou *art* my sister; and call understanding *thy* kinswoman: that they may keep thee from the strange woman, from the stranger *which* flattereth with her words.

For at the window of my house I looked through my casement, and beheld among the simple ones, I discerned among the youths, a young man void of understanding, passing through the street near her corner; and he went the way to her house, in the twilight, in the evening, in the black and dark night: for she hath cast down many wounded: yea, many strong *men* have been slain by her. Her house *is* the way to hell, going down to the chambers of death (Prov 7:4–27).

A foolish woman *is* clamorous: *she is* simple, and knoweth nothing. For she sitteth at the door of her house, on a seat in the high places of the city, to call passengers who go right on their ways: whoso *is* simple, let him turn in hither: and *as for* him that wanteth understanding, she saith to him, stolen waters are sweet, and bread *eaten* in secret is pleasant.

But he knoweth not that the dead *are* there; *and that* her guests *are* in the depths of hell (Prov 9:13–18).

Biblical Examples: Gen 19:30–35, 2 Sam 13:1–14.

Further References: Deut 27:20; 2 Tim 3:6, 13.

SEGREGATION (See Race Relations)

SELF-CONTROL (See also Temperance)

He that *hath* no rule over his own spirit *is like* a city *that is* broken down, *and* without walls (Prov 25:28).

And as he reasoned of righteousness, temperance, and judgment to come, Felix trembled, and answered, Go thy way for this time; when I have a convenient season, I will call for thee (Acts 24:25).

But if they cannot contain, let them marry: for it is better to marry than to burn (1 Cor 7:9).

And every man that striveth for the mastery is temperate in all things. Now they *do it* to obtain a corruptible crown; but we an incorruptible (1 Cor 9:25).

Stand fast therefore in the liberty wherewith Christ hath made us free, and be not entangled again with the yoke of bondage. . . . For, brethren, ye have been

called unto liberty; only *use* not liberty for an occasion to the flesh, but by love serve one another (Gal 5:1, 13).

For the flesh lusteth against the Spirit, and the Spirit against the flesh: and these are contrary the one to the other: so that ye cannot do the things that ye would (Gal 5:17).

But the fruit of the Spirit is love, joy, peace, longsuffering, gentleness, goodness, faith, meekness, temperance: against such there is no law (Gal 5:22, 23).

But refuse profane and old wives' fables, and exercise thyself *rather* unto godliness. For bodily exercise profiteth little: but godliness is profitable unto all things, having promise of the life that now is, and of that which is to come (1 Tim 4:7, 8).

For a bishop must be blameless, as the steward of God; not selfwilled, not soon angry, not given to wine, no striker, not given to filthy lucre; but a lover of hospitality, a lover of good men, sober, just, holy, temperate (Titus 1:7, 8).

And beside this, giving all diligence, add to your faith virtue; and to virtue knowledge; and to knowledge temperance; and to temperance patience, and to patience godliness (2 Peter 1:5, 6).

Biblical Examples: Gen 43:31; 1 Sam 10:27; 24:1–15; 26:1–20; Matt 26:62, 63; 27:12–14.

SELF-DENIAL

And he said, Lay not thine hand upon the lad, neither do thou any thing unto him: for now I know that thou fearest God, seeing thou hast not withheld thy son, thine only *son* from me (Gen 22:12).

He *that is* slow to anger *is* better than the mighty; and he that ruleth his spirit than he that taketh a city (Prov 16:32).

And put a knife to thy throat, if thou *be* a man given to appetite (Prov 23:2).

And if thy right eye offend thee, pluck it out, and cast *it* from thee: for it is profitable for thee that one of thy members should perish, and not *that* thy whole body should be cast into hell. And if thy right hand offend thee, cut it off, and cast *it* from thee: for it is profitable for thee that one of thy members should perish, and not *that* thy whole body should be cast into hell (Matt 5:29, 30).

And a certain scribe came, and said unto him, Master, I will follow thee whithersoever thou goest. And Jesus said unto him, The foxes have holes, and the birds of the air *have* nests; but the Son of man hath not where to lay *his* head. And another of his disciples said unto him, Lord, suffer me first to go and bury my father. But Jesus said unto him, Follow me; and let the dead bury their dead (Matt 8:19–22).

He that loveth father or mother more than me is not worthy of me: and he that loveth son or daughter more than me is not worthy of me. And he that taketh not his cross, and followeth after me is not worthy of me. He that findeth his life shall lose it: and he that loseth his life for my sake shall find it (Matt 10:37–39).

Then said Jesus unto his disciples, If any *man* will come after me, let him deny himself, and take up his cross, and follow me. For whosoever will save his life shall lose it: and whosoever will lose his life for my sake shall find it. For what is a man profited, if he shall gain the whole world, and lose his own soul? or what shall a man give in exchange for his soul? (Matt 16:24–26).

And if thy hand offend thee, cut it off: it is better for thee to enter into life maimed, than having two hands to go into hell, into the fire that never shall be quenched: where their worm dieth not, and the fire is not quenched.

And if thy foot offend thee, cut it off: it is better for thee to enter halt into life, than having two feet to be cast into hell, into the fire that never shall be quenched: where their worm dieth not, and the fire is not quenched. And if thine eye offend thee, pluck it out: it is better for thee to enter into the kingdom of God with one eye, than having two eyes to be cast into hell fire: where their worm dieth not, and the fire is not quenched. (Mark 9:43–48).

And Jesus answered and said, Verily I say unto you, There is no man that hath left house, or brethren, or sisters, or father, or mother, or wife, or children, or lands, for my sake, and the gospel's, but he shall receive an hundredfold now in this time, houses, and brethren, and sisters, and mothers, and children, and lands, with persecutions; and in the world to come eternal life. But many *that are* first shall be last; and the last first (Mark 10:29–31).

I beseech you therefore, brethren, by the mercies of God, that ye present your bodies a living sacrifice, holy, acceptable unto God, *which is* your reasonable service. And be not conformed to this world: but be ye transformed by the renewing of your mind, that ye may prove what *is* that good, and acceptable, and perfect, will of God (Rom 12:1, 2).

We then that are strong ought to bear the infirmities of the weak, and not to please ourselves. Let every one of us please *his* neighbour for *his* good to edification. For even Christ pleased not himself; but, as it is written, The reproaches of them that reproached thee fell on me. For whatsoever things were written aforetime were written for our learning, that we through patience and comfort of the scriptures might have hope. Now the God of patience and consolation grant you to be likeminded one toward another according to Christ Jesus (Rom 15:1–5).

For if any man see thee which hast knowledge sit at meat in the idol's temple, shall not the conscience of him which is weak be emboldened to eat those things which are offered to idols; and through thy knowledge shall the weak brother perish, for whom Christ died? But when ye sin so against the brethren, and wound their weak conscience, ye sin against Christ (1 Cor 8:10–12).

If others be partakers of *this* power over you, *are* not we rather? Nevertheless we have not used this power; but suffer all things, lest we should hinder the gospel of Christ (1 Cor 9:12).

But I have used none of these things: neither have I written these things, that it should be so done unto me: for *it were* better for me to die, than that any man should make my glorying void (1 Cor 9:15).

What is my reward then? *Verily* that, when I preach the gospel, I may make the gospel of Christ without charge, that I abuse not my power in the gospel. For though I be free from all *men*, yet have I made myself servant unto all, that I might gain the more. And unto the Jews I became as Jew, that I might gain the Jews; to them that are under the law, as under the law, that I might gain them that are under the law; to them that are without law, as without law, (being not without law to God, but under the law to Christ,) that I might gain them that are without law.

To the weak became I as weak, that I might gain the weak: I am made all things to all *men*, that I might by all means save some. And this I do for the gospel's sake, that I might be partaker thereof with *you* (1 Cor 9:18–23).

And every man that striveth for the mastery is temperate in all things. Now they *do it* to obtain a corruptible crown; but we an incorruptible. I therefore so run, not as uncertainly; so fight I, not as one that beateth the air: but I keep under my body, and bring *it* into subjection: lest that by any means, when I have preached to others, I myself should be a castaway (1 Cor 9:25–27).

I am crucified with Christ: nevertheless I live; yet not I, but Christ liveth in me: and the life which I now live in the flesh I live by the faith of the Son of God, who loved me, and gave himself for me (Gal 2:20).

But God forbid that I should glory, save in the cross of our Lord Jesus Christ, by whom the world is crucified unto me, and I unto the world (Gal 6:14).

Let nothing *be done* through strife or vainglory; but in lowliness of mind let each esteem other better than themselves. Look not every man on his own things, but every man also on the things of others. Let this mind be in you, which was also in Christ Jesus: who, being in the form of God, thought it not robbery to be equal with God: but made himself of no reputation, and took upon him the form of a servant, and was made in the likeness of men (Phil 2:3–7).

But what things were gain to me, those I counted loss for Christ. Yea doubtless, and I count all things *but* loss for the excellency of the knowledge of Christ Jesus my Lord: for whom I have suffered the loss of all things, and do count them *but* dung, that I may win Christ, and be found in

him, not having mine own righteousness, which is of the law, but that which is through the faith of Christ, the righteousness which is of God by faith (Phil 3:7–9).

Wherefore if ye be dead with Christ from the rudiments of the world, why, as though living in the world, are ye subject to ordinances, (touch not; taste not; handle not; which all are to perish with the using;) after the commandments and doctrines of men? Which things have indeed a shew of wisdom in will-worship, and humility, and neglecting of the body; not in any honour to the satisfying of the flesh (Col 2:20–23).

Mortify therefore your members which are upon the earth; fornication, uncleanness, inordinate affection, evil concupiscence, and covetousness, which is idolatry (Col 3:5).

No man that warreth entangleth himself with the affairs of *this* life; that he may please him who hath chosen him to be a soldier (2 Tim 2:4).

Forasmuch then as Christ hath suffered for us in the flesh, arm yourselves likewise with the same mind: for he that hath suffered in the flesh hath ceased from sin; that he no longer should live the rest of *his* time in the flesh to the lusts of men, but to the will of God (1 Peter 4:1, 2).

And they overcame him by the blood of the Lamb, and by the word of their testimony; and they loved not their lives unto the death (Rev 12:11).

Biblical Examples: 2 Sam 24:24; 1 Kings 17:12–15; Esth 4:16; Ps 132:3–5; Dan 1:8; 5:16, 17; 10:3; Matt 19:27; Mark 2:14; 10:28; 12:43, 44; Luke 5:11, 27, 28; 21:2–4; Acts 4:36, 37; 20:22–24; 21:13; Heb 11:25.

Further References: Matt 13:44–46; 18:8, 9; 19:12, 21; Mark 8:34, 35; Luke 9:23, 24, 59, 60; 12:33; 14:26–33; 18:27–30; John 12:25; Rom 13:14; 14:1–22; 1 Cor 6:12; Gal 5:16, 17, 24; 1 Peter 2:11–16.

SELFISHNESS

And the LORD said unto Cain, Where *is* Abel thy brother? And he said, I know not: *Am* I my brother's keeper? (Gen 4:9).

He that withholdeth corn, the people shall curse him: but blessing *shall be* upon the head of him that selleth *it* (Prov 11:26).

Speak unto all the people of the land, and to the priests, saying, When ye fasted and mourned in the fifth and seventh *month,* even those seventy years, did ye at all fast unto me, *even* to me? And when ye did eat, and when ye did drink, did not ye eat *for yourselves,* and drink *for yourselves?* (Zech 7:5, 6).

Jesus said unto him, If thou wilt be perfect, go *and* sell that thou hast, and give to the poor, and thou shalt have treasure in heaven: and come *and* follow me. But when the young man heard that saying, he went away sorrowful: for he had great possessions (Matt 19:21, 22).

For if ye love them which love you, what thank have ye? for sinners also love those that love them. And if ye do good to them which do good to you, what thank have ye? for sinners also do even the same. And if ye lend *to them* of whom ye hope to receive, what thank have ye? for sinners also lend to sinners, to receive as much again (Luke 6:32–34).

We then that are strong ought to bear the infirmities of the weak, and not to please ourselves. Let every one of us please *his* neighbour for *his* good to edification. For even Christ pleased not himself; but, as it is written, The reproaches of them that reproached thee fell on me (Rom 15:1–3).

Let no man seek his own, but every man another's *wealth* (1 Cor 10:24).

And *that* he died for all, that they which live should not henceforth live unto themselves, but unto him which died for them, and rose again (2 Cor 5:15).

Bear ye one another's burdens, and so fulfil the law of Christ (Gal 6:2).

Look not every man on his own things, but every man also on the things of others (Phil 2:4).

For men shall be lovers of their own selves, covetous, boasters, proud, blasphemers, disobedient to parents, unthankful, unholy, without natural affection, trucebreakers, false accusers, incontinent, fierce, despisers of those that are good, traitors, heady, highminded, lovers of pleasure more than lovers of God (2 Tim 3:2–4).

But whoso hath this world's good, and seeth his brother have need, and shutteth up his bowels *of compassion* from him, how dwelleth the love of God in him? (1 John 3:17).

Biblical Examples: Num 32:6; Ezek 34:18; Mic 3:11; Hag 1:4, 9, 10; Phil 2:20, 21.

Further References: Prov 28:27; James 2:15, 16.

SELF-RIGHTEOUSNESS (See also Pride)

Can a man be profitable unto God, as he that is wise may be profitable unto himself? *Is it* any pleasure to the Almighty, that thou art righteous? or *is it* gain *to him,* that thou makest thy ways perfect? (Job 22:2, 3).

The way of a fool *is* right in his own eyes: but he that hearkeneth unto counsel *is* wise (Prov 12:15).

There is a way which seemeth right unto a man, but the end thereof *are* the ways of death. Even in laughter the heart is sorrowful; and the end of that mirth *is* heaviness (Prov 14:12, 13).

Most men will proclaim every one his own goodness: but a faithful man who can find? (Prov 20:6).

Seest thou a man wise in his own conceit? *there is* more hope of a fool than of him (Prov 26:12).

Let another man praise thee, and not thine own mouth; a stranger, and not thine own lips (Prov 27:2).

He that covereth his sins shall not prosper: but whoso confesseth and forsaketh *them* shall have mercy (Prov 28:13).

He that trusteth in his own heart is a fool: but whoso walketh wisely, he shall be delivered (Prov 28:26).

Woe unto *them that are* wise in their own eyes, and prudent in their own sight! (Isa 5:21).

Thus saith the LORD; Cursed *be* the man that trusteth in man, and maketh flesh his arm, and whose heart departeth from the LORD (Jer 17:5).

In that day shalt thou not be ashamed for all thy doings, where in thou hast transgressed against me: for then I will take away out of the midst of thee them that rejoice in thy pride, and thou shalt no more be haughty because of my holy mountain (Zeph 3:11).

Many will say to me in that day, Lord, Lord, have we not prophesied in thy name? and in thy name have cast out devils? and in thy name done many wonderful works? And then will I profess unto them, I never knew you: depart from me, ye that work iniquity (Matt 7:22, 23).

Woe unto you, scribes and Pharisees, hypocrites! because ye build the tombs of the prophets, and garnish the sepulchres of the righteous, and say, If we had been in the days of our fathers, we would not have been partakers with them in the blood of the prophets. Wherefore ye be witnesses unto yourselves, that ye are the children of them which killed the prophets (Matt 23:29–31).

And the Pharisees and scribes murmured, saying, This man receiveth sinners, and eateth with them. Now his elder son was in the field: and as he came and drew nigh to the house, he heard music and dancing. And he called one of the servants, and asked what these things meant. And he said unto him, Thy brother is come; and thy father hath killed the fatted calf, because he hath received him safe and sound. And he was angry, and would not go in: therefore came his father out, and entreated him. And he answering said to *his* father, Lo, these many years do I serve thee, neither transgressed I at any time thy commandment: and yet thou never gavest me a kid, that I might make merry with my friends: but as soon as this thy son was come, which hath devoured thy living with harlots, thou hast killed for him the fatted calf. And he said unto him, Son, thou art ever with me, and all that I have is thine. It was meet that we should make merry, and be glad: for this thy brother was dead, and is alive again; and was lost, and is found (Luke 15:2, 25–32).

And the Pharisees also, who were covetous, heard all these things: and they derided him. And he said unto them, Ye are they which justify yourselves before men; but God knoweth your hearts: for that which is highly esteemed among men is abomination in the sight of God (Luke 16:14, 15).

And he spake this parable unto certain which trusted in themselves that they were righteous, and despised others: two men went up into the temple to pray; the one a Pharisee, and the other a publican.

The Pharisee stood and prayed thus with himself, God, I thank thee, that I am not as other men *are*, extortioners, unjust, adulterers, or even as this publican. I fast twice in the week, I give tithes of all that I possess (Luke 18:9–12).

For they being ignorant of God's righteousness, and going about to establish their own righteousness, have not submitted themselves unto the righteousness of God (Rom 10:3).

But he that glorieth, let him glory in the Lord (2 Cor. 10:17).

For if a man think himself to be something, when he is nothing, he deceiveth himself (Gal 6:3).

Biblical Examples: Num 16:3; Deut 9:4–6; 1 Sam 15:13–31; Job 11:4–6; 13:3, 13–16, 18, 19; 32:1, 2; 33:8, 9; Prov 30:12, 13; Isa 65:3–5; Jer 2:13, 22, 23, 34, 35; Ezek 33:24–26; Hos 12:8; Matt 9:10–13; 19:16–22; Mark 2:16; 10:17–22; Luke 5:30; 7:36–50; 18:18–23; John 9:34, 39–41; Rev 3:17, 18.

Further References: Ps 10:5, 6; Prov 16:2; 21:2; 25:14–27; Isa 64:6; Rom 11:19–21; 2 Cor 1:9.

SENSUALITY (See Pleasure, Lover of)

SERVICE (See Ministry)

SEX AND SEXUALITY (See also Adultery; Bestiality; Birth Control; Birth Out of Wedlock; Body, Human; Celibacy; Chastity; Fornication; Homosexuality; Husband-Wife Relations; Incest; Lust; Marriage; Monogamy; Pleasure, Lover of; Purity; Rape; Seduction; Virginity)

And God blessed them, and God said unto them, Be fruitful, and multiply, and replenish the earth, and subdue it: and have dominion over the fish of the sea, and over the fowl of the air, and over every living thing that moveth upon the earth (Gen 1:28).

Therefore shall a man leave his father and his mother, and shall cleave unto his wife: and they shall be one flesh (Gen 2:24).

Thou shalt not commit adultery (Exod 20:14).

And if a man entice a maid that is not betrothed, and lie with her, he shall surely endow her to be his wife (Exod 22:16).

Whosoever lieth with a beast shall surely be put to death. (Exod 22:19).

And if a woman have an issue, *and* her issue in her flesh be blood, she shall be put apart seven days: and whosoever toucheth her shall be unclean until the even. And every thing that she lieth upon in her separation shall be unclean: every thing also that she sitteth upon shall be unclean. And whosoever toucheth her bed shall wash his clothes, and bathe *himself* in water, and be unclean until the even. And whosoever toucheth any thing that she sat upon shall wash his clothes, and bathe *himself* in water, and be unclean until the even. And if it *be* on *her* bed, or on any thing whereon she sitteth, when he toucheth it, he shall be unclean until the even. And if any man lie with her at all, and her flowers be upon him, he shall be unclean seven days; and all the bed whereon he lieth shall be unclean (Lev 15:19–24).

None of you shall approach to any that is near of kin to him, to uncover *their* nakedness: I *am* the LORD (Lev 18:6).

Moreover thou shalt not lie carnally with thy neighbour's wife, to defile thyself with her (Lev 18:20).

Thou shalt not lie with mankind, as with womankind: it *is* abomination (Lev 18:22).

And whosoever lieth carnally with a woman, that *is* a bondmaid, betrothed to an husband, and not at all redeemed, nor freedom given her; she shall be scourged; they shall not be put to death, because she was not free (Lev 19:20).

Do not prostitute thy daughter, to cause her to be a whore; lest the land fall to whoredom, and the land become full of wickedness (Lev 19:29).

And the man that committeth adultery with *another* man's wife, *even he* that committeth adultery with his neighbour's wife, the adulterer and the adulteress shall surely be put to death (Lev 20:10).

If any man take a wife, and go in unto her, and hate her, and give occasions of speech against her, and bring up an evil name upon her, and say, I took this woman, and when I came to her, I found her not a maid: then shall the father of the damsel, and her mother, take and bring forth *the tokens* of the damsel's vir-

ginity unto the elders of the city in the gate: and the damsel's father shall say unto the elders, I gave my daughter unto this man to wife, and he hateth her; and, lo, he hath given occasions of speech *against her*, saying, I found not thy daughter a maid; and yet these *are the tokens of* my daughter's virginity. And they shall spread the cloth before the elders of the city. And the elders of that city shall take that man and chastise him; and they shall amerce him in an hundred *shekels* of silver, and give *them* unto the father of the damsel, because he hath brought up an evil name upon a virgin of Israel: and she shall be his wife; he may not put her away all his days. But if this thing be true, *and the tokens of* virginity be not found for the damsel: then they shall bring out the damsel to the door of her father's house, and the men of her city shall stone her with stones that she die: because she hath wrought folly in Israel, to play the whore in her father's house: so shalt thou put evil away from among you.

If a man be found lying with a woman married to an husband, then they shall both of them die, *both* the man that lay with the woman, and the woman: so shalt thou put away evil from Israel (Deut 22:13–22).

There shall be no whore of the daughters of Israel, nor a sodomite of the sons of Israel (Deut 23:17).

Cursed *be* he that lieth with his father's wife; because he uncovereth his father's skirt. And all the people shall say, Amen. Cursed *be* he that lieth with any manner of beast. And all the people shall say, Amen. Cursed *be* he that lieth with his sister, the daughter of his father, or the daughter of his mother. And all the people shall say, Amen. Cursed *be* he that lieth with his mother in law. And all the people shall say, Amen (Deut 27:20–23).

Ye have heard that it was said by them of old time, Thou shalt not commit adultery: but I say unto you, That whosoever looketh on a woman to lust after her hath committed adultery with her already in his heart (Matt 5:27, 28).

For out of the heart proceed evil thoughts, murders, adulteries, fornications, thefts, false witness, blasphemies:

these are *the things* which defile a man: but to eat with unwashen hands defileth not a man (Matt 15:19, 20).

And it came to pass, *that* when Jesus had finished these sayings, he departed from Galilee, and came into the coasts of Judaea beyond Jordan; and great multitudes followed him; and he healed them there.

The Pharisees also came unto him, tempting him, and saying unto him, Is it lawful for a man to put away his wife for every cause? And he answered and said unto them, Have ye not read, that he which made *them* at the beginning made them male and female, and said, For this cause shall a man leave father and mother, and shall cleave to his wife: and they twain shall be one flesh? Wherefore they are no more twain, but one flesh. What therefore God hath joined together, let no man put asunder. They say unto him, Why did Moses then command to give a writing of divorcement, and to put her away? He saith unto them, Moses because of the hardness of your hearts suffered you to put away your wives: but from the beginning it was not so. And I say unto you, Whosoever shall put away his wife, except *it be* for fornication, and shall marry another, committeth adultery: and whoso marrieth her which is put away doth commit adultery.

His disciples say unto him, If the case of the man be so with *his* wife, it is not good to marry. But he said unto them, All *men* cannot receive this saying, save *they* to whom it is given. For there are some eunuchs, which were so born from *their* mother's womb: and there are some eunuchs, which were made eunuchs of men: and there be eunuchs, which have made themselves eunuchs for the kingdom of heaven's sake. He that is able to receive *it*, let him receive *it* (Matt 19:1–12).

For this cause God gave them up unto vile affections: for even their women did change the natural use into that which is against nature: and likewise also the men, leaving the natural use of the woman, burned in their lust one toward another; men with men working that which is unseemly, and receiving in themselves that recompence of their error which was meet (Rom 1:26, 27).

I beseech you therefore, brethren, by the mercies of God, that ye present your bodies a living sacrifice, holy, acceptable unto God, *which is* your reasonable service (Rom 12:1).

It is reported commonly *that there is* fornication among you, and such fornication as is not so much as named among the Gentiles, that one should have his father's wife. And ye are puffed up, and have not rather mourned, that he that hath done this deed might be taken away from among you. For I verily, as absent in body, but present in spirit, have judged already, as though I were present, *concerning* him that hath so done this deed, in the name of our Lord Jesus Christ, when ye are gathered together, and my spirit, with the power of our Lord Jesus Christ, to deliver such an one unto Satan for the destruction of the flesh, that the spirit may be saved in the day of the Lord Jesus. Your glorying *is* not good. Know ye not that a little leaven leaveneth the whole lump? Purge out therefore the old leaven, that ye may be a new lump, as ye are unleavened. For even Christ our passover is sacrificed for us: therefore let us keep the feast, not with old leaven, neither with the leaven of malice and wickedness; but with the unleavened *bread* of sincerity and truth. I wrote unto you in an epistle not to company with fornicators: yet not altogether with the fornicators of this world, or with the covetous, or extortioners, or with idolaters; for then must ye needs go out of the world. But now I have written unto you not to keep company, if any man that is called a brother be a fornicator, or covetous, or an idolater, or a railer, or a drunkard, or an extortioner; with such an one no not to eat. For what have I to do to judge them also that are without? do not ye judge them that are within? But them that are without God judgeth. Therefore put away from among yourselves that wicked person (1 Cor 5:1–13).

Know ye not that the unrighteous shall not inherit the kingdom of God? Be not deceived: neither fornicators, nor idolaters, nor adulterers, nor effeminate, nor abusers of themselves with mankind, nor thieves, nor covetous, nor drunkards, nor revilers, nor extortioners, shall inherit the kingdom of God. And such were some of you: but ye are washed, but ye are sanctified, but ye are justified in the name of the Lord Jesus, and by the Spirit of our God. All things are lawful unto me, but all things are not expedient: all things are lawful for me, but I will not be brought under the power of any. Meats for the belly, and the belly for meats: but God shall destroy both it and them. Now the body *is* not for fornication, but for the Lord; and the Lord for the body. And God hath both raised up the Lord, and will also raise up us by his own power. Know ye not that your bodies are the members of Christ? shall I then take the members of Christ, and make *them* the members of an harlot? God forbid. What? know ye not that he which is joined to an harlot is one body? for two, saith he, shall be one flesh. But he that is joined unto the Lord is one spirit. Flee fornication. Every sin that a man doeth is without the body; but he that committeth fornication sinneth against his own body. What? know ye not that your body is the temple of the Holy Ghost *which is* in you, which ye have of God, and ye are not your own? For ye are bought with a price: therefore glorify God in your body, and in your spirit, which are God's (1 Cor 6:9–20).

Nevertheless, *to avoid* fornication, let every man have his own wife, and let every woman have her own husband. Let the husband render unto the wife due benevolence: and likewise also the wife unto the husband. The wife hath not power of her own body, but the husband: and likewise also the husband hath not power of his own body, but the wife. Defraud ye not one the other, except *it be* with consent for a time, that ye may give yourselves to fasting and prayer; and come together again, that Satan tempt you not for your incontinency. But I speak this by permission, *and* not of commandment. For I would that all men were even as I myself. But every man hath his proper gift of God, one after this manner, and another after that. I say therefore to the unmarried and widows, It is good for them if they abide even as I. But if they cannot contain, let them marry: for it is better to marry than to burn (1 Cor 7:2–9).

Wives, submit yourselves unto your own husbands, as unto the Lord. For the husband is the head of the wife, even as Christ is the head of the church: and he is the saviour of the body. Therefore as the church is subject unto Christ, so *let* the wives *be* to their own husbands in every thing. Husbands, love your wives, even as Christ also loved the church, and gave himself for it; that he might sanctify and cleanse it with the washing of water by the word, that he might present it to himself a glorious church, not having spot, or wrinkle, or any such thing; but that it should be holy and without blemish. So ought men to love their wives as their own bodies. He that loveth his wife loveth himself. For no man ever yet hated his own flesh; but nourisheth and cherisheth it, even as the Lord the church: for we are members of his body, of his flesh, and of his bones. For this cause shall a man leave his father and mother, and shall be joined unto his wife, and they too shall be one flesh. This is a great mystery: but I speak concerning Christ and the church. Nevertheless let every one of you in particular so love his wife even as himself; and the wife *see* that she reverence *her* husband (Eph 5:22–33).

For this is the will of God, *even* your sanctification, that ye should abstain from fornication: that every one of you should know how to possess his vessel in sanctification and honour; not in the lust of concupiscence, even as the Gentiles which know not God: that no *man* go beyond and defraud his brother in *any* matter: because that the Lord *is* the avenger of all such, as we also have forewarned you and testified. For God hath not called us unto uncleanness, but unto holiness. He therefore that despiseth, despiseth not man, but God, who hath also given unto us his holy Spirit (1 Thess 4:3–8).

Forbidding to marry, *and commanding* to abstain from meats, which God hath created to be received with thanksgiving of them which believe and know the truth. For every creature of God *is* good, and nothing to be refused, if it be received with thanksgiving (1 Tim 4:3, 4).

Marriage *is* honourable in all, and the bed undefiled: but whoremongers and adulterers God will judge (Heb 13:4).

Blessed *are* they that do his commandments, that they may have right to the tree of life, and may enter in through the gates into the city. For without *are* dogs, and sorcerers, and whoremongers, and murderers, and idolaters, and whosoever loveth and maketh a lie (Rev 22:14, 15).

Biblical Examples: (see separate related topics).

Further References: (see separate related topics).

SICK, CARE OF (See Ministry)

SINCERITY (See also Honesty, Lying)

Now therefore fear the LORD, and serve him in sincerity and in truth: and put away the gods which your fathers served on the other side of the flood, and in Egypt; and serve ye the LORD (Josh 24:14).

Blessed *is* the man unto whom the LORD imputeth not iniquity, and in whose spirit *there is* no guile (Ps 32:2).

So likewise shall my heavenly Father do also unto you, if ye from your hearts forgive not every one his brother their trespasses (Matt 18:35).

Let love be without dissimulation. Abhor that which is evil; cleave to that which is good (Rom 12:9).

Therefore let us keep the feast, not with old leaven, neither with the leaven of malice and wickedness; but with the unleavened *bread* of sincerity and truth (1 Cor 5:8).

Whether therefore ye eat, or drink, or whatsoever ye do, do all to the glory of God (1 Cor 10:31).

For our rejoicing is this, the testimony of our conscience, that in simplicity and godly sincerity, not with fleshly wisdom, but by the grace of God, we have had our conversation in the world, and more abundantly to you-ward (2 Cor 1:12).

I speak not by commandment, but by occasion of the forwardness of others, and to prove the sincerity of your love. . . .

Wherefore shew ye to them, and before the churches, the proof of your love, and of our boasting on your behalf (2 Cor 8:8, 24).

Servants, be obedient to them that are *your* masters according to the flesh, with fear and trembling, in singleness of your heart, as unto Christ; not with eye-service, as men-pleasers; but as the servants of Christ, doing the will of God from the heart; with good will doing service, as to the Lord, and not to men: grace *be* with all them that love our Lord Jesus Christ in sincerity. Amen (Eph 6:5–7, 24).

For our exhortation *was* not of deceit, nor of uncleanness, nor in guile: but as we were allowed of God to be put in trust with the gospel, even so we speak; not as pleasing men, but God, which trieth our hearts. For neither at any time used we flattering words, as ye know, nor a cloak of covetousness; God *is* witness (1 Thess 2:3–5).

Now the end of the commandment is charity out of a pure heart, and *of* a good conscience, and *of* faith unfeigned (1 Tim 1:5).

In all things shewing thyself a pattern of good works: in doctrine *shewing* uncorruptness, gravity, sincerity, sound speech, that cannot be condemned; that he that is of the contrary part may be ashamed, having no evil thing to say of you (Titus 2:7, 8).

Seeing ye have purified your souls in obeying the truth through the Spirit unto unfeigned love of the brethren, *see that ye* love one another with a pure heart fervently (1 Peter 1:22).

Who did no sin, neither was guile found in his mouth (1 Peter 2:22).

Biblical Examples: 1 Chron 12:33; Isa 38:3; John 1:47; 2 Cor 1:12; 2 Tim 1:5; 1 Peter 2:22.

Further References: Ps 5:9; 32:2; 55:21; 1 Cor 5:8; 2 Cor 2:17; Phil 1:16; 1 Peter 2:1.

SLANDER (See also Gossip, Tongue)

If a false witness rise up against any man to testify against him *that which is* wrong; then both the men, between whom the controversy *is,* shall stand before the

LORD, before the priests and the judges, which shall be in those days; and the judges shall make diligent inquisition: and, behold, *if* the witness *be* a false witness, *and* hath testified falsely against his brother; then shall ye do unto him, as he had thought to have done unto his brother: so shalt thou put the evil away from among you. And those which remain shall hear, and fear, and shall henceforth commit no more any such evil among you. And thine eye shall not pity; *but* life *shall go* for life, eye for eye, tooth for tooth, hand for hand, foot for foot (Deut 19:16–21).

Thou shalt be hid from the scourge of the tongue: neither shalt thou be afraid of destruction when it cometh (Job 5:21).

Lord, who shall abide in thy tabernacle? who shall dwell in thy holy hill? He that walketh uprightly, and worketh righteousness, and speaketh the truth in his heart. He *that* backbiteth not with his tongue, nor doeth evil to his neighbour, nor taketh up a reproach against his neighbour (Ps 15:1–3).

They compassed me about also with words of hatred; and fought against me without a cause (Ps 109:3).

A false witness *that* speaketh lies, and he that soweth discord among brethren (Prov 6:19).

An hypocrite with *his* mouth destroyeth his neighbour: but through knowledge shall the just be delivered (Prov 11:9).

The north wind driveth away rain: so *doth* an angry countenance a backbiting tongue (Prov 25:23).

But I say unto you, That every idle word that men shall speak, they shall give account thereof in the day of judgment (Matt 12:36).

A good man out of the good treasure of his heart bringeth forth that which is good; and an evil man out of the evil treasure of his heart bringeth forth that which is evil: for of the abundance of the heart his mouth speaketh (Luke 6:45).

And withal they learn *to be* idle, wandering about from house to house; and not only idle, but tattlers also and busybodies, speaking things which they ought not (1 Tim 5:13).

If any man teach otherwise, and consent not to wholesome words, *even* the words of our Lord Jesus Christ, and to the doctrine which is according to godliness; he is proud, knowing nothing, but doting about questions and strifes of words, whereof cometh envy, strife, railing, evil surmisings, perverse disputings of men of corrupt minds, and destitute of the truth, supposing that gain is godliness: from such withdraw thyself (1 Tim 6:3–5).

The aged women likewise, that *they be* in behavior as becometh holiness, not false accusers, not given to much wine, teachers of good things (Titus 2:3).

Put them in mind to be subject to principalities and powers, to obey magistrates, to be ready to every good work, to speak evil of no man, to be no brawlers, *but* gentle, shewing all meekness unto all men (Titus 3:1, 2).

Having your conversation honest among the Gentiles: that, whereas they speak against you as evildoers, they may by *your* good works, which they shall behold, glorify God in the day of visitation. . . . Having a good conscience; that, whereas they speak evil of you, as of evildoers, they may be ashamed that falsely accuse your good conversation in Christ (1 Peter 2:12; 3:16).

Not rendering evil for evil, or railing for railing: but contrariwise blessing; knowing that ye are thereunto called, that ye should inherit a blessing (1 Peter 3:9).

And I heard a loud voice saying in heaven, Now is come salvation, and strength, and the kingdom of our God, and the power of his Christ: for the accuser of our brethren is cast down, which accused them before our God day and night (Rev 12:10).

Biblical Examples: Gen 39:14–18; 2 Sam 16:3; 1 Kings 21:9–14; Ps 31:13; 41:6–9; Jer 18:18; Matt 11:19; 26:60; Mark 14:64; Luke 22:65; John 5:18; 8:48–52; Rom 3:8; 1 Cor 4:13; 2 Cor 4:13; 6:8; 1 Peter 4:4.

Further References: Deut 22:13–19; 1 Sam 24:9; Ps 31:13; 34:13; 35:11; 38:12; 50:20; 101:5; Prov 10:18; 11:9; Jer 6:28; 9:4; Matt 5:11; 1 Cor 10:30; 1 Peter 3:10.

SLAVERY (See also Race Relations)

He that is born in thy house, and he that is bought with thy money, must needs be circumcised: and my covenant shall be in your flesh for an everlasting covenant (Gen 17:13).

Now these *are* the judgments which thou shalt set before them. If thou buy an Hebrew servant, six years he shall serve: and in the seventh he shall go out free for nothing. If he came in by himself, he shall go out by himself: if he were married, then his wife shall go out with him. If his master have given him a wife, and she have borne him sons or daughters; the wife and her children shall be her master's, and he shall go out by himself. And if the servant shall plainly say, I love my master, my wife, and my children; I will not go out free: then his master shall bring him unto the judges; he shall also bring him to the door, or unto the door post; and his master shall bore his ear through with an awl; and he shall serve him for ever.

And if a man sell his daughter to be a maidservant, she shall not go out as the menservants do. If she please not her master, who hath betrothed her to himself, then shall he let her be redeemed: to sell her unto a strange nation he shall have no power, seeing he hath dealt deceitfully with her. And if he have betrothed her unto his son, he shall deal with her after the manner of daughters. If he take him another *wife;* her food, her raiment, and her duty of marriage, shall he not diminish. And if he do not these three unto her, then shall she go out free without money (Exod 21:1–11).

And if a man smite his servant, or his maid, with a rod, and he die under his hand; he shall be surely punished. Notwithstanding, if he continue a day or two, he shall not be punished: for he *is* his money.

If men strive, and hurt a woman with child, so that her fruit depart *from her,* and yet no mischief follow: he shall be surely punished, according as the woman's husband will lay upon him; and he shall pay as the judges *determine.* And if *any* mischief follow, then thou shalt give life for life, eye for eye, tooth for tooth, hand for hand, foot for foot, burning for burning, wound for wound, stripe for stripe. And if a man smite the eye of his ser-

vant, or the eye of his maid, that it perish; he shall let him go free for his eye's sake. And if he smite out his manservant's tooth, or his maidservant's tooth; he shall let him go free for his tooth's sake.

If an ox gore a man or a woman, that they die: then the ox shall be surely stoned, and his flesh shall not be eaten; but the owner of the ox *shall be* quit. But if the ox were wont to push with his horn in time past, and it hath been testified to his owner, and he hath not kept him in, but that he hath killed a man or a woman; the ox shall be stoned, and his owner also shall be put to death. If there be laid on him a sum of money, then he shall give for the ransom of his life whatsoever is laid upon him. Whether he have gored a son, or have gored a daughter, according to this judgment shall it be done unto him. If the ox shall push a manservant or a maidservant; he shall give unto their master thirty shekels of silver, and the ox shall be stoned (Exod 21:20–32).

And whosoever lieth carnally with a woman, that *is* a bondmaid, betrothed to an husband, and not at all redeemed, nor freedom given her; she shall be scourged; they shall not be put to death, because she was not free. And he shall bring his trespass offering unto the LORD, unto the door of the tabernacle of the congregation, *even* a ram for a trespass offering. And the priest shall make an atonement for him with the ram of the trespass offering before the LORD for his sin which he hath done: and the sin which he hath done shall be forgiven him (Lev 19:20–22).

But if the priest buy *any* soul with his money, he shall eat of it, and he that is born in his house: they shall eat of his meat (Lev 22:11).

Both thy bondmen, and thy bondmaids, which thou shalt have, *shall be* of the heathen that are round about you; of them shall ye buy bondmen and bondmaids. Moreover of the children of the strangers that do sojourn among you, of them shall ye buy, and of their families that *are* with you, which they begat in your land: and they shall be your possession (Lev 25:44, 45).

And if thy brother, an Hebrew man, or an Hebrew woman, be sold unto thee, and serve thee six years; then in the seventh year thou shalt let him go free from thee. And when thou sendest him out free from thee, thou shalt not let him go away empty: thou shalt furnish him liberally out of thy flock, and out of thy floor, and out of thy winepress: *of that* wherewith the LORD thy God hath blessed thee thou shalt give unto him. And thou shalt remember that thou wast a bondman in the land of Egypt, and the LORD thy God redeemed thee: therefore I command thee this thing today. And it shall be, if he say unto thee, I will not go away from thee; because he loveth thee and thine house, because he is well with thee; then thou shalt take an awl, and thrust *it* through his ear unto the door, and he shall be thy servant for ever. And also unto thy maidservant thou shalt do likewise. It shall not seem hard unto thee, when thou sendest him away free from thee; for he hath been worth a double hired servant *to thee*, in serving thee six years: and the LORD thy God shall bless thee in all that thou doest (Deut 15:12–18).

If a man be found stealing any of his brethren of the children of Israel, and maketh merchandise of him, or selleth him; then that thief shall die; and thou shalt put evil away from among you (Deut 24:7).

And the LORD shall bring thee into Egypt again with ships, by the way whereof I spake unto thee, Thou shalt see it no more again: and there ye shall be sold unto your enemies for bondmen and bondwomen, and no man shall buy *you* (Deut 28:68).

Hear this, O ye that swallow up the needy, even to make the poor of the land to fail, saying, When will the new moon be gone, that we may sell corn? and the sabbath, that we may set forth wheat, making the ephah small, and the shekel great, and falsifying the balances by deceit? That we may buy the poor for silver, and the needy for a pair of shoes; *yea*, and sell the refuse of the wheat? (Amos 8:4–6).

Paul, a prisoner of Jesus Christ, and Timothy *our* brother, unto Philemon our dearly beloved, and fellow-labourer, and even as they did not like to retain God

in *their* knowledge, God gave them over to a reprobate mind, to do those things which are not convenient; being filled with all unrighteousness, fornication, wickedness, covetousness, maliciousness; full of envy, murder, debate, deceit, malignity; whisperers, backbiters, haters of God, despiteful, proud, boasters, inventors of evil things, disobedient to parents, without understanding, covenant-breakers, without natural affection, implacable, unmerciful (Rom 1:28–31).

But now I have written unto you not to keep company, if any man that is called a brother be a fornicator, or covetous, or an idolater, or a railer, or a drunkard, or an extortioner; with such an one no not to eat (1 Cor 5:11).

For I fear, lest, when I come, I shall not find you such as I would, and *that* I shall be found unto you such as ye would not: lest *there be* debates, envyings, wraths, strifes, backbitings, whisperings, swellings, tumults (2 Cor 12:20).

Let all bitterness, and wrath, and anger, and clamour, and evil speaking, be put away from you, with all malice (Eph 4:31).

Even so *must their* wives *be* grave, not slanderers, sober, faithful in all things (1 Tim 3:11).

And to *our* beloved Apphia, and Archippus our fellow-soldier, and to the church in thy house: grace to you, and peace, from God our Father and the Lord Jesus Christ. I thank my God, making mention of thee always in my prayers, hearing of thy love and faith, which thou hast toward the Lord Jesus, and toward all saints; that the communication of thy faith may become effectual by the acknowledging of every good thing which is in you in Christ Jesus. For we have great joy and consolation in thy love, because the bowels of the saints are refreshed by thee, brother. Wherefore, though I might be much bold in Christ to enjoin thee that which is convenient, yet for love's sake I rather beseech *thee*, being such an one as Paul the aged, and now also a prisoner of Jesus Christ. I beseech thee for my son Onesimus, whom I have begotten in my bonds: which in time past was to thee unprofitable, but now profitable to thee and to me: whom I have sent again: thou therefore receive him, that is, mine own bowels: whom I would have retained with me, that in thy stead he might have ministered unto me in the bonds of the gospel: but without thy mind would I do nothing; that thy benefit should not be as it were of necessity, but willingly. For perhaps he therefore departed for a season, that thou shouldest receive him for ever; not now as a servant, but above a servant, a brother beloved, specially to me, but how much more unto thee, both in the flesh, and in the Lord? If thou count me therefore a partner, receive him as myself. If he hath wronged thee, or oweth *thee* aught, put that on mine account; I Paul have written *it* with mine own hand, I will repay *it:* albeit I do not say to thee how thou owest unto me even thine own self besides. Yea, brother, let me have joy of thee in the Lord: refresh my bowels in the Lord. Having confidence in thy obedience I wrote unto thee, knowing that thou wilt also do more than I say. But withal prepare me also a lodging: for I trust that through your prayers I shall be given unto you. There salute thee Epaphras, my fellow-prisoner in Christ Jesus; Marcus, Aristarchus, Demas, Lucas, my fellow-labourers. The grace of our Lord Jesus Christ *be* with your spirit. Amen (Philem 1:25).

Biblical Examples: Gen 17:27; 37:23–36; Esth 7:4; Ezek 27:13; Joel 3:6.

SLOTH (See Idleness; Procrastination)

SOCIAL ACTION (See Ministry)

SOCIAL CLASS (See Poverty; Wealth)

SODOMY (See Homosexuality)

SORCERY (See also Astrology; Magic; Witchcraft)

Thou shalt not suffer a witch to live (Exod 22:18).

Ye shall not eat *any thing* with the blood: neither shall ye use enchantment, nor observe times. Ye shall not round the corners of your heads, neither shalt thou mar the corners of thy beard. Ye shall not make any cuttings in your flesh for the dead, nor print any marks upon you: I *am* the LORD (Lev 19:26–28).

Regard not them that have familiar spirits, neither seek after wizards, to be defiled by them: I *am* the LORD your God (Lev 19:31).

A man also or woman that hath a familiar spirit, or that is a wizard, shall surely be put to death: they shall stone them with stones: their blood *shall be* upon them (Lev 20:27).

When thou art come into the land which the LORD thy God giveth thee, thou shalt not learn to do after the abominations of those nations. There shall not be found among you *any one* that maketh his son or his daughter to pass through the fire, *or* that useth divination, *or* an observer of times, or an enchanter, or a witch, or a charmer, or a consulter with familiar spirits, or a wizard, or a necromancer. For all that do these things *are* an abomination unto the LORD: and because of these abominations the LORD thy God doth drive them out from before thee. Thou shalt be perfect with the LORD thy God. For these nations, which thou shalt possess, hearkened unto observers of times, and unto diviners: but as for thee, the LORD thy God hath not suffered thee so *to do* (Deut 18:9–14).

For rebellion *is as* the sin of witchcraft, and stubbornness *is as* iniquity and idolatry. Because thou hast rejected the word of the LORD, he hath also rejected thee from *being* king (1 Sam 15:23).

Moreover the *workers with* familiar spirits, and the wizards, and the images, and the idols, and all the abominations that were spied in the land of Judah and in Jerusalem, did Josiah put away, that he might perform the words of the law which were written in the book that Hilkiah the priest found in the house of the LORD (2 Kings 23:24).

And when they shall say unto you, Seek unto them that have familiar spirits, and unto wizards that peep, and that mutter: should not a people seek unto their God? for the living to the dead? (Isa 8:19).

And the word of the LORD came unto me, saying, Son of man, what *is* that proverb *that* ye have in the land of Israel, saying, The days are prolonged, and every vision faileth? Tell them therefore, Thus saith the Lord GOD; I will make this proverb to cease, and they shall no more use it as a proverb in Israel; but say unto them, The days are at hand, and the effect of every vision. For there shall be no more any vain vision nor flattering divination within the house of Israel (Ezek 12:21–24).

And I will come near to you to judgment; and I will be a swift witness against the sorcerers, and against the adulterers, and against false swearers, and against those that oppress the hireling in *his* wages, the widow, and the fatherless, and that turn aside the stranger *from his right,* and fear not me, saith the LORD of hosts (Mal 3:5).

Many of them also which used curious arts brought their books together, and burned them before all *men:* and they counted the price of them, and found *it* fifty thousand *pieces* of silver (Acts 19:19).

Now the works of the flesh are manifest, which are *these;* Adultery, fornication, uncleanness, lasciviousness, idolatry, witchcraft, hatred, variance, emulations, wrath, strife, seditions, heresies, envyings, murders, drunkenness, revellings, and such like: of the which I tell you before, as I have also told *you* in time past, that they which do such things shall not inherit the kingdom of God (Gal 5:19–21).

But the fearful, and unbelieving, and the abominable, and murderers, and whoremongers, and sorcerers, and idolaters, and all liars, shall have their part in the lake which burneth with fire and brimstone: which is the second death (Rev 21:8).

Biblical Examples: Exod 7:11, 22; 8:7, 18; Num 22:6; 23:23; 1 Sam 28:7–25; 2 Kings 9:22; 23:24; Isa 19:3, 11, 12; 47:9–13; Jer 10:2; 14:14; Ezek 13:6–9; 21:21, 22, 29; 22:28; Dan 2:2, 10, 27; 5:7, 15; Hos 4:12; Mic 3:6, 7; Nah 3:4, 5; Matt 24:24; Acts 8:9–11; 13:8; 16:16; 19:13–15.

Further References: Lev 20:6; Deut 13:5; 1 Chron 10:13; 2 Chron 33:6; Isa 8:19; 44:25; Mic 5:10–14; Zech 10:2; 2 Thess 2:9.

STEWARDSHIP (See also Daily Work; Ecology; Economics; Property; Poverty; Wealth)

And all the tithe of the land, *whether* of the seed of the land, *or* of the fruit of the tree, *is* the LORD'S: *it is* holy unto the LORD. And if a man will at all redeem *aught* of his tithes, he shall add thereto the fifth *part* thereof. And concerning the tithe of the herd, or of the flock, *even* of whatsoever passeth under the rod, the tenth shall be holy unto the LORD (Lev 27:30–32).

Honour the LORD with thy substance, and with the firstfruits of all thine increase: so shall thy barns be filled with plenty, and thy presses shall burst out with new wine (Prov 3:9, 10).

Will a man rob God? Yet ye have robbed me. But ye say, Wherein have we robbed thee? In tithes and offerings. Ye *are* cursed with a curse: for ye have robbed me, *even* this whole nation. Bring ye all the tithes into the storehouse, that there may be meat in mine house, and prove me now herewith, saith the LORD of hosts, if I will not open you the windows of heaven, and pour you out a blessing, that *there shall* not *be room* enough *to receive it* (Mal 3:8–10).

And he spake a parable unto them, saying, The ground of a certain rich man brought forth plentifully: and he thought within himself, saying, What shall I do, because I have no room where to bestow my fruits? And he said, This will I do: I will pull down my barns, and build greater; and there will I bestow all my fruits and my goods. And I will say to my soul, Soul, thou hast much goods laid up for many years; take thine ease, eat, drink, *and* be merry. But God said unto him, *Thou* fool, this night thy soul shall be required of thee: then whose shall those things be, which thou hast provided? So *is* he that layeth up treasure for himself, and is not rich toward God (Luke 12:16–21).

He that is faithful in that which is least is faithful also in much: and he that is unjust in the least is unjust also in much (Luke 16:10).

What then? shall we sin, because we are not under the law, but under grace? God forbid. Know ye not, that to whom ye yield yourselves servants to obey, his servants ye are to whom ye obey; whether of sin unto death, or of obedience unto righteousness? But God be thanked, that ye were the servants of sin, but ye have obeyed from the heart that form of doctrine which was delivered you. Being then made free from sin, ye became the servants of righteousness. I speak after the manner of men because of the infirmity of your flesh: for as ye have yielded your members servants to uncleanness and to iniquity unto iniquity; even so now yield your members servants to righteousness unto holiness (Rom 6:15–19).

Let a man so account of us, as of the ministers of Christ, and stewards of the mysteries of God. Moreover it is required in stewards, that a man be found faithful (1 Cor 4:1, 2).

Now concerning the collection for the saints, as I have given order to the churches of Galatia, even so do ye. Upon the first *day* of the week let every one of you lay by him in store, as *God* hath prospered him, that there be no gatherings when I come (1 Cor 16:1, 2).

Therefore, as ye abound in every *thing, in* faith, and utterance, and knowledge, and *in* all diligence, and *in* your love to us, *see* that ye abound in this grace also. I speak not by commandment, but by occasion of the forwardness of others, and to prove the sincerity of your love. For ye know the grace of our Lord Jesus Christ, that, though he was rich, yet for your sakes he became poor, that ye through his poverty might be rich. For *I mean* not that other men be eased, and ye burdened: but by an equality, *that* now at this time your abundance *may be a supply* for their want, that their abundance also may be *a supply* for your want: that there may be equality: as it is written, He that *had gathered* much had nothing over; and he that *had gathered* little had no lack (2 Cor 8:7–9, 13–15).

But this *I say,* He which soweth sparingly shall reap also sparingly; and he which soweth bountifully shall reap also bountifully. Every man according as he purposeth in his heart, *so let him give;* not grudgingly, or of necessity: for God loveth a cheerful giver. And God *is* able to make all grace abound toward you; that ye, always having all sufficiency in all *things,* may abound to every good work: (as it is written, He hath dispersed abroad; he hath given to the poor: his righteousness remaineth for ever. Now he that ministereth seed to the sower both minister bread for *your* food, and multiply your seed sown, and increase the fruits of your righteousness;) being enriched in every thing to all bountifulness, which causeth through us thanksgiving to God (2 Cor 9:6–11).

For a bishop must be blameless, as the steward of God; not selfwilled, not soon angry, not given to wine, no striker, not given to filthy lucre (Titus 1:7).

As every man hath received the gift, *even so* minister the same one to another, as good stewards of the manifold grace of God (1 Peter 4:10).

Biblical Examples: Luke 12:35–48; 2 Cor 8:1–5.

Further References: Gen 1:1–31; Matt 23:23; 25:14–30; Luke 16:1–8; 19:12–27; John 14:15.

STRIFE

How can I myself alone bear your cumbrance, and your burden, and your strife? (Deut 1:12).

Thou shalt hide them in the secret of thy presence from the pride of man: thou shalt keep them secretly in a pavilion from the strife of tongues (Ps 31:20).

Destroy, O Lord, *and* divide their tongues: for I have seen violence and strife in the city (Ps 55:9).

Strive not with a man without cause, if he have done thee no harm (Prov 3:30).

A naughty person, a wicked man, walketh with a froward mouth. He winketh with his eyes, he speaketh with his feet, he teacheth with his fingers; frowardness *is* in his heart, he deviseth mischief continually; he soweth discord.

These six *things* doth the LORD hate: yea, seven *are* an abomination unto him: a proud look, a lying tongue, and hands that shed innocent blood, an heart that deviseth wicked imaginations, feet that be swift in running to mischief, a false witness *that* speaketh lies, and he that soweth discord among brethren (Prov 6:12–14, 16–19).

A wrathful man stirreth up strife: but *he that is* slow to anger appeaseth strife (Prov 15:18).

Better *is* a dry morsel, and quietness therewith, than an house full of sacrifices *with* strife (Prov 17:1).

It is an honour for a man to cease from strife: but every fool will be meddling (Prov 20:3).

He that passeth by, *and* meddleth with strife *belonging* not to him, *is like* one that taketh a dog by the ears. Where no wood is, *there* the fire goeth out: so where *there is* no talebearer, the strife ceaseth. *As* coals *are* to burning coals, and wood to fire; so *is* a contentious man to kindle strife (Prov 26:17, 20, 21).

An angry man stirreth up strife, and a furious man aboundeth in transgression (Prov 29:22).

Surely the churning of milk bringeth forth butter, and the wringing of the nose bringeth forth blood: so the forcing of wrath bringeth forth strife (Prov 30:33).

Behold, ye fast for strife and debate, and to smite with the fist of wickedness: ye shall not fast as *ye do this* day, to make your voice to be heard on high (Isa 58:4).

Why dost thou shew me iniquity, and cause *me* to behold grievance? for spoiling and violence *are* before me: and there are *that* raise up strife and contention (Hab 1:3).

Agree with thine adversary quickly, whiles thou art in the way with him; lest at any time the adversary deliver thee to the judge, and the judge deliver thee to the officer, and thou be cast into prison. . . . But I say unto you, That ye resist not evil: but whosoever shall smite thee on thy right cheek, turn to him the other also. And if any man will sue thee at the law, and take away thy coat, let him have *thy* cloak also. And whosoever shall compel thee to go a mile, go with him twain (Matt 5:25, 39–41).

Think not that I am come to send peace on earth: I came not to send peace, but a sword. For I am come to set a man at variance against his father, and the daughter against her mother, and the daughter in law against her mother in law. And a man's foes *shall be* they of his own household (Matt 10:34–36).

Moreover if thy brother shall trespass against thee, go and tell him his fault be-tween thee and him alone: if he shall hear thee, thou hast gained thy brother. But if he will not hear *thee, then* take with thee one or two more, that in the mouth of two or three witnesses every word may be established. And if he shall neglect to hear them, tell *it* unto the church: but if he neglect to hear the church, let him be unto thee as an heathen man and a publican (Matt 18:15–17).

Suppose ye that I am come to give peace on earth? I tell you, Nay; but rather division: for from henceforth there shall be five in one house divided, three against two, and two against three. The father shall be divided against the son, and the son against the father; the mother against the daughter, and the daughter against the mother; the mother in law against her daughter in law, and the daughter in law against her mother in law.

When thou goest with thine adversary to the magistrate, *as thou art* in the way, give diligence that thou mayest be delivered from him; lest he hale thee to the judge, and the judge deliver thee to the officer, and the officer cast thee into prison. I tell thee, thou shalt not depart thence, till thou hast paid the very last mite (Luke 12:51–53, 58, 59).

Let us walk honestly, as in the day; not in rioting and drunkenness, not in chambering and wantonness, not in strife and envying (Rom 13:13).

Him that is weak in the faith receive ye, *but* not to doubtful disputations. . . . Let us therefore follow after the things which make for peace, and things wherewith one may edify another. For meat destroy not the work of God. All things indeed *are* pure; but *it is* evil for that man who eateth with offence. *It is* good neither to eat flesh, nor to drink wine, nor *any thing* whereby thy brother stumbleth, or is offended, or is made weak (Rom 14:1, 19–21).

And I, brethren, could not speak unto you as unto spiritual, but as unto carnal, *even* as unto babes in Christ. I have fed you with milk, and not with meat: for hitherto ye were not able *to bear it*, neither yet now are ye able. For ye are yet carnal: for whereas *there is* among you envying, and strife, and divisions, are ye not carnal, and walk as men? For while one saith, I am of Paul; and another, I *am* of Apollos; are ye not carnal? (1 Cor 3:1–4).

For I fear, lest, when I come, I shall not find you such as I would, and *that* I shall be found unto you such as ye would not: lest *there be* debates, envyings, wraths, strifes, backbitings, whisperings, swellings, tumults (2 Cor 12:20).

I have confidence in you through the Lord, that ye will be none otherwise minded: but he that troubleth you shall bear his judgment, whosoever he be. . . . But if ye bite and devour one another, take heed that ye be not consumed one of another. . . . But if ye be led of the Spirit, ye are not under the law. Now the works of the flesh are manifest, which are *these;* Adultery, fornication, uncleanness, lasciviousness, idolatry, witchcraft, hatred, variance, emulations, wrath, strife, seditions, heresies, envyings, murders, drunkenness, revellings, and such like: of the which I tell you before, as I have also told *you* in time past, that they which do such things shall not inherit the kingdom of God (Gal 5:10, 15, 18–21).

Let nothing *be done* through strife or vainglory; but in lowliness of mind let each esteem other better than themselves. . . . Do all things without murmurings and disputings: that ye may be blameless and harmless, the sons of God, without rebuke, in the midst of a crooked and perverse nation, among whom ye shine as lights in the world (Phil 2:3, 14, 15).

Of these things put *them* in remembrance, charging *them* before the Lord that they strive not about words to no profit, *but* to the subverting of the hearers. . . . But foolish and unlearned questions avoid, knowing that they do gender strifes. And the servant of the Lord must not strive; but be gentle unto all *men,* apt to teach, patient, in meekness instructing those that oppose themselves; if God peradventure will give them repentance to the acknowledging of the truth (2 Tim 2:14, 23–25).

But if ye have bitter envying and strife in your hearts, glory not, and lie not against the truth. This wisdom descendeth not from above, but *is* earthly, sensual, devilish. For where envying and strife *is,* there *is* confusion and every evil work (James 3:14–16).

Biblical Examples: Gen 13:6, 7; 31:36; Deut 1:12; Judg 11:2; 12:1–6; 2 Sam 19:41–43; Mark 9:34; John 10:19; Acts 15:2, 38, 39; 23:7–10; Rom 16:17, 18; 1 Cor 1:10–13; 6:1–7; 11:16–19, Phil 1:15, 16.

Further References: Gen 13:8; 45:24; Ps 80:6; Prov 10:12; 16:28; 22:10; 23:29, 30; 28:25; Matt 12:25; Mark 3:24, 25; Luke 11:17; 1 Tim 3:2, 3; 6:3–5, 20, 21; Titus 3:1–3, 9.

SUFFERING AND DEATH (See also Ministry)

In the sweat of thy face shalt thou eat bread, till thou return unto the ground; for out of it wast thou taken: for dust thou *art,* and unto dust shalt thou return (Gen 3:19).

The LORD killeth, and maketh alive: he bringeth down to the grave, and bringeth up (1 Sam 2:6).

For now should I have lain still and been quiet, I should have slept: then had I been at rest, with kings and counsellors of the earth, which built desolate places for themselves; or with princes that had gold, who filled their houses with silver: or as an hidden untimely birth I had not been; as infants *which* never saw light. There the wicked cease *from* troubling; and there the weary be at rest. *There* the prisoners rest together; they hear not the voice of the oppressor. The small and great are there; and the servant *is* free from his master (Job 3:13–19).

One dieth in his full strength, being wholly at ease and quiet. His breasts are full of milk, and his bones are moistened with marrow. And another dieth in the bitterness of his soul, and never eateth with pleasure. They shall lie down alike in the dust, and the worms shall cover them (Job 21:23–26).

Yea, though I walk through the valley of the shadow of death, I will fear no evil: for thou *art* with me; thy rod and thy staff they comfort me (Ps 23:4).

LORD, make me to know mine end, and the measure of my days, what it *is;*

that I may know how frail I *am* (Ps 39:4).

As for man, his days *are* as grass: as a flower of the field, so he flourisheth. For the wind passeth over it, and it is gone; and the place thereof shall know it no more (Ps 103:15, 16).

Give strong drink unto him that is ready to perish, and wine unto those that be of heavy hearts (Prov. 31:6).

The wise man's eyes *are* in his head; but the fool walketh in darkness: and I myself perceived also that one event happeneth to them all. Then said I in my heart, As it happened to the fool, so it happeneth even to me; and why was I then more wise? Then I said in my heart, that this also *is* vanity. For *there is* no remembrance of the wise more than of the fool for ever; seeing that which now *is* in the days to come shall all be forgotten. And how dieth the wise *man?* as the fool. Therefore I hated life; because the work that is wrought under the sun *is* grievous unto me: for all *is* vanity and vexation of spirit.

Yea, I hated all my labour which I had taken under the sun: because I should leave it unto the man that shall be after me (Eccl 2:14–18).

A time to be born, and a time to die; a time to plant, and a time to pluck up *that which is* planted (Eccl 3:2).

For that which befalleth the sons of men befalleth beasts; even one thing befalleth them: as the one dieth, so dieth the other; yea, they have all one breath; so that a man hath no preeminence above a beast: for all *is* vanity. All go unto one place; all are of the dust, and all turn to dust again. Who knoweth the spirit of man that goeth upward, and the spirit of the beast that goeth downward to the earth? (Eccl 3:19–21).

As he came forth of his mother's womb, naked shall he return to go as he came, and shall take nothing of his labour, which he may carry away in his hand (Eccl 5:15).

There is no man that hath power over the spirit to retain the spirit; neither *hath he* power in the day of death: and *there is* no discharge in *that* war; neither shall wickedness deliver those that are given to it (Eccl 8:8).

He will swallow up death in victory; and the Lord GOD will wipe away tears from off all faces; and the rebuke of his people shall he take away from off all the earth: for the LORD hath spoken *it* (Isa 25:8).

For I have no pleasure in the death of him that dieth, saith the Lord GOD: wherefore turn *yourselves,* and live ye (Ezek 18:32).

Blessed *are* they which are persecuted for righteousness' sake: for theirs is the kingdom of heaven. Blessed are ye, when *men* shall revile you, and persecute *you,* and shall say all manner of evil against you falsely, for my sake. Rejoice, and be exceeding glad: for great *is* your reward in heaven: for so persecuted they the prophets which were before you (Matt 5:10–12).

But beware of men: for they will deliver you up to the councils, and they will scourge you in their synagogues; and ye shall be brought before governors and kings for my sake, for a testimony against them and the Gentiles. But when they deliver you up, take no thought how or what ye shall speak: for it shall be given you in that same hour what ye shall speak. For it is not ye that speak, but the Spirit of your Father which speaketh in you. And the brother shall deliver up the brother to death, and the father the child: and the children shall rise up against *their* parents, and cause them to be put to death. And ye shall be hated of all *men* for my name's sake: but he that endureth to the end shall be saved. But when they persecute you in this city, flee ye into another for verily I say unto you, ye shall not have gone over the cities of Israel, till the Son of man be come. The disciple is not above *his* master, nor the servant above his lord. It is enough for the disciple that he be as his master, and the servant as his lord. If they have called the master of the house Beelzebub, how much more *shall they call* them of his household? (Matt 10:17–25).

And fear not them which kill the body, but are not able to kill the soul: but rather fear him which is able to destroy both soul and body in hell (Matt 10:28).

And Jesus answering said unto them, The children of this world marry, and are given in marriage: but they which shall be accounted worthy to obtain that world, and the resurrection from the dead, neither marry, nor are given in marriage: neither can they die any more: for they are equal unto the angels; and are the children of God, being the children of the resurrection. Now that the dead are raised, even Moses shewed at the bush, when he calleth the Lord the God of Abraham, and the God of Isaac and the God of Jacob. For he is not a God of the dead, but of the living: for all live unto him (Luke 20:34–38).

And as *Jesus* passed by, he saw a man which was blind from *his* birth. And his disciples asked him, saying, Master, who did sin, this man, or his parents, that he was born blind? Jesus answered, Neither hath this man sinned, nor his parents: but that the works of God should be made manifest in him (John 9:1–3).

Let not your heart be troubled: ye believe in God, believe also in me. In my Father's house are many mansions: if *it were* not *so,* I would have told you. I go to prepare a place for you. And if I go and prepare a place for you, I will come again, and receive you unto myself; that where I am, *there* ye may be also. And whither I go ye know, and the way ye know (John 14:1–4).

Wherefore, as by one man sin entered into the world, and death by sin; and so death passed upon all men, for that all have sinned: (for until the law sin was in the world: but sin is not imputed when there is no law. Nevertheless death reigned from Adam to Moses, even over them that had not sinned after the similitude of Adam's transgression, who is the figure of him that was to come (Rom 5:12–14).

Therefore we are buried with him by baptism into death: that like as Christ was raised up from the dead by the glory of the Father, even so we also should walk in newness of life. For if we have been planted together in the likeness of his death, we shall be also *in the likeness of his* resurrection: knowing this, that our old man is crucified with *him,* that the body of sin might be destroyed, that henceforth we should not serve sin. For he that is dead is freed from sin. Now if we be dead

with Christ, we believe that we shall also live with him: knowing that Christ being raised from the dead dieth no more; death hath no more dominion over him. For in that he died, he died unto sin once: but in that he liveth, he liveth unto God. Likewise reckon ye also yourselves to be dead indeed unto sin, but alive unto God through Jesus Christ our Lord (Rom 6:4–11).

For the wages of sin *is* death; but the gift of God *is* eternal life through Jesus Christ our Lord (Rom 6:23).

For whether we live, we live unto the Lord; and whether we die, we die unto the Lord: whether we live therefore, or die, we are the Lord's (Rom 14:8).

Now if Christ be preached that he rose from the dead, how say some among you that there is no resurrection of the dead? But if there be no resurrection of the dead, then is Christ not risen: and if Christ be not risen, then *is* our preaching vain, and your faith *is* also vain. Yea, and we are found false witnesses of God; because we have testified of God that he raised up Christ: whom he raised not up, if so be that the dead rise not. For if the dead rise not, then is not Christ raised: and if Christ be not raised, your faith *is* vain; ye are yet in your sins. Then they also which are fallen asleep in Christ are perished. If in this life only we have hope in Christ, we are of all men most miserable.

But now is Christ risen from the dead, *and* become the firstfruits of them that slept. For since by man *came* death, by man *came* also the resurrection of the dead. For as in Adam all die, even so in Christ shall all be made alive. But every man in his own order: Christ the firstfruits; afterward they that are Christ's at his coming. Then *cometh* the end, when he shall have delivered up the kingdom to God, even the Father; when he shall have put down all rule and all authority and power. For he must reign, till he hath put all enemies under his feet. The last enemy *that* shall be destroyed *is* death (1 Cor 15:12–26).

O death, where *is* thy sting? O grave, where *is* thy victory? The sting of death *is* sin; and the strength of sin *is* the law. But thanks *be* to God, which giveth us the victory through our Lord Jesus Christ (1 Cor 15:55–57).

But if the ministration of death, written *and* engraven in stones, was glorious, so that the children of Israel could not stedfastly behold the face of Moses for the glory of his countenance; which *glory* was to be done away (2 Cor 3:7).

But we have this treasure in earthen vessels, that the excellency of the power may be of God, and not of us. *We are* troubled on every side, yet not distressed; *we are* perplexed, but not in despair; persecuted, but not forsaken; cast down, but not destroyed; always bearing about in the body the dying of the Lord Jesus that the life also of Jesus might be made manifest in our body. For we which live are alway delivered unto death for Jesus' sake, that the life also of Jesus might be made manifest in our mortal flesh. So then death worketh in us, but life in you.

We having the same spirit of faith, according as it is written, I believed, and therefore have I spoken; we also believe, and therefore speak; knowing that he which raised up the Lord Jesus shall raise up us also by Jesus, and shall present *us* with you. For all things *are* for your sakes, that the abundant grace might through the thanksgiving of many redound to the glory of God.

For which cause we faint not; but through our outward man perish, yet the inward *man* is renewed day by day. For our light affliction, which is but for a moment, worketh for us a far more exceeding *and* eternal weight of glory (2 Cor 4:7–17).

For to me to live *is* Christ, and to die *is* gain (Phil 1:21).

Let this mind be in you, which was also in Christ Jesus: who, being in the form of God, thought it not robbery to be equal with God: but made himself of no reputation, and took upon him the form of a servant, and was made in the likeness of men: and being found in fashion as a man, he humbled himself, and became obedient unto death, even the death of the cross (Phil 2:5–8).

For we brought nothing into *this* world, *and it is* certain we can carry nothing out (1 Tim 6:7).

And ye have forgotten the exhortation which speaketh unto you as unto children, My son, despise not thou the chastening of the Lord, nor faint when thou art rebuked of him: for whom the Lord loveth he chasteneth, and scourgeth every son whom he receiveth (Heb 12:5, 6).

Is any among you afflicted? let him pray. Is any merry? let him sing psalms. Is any sick among you? let him call for the elders of the church; and let them pray over him, anointing him with oil in the name of the Lord: and the prayer of faith shall save the sick, and the Lord shall raise him up; and if he have committed sins, they shall be forgiven him (James 5:13–15).

For this *is* thankworthy, if a man for conscience toward God endure grief, suffering wrongfully. For what glory *is it*, if, when ye be buffeted for your faults, ye shall take it patiently? but if, when ye do well, and suffer *for it*, ye take it patiently, this *is* acceptable with God. For even hereunto were ye called: because Christ also suffered for us, leaving us an example, that ye should follow his steps: who did no sin, neither was guile found in his mouth: who, when he was reviled, reviled not again; when he suffered, he threatened not; but committed *himself* to him that judgeth righteously: who his own self bare our sins in his own body on the tree, that we, being dead to sins, should live unto righteousness: by whose stripes ye were healed. For ye were as sheep going astray; but are now returned unto the Shepherd and Bishop of your souls (1 Peter 2:19–25).

But and if ye suffer for righteousness' sake, happy *are ye:* and be not afraid of their terror, neither be troubled; but sanctify the Lord God in your hearts: and *be* ready always to *give* an answer to every man that asketh you a reason of the hope that is in you with meekness and fear: having a good conscience; that, whereas they speak evil of you, as of evildoers, they may be ashamed that falsely accuse your good conversation in Christ. For *it is* better, if the will of God be so, that ye suffer for well-doing, than for evil-doing (1 Peter 3:14–17).

Beloved, think it not strange concerning the fiery trial which is to try you, as though some strange thing happened unto you: but rejoice, inasmuch as ye are partakers of Christ's sufferings; that, when his glory shall be revealed, ye may be glad also with exceeding joy. If ye be reproached for the name of Christ, happy *are ye;* for the spirit of glory and of God resteth upon you: on their part he is evil spoken of, but on your part he is glorified. But let none of you suffer as a murderer, or *as* a thief, or *as* an evildoer, or as a busybody in other men's matters. Yet if *any man suffer* as a Christian, let him not be ashamed; but let him glorify God on this behalf. For the time *is come* that judgment must begin at the house of God: and if *it* first *begin* at us, what shall the end *be* of them that obey not the gospel of God? And if the righteous scarcely be saved, where shall the ungodly and the sinner appear? Wherefore let them that suffer according to the will of God commit the keeping of their souls *to him* in well-doing, as unto a faithful Creator (1 Peter 4:12–19).

The Lord is not slack concerning his promise, as some men count slackness; but is longsuffering to us-ward, not willing that any should perish, but that all should come to repentance (2 Peter 3:9).

And when I saw him, I fell at his feet as dead. And he laid his right hand upon me, saying unto me, Fear not; I am the first and the last: I *am* he that liveth, and was dead; and, behold, I am alive for evermore, Amen; and have the keys of hell and of death (Rev 1:17, 18).

And I saw the dead, small and great, stand before God; and the books were opened: and another book was opened, which is *the book* of life: and the dead were judged out of those things which were written in the books, according to their works. And the sea gave up the dead which were in it; and death and hell delivered up the dead which were in them: and they were judged every man according to their works. And death and hell were cast into the lake of fire. This is the second death (Rev 20:12–14).

And God shall wipe away all tears from their eyes; and there shall be no more death, neither sorrow, nor crying, neither shall there be any more pain: for the former things are passed away (Rev 21:4).

But the fearful, and unbelieving, and the abominable, and murderers, and whoremongers, and sorcerers, and idolaters, and all liars, shall have their part in the lake which burneth with fire and brimstone: which is the second death (Rev 21:8).

Biblical Examples: Gen 5:24; Josh 7:1–26; 2 Kings 2: Matt 27:23–25; Mark 15:23; Luke 16:19–31; 2 Cor 11:23–30.

Further References: Gen 2:16–3:19; Job 14:2–21; Ps 9:12; 22:26.

SUICIDE

Thou shalt not kill (Exod 20:13).

Then said Saul unto his armour-bearer, Draw thy sword, and thrust me through therewith; lest these uncircumcised come and thrust me through, and abuse me. But his armour-bearer would not; for he was sore afraid. Therefore Saul took a sword, and fell upon it (1 Sam 31:4).

Then the devil taketh him up into the holy city, and setteth him on a pinnacle of the temple, and saith unto him, If thou be the Son of God, cast thyself down: for it is written, He shall give his angels charge concerning thee: and in *their* hands they shall bear thee up, lest at any time thou dash thy foot against a stone (Matt 4:5, 6).

He saith unto him, Which? Jesus said, Thou shalt do no murder, Thou shalt not commit adultery, Thou shalt not steal, Thou shalt not bear false witness (Matt 19:18).

And the keeper of the prison awaking out of his sleep, and seeing the prison doors open, he drew out his sword, and would have killed himself, supposing that the prisoners had been fled (Acts 16:27).

And in those days shall men seek death, and shall not find it; and shall desire to die, and death shall flee from them (Rev 9:6).

Biblical Examples: Judg 16:29–30; 2 Sam 17:23; 1 Chron 10:4, 5; 1 Kings 16:18; Matt 27:5; Acts 1:18.

- T -

TAXES (See also Citizenship; Economics; Government)

And the LORD spake unto Moses, saying, When thou takest the sum of the children of Israel after their number, then shall they give every man a ransom for his soul unto the LORD, when thou numberest them; that there be no plague among them, when *thou* numberest them. This they shall give, every one that passeth among them that are numbered, half a shekel after the shekel of the sanctuary: (a shekel *is* twenty gerahs:) an half shekel *shall be* the offering of the LORD. Every one that passeth among them that are numbered, from twenty years old and above, shall give an offering unto the LORD. The rich shall not give more, and the poor shall not give less than half a shekel, when *they* give an offering unto the LORD, to make an atonement for your souls. And thou shalt take the atonement money of the children of Israel, and shalt appoint it for the service of the tabernacle of the congregation; that it may be a memorial unto the children of Israel before the LORD, to make an atonement for your souls (Exod 30:11–16).

Some also there were that said, We have mortgaged our lands, vineyards, and houses, that we might buy corn, because of the dearth. There were also that said, We have borrowed money for the king's tribute, *and that upon* our lands and vineyards (Neh 5:3, 4).

And when they were come to Capernaum, they that received tribute *money* came to Peter, and said, Doth not your master pay tribute? He saith, Yes. And when he was come into the house, Jesus prevented him, saying, What thinkest thou, Simon? of whom do the kings of the earth take custom or tribute? of their own children, or of strangers? Peter saith unto him, Of strangers. Jesus saith unto him, Then are the children free. Notwithstanding, lest we should offend them, go thou to the sea, and cast an hook, and take up the fish that first cometh up; and when thou hast opened his mouth, thou shalt find a piece of money: that take, and give unto them for me and thee (Matt 17:24–27).

And when they were come, they say unto him, Master, we know that thou art true, and carest for no man: for thou regardest not the person of men, but teachest the way of God in truth: Is it lawful to give tribute to Cæsar, or not? (Mark 12:14).

For for this cause pay ye tribute also: for they are God's ministers, attending continually upon this very thing. Render therefore to all their dues: tribute to whom tribute *is due;* custom to whom custom; fear to whom fear; honour to whom honour (Rom 13:6, 7).

Biblical Examples: Gen 41:34, 46–57; 1 Kings 4:7–28; 9:15; 2 Kings 15:19, 20; 23:35; Amos 5:11; Luke 2:1–3.

Further References: Exod 38:26; 2 Sam 20:24; 1 Kings 12:18; 2 Chron 10:18; Neh 10:32; Dan 11:20; Matt 5:46; 9:11; 22:17; Mark 2:14; Luke 3:13; 20:21–25.

TEMPERANCE (See also Self-control)

When thou sittest to eat with a ruler, consider diligently what *is* before thee: and put a knife to thy throat, if thou *be* a man given to appetite. Be not desirous of his dainties: for they *are* deceitful meat (Prov 23:1–3).

Hast thou found honey? eat so much as is sufficient for thee, lest thou be filled therewith, and vomit it (Prov 25:16).

But put ye on the Lord Jesus Christ, and make not provision for the flesh, to *fulfil* the lusts *thereof* (Rom 13:14).

And every man that striveth for the mastery is temperate in all things. Now they *do it* to obtain a corruptible crown; but we an incorruptible. I therefore so run, not as uncertainly; so fight I, not as one that beateth the air: but I keep under my body, and bring *it* into subjection: lest that by any means, when I have preached to others, I myself should be a castaway (1 Cor 9:25–27).

Conscience, I say, not thine own, but of the other: for why is my liberty judged of another *man's* conscience? For if I by grace be a partaker, why am I evil spoken of for that for which I give thanks? Whether therefore ye eat, or drink, or whatsoever ye do, do all to the glory of God. Give none offence, neither to the Jews, nor to the Gentiles, nor to the church of God (1 Cor 10:29–32).

Let your moderation be known unto all men. The Lord *is* at hand (Phil 4:5).

That the aged men be sober, grave, temperate, sound in faith, in charity, in patience. The aged women likewise, that *they be* in behaviour as becometh holiness, not false accusers, not given to much wine, teachers of good things. . . . Teaching us that, denying ungodliness and worldly lusts, we should live soberly, righteously, and godly, in this present world (Titus 2:2, 3, 12).

And beside this, giving all diligence, add to your faith virtue; and to virtue knowledge; and to knowledge temperance; and to temperance patience; and to patience godliness (2 Peter 1:5, 6).

Biblical Examples: Dan 1:3, 12–16; 1 Cor 8:10–13; 9:22.

Further References: 1 Thess 5:6–8; 1 Tim 3:2, 3, 8; Titus 1:7, 8.

TEMPTATION

Take heed to thyself, lest thou make a covenant with the inhabitants of the land whither thou goest, lest it be for a snare in the midst of thee (Exod 34:12).

The graven images of their gods shall ye burn with fire: thou shalt not desire the silver or gold *that is* on them, nor take *it* unto thee, lest thou be snared therein: for it *is* an abomination to the LORD thy God (Deut 7:25).

When thou hast eaten and art full, then thou shalt bless the LORD thy God for the good land which he hath given thee. Beware that thou forget not the LORD thy God, in not keeping his commandments, and his judgments, and his statutes, which I command thee this day: lest *when* thou hast eaten and art full, and hast built goodly houses, and dwelt *therein;* and *when* thy herds and thy flocks multiply, and thy silver and thy gold is multiplied, and all that thou hast is multiplied; then thine heart be lifted up, and thou forget the LORD thy God, which brought thee forth out of the land of Egypt, from the house of bondage. . . . And thou say in thine heart, My power and the might of *mine* hand hath gotten me this wealth. But thou shalt remember the LORD thy God: for *it is* he that giveth thee power to get wealth, that he may establish his covenant which he sware unto thy fathers, as *it is* this day (Deut 8:10–14, 17, 18).

Thou shalt not hearken unto the words of that prophet, or that dreamer of dreams: for the LORD your God proveth you, to know whether ye love the LORD your God with all your heart and with all your soul (Deut 13:3).

My son, if sinners entice thee, consent thou not. If they say, Come with us, let us lay wait for blood, let us lurk privily for the innocent without cause: let us swallow them up alive as the grave; and whole, as those that go down into the pit: we shall find all precious substance, we shall fill our houses with spoil: cast in thy lot among us; let us all have one purse; my son, walk not thou in the way with them; refrain thy foot from their path: for their feet run to evil, and make haste to shed blood. Surely in vain the net is spread in the sight of any bird (Prov 1:10–17).

When wisdom entereth into thine heart, and knowledge is pleasant unto thy soul; discretion shall preserve thee, understanding shall keep thee: to deliver thee from the way of the evil *man*, from the man that speaketh froward things; to deliver thee from the strange woman, *even* from the stranger *which* flattereth with her words (Prov 2:10–12, 16).

Enter not into the path of the wicked, and go not in the way of evil *men*. Avoid it, pass not by it, turn from it, and pass away (Prov 4:14, 15).

Drink waters out of thine own cistern, and running waters out of thine own well. Let thy fountains be dispersed abroad, *and* rivers of waters in the streets. Let them be only thine own, and not strangers' with thee. Let thy fountain be blessed: and rejoice with the wife of thy youth. *Let her be as* the loving hind and pleasant roe; let her breasts satisfy thee at all times; and be thou ravished always with her love. And why wilt thou, my son, be ravished with a strange woman, and embrace the bosom of a stranger? For the ways of man *are* before the eyes of the LORD, and he pondereth all his goings (Prov 5:15–21).

Can a man take fire in his bosom, and his clothes not be burned? Can one go upon hot coals, and his feet not be burned? (Prov 6:27, 28).

A violent man enticeth his neighbour, and leadeth him into the way *that is* not good (Prov 16:29).

Cease, my son, to hear the instruction *that causeth* to err from the words of knowledge (Prov 19:27).

And I find more bitter than death the woman, whose heart *is* snares and nets, *and* her hands *as* bands: whoso pleaseth God shall escape from her; but the sinner shall be taken by her (Eccl 7:26).

Whosoever therefore shall break one of these least commandments, and shall teach men so, he shall be called the least in the kingdom of heaven: but whosoever shall do and teach *them*, the same shall be called great in the kingdom of heaven (Matt 5:19).

But whoso shall offend one of these little ones which believe in me, it were better for him that a millstone were hanged about his neck, and *that* he were drowned in the depth of the sea.

Woe unto the world because of offences! for it must needs be that offences come; but woe to that man by whom the offence cometh! Wherefore if thy hand or thy foot offend thee, cut them off, and cast *them* from thee: it is better for thee to enter into life halt or maimed, rather than having two hands or two feet to be cast into everlasting fire. And if thine eye offend thee, pluck it out, and cast *it* from thee: it is better for thee to enter into life with one eye, rather than having two eyes to be cast into hell fire (Matt 18:6–9).

Then saith Jesus unto them, All ye shall be offended because of me this night: for it is written, I will smite the shepherd, and the sheep of the flock shall be scattered abroad. . . .

Watch and pray, that ye enter not into temptation: the spirit indeed *is* willing, but the flesh *is* weak (Matt 26:31, 41).

And forgive us our sins; for we also forgive every one that is indebted to us. And lead us not into temptation; but deliver us from evil (Luke 11:4).

And said unto them, Why sleep ye? rise and pray, lest ye enter into temptation (Luke 22:46).

Let us not therefore judge one another any more: but judge this rather, that no man put a stumblingblock or an occasion to fall in *his* brother's way. I know, and am persuaded by the Lord Jesus, that *there is* nothing unclean of itself: but to him that esteemeth any thing to be unclean, to him *it is* unclean. But if thy brother be grieved with *thy* meat, now walkest thou not charitably. Destroy not him with thy meat, for whom Christ died. . . .

It is good neither to eat flesh, nor to drink wine, nor *any thing* whereby thy brother stumbleth, or is offended, or is made weak (Rom 14:13–15, 21).

Defraud ye not one the other, except *it be* with consent for a time, that ye may give yourselves to fasting and prayer; and come together again, that Satan tempt you not for your incontinency (1 Cor 7:5).

But take heed lest by any means this liberty of yours become a stumblingblock to them that are weak. For if any man see thee which hast knowledge sit at meat in the idol's temple, shall not the conscience of him which is weak be emboldened to eat those things which are offered to idols; and through thy knowledge shall the weak brother perish, for whom Christ died? But when ye sin so against the brethren, and wound their weak conscience, ye sin against Christ. Wherefore, if meat make my brother to offend, I will eat no flesh while the world standeth, lest I make my brother to offend (1 Cor 8:9–13).

There hath no temptation taken you but such as is common to man: but God *is* faithful, who will not suffer you to be tempted above that ye are able; but will with the temptation also make a way to escape, that ye may be able to bear *it.* But if any man say unto you, This is offered in sacrifice unto idols, eat not for his sake that shewed it, and for conscience sake: for the earth *is* the Lord's and the fulness thereof: conscience, I say, not thine own, but of the other: for why is my liberty judged of another *man's* conscience? For if I by grace be a partaker, why am I evil spoken of for that for which I give thanks? Whether therefore ye eat, or drink, or whatsoever ye do, do all to the glory of God. Give none offence, neither to the Jews, nor to the Gentiles, nor to the church of God (1 Cor 10:13, 28–32).

Neither give place to the devil (Eph 4:27).

But they that will be rich fall into temptation and a snare, and *into* many foolish and hurtful lusts, which drown men in destruction and perdition. For the love of money is the root of all evil: which while some coveted after, they have erred from the faith, and pierced themselves through with many sorrows (1 Tim 6:9–10).

For in that he himself hath suffered being tempted, he is able to succour them that are tempted (Heb 2:18).

For we have not an high priest which cannot be touched with the feeling of our infirmities; but was in all points tempted like as *we are, yet* without sin (Heb 4:15).

My brethren, count it all joy when ye fall into divers temptations; knowing *this,* that the trying of your faith worketh patience. But let patience have *her* perfect work, that ye may be perfect and entire, wanting nothing. . . .

Blessed *is* the man that endureth temptation: for when he is tried, he shall receive the crown of life, which the Lord hath promised to them that love him. Let no man say when he is tempted, I am tempted of God: for God cannot be tempted with evil, neither tempteth he any man: but every man is tempted, when he is drawn away of his own lust, and enticed. Then when lust hath conceived, it bringeth forth sin: and sin, when it is finished, bringeth forth death. Do not err, my beloved brethren (James 1:2–4, 12–16).

Wherein ye greatly rejoice, though now for a season, if need be, ye are in heaviness through manifold temptations: that the trial of your faith, being much more precious than of gold that perisheth, though it be tried with fire, might be found unto praise and honour and glory at the appearing of Jesus Christ (1 Peter 1:6–7).

The Lord knoweth how to deliver the godly out of temptations, and to reserve the unjust unto the day of judgment to be punished (2 Peter 2:9).

Because thou hast kept the word of my patience, I also will keep thee from the hour of temptation, which shall come upon all the world, to try them that dwell upon the earth (Rev. 3:10).

Biblical Examples: Gen 3:1–13; 18:13–15; 20:6; 39:7–10; Num 22:7–18; 1 Sam 26:5–25; 2 Sam 11:2–5; 1 Kings 13:7–9; Job 2:3–10; Jer 35:5–7; Amos 2:12; Matt 4:1–11; Luke 4:1–13; 1 Tim 5:15; 1 Peter 4:12.

Further References: Gen 22:11; Deut 13:1–3; 2 Chron 32:31; Job 1:1–22; 31; Prov 7:7–23; 12:26; 14:27; Matt 13:22; Mark 4:15–17; 13:21, 22; 14:37, 38; Luke 22:40; 2 Cor 2:11; 11:3, 14, 15; Eph 6:11–17; 2 Tim 3:13; James 4:7; 1 Peter 5:8, 9; 2 Peter 3:17; 1 John 2:26; 4:4.

THEFT (See also Dishonesty)

Thou shalt not steal (Exod 20:15).

And he that stealeth a man, and selleth him, or if he be found in his hand, he shall surely be put to death (Exod 21:16).

If a man shall steal an ox, or a sheep, and kill it, or sell it; he shall restore five oxen for an ox, and four sheep for a sheep.

If a thief be found breaking up, and be smitten that he die, *there shall* no blood *be shed* for him. If the sun be risen upon him, *there shall be* blood *shed* for him; *for* he should make full restitution; if he have nothing, then he shall be sold for his theft. If the theft be certainly found in his hand alive, whether it be ox, or ass, or sheep; he shall restore double. . . .

If a man deliver unto his neighbour an ass, or an ox, or a sheep, or any beast, to keep; and it die, or be hurt, or driven away, no man seeing *it: then* shall an oath of the LORD be between them both, that he hath not put his hand unto his neighbour's goods; and the owner of it shall accept *thereof*, and he shall not make *it* good. And if it be stolen from him, he shall make restitution unto the owner thereof. If it be torn in pieces, *then* let him bring it *for* witness, *and* he shall not make good that which was torn.

And if a man borrow *aught* of his neighbour, and it be hurt, or die, the owner thereof *being* not with it, he shall surely make *it* good. *But* if the owner thereof *be* with it, he shall not make *it* good: if it *be* an hired *thing*, it came for his hire (Exod 22:1–4, 10–15).

If a soul sin, and commit a trespass against the LORD, and lie unto his neighbour in that which was delivered him to keep, or in fellowship, or in a thing taken away by violence, or hath deceived his neighbour; or have found that which was lost, and lieth concerning it, and sweareth falsely; in any of all these that a man doeth, sinning therein: then it shall be, because he hath sinned, and is guilty, that he shall restore that which he took violently away, or the thing which he hath deceitfully gotten, or that which was delivered him to keep, or the lost thing which he found, or all that about which he hath sworn falsely; he shall even restore it in the principal, and shall add the fifth part more thereto, *and* give it unto him to whom it appertaineth, in the day of his trespass offering. And he shall bring his trespass offering unto the LORD, a ram without blemish out of the flock, with thy estimation, for a trespass offering, unto the

priest: and the priest shall make an atonement for him before the LORD: and it shall be forgiven him for any thing of all that he hath done in trespassing therein (Lev 6:2–7).

Ye shall not steal, neither deal falsely, neither lie one to another.

And ye shall not swear by my name falsely, neither shalt thou profane the name of thy God: I *am* the LORD.

Thou shalt not defraud thy neighbour, neither rob *him:* the wages of him that is hired shall not abide with thee all night until the morning (Lev 19:11–13).

When thou comest into thy neighbour's vineyard, then thou mayest eat grapes thy fill at thine own pleasure; but thou shalt not put *any* in thy vessel. When thou comest into the standing corn of thy neighbour, then thou mayest pluck the ears with thine hand; but thou shalt not move a sickle unto thy neighbour's standing corn (Deut 23:24, 25).

When thou sawest a thief, then thou consentedst with him, and hast been partaker with adulterers (Ps 50:18).

Trust not in oppression, and become not vain in robbery: if riches increase, set not your heart *upon them* (Ps 62:10).

The robbery of the wicked shall destroy them; because they refuse to do judgment (Prov 21:7).

Then said he unto me, This *is* the curse that goeth forth over the face of the whole earth: for every one that stealeth shall be cut off *as* on this side according to it; and every one that sweareth shall be cut off *as* on that side according to it (Zech 5:3).

Lay not up for yourselves treasures upon earth, where moth and rust doth corrupt, and where thieves break through and steal: but lay up for yourselves treasures in heaven, where neither moth nor rust doth corrupt, and where thieves do not break through nor steal (Matt 6:19–20).

For out of the heart proceed evil thoughts, murders, adulteries, fornications, thefts, false witness, blasphemies (Matt 15:19).

And he taught, saying unto them, Is it not written, My house shall be called of all nations the house of prayer? but ye have made it a den of thieves (Mark 11:17).

And with him they crucify two thieves; the one on his right hand, and the other on his left (Mark 15:27).

Verily, verily, I say unto you, He that entereth not by the door into the sheepfold, but climbeth up some other way, the same is a thief and a robber (John 10:1).

Thou therefore which teachest another, teachest thou not thyself? thou that preachest a man should not steal, dost thou steal? (Rom 2:21).

Nay, ye do wrong, and defraud, and that *your* brethren. Know ye not that the unrighteous shall not inherit the kingdom of God? Be not deceived: neither fornicators, nor idolaters, nor adulterers, nor effeminate, nor abusers of themselves with mankind, nor thieves, nor covetous, nor drunkards, nor revilers, nor extortioners, shall inherit the kingdom of God (1 Cor 6:8–10).

Let him that stole steal no more: but rather let him labour, working with *his* hands the thing which is good, that he may have to give him that needeth (Eph 4:28).

Not purloining, but shewing all good fidelity; that they may adorn the doctrine of God our Saviour in all things (Titus 2:10).

But let none of you suffer as a murderer, or *as* a thief, or *as* an evildoer, or as a busybody in other men's matters (1 Peter 4:15).

Biblical Examples: Gen 31:19, 34, 35; Josh 7:11; Judg 17:2; 18:14–27; Jer 7:9, 10; Ezek 22:29; Hos 4:1, 2; Nah 3:1; John 12:6; Rev 9:21.

Further References: Deut 5:19; 24:7; Ps 119:61; Prov 6:30, 31; Isa 61:8; Jer 2:26; Matt 19:18; 21:13; 27:38–44; Mark 7:21, 22; Luke 18:20; 19:45, 46; Rom 13:9.

TONGUE (See also Blasphemy; Cursing; Flattery; Gossip; Lying; Oaths; Perjury; Scoffing; Slander)

Thou shalt not revile the gods, nor curse the ruler of thy people (Exod 22:28).

My lips shall not speak wickedness, nor my tongue utter deceit (Job 27:4).

His mouth is full of cursing and deceit and fraud: under his tongue *is* mischief and vanity. He sitteth in the lurking places of the villages: in the secret places doth he murder the innocent: his eyes are privily set against the poor (Ps 10:7, 8).

The LORD shall cut off all flattering lips, *and* the tongue that speaketh proud things: who have said, With our tongue will we prevail; our lips *are* our own: who *is* lord over us? (Ps 12:3, 4).

LORD, who shall abide in thy tabernacle? who shall dwell in thy holy hill? He that walketh uprightly, and worketh righteousness, and speaketh the truth in his heart. *He that* backbiteth not with his tongue, nor doeth evil to his neighbour, nor taketh up a reproach against his neighbour (Ps 15:1–3).

Keep thy tongue from evil, and thy lips from speaking guile (Ps 34:13).

I said, I will take heed to my ways, that I sin not with my tongue: I will keep my mouth with a bridle, while the wicked is before me (Ps 39:1).

Why boastest thou thyself in mischief, O mighty man? the goodness of God *endureth* continually. Thy tongue deviseth mischiefs; like a sharp razor, working deceitfully. Thou lovest evil more than good; *and* lying rather than to speak righteousness. Selah. Thou lovest all devouring words, O *thou* deceitful tongue (Ps 52:1–4).

For the sin of their mouth *and* the words of their lips let them even be taken in their pride: and for cursing and lying *which* they speak (Ps 59:12).

I will meditate also of all thy work, and talk of thy doings (Ps 77:12).

My tongue shall speak of thy word: for all thy commandments *are* righteousness (Ps 119:172).

In my distress I cried unto the LORD, and he heard me. Deliver my soul, O LORD, from lying lips, *and* from a deceitful tongue. What shall be given unto thee? or what shall be done unto thee, thou false tongue? Sharp arrows of the mighty, with coals of juniper. Woe is me, that I sojourn in Mesech, *that* I dwell in the tents of Kedar! My soul hath long dwelt with him that hateth peace. I *am for* peace: but when I speak, they *are* for war (Ps 120: 1–7).

They have sharpened their tongues like

a serpent; adders' poison *is* under their lips. Selah. . . .

Let not an evil speaker be established in the earth: evil shall hunt the violent man to overthrow *him* (Ps 140:3, 11).

Set a watch, O LORD, before my mouth; keep the door of my lips (Ps 141:3).

I will speak of the glorious honour of thy majesty, and of thy wondrous works. And *men* shall speak of the might of thy terrible acts: and I will declare thy greatness. They shall abundantly utter the memory of thy great goodness, and shall sing of thy righteousness (Ps 145:5–7).

Put away from thee a froward mouth, and perverse lips put far from thee (Prov 4:24).

These six *things* doth the LORD hate: yea, seven *are* an abomination unto him: a proud look, a lying tongue, and hands that shed innocent blood, an heart that deviseth wicked imaginations, feet that be swift in running to mischief, a false witness *that* speaketh lies, and he that soweth discord among brethren (Prov 6:16–19).

The mouth of a righteous *man is* a well of life: but violence covereth the mouth of the wicked. . . .

In the multitude of words there wanteth not sin: but he that refraineth his lips *is* wise. . . .

The mouth of the just bringeth forth wisdom: but the froward tongue shall be cut out. The lips of the righteous know what is acceptable: but the mouth of the wicked *speaketh* frowardness (Prov 10:11, 19, 31, 32).

He that is void of wisdom despiseth his neighbour: but a man of understanding holdeth his peace. A talebearer revealeth secrets: but he that is of a faithful spirit concealeth the matter. Where no counsel *is*, the people fall: but in the multitude of counsellors *there is* safety (Prov 11:12–14).

He that speaketh truth sheweth forth righteousness: but a false witness deceit. There is that speaketh like the piercings of a sword: but the tongue of the wise *is* health. The lip of truth shall be established for ever: but a lying tongue *is* but for a moment (Prov 12:17–19).

A true witness delivereth souls: but a deceitful *witness* speaketh lies (Prov 14:25).

A soft answer turneth away wrath: but grievous words stir up anger. The tongue of the wise useth knowledge aright: but the mouth of fools poureth out foolishness. The eyes of the LORD *are* in every place, beholding the evil and the good. A wholesome tongue *is* a tree of life: but perverseness therein *is* a breach of the spirit (Prov 15:1–4).

He that hath a froward heart findeth no good: and he that hath a perverse tongue falleth into mischief (Prov 17:20).

Death and life *are* in the power of the tongue: and they that love it shall eat the fruit thereof (Prov 18:21).

Whoso keepeth his mouth and his tongue keepeth his soul from troubles (Prov 21:23).

A word fitly spoken *is like* apples of gold in pictures of silver. . . .

The north wind driveth away rain: so *doth* an angry countenance a backbiting tongue (Prov 25:11, 23).

Where no wood is, *there* the fire goeth out: so where *there is* no talebearer, the strife ceaseth. *As* coals *are* to burning coals, and wood to fire; so *is* a contentious man to kindle strife. The words of a talebearer *are* as wounds, and they go down into the innermost parts of the belly. Burning lips and a wicked heart *are like* a potsherd covered with silver dross (Prov 26:20–23).

A time to rend, and a time to sew; a time to keep silence, and a time to speak (Eccl 3:7).

For the vile person will speak villainy, and his heart will work iniquity, to practise hypocrisy, and to utter error against the LORD, to make empty the soul of the hungry, and he will cause the drink of the thirsty to fail. The instruments also of the churl *are* evil: he deviseth wicked devices to destroy the poor with lying words, even when the needy speaketh right (Isa 32:6, 7).

These *are* the things that ye shall do; Speak ye every man the truth to his neighbour; execute the judgment of truth and peace in your gates (Zech 8:16).

But I say unto you, That whosoever is angry with his brother without a cause shall be in danger of the judgment: and whosoever shall say to his brother, Raca, shall be in danger of the council: but whosoever shall say, Thou fool, shall be in danger of hell fire (Matt 5:22).

But let your communication be, Yea, yea; Nay, nay: for whatsoever is more than these cometh of evil (Matt 5:37).

O generation of vipers, how can ye, being evil, speak good things? for out of the abundance of the heart the mouth speaketh. A good man out of the good treasure of the heart bringeth forth good things: and an evil man out of the evil treasure bringeth forth evil things. But I say unto you, That every idle word that men shall speak, they shall give account thereof in the day of judgment. For by thy words thou shalt be justified, and by thy words thou shalt be condemned (Matt 12:34–37).

A good man out of the good treasure of his heart bringeth forth that which is good; and an evil man out of the evil treasure of his heart bringeth forth that which is evil: for of the abundance of the heart his mouth speaketh (Luke 6:45).

Their throat *is* an open sepulchre; with their tongues they have used deceit; the poison of asps *is* under their lips: whose mouth *is* full of cursing and bitterness (Rom 3:13, 14).

That ye put off concerning the former conversation the old man, which is corrupt according to the deceitful lusts; and be renewed in the spirit of your mind; and that ye put on the new man, which after God is created in righteousness and true holiness. Wherefore putting away lying, speak every man truth with his neighbour: for we are members one of another. Be ye angry, and sin not: let not the sun go down upon your wrath: Neither give place to the devil. Let him that stole steal no more: but rather let him labour, working with *his* hands the thing which is good, that he may have to give to him that needeth. Let no corrupt communication proceed out of your mouth, but that which is good to the use of edifying, that it may minister grace unto the hearers. And grieve not the holy Spirit of God, whereby ye are sealed unto the day of redemption. Let all bitterness, and wrath, and anger, and clamour, and evil speaking, be put away from you, with all malice (Eph 4:22–31).

Neither filthiness, nor foolish talking, nor jesting, which are not convenient: but rather giving of thanks (Eph 5:4).

Only let your conversation be as it becometh the gospel of Christ: that whether I come and see you, or else be absent, I may hear of your affairs, that ye stand fast in one spirit, with one mind striving together for the faith of the gospel (Phil 1:27).

Let your speech *be* alway with grace, seasoned with salt, that ye may know how ye ought to answer every man (Col 4:6).

For there are many unruly and vain talkers and deceivers, specially they of the circumcision: whose mouths must be stopped, who subvert whole houses, teaching things which they ought not, for filthy lucre's sake (Titus 1:10, 11).

Wherefore, my beloved brethren, let every man be swift to hear, slow to speak, slow to wrath. . . .

If any man among you seem to be religious, and bridleth not his tongue, but deceiveth his own heart, this man's religion *is* vain (James 1:19, 26).

For in many things we offend all. If any man offend not in word, the same *is* a perfect man, *and* able also to bridle the whole body (James 3:2).

Even so the tongue is a little member, and boasteth great things. Behold, how great a matter a little fire kindleth! And the tongue *is* a fire, a world of iniquity: so is the tongue among our members, that it defileth the whole body, and setteth on fire the course of nature; and it is set on fire of hell. For every kind of beasts, and of birds, and of serpents, and of things in the sea, is tamed, and hath been tamed of mankind: but the tongue can no man tame; *it is* an unruly evil, full of deadly poison. Therewith bless we God, even the Father; and therewith curse we men, which are made after the similitude of God. Out of the same mouth proceedeth blessing and cursing. My brethren, these things ought not so to be. . . .

Who *is* a wise man and endued with knowledge among you? let him shew out of a good conversation his works with meekness of wisdom (James 3:5–10, 13).

Wherefore laying aside all malice, and all guile, and hypocrisies, and envies, and all evil speakings. . . .

Having your conversation honest among the Gentiles: that, whereas they speak against you as evildoers, they may by *your* good works, which they shall behold, glorify God in the day of visitation (1 Peter 2:1, 12).

Not rendering evil for evil, or railing for railing: but contrariwise blessing; knowing that ye are thereunto called, that ye should inherit a blessing. For he that will love life, and see good days, let him refrain his tongue from evil, and his lips that they speak no guile. . . .

But sanctify the Lord God in your hearts: and *be* ready always to *give* an answer to every man that asketh you a reason of the hope that is in you with meekness and fear: having a good conscience; that, whereas they speak evil of you, as of evildoers, they may be ashamed that falsely accuse your good conversation in Christ (1 Peter 3:9, 10, 15, 16).

Likewise also these *filthy* dreamers defile the flesh, despise dominion, and speak evil of dignities. Yet Michael the archangel, when contending with the devil he disputed about the body of Moses, durst not bring against him a railing accusation, but said, The Lord rebuke thee. But these speak evil of those things which they know not: but what they know naturally, as brute beasts, in those things they corrupt themselves (Jude 8–10).

Biblical Examples: Job 19:18; Ps 41:5–9; 106:33; 119:23; Eccl 12:9–11; Rom 1:29, 30; Rev 14:5.

Further References: Ps 64:2–5; 69:12; 70:3; Prov 8:13; 11:11; 12:6, 14, 23; 13:3; 14:3; 15:7, 14, 23–28; 16:27, 28; 17:4, 7, 9, 20, 27, 28; 18:4, 8, 23; 19:1, 22–28; 24:2; 26:4–9, 28; 29:11, 20; Eccl 7:22; 9:17; 10:11, 12, 20; Isa 6:5; Amos 5:13; Zeph 3:13; 1 Cor 6:10; 2 Cor 12:20; James 4:11; 2 Peter 2:7–10.

TRUTH (See also Honesty)

Moreover thou shalt provide out of all the people able men, such as fear God, men of truth, hating covetousness; and place *such* over them, *to be* rulers of thousands, *and* rulers of hundreds, rulers of fifties, and rulers of tens (Exod 18:21).

He is the Rock, his work *is* perfect: for all his ways *are* judgment: a God of truth and without iniquity, just and right *is* he (Deut 32:4).

Now therefore fear the Lord, and serve him in sincerity and in truth: and put away the gods which your fathers served on the other side of the flood, and in Egypt; and serve ye the Lord (Josh 24:14).

Only fear the Lord, and serve him in truth with all your heart; for consider how great *things* he hath done for you (1 Sam 12:24).

That the Lord may continue his word which he spake concerning me, saying, If thy children take heed to their way, to walk before me in truth with all their heart and with all their soul, there shall not fail thee (said he) a man on the throne of Israel (1 Kings 2:4).

I beseech thee, O Lord, remember now how I have walked before thee in truth and with a perfect heart, and have done *that which is* good in thy sight. And Hezekiah wept sore (2 Kings 20:3).

Into thine hand I commit my spirit: thou hast redeemed me, O Lord God of truth. (Ps 31:5).

Behold, thou desirest truth in the inward parts: and in the hidden *part* thou shalt make me to know wisdom (Ps 51:6).

He shall send from heaven, and save me *from* the reproach of him that would swallow me up. Selah. God shall send forth his mercy and his truth. . . . For thy mercy *is* great unto the heavens, and thy truth unto the clouds (Ps 57:3, 10).

Mercy and truth are met together; righteousness and peace have kissed *each other.* Truth shall spring out of the earth; and righteousness shall look down from heaven (Ps 85:10, 11).

For the Lord *is* good; his mercy *is* everlasting; and his truth *endureth* to all generations (Ps 100:5).

Let not mercy and truth forsake thee: bind them about thy neck; write them upon the table of thine heart (Prov 3:3).

He that speaketh truth sheweth forth righteousness: but a false witness deceit. . . . The lip of truth shall be established for ever: but a lying tongue *is* but for a moment. . . . Lying lips *are* abomination to the LORD: but they that deal truly *are* his delight (Prov 12:17, 19, 22).

Mercy and truth preserve the king: and his throne is upholden by mercy (Prov 20:28).

Buy the truth, and sell *it* not; *also* wisdom, and instruction, and understanding (Prov 23:23).

O LORD, thou *art* my God; I will exalt thee, I will praise thy name; for thou hast done wonderful things; *thy* counsels of old *are* faithfulness *and* truth (Isa 25:1).

O LORD, *are* not thine eyes upon the truth? thou hast stricken them, but they have not grieved; thou hast consumed them, *but* they have refused to receive correction: they have made their faces harder than a rock; they have refused to return (Jer 5:3).

Now I Nebuchadnezzar praise and extol and honour the King of heaven, all whose works *are* truth, and his ways judgment: and those that walk in pride he is able to abase (Dan 4:37).

These *are* the things that ye shall do; Speak ye every man the truth to his neighbour; execute the judgment of truth and peace in your gates: and let none of you imagine evil in your hearts against his neighbour; and love no false oath: for all these *are things* that I hate, saith the LORD.

And the word of the LORD of hosts came unto me, saying, Thus saith the LORD of hosts; The fast of the fourth *month,* and the fast of the fifth, and the fast of the seventh, and the fast of the tenth, shall be to the house of Judah joy and gladness, and cheerful feasts; therefore love the truth and peace (Zech 8:16–19).

And the Word was made flesh, and dwelt among us, (and we beheld his glory, the glory as of the only begotten of the Father,) full of grace and truth. . . . For the law was given by Moses, *but* grace and truth came by Jesus Christ (John 1:14, 17).

Ye sent unto John, and he bare witness unto the truth. (John 5:33).

Then said Jesus to those Jews which believed on him, If ye continue in my word, *then* are ye my disciples indeed; and ye shall know the truth, and the truth shall make you free. . . .

Ye are of *your* father the devil, and the lusts of your father ye will do. He was a murderer from the beginning, and abode not in the truth, because there is no truth in him. When he speaketh a lie, he speaketh of his own: for he is a liar, and the father of it (John 8:31, 32, 44).

Jesus saith unto him, I am the way, the truth, and the life: no man cometh unto the Father, but by me (John 14:6).

Howbeit when he, the Spirit of truth, is come, he will guide you into all truth: for he shall not speak of himself; but whatsoever he shall hear, *that* shall he speak: and he will shew you things to come (John 16:13).

Sanctify them through thy truth: thy word *is* truth. As thou hast sent me into the world, even so have I also sent them into the world. And for their sakes I sanctify myself, that they also might be sanctified through the truth (John 17:17–19).

Pilate therefore said unto him, Art thou a king then? Jesus answered, Thou sayest that I am a king. To this end was I born, and for this cause came I into the world, that I should bear witness unto the truth. Every one that is of the truth heareth my voice. Pilate said unto him, What is truth? And when he had said this, he went out again unto the Jews, and saith unto them, I find in him no fault *at all* (John 18:37, 38).

But we are sure that the judgment of God is according to truth against them which commit such things. . . . But unto them that are contentious, and do not obey the truth, but obey unrighteousness, indignation and wrath (Rom 2:2, 8).

Rejoiceth not in iniquity, but rejoiceth in the truth (1 Cor 13:6).

By the word of truth, by the power of God, by the armour of righteousness on the right hand and on the left, by honour and dishonour, by evil report and good report: as deceivers, and *yet* true (2 Cor 6:7, 8).

For though I would desire to glory, I shall not be a fool; for I will say the truth: but *now* I forbear, lest any man should think of me above that which he seeth me *to be,* or *that* he heareth of me. (2 Cor 12:6).

Where is then the blessedness ye spake of? for I bear you record, that, if *it had been* possible, ye would have plucked out your own eyes, and have given them to me. Am I therefore become your enemy, because I tell you the truth? (Gal 4:15, 16).

Wherefore putting away lying, speak every man truth with his neighbour: for we are members one of another (Eph 4:25).

(For the fruit of the Spirit *is* in all goodness and righteousness and truth) (Eph 5:9).

Stand therefore, having your loins girt about with truth, and having on the breastplate of righteousness (Eph 6:14).

Finally, brethren, whatsoever things are true, whatsoever things *are* honest, whatsoever things *are* just, whatsoever things *are* pure, whatsoever things *are* lovely, whatsoever things *are* of good report; if *there be* any virtue, and if *there be* any praise, think on these things (Phil 4:8).

And with all deceivableness of unrighteousness in them that perish; because they received not the love of the truth, that they might be saved. . . . That they all might be damned who believed not the truth, but had pleasure in unrighteousness. But we are bound to give thanks always to God for you, brethren beloved of the Lord, because God hath from the beginning chosen you to salvation through sanctification of the Spirit and belief of the truth (2 Thess 2:10, 12, 13).

Whereunto I am ordained a preacher, and an apostle, (I speak the truth in Christ, *and* lie not;) a teacher of the Gentiles in faith and verity (1 Tim 2:7).

But if I tarry long, that thou mayest know how thou oughtest to behave thyself in the house of God, which is the church of the living God, the pillar and ground of the truth (1 Tim 3:15).

Forbidding to marry, *and commanding* to abstain from meats, which God hath created to be received with thanksgiving of them which believe and know the truth. (1 Tim 4:3).

Study to shew thyself approved unto God, a workman that needeth not to be ashamed, rightly dividing the word of truth (2 Tim 2:15).

Paul, a servant of God, and an apostle of Jesus Christ, according to the faith of God's elect, and the acknowledging of the truth which is after godliness (Titus 1:1).

He that saith, I know him, and keepeth not his commandments, is a liar, and the truth is not in him (1 John 2:4).

Biblical Examples: Isa 59:14, 15; Amos 2:4.

Further References: Ps 33:4; 86:15; 89:14; 96:13; 108:4; Prov 16:13; Isa 65:16; Jer 9:5–9; 33:6; Hos 4:1–3; 2 Cor 4:2; Gal 3:1; 1 Tim 6:5; 2 Tim 2:25; 3:8; 4:4; 1 Peter 1:22; 2 John 2.

– U –

UNSELFISHNESS (See also Altruism)

Let love be without dissimulation. Abhor that which is evil; cleave to that which is good. Be kindly affectioned one to another with brotherly love; in honour preferring one another (Rom 12:9, 10).

We then that are strong ought to bear the infirmities of the weak, and not to please ourselves. Let every one of us please *his* neighbour for *his* good to edification. For even Christ pleased not himself; but, as it is written; The reproaches of them that reproached thee fell on me (Rom 15:1–3).

For though I be free from all *men,* yet have I made myself servant unto all, that I might gain the more. And unto the Jews I became as a Jew, that I might gain the Jews; to them that are under the law, as under the law, that I might gain them that are under the law; to them that are without law, as without law, (being not without law to God, but under the law to Christ,) that I might gain them that are without law. To the weak became I as weak, that I might gain the weak: I am made all things to all *men,* that I might by all means save some. And this I do for the gospel's sake, that I might be partaker thereof with *you* (1 Cor 9:19–23).

Let no man seek his own, but every man another's *wealth.* . . . Even as I please all *men* in all *things,* not seeking mine own profit, but the *profit* of many, that they may be saved. (1 Cor 10: 24, 33).

Charity suffereth long, *and* is kind; charity envieth not; charity vaunteth not itself, is not puffed up, doth not behave itself unseemly, seeketh not her own, is not easily provoked, thinketh no evil (1 Cor 13:4, 5).

For ye know the grace of our Lord Jesus Christ, that, though he was rich, yet for your sakes he became poor, that ye through his poverty might be rich (2 Cor 8:9).

Biblical Examples: Gen 13:9; 14:21–24; Num 11:29; 14:12–19; 1 Sam 11:12; 23:17, 18; 2 Sam 15:19, 20; 23:16, 17; Dan 5:17; Jonah 1:12; Matt 1:19; Acts 4:34, 35; Rom 16: 3, 4; 1 Cor 10:33; Philem 13, 14.

Further References: 2 Cor 5:14, 15; Phil 2:3, 4; James 2:8.

USURY AND INTEREST (See also Debt and Debtor; Economics)

If thou lend money to *any of* my people *that is* poor by thee (Exod 22:25).

And if thy brother be waxen poor, and fallen in decay with thee; then thou shalt relieve him: *yea, though he be* a stranger, or a sojourner; that he may live with thee. Take thou no usury of him, or increase: but fear thy God; that thy brother may live with thee. Thou shalt not give him thy money upon usury, nor lend him thy victuals for increase (Lev 25:35–37).

Thou shalt not lend upon usury to thy brother; usury of money, usury of victuals, usury of any thing that is lent upon usury: unto a stranger thou mayest lend upon usury; but unto thy brother thou shalt not lend upon usury: that the LORD thy God may bless thee in all that thou settest thine hand to in the land whither thou goest to possess it (Deut 23:19, 20).

He that sweareth to *his own* hurt, and changeth not. He *that* putteth not out his money to usury, nor taketh reward against the innocent. He that doeth these *things* shall never be moved (Ps 15:4b, 5).

He that by usury and unjust gain increaseth his substance, he shall gather it for him that will pity the poor (Prov 28:8).

Woe is me, my mother, that thou hast borne me a man of strife and a man of contention to the whole earth! I have neither lent on usury, nor men have lent to me on usury; *yet* every one of them doth curse me (Jer 15:10).

He *that* hath not given forth upon usury, neither hath taken any increase, *that* hath withdrawn his hand from iniquity, hath executed true judgment between man and man, hath walked in my statutes, and hath kept my judgments, to deal truly; he *is* just, he shall surely live, saith the Lord GOD.

If he beget a son *that is* a robber, a shedder of blood, and *that* doeth the like to *any* one of these *things,* and that doeth not any of those *duties,* but even hath eaten upon the mountains, and defiled his neighbour's wife, hath oppressed the poor and needy, hath spoiled by violence, hath not restored the pledge, and hath lifted up his eyes to the idols, hath committed abomination, hath given forth upon usury, and hath taken increase: shall he then live? he shall not live: he hath done all these abominations; he shall surely die; his blood shall be upon him.

Now, lo, *is* he beget a son, that seeth all his father's sins which he hath done, and considereth, and doeth not such like, *That* hath not eaten upon the mountains, neither hath lifted up his eyes to the idols of the house of Israel, hath not defiled his neighbour's wife, neither hath oppressed any, hath not withholden the pledge, neither hath spoiled by violence, *but* hath given his bread to the hungry, and hath covered the naked with a garment, *that* hath taken off his hand from the poor, *that* hath not received usury nor increase, hath executed my judgments, hath walked in my statutes; he shall not die for the iniquity of his father, he shall surely live (Ezek 18:8–17).

In thee have they taken gifts to shed blood; thou hast taken usury and increase, and thou hast greedily gained of thy neighbours by extortion, and hast forgotten me, saith the Lord GOD (Ezek 22:12).

And there was a great cry of the people and of their wives against their brethren the Jews. For there were that said, We, our sons, and our daughters, *are* many: therefore we take up corn *for them,* that we may eat, and live. *Some* also there were that said, We have mortgaged our lands, vineyards, and houses, that we might buy corn, because of the dearth. There were also that said, We have borrowed money for the king's tribute, *and that upon* our lands and vineyards. Yet now our flesh *is* as the flesh of our brethren, our children as their children: and, lo, we bring into bondage our sons and our daughters to be servants, and *some* of our daughters are brought unto bondage *already:* neither *is it* in our power *to redeem them;* for other men have our lands and vineyards.

And I was very angry when I heard their cry and these words. Then I consulted with myself, and I rebuked the nobles, and the rulers, and said unto them, Ye exact usury, every one of his brother. And I set a great assembly against them. And I said unto them, We after our ability have redeemed our brethren the Jews, which were sold unto the heathen; and will ye even sell your brethren? or shall they be sold unto us? Then held they their peace, and found nothing *to answer.* Also I said, It *is* not good that ye do: ought ye not to walk in the fear of our God because of the reproach of the heathen our enemies? I likewise, *and* my brethren, and my servants, might exact of them money and corn: I pray you, let us leave off this usury. Restore, I pray you, to them, even this day, their lands, their vineyards, their oliveyards, and their houses, also the hundredth *part* of the money, and of the corn, the wine, and the oil, that ye exact of them. Then said they, We will restore *them,* and will require nothing of them; so will we do as thou sayest. Then I called the priests, and took an oath of them, that they should do according to this promise. Also I shook my lap, and said, So God shake out every man from his house, and from his labour, that performeth not his promise, even thus be he shaken out, and emptied. And all the congregation said, Amen, and praised the LORD. And the people did according to this promise (Neh 5:1–13).

His lord answered and said unto him, *Thou* wicked and slothful servant, thou knewest that I reap where I sowed not, and gather where I have not strawed: thou oughtest therefore to have put my money to the exchangers, and *then* at my coming I should have received mine own with usury. (Matt 25:26, 27).

And if ye lend *to them* of whom ye hope to receive, what thank have ye? for sinners also lend to sinners, to receive as much again (Luke 6:34).

Further References: Ps 109:1–11; Isa 24:2; Luke 19:11–26.

– V –

VANITY (See Flattery; Pride)

VENGEANCE

And if *any* mischief follow, then thou shalt give life for life, eye for eye, tooth for tooth, hand for hand, foot for foot, burning for burning, wound for wound, stripe for stripe (Exod 21:23–25).

Thou shalt not hate thy brother in thine heart: thou shalt in any wise rebuke thy neighbour, and not suffer sin upon him. Thou shalt not avenge, nor bear any grudge against the children of thy people, but thou shalt love thy neighbour as thyself: I *am* the LORD (Lev 19:17, 18).

And if a man cause a blemish in his neighbour; as he hath done, so shall it be done to him; breach for breach, eye for eye, tooth for tooth: as he hath caused a blemish in a man, so shall it be done to him *again*. And he that killeth a beast, he shall restore it: and he that killeth a man, he shall be put to death (Lev 24:19–21).

And thine eye shall not pity; *but* life *shall go* for life, eye for eye, tooth for tooth, hand for hand, foot for foot (Deut 19:21).

And Samson said unto them, Though ye have done this, yet will I be avenged of you, and after that I will cease (Judg 15:7).

O LORD God, to whom vengeance belongeth; O God, to whom vengeance belongeth, shew thyself (Ps 94:1).

Say not thou, I will recompense evil; *but* wait on the LORD, and he shall save thee (Prov 20:22).

Say not, I will do so to him as he hath done to me: I will render to the man according to his work (Prov 24:29).

But, O LORD of hosts, that judgest righteously, that triest the reins and the heart, let me see thy vengeance on them: for unto thee have I revealed my cause (Jer 11:20).

But, O LORD of hosts, that triest the righteous, *and* seest the reins and the heart, let me see thy vengeance on them: for unto thee have I opened my cause (Jer 20:12).

Thus saith the Lord GOD; Because the Philistines have dealt by revenge, and have taken vengeance with a despiteful heart, to destroy *it* for the old hatred; therefore thus saith the Lord GOD; Behold, I will stretch out mine hand upon the Philistines, and I will cut off the Cherethims, and destroy the remnant of the sea coast. And I will execute great vengeance upon them with furious rebukes; and they shall know that I *am* the LORD, when I shall lay my vengeance upon them (Ezek 25:15–17).

Thus saith the LORD; For three transgressions of Edom, and for four, I will not turn away *the punishment* thereof; because he did pursue his brother with the sword, and did cast off all pity, and his anger did tear perpetually, and he kept his wrath for ever: but I will send a fire upon Teman, which shall devour the palaces of Bozrah (Amos 1:11, 12).

Ye have heard that it hath been said, An eye for an eye, and a tooth for a tooth: but I say unto you, That ye resist not evil: but whosoever shall smite thee on thy right cheek, turn to him the other also. And if any man will sue thee at the law, and take away thy coat, let him have *thy* cloak also. And whosoever shall compel thee to go a mile, go with him twain. Give to him that asketh thee, and from him that would borrow of thee turn not thou away.

Ye have heard that it hath been said, Thou shalt love thy neighbour, and hate thine enemy. But I say unto you, Love your enemies, bless them that curse you, do good to them that hate you, and pray for them which despitefully use you, and persecute you (Matt 5:38–44).

And unto him that smiteth thee on the *one* cheek offer also the other; and him that taketh away thy cloak forbid not *to take thy* coat also (Luke 6:29).

And when his disciples James and John saw *this,* they said, Lord, wilt thou that we command fire to come down from heaven, and consume them, even as Elias did? But he turned, and rebuked them, and said, Ye know not what manner of spirit ye are of (Luke 9:54, 55).

Recompense to no man evil for evil. Provide things honest in the sight of all men. If it be possible, as much as lieth in you, live peaceably with all men. Dearly beloved, avenge not yourselves, but *rather* give place unto wrath: for it is written, Vengeance *is* mine; I will repay, saith the Lord. Therefore if thine enemy hunger, feed him; if he thirst, give him drink: for in so doing thou shalt heap coals of fire on his head. Be not overcome of evil, but overcome evil with good (Rom 12:17–21).

See that none render evil for evil unto any *man;* but ever follow that which is good, both among yourselves, and to all *men* (1 Thess 5:15).

Not rendering evil for evil, or railing for railing: but contrariwise blessing; knowing that ye are thereunto called, that ye should inherit a blessing (1 Peter 3:9).

Biblical Examples: Gen 34:20–31; Deut 25:17–19; Judg 15:7, 8; 16:28–30; 1 Sam 15:1–9; 2 Sam 3:27; 13:23–29; 1 Kings 22:27; Luke 9:52–54; Acts 7:54–59.

Further References: Prov 26:27; Isa 33:1; Matt 7:1, 2; 1 Cor 6:7, 8.

VICES AND VIRTUES (See also index for specific vices and virtues)

Blessed *is* the man that walketh not in the counsel of the ungodly, nor standeth in the way of sinners, nor sitteth in the seat of the scornful. But his delight *is* in the law of the LORD; and in his law doth he mediate day and night. And he shall be like a tree planted by the rivers of water, that bringeth forth his fruit in his season; his leaf also shall not wither; and whatsoever he doeth shall prosper (Ps 1:1–3).

Lord, who shall abide in the tabernacle? who shall dwell in thy holy hill? He that walketh uprightly, and worketh righteousness, and speaketh the truth in his heart. *He that* backbiteth not with his tongue, nor doeth evil to his neighbour, nor taketh up a reproach against his neighbour. In whose eyes a vile person is contemned; but he honoureth them that fear the LORD. *He that* sweareth to *his own* hurt, and changeth not. *He that* putteth not out his money to usury, nor taketh reward against the innocent. He that doeth these *things* shall never be moved (Ps 15).

The earth *is* the LORD'S, and the fulness thereof; the world, and they that dwell therein. For he hath founded it upon the seas, and established it upon the floods. Who shall ascend into the hill of the LORD? or who shall stand in his holy place? He that hath clean hands, and a pure heart; who hath not lifted up his soul unto vanity, nor sworn deceitfully. He shall receive the blessing from the LORD, and righteousness from the God of his salvation. This *is* the generation of them that seek him, that seek thy face, O Jacob. Selah (Ps 24:1–6).

Blessed *are* the poor in spirit: for theirs is the kingdom of heaven. Blessed *are* they that mourn: for they shall be comforted. Blessed *are* the meek: for they shall inherit the earth. Blessed *are* they which do hunger and thirst after righteousness: for they shall be filled. Blessed *are* the merciful: for they shall obtain mercy. Blessed *are* the pure in heart: for they shall see God. Blessed *are* the peacemakers: for they shall be called the children of God.

Blessed *are* they which are persecuted for righteousness' sake: for theirs is the kingdom of heaven. Blessed are ye, when *men* shall revile you, and persecute *you,* and shall say all manner of evil against you falsely, for my sake (Matt 5:3–11).

Let love be without dissimulation. Abhor that which is evil; cleave to that which is good. *Be* kindly affectioned one to another with brotherly love; in honour preferring one another (Rom 12:9, 10).

For the flesh lusteth against the Spirit, and the Spirit against the flesh: and these are contrary the one to the other; so that ye cannot do the things that ye would. But if ye be led of the Spirit, ye are not under the law. Now the works of the flesh are manifest, which are *these;* Adultery, fornication, uncleanness, lasciviousness, idolatry, witchcraft, hatred, variance, emulations, wrath, strife, seditions, heresies, envyings, murders, drunkenness, revellings, and such like: of the which I tell you before, as I have also told *you* in time past, that they which do such things shall not inherit the kingdom of God. But the fruit of the Spirit is love, joy, peace, long-suffering, gentleness, goodness, faith, meekness, temperance: against such there is no law (Gal 5:17–23).

This I say therefore, and testify in the Lord, that ye henceforth walk not as other Gentiles walk, in the vanity of their mind, having the understanding darkened, being alienated from the life of God through the ignorance that is in them, because of the blindness of their heart: who being past feeling have given themselves over unto lasciviousness, to work all uncleanness with greediness. But ye have not so learned Christ; if so be that ye have heard him, and have been taught by him, as the truth is in Jesus: that ye put off concerning the former conversation the old man, which is corrupt according to the deceitful lusts (Eph 4:17–22).

Finally, brethren, whatsoever things are true, whatsoever things *are* honest, whatsoever things *are* just, whatsoever things *are* pure, whatsoever things *are* lovely, whatsoever things *are* of good report; if *there be* any virtue, and if *there be* any praise, think on these things (Phil 4:8).

Mortify therefore your members which are upon the earth; fornication, uncleanness, inordinate affection, evil concupiscence, and covetousness, which is idolatry: for which things' sake the wrath of God cometh on the children of disobedience: in the which ye also walked some time, when ye lived in them. But now ye also put off all these; anger, wrath, malice, blasphemy, filthy communication out of your mouth. Lie not one to another, seeing that ye have put off the old man with his deeds; and have put on the new *man,* which is renewed in knowledge after the image of him that created him (Col 3:5–10).

Abstain from all appearance of evil (1 Thess 5:22).

But thou, O man of God, flee these things; and follow after righteousness, godliness, faith, love, patience, meekness (1 Tim 6:11).

For we ourselves also were sometimes foolish, disobedient, deceived, serving divers lusts and pleasures, living in malice and envy, hateful, *and* hating one another (Titus 3:3)

Further References: Job 31; Ezek 18; Col 3:1–17.

VIOLENCE (see also Crime and Punishment; Revenge; Vengeance; War)

The earth also was corrupt before God, and the earth was filled with violence. And God looked upon the earth, and, behold, it was corrupt; for all flesh had corrupted his way upon the earth. And God said unto Noah, The end of all flesh is come before me; for the earth is filled with violence through them; and, behold, I will destroy them with the earth (Gen 6:11–13).

And he that smiteth his father, or his mother, shall be surely put to death. And he that stealeth a man, and selleth him, or if he be found in his hand, he shall surely be put to death. And he that curseth his father, or his mother, shall surely be put to death (Exod 21:15–17).

Happy *shall he be,* that taketh and dasheth thy little ones against the stones (Ps 137:9).

Let not an evil speaker be established in the earth: evil shall hunt the violent man to overthrow *him* (Ps 140:11)

Their webs shall not become garments, neither shall they cover themselves with their works: their works *are* works of iniquity, and the act of violence *is* in their hands. Their feet run to evil, and they make haste to shed innocent blood: their thoughts *are* thoughts of iniquity; wasting and destruction *are* in their paths. The way of peace they know not; and *there is* no judgment in their goings: they have made them crooked paths: whosoever goeth therein shall not know peace (Isa 59:6–8).

Thus saith the Lord GOD; Let it suffice you, O princes of Israel: remove violence and spoil, and execute judgment and justice, take away your exactions from my people, saith the Lord GOD (Ezek 45:9).

Thus saith the LORD; For three transgressions of Damascus, and for four, I will not turn away *the punishment* thereof; because they have threshed Gilead with threshing instruments of iron: but I will send a fire into the house of Hazael, which shall devour the palaces of Ben-hadad. I will break also the bar of Damascus, and cut off the inhabitant from the plain of Aven, and him the holdeth the sceptre from the house of Eden: and the people of Syria shall go into capitivity unto Kir, saith the LORD.

Thus saith the LORD; For three transgressions of Gaza, and for four, I will not turn away *the punishment* thereof; because they carried away captive the whole captivity, to deliver *them* up to Edom: but I will send a fire on the wall of Gaza, which shall devour the palaces thereof: and I will cut off the inhabitant from Ashdod, and him that holdeth the sceptre from Ashkelon, and I will turn mine hand against Ekron: and the remnant of the Philistines shall perish, saith the Lord GOD.

Thus saith the LORD; For three transgressions of Tyrus, and for four, I will not turn away *the punishment* thereof; because they delivered up the whole captivity to Edom, and remembered not the brotherly covenant: but I will send a fire on the wall of Tyrus, which shall devour the palaces thereof.

Thus saith the LORD; For three transgressions of Edom, and for four, I will not turn away *the punishment* thereof; because he did pursue his brother with the sword, and did cast off all pity, and his anger did tear perpetually, and he kept his wrath for ever: but I will send a fire upon Teman, which shall devour the palaces of Bozrah.

Thus saith the LORD; For three transgressions of the children of Ammon, and for four, I will not turn away *the punishment* thereof; because they have ripped up the women with child of Gilead, that they might enlarge their border: but I will kindle a fire in the wall of Rabbah, and it shall devour the palaces thereof, with shouting in the day of battle, with a tempest in the day of the whirlwind: And their king shall go into captivity, he and his princes together, saith the LORD.

Thus saith the LORD; For three transgressions of Moab, and for four, I will not turn away *the punishment* thereof; because he burned the bones of the king of Edom into lime: but I will send a fire upon Moab, and it shall devour the palaces of Kirioth: and Moab shall die with tumult, with shouting, *and* with the sound of the trumpet: And I will cut off the judge from the midst thereof, and will slay all the princes thereof with him, saith the LORD.

Thus saith the LORD; For three transgressions of Judah, and for four, I will not turn away *the punishment* thereof; because they have despised the law of the LORD, and have not kept his commandments, and their lies caused them to err, after the which their fathers have walked: but I will send a fire upon Judah, and it shall devour the palaces of Jerusalem (Amos 1:3–2:5).

For they know not to do right, saith the LORD, who store up violence and robbery in their palaces (Amos 3:10).

Ye have heard that it hath been said, An eye for an eye, and a tooth for a tooth: but I say unto you, That ye resist not evil: but whosoever shall smite thee on thy right cheek, turn to him the other also (Matt 5:38, 39).

And fear not them which kill the body, but are not able to kill the soul: but rather fear him which is able to destroy both soul and body in hell (Matt 10:28).

I exhort therefore, that, first of all, supplications, prayers, intercessions, *and* giving of thanks, be made for all men; for kings, and *for* all that are in authority; that we may lead a quiet and peaceable life in all godliness and honesty. For this *is* good and acceptable in the sight of God our Saviour (1 Tim 2:1–3).

This *is* a true saying, If a man desire the office of a bishop, he desireth a good work. A bishop then must be blameless, the husband of one wife, vigilant, sober, of good behavior, given to hospitality, apt to teach; not given to wine, no striker, not greedy of filthy lucre; but patient, not a brawler, not covetous (1 Tim 3:1–3).

For a bishop must be blameless, as the steward of God; not selfwilled, not soon angry, not given to wine, no striker, not given to filthy lucre; but a lover of hospitality, a lover of good men, sober, just, holy, temperate; holding fast the faithful word as he hath been taught, that he may be able by sound doctrine both to exhort and to convince the gainsayers. For there are many unruly and vain talkers and deceivers, specially they of the circumcision (Titus 1:7–10).

Biblical Examples: Gen 4:1–16; Judg 3:15–22; 1 Sam 15; 2 Sam 3:27; 4:5–12; 20:9, 10; 2 Kings 12:20; 19:37; Matt 21:12; 27:17–23.

Further References: Mic 6:12; Zeph 1:7–9; Luke 3:14.

VIRGINITY (See also Chastity; Purity)

If her father utterly refuse to give her unto him, he shall pay money according to the dowry of virgins.

Thou shalt not suffer a witch to live.

Whosoever lieth with a beast shall surely be put to death.

He that sacrificeth unto *any* god, save unto the LORD only, he shall be utterly destroyed.

Thou shalt neither vex a stranger, nor oppress him: for ye were strangers in the land of Egypt.

Ye shall not afflict any widow, or fatherless child. If thou afflict them in any wise, and they cry at all unto me, I will surely hear their cry; and my wrath shall wax hot, and I will kill you with the sword; and your wives shall be widows, and your children fatherless (Exod 22:17–24).

A widow, or a divorced woman, or profane, *or* an harlot, these shall he not take: but he shall take a virgin of his own people to wife (Lev. 21:14).

If any man take a wife, and go in unto her, and hate her, and give occasions of speech against her, and bring up an evil name upon her, and say, I took this woman, and when I came to her, I found her not a maid: then shall the father of

the damsel, and her mother, take and bring forth *the tokens of* the damsel's virginity unto the elders of the city in the gate: and the damsel's father shall say unto the elders, I gave my daughter unto this man to wife, and he hateth her; and, lo, he hath given occasions of speech *against her,* saying, I found not thy daughter a maid; and yet these *are the tokens of* my daughter's virginity. And they shall spread the cloth before the elders of the city. And the elders of that city shall take that man and chastise him; and they shall amerce him in an hundred *shekels* of silver, and give *them* unto the father of the damsel, because he hath brought up an evil name upon a virgin of Israel: and she shall be his wife; he may not put her away all his days. But if this thing be true, *and the tokens of* virginity be not found for the damsel: then they shall bring out the damsel to the door of her father's house, and the men of her city shall stone her with stones that she die: because she hath wrought folly in Israel, to play the whore in her father's house: so shalt thou put evil away from among you (Deut 22:13–21).

And *she had* a garment of divers colours upon her: for with such robes were the king's daughters *that were* virgins apparelled. Then his servant brought her out, and bolted the door after her (2 Sam 13:18).

Therefore the Lord himself shall give you a sign; Behold, a virgin shall conceive, and bear a son, and shall call his name Immanuel (Isa 7:14).

The ways of Zion do mourn, because none come to the solemn feasts: all her gates are desolate: her priests sigh, her virgins are afflicted, and she *is* in bitterness (Lam 1:4).

The elders of the daughters of Zion sit upon the ground, *and* keep silence: they have cast up dust upon their heads; they have girded themselves with sackcloth: the virgins of Jerusalem hang down their heads to the ground (Lam 2:10).

I say therefore to the unmarried and widows, It is good for them if they abide even as I. . . .

Now concerning virgins I have no commandment of the Lord: yet I give my judgment, as one that hath obtained mercy of the Lord to be faithful. I suppose therefore that this is good for the present distress, I *say*, that *it is* good for a man so to be. Art thou bound unto a wife? seek not to be loosed. Art thou loosed from a wife? seek not a wife. But and if thou marry, thou hast not sinned; and if a virgin marry, she hath not sinned. Nevertheless such shall have trouble in the flesh: but I spare you. . . .

There is difference *also* between a wife and a virgin. The unmarried woman careth for the things of the Lord, that she may be holy both in body and in spirit: but she that is married careth for the things of the world, how she may please *her* husband. . . . But if any man think that he behaveth himself uncomely toward his virgin, if she pass the flower of *her* age, and need so require, let him do what he will, he sinneth not; let them marry. Nevertheless he that standeth stedfast in his heart, having no necessity, but hath power over his own will, and hath so decreed in his heart that he will keep his virgin, doeth well. So then he that giveth *her* in marriage doeth well; but he that giveth *her* not in marriage doeth better (1 Cor 7:8, 25–28, 34, 36–38).

Biblical Examples: Judg 11:37–39; Matt 1:23; 25:1–13; Luke 1:27.

Further References: Isa 62:5; Jer 14:17; 31:4, 13; 1 Cor 7:25, 37; 2 Cor 11:2; Rev 14:4.

VOCATION, CALLING

He sent Moses his servant; *and* Aaron whom he had chosen (Ps 105:26).

Look unto Abraham your father, and unto Sarah *that* bare you: for I called him alone, and blessed him and increased him (Isa 51:2).

Ye have not chosen me, but I have chosen you, and ordained you, that ye should go and bring forth fruit, and *that* your fruit should remain: that whatsoever ye shall ask of the Father in my name, he may give it to you (John 15:16).

I have seen, I have seen the affliction of my people which is in Egypt, and I have heard their groaning, and am come down to deliver them. And now come, I will send thee into Egypt. This Moses whom they refused, saying, Who made thee a ruler and a judge? the same did God send *to be* a ruler and a deliverer by the hand of the angel which appeared to him in the bush (Acts 7:34, 35).

Paul, a servant of Jesus Christ, called *to be* an apostle, separated unto the gospel of God (Rom 1:1).

Moreover whom he did predestinate, them he also called: and whom he called, them he also justified: and whom he justified, them he also glorified (Rom 8:30).

Unto the church of God which is at Corinth, to them that are sanctified in Christ Jesus, called *to be* saints, with all that in every place call upon the name of Jesus Christ our Lord, both theirs and ours: grace *be* unto you, and peace, from God our Father, and *from* the Lord Jesus Christ. I thank my God always on your behalf, for the grace of God which is given you by Jesus Christ; that in every thing ye are enriched by him, in all utterance, and *in* all knowledge; even as the testimony of Christ was confirmed in you: so that ye come behind in no gift; waiting for the coming of our Lord Jesus Christ: who shall also confirm you unto the end, *that ye may be* blameless in the day of our Lord Jesus Christ. God *is* faithful, by whom ye were called unto the fellowship of his Son Jesus Christ our Lord (1 Cor 1:2–9).

But unto them which are called, both Jews and Greeks, Christ the power of God, and the wisdom of God (1 Cor 1:24).

Let every man abide in the same calling wherein he was called. . . . Brethren, let every man wherein he is called, therein abide with God (1 Cor 7:20, 24).

Now there are diversities of gifts, but the same Spirit. And there are differences of administrations, but the same Lord. And there are diversities of operations, but it is the same God which worketh all in all. But the manifestation of the Spirit is given to every man to profit withal. For to one is given by the Spirit the word of wisdom; to another the word of knowledge by the same Spirit; to another faith by the same Spirit; to another the gifts of healing by the same Spirit; to another the working of miracles; to another prophecy; to another discerning of spirits; to another *divers* kinds of tongues; to another the interpretation of tongues (1 Cor 12:4–10).

And God hath set some in the church, first apostles, secondarily prophets, thirdly teachers, after that miracles, then gifts of healings, helps, governments, diversities of tongues. *Are* all apostles? *are* all prophets? *are* all teachers? *are* all workers of miracles? Have all the gifts of healing? do all speak with tongues? do all interpret? (1 Cor 12:28–30).

I therefore, the prisoner of the Lord, beseech you that ye walk worthy of the vocation wherewith ye are called, with all lowliness and meekness, with longsuffering, forbearing one another in love; endeavouring to keep the unity of the Spirit in the bond of peace (Eph 4:1–3).

And he gave some, apostles; and some, prophets; and some, evangelists; and some, pastors and teachers; for the perfecting of the saints, for the work of the ministry, for the edifying of the body of Christ (Eph 4:11, 12).

As ye know how we exhorted and comforted and charged every one of you, as a father *doth* his children, that ye would walk worthy of God, who hath called you unto his kingdom and glory (1 Thess 2:11, 12).

Wherefore also we pray always for you, that our God would count you worthy of *this* calling, and fulfil all the good pleasure of *his* goodness, and the work of faith with power (2 Thess 1:11).

Wherefore, holy brethren, partakers of the heavenly calling, consider the Apostle and High Priest of our profession, Christ Jesus; who was faithful to him that appointed him, as also Moses *was faithful* in all his house. . . .

Wherefore (as the Holy Ghost saith, To-day if ye will hear his voice, harden not your hearts, as in the provocation, in the day of temptation in the wilderness (Heb 3:1, 2, 7, 8).

And no man taketh this honour unto himself, but he that is called of God, *as was* Aaron (Heb 5:4).

By faith Abraham, when he was called to go out into a place which he should after receive for an inheritance, obeyed; and he went out, not knowing whither he went (Heb 11:8).

But ye *are* a chosen generation, a royal priesthood, an holy nation, a peculiar people; that ye should shew forth the praises of him who hath called you out of darkness into his marvellous light (1 Peter 2:9).

As every man hath received the gift, *even so* minister the same one to another, as good stewards of the manifold grace of God. If any man speak, *let him speak* as the oracles of God; if any man minister, *let him do it* as of the ability which God giveth: that God in all things may be glorified through Jesus Christ, to whom be praise and dominion for ever and ever. Amen (1 Peter 4:10, 11).

According as his divine power hath given unto us all things that *pertain* unto life and godliness, through the knowledge of him that hath called us to glory and virtue. . . . Wherefore the rather, brethren, give diligence to make your calling and election sure: for if ye do these things, ye shall never fall (2 Peter 1:3, 10).

And he saith unto me, Write, Blessed *are* they which are called unto the marriage supper of the Lamb. And he saith unto me, These are the true sayings of God (Rev 19:9).

Biblical Examples: Gen 12:1–3, Exod 3:2–10; 4:1–16; Num 27:18–23; Deut 31:14–23; Josh 1:1–9; Judg 6:11–16; 1 Sam 3:1–10; 2 Kings 9:6, 7; 1 Chron 28:6–10; Isa 6; Amos 7:14, 15; Matt 4:18–22; Mark 1:16, 17; 2:14; 10:21, 22; Acts 9:1–18; 10:25–34; 13:2, 3; 16:9, 10.

Further References: 2 Chron 22:7; Isa 42:6, 7; 45:1–4; Matt 9:9; Mark 3:13–19; Luke 5:27; 6:13–15; Rom 12:6–8; 1 Cor 1:1; 2 Cor 1:1; Gal 1:1; Eph 1:1; Col 1:1; 2 Thess 2:13, 14; 1 Tim 1:1; 2 Tim 1:1, 9; 1 Peter 5:10; Jude 1.

– W –

WAGES (See also Economics; Labor Relations)

Thou shalt not defraud thy neighbour, neither rob *him:* the wages of him that is hired shall not abide with thee all night until the morning (Lev 19:13).

Thou shalt not oppress an hired servant *that is* poor and needy, *whether he be* of thy brethren, or of thy strangers that *are* in thy land within thy gates: at his day thou shalt give *him* his hire, neither shall the sun go down upon it; for he *is* poor, and setteth his heart upon it: lest he cry against thee unto the LORD, and it be sin unto thee (Deut 24:14, 15).

Thou shalt not muzzle the ox when he treadeth out *the corn* (Deut 25:4).

Woe unto him that buildeth his house by unrighteousness, and his chambers by wrong; *that* useth his neighbour's service without wages, and giveth him not for his work (Jer 22:13).

Ye have sown much, and bring in little; ye eat, but ye have not enough; ye drink, but ye are not filled with drink; ye clothe you, but there is none warm; and he that earneth wages earneth wages *to put it* into a bag with holes (Hag 1:6).

And I will come near to you to judgment; and I will be a swift witness against the sorcerers, and against the adulterers, and against false swearers, and against those that oppress the hireling in *his* wages, the widow, and the fatherless, and that turn aside the stranger *from his right,* and fear not me, saith the LORD of hosts (Mal 3:5).

For the kingdom of heaven is like unto a man *that is* an householder, which went out early in the morning to hire labourers into his vineyard. And when he had agreed with the labourers for a penny a day, he sent them into his vineyard. And he went out about the third hour, and saw others standing idle in the marketplace, and said unto them; Go ye also into the vineyard, and whatsoever is right I will give you. And they went their way. Again he went out about the sixth and ninth hour, and did likewise.

And about the eleventh hour he went out, and found others standing idle, and saith unto them, Why stand ye here all the day idle? They say unto him, Because no man hath hired us. He saith unto them, Go ye also into the vineyard; and whatsoever is right, *that* shall ye receive. So when even was come, the lord of the vineyard saith unto his steward, Call the labourers, and give them *their* hire, beginning from the last unto the first. And when they came that *were hired* about the eleventh hour, they received every man a penny. But when the first came, they supposed that they should have received more; and they likewise received every man a penny. And when they had received *it,* they murmured against the goodman of the house, saying, These last have wrought *but* one hour, and thou hast made them equal unto us, which have borne the burden and heat of the day. But he answered one of them, and said, Friend, I do thee no wrong: didst thou agree with me for a penny? Take *that* thine *is,* and go thy way: I will give unto this last, even as unto thee. Is it not lawful for me to do what I will with mine own? Is thine eye evil, because I am good? (Matt 20:1–15).

And the soldiers likewise demanded of

him, saying, And what shall we do? And he said unto them, Do violence to no man, neither accuse *any* falsely; and be content with your wages (Luke 3:14).

And in the same house remain, eating and drinking such things as they give: for the labourer is worthy of his hire. Go not from house to house (Luke 10:7).

Masters, give unto *your* servants that which is just and equal; knowing that ye also have a Master in heaven (Col 4:1).

Behold, the hire of the labourers who have reaped down your fields, which is of you kept back by fraud, crieth: and the cries of them which have reaped are entered into the ears of the Lord of sabaoth (James 5:4).

Biblical Examples: Gen 29:15-30; 30:28-34; 31:7, 41.

Further References: Rom 4:4; 6:23.

WAR (See also Conscientious Objection; Violence)

And Moses said unto the people, Fear ye not, stand still, and see the salvation of the LORD, which he will shew to you today: for the Egyptians whom ye have seen today, ye shall see them again no more for ever. The LORD shall fight for you, and ye shall hold your peace (Exod 14:13, 14).

Thou shalt not kill (Exod 20:13).

Thou shalt not bow down to their gods, nor serve them, nor do after their works: but thou shalt utterly overthrow them, and quite break down their images (Exod 23:24).

And if ye walk contrary unto me, and will not hearken unto me; I will bring seven times more plagues upon you according to your sins. I will also send wild beasts among you, which shall rob you of your children, and destroy your cattle, and make you few in number; and your *high* ways shall be desolate. And if ye will not be reformed by me by these things, but will walk contrary unto me; then will I also walk contrary unto you, and will punish you yet seven times for your sins. And I will bring a sword upon you, that shall avenge the quarrel of *my* covenant: and when ye are gathered together within your cities, I will send the pestilence among you; and ye shall be delivered into the hand of the enemy (Lev 26:21-25).

The LORD your God which goeth before you, he shall fight for you, according to all that he did for you in Egypt before your eyes (Deut 1:30).

How should one chase a thousand, and two put ten thousand to flight, except their Rock had sold them, and the LORD had shut them up? (Deut 32:30).

He teacheth my hands to war; so that a bow of steel is broken by mine arms (2 Sam 22:35).

For there fell down many slain, because the war *was* of God. And they dwelt in their steads until the captivity. . . . And the God of Israel stirred up the spirit of Pul king of Assyria, and the spirit of Tilgath-pilneser king of Assyria, and he carried them away, even the Reubenites, and the Gadites, and the half tribe of Manasseh, and brought them unto Halah, and Harbor, and Hara, and to the river Gozen, unto this day (1 Chron 5:22, 26).

But the word of the LORD came to me, saying, Thou hast shed blood abundantly, and hast made great wars: thou shalt not build an house unto my name, because thou hast shed much blood upon the earth in my sight. Behold, a son shall be born to thee, who shall be a man of rest; and I will give him rest from all his enemies round about: for his name shall be Solomon, and I will give peace and quietness unto Israel in his days (1 Chron 22:8, 9).

Then David the king stood up upon his feet, and said, Hear me, my brethren, and my people: *As for me,* I *had* in mine heart to build an house of rest for the ark of the covenant of the LORD, and for the footstool of our God, and had made ready for the building: but God said unto me, Thou shalt not built an house for my name, because thou *hast been* a man of war, and hast shed blood (1 Chron 28:2, 3).

Be ye afraid of the sword: for wrath *bringeth* the punishments of the sword, that ye may know *there is* a judgment (Job 19:29).

Depart from evil, and do good; seek peace, and pursue it (Ps 34:14).

But thou hast cast off, and put us to shame; and goest not forth with our armies. Thou makest us to turn back from the enemy: and they which hate us spoil for themselves. Thou hast given us like sheep *appointed* for meat; and hast scattered us among the heathen. Thou sellest thy people for nought, and dost not increase *thy wealth* by their price. Thou makest us a reproach to our neighbours, a scorn and a derision to them that are round about us. Thou makest us a byword among the heathen, a shaking of the head among the people. My confusion *is* continually before me, and the shame of my face hath covered me, for the voice of him that reproacheth and blasphemeth; by reason of the enemy and avenger (Ps 44:9–16).

Come, behold the works of the LORD, what desolations he hath made in the earth. He maketh wars to cease unto the end of the earth; he breaketh the bow, and cutteth the spear in sunder; he burneth the chariot in the fire (Ps 46:8, 9).

O God, thou hast cast us off, thou hast scattered us, thou hast been displeased; O turn thyself to us again. Thou hast made the earth to tremble; thou hast broken it: heal the breaches thereof; for it shaketh. Thou hast shewed thy people hard things: thou hast made us to drink the wine of astonishment (Ps 60:1–3).

Thy God hath commanded thy strength: strengthen, O God, that which thou hast wrought for us. Because of thy temple at Jerusalem shall kings bring presents unto thee. Rebuke the company of spearmen, the multitude of the bulls, with the calves of the people, *till every one* submit himself with pieces of silver: scatter thou the people *that* delight in war (Ps 68:28–30).

There brake he the arrows of the bow, the shield, and the sword, and the battle. Selah (Ps 76:3).

My soul hath long dwelt with him that hateth peace. I *am for* peace: but when I speak, they *are* for war (Ps 120:6, 7).

Happy *shall he be,* that taketh and dasheth thy little ones against the stones (Ps 137:9).

A wise *man* scaleth the city of the mighty, and casteth down the strength of the confidence thereof (Prov 21:22).

For by wise counsel thou shalt make thy war: and in multitude of counsellors *there is* safety (Prov 24:6).

There was a little city, and few men within it; and there came a great king against it, and besieged it, and built great bulwarks against it: now there was found in it a poor wise man, and he by his wisdom delivered the city; yet no man remembered that same poor man. Then said I, Wisdom *is* better than strength: nevertheless the poor man's wisdom *is* despised, and his words are not heard. The words of wise *men are* heard in quiet more than the cry of him that ruleth among fools. Wisdom *is* better than weapons of war: but one sinner destroyeth much good (Eccl 9:14–18).

And he shall judge among the nations, and shall rebuke many people: and they shall beat their swords into plowshares, and their spears into pruninghooks: nation shall not lift up sword against nation, neither shall they learn war any more (Isa 2:4).

Now will I sing to my well-beloved a song of my beloved touching his vineyard. My well-beloved hath a vineyard in a very fruitful hill: and he fenced it, and gathered out the stones thereof, and planted it with the choicest vine, and built a tower in the midst of it, and also made a winepress therein: and he looked that it should bring forth grapes, and it brought forth wild grapes. And now, O inhabitants of Jerusalem, and men of Judah, judge, I pray you, betwixt me and my vineyard. What could have been done more to my vineyard, that I have not done in it? wherefore, when I looked that it should bring forth grapes, brought it forth wild grapes? And now go to; I will tell you what I will do to my vineyard: I will take away the hedge thereof, and it shall be eaten up; *and* break down the wall thereof, and it shall be trodden down: and I will lay it waste: it shall not be pruned, nor digged; but there shall come up briers and thorns: I will also command the clouds that they rain no rain upon it. For the vineyard of the LORD of hosts *is* the house of Israel, and the men of Judah his pleasant plant: and he looked for judgment, but behold oppression; for righteousness, but behold a cry.

Woe unto them that join house to house, *that* lay field to field, till *there be* no place, that they may be placed alone in the midst of the earth! (Isa 5:1–8).

The LORD hath opened his armoury, and hath brought forth the weapons of his indignation: for this *is* the work of the Lord GOD of hosts in the land of the Chaldeans (Jer 50:25).

Therefore, O Aholibah, thus saith the Lord GOD; Behold, I will raise up thy lovers against thee, from whom thy mind is alienated, and I will bring them against thee on every side; the Babylonians, and all the Chaldeans, Pekod, and Shoa, and Koa, *and* all the Assyrians with them: all of them desirable young men, captains and rulers, great lords and renowned, all of them riding upon horses. And they shall come against thee with chariots, wagons, and wheels, and with an assembly of people, *which* shall set against thee buckler and shield and helmet round about: and I will set judgment before them, and they shall judge thee according to their judgments. And I will set my jealousy against thee, and they shall deal furiously with thee: they shall take away thy nose and thine ears; and thy remnant shall fall by the sword: they shall take thy sons and thy daughters; and thy residue shall be devoured by the fire (Ezek 23:22–25).

Shall a trumpet be blown in the city, and the people not be afraid? shall there be evil in a city, and the LORD hath not done *it?* (Amos 3:6).

I have overthrown *some* of you, as God overthrew Sodom and Gomorrah, and ye were as a firebrand plucked out of the burning: yet have ye not returned unto me, saith the LORD (Amos 4:11).

Hold thy peace at the presence of the Lord GOD: for the day of the LORD *is* at hand: for the LORD hath prepared a sacrifice, he hath bid his guests. And it shall come to pass in the day of the LORD's sacrifice, that I will punish the princes, and the king's children, and all such as are clothed with strange apparel. In the same day also will I punish all those that leap on the threshold, which fill their masters' houses with violence and deceit. And it shall come to pass in that day, saith the LORD, *that there shall be* the noise of a cry from the fish gate, and an howling from the second, and a great crashing

from the hills. Howl, ye inhabitants of Maktesh, for all the merchant people are cut down; all they that bear silver are cut off. And it shall come to pass at that time, *that* I will search Jerusalem with candles, and punish the men that are settled on their lees: that say in their heart, The LORD will not do good, neither will he do evil. Therefore their goods shall become a booty, and their houses a desolation: they shall also build houses, but not inhabit *them;* and they shall plant vineyards, but not drink the wine thereof. The great day of the LORD *is* near, *it is* near, and hasteth greatly, *even* the voice of the day of the LORD: the mighty man shall cry there bitterly. That day *is* a day of wrath, a day of trouble and distress, a day of wasteness and desolation, a day of darkness and gloominess, a day of clouds and thick darkness, a day of the trumpet and alarm against the fenced cities, and against the high towers. And I will bring distress upon men, that they shall walk like blind men, because they have sinned against the LORD: and their blood shall be poured out as dust, and their flesh as the dung. Neither their silver nor their gold shall be able to deliver them in the day of the LORD's wrath; but the whole land shall be devoured by the fire of his jealousy: for he shall make even a speedy riddance of all them that dwell in the land (Zeph 1:7–18).

For before these days there was no hire for man, nor any hire for beast; neither *was there any* peace to him that went out or came in because of the affliction: for I set all men every one against his neighbour (Zech 8:10).

Blessed *are* the peacemakers: for they shall be called the children of God (Matt 5:9).

But I say unto you, Love your enemies, bless them that curse you, do good to them that hate you, and pray for them which despitefully use you, and persecute you; that ye may be the children of your Father which is in heaven: for he maketh his sun to rise on the evil and on the good, and sendeth rain on the just and on the unjust (Matt 5:44, 45).

And when ye shall hear of wars and rumours of wars, be ye not troubled: for *such things* must needs be; but the end *shall* not *be* yet (Mark 13:7).

Or what king, going to make war against another king, sitteth not down first, and consulteth whether he be able with ten thousand to meet him that cometh against him with twenty thousand? Or else, while the other is yet a great way off, he sendeth an ambassage, and desireth conditions of peace (Luke 14:31, 32).

And when ye shall see Jerusalem compassed with armies, then know that the desolation thereof is nigh. Then let them which are in Judæa flee to the mountains; and let them which are in the midst of it depart out; and let not them that are in the countries enter thereinto. For these be the days of vengeance, that all things which are written may be fulfilled. But woe unto them that are with child, and to them that give suck, in those days! for there shall be great distress in the land, and wrath upon this people. And they shall fall by the edge of the sword, and shall be led away captive into all nations: and Jerusalem shall be trodden down of the Gentiles, until the times of the Gentiles be fulfilled.

And there shall be signs in the sun, and in the moon, and in the stars; and upon the earth distress of nations, with perplexity; the sea and the waves roaring; men's hearts failing them for fear, and for looking after those things which are coming on the earth: for the powers of heaven shall be shaken (Luke 21:20–26).

Recompense to no man evil for evil. Provide things honest in the sight of all men. If it be possible, as much as lieth in you, live peaceably with all men. Dearly beloved, avenge not yourselves, but *rather* give place unto wrath: for it is written, Vengeance *is* mine; I will repay, saith the Lord. Therefore if thine enemy hunger, feed him; if he thirst, give him drink: for in so doing thou shalt heap coals of fire on his head. Be not overcome of evil, but overcome evil with good (Rom 12:17–21).

Let us therefore follow after the things which make for peace, and things wherewith one may edify another (Rom 14:19).

From whence *come* wars and fightings among you? *come they* not hence, *even*

of your lusts that war in your members? Ye lust, and have not: ye kill, and desire to have, and cannot obtain: ye fight and war, yet ye have not, because ye ask not (James 4:1, 2).

He that leadeth into captivity shall go into captivity: he that killeth with the sword must be killed with the sword. Here is the patience and the faith of the saints (Rev 13:10).

And I saw an angel standing in the sun; and he cried with a loud voice, saying to all the fowls that fly in the midst of heaven, Come and gather yourselves together unto the supper of the great God; that ye may eat the flesh of kings, and the flesh of captains, and the flesh of mighty men, and the flesh of horses, and of them that sit on them, and the flesh of all *men, both* free and bond, both small and great (Rev 19:17, 18).

Biblical Examples: Exod 17:14; Num 31:7–17; Deut 2:33, 34; 3:6; 20:13–18; 25:19; 32:25; Josh 6:21–24; 7:12, 13; 8:24, 25; 10:2–40; 11:11–23; Judg 12:1–6; 20; 1 Sam 2:10; 15:3–9; 27:8–11; 2 Sam 2:12–31; 3:1; 20; 1 Kings 14:30; 16:21, 22; 2 Kings 18:19–36; 2 Chron 11:14; 12:5–8; 13:4–12; 18:12–16; 24:23, 24; Isa 14:19; 18:6; 19:2; 30:15–17; Ezek 15:6–8; 21:9–17; Amos 2:2.

Further References: Deut 3:21, 22; 7:17–24; 13:12–18; 20:1–4; 28:25–68; 31:6–8; 32:29, 30; Josh 1:1–9; 22:10–34; Judg 1:2; 2:11–15; 6:16; 7:9–11; 11:29; 1 Sam 17:45–47; 19:5; 30:7, 8; 2 Sam 5:22–24; 16:20; 22:18; 1 Kings 20:28; 2 Kings 15:37; 1 Chron 21:12; 2 Chron 12:1–12; 15:6; 24:23, 24; 33:11; Ps 18:34; 48:4–7; 78:62; 79:1–3, 10; 105:25; Isa 3:5, 25, 26; 5:25–30; 6:11, 12; 9:3–12, 19–21; 13:3–9, 15, 16; 16:9, 10; 18:6; 19:2–16; 32:13, 14; 34:2–15; 43:28; 45:7; Jer 4:19–31; 5:16, 17; 6:24–26; 7:33, 34; 8:16, 17; 9:10–21; 10:20; 12:7–12; 13:14; 14:18; 15:8, 9; 19:7–9; 46:3–21; 47:3–7; 48:10, 28, 33; 49:5; 51:30–58; Lam 1–5; Ezek 33:27; 39:17–19; Hos 10:14; 13:16; Joel 2:2–10; Amos 1:13; 5:8, 9; 6:9, 10; 8:3; Mic 4:3; Nah 2:10; 3:3–10; Zech 14:2; Matt 6:14, 15; 10:34–36; Mark 12:17; John 14:27; Eph 2:14–18; 6:15.

WASTEFULNESS (See Extravagance; Stewardship)

WEALTH (See also Economics; Extravagance; Materialism; Property; Stewardship)

And it shall be, when the LORD thy God shall have brought thee into the land which he sware unto thy fathers, to Abraham, to Isaac, and to Jacob, to give thee great and goodly cities, which thou buildedst not, and houses full of all good *things,* which thou filledst not, and wells digged, which thou diggedst not, vineyards and olive trees, which thou plantedst not; when thou shalt have eaten and be full; *then* beware lest thou forget the LORD, which brought thee forth out of the land of Egypt, from the house of bondage (Deut 6:10–12).

And thou say in thine heart, My power and the might of *mine* hand hath gotten me this wealth. But thou shalt remember the LORD thy God: for *it is* he that giveth thee power to get wealth, that he may establish his covenant which he sware unto thy fathers, as *it is* this day (Deut 8:17, 18).

The LORD maketh poor, and maketh rich: he bringeth low, and lifteth up (1 Sam 2:7).

Wherefore do the wicked live, become old, yea, are mighty in power? Their seed is established in their sight with them, and their offspring before their eyes. Their houses *are* safe from fear, neither *is* the rod of God upon them. Their bull gendereth, and faileth not; their cow calveth, and casteth not her calf. They send forth their little ones like a flock, and their children dance. They take the timbrel and harp, and rejoice at the sound of the organ. They spend their days in wealth, and in a moment go down to the grave. Therefore they say unto God, Depart from us; for we desire not the knowledge of thy ways. What *is* the Almighty, that we should serve him? and what profit should we have, if we pray unto him? (Job 21:7–15).

This *is* the portion of a wicked man with God, and the heritage of oppressors, *which* they shall receive of the Almighty. If his children be multiplied, *it is* for the sword: and his offspring shall not be satisfied with bread. Those that remain of him shall be buried in death: and his widows shall not weep. Though he heap up silver

as the dust, and prepare raiment as the clay; he may prepare *it,* but the just shall put *it* on, and the innocent shall divide the silver. He buildeth his house as a moth, and as a booth *that* the keeper maketh. The rich man shall lie down, but he shall not be gathered: he openeth his eyes, and he *is* not. Terrors take hold on him as waters, a tempest stealeth him away in the night. The east wind carrieth him away, and he departeth: and as a storm hurleth him out of his place. For *God* shall cast upon him, and not spare: he would fain flee out of his hand. *Men* shall clap their hands at him, and shall hiss him out of his place (Job 27:13–23).

If I have made gold my hope, or have said to the fine gold, *Thou art* my confidence; if I rejoiced because my wealth *was* great, and because mine hand had gotten much; this also *were* an iniquity *to be punished by* the judge: for I should have denied the God *that is* above (Job 31:24, 25, 28).

A little that a righteous man hath *is* better than the riches of many wicked (Ps 37:16).

Be not thou afraid when one is made rich, when the glory of his house is increased; for when he dieth he shall carry nothing away: his glory shall not descend after him. Though while he lived he blessed his soul: and *men* will praise thee, when thou doest well to thyself (Ps 49:16–18).

Why boastest thou thyself in mischief, O mighty man? the goodness of God *endureth* continually. Thy tongue deviseth mischiefs; like a sharp razor, working deceitfully. Thou lovest evil more than good; *and* lying rather than to speak righteousness. Selah. Thou lovest all devouring words, O *thou* deceitful tongue. God shall likewise destroy thee for ever, he shall take thee away, and pluck thee out of *thy* dwelling place, and root thee out of the land of the living. Selah. The righteous also shall see, and fear, and shall laugh at him: lo, *this is* the man *that* made not God his strength; but trusted in the abundance of his riches, *and* strengthened himself in his wickedness (Ps 52:1–7).

There is that scattereth, and yet increaseth; and *there is* that withholdeth more than is meet, but *it tendeth* to poverty (Prov 11:24).

The slothful *man* roasteth not that which he took in hunting: but the substance of a diligent man *is* precious (Prov 12:27).

Wealth *gotten* by vanity shall be diminished: but he that gathereth by labour shall increase (Prov 13:11).

Pride *goeth* before destruction, and an haughty spirit before a fall (Prov 16:18).

Wealth maketh many friends; but the poor is separated from his neighbour (Prov 19:4).

Labour not to be rich: cease from thine own wisdom. Wilt thou set thine eyes upon that which is not? for *riches* certainly make themselves wings; they fly away as an eagle toward heaven (Prov 23:4, 5).

Be thou diligent to know the state of thy flocks, *and* look well to thy herds. For riches *are* not for ever: and doth the crown *endure* to every generation? (Prov 27:23, 24).

The rich man *is* wise in his own conceit; but the poor that hath understanding searcheth him out (Prov 28:11).

Remove far from me vanity and lies: give me neither poverty nor riches; feed me with food convenient for me: lest I be full, and deny *thee,* and say, Who *is* the LORD? or lest I be poor, and steal, and take the name of my God *in vain* (Prov 30:8, 9).

There is a sore evil *which* I have seen under the sun, *namely,* riches kept for the owners thereof to their hurt. But those riches perish by evil travail: and he begetteth a son, and *there is* nothing in his hand (Eccl 5:13, 14).

There is an evil which I have seen under the sun, and it *is* common among men: a man to whom God hath given riches, wealth, and honour, so that he wanteth nothing for his soul of all that he desireth, yet God giveth him not power to eat thereof, but a stranger eateth it: this *is* vanity, and it *is* an evil disease (Eccl 6:1, 2).

Woe unto them that join house to house, *that* lay field to field, till *there be* no place, that they may be placed alone in the midst of the earth! (Isa 5:8).

Thus saith the LORD, Let not the wise *man* glory in his wisdom, neither let the mighty *man* glory in his might, let not the rich *man* glory in his riches (Jer 9:23).

As the partridge sitteth *on eggs,* and hatcheth *them* not; *so* he that getteth riches, and not by right, shall leave them in the midst of his days, and at his end shall be a fool (Jer 17:11).

They shall cast their silver in the streets, and their gold shall be removed: their silver and their gold shall not be able to deliver them in the day of the wrath of the LORD: they shall not satisfy their souls, neither fill their bowels: because it is the stumblingblock of their iniquity (Ezek 7:19).

For the rich men thereof are full of violence, and the inhabitants thereof have spoken lies, and their tongue *is* deceitful in their mouth (Mic 6:12).

Neither their silver nor their gold shall be able to deliver them in the day of the LORD'S wrath; but the whole land shall be devoured by the fire of his jealousy: for he shall make even a speedy riddance of all them that dwell in the land (Zeph 1:18).

Lay not up for yourselves treasures upon earth, where moth and rust doth corrupt, and where thieves break through and steal: but lay up for yourselves treasures in heaven, where neither moth nor rust doth corrupt, and where thieves do not break through nor steal: for where your treasure is, there will your heart be also (Matt 6:19–21).

Or what man is there of you, whom if his son ask bread, will he give him a stone? Or if he ask a fish, will he give him a serpent? If ye then, being evil, know how to give good gifts unto your children, how much more shall your Father which is in heaven give good things to them that ask him? (Matt 7:9–11).

He also that received seed among the thorns is he that heareth the word; and the care of this world, and the deceitfulness of riches, choke the word, and he becometh unfruitful (Matt 13:22).

And again I say unto you, It is easier for a camel to go through the eye of a needle, than for a rich man to enter into the kingdom of God (Matt 19:24).

And the cares of this world, and the deceitfulness of riches, and the lusts of other things entering in, choke the word, and it becometh unfruitful (Mark 4:19).

But woe unto you that are rich! for ye have received your consolation. Woe unto you that are full! for ye shall hunger. Woe unto you that laugh now! for ye shall mourn and weep (Luke 6:24, 25).

And he said unto them, Take heed, and beware of covetousness: for a man's life consisteth not in the abundance of the things which he possesseth. And he spake a parable unto them, saying, The ground of a certain rich man brought forth plentifully: and he thought within himself, saying, What shall I do, because I have no room where to bestow my fruits? And he said, This will I do: I will pull down my barns, and build greater; and there will I bestow all my fruits and my goods. And I will say to my soul, Soul, thou hast much goods laid up for many years; take thine ease, eat, drink, *and* be merry. But God said unto him, *Thou* fool, this night thy soul shall be required of thee: then whose shall those things be, which thou hast provided? So *is* he that layeth up treasure for himself, and is not rich toward God (Luke 12:15–21).

No servant can serve two masters: for either he will hate the one, and love the other; or else he will hold to the one, and despise the other. Ye cannot serve God and mammon. And the Pharisees also, who were covetous, heard all these things: and they derided him (Luke 16:13, 14).

There was a certain rich man, which was clothed in purple and fine linen, and fared sumptuously every day: and there was a certain beggar named Lazarus, which was laid at his gate, full of sores, and desiring to be fed with the crumbs which fell from the rich man's table: moreover the dogs came and licked his sores. And it came to pass, that the beggar died, and was carried by the angels into Abraham's bosom: the rich man also died, and was buried; and in hell he lift up his eyes, being in torments, and seeth Abraham afar off, and Lazarus in his bosom. And he cried and said, Father Abraham, have mercy on me, and send Lazarus, that he may dip the tip of his finger in water, and cool my tongue; for I am tormented in this flame. But Abraham said, Son, remem-

ber that thou in thy lifetime receivedst thy good things, and likewise Lazarus evil things: but now he is comforted, and thou art tormented. And beside all this, between us and you there is a great gulf fixed: so that they which would pass from hence to you cannot; neither can they pass to us, that *would come* from thence. Then he said, I pray thee therefore, father, that thou wouldest send him to my father's house: for I have five brethren; that he may testify unto them, lest they also come into this place of torment. Abraham saith unto him, They have Moses and the prophets; let them hear them. And he said, Nay, father Abraham: but if one went unto them from the dead, they will repent. And he said unto him, If they hear not Moses and the prophets, neither will they be persuaded, though one rose from the dead (Luke 16:19–31).

I have shewed you all things, how that so labouring ye ought to support the weak, and to remember the words of the Lord Jesus, how he said, It is more blessed to give than to receive (Acts 20:35).

Charge them that are rich in this world, that they be not highminded, nor trust in uncertain riches, but in the living God, who giveth us richly all things to enjoy; that they do good, that they be rich in good works, ready to distribute, willing to communicate; laying up in store for themselves a good foundation against the time to come, that they may lay hold on eternal life (1 Tim 6:17–19).

Let the brother of low degree rejoice in that he is exalted: but the rich, in that he is made low: because as the flower of the grass he shall pass away. For the sun is no sooner risen with a burning heat, but it withereth the grass, and the flower thereof falleth, and the grace of the fashion of it perisheth: so also shall the rich man fade away in his ways (James 1:9–11).

Go to now, *ye* rich men, weep and howl for your miseries that shall come upon *you*. Your riches are corrupted, and your garments are motheaten. Your gold and silver is cankered; and the rust of them shall be a witness against you, and shall eat your flesh as it were fire. Ye have heaped treasure together for the last days. Behold, the hire of the labourers who have reaped down your fields, which is of you kept back by fraud, crieth: and the cries of them which have reaped are entered into the ears of the Lord of sabaoth. Ye have lived in pleasure on the earth, and been wanton; ye have nourished your hearts, as in a day of slaughter. Ye have condemned *and* killed the just; *and* he doth not resist you (James 5:1–6).

But whoso hath this world's good, and seeth his brother have need, and shutteth up his bowels *of compassion* from him, how dwelleth the love of God in him? (1 John 3:17).

Biblical Examples: Gen 13:2; 24:35; 1 Kings 10:23; 2 Kings 20:12–18; Job 1:3; Jer 5:7–9, 27–29; 48:36; Hos 12:8; Amos 6:1–6; Matt 25:14–30; 27:57; Mark 10:17–25; Luke 12:42; 16:8; 19:2; James 2:6, 7.

Further References: Deut 8:10–16; 31:20; Neh 5:1–13; Ps 73:3–22; Prov 11:4, 28; 13:7, 8; 14:20; 15:6, 16, 17; 18:11, 23; 21:6; Eccl 5:9–20; 7:11, 12; Jer 22:13–19; Ezek 28:5; Matt 17:24–27; 19:16–29; 25:35–46; Mark 10:17–25; Luke 18:18–25; Eph 4:28; 1 Tim 6:4–11.

WHOREDOM (See Adultery; Fornication; Sex and Sexuality)

WIDOWS (See also Ministry)

Ye shall not afflict any widow, or fatherless child. If thou afflict them in any wise, and they cry at all unto me, I will surely hear their cry; and my wrath shall wax hot, and I will kill you with the sword; and your wives shall be widows, and your children fatherless (Exod 22:22–24).

A widow, or a divorced woman, or profane, *or* an harlot, these shall he not take: but he shall take a virgin of his own people to wife (Lev 21:14).

He doth execute the judgment of the fatherless and widow, and loveth the stranger, in giving him food and raiment (Deut 10:18).

At the end of three years thou shalt bring forth all the tithe of thine increase the same year, and shalt lay *it* up within thy gates: and the Levite, (because he hath no part nor inheritance with thee,) and the stranger, and the fatherless, and the widow, which *are* within thy gates, shall come, and shall eat and be satisfied; that the LORD thy God may bless thee in all

the work of thine hand which thou doest (Deut 14:28, 29).

Thou shalt not pervert the judgment of the stranger, *nor* of the fatherless; nor take a widow's raiment to pledge: when thou cuttest down thine harvest in thy field, and hast forgot a sheaf in the field, thou shalt not go again to fetch it: it shall be for the stranger, for the fatherless, and for the widow: that the LORD thy God may bless thee in all the work of thine hands. When thou beatest thine olive tree, thou shalt not go over the boughs again: it shall be for the stranger, for the fatherless, and for the widow. When thou gatherest the grapes of thy vineyard, thou shalt not glean *it* afterward: it shall be for the stranger, for the fatherless, and for the widow (Deut 24:17, 19–21).

If brethren dwell together, and one of them die, and have no child, the wife of the dead shall not marry without unto a stranger: her husband's brother shall go in unto her, and take her to him to wife, and perform the duty of an husband's brother unto her (Deut 25:5).

Cursed *be* he that perverteth the judgment of the stranger, fatherless, and widow. And all the people shall say, Amen (Deut 27:19).

Is not thy wickedness great? and thine iniquities infinite? . . . Thou hast sent widows away empty, and the arms of the fatherless have been broken (Job 22:5, 9).

A father of the fatherless, and a judge of the widows, *is* God in his holy habitation (Ps 68:5).

The LORD preserveth the strangers; he relieveth the fatherless and widow: but the way of the wicked he turneth upside down (Ps 146:9).

The LORD will destroy the house of the proud: but he will establish the border of the widow (Prov 15:25).

Woe unto them that decree unrighteous decrees, and that write grievousness *which* they have prescribed; to turn aside the needy from judgment, and to take away the right from the poor of my people, that widows may be their prey, and *that* they may rob the fatherless! (Isa 10:1, 2).

Fear not; for thou shalt not be ashamed: neither be thou confounded; for thou shalt not be put to shame: for thou shalt forget the shame of thy youth, and shalt not remember the reproach of thy widowhood any more (Isa 54:4).

If ye oppress not the stranger, the fatherless, and the widow, and shed not innocent blood in this place, neither walk after other gods to your hurt: then will I cause you to dwell in this place, in the land that I gave to your fathers, for ever and ever (Jer 7:6, 7).

Leave thy fatherless children, I will preserve *them* alive; and let thy widows trust in me (Jer 49:11).

Woe unto you, scribes and Pharisees, hypocrites! for ye devour widows' houses, and for a pretence make long prayer: therefore ye shall receive the greater damnation (Matt 23:14).

So then if, while *her* husband liveth, she be married to another man, she shall be called an adulteress: but if her husband be dead, she is free from that law; so that she is no adulteress, though she be married to another man (Rom 7:3).

The wife is bound by the law as long as her husband liveth; but if her husband be dead, she is at liberty to be married to whom she will; only in the Lord (1 Cor 7:39).

Honour widows that are widows indeed. But if any widow have children or nephews, let them learn first to shew piety at home, and to requite their parents: for that is good and acceptable before God. Now she that is a widow indeed, and desolate, trusteth in God, and continueth in supplications and prayers night and day. But she that liveth in pleasure is dead while she liveth. And these things give in charge, that they may be blameless. But if any provide not for his own, and specially for those of his own house, he hath denied the faith, and is worse than an infidel. Let not a widow be taken into the number under threescore years old, having been the wife of one man, well reported of for good works; if she have brought up children, if she have lodged strangers, if she have washed the saints' feet, if she have relieved the afflicted, if she have diligently followed every good work. But the younger widows refuse: for when they have begun to wax wanton against Christ, they will marry; having

damnation, because they have cast off their first faith. And withal they learn *to be* idle, wandering about from house to house; and not only idle, but tattlers also and busybodies, speaking things which they ought not. I will therefore that the younger women marry, bear children, guide the house, give none occasion to the adversary to speak reproachfully. For some are already turned aside after Satan. If any man or woman that believeth have widows, let them relieve them, and let not the church be charged; that it may relieve them that are widows indeed (1 Tim 5:3–16).

Pure religion and undefiled before God and the Father is this, To visit the fatherless and widows in their affliction, *and* to keep himself unspotted from the world (James 1:27).

Biblical Examples: Ruth 1:3; 1–4; 1 Kings 17; 2 Kings 4:1–7; Mark 12:41–44; Luke 2:36, 37; 7:11–15; 21:2; Acts 6:1.

Further References: Lev 22:13; Num 30:9; Deut 16:11–14; 25:5–10; Job 24:3, 21; 29:13; 31:16, 21; Ps 94:6; Isa 1:17, 23; Jer 22:3; Zech 7:10; Mal 3:5; Mark 12:40; Luke 20:47.

WIFE (See also Husband-Wife Relations)

And the LORD God said, *It is* not good that the man should be alone; I will make him an help meet for him. And out of the ground the LORD God formed every beast of the field, and every fowl of the air; and brought *them* unto Adam to see what he would call them: and whatsoever Adam called every living creature, that *was* the name thereof. And Adam gave names to all cattle, and to the fowl of the air, and to every beast of the field; but for Adam there was not found an help meet for him. And Adam said, This *is* now bone of my bones, and flesh of my flesh: she shall be called Woman, because she was taken out of Man. Therefore shall a man leave his father and his mother, and shall cleave unto his wife: and they shall be one flesh (Gen 2:18–20, 23–24).

Unto the woman he said, I will greatly multiply thy sorrow and thy conception; in sorrow thou shalt bring forth children; and the desire *shall be* to thy husband, and he shall rule over thee (Gen 3:16).

And Abraham hastened into the tent unto Sarah, and said, Make ready quickly three measures of fine meal, knead *it*, and make cakes upon the hearth (Gen 18:6).

Thy wife *shall be* as a fruitful vine by the sides of thine house: thy children like olive plants round about thy table. Behold, that thus shall the man be blessed that feareth the LORD (Ps 128:3, 4).

A virtuous woman *is* a crown to her husband: but she that maketh ashamed *is* as rottenness in his bones (Prov 12:4).

Whoso findeth a wife findeth a good *thing*, and obtaineth favour of the LORD (Prov 18:22).

Who can find a virtuous woman? for her price *is* far above rubies. The heart of her husband doth safely trust in her, so that he shall have no need of spoil. She will do him good and not evil all the days of her life. She seeketh wool, and flax, and worketh willingly with her hands. She is like the merchants' ships; she bringeth her food from afar. She riseth also while it is yet night, and giveth meat to her household, and a portion to her maidens. She considereth a field, and buyeth it: with the fruit of her hands she planteth a vineyard. She girdeth her loins with strength, and strengtheneth her arms. She perceiveth that her merchandise *is* good: her candle goeth not out by night. She layeth her hands to the spindle, and her hands hold the distaff. She stretcheth out her hand to the poor; yea, she reacheth forth her hands to the needy. She is not afraid of the snow for her household: for all her household *are* clothed with scarlet. She maketh herself coverings of tapestry; her clothing *is* silk and purple. Her husband is known in the gates, when he sitteth among the elders of the land. She maketh fine linen, and selleth *it;* and delivereth girdles unto the merchant. Strength and honour *are* her clothing; and she shall rejoice in time to come. She openeth her mouth with wisdom; and in her tongue *is* the law of kindness. She looketh well to the ways of her household, and eateth not the bread of idleness. Her children arise up, and call her blessed; her husband *also,* and he praiseth her. Many daughters have done virtuously, but thou excellest them all. Favour *is* deceitful, and beauty *is* vain: *but* a woman *that* feareth the LORD, she shall be praised. Give her of the fruit of her hands; and let her own works praise her in the gates (Prov 31:10–31).

Nevertheless, *to avoid* fornication, let every man have his own wife, and let every woman have her own husband. Let the husband render unto the wife due benevolence: and likewise also the wife unto the husband. The wife hath not power of her own body, but the husband: and likewise also the husband hath not power of his own body, but the wife. Defraud ye not one the other, except *it be* with consent for a time, that ye may give yourselves to fasting and prayer; and come together again, that Satan tempt you not for your incontinency. But I speak this by permission, *and* not of commandment (1 Cor 7:2–6).

But and if she depart, let her remain unmarried, or be reconciled to *her* husband: and let not the husband put away *his* wife. But to the rest speak I, not the Lord: If any brother hath a wife that believeth not, and she be pleased to dwell with him, let him not put her away. And the woman which hath an husband that believeth not, and if he be pleased to dwell with her, let her not leave him. For the unbelieving husband is sanctified by the wife, and the unbelieving wife is sanctified by the husband: else were your children unclean; but now are they holy. But if the unbelieving depart, let him depart. A brother or a sister is not under bondage in such *cases:* but God hath called us to peace. For what knowest thou, O wife, whether thou shalt save *thy* husband? or how knowest thou, O man, whether thou shalt save *thy* wife? (1 Cor 7:11–16).

Art thou bound unto a wife? seek not to be loosed. Art thou loosed from a wife? seek not a wife. But and if thou marry, thou hast not sinned; and if a virgin marry, she hath not sinned. Nevertheless such shall have trouble in the flesh: but I spare you. But this I say, brethren, the time *is* short: it remaineth, that both they that have wives be as though they had none; and they that weep, as though they wept not; and they that rejoice, as though they rejoiced not; and they that buy, as though they possessed not; and they that use this world as not abusing *it:* for the fashion of this world passeth away. But I would have you without carefulness. He that is unmarried careth for the things that belong to the Lord, how he may please the Lord: but he that is married careth for the things that are of the world, how he may please *his* wife. There is difference *also* between a wife and a virgin. The unmarried woman careth for the things of the Lord, that she may be holy both in body and in spirit: but she that is married careth for the things of the world, how she may please *her* husband (1 Cor 7:27–34).

So then he that giveth *her* in marriage doeth well; but he that giveth *her* not in marriage doeth better. The wife is bound by the law as long as her husband liveth; but if her husband be dead, she is at liberty to be married to whom she will; only in the Lord. But she is happier if she so abide, after my judgment: and I think also that I have the Spirit of God (1 Cor 7:38–40).

But I would have you know, that the head of every man is Christ; and the head of the woman *is* the man; and the head of Christ *is* God. Every man praying or prophesying, having *his* head covered, dishonoureth his head. But every woman that prayeth or prophesieth with *her* head uncovered dishonoureth her head: for that is even all one as if she were shaven. For if the woman be not covered, let her also be shorn: but if it be a shame for a woman to be shorn or shaven, let her be covered. For a man indeed ought not to cover *his* head, forasmuch as he is the image and glory of God: but the woman is the glory of the man. For the man is not of the woman; but the woman of the man. Neither was the man created for the woman; but the woman for the man. For this cause ought the woman to have power on *her* head because of the angels. Nevertheless neither is the man without the woman, neither the woman without the man, in the Lord. For as the woman *is* of the man, even so *is* the man also by the woman; but all things of God (1 Cor 11:3–12).

Let your women keep silence in the churches: for it is not permitted unto them to speak; but *they are commanded* to be under obedience, as also saith the law. And if they will learn any thing, let them ask their husbands at home: for it is a shame for women to speak in the church (1 Cor 14:34, 35).

Wives, submit yourselves unto your own husbands, as unto the Lord. For the husband is the head of the wife, even as Christ is the head of the church: and he is the saviour of the body. Therefore as the church is subject unto Christ, so *let* the wives *be* to their own husbands in every thing. Husbands, love your wives, even as Christ also loved the church, and gave himself for it; that he might sanctify and cleanse it with the washing of water by the word, that he might present it to himself a glorious church, not having spot, or wrinkle, or any such thing; but that it should be holy and without blemish. So ought men to love their wives as their own bodies. He that loveth his wife loveth himself. For this cause shall a man leave his father and mother, and shall be joined unto his wife, and they two shall be one flesh. This is a great mystery: but I speak concerning Christ and the church. Nevertheless let every one of you in particular so love his wife even as himself; and the wife *see* that she reverence *her* husband (Eph 5:22–28, 31–33).

Even so *must their* wives *be* grave, not slanderers, sober, faithful in all things (1 Tim 3:11).

Likewise, ye wives, *be* in subjection to your own husbands; that, if any obey not the word, they also may without the word be won by the conversation of the wives; while they behold your chaste conversation *coupled* with fear. Whose adorning let it not be that outward *adorning* of plaiting of the hair, and of wearing of gold, or of putting on of apparel; but *let it be* the hidden man of the heart, in that which is not corruptible, *even the ornament* of a meek and quiet spirit, which is in the sight of God of great price. For after this manner in the old time the holy women also, who trusted in God, adorned themselves, being in subjection unto their own husbands: even as Sara obeyed Abraham, calling him lord: whose daughters ye are, as long as ye do well, and are not afraid with any amazement. Likewise, ye husbands, dwell with *them* according to knowledge, giving honour unto the wife, as unto the weaker vessel, and as being heirs together of the grace of life; that your prayers be not hindered (1 Peter 3:1–7).

Biblical Examples: Gen 3:16; 24:67; 29:30; 31:14–16; 39:7; Exod 21:7–11; Num 5:14–31; 30:6–16; Judg 21; 1 Sam 25:3, 14–42; 2 Sam 11:2–5; 1 Kings 11:4–8; 21; 2 Kings 9:30–37.

Further References: Esth 1:20–22; Prov 14:1; 19:13, 14; 25:24; 30:21–23; Ezek 24:16; Col 3:12–19.

WILL OF GOD (See also Decision-making)

I delight to do thy will, O my God: yea, thy law *is* within my heart (Ps 40:8).

Teach me to do thy will; for thou *art* my God; thy spirit *is* good; lead me into the land of uprightness (Ps 143:10).

There are many devices in a man's heart; nevertheless the counsel of the LORD, that shall stand (Prov 19:21).

For whosoever shall do the will of my Father which is in heaven, the same is my brother, and sister, and mother (Matt 12:50).

And he went a little farther, and fell on his face, and prayed, saying, O my Father, if it be possible, let this cup pass from me: nevertheless not as I will, but as thou *wilt* (Matt 26:39).

He went away again the second time, and prayed, saying, O my Father, if this cup may not pass away from me, except I drink it, thy will be done (Matt 26:42).

And he said unto them, When ye pray, say, Our Father which art in heaven, Hallowed be thy name. Thy kingdom come. Thy will be done, as in heaven, so in earth. Give us day by day our daily bread. And forgive us our sins; for we also forgive every one that is indebted to us. And lead us not into temptation; but deliver us from evil (Luke 11:2–4).

Jesus saith unto them, My meat is to do the will of him that sent me, and to finish his work (John 4:34).

I can of mine own self do nothing: as I hear, I judge: and my judgment is just; because I seek not mine own will, but the will of the Father which hath sent me (John 5:30).

For I came down from heaven, not to do mine own will, but the will of him that sent me. And this is the Father's will which hath sent me, that of all which he hath given me I should lose nothing, but should raise it up again at the last day. And this is the will of him that sent me, that every one which seeth the Son, and believeth on him, may have everlasting life: and I will raise him up at the last day (John 6:38–40).

Jesus answered them, and said, My doctrine is not mine, but his that sent me. If any man will do his will, he shall know of the doctrine, whether it be of God, or *whether* I speak of myself (John 7:16, 17).

When they desired *him* to tarry longer time with them, he consented not; but bade them farewell, saying, I must by all means keep this feast that cometh in Jerusalem: but I will return again unto you, if God will. And he sailed from Ephesus (Acts 18:20, 21).

And be not conformed to this world: but be ye transformed by the renewing of your mind, that ye may prove what *is* that good, and acceptable, and perfect, will of God (Rom 12:2).

That I may come unto you with joy by the will of God, and may with you be refreshed (Rom 15:32).

But I will come to you shortly, if the Lord will, and will know, not the speech of them which are puffed up, but the power (1 Cor 4:19).

For I will not see you now by the way; but I trust to tarry a while with you, if the Lord permit (1 Cor 16:7).

Servants, be obedient to them that are *your* masters according to the flesh, with fear and trembling, in singleness of your heart, as unto Christ; not with eye-service, as men-pleasers; but as the servants of Christ, doing the will of God from the heart (Eph 6:5, 6).

Wherefore, my beloved, as ye have always obeyed, not as in my presence only, but now much more in my absence, work out your own salvation with fear and trembling. For it is God which worketh in you both to will and to do of *his* good pleasure (Phil 2:12, 13).

And this will we do, if God permit (Heb 6:3).

Now the God of peace, that brought again from the dead our Lord Jesus, that great shepherd of the sheep, through the blood of the everlasting covenant, make you perfect in every good work to do his will, working in you that which is well-pleasing in his sight, through Jesus Christ; to whom *be* glory for ever and ever. Amen (Heb 13:20, 21).

Go to now, ye that say, Today or tomorrow we will go into such a city, and continue there a year, and buy and sell, and get gain: whereas ye know not what *shall be* on the morrow. For what *is* your life? It is even a vapour, that appeareth for a little time, and then vanisheth away. For that ye *ought* to say, If the Lord will, we shall live, and do this, or that (James 4:13–15).

For *it is* better, if the will of God be so, that ye suffer for well-doing, than for evil-doing (1 Peter 3:17).

Biblical Examples: Scriptures setting forth God's commands, guidance, character, and instruction are patterns of the expression of God's will.

Further References: Matt 6:10; Mark 3:35; 14:36; Luke 22:42; Rom 8:3, 4; Eph 4:3.

WINE (See also Alcohol and Alcoholism; Drunkenness)

And with the one lamb a tenth deal of flour mingled with the fourth part of an hin of beaten oil; and the fourth part of an hin of wine *for* a drink offering (Exod 29:40).

Do not drink wine nor strong drink, thou, nor thy sons with thee, when ye go into the tabernacle of the congregation, lest ye die: *it shall be* a statute for ever throughout your generations (Lev 10:9).

Speak unto the children of Israel, and say unto them, When either man or woman shall separate *themselves* to vow a vow of a Nazarite, to separate *themselves* unto the LORD: he shall separate *himself* from wine and strong drink, and shall drink no vinegar of wine, or vinegar of strong drink, neither shall he drink any liquor of grapes, nor eat moist grapes, or dried (Num 6:2, 3).

Thou shalt truly tithe all the increase of thy seed, that the field bringeth forth year by year. And thou shalt eat before the LORD thy God, in the place which he shall choose to place his name there, the tithe of thy corn, of thy wine, and of thine oil, and the firstlings of thy herds and of thy flocks; that thou mayest learn to fear the LORD thy God always. And if the way be too long for thee, so that thou art not able to carry it; *or* if the place be too far from thee, which the LORD thy God shall choose to set his name there, when the LORD thy God hath blessed thee: then shalt thou turn *it* into money, and bind up the money in thine hand, and shalt go unto the place which the LORD thy God shall choose: and thou shalt bestow that money for whatsoever thy soul lusteth after, for oxen, or for sheep, or for wine, or for strong drink, or for whatsoever thy soul desireth: and thou shalt eat there before the LORD thy God, and thou shalt rejoice, thou, and thine household (Deut 14:22–26).

He causeth the grass to grow for the cattle, and herb for the service of man: that he may bring forth food out of the earth; and wine *that* maketh glad the heart of man, *and* oil to make *his* face to shine, and bread *which* strengtheneth man's heart (Ps 104:14, 15).

For they eat the bread of wickedness, and drink the wine of violence (Prov 4:17).

Wine *is* a mocker, strong drink *is* raging: and whosoever is deceived thereby is not wise (Prov 20:1).

He that loveth pleasure *shall be* a poor man: he that loveth wine and oil shall not be rich (Prov 21:17).

Who hath woe? who hath sorrow? who hath contentions? who hath babbling? who hath wounds without cause? who hath redness of eyes? They that tarry long at the wine; they that go to seek mixed wine. Look not thou upon the wine when it is red, when it giveth his colour in the cup, *when* it moveth itself aright. At the last it biteth like a serpent, and stingeth like an adder. Thine eyes shall behold strange women, and thine heart shall utter perverse things. Yea, thou shalt be as he that lieth down in the midst of the sea, or as he that lieth upon the top of a mast.

They have stricken me, *shalt thou say, and* I was not sick; they have beaten me, *and* I felt *it* not: when shall I awake? I will seek it yet again (Prov 23:29–35).

It is not for kings, O Lemuel, *it is* not for kings to drink wine; nor for princes strong drink: lest they drink, and forget the law, and pervert the judgment of any of the afflicted. Give strong drink unto him that is ready to perish, and wine unto those that be of heavy hearts. Let him drink, and forget his poverty, and remember his misery no more (Prov 31:4–7).

I sought in mine heart to give myself unto wine, yet acquainting mine heart with wisdom; and to lay hold on folly, till I might see what *was* that good for the sons of men, which they should do under the heaven all the days of their life. . . . Then I looked on all the works that my hands had wrought, and on the labour that I had laboured to do: and, behold, all *was* vanity and vexation of spirit, and *there was* no profit under the sun (Eccl 2:3, 11).

Go thy way, eat thy bread with joy, and drink thy wine with a merry heart; for God now accepteth thy works (Eccl 9:7).

Woe unto them that rise up early in the morning, *that* they may follow strong drink; that continue until night, *till* wine inflame them! . . . Woe unto *them that are* mighty to drink wine, and men of strength to mingle strong drink (Isa 5:11, 22).

Come ye, *say they,* I will fetch wine, and we will fill ourselves with strong drink; and tomorrow shall be as this day, *and* much more abundant (Isa 56:12).

Neither shall any priest drink wine, when they enter into the inner court (Ezek 44:21).

And they have cast lots for my people; and have given a boy for an harlot, and sold a girl for wine, that they might drink (Joel 3:3).

That drink wine in bowls, and anoint themselves with the chief ointments: but they are not grieved for the affliction of Joseph (Amos 6:6).

For how great *is* his goodness, and how great *is* his beauty! corn shall make the young men cheerful, and new wine the maids (Zech 9:17).

And he took the cup, and gave thanks, and gave *it* to them, saying, Drink ye all of it; for this is my blood of the new testament, which is shed for many for the remission of sins. But I say unto you, I will not drink henceforth of this fruit of the vine, until that day when I drink it new with you in my Father's kingdom (Matt 26:27–29).

And straightway one of them ran, and took a sponge, and filled *it* with vinegar, and put *it* on a reed, and gave him to drink (Matt 27:48).

For he shall be great in the sight of the Lord, and shall drink neither wine nor strong drink; and he shall be filled with the Holy Ghost, even from his mother's womb (Luke 1:15).

And the third day there was a marriage in Cana of Galilee; and the mother of Jesus was there: and both Jesus was called, and his disciples, to the marriage. And when they wanted wine, the mother of Jesus saith unto him, They have no wine. Jesus saith unto her, Woman, what have I to do with thee? mine hour is not yet come. His mother saith unto the servants, Whatsoever he saith unto you, do *it.* And there were set there six waterpots of stone, after the manner of the purifying of the Jews, containing two or three firkins apiece. Jesus saith unto them, Fill the waterpots with water. And they filled them up to the brim. And he saith unto them, Draw out now, and bear unto the governor of the feast. And they bare *it.* When the ruler of the feast had tasted the water that was made wine, and knew not whence it was: (but the servants which drew the water knew;) the governor of the feast called the bridegroom, and saith unto him, Every man at the beginning doth set forth good wine; and when men have well drunk, then that which is worse: *but* thou hast kept the good wine until now. This beginning of miracles did Jesus in Cana of Galilee, and manifested forth his glory; and his disciples believed on him.

After this he went down to Capernaum, he, and his mother, and his brethren, and his disciples: and they continued there not many days (John 2:1–12).

It is good neither to eat flesh, nor to drink wine, nor *any thing* whereby thy brother stumbleth, or is offended, or is made weak (Rom 14:21).

And be not drunk with wine, wherein is excess; but be filled with the Spirit (Eph 5:18).

Drink no longer water, but use a little wine for thy stomach's sake and thine often infirmities (1 Tim 5:23).

Biblical Examples: Gen 9:20, 21; 14:18; 40:11; 43:34; 49:11, 12; Deut 29:6; Josh 9:4–13; Judg 13:4, 5; 1 Sam 25:36–38; 2 Sam 13:28, 29; 1 Chron 27:27; 2 Chron 32:28; Job 32:19; Prov 9:2–6; Isa 25:6; 28:1–3; Jer 13:12; 40:10–12; Dan 1:5–16; 10:3; Hos 2:8, 22; 7:5, 14; Joel 2:24; Matt 9:17; Luke 5:37–39.

Further References: Deut 33:28; 2 Kings 18:32; Neh 10:39; Ps 4:7; 60:1–3; Isa 24:6–10; 28:1–7; 55:1; Jer 23:9; 35:2–19; Hos 4:11; Amos 6:4–6; Zech 10:7; Mark 14:23; 15:23; Luke 22:17–20; 23:36; John 19:29; Rom 13:13; 1 Tim 3:3–8; Titus 1:7; 2:3.

WITCHCRAFT (See also Astrology; Demons; Sorcery)

Thou shalt not suffer a witch to live (Exod 22:18).

Ye shall not eat *any thing* with the blood: neither shall ye use enchantment, nor observe times (Lev 19:26).

And the soul that turneth after such as have familiar spirits, and after wizards, to go a-whoring after them, I will even set my face against that soul, and will cut him off from among his people.

Sanctify yourselves therefore, and be ye holy: for I *am* the LORD your God (Lev 20:6, 7).

A man also or woman that hath a familiar spirit, or that is a wizard, shall surely be put to death: they shall stone them with stones: their blood *shall be* upon them (Lev 20:27).

When thou art come into the land which the LORD thy God giveth thee, thou shalt not learn to do after the abominations of those nations. There shall not be found among you *any one* that maketh his son or his daughter to pass through the fire, *or* that useth divination, *or* an observer of times, or an enchanter, or a witch, or a charmer, or a consulter with familiar spirits, or a wizard, or a necromancer. For all that do these things *are* an abomination unto the LORD: and because of these

abominations the LORD thy God doth drive them out from before thee. Thou shalt be perfect with the LORD thy God. For these nations, which thou shalt possess, hearkened unto observers of times, and unto diviners: but as for thee, the LORD thy God hath not suffered thee so *to do* (Deut 18:9–14).

Moreover the *workers with* familiar spirits, and the wizards, and the images, and the idols, and all the abominations that were spied in the land of Judah and in Jerusalem, did Josiah put away, that he might perform the words of the law which were written in the book that Hilkiah the priest found in the house of the LORD (2 Kings 23:24).

And when they shall say unto you, Seek unto them that have familiar spirits, and unto wizards that peep, and that mutter: should not a people seek unto their God? for the living to the dead? (Isa 8:19).

But the fearful, and unbelieving, and the abominable, and murderers, and whoremongers, and sorcerers, and idolaters, and all liars, shall have their part in the lake which burneth with fire and brimstone: which is the second death (Rev 21:8).

Biblical Examples: 1 Sam 15:23; 2 Chron 33:1–6; Acts 8:9; 13:8; 19:18, 19.

WOMEN

So God created man in his *own* image, in the image of God created he him; male and female created he them (Gen 1:27).

And the LORD God said, *It is* not good that the man should be alone; I will make him an help meet for him. And out of the ground the LORD God formed every beast of the field, and every fowl of the air; and brought *them* unto Adam to see what he would call them: and whatsoever Adam called every living creature, that *was* the name thereof. And Adam gave names to all cattle, and to the fowl of the air, and to every beast of the field; but for Adam there was not found an help meet for him. And the LORD God caused a deep sleep to fall upon Adam, and he slept: and he took one of his ribs, and closed up the flesh instead thereof; and the rib, which the LORD God had taken from man, made he a woman, and brought her unto the man. And Adam said, This *is* now bone of my bones, and flesh of my flesh: she shall be called Woman, because she was taken out of Man. Therefore shall a man leave his father and his mother, and shall cleave unto his wife: and they shall be one flesh. And they were both naked, the man and his wife, and were not ashamed (Gen 2:18–25).

And I will put enmity between thee and the woman, and between thy seed and her seed; it shall bruise thy head, and thou shalt bruise his heel. Unto the woman he said, I will greatly multiply thy sorrow and thy conception; in sorrow thou shalt bring forth children; and thy desire *shall be* to thy husband, and he shall rule over thee (Gen 3:15, 16).

And I will make thee swear by the LORD, the God of heaven, and the God of the earth, that thou shalt not take a wife unto my son of the daughters of the Canaanites, among whom I dwell: but thou shalt go unto my country, and to my kindred, and take a wife unto my son Isaac (Gen 24:3–4).

And they came, both men and women, as many as were willing-hearted, *and* brought bracelets, and earrings, and rings, and tablets, all jewels of gold: and every man that offered *offered* an offering of gold unto the LORD (Exod 35:22).

And if a woman have an issue, *and* her issue in her flesh be blood, she shall be put apart seven days: and whosoever toucheth her shall be unclean until the even. And every thing that she lieth upon in her separation shall be unclean: every thing also that she sitteth upon shall be unclean. And whosoever toucheth her bed shall wash his clothes, and bathe *himself* in water, and be unclean until the even. And whosoever toucheth anything that she sat upon shall wash his clothes, and bathe *himself* in water, and be unclean until the even. And if it *be* on *her* bed, or on any thing whereon she sitteth, when he toucheth it, he shall be unclean until the even. And if any man lie with her at all, and her flowers be upon him, he shall be unclean seven days; and all the bed whereon he lieth shall be unclean. And if a woman have an issue of her blood many days out of the time of her separation, or if it run beyond the time of her separation; all the days of the issue of

her uncleanness shall be as the days of her separation: she *shall be* unclean. Every bed whereon she lieth all the days of her issue shall be unto her as the bed of her separation: and whatsoever she sitteth upon shall be unclean, as the uncleanness of her separation. And whosoever toucheth those things shall be unclean, and shall wash his clothes, and bathe *himself* in water, and be unclean until the even. But if she be cleansed of her issue, then she shall number to herself seven days, and after that she shall be clean. And on the eighth day she shall take unto her two turtles, or two young pigeons, and bring them unto the priest, to the door of the tabernacle of the congregation. And the priest shall offer the one *for* a sin offering, and the other *for* a burnt offering; and the priest shall make an atonement for her before the LORD for the issue of her uncleanness. Thus shall ye separate the children of Israel from their uncleanness; that they die not in their uncleanness, when they defile my tabernacle that *is* among them. This *is* the law of him that hath an issue, and *of him* whose seed goeth from him, and is defiled therewith; and of her that is sick of her flowers, and of him that hath an issue, of the man, and of the woman, and of him that lieth with her that is unclean (Lev 15:19–33).

The woman shall not wear that which pertaineth unto a man, neither shall a man put on a woman's garment: for all that do so *are* abomination unto the LORD thy God (Deut 22:5).

Now Eli was very old, and heard all that his sons did unto all Israel; and how they lay with the women that assembled *at* the door of the tabernacle of the congregation (1 Sam 2:22).

All these *were* the sons of Heman the king's seer in the words of God, to lift up the horn. And God gave to Heman fourteen sons and three daughters. All these *were* under the hands of their father for song *in* the house of the LORD, with cymbals, psalteries, and harps, for the service of the house of God, according to the king's order to Asaph, Jeduthun, and Heman (1 Chron 25:5, 6).

A gracious woman retaineth honour, and strong *men* retain riches. *As a* jewel of gold in a swine's snout, *so is* a fair woman which is without discretion (Prov 11:16, 22).

Who can find a virtuous woman? for her price *is* far above rubies. The heart of her husband doth safely trust in her, so that he shall have no need of spoil. She will do him good and not evil all the days of her life. She seeketh wool, and flax, and worketh willingly with her hands. She is like the merchants' ships; she bringeth her food from afar. She riseth also while it is yet night, and giveth meat to her household, and a portion to her maidens. She considereth a field, and buyeth it: with the fruit of her hands she planteth a vineyard. She girdeth her loins with strength, and strengtheneth her arms. She perceiveth that her merchandise *is* good: her candle goeth not out by night. She layeth her hands to the spindle, and her hands hold the distaff. She stretcheth out her hand to the poor; yea, she reacheth forth her hands to the needy. She is not afraid of the snow for her household: for all her household *are* clothed with scarlet. She maketh herself coverings of tapestry; her clothing *is* silk and purple. Her husband is known in the gates, when he sitteth among the elders of the land. She maketh fine linen, and selleth *it;* and delivereth girdles unto the merchant. Strength and honour *are* her clothing; and she shall rejoice in time to come. She openeth her mouth with wisdom; and in her tongue *is* the law of kindness. She looketh well to the ways of her household, and eateth not the bread of idleness. Her children arise up, and call her blessed; her husband *also,* and he praiseth her. Many daughters have done virtuously, but thou excellest them all. Favour *is* deceitful, and beauty *is* vain: *but* a woman *that* feareth the LORD, she shall be praised. Give her of the fruit of her hands; and let her own works praise her in the gates (Prov 31:10–31).

And I find more bitter than death the woman, whose heart *is* snares and nets, *and* her hands as bands: whoso pleaseth God shall escape from her; but the sinner shall be taken by her. Behold, this have I found, saith the preacher, *counting* one by one, to find out the account: which yet my soul seeketh, but I find not: one man among a thousand have I found; but a woman among all those have I not found (Eccl 7:26–28).

Moreover the LORD saith, Because the daughters of Zion are haughty, and walk with stretched forth necks and wanton eyes, walking and mincing *as* they go, and making a tinkling with their feet: therefore the Lord will smite with a scab the crown of the head of the daughters of Zion, and the LORD will discover their secret parts. In that day the Lord will take away the bravery of *their* tinkling ornaments *about their feet,* and *their* cauls, and *their* round tires like the moon, the chains, and the bracelets, and the mufflers, the bonnets, and the ornaments of the legs, and the headbands, and the tablets, and the earrings, the rings, and nose jewels, the changeable suits of apparel, and the mantles, and the wimples, and the crisping pins, the glasses, and the fine linen, and the hoods, and the veils (Isa 3:16–23).

Rise up, ye women that are at ease; hear my voice, ye careless daughters; give ear unto my speech. Many days and years shall ye be troubled, ye careless women: for the vintage shall fail, the gathering shall not come. Tremble, ye women that are at ease; be troubled, ye careless ones: strip you, and make you bare, and gird *sackcloth* upon *your* loins. They shall lament for the teats, for the pleasant fields, for the fruitful vine (Isa 32:9–12).

And when he had considered *the thing,* he came to the house of Mary the mother of John, whose surname was Mark; where many were gathered together praying. And as Peter knocked at the door of the gate, a damsel came to hearken, named Rhoda (Acts 12:12, 13).

But I would have you know, that the head of every man is Christ; and the head of the woman *is* the man; and the head of Christ *is* God. Every man praying or prophesying, having *his* head covered, dishonoureth his head. But every woman that prayeth or prophesieth with *her* head uncovered dishonoureth her head: for that is even all one as if she were shaven. For if the woman be not covered, let her also be shorn: but if it be a shame for a woman to be shorn or shaven, let her be covered. For a man indeed ought not to cover *his* head, forasmuch as he is the image and glory of God: but the woman is the glory of the man. For the man is not of the woman; but the woman of the man. Neither was the man created for the woman; but the woman for the man. For this cause ought the woman to have power on *her* head because of the angels. Nevertheless neither is the man without the woman, neither the woman without the man, in the Lord. For as the woman *is* of the man, even so *is* the man also by the woman; but all things of God. Judge in yourselves: is it comely that a woman pray unto God uncovered? Doth not even nature itself teach you, that, if a man have long hair, it is a shame unto him? But if a woman have long hair, it is a glory to her: for *her* hair is given her for a covering (1 Cor 11:3–15).

For God is not *the author* of confusion, but of peace, as in all churches of the saints. Let your women keep silence in the churches: for it is not permitted unto them to speak; but *they are commanded* to be under obedience, as also saith the law. And if they will learn any thing, let them ask their husbands at home: for it is a shame for women to speak in the church (1 Cor 14:33–35).

But I fear, lest by any means, as the serpent beguiled Eve through his subtilty, so your minds should be corrupted from the simplicity that is in Christ (2 Cor 11:3).

I will therefore that men pray every where, lifting up holy hands, without wrath and doubting. In like manner also, that women adorn themselves in modest apparel, with shamefacedness and sobriety; not with broided hair, or gold, or pearls, or costly array; but (which becometh women professing godliness) with good works. Let the woman learn in silence with all subjection. But I suffer not a woman to teach, nor to usurp authority over the man, but to be in silence. For Adam was first formed, then Eve. And Adam was not deceived, but the woman being deceived was in the transgression. Notwithstanding, she shall be saved in childbearing, if they continue in faith and charity and holiness with sobriety (1 Tim 2:8–15).

The aged women likewise, that *they be* in behaviour as becometh holiness, not false accusers, not given to much wine, teachers of good things; that they may teach the young women to be sober, to love their husbands, to love their children, *to be* discreet, chaste, keepers at home, good, obedient to their own husbands, that the word of God be not blasphemed (Titus 2:3–5).

Whose adorning let it not be that outward *adorning* of plaiting the hair, and of wearing of gold, or of putting on of apparel; but *let it be* the hidden man of the heart, in that which is not corruptible, *even the ornament* of a meek and quiet spirit, which is in the sight of God of great price. For after this manner in the old time the holy women also, who trusted in God, adorned themselves, being in subjection unto their own husbands: even as Sara obeyed Abraham, calling him lord: whose daughters ye are, as long as ye do well, and are not afraid with any amazement (1 Pet 3:3–6).

Biblical Examples: (of various roles of women): Gen 18:6; 19:26, 31–38; 24:11–20; 30:1; 39:7–20; Exod 15:20, 21; 35:25, 26; Num 12; 31:15; Deut 31:12; 32:25; Josh 8:35; Judg 4, 5; 9:53; 13:23; Ruth 1:4; 2–4; 2:8; 2 Sam 1:20–26; 1 Kings 10:1–13; 17:8–24; 2 Kings 4:8–37; 11:1–16; 22:14–20; 1 Chron 25:5, 6; Neh 2:6; 6:14; Esth 1:10–22; 4:15–17; Ps 78:63; Isa 3:12; 27:11; 49:15; Jer 31:13; Dan 5:1–12; Matt 14:3–8; 24:41; 26:69; 27:19, 55, 56; Mark 12:41–44; 14:3–9; 15:26, 27; 16:1, 9; Luke 1:42–45; 2:36–38; Acts 1:14; 8:27; 9:36–39; 16:14, 15; 17:4, 12, 34; 18:18–26; 21:9; 24:24; 25:13; 26:30; Rom 1:26; 16:1–3, 15; 2 Tim 1:5; 3:6, 7.

Further References: Gen 3:1–16; 30:1, 9–18; 34:1, 2; 38:14–24; Exod 4:25, 26; Lev 12; Num 27:1–11; Josh 2:1; Judg 16:4–20; 1 Sam 1:4–8; 2 Sam 6:16, 20–23; 11:4, 5, 27; 12:9–10; 1 Kings 11:1–11; 14:6; 21:11–16; 2 Kings 6:28, 29; 23:7; Esth 5:14; Job 2:9; Prov 14:1; 27:15, 16; Ezek 13:17–23; Hos 1:2, 3; Mark 16:1–6; Luke 8:2; 10:42; 21:2–4; 23:27, 28, 49–56; John 8:1–11; 20:14–18; Acts 5:2–10; 1 Tim 5:1–16.

WORK (See Daily Work)

WORLDLINESS

Nevertheless the people refused to obey the voice of Samuel; and they said, Nay; but we will have a king over us; that we also may be like all the nations; and that our king may judge us, and go out before us, and fight our battles (1 Sam 8:19, 20).

They send forth their little ones like a flock, and their children dance. They take the timbrel and harp, and rejoice at the sound of the organ. They spend their days in wealth, and in a moment go down to the grave. Therefore they say unto God, Depart from us; for we desire not the knowledge of thy ways. What *is* the Almighty, that we should serve him? and what profit should we have, if we pray unto him? (Job 21:11–15).

But as for me, my feet were almost gone; my steps had well nigh slipped. For I was envious at the foolish, *when* I saw the prosperity of the wicked. For *there are* no bands in their death: but their strength *is* firm. They *are* not in trouble *as other* men; neither are they plagued like *other* men. Therefore pride compasseth them about as a chain; violence covereth them *as* a garment. Their eyes stand out with fatness: they have more than heart could wish. They are corrupt, and speak wickedly *concerning* oppression: they speak loftily. They set their mouth against the heavens, and their tongue walketh through the earth. Therefore his people return hither: and waters of a full *cup* are wrung out of them. And they say, How doth God know? and is there knowledge in the most High? Behold, these *are* the ungodly, who prosper in the world; they increase *in* riches. Verily I have cleansed my heart *in* vain, and washed my hands in innocency. For all the day long have I been plagued, and chastened every morning. If I say, I will speak thus; behold, I should offend *against* the generation of thy children. When I thought to know this, it *was* too painful for me; until I went into the sanctuary of God; *then* understood I their end. Surely thou didst set them in slippery places: thou castedst them down into destruction. How are they *brought* into desolation, as in a moment! they are utterly consumed with terrors. As a dream when *one* awaketh; *so,* O Lord, when thou awakest, thou shalt despise their image. Thus my heart was grieved, and I was pricked in my reins. So foolish *was* I, and ignorant: I was *as* a beast before thee (Ps 73:2–22).

He that loveth pleasure *shall be* a poor man: he that loveth wine and oil shall not be rich (Prov 21:17).

Be not among winebibbers; among riotous eaters of flesh: for the drunkard and the glutton shall come to poverty: and drowsiness shall clothe *a man* with rags (Prov 23:20, 21).

I said in mine heart, Go to now, I will prove thee with mirth, therefore enjoy pleasure: and, behold, this also *is* vanity. I said of laughter, *It is* mad: and of mirth, What doeth it? I sought in mine heart to give myself unto wine, yet acquainting mine heart with wisdom; and to lay hold on folly, till I might see what *was* that good for the sons of men, which they should do under the heaven all the days of their life. I made me great works; I builded me houses; I planted me vineyards: I made me gardens and orchards, and I planted trees in them of all *kind of* fruits: I made me pools of water, to water therewith the wood that bringeth forth trees: I got *me* servants and maidens, and had servants born in my house; also I had great possessions of great and small cattle above all that were in Jerusalem before me: I gathered me also silver and gold, and the peculiar treasure of kings and of the provinces: I gat me men singers and women singers, and the delights of the sons of men, *as* musical instruments, and that of all sorts. So I was great, and increased more than all that were before me in Jerusalem: also my wisdom remained with me. And whatsoever mine eyes desired I kept not from them, I withheld not my heart from any joy; for my heart rejoiced in all my labour: and this was my portion of all my labour. Then I looked on all the works that my hands had wrought, and on the labour that I had laboured to do: and, behold, all *was* vanity and vexation of spirit, and *there was* no profit under the sun.

And I turned myself to behold wisdom, and madness, and folly: for what *can* the man *do* that cometh after the king? *even* that which hath been already done (Eccl 2:1–12).

Then I commended mirth, because a man hath no better thing under the sun, than to eat, and to drink, and to be merry:

for that shall abide with him of his labour the days of his life, which God giveth him under the sun.

When I applied mine heart to know wisdom, and to see the business that is done upon the earth: (for also *there is that* neither day nor night seeth sleep with his eyes:) then I beheld all the work of God, that a man cannot find out the work that is done under the sun: because though a man labour to seek *it* out, yet he shall not find *it;* yea farther; though a wise *man* think to know *it,* yet shall he not be able to find *it* (Eccl 8:15–17).

And in that day did the Lord GOD of hosts call to weeping, and to mourning, and to baldness, and to girding with sackcloth: and behold joy and gladness, slaying oxen, and killing sheep, eating flesh, and drinking wine: let us eat and drink; for tomorrow we shall die (Isa 22:12, 13).

Ye that put far away the evil day, and cause the seat of violence to come near; that lie upon beds of ivory, and stretch themselves upon their couches, and eat the lambs out of the flock, and the calves out of the midst of the stall; that chant to the sound of the viol, *and* invent to themselves instruments of music, like David; that drink wine in bowls, and anoint themselves with the chief ointments: but they are not grieved for the affliction of Joseph.

Therefore now shall they go captive with the first that go captive, and the banquet of them that stretched themselves shall be removed (Amos 6:3–7).

Ye have sown much, and bring in little; ye eat, but ye have not enough; ye drink, but ye are not filled with drink; ye clothe you, but there is none warm; and he that earneth wages earneth wages *to put it* into a bag with holes (Hag 1:6).

Therefore I say unto you, Take no thought for your life, what ye shall eat, or what ye shall drink; nor yet for your body, what ye shall put on. Is not the life more than meat, and the body than raiment? Behold the fowls of the air: for they sow not, neither do they reap, nor gather into barns; yet your heavenly Father feedeth them. Are ye not much better than they? Which of you by taking thought can add one cubit unto his stature? And why

take ye thought for raiment? Consider the lilies of the field, how they grow; they toil not, neither do they spin; and yet I say unto you, That even Solomon in all his glory was not arrayed like one of these. Wherefore, if God so clothe the grass of the field, which today is, and tomorrow is cast into the oven, *shall he* not much more *clothe* you, O ye of little faith? Therefore take no thought, saying, What shall we eat? or, What shall we drink? or, Wherewithal shall we be clothed? (For after all these things do the Gentiles seek:) for your heavenly Father knoweth that ye have need of all these things. But seek ye first the kingdom of God, and his righteousness; and all these things shall be added unto you. Take therefore no thought for the morrow: for the morrow shall take thought for the things of itself. Sufficient unto the day *is* the evil thereof (Matt 6:25–34).

For as in the days that were before the flood they were eating and drinking, marrying and giving in marriage, until the day that Noe entered into the ark, and knew not until the flood came, and took them all away; so shall also the coming of the Son of man be (Matt 24:38, 39).

For whosoever will save his life shall lose it; but whosoever shall lose his life for my sake and the gospel's, the same shall save it. For what shall it profit a man, if he shall gain the whole world, and lose his own soul? (Mark 8:35, 36).

And that which fell among thorns are they, which, when they have heard, go forth, and are choked with cares and riches and pleasures of *this* life, and bring no fruit to perfection (Luke 8:14).

And I will say to my soul, Soul, thou hast much goods laid up for many years; take thine ease, eat, drink, *and* be merry (Luke 12:19).

And sent his servant at supper time to say to them that were bidden, Come; for all things are now ready. And they all with one *consent* began to make excuse. The first said unto him, I have bought a piece of ground, and I must needs go and see it: I pray thee have me excused. And another said, I have bought five yoke of oxen, and I go to prove them: I pray thee have me excused. And another said, I have married a wife, and therefore I cannot come. So that servant came, and shewed his lord these things. Then the master of the house being angry said to his servant, Go out quickly into the streets and lanes of the city, and bring in hither the poor, and the maimed, and the halt, and the blind. And the servant said, Lord, it is done as thou hast commanded, and yet there is room. And the lord said unto the servant, Go out into the highways and hedges, and compel *them* to come in, that my house may be filled. For I say unto you, That none of those men which were bidden shall taste of my supper (Luke 14:17–24).

And he said also unto his disciples, There was a certain rich man, which had a steward; and the same was accused unto him that he had wasted his goods. And he called him, and said unto him, How is it that I hear this of thee? give an account of thy stewardship; for thou mayest be no longer steward. Then the steward said within himself, What shall I do? for my lord taketh away from me the stewardship: I cannot dig; to beg I am ashamed. I am resolved what to do, that, when I am put out of the stewardship, they may receive me into their houses. So he called every one of his lord's debtors *unto him,* and said unto the first, How much owest thou unto my lord? And he said, An hundred measures of oil. And he said unto him, Take thy bill, and sit down quickly, and write fifty. Then said he to another, And how much owest thou? And he said, An hundred measures of wheat. And he said unto him, Take thy bill, and write fourscore. And the lord commended the unjust steward, because he had done wisely: for the children of this world are in their generation wiser than the children of light. And I say unto you, Make to yourselves friends of the mammon of unrighteousness; that, when ye fail, they may receive you into everlasting habitations. He that is faithful in that which is least is faithful also in much: and he that is unjust in the least is unjust also in much. If therefore ye have not been faithful in the unrighteous mammon, who will commit to your trust the true *riches?* And if ye have not been faithful in that which

is another man's, who shall give you that which is your own?

No servant can serve two masters: for either he will hate the one, and love the other; or else he will hold to the one, and despise the other. Ye cannot serve God and mammon (Luke 16:1–13).

And take heed to yourselves, lest at any time your hearts be overcharged with surfeiting, and drunkenness, and cares of this life, and *so* that day come upon you unawares (Luke 21:34).

For they loved the praise of men more than the praise of God (John 12:43).

If ye were of the world, the world would love his own: but because ye are not of the world, but I have chosen you out of the world, therefore the world hateth you (John 15:19).

And be not conformed to this world: but be ye transformed by the renewing of your mind, that ye may prove what *is* that good, and acceptable, and perfect, will of God (Rom 12:2).

But this I say, brethren, the time *is* short: it remaineth, that both they that have wives be as though they had none; and they that weep, as though they wept not; and they that rejoice, as though they rejoiced not; and they that buy, as though they possessed not; and they that use this world, as not abusing it: for the fashion of this world passeth away (1 Cor 7:29–31).

(For many walk, of whom I have told you often, and now tell you even weeping, *that they are* the enemies of the cross of Christ: whose end *is* destruction, whose God *is their* belly, and *whose* glory *is* in their shame, who mind earthly things) (Phil 3:18, 19).

Set your affection on things above, not on things on the earth. For ye are dead, and your life is hid with Christ in God. When Christ, *who is* our life, shall appear, then shall ye also appear with him in glory. Mortify therefore your members which are upon the earth; fornication, uncleanness, inordinate affection, evil concupiscence, and covetousness, which is idolatry (Col 3:2–5).

But she that liveth in pleasure is dead while she liveth (1 Tim 5:6).

No man that warreth entangleth himself with the affairs of *this* life; that he may please him who hath chosen him to be a soldier. . . .

Flee also youthful lusts: but follow righteousness, faith, charity, peace, with them that call on the Lord out of a pure heart (2 Tim 2:4, 22).

For men shall be lovers of their own selves, covetous, boasters, proud, blasphemers, disobedient to parents, unthankful, unholy, without natural affection, trucebreakers, false accusers, incontinent, fierce, despisers of those that are good, traitors, heady, highminded, lovers of pleasures more than lovers of God; having a form of godliness, but denying the power thereof: from such turn away. For of this sort are they which creep into houses, and lead captive silly women laden with sins, led away with divers lusts, ever learning, and never able to come to the knowledge of the truth (2 Tim 3:2–7).

Teaching us that, denying ungodliness and worldly lusts, we should live soberly, righteously, and godly, in this present world (Titus 2:12).

By faith Moses, when he was come to years, refused to be called the son of Pharaoh's daughter; choosing rather to suffer affliction with the people of God, than to enjoy the pleasures of sin for a season; esteeming the reproach of Christ greater riches than the treasures in Egypt: for he had respect unto the recompence of the reward (Heb 11:24–26).

Ye adulterers and adulteresses, know ye not that the friendship of the world is enmity with God? whosoever therefore will be a friend of the world is the enemy of God. . . .

Be afflicted, and mourn, and weep: let your laughter be turned to mourning, and *your* joy to heaviness (James 4:4, 9).

Dearly beloved, I beseech *you* as strangers and pilgrims, abstain from fleshly lusts, which war against the soul (1 Peter 2:11).

For the time past of *our* life may suffice us to have wrought the will of the Gentiles, when we walked in lasciviousness, lusts, excess of wine, revellings, banquet-ings, and abominable idolatries: wherein they think it strange that ye run not with *them* to the same excess of riot, speaking evil of *you* (1 Peter 4:3, 4).

Love not the world, neither the things *that are* in the world. If any man love the world, the love of the Father is not in him. For all that *is* in the world, the lust of the flesh, and the lust of the eyes, and the pride of life, is not of the Father, but is of the world. And the world passeth away, and the lust thereof: but he that doeth the will of God abideth for ever (1 John 2:15–17).

Woe unto them! for they have gone in the way of Cain, and ran greedily after the error of Balaam for reward, and perished in the gainsaying of Core. These are spots in your feasts of charity, when they feast with you, feeding themselves without fear: clouds *they are* without water, carried about of winds; trees whose fruit withereth, without fruit, twice dead, plucked up by the roots; raging waves of the sea, foaming out their own shame; wandering stars, to whom is reserved the blackness of darkness for ever. . . .

These are murmurers, complainers, walking after their own lusts; and their mouth speaketh great swelling *words*, having men's persons in admiration because of advantage. But, beloved, remember ye the words which were spoken before of the apostles of our Lord Jesus Christ; how that they told you there should be mockers in the last time, who should walk after their own ungodly lusts. These be they who separate themselves, sensual, having not the Spirit (Jude 11–13, 16–19).

Biblical Examples: Gen 25:30–34; 37:26, 27; Num 11:33, 34; 1 Sam 2:12–17; 2 Kings 5:21–27; Matt 14:6, 7; Titus 1:12; 2 Peter 2:15.

Further References: Job 20:4–29; Ps 49:16–18; 78:18; Prov 14:12, 13; Isa 32:9–11; Hos 9:1, 11–13; Matt 10:39; 13:22; 16:26; 22:2–6; Mark 4:19; Luke 17:26–29, 33; John 12:25; 1 Cor 15:32; Titus 3:3; Heb 12:6; James 2:1–4; 5:5; 1 Peter 1:14, 24.

– Y –

YOUTH (See also Children; Family; Parent-Child Relations)

Wherewithal shall a young man cleanse his way? by taking heed *thereto* according to thy word (Ps 119:9).

Both young men, and maidens; old men, and children: let them praise the name of the LORD: for his name alone is excellent; his glory *is* above the earth and heaven (Ps 148:12, 13).

The proverbs of Solomon the son of David, king of Israel; to know wisdom and instruction; to perceive the words of understanding; to receive the instruction of wisdom, justice, and judgment, and equity; to give subtilty to the simple, to the young man knowledge and discretion. A wise *man* will hear, and will increase learning; and a man of understanding shall attain unto wise counsels: to understand a proverb, and the interpretation; the words of the wise, and their dark sayings.

The fear of the LORD *is* the beginning of knowledge: *but* fools despise wisdom and instruction. My son, hear the instruction of thy father, and forsake not the law of thy mother: for they *shall be* an ornament of grace unto thy head, and chains about thy neck.

My son, if sinners entice thee, consent thou not. If they say, Come with us, let us lay wait for blood, let us lurk privily for the innocent without cause: let us swallow them up alive as the grave; and whole, as those that go down into the pit: we shall find all precious substance, we shall fill our houses with spoil: cast in thy lot among us; let us all have one purse: my son, walk not thou in the way with them; refrain thy foot from their path: for their feet run to evil, and make haste to shed blood. Surely in vain the net is spread in the sight of any bird. And they lay wait for their *own* blood; they lurk privily for their *own* lives. So *are* the ways of every one that is greedy of gain; *which* taketh away the life of the owners thereof.

Wisdom crieth without; she uttereth her voice in the streets: she crieth in the chief place of concourse, in the openings of the gates: in the city she uttereth her words, *saying,* How long, ye simple ones, will ye love simplicity? and the scorners delight in their scorning, and fools hate knowledge? Turn you at my reproof: behold, I will pour out my spirit unto you, I will make known my words unto you.

Because I have called, and ye refused; I have stretched out my hand, and no man regarded; but ye have set at nought all my counsel, and would none of my reproof: I also will laugh at your calamity; I will mock when your fear cometh; when your fear cometh as desolation, and your destruction cometh as a whirlwind; when distress and anguish cometh upon you. Then shall they call upon me, but I will not answer; they shall seek me early, but they shall not find me: for that they hated knowledge, and did not choose the fear of the LORD: they would none of my counsel: they despised all my reproof. Therefore shall they eat of the fruit of their own way, and be filled with their own devices. For the turning away of the simple shall slay them, and the prosperity of fools shall destroy them. But whoso hearkeneth unto me shall dwell safely, and shall be quiet from fear of evil (Prov 1:1–33).

Hear, ye children, the instruction of a father, and attend to know understanding. For I give you good doctrine, forsake ye not my law. For I was my father's son, tender and only *beloved* in the sight of my mother. He taught me also, and said unto me, Let thine heart retain my words: keep my commandments, and live. Get wisdom, get understanding: forget *it* not; neither decline from the words of my mouth. Forsake her not, and she shall preserve thee: love her, and she shall keep thee. Wisdom *is* the principal thing; *therefore* get wisdom: and with all thy getting get understanding. Exalt her, and she shall promote thee: she shall bring thee to honour, when thou dost embrace her. She shall give to thine head an ornament of grace: a crown of glory shall she deliver to thee. Hear, O my son, and receive my sayings; and the years of thy life shall be many. I have taught thee in the way of wisdom; I have led thee in right paths. When thou goest, thy steps shall not be straitened; and when thou runnest, thou shalt not stumble. Take fast hold of instruction; let *her* not go: keep her; for she *is* thy life.

Enter not into the path of the wicked, and go not in the way of evil *men*. Avoid it, pass not by it, turn from it, and pass away. For they sleep not, except they have done mischief; and their sleep is taken away, unless they cause *some* to fall. For they eat the bread of wickedness, and drink the wine of violence. But the path of the just *is* as the shining light, that shineth more and more unto the perfect day. The way of the wicked *is* as darkness: they know not at what they stumble.

My son, attend to my words; incline thine ear unto my sayings. Let them not depart from thine eyes; keep them in the midst of thine heart. For they *are* life unto those that find them, and health to all their flesh.

Keep thy heart with all diligence; for out of it *are* the issues of life. Put away from thee a froward mouth, and perverse lips put far from thee. Let thine eyes look right on, and let thine eyelids look straight before thee. Ponder the path of thy feet, and let all thy ways be established. Turn not to the right hand nor to the left: remove thy foot from evil (Prov 4:1–27).

The proverbs of Solomon. A wise son maketh a glad father: but a foolish son *is* the heaviness of his mother (Prov 10:1).

A wise son *heareth* his father's instruction: but a scorner heareth not rebuke (Prov 13:1).

A foolish son *is* a grief to his father, and bitterness to her that bare him (Prov 17:25).

The glory of young men *is* their strength: and the beauty of old men *is* the grey head (Prov 20:29).

My son, be wise, and make my heart glad, that I may answer him that reproacheth me (Prov 27:11).

Whoso keepeth the law *is* a wise son: but he that is a companion of riotous *men* shameth his father (Prov 28:7).

And he said, A certain man had two sons: and the younger of them said to *his* father, Father, give me the portion of goods that falleth *to me*. And he divided unto them *his* living. And not many days after the younger son gathered all together, and took his journey into a far country, and there wasted his substance with riotous living. And when he had spent all, there arose a mighty famine in that land; and he began to be in want. And he went and joined himself to a citizen of that country; and he sent him into his fields to feed swine. And he would fain have filled his belly with the husks that the swine did eat: and no man gave unto him. And when he came to himself, he said, How many hired servants of my father's have bread enough and to spare, and I perish with hunger! I will arise and go to my father, and will say unto him, Father, I have sinned against heaven, and before thee, and am no more worthy to be called thy son: make me as one of thy hired servants. And he arose, and came to his father. But when he was yet a great way off, his father saw him, and had compassion, and ran, and fell on his neck, and kissed him. And the son said unto him, Father, I have sinned against heaven, and in thy sight, and am no more worthy to be called thy son. But the father said to his servants, Bring forth the best robe, and put *it* on him; and put a ring on his hand, and shoes on *his* feet: and bring hither the fatted calf, and kill *it;* and let us eat, and be merry: for this my son was dead, and is alive again; he was lost, and is found. And they began to be merry. Now his elder son was in the field: and as he came and drew nigh to the house, he heard music and dancing. And he called one of the servants, and asked what these things meant. And he said unto him, Thy brother is come; and thy father hath killed the fatted calf, because he hath received him safe and sound. And he was angry, and would not go in: therefore came his father out, and entreated him. And he answering said to *his* father, Lo, these many years do I serve thee, neither transgressed I at any time thy commandment: and yet thou never gavest me a kid, that I might make merry with my friends: but as soon as this thy son was come, which hath devoured thy living with harlots, thou hast killed for him the fatted calf. And he said unto him, Son, thou art ever with me, and all that I have is thine. It was meet that we should make merry, and be glad: for this thy brother was dead, and is alive again; and was lost, and is found (Luke 15:11–32).

Let no man despise thy youth; but be thou an example of the believers in word, in conversation, in charity, in spirit, in faith, in purity (1 Tim 4:12).

Flee also youthful lusts: but follow righteousness, faith, charity, peace, with them that call on the Lord out of a pure heart. But foolish and unlearned questions avoid, knowing that they do gender strifes (2 Tim 2:22, 23).

The aged women likewise, that *they be* in behaviour as becometh holiness, not false accusers, not given to much wine, teachers of good things; that they may teach the young women to be sober, to love their husbands, to love their children, *to be* discreet, chaste, keepers at home, good, obedient to their own husbands, that the word of God be not blasphemed. Young men likewise exhort to be sober minded (Titus 2:3–6).

I write unto you, fathers, because ye have known him *that is* from the beginning. I write unto you, young men, because ye have overcome the wicked one. I write unto you, little children, because ye have known the Father. I have written unto you, fathers, because ye have known him *that is* from the beginning. I have written unto you, young men, because ye are strong, and the word of God abideth in you, and ye have overcome the wicked one. Love not the world, neither the things *that are* in the world. If any man love the world, the love of the Father is not in him. For all that *is* in the world, the lust of the flesh, and the lust of the eyes, and the pride of life, is not of the Father, but is of the world. And the world passeth away, and the lust thereof: but he that doeth the will of God abideth for ever (1 John 2:13–17).

Biblical Examples: Gen 37:4–11, 18–28; Exod 24:3–5; 1 Sam 3; 16–18; 1 Kings 12:6–15; Jer 22:18–21; Matt 19:16–22; Luke 2:1–52; Heb 11:24–26.

Further References: Prov 2:1–22; 3:1–35; 5:1–23; 6:1–35; 7:1–27; 15:5; 17:2; 19:13, 26, 27; 23:15–35; 24:1–34; Mark 10:17–22; Luke 18:18–23.

– Z –

ZEAL

As the hart panteth after the water brooks, so panteth my soul after thee, O God. My soul thirsteth for God, for the living God: when shall I come and appear before God? (Ps 42:1, 2).

Because for thy sake I have borne reproach; shame hath covered my face. I am become a stranger unto my brethren, and an alien unto my mother's children. For the zeal of thine house hath eaten me up; and the reproaches of them that reproached thee are fallen upon me (Ps 69:7–9).

Sing unto the LORD, bless his name; shew forth his salvation from day to day. Declare his glory among the heathen, his wonders among all people. . . .

Say among the heathen *that* the LORD reigneth: the world also shall be established that it shall not be moved: he shall judge the people righteously (Ps 96:2, 3, 10).

My zeal hath consumed me, because mine enemies have forgotten thy words (Ps 119:139).

Whatsoever thy hand findeth to do, do *it* with thy might; for *there is* no work, nor device, nor knowledge, nor wisdom, in the grave, whither thou goest (Eccl 9:10).

Ye are the salt of the earth: but if the salt have lost his savour, wherewith shall it be salted? it is thenceforth good for nothing, but to be cast out, and to be trodden under foot of men. Ye are the light of the world. A city that is set on an hill cannot be hid. Neither do men light a candle, and put it under a bushel, but on a candlestick; and it giveth light unto all that are in the house. Let your light so shine before men, that they may see your good works, and glorify your Father which is in heaven (Matt 5:13–16).

Not slothful in business; fervent in spirit; serving the Lord (Rom 12:11).

Even so ye, forasmuch as ye are zealous of spiritual *gifts*, seek that ye may excel to the edifying of the church (1 Cor 14:12).

Therefore, my beloved brethren, be ye stedfast, unmoveable, always abounding in the work of the Lord, forasmuch as ye know that your labour is not in vain in the Lord (1 Cor 15:58).

But *it is* good to be zealously affected always in *a* good *thing*, and not only when I am present with you (Gal 4:18).

And let us not be weary in well-doing: for in due season we shall reap, if we faint not (Gal 6:9).

Stand therefore, having your loins girt about with truth, and having on the breastplate of righteousness; and your feet shod with the preparation of the gospel of peace; above all, taking the shield of faith, wherewith ye shall be able to quench all the fiery darts of the wicked. And take the helmet of salvation, and the sword of the Spirit, which is the word of God: praying always with all prayer and supplication in the Spirit, and watching thereunto with all perseverance and supplication for all saints; and for me, that utterance may be given unto me, that I may open my mouth boldly, to make known the mystery of the gospel, for which I am an ambassador in bonds: that therein I may speak boldly, as I ought to speak (Eph 6:14–20).

Who gave himself for us, that he might redeem us from all iniquity, and purify unto himself a peculiar people, zealous of good works (Titus 2:14).

Beloved, when I gave all diligence to write unto you of the common salvation, it was needful for me to write unto you, and exhort *you* that ye should earnestly contend for the faith which was once delivered unto the saints.

And of some have compassion, making a difference: and others save with fear, pulling *them* out of the fire; hating even the garment spotted by the flesh (Jude 3, 22, 23).

As many as I love, I rebuke and chasten: be zealous therefore, and repent (Rev 3:19).

Biblical Examples: Exod 32:31, 32; Deut 9:18; Josh 24:15, 16; 1 Sam 17:26; 2 Sam 24:24, 25; 1 Kings 22:14; Ezra 7:10; Neh 4–8; 13:7–9; Ps 71:17, 18; Isa 6:8; Jer 13:17; Dan 3:17, 18; Mark 14:29–31; Luke 22:32, 33; John 4:28–30, 34, 35; Acts 4:18–33; 5:42; 6:4, 10; 8:4, 35; 18:25–28; 26:19–29; Rom 15:18–21; 2 Cor 4:8–10, 13–18; 7:11; 8:1–5, 16–18; 9:2; Phil 1:18–27; 2:22, 26–30; 3:4–14; 1 Thess 1:2–8; 2:2–6, 8–11; Heb 11:15–27.

Further References: 2 Chron 15:15; Isa 59:17; 60:1; 62:6, 7; Jer 9:1–3; 20:9; Mark 4:21, 22; Luke 8:16, 17; John 9:4; Rom 10:1; 1 Cor 7:29–34; Eph 5:15, 16; Heb 13:13–15; 2 Peter 3:14; 3 John 4–7.